John Kersey

A New English Dictionary

Anglistica & Americana

A Series of Reprints Selected by
Bernhard Fabian, Edgar Mertner,
Karl Schneider and Marvin Spevack
120

1974

Georg Olms Verlag
Hildesheim · New York

JOHN KERSEY

A New English Dictionary

(1702)

1974

Georg Olms Verlag
Hildesheim · New York

Note

The present facsimile is reproduced from a copy in the possession of the University Library, Edinburgh.
Shelfmark: 83668

K. S.

Reprographischer Nachdruck der Ausgabe London 1702
Printed in Germany
Herstellung: Druckerei Anton Hain KG, Meisenheim/Glan
ISBN: 3 487 05349 7

A NEW
English Dictionary:

Or, a Compleat
COLLECTION
Of the Most
Proper and Significant Words,
Commonly used in the
LANGUAGE;

With a Short and Clear Exposition of

Difficult Words and Terms of Art.

The whole digested into Alphabetical Order; and chiefly designed for the benefit of Young *Scholars*, *Tradesmen*, *Artificers*, and the *Female Sex*, who would learn to spell truely; being so fitted to every Capacity, that it may be a continual help to all that want an Instructer.

By *J. K.*

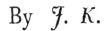

LONDON:
Printed for Henry Bonwicke, at the *Red Lion*, and Robert Knaplock, at the *Angel* in St. *Paul*'s Church-Yard. 1702.

THE
PREFACE.

ALTHOUGH it may be needless to insist on the usefulness of Dictionaries in general, in regard that Words are introductory to the knowledge of Things, and no Arts or Sciences can be attain'd without a right understanding of their peculiar Terms; yet we think it expedient to give some account of our present undertaking: The main design of which, is to instruct Youth, and even adult Persons, who are ignorant of the Learned Languages, in the *Orthography*, or true and most accurate manner of Spelling, Reading and Writing the genuine Words of their own Mother-tongue. For that purpose, we have taken care to make a Collection of all the most proper and significant *English* Words, that are now commonly us'd either in Speech, or in the familiar way of Writing Letters, *&c*; omitting at the same time, such as are obsolete, barbarous, foreign or peculiar to the several Counties of *England*; as also many difficult, abstruse and uncouth Terms of Art, as altogether unnecessary, nay even prejudicial to the endeavours of young Beginners, and unlearned Persons, and whereof seldom any use does occur: However, the most useful Terms in all Faculties are briefly explain'd; more especially those that relate to Divinity, Ecclesiastical Affairs, the Statute-Laws of this Nation, History, Geography, Maritime Affairs, Plants, Gardening, Husbandry, Mechanicks; Handicrafts, Hunting, Fowling, Fishing, *&c*.

The whole Work is digested into Alphabetical order, in which the different senses of Original Words are set down, and where 'tis needful they are also illustrated with a clear and short Exposition; so as the true meaning of their reſpective Derivatives and Compounds may be eaſily diſcover'd. But to prevent the bulk of the Volume from ſwelling beyond its due Bounds, 'tis judg'd expedient only to leave out the common Terminations of Verbs and Adverbs, that may be form'd from their Primitives, with a very little application; and of which an Example or two, may ſerve for the Reader's future Direction: Thus from the Verb *To love*, it is caſy to deduce the Participles *loved* and *loving*, and from the latter, the Adverb *lovingly*, by adding to the Primitive, the uſual Terminations of *ed*, *ing*, and *ly*. Again, the Participles *diſpoſed* and *diſpoſing* are naturally deriv'd from the Verb to diſpoſe; in like manner the Adverb *delicioſly*, takes its riſe from the Adjective *delicious* and ſo of the reſt: Moreover, the Poſitive, or firſt degree of Compariſon of all Adjectives, that are regularly compar'd is only inſerted; it being no difficult matter to add the proper Terminations of *er* and *eſt*; as *rich*, *richer*, *richeſt*; *wiſe*, *wiſer*, *wiſeſt*; *noble*, *nobler*, *nobleſt*; &c. Theſe few Rules being duely obſerv'd, the Work will appear uninterrupted, and altogether conformable to the uſual method of Dictionaries.

And it may be affirm'd, That no other Book of the ſame nature, is as yet extant; altho' there are two, which ſeem to come near our preſent Deſign; *Viz.* a little Tract firſt ſet forth by *John Bulloker* Doctor of Phyſick, under the Title of *An Engliſh Expoſiter*, and Mr. *E. Coles*'s *Engliſh Dictionary*. The former is defective in ſeveral reſpects, and yet abounds with difficult Terms, which are here purpoſely avoided, for the above-mention'd Reaſons; neither is the latter free from the like unprofitable Redundancy. For it is obſervable, That Mr. *Coles* in his elaborate Work, has inſerted ſeveral Words purely *Latin*, without any alteration, as *Dimidietas* for an half; *Sufflamen*, for a Trigger, and ſome hundreds only vary'd with an *Engliſh* Termination, which are ſcarce ever us'd by any ancient or modern Writer, even in a Figurative, Philoſophical, or Poetical Senſe; ſuch as *Ægrimony* and *Ægroting* for Sickneſs; *Beneplacity*, well pleaſing; *Egeſtuoſity*, extreme poverty; *Elingued*, tongue-tied; To *egurgitate* or diſgorge; *Graveolence*, a rank or ſtrong ſcent; *Gynecocracy*, a *Greek* Term denoting Feminine Government; *Horripilation*, the ſtanding up of the Hair

for

for fear; *Horrisonant*, making a terrible noise; *Ignifluous*, flowing with Fire; *Ignipotent*, mighty by Fire; *Impluvious*, without Rain; *Innubilous*, without Clouds; *Internecion*, an universal slaughter; *Largifical*, bountiful; *Nidifice*, a Nest; *Odoraminous*, sweet-smelled; To *offuscate*, or darken; A *Pronephew*, from *Pronepos*, for a Nephew's Son; *Receptitious*, received; *Scaturiginous*, full of Springs; *Scelestique*, wicked; *Sevidical*, speaking cruelly; To *sufflaminate*, or skatch a wheel; *Sulcation*, a making Furrows; *Supplice*, Punishment; *Susurration*, a whispering, *&c.* Likewise many other Terms that are very uncouth and unintelligible; as *Amexation Dapocaginous*, To *elacerate*, To *eglomerate*, *Fritiniancy*, *Helaution*, *Umbiligality*, *Yvernagium*, &c Besides an innumerable multitude of *Greek*, *Latin*, *French*, *Italian*, *Spanish*, *British*, *Saxon*, and old *English* Words that are often introduc'd even without changing their Original Terminations, and which are never used in *English*; with others that are peculiar to distinct Counties of *England*, *Scotland*, and *Ireland*, and never us'd or understood any where else. So that a plain Country-man, in looking for a common *English* Word, amidst so vast a Wood of such as are above the reach of his Capacity, must needs lose the sight of it, and be extremely discouraged, if not forc'd to give over the search.

Neither are Mr. *Coles's* Expositions always proper, or pertinent, particularly, of the Word *Revolution*, which he only defines to be *a turning round to the first point*; but this Term, which simply denotes *a whirling round*, is us'd in Astronomy, for a certain Course of the Planets, Time, *&c.* and in common acceptation, for some notable change, especially of Government. Moreover, in the explaining of *English* Words deriv'd from the *Latin*, he makes no scruple of producing such senses as are only peculiar to the Original; as will plainly appear from an instance or two, *viz.* The Term *Insolent* is rightly Interpreted by our Author, *Proud* or *Arrogant*; but he also adds, *contrary to common Custom*, which last sense is never used in *English*; altho' *Insolens* in *Latin* admits of both significations: Again, he renders the Word Personate, *to represent one's Person*, also *to sound aloud*; whereas the latter sense only belongs to the Latin Verb *Persono*. We cannot forbear adding a third instance, which is very remarkable, *viz.* Villication, *the Rule of Husbandry, under the Master of a*

Mannour

Manneur; a ſtrange Term, explain'd by a no leſs odd Definition: Indeed we meet with the *Latin* Word *Villicatio* in *Columella* & other Authors, which may well be interpreted, *A Stewardſhip* or *Bailyſhip in the Country*; alſo *the Hiring* or *managing of a Farm.* However, it muſt be acknowledged, That the Deſign of this Ingenious Author (from whoſe Merit it is not our intention in the leaſt to derogate) is very different from ours; That apparently being to oblige the Publick, with as large a Collection as poſſibly could be made, of all ſorts of hard and obſolete Words, both domeſtick and foreign, as well Proper Names, as the Terms of all Arts and Sciences, Poetical Fictions, *&c.* Whereas, ours is intended only to explain ſuch *Engliſh* Words as are genuine, and uſed by Perſons of clear Judgment and good Style; leaving out all thoſe foreign Terms, that in Mr. *Coles*'s time were viciouſly introduc'd into our Language, by thoſe who ſought to approve themſelves Learned rather by unintelligible Words than by proper Language.

Laſtly, it ought to be obſerv'd, That very few of the genuine and common ſignificant Words of the *Engliſh* Tongue are contain'd in either of the two Dictionaries but now cited, or in any other particular Work of the like nature, hitherto publiſhed; as has been already hinted. To conclude, the uſefulneſs of this Manual to all Perſons not perfectly Maſters of the *Engliſh* Tongue, and the aſſiſtance it gives to young Scholars, Tradeſmen, Artificers and others, and particularly, the more ingenious Practitioners of the Female Sex; in attaining to the true manner of Spelling of ſuch Words, as from time to time they have occaſion to make uſe of, will, we hope procure it a favourable Reception. The Author does not expect a Recompence proportioned to the great Trouble and Pains he has taken, but will have full ſatisfaction, if the Publick reap as much Benefit by his Work, as he has beſtow'd Labour in Compiling it.

Books Printed for Robert Knaplock, *at the* Angel *in* St. *Paul's Church-yard.*

1. THE Remains of Arch Bishop *Laud*, containing his Answer to the Lord *Say*'s Speech against the Bishops; his Speech at the Censure of *Bastwick*, *Prynn*, and *Burton*, and his History of his Chancellorship of *Oxford*, Published by the Reverend Mr. *Wharton.* in *Folio.*

2. Mr. *Tyrrell*'s General History of *England*, both Ecclesiastical and Civil; taken from the most Ancient Records, Manuscripts, and Printed Historians, Three Vol. In *Folio.*

3. *Romæ Antiquæ Notitia*; or, the Antiquities of *Rome*, in two Parts. I. A short History of the Rise, Progress, and Decay of the Common-wealth. II. A Description of the City, an Account of the Religion, Civil Government, and Art of War; with the Remarkable Customs and Ceremonies, Publick and Private: Also Copper Cuts of the Principal Buildings, &c. By *Basil Kennet*, of C. C. Coll. *Oxon.* The second Edition, with large Additions.

4. Fifteen Sermons upon several Occasions. By *George Stanhope*, D. D. Chaplain in Ordinary to His Majesty.

5. *Joannis Clerici Physica, sive de Rebus Corporeis, Libri quinq; In quibus, præmissis potissimis Corporearum Naturarum phænomenis & proprietatibus, Veterum & Recentiorum de eorum causis celeberrimæ conjecturæ traduntur. Editio Novissima Prioribus Correctior. Cantabrigiæ, Typis Academicis*, 1700. in 12°.

6. *Mathesis Enucleata*: Or, The Elements of the Mathematicks. By *J. Christ. Sturmius*, Professor of Philosophy and Mathematicks, in the University of *Altorf*. Made English: By *J. Ralphson*, M. A. and Fellow of the *Royal Society*.

Short, but yet plain Elements of Geometry and plain Trigonometry: Shewing, how by a brief and easie Method, all that's necessary and useful in *Euclid, Archimedes, Apollonius* and other excellent Geometricians, both Ancient and Modern, may be understood. Written in *French*. By *F. Pardies*; and now Render'd into *English* from the 4th and last Edition: By *J. Harris*, A. M. and Fellow of the *Royal Society* With many Additions, and Improvements, the whole being accommodated to the Capacities of young Beginners. 8vo.

A B

AN Abaisance, or *low-Congee.*
To abandon, *cast off, or utterly forsake.*
To abase, or *bring low.*
An Abasement.
To be abashed, or *ashamed.*
To abate, *diminish,* or *grow less.*
An Abatement.
An Abbess, *she that Governs*
An Abbey, or *Monastery.*
An Abbot, *the Ruler of an Abbey.*
An Abbotship, or *Abbot's Dignity.*
To Abbreviate, or *shorten.*
An Abbreviation.
To abbridge, *epitomize, lessen, or keep short.*
An Abbridgment.
A-bed, or *in Bed.*
To Abet, *set one on, aid,* or *take his part.*
An Abetter.
To abhor, or *loath.*
An Abhorrence, *or* abhorrency.
An Abhorrer.
To Abide, *stay, tarry, last, or endure.*
Abject, *vile, or of no esteem.*
Ability, or *power.*
An Abjuration, or *solemn recanting.*
To abjure, *forswear,* or *abandon the Realm.*
Able, or *powerful in strength, or skill.*
Ableness, or *ability.*
Ablution, or *washing used by Popish-Priests.*
A-board, as *a-board a ship*
An Abode, *dwelling,* or *continuance in a place.*
To Abolish, *repeal, deface, or utterly destroy.*
Abominable, or *hateful.*
To Abominate, *hate,* or *loath.*
An Abomination.
Abortive, or *born out of due time.*
Above, as *above an Hour.*
To be above, or *to excell.*
To abound with, or *have plenty of.*
About, as *about Noon.*
Abraham's balm, or *hemp-tree, a kind of Willow.*
A-breast, or *in front.*
A-broach, as *a vessel a-broach.*
Abroad, or *without doors.*
To abrogate, *or repeal.*
An Abrogation.
To sit abrood *upon eggs, as a bird does.*
Abrupt, *rough, uneven, cragged,* or *hasty.*
Abruptness.
To abscond, or *hide himself.*
Absence, or *being away.*
Absent, or *out of the way.*
To absent himself.
To absolve, *to acquit,* or *to bring to perfection.*
Absolute, *perfect,* or *not depending.*
Absoluteness, or *absolute power.*
The Absolution, or *remission of sins.*
To abstain, or *forbear.*
Abstemious, *that abstains from Wine,* &c.
Abstemiousness, or *sobriety*
Abstinence, or *forbearance.*
Abstinent, *forbearing meat, drink,* &c.
An Abstract, or *short draught of a thing.*
To abstract, or *abbridge.*
Abstruse, *close,* or *secret.*
Absurd, *foolish, improper,* or *aukward.*
An Absurdity.
Abundance, *plenty,* or *good store.*
Abundant, or *plentifull.*
An Abuse, or *affront.*
To abuse, *misuse,* or *do one an injury.*
Abusive, or *apt to abuse.*
Abusiveness.
To Abut, or *border upon.*
An Abyss, or *bottomless pit*

A C

Academical, *belonging to*
An Academy, or *University.*
An Accent, or *mark over a letter, for the right founding of a Syllable.*
To Accent *words.*
To accept, *allow* or *take in good part.*
Acceptable.
Acceptableness.
Acceptance, *or* acceptation
The acception, or *meaning of a word.*
Access, or *admittance.*
Accessible, or *that may be approached.*
An Accession, *additional advantage, or a coming.*
An Accessory, or *partaker in the guilt of a crime.*
The Accidence, or *introduction to the* Latin *Grammar.*
An Accident, or *chance.*
Accidental, or *casual.*
An Acclamation, *or shout.*
An Accommodate, *fit, or furnish*; or *to compose a difference.*
An Accommodation.
To accompany, *keep company with, or attend.*
An Accomplice, or *accessory.*
To Accomplish, *perform,* or *finish.*
An Accomplishment.
Accord, as *with one accord.*
To Accord, or *agree.*
According as, according to, &c.
To accost, *come up to, set upon,* or *salute.*
An Account, or *reckoning.*
To Account, *reckon,* or *esteem of.*
Accountable.
An Accountant.
To accouter, *dress,* or *trim up.*

Accoutrements.
Accuracy, or *neatneſs.*
Accurate, *exact*, or *neat.*
Accurſed, *lying under a curſe.*
An Accuſation, or *charge.*
To accuſe, *impeach*, or *charge with.*
An Accuſer.
To accuſtom, *himſelf to a thing.*
Ambs-ace, *or* amms-ace.
An Ache, or *pain.*
The Ache-*bone.*
Acid, or *ſharp as vinegar.*
To acknowledge, *own*, or *confeſs.*
An Acknowledgment.
An Acorn, *the fruit of an oak.*
To acquaint, *inform*, or *become familiar with.*
Acquaintance.
To acquieſce, or *reſt ſatiſfied.*
To acquire, or *get.*
An Acquiſition.
To acquit, or *diſcharge.*
An Acquittal.
An Acquittance, *for money.*
An Acre, *of land.*
The Acrimony, or *ſharpneſs of humours.*
A-croſs, as *arms folded a-croſs.*
An Act, *deed*, *or decree.*
To act, or *do.*
An Action, *deed*, *geſture*, or *ſuit at law.*
Actionable, *that will bear an action at Law.*
Active, *quick*, or *nimble.*
Activity, or *nimbleneſs.*
An Actor, *or Stage-player.*
An Actreſs, or *female actor.*
Actual, *that is brought to effect.*
Acute, *keen*, or *ſharp.*

A D

An Adamant-*ſtone.*
To adapt, or *fit.*
To add, *put to*, or *reckon to.*
An Adder, *a kind of ſerpent.*
A Water-adder.
Adders-graſs } *herbs.*
Adders-tongue } *herbs.*
Adder-wort, or *Snakeweed.*
An Addice, or Adze, *a Cooper's tool.*
To addict, or *give himſelf to.*
An Addition, or *adding.*
Additional.
Addle, as, *an addle egg.*
Addle-headed.
Addle, *coming from Wine-lees.*
To addreſs, *petition*, or *make application to.*
An Addreſs, or *petition.*
Addreſſers, or *petitioners.*
Adequate, or *proportionable.*
To adhere, or *ſtick to.*
An Adherence.
An Adherent, or *abetter.*
Adjacent, or *lying near.*
A-dieu, or *farewell.*
Adjoining, *neighbouring*, or *lying next to.*
To adjourn, *or put off to another day.*
An Adjournment.
To adjudge, or *determine of.*
An Adjunct, or *circumſtance.*
An Adjuration, or *earneſt charging.*
To adjure, *to exact an oath*, or *give a ſtrict charge.*
To adjuſt, *make fit*, *order*, or *regulate.*
An Adjutant, *a military Officer, that aſſiſts the General.*
To adminiſter, *to govern*, *to give*, *diſpenſe*, &c.
An Adminiſtration.
An Adminiſtrator.
An Adminiſtratrix.
Admirable, or *worthy of admiration.*
An Admiral, *or chief Commander at Sea.*
A Reer-Admiral.
A Vice-Admiral.
The *Lord-high* Admiral *of England.*
The Admiralſhip, or *admiral's Office.*
The Admiralty-Court.
An Admiration, *from*
To admire, or *wonder at.*
An Admirer.
An Admiſſion, or *admittance.*
To admit, or *take unto.*
To admoniſh, or *warn.*
An Admoniſhment, *or* admonition.
A-doe, as *with much adoe.*
Adonis-*flower.*
To adopt, or *chooſe one for an heir.*
An Adopter.
An Adoption.
Adoptive.
Adorable, *and*
Adoration, *from*
To adore, or *worſhip.*
An Adorer.
To adorn, *trim*, or *deck.*
To advance, *lift up*, *prefer*, *go forward*, &c.
An Advancement.
Advantage, *gain*, or *over-meaſure.*
To advantage, or *avail.*
Advantagious, or *profitable.*
Advent, *i. e.* Coming; *the time ſet a-part by the Church to prepare for the approaching Feſtival of Chriſtmas.* Advent Sundays, *four in number.*
Adventitious, *that comes by chance.*
To adventure, *enterprize*, *try*, *hazard*, &c.
An Adventure, or *chance.*
An Adventurer.
Adventurous, or *bold.*
An Adverſary, or *he that is againſt one.*
Adverſe, *croſs*, or *contrary.*
Adverſity, or *calamity.*
To advert, or *mark.*
Advertency.
To advertiſe, *warn*, or *give notice.*
An Advertiſer.
An Advertiſement.
Advice, or *counſel.*

Ad-

Advisable.
To advise, *to give counsel, or to consider.*
Advisedness.
An Adviser.
Adulatory, or *apt to flatter.*
Adult, or *grown to full age.*
Adulterate, *or* adulterated.
To adulterate, or *corrupt.*
An Adulterer, or *Whoremonger.*
An Adulteress.
Adulterous, *given to*
Adultery, or *incontinency, properly of married persons.*
An Advocate, *an intercessor*, or *counsellor at Law.*
An Advocateship.
An Advowson, or *right to present to a Benefice.*

A E A F

Aerial, *or airy.*
Æthereal, or *heavenly.*
Afar, or afar off.
Affability, *from*
Affable, *easy to be spoken to*, or *courteous.*
An Affair, *business*, or *concern.*
To affect, *work upon*, or *set one's mind upon.*
Affectation, *an over-nice imitation.*
Affectedness.
Affection, *love*, or *kindness.*
Affectionate, or *full of affection.*
Affiance, *confidence*, or *relying upon.*
An Affidavit, or *deposition upon Oath.*
Affinity; *alliance*, or *kin by marriage*, or *likeness.*
To affirm, *assure*, or *assert.*
Affirmable.
An Affirmation.
Affirmative.
To affix, or *fasten to.*
To afflict, *grieve*, or *trouble.*
Affliction.
Afflictive.
Affluence, or *great plenty.*
To afford, *yield*, or *give.*
To afforest, or *turn ground into forest.*
To affright, or *terrify.*
To affront, *insult over*, or *injure one.*
An Affront, or *injury.*
Affrontive, or *injurious.*
A-float, as, *a Ship set afloat.*
Afore, afore-hand.
Afraid, or *fearfull.*
A-fresh, or *new again.*
Africans, or *French marygolds.*
After, as *after dinner.*
After-ages.
The After-birth, or *after-burden.*
An After-clap.
The Afternoon.
Afterwards.

A G

Again, to and again.
Against, or *contrary to.*
An Agate-*stone.*
Age, *the duration of time*, or *the space of* 100 *years.*
Non-age, or *Minority.*
Aged, or *advanc'd in years.*
An Agent, *a doer, Factor*, or *Resident.*
To aggrandize, or *make* great.
To aggravate, *to make more heinous*, or *worse.*
An Aggravation.
An Aggressour, *or assaulter.*
Aggrieved, or troubled.
Agility, or nimbleness.
To agitate, or *manage a business.*
An Agitation.
Agoe, or before this time.
An Agony, *extremity of anguish*, *or pangs of death.*
A-great, *or* by the great; *as work taken a-great.*
To agree, *assent*, or *yield to; to suit*, *or be fit.*
Agreeable.
Agreeableness.
An Agreement.
Agriculture, or *the Art of Husbandry.*
Agrimony, *or* liver-wort.
The Agriot, or *tart cherry.*
A-ground, as *to run aground.*
An Ague, a Disease.
The Ague-tree, *a plant.*
Aguish, or *feavourish.*

A H A I

Ah! alass!
To aid, *help*, or *assist.*
Aid, or *assistance.*
To ail, as, *what ails you?*
An ailment, or *indisposition.*
To aim at, or *take aim at.*
An Aim, or *level.*
The Air, *an element.*
An Air, in *Musick*, &c.
To air, or dry a thing.
Airiness.
Airy.
An Airy, or *young brood of Hawks*, &c.
Aise, or *axweed*, an *herb.*

A K

To ake, as, *my head akes.*
The Head-ake.
The Tooth-ake.
A Aker-staff, *to cleanse the plough-coulter.*

A L

Alabaster, *a sort of stone.*
An Alabaster-box.
Alack!, *or* alass!
Alacrity, or *cheerfulness.*
An Alarm, or alarum; *a sudden outcry to arms.*
To alarm, or *give the alarm.*
An Alarm-bell.
An Alarm-watch.
Alass, for shame!
A-late, or *of late.*
Alchymy, or *Chymistry.*
The Alcoran, *the Law of* Mahomet, or *Turks Bible*
An Alcove, or *by-place for a bed.*
An Alder, *a tree.*

An Alderman, *of a Ward.*
Ale, *a well known drink.*
An Ale-conner, *or ale-taster.*
Ale-coſt, *an herb.*
Ale-hoof, or *ground-ivy.*
An Ale-houſe, or *victualling-houſe.*
Aleſſander } *herbs.*
Alexander's foot } *herbs.*
Algebra, or *the Art of figurative numbers.*
Alicant-Wine.
An Alien, *foreigner,* or *ſtranger.*
To alienate, eſtrange, put away, or ſell.
An Alienation.
To alight *off an horſe,* or *as a bird does.*
Alike, as, *all alike.*
Aliment, or *nouriſhment.*
Alimony, or *ſeparate maintenance for a Wife.*
Aliſanders, or *lovage, an herb.*
Alive, *or living.*
Alkanet, *or* orchanet, *an herb.*
All, as, *all the world.*
All-good, } *herbs.*
All-heal, } *herbs.*
All-ſeed, } *herbs.*
To allay, *to aſſwage,* or *to temper metals.*
The Allay, *or* alloy of coin.
To alledge, *cite,* or *ſay for himſelf.*
An Allegation.
An Allegator, *a kind of* Indian *Crocodile.*
Allegiance, or *loyalty to the King.*
Allegorical.
To allegorize, to uſe
An Allegory, or *figurative expreſſion.*
Allelujah, i. e. *praiſe the Lord*; alſo, *wood-ſorrel, an herb.*
To alleviate, *lighten, diminiſh,* or *give eaſe.*
An Alleviation.
An Alley, *in a garden,* or *in the ſtreets.*
Alliance.
Allies, or *Confederates.*
To ally, or *aſſociate.*
To allot, *aſſign,* or *appoint.*
An Allotment.
To allow, *approve,* or *grant.*
Allowable.
An Allowance.
The Alloy, *of gold, or ſilver-coin.*
To allude, or *ſpeak with reſpect to another thing.*
Allum, *a mineral.*
Roch-allum.
To allure, *decoy,* or *entice.*
An Allurement.
An Allurer.
An Alluſion, (*from* to allude)
An Almanack, or *Calendar.*
An Almandine, *a kind of Ruby.*
Almightineſs.
Almighty, or *all-powerful*
An Almond, *a fruit.*
The Almonds *of the ears.*
An Almoner, *or* almner, *the diſtributer of the Royal Alms.*
An Almonry, *or* aumry; *the Almoner's lodgings,* or *place where alms are given.*
Almoſt, or *well near.*
Alms, or *benevolence to the poor.*
An Alms-houſe.
An Alneger, *an Officer that looks to the aſſize of woollen-cloth.*
Aloes, *a bitter, purging Gum.*
Aloft, or *on high.*
Alone, or *ſolitary.*
Along, all along.
Aloof off, or *at a diſtance.*
Aloud, or *with a loud voice.*
An Alphabet, or *collection of the letters of any language.*
Alphabetical, *according to the order of the Alphabet.*
Alſo, as alſo, but alſo.
Alſines, or *mouſe-ear, an herb.*
An Altar, *for ſacrifices.*
To alter, or *change.*
Alterable.
An Alteration.
An Altercation, or *wrangling.*
An Alternation, or *changing by turns.*
Alternate, *or* alternative, *done by turns.*
Although.
Altitude, or *height.*
Altogether, or *utterly.*
Alway, *or* always.

A M

Amain, or *with main force*
To amaſs, or *heap up.*
To amaze, *daunt,* or *aſtoniſh.*
An Amazement.
An Ambaſſador, *a Commiſſioner ſent by one Prince to another, to treat about ſtate-affairs.*
An Ambaſſadreſs.
An Ambaſſage, *or* Embaſſy.
Amber, *a kind of hard yellow-gum.*
Ambergreece, *a ſweet clammy juice, or perfume found on the ſea-ſhore.*
Ambidexter, *one that uſes both hands alike, a Jack on both ſides.*
Ambiguity.
Ambiguous, or *doubtfull.*
Ambition, or *an immoderate deſire of honour.*
Ambitious.
To amble, or *pace.*
Ambroſe, *an herb.*
Ambury, *a horſe-diſeaſe.*
An Ambuſcado, or *Ambuſh; a lying in wait.*
Amel-corn, *a ſort of grain.*
Amen, *ſo be it.*
To amend, *to repair; to make, or grow better.*
An Amendment.
Amends, or *ſatisfaction.*
To Amerce, or *ſet a fine upon.*
An Amercement, *or* amerciament; *a fine at pleaſure.*
An Amethyſt, *a precious ſtone.*

Amiable, or *lovely*.
Amiableness.
Amicable, or *friendly*.
Amidst, or *in the middle*.
Amiss, *not rightly*, or *improperly*.
Amity, or *friendship*.
Ammunition, or *warlike provision*.
An Amnesty, or *act of oblivion*.
Among, or amongst.
Amorous, *deep in love*.
Amort, *dead-hearted*, or *sorrowfull*.
To amount, or *rise up to*.
An Amour, or *love-intrigue*.
Amphibious, *that lives both on land and water*.
An Amphitheater, *a round theater, or stage for plays*.
Ample, or *large*.
An Amplification.
To amplify, or *enlarge*.
Amputation, or *the cutting off a limb*.
An Amulet, *a kind of charm against poison, or witchcraft*.
To amuse, *to keep at a bay, delude, or sham*.
An Amusement.

AN

Anabaptists, i. e. *baptizers again, whose peculiar Tenet is to oppose Infant-baptism*.
An Anagram, *a short sentence made by transposing the letters of one's Name*.
Analogical, *belonging to*
Analogy, or *proportion*.
An Analysis, *explication*, or *unfolding*.
Anarchy, *want of government*, or *confusion*.
An Anathema, *curse*, or *excommunication*.
To Anathematize.
Anatomical.
An Anatomist.
To Anatomize, *from*
Anatomy, or *the art of dissecting bodies*.

Ancestors, or *fore-fathers*.
An Anchor *of a Ship*.
Anchorage, *a duty paid for Ships riding at anchor in a Port*.
An Anchoret, or *Hermit*.
An Anchove, *a fish*.
Ancient, or *old*.
An Ancient, or *Flag in a Ship*, &c.
Ancientness.
And, and if, and not.
An Andiron, or *cob-iron*.
An Anemone, or *wind-flower*.
A-new; as, *to begin anew*.
An Angel, or *messenger from Heaven*.
An Angel, *a gold-coin worth ten shillings*.
Angelica, *an herb*.
Angelical, *belonging to*, or *like an angel*.
To anger, *provoke to wrath*, or *exasperate*.
Anger, or *wrath*.
An Angle, or *corner*.
An Angle, or *fishing-rod*.
To Angle, or *fish with a rod*.
An Angler.
An Anglicism, or *propriety of the English Speech*.
Angry, or *passionate*.
Anguish, or *great trouble of body*, or *mind*.
An Animadversion, or *remark*.
To animadvert, or *take notice of*.
An Animal, or *living creature*.
To animate, or *encourage*.
Animosity, *heart-burning* or *grudge*.
Anis, *an herb*.
The Ankle, *of the leg*.
The Ankle-bone.
An Annalist, or *writer of*
Annals, or *yearly Chronicles*.
Annates, or *first-fruits of Church-livings*.
To anneal, or *bake colours thro' painted glass*.
To annex, or *join to*.

To annihilate, or *reduce to nothing*.
An Annihilation.
Anniversary, *that which returns yearly, at a certain time*.
An Annotation, or *expounding Note*.
To annoy, *hurt*, or *prejudice*.
An Annoyance.
Annual, or *yearly*.
An Annuity, or *yearly pension*.
To annul, or *make void*.
The Annunciation *of the Virgin* Mary; or *Lady-day*.
To Anoint, or *besmear*.
An Anointer.
Anon, *by and by*, or *presently*.
Anonymous, or *nameless*.
Another, one another.
To answer, *to reply*, or *to accord to*.
An Answer, or *reply*.
Answerable.
An Answerer *for another*.
An Ant, *emmet*, or *pismire*.
An Ant-hillock.
An Antagonist, or *Adversary*.
Antecedent, or *foregoing*.
To antedate, or *date before the time*.
An Anthem, or *hymn sung in a quire*.
An Anti-chamber.
Antichrist, *the enemy of Christ*.
An antichristian *doctrine*.
To Anticipate, or *prevent*.
An Anticipation.
Anticks, *in building and dancing*.
An Antidote, or *remedy against poison*.
An Antilope, *a kind of Goat*.
Antimonarchical, *that is against Kingly government*.
Antimony, *a mineral*.
An Antipathy, or *natural contrariety*.

Antipodes, *those that dwell on the other side of the Globe, having their feet directly opposite to ours.*
An Antiquary, *one that is well vers'd in antiquities.*
Antiquated, or *grown out of date.*
Antiquity, or *ancientness.*
Antlers, or *brow-antlers in deer.*
An Anvil, *a Smith's tool.*
Anxiety, or *trouble of mind.*
Anxious, or *carefull.*
Any, any one, any where, *&c.*

A P

A-pace, *in haste,* or *with speed.*
A-part, or *separately.*
An Ape, *a beast.*
To ape, or *imitate one.*
An Aphorism, *a short definition, or general rule; more especially in Physick.*
Apish, *like an ape, foolish.*
Apishness.
The Apocalypse, or *St. John's Revelation.*
Apocrypha, *i. e. hidden; certain Books of doubtfull authority, annexed to the Bible.*
Apocryphal, *belonging to those Books.*
An Apologetick *oration.*
An Apologist, *one that makes an Apology.*
To apologize, or *make one's defence.*
An Apologue, or *moral fable.*
An Apology, *a defence,* or *excuse in words and arguments.*
An Apophthegm, *a short and witty saying.*
Apoplectical, or Apoplectick; *of, or belonging to*
The Apoplexy, *a disease that suddenly surprizes the brain, and takes away all manner of sense and life.*
Apostacy, *a defection,* or *falling away from the true Religion.*
An Apostate, *such a revolter.*
To Apostatize *from the Faith.*
An Apostle, *one sent as a messenger, or ambassadour to preach the Gospel.*
An Apostleship, *the office,* &c.
Apostolical, or Apostolick, *belonging to an Apostle.*
An Apostrophe, *the mark of a vowel cut off.*
An Apothecary, *a seller of medicines, drugs,* &c.
An Apozeme, or *physical decoction of herbs, drugs,* &c.
Apparel, *habit,* or *furniture.*
Apparelled, or *cloathed.*
Apparent, or *manifest.*
Apparentness.
An Apparition, or *Ghost.*
An Apparitor, or *summoner to appear in the Spiritual Court.*
An Appartment, or *separate lodging in a House.*
To appeal, *to an higher Court.*
An Appeal, *removing a cause from an inferior to a higher Judge.*
An Appealer, or appellant.
To appear, or *present himself,* or *to be in sight.*
An Appearance.
To appease, *pacify,* or *quiet,*
An Appellour, or *challenger.*
Appendant, *depending on,* or *belonging to.*
An Appendix, or *separate addition to a Book.*
To appertain, or *belong.*
Appertinencies, or *dependencies.*
An Appetency, or *earnest desire.*
An Appetite, *a desire of victuals,* &c.
To applaud, or *highly commend, as it were by the clapping of hands.*
An Applauder.
Applause.
An Apple, *a known fruit.*
Apple of love, *an herb.*
The Apple of the Eye.
An Apple-loft.
An Apple-pie, *&c.*
Appliable, or applicable.
An Application, or *applying.*
To apply, *to put one thing to another;* or *to addict himself to.*
To appoint, *order,* or *design.*
An Appointment.
To apportion, or *divide into convenient portions.*
An Apportionment, *the dividing of a Rent into parts.*
Apposite, or *pat.*
To apprehend, *to lay hold on, to understand, to fear,* or *suspect.*
An Apprehension.
Apprehensive.
Apprehensiveness.
An Apprentice, *a learner of a trade, art,* &c.
An Apprenticeship.
To approach, or *draw near.*
An Approach, or *coming near.*
Approachable.
An Approbation, or *approving.*
To appropriate, *apply,* or *take to himself.*
An Appropriation, *when the profits of a Church-living are made over to a lay-man, or to a body corporate; only maintaining a Vicar.*
To approve, *like, allow,* or *render himself recommendable.*
An Approver.
An Apricock, *a fruit.*
April, *one of the* 12 *months.*

An

An Apron, *for a Woman*, &c.
The Apron of a roasted goose.
Apt, *meet*, *fit*, or *forwardly inclined to*.
Aptness.

A Q

Aqua fortis, *a strong corroding liquor made of allum, vitriol, saltpeter*, &c.
Aqua vitæ, *a sort of strong water*.
An Aqueduct, *a conduit* or *passage for water*.
Aqueous, or *waterish*.

A R

Arable land, *fit to be plough'd*.
Arbitrable.
Arbitrary, or *absolute*.
To arbitrate, or *decide a controversy between two parties, by way of umpirage*.
An Arbitration, or arbitrement.
An Arbitrator.
An Arbitratrix.
An Arbour, *in a garden*.
An Arbut-tree, or *strawberry-tree*.
An Arch, *of a bridge*, &c.
To arch, or *make an arch*.
The Court of Arches.
Arch, or *chief* (in composition) *as*,
An Archangel, or *chief of angels*.
Archangel, or *dead nettles an herb*.
An Archbishop.
An Archbishoprick.
An Arch-deacon, *the Bishop's Vicar*.
An Archdeaconry.
An Archduke.
The Archdukedom of Austria.
An Archdutchess.
An Archpriest.
An Archer, or *shooter with a bow and arrows*.
Water-archer, *an herb*.
An Arch-heretick.
An Architect, or *Master-builder*.
Architecture, or *the Art of building*.
An Architrave, or *Master-beam*; *also the chapiter of a pillar*.
An Archive, *the place where old records are kept*
Ardent, *very hot*, *vehement*, or *eager*.
Ardentness, ardency, or ardour.
Argent, *silver-colour*, or *white in Heraldry*.
Argentine, or *wild tansey, an herb*.
To argue, or *debate*.
An Argument, *reason*, or *proof*; *also the subject of a discourse*, *Treatise*, &c.
Arianism, *the Heresy of* Arius, *who deny'd the Son of God to be of the same substance with the Father*.
A-right, or *rightly*.
To arise, as, *the Sun does*, or *to get up*.
Aristocracy, or *the government of a commonwealth by the Nobility*.
Aristrocratical, *belonging to such a government*.
Arithmetical.
An Arithmetician, *a professour of*
Arithmetick, or *the Art of numbering*.
An Ark, *as* Noah's *Ark*, or *ship*.
The Ark *of the Testament*, or *the chest in which the Tables of the Levitical Law were kept*.
An Arm of a man's body, *of a tree*, or *of the sea*.
The Arm-pit, or *arm-hole*.
To arm, or *furnish with arms*.
An Armada, or *Spanish Fleet of men of War*.
An Armadillio, *a little West-Indian beast, with skin like armour*.
Armour, or *warlike harness*.
An Armourer; or *maker of armour*.
An Armoury, *a storehouse of*
Arms, or *weapons*.
A Coat of arms.
Fire-arms.
An Army, or *military forces*.
Aromatical, *or* aromatick; *spicy*.
An Arquebuss, *a sort of great musket*.
To arraign *a criminal*, or *bring him to a tryal*.
An Arraignment.
Arras-hangings, *a sort of rich tapestry made at* Arras *in* Flanders.
Arrant *for very*; as, *an arrant knave*, *cheat*, *thief*, &c.
An Array, or *ranking of soldiers in battel*.
Battel-array.
Arrayers, or *Commissioners of* array; *certain Officers that look after the soldiers armour*.
Arrearage, or arrears; *a debt remaining on an old account*.
To arrest, *stop*, or *seize upon*.
An Arrest, *stop*, or *seizure*; *also a court-decree*.
Arrierban, *the Gentlemen of a Country, summon'd to serve in the War*.
An Arrival, *from*
To arrive, or *come to a place*.
Arrogancy, or *presumption*.
Arrogant, or *saucy*.
To arrogate, or *take too much to himself*.
An Arrow, *to shoot with*.
Arrow-head, *an herb*.
The Arse, or *fundament*.
An Arse-foot, or *little didapper, a bird*.
Arse-smart, *an herb*.
An Arsenal, *or magazine of arms and ammunition*
Arsenick, *a sort of strong poison*.

Arse-versy, *topsy-turvy*, or *preposterously*.
An Art, or *science*.
Arterial, *belonging to*
An Artery, *a vessel that conveys the thinnest blood with the vital spirits*.
Artfull, or *artificial*.
An Artichoke, *a plant*.
An Article, *condition, chief head in a discourse, clause*, &c.
To Article, or *draw up articles*.
Articulate, or *distinct*.
An Artifice, *a cunning fetch*, or *crafty device*.
An Artificer, or *handy-crafts-man*.
Artificial, *done according to the rules of Art*.
Artificialness.
Artillery, *pieces of Ordinance, and other warlike Instruments*.
A Train of Artillery.
The Artillery-Company.
An Artisan, or artist.
Artless, *not artificial*; or *plain*.

A S

As, even as, like as, &c.
To ascend, or *go up*.
The Ascendant *of a Nativity*; i.e. *that point of the Ecliptick, which rises at one's birth*.
To gain the Ascendant upon one; *to have a power, or influence over him*.
The Ascension *of our Lord and Saviour Jesus Christ into Heaven*.
An Ascent, or *rising ground*, &c.
To ascertain, or *assure*.
To ascribe, *attribute*, or *impute*.
An Ash, or *ash-tree*.
A *Wild* ash.
Ash-weed, *an herb*.
Ashamed, or *out of countenance*.
Ashen, *belonging to*, or *made of Ash*.
Ashes of *coals*, *wood*, &c.
Lye-ashes.
A-shore; as, *to go a-shore*.
Ashy, or *full of ashes*.
Aside, or *a-part*.
To ask, *desire*, or *demand*.
An Asker.
A-skew, awry, *or* on one side.
A-sleep, fast a-sleep.
An Asp, or aspick; *a venomous sort of serpent*.
An Asp, or aspin-tree.
Asparagus, *an herb*.
An Aspect, or *look*; *the air of one's countenance*; *or the position of the Stars*.
An Aspen-leaf.
An Asper, *a Turkish coin, worth about five farthings*
To asperse, or *slander one*.
An Aspersion.
An Aspiration, or *breathing*; *also the Greek mark* (ʽ) *for* h.
To aspire, *aim at*, or *seek ambitiously*.
A-squint; as, *to look a-squint*.
An Ass, *a beast*.
An Assailant, *one that assaults another*.
Assaraback, or *wild spikenard*.
To Assassinate, *or kill treacherously*.
An Assassination.
An Assassine, *one that kills another for gain*, or *upon hope*, or *promise of reward*.
An Assault, or *onset*.
To assault, *set upon*, or *attack*.
An Assaulter.
To assay, or *try metals*, &c.
An Assay, or *examination of weights and measures*.
An Assayer, *an Officer of the Mint*.
To assemble, *to call*, or *come together*.
An Assembly.
To assent, or *agree to*.
An Assent, or *consent*.
To assert, *maintain*, or *affirm*.
An Assertion.
An Asserter.
To assess, or *tax*.
An Assesser.
An Assessment.
An Assessor, or *assistant to a Judge*.
Assets, *effects sufficient to discharge debts, legacies*, &c.
An Asseveration, or *earnest affirming*.
Assiduity, or *diligence*.
Assiduous, *diligent*, or *close at business*.
To assign, *appoint*, or *make over*.
An Assign, *or* assignee, *one appointed by another, to transact any business*.
An Assignment.
To assimilate, or *liken*.
To assist, *aid*, or *help*.
Assistance.
An Assistant.
The Assize, or *set price of any commodity*.
To Assize, or *regulate such rates*.
An Assizer *of weights and measures*.
The Assizes, or *sitting of Justices upon their Commission*.
To associate himself, *or keep company*.
An Associate, or *companion*.
An Association.
To assume, or *take to himself*.
An Assumption.
An Assurance, *from*
To assure, *to make sure*, or *to avouch*.
Assuredness, or *certainty*.
To asswage, *allay*, or *appease*.
An Asswager.
An Asterick, or *mark like a star*.
An Asthma, *shortness*, or *difficulty of breathing*.
Asthmatick, or *pursy*.
To astonish, or *amaze*.
An Astonishment.

A-stride, or *a-straddle.*
Astrologe, or *hart-wort.*
An *Astrologer.*
Astrological, belonging to
Astrology, or *the Art of foretelling future events by the knowledge of the Stars.*
An Astronomer, *one skilled in the*
Astronomical *Art*, *or*
Astronomy, *a Science, that shews the measure and motion of the Stars and other heavenly Bodies.*
Asunder, or *separately.*

A T

At, *as, at first sight.*
To Achieve, or *perform some notable Enterprize.*
An Atchievement, or *exploit; also a coat of Arms fully set out.*
Atheism, *the Opinion of*
An Atheist, *who denies the Being of a God.*
Atheistical, *belonging to such an Opinion*
A-thwart, or *a-cross.*
An Atome, *a thing so small that it can't be divided, as a mote in the Sun,* &c.
To Atone, *appease*, or *reconcile.*
An Atonement,
Atriplex, *an herb.*
To Attach, or *seize on one's body*, or *goods.*
An Attachment.
To Attack, or *set upon.*
An Attack, or *onset.*
To attain to, *come to*, or *get.*
An Attainment.
Attaint, *a Term us'd by Farriers, to denote a hurt in a horses Leg.*
To Attaint, or *convict one of a crime, to corrupt the blood, as high Treason does.*
A Bill of Attainder.
Attainture, or *corruption of blood.*

To attempt, *enterprize*, or *endeavour.*
An Attempt, or *effort.*
An Attempter.
To attend, *to hearken to, to wait for*, or *upon.*
Attendance, *service, waiting for one*, or *a Train of*
Attendants, *servants*, or *followers.*
Attention, *heed, carefulness*, or *diligence.*
Attentive, *heedfull*, or *diligently hearkning.*
Attentiveness.
To Attest, or *witness.*
An Attestation.
Attire, or *Womens apparel, and furniture.*
Attired, or *dress'd.*
The Attires, or *large horns of a Stag in Heraldry.*
An Attorney, *at Law.*
The King's Attorney-General.
To attract, *draw to one's self*, or *entice.*
Attraction.
Attractive.
Bravely attraped, or *well accoutred.*
To attribute, *ascribe, impute; or give to.*
The Divine Attributes.
An Attribution, *assignment*, or *delivery.*
Attrition *(in Divinity) an imperfect contrition*, or *sorrow for Sin.*

A V

To Avail, *profit*, or *conduce to.*
Availableness.
Of little Availment.
Avarice, or *covetousness.*
Auburn, *dark* or *brown coloured.*
An Auction, or *publick Sale, in which the highest bidder is the buyer.*
Audacious, or *over-bold.*
Audaciousness, or *audacity.*
Audible, *that may be heard.*

Audience, *hearing, or being heard; also the company of Hearers.*
The Audience *of an Ambassador.*
Audience-Court, *belonging to the Archbishop of* Canterbury.
An Audit *of accounts in a Chapter.*
To audit, or *examine an account.*
An Auditor, *an hearer*, or *a settler of accounts.*
An Auditor *of the Exchequer.*
An Auditory, *an assembly of Hearers*, or *the hearing-place.*
An Ave-Mary, or *prayer to the Virgin* Mary.
Avenage, *a certain quantity of Oats given to a Landlord, for some other Duties.*
An Avener, *an Officer that provides Oats for the King's Horses.*
To avenge, or *be avenged on one.*
An Avenger.
Avens, *an herb.*
An Avenue, or *passage lying open to a place.*
An Averment. *from*
To aver, *assert*, or *avouch.*
Averse, *that abhors*, or *dislikes a thing.*
Averseness, or *aversion.*
To avert, or *turn aside.*
An Avery, *the place where Oats* or *provender is kept for the King's Horses.*
An Auff, or *elf; a fool*, or *sot.*
An Auger, or *wimble, a boring tool.*
To augment, *encrease, enlarg* or *improve.*
An Augmentation.
An Augmenter.
An Augur, or *Roman Soothsayer.*
Augury, or *divination by birds.*

August, *venerable*, or *majestick*; as *an august Assembly*.
August, *the Month so called*.
An Aviary, or *large Bird-Cage*.
Aukward, *untoward*, or *unhandy*.
Aukwardness.
An Aumbry, or *Cupboard to keep victuals in*; also, *the place where the Almoner lives*.
An Aume of *Rhenish Wine*, *containing* 40 *Gallons*.
An Aunt, *a Father's* or *Mother's sister*.
An Avocation, *let*, or *hindrance*.
To avoid, *eschew*, or *shun*.
An Avoidance, *a Spiritual living become void*.
An Avoider.
Avoir-du-pois, *or* averdupois-*weight*, i. e. *to have full weight*; *allowing* 16 *Ounces to the pound*.
To avouch, *to affirm resolutely*, *or to pass one's word for another*.
An Avoucher.
To avow, or *justify*.
An Avowee, *he that has the right of Advowson*, or *presenting to a Benefice, in his own Name*.
An Avowry, *or* Advowry; *the justifying of an Act already done*; *as of distress for Rent*, &c.
Auricular, *belonging to the ear*; *as auricular Confession made to a Priest*.
Auspicious, or *lucky*.
Austere, *harsh*, *crabbed*, *stern*, or *severe*.
Austereness, *or* austerity.
Authentical, *or* authentick, *of good authority*, *original*, or *valid*.
An Author, *maker*, *contriver*, or *ring-leader*.
Authoritative, *done*, or *exerted by*
Authority, *power*, *privilege*, or *preheminence*.
To authorize, or *give power to*.
Autumnal, *belonging to* Autumn, *the season for Harvest and Vintage*.
Auxiliary, *helpful*, *that comes to aid*, *succour*, or *assist*.
The auxiliary *forces*, or Auxiliaries.

A W

Aw, or *fear*.
To aw, *or keep in* aw.
Awake, *or* awaked.
To awake, *out of sleep*.
An Awaker.
An Award, *or* Judgement, *chiefly in arbitration*.
To award, *or judge to*.
Aware of, *perceiving before-hand*, or *fore-seeing*.
Away, as, *to get away*.
Awful, *to be feared*, *reverend*, or *terrible*.
Awfulness.
An Awl, *a Shoomaker's Tool*.
An Awning, *a piece of Tarpawling*, or *Canvas-sail spread over the deck of a Ship*, &c. or *a shelter from the injury of the Weather*.
Awry, *crooked*, or *inclining on one side*.

AX AY AZ

An Ax, or *hatchet*.
A Battel-ax, or *pole-ax*.
A Chip-ax.
A Pick-ax.
Ax-vetch, or ax-wort, } *herbs*.
Ax-weed, } *herbs*.
An Axiom, *a maxime principle*, or *general Rule of any Art*, or *Science*.
An Axle-tree, *of a Coach*, *Waggon*, *Cart*, &c.
An Axle-pin.
Ay, *or* Yes.
Azure, *sky-coloured*, or *blew*.
The Azure-stone.

B A

BAbble, *or* silly talk.
To babble, *or* prate.
A Babe, *or* Infant.
A Baboon, *a kind of Ape*.
A Bacheler, *or* Bachelour a single-man.
A Bacheler of Arts.
Bacheler's-button, *an herb*.
Bachelourship.
Back, *as to give back*, or *recoil*.
A Back-blow, *or* back-stroak.
The Back-bone.
A Back-door.
A Back-friend.
A Back *of a Man Beast*, &c.
A Back-swanked Horse.
To Back an Horse.
To Back, *abet*, or *assist*.
To Backbite, or *slander one behind his back*.
A Backbiter.
Backsliding, or *revolting*.
Backward, or Backwards.
Backwardness, *slowness*, or *aversion*.
Bacon, *as a flitch of bacon*.
Bad, *evil*, or *naught*.
A Badge, *cognizance*, or *token*.
A Badger, *a beast*.
A Badger, or *engrosser of Corn*.
Badness, or *naughtiness*.
To baffle, *delude*, *disappoint*, or *confute*.
A Baffler.
A Bag, or *sack*.
A Cloak-bag.
A Bag-pipe.
A Bag-pudding.
Bag, and baggage.
A Baggage, or *Soldier's punk*.

A Bagnio, or *Sweating-house.*
Bail, or *security for one's personal appearance.*
To Bail *one.*
A Bailiff, or *overseer of Lands.*
A Bailiff, or *Serjeant to arrest.*
A Bailliwick, *the Jurisdiction of a Bailiff.*
A Bait *for fish.* &c.
To Bait a hook.
To bait, or *refresh himself at an Inn.*
To bait *a Bear, Bull,* &c.
The Hawk baits, or *shakes her wings.*
Baize, *a sort of stuff.*
To Bake *in an Oven.*
A Bake-house.
A Baker.
A Bisket-baker.
A Sugar-baker.
Baker-legg'd, *or* bandy-legg'd.
A Baking-pan.
A Balass, *a kind of Ruby.*
A Balcony *of a House.*
Bald, *bare,* or *thin.*
A Bald Buzzard, *a bird.*
Baldmony, *an herb.*
Balderdash, *a confused mixture.*
Baldness, *(from bald.)*
A Bale, or *pack of Cloth. Silk, Books,* &c.
A Balk, or *great beam.*
A Balk, or *furrow.*
To balk, *pass by, neglect,* or *discourage.*
Balkers, or *conders, that shew the passage of Herrings.*
A Ball, *(in all senses.)*
A Fire-ball.
A Foot-ball.
A Snow-ball.
A Tennis-ball.
A Wash-ball.
A Ballad, or *song, sung up and down the streets.*
A Ballance, *a pair of Scales;* or *even weight.*
To ballance, or *even an Account.*

A Ballance-wheel.
Ballast, *for Ships.*
Ballisters, or *rails.*
To ballister, or *enclose with ballisters.*
Balloting, *an Election by casting lots with Balls, as at* Venice.
Balm, }
Balm-gentle, } *herbs.*
Assyrian-balm, }
The Balm-tree.
Balsam, *a medicinal composition.*
Balsam-mint, *an herb.*
Balsamick.
A Band *(in several senses)*
A Head-band, for a book.
A Hat-band.
Banditi, or *Italian Robbers.*
A Bandoe, or *Widow's peak.*
Bandoleers *to hold Gunpowder.*
A Bandy, or *crooked stick to strike a Ball with.*
To bandy *at Tennis;* or *to make a party.*
Bandy-legg'd.
Bane, *poison,* or *mischief.*
Rats-bane, *or* Arsenick.
Wolf-bane, }
Bane-berry, } *herbs.*
Bane-wort, }
The Banes *of Matrimony.*
A Bang, or *blow.*
To bang, or *beat one.*
Bangle-ear'd
To banish, or *confine to a place at a distance.*
Banishment, *or* Exile.
A Bank *(in all senses.)*
Bank-cresses, *an herb.*
A Banker, *that deals in Money.*
A Bankrupt, or *broken Merchant.*
To bann, or *curse.*
A Banner, or *standard.*
A Knight-banneret, *made in the field.*
A Banquet, or *entertainment.*
To Banquet, or *feast.*
A Banqueting-house.

A Banstickle, or *stickle-back, a fish.*
To banter, *amuse,* or *fool one.*
A Banterer.
Baptism, or *the Sacrament of Baptism.*
Baptismal.
Baptist, *as St.* John *Baptist.*
To Baptize, or *christen.*
A Bar, *and to* bar *(in all senses.)*
To barb, or *trim.*
A Barber.
St Barbara's *herb.*
Barbarians, or *barbarous People.*
A Barbarism, *in Speech.*
Barbarity, or *cruelty.*
Barbarous, *uncouth, cruel,* or *inhumane.*
Barbarousness.
A Barbary-Horse.
A Barbel, *a Fish.*
A Barbed arrow.
A Barber *(from to barb.)*
A Barberry, *a fruit.*
The Barbles, *a disease in Cattel.*
Barbs, *for Horses.*
A Bard, or *old British Poet.*
To bard, *or* beard *Wooll.*
Bare, or *naked.*
To bare, or *make bare.*
Thread-bare.
Bare-faced.
Bare-footed.
Bare-headed.
Bareness.
A Bargain, or *contract.*
To Bargain, or make a bargain.
A Barge, *a kind of boat.*
A Barge-man.
A Bark, or *little ship.*
The bark, or *rind of a Tree.*
To bark, or *pill Trees.*
To bark *like a Dog,* or *Fox.*
A Barker *of Trees.*
Barley, *a sort of Grain.*
Great-barley, or *Beer-barley.*

A Barley-corn, *in measure.*
Barm, or *yest.*
A Barn, or *granary.*
The Barn-owl.
A Barnacle, or *brake for a Horse's nose; also a kind of bird.*
A Baron, *a noble-man.*
A Baron *of the Exchequer.*
The Lord chief Baron.
A Baroness, *or* Baron's Lady.
A Baronet.
A Knight and Baronet.
A Barony, or *Lordship.*
Barracan, *a sort of stuff.*
A Barrel *of ale, beer,* &c.
The Barrel of a Gun.
To barrel up, or *put into a barrel.*
Barrel-cod.
Barren, or *unfruitful.*
Barrenness.
Barren, *or* creeping Ivy.
Barren-weed.
A Barretor, or *common Wrangler.*
A Barricado, *a kind of warlike defence, made of barrels fill'd with Earth,* &c.
To Barricado, or *block up.*
A Barrister, or *Lawyer admitted to plead at Bar.*
A Barrow *to carry out dung,* &c.
A Hand-barrow.
A Wheel-barrow.
Barrow-grease.
A Barrow-hog.
Barter, or *traffick.*
To barter, or *exchange one Commodity for another.*
Base, *mean, vile,* or *counterfeit.*
Base-born, or bastardly.
A Base, or *Sea-wolf.*
The base, or *pedestal of a pillar.*
Baseness.
Bashful, *shame-fac'd, demure,* or *modest.*
Bashfulness.
Basil, *or* sweet-basil, *an herb.*
Cow-basil.
Stone-basil.
A Basilisk, *or Cockatrice.*
Basinets, *an herb.*
The Basis, or *base of a Pillar.*
The Bases *of a Bed.*
To bask, or *warm himself in the Sun.*
A Basket.
A Bread-Basket.
A Hand-basket.
A Table-basket.
A Wicker-basket.
A Basket-hilt.
A Basket-maker.
A Bason, *to wash one's hands* in.
Venus-bason, or *fuller's teazel, an herb.*
The Bass, *in Musick.*
A Bass-viol.
The Thorough-bass.
A Bass, or *bassock, to kneel upon.*
A Bassa, *or* Basha, *a Turkish Commander.*
Baste, or *the bark of twigs.*
A Basten-rope.
To baste, *or beat one.*
To baste *meat.*
A Basting-ladle.
A Bastard, or *base-born person.*
To bastardize, *corrupt,* or *spoil.*
Bastardy.
A Bastinado, *a banging,* or *cudgelling.*
To bastinado *one,* or *give him the bastinado.*
A Bastion, or *bulwark.*
A Baston, *an Officer of the Fleet, who attends the Court with a red staff.*
A Bat, or *rere-mouse.*
A Bat, or *club.*
A Brick-bat.
A Whorle-bat.
A Batch *of Bread.*
A Batcheler, *or* Bacheler.
Bate, or *strife.*
To make bate.
To bate, or *abate of the price.*
To bate, or *flutter, as a Hawk does.*
A Bath, *or* bain *to wash in.*
The Bath-fly.
A Bath-keeper.
To bathe, *wash,* or *soak.*
A Bathing-tub.
A Batoon, or *short club.*
In Battalia, or *battel-aray.*
A Battalion, *a body of Infantry.*
A Battel, battle, or *fight.*
A Battel-ax.
To batten, or *roll as a Sow does, in her own dung.*
Batter, *for pancakes, puddings,* &c.
To batter, *bruise,* or *beat down.*
A Battery, *of Ordinance.*
An action for assault and battery.
A Batting-staff, *used by Laundresses.*
To battle, or *score for diet in a College-book* at Oxford.
A Battler *(in such a sense)*
A Battledore, *to play at Shittlecock with.*
The Battlements *of a building.*
Bavins, or *brush-wood.*
A Bawble, or *toy.*
A Bawd, *pander,* or *procurer of whores.*
Bawdry, or *ribaldry.*
Bawdy, *obscene,* or *filthy.*
A Bawdy-house.
To bawl, or *cry out.*
A Bawler.
A Bay, or *road for Ships.*
To hold one at a Bay.
To Bay, or *bleet like a Lamb.*
The Bay-colour.
A Bay-tree.
A dwarf Bay-tree, *or* wild-Bay Tree.
The Cherry-Bay Tree.
The Rose-bay Tree.
Bayz, *or* Baiz, *a kind of Stuff.*

B E

To be, or *exist.*
A Beach, *a shore,* or *point*

point of Land jutting into the Sea.
A Beach, *a kind of shrub.*
A Beacon, *or signal by fire set up on high, to give notice of an Invasion, &c.*
Beaconage; *money for the maintenance of a beacon.*
A Bead *of a Necklace, &c.*
A Glass-bead.
Bead-cuffs.
The Bead-tree, *with white berries.*
A Beadle; *an Officer in a Corporation, Parish, Company, &c.*
A Beagle, *a sort of hunting-dog.*
A Beak *of a Bird,* or *Ship.*
The beak-head *of a Ship.*
A Beaker, *a kind of Cup.*
A Beam, *(in all senses.)*
The Beam-antlers, *of a Stag.*
The Beam-fish, *like a Pike, a most cruel enemy to Mankind.*
A Draw-beam.
The Sun-beams.
The Horn-beam-tree.
The white Beam-tree. *or* Cumberland Haw-thorn.
A Bean, *a kind of pulse.*
The French-bean, or Kidney-bean.
The Scarlet-bean.
The Bean-caper, *a fruit.*
Bean-straw, or *holm.*
The Bean-tree.
Bean-trefoil, *an herb.*
A Bear, *a wild beast.*
A Sea-bear, *a shell-fish.*
Bears-breach, Bears-ears, Bears-foot, Bears-garlick, Bears-wort, } *herbs.*
To bear. *carry, suffer, bring forth, support, &c.*
A Bearer.
A Beard, *of Man, or beast.*
To beard, or *affront one.*
To beard, or bard *Wooll.*
Bearded, *that has a beard*
The bearded-creeper, *an herb.*
Beardless, *without a beard*
A Beast, or *brute-beast.*
Beastliness.
Beastly, *brutish,* or *filthy.*
The Beat *of a Drum.*
To beat, *strike, knock,* or *bang.*
Beaten.
A Beater, or *rammer.*
Beatifick, *that makes blessed.*
Beatitude, or *blessedness.*
A Beau, *Fop,* or *finical fellow.*
A Beaver, *a beast.*
A Beaver-hat.
Beauteous, or beautiful.
Beautifulness.
To beautify, or *adorn.*
Beauty, or *comliness.*
To becalm, or *cause a calm.*
Because, *because of.*
Beccafigo, *a bird like a Wheat-ear.*
A Beck, *nod,* or *sign.*
To becken, or *make a sign.*
To become, or *beseem.*
Becomingness.
A Bed, *to lie in.*
To bed *with one.*
A Bride-bed.
A Feather-bed.
A Flock-bed.
A Pallet-bed.
A Press-bed.
A Settle-bed.
A Straw-bed.
A Table-bed.
A Truckle-bed.
A Trundle-bed.
A Bedfellow.
A Bed-stead.
Beds-foot, *an herb.*
Bed-straw, *an herb.*
To bedaggle, or *dirty the skirts of one's cloaths.*
To bedew, or *wet with dew.*
Bedlam, or Bethlem, *a place where mad people are kept.*
A Bedlam, or *mad person.*
Bed-rid, *that keeps his bed.*
A Bee, *an insect.*
A Bumble-bee, *or* Humble-bee.
A Drone-bee.
A Gad-bee.
A Bee-eater, *a bird.*
Bee-flower, Bees-nest, Bee-wort, } *herbs.*
A Beech-tree.
Beech-mast.
Beechen, *or made of* beech-wood.
Beef, *the flesh of an Ox,* or *Cow.*
Martlemas-beef.
Beer, or *drink.*
A Beesom, or *Broom.*
Beesom-weed.
Beastings, *or* Brestlings, *the first milk of a Cow after calving.*
Beet, *an herb; either white,* or *red.*
A Beetle, *an insect.*
The Dung-Beetle.
The knobb'd horned Beetle.
The Beetle-fish.
A Beetle, or *hammer.*
Beetle-brow'd.
Beetle-headed.
To befal, or *happen.*
Befitting, or *convenient.*
To befool, or *mock one.*
Before, *long before.*
Before-hand, in the World.
To befriend *one,* or *treat him as a friend.*
To beg, *humbly entreat,* or *earnestly desire.*
A Begger.
To begger, or *reduce to beggery.*
Beggerliness.
Beggery, or *extreme poverty.*
To beget, *engender,* or *procure.*
A Begetter.
To begin, or *commence.*
A Beginner.
A Beglerbeg (i. e. *lord of lords) a Turkish Governour of a Province.*
Begotten *(from to beget.)*

To beguile, or *deceive.*
A Beguiler.
Begun, (*from to begin.*)
In my behalf, *&c.*
To behave, or *demean himself.*
Behaviour.
To behead, or *cut off one's head.*
Beheld (*from to behold.*)
Behind, *as, there is so much behind.*
Behind-hand in the world
To behold, *look upon*, or *view.*
Beholden, beholding, or *oblig'd to one.*
A Beholder.
Beholdingness.
Behoof, *interest, advantage*, or *convenience.*
Behovefull.
It behoves.
A Being, or *existence.*
To belabour, or *belam one soundly.*
Belagged, or *left behind.*
Belated, *detain'd till it grows late.*
A Belch.
To belch, or *break wind upwards.*
A Belcher.
A Beldame, or *old Woman.*
A Belfry, *to hang Bells in*
Belief, *trust*, or *credit.*
The Belief, or *Apostles-Creed.*
To believe, *think, suppose*, or *confide in.*
A Believer.
Belike, or *as it seems.*
A Bell, (*in several senses*)
An Alarum-bell.
Canterbury bells, *a flower*
Hedge-bells, *a flower.*
A Low-bell.
A Passing-bell.
A Bell-bit, *for a Horse.*
Bell-flowers, *or* blew bells.
A Bell-founder.
A Bell-weather Sheep.
To bellow, *like an Ox*, or *Cow.*
A pair of Bellows.
Bellied, or *full-bellied.*
Great-bellied, *&c.*
A Belly, or *paunch.*
A Gore-belly, or paunch-belly.
To belong, or *appertain to*
Beloved, *dearly beloved.*
Below, or *beneath.*
A Belt.
A Shoulder-belt.
A Waste-belt.
A Belt-maker.
To bely, *to tell lyes of*, or *to slander one.*
To bemire, *dawb*, or *defile.*
To bemoan, *lament*, or *condole.*
Ben, *a kind of aromatick Nut.*
A Bench *to sit on.*
A Bench of Justice.
The King's-bench.
A Bencher, or *eminent Lawyer.*
The Benchers *in a Barge*, or *Ship.*
A Bend, or *fold.*
To bend, *crook*, or *bow.*
Bendwith, *a plant.*
Beneath, or *below.*
A Benediction, or *blessing.*
A Benefactor, *he that does one a good turn.*
Benefacture, *or* benefaction.
A Benefice, or *Church-living.*
Beneficence, or *doing of good turns.*
Beneficial, *profitable*, or *advantageous.*
A Benefit, *a good turn, advantage*, or *profit.*
To benefit, *to profit one*, or *profit by him.*
Benevolence, or *good-will.*
Benjamin, *or* benzoin, *a Gum; also an herb.*
Benighted, or *overtaken with Night.*
Benign, *kind*, or *courteous.*
Benignity.
Bennet, *an herb.*
Bent, or *bow'd* (*from to* bend.)
A Bent, or *rush.*
The bent-grass.
To benum, or *stupify.*
Benummedness.
To bepiss, or *piss upon.*
To bequeath, or *leave by Will.*
To beray, *defile*, or *fill with ordure.*
To bereave, or *deprive.*
Bereft, *or* bereaved.
A Bergamot-pear.
A Bergander, *a fowl.*
A Berry.
A Bay-berry.
A Bill-berry.
A Black-berry, *or* bramble-berry.
An Elder-berry.
A Goose-berry.
A Juniper-berry.
An Ivy-berry.
One-berry, or *the herb true-love.*
A Rasberry, or *raspis-berry.*
A Service-berry.
A Strawberry.
A White-thorn berry.
Bertram, or *wild-pellitory, an herb.*
A Beryl, *a precious stone.*
To beseech, or *entreat.*
Beseeming, or *becoming.*
To beset, or *surround.*
To beshit, or *dawb with ordure.*
Beside, *or* besides.
To besige, or *lay siege to a Town.*
A Besieger.
To besmear, *anoint*, or *dawb over.*
Besmoaked, or *befit with smoak.*
Besmutted, or *defil'd with smut.*
To besot, or *infatuate.*
Besought (*from to* beseech.)
To bespatter, *dawb, slander*, or *defame.*
To bespawl, or *defile with spittle.*

To

To bespeak, (*in several senses.*)
Bespeckled, or *marked with specks.*
To bespew, or *spew upon.*
To bespit or *bespawl.*
Bespoke, (*from to* bespeak.)
To bespot, or *defile with spots.*
To besprinkle, or *sprinkle upon.*
Best, *beyond compare.*
To bestead *one*, or *stand his friend.*
Bestial, or *beastly.*
To Bestink, or *fill with stink.*
To bestir *himself*, or *take a great deal of pains.*
To bestow, *give*, or *lay out.*
To bestride, or *sit a-stride.*
A Bet, or *stake.*
To bet, *to wager*, or *lay down a stake.*
A Better.
To betake, or *apply himself to.*
To bethink, *to muse upon*, or *to recollect.*
To betide, or *happen.*
Betimes, or *very early.*
To betoken, or *fore-shew.*
Betony, *an herb.*
Water-betony.
Wild running Betony.
To betray, *discover*, or *deliver up.*
A Betrayer,
To betroth *one for a Wife.*
Better, or *of more worth.*
To better, or *make better.*
Between, or betwixt.
A Bever, or *small collation between meals.*
The Bever *of an helmet.*
Beverage, *a sort of drink.*
A Bevy, or *flock of Quails* &c.
To bewail, or *lament.*
To beware, or *take heed.*
Bewilder'd, *that has a wild look.*
To bewitch, or *inchant.*
To bewray, or *discover a secret.*
To bewray, or *foul his hose.*
Beyond, or *on the farther side.*
The Bezel, or bezil *of a Ring.*
A Bezantler, *the second branch of a Stag's horn.*
Bezoar, *a sort of precious stone.*
To bezzle, or *tipple.*

BI

The Bias *of a bowl*, &c.
To bias, or *incline one to.*
A Bib, or *slabbering-bib, for a Child.*
To bib, or *sip.*
A Bibber.
A Wine-bibber.
The Bible, or *books of Holy Scripture.*
To bicker, *quarrel*, or *strive with.*
A Bickerer.
To bid, *proffer*, *invite*, *enjoin*, or *proclaim.*
Bidden.
A Bidder.
Biennial, or *of two years continuance.*
A Bier, or bear *to carry a Corps on.*
Bifoil, or *Tway-blade, an herb.*
Big, or *great.*
Bigamy, *the having two Wives at once.*
A Biggin, or *coif, for a Child.*
Bigness, *greatness*, or *largeness.*
A Bigot, or *superstitious person.*
Bigotted, *grown a Bigot.*
A Bilander, or *small coasting Vessel.*
The Bilboes, *a sort of punishment at Sea.*
A Bile, or *sore.*
A Bilberry, *a fruit.*
Bilk, *at cribbage.*
Bilked, or *disappointed.*
A Bill (*in all senses.*)
To bill, *as Pigeons do.*
Cranes-bill, *an herb.*
A Billet, *of Wood.*
A Billet, or *ticket for Soldiers quarters.*
Billiards, *a sort of game.*
A Billiard-ball.
A Billiard-stick.
A Billiard-table.
A Billow, or *great wave.*
A Bind of Eels, or *skins.*
To bind, (*in all senses.*)
Wood-bind, *a shrub.*
A Binder.
A Book-binder.
Bind-weed, or *withy-wind.*
Sea-bind-weed.
A Birch-tree.
The Birch-cock.
Birchen, or *made of birch.*
A Bird, or *fowl.*
A Bird-cage.
A Bird-call.
Bird-lime.
A Birder, or *fowler.*
Birds-cherry, Birds-eye, Birds-foot, Birds-nest, Birds-tares, Birds-tongue, } *herbs.*
Birth, *nativity*, *parentage*, or *extraction.*
The After-birth.
A Birth-day.
Birth-right.
Birth-wort, *an herb.*
A Bishop, *of a Diocess.*
An Arch-bishop.
A Bishoprick.
Bishops-leaves, *an herb.*
Bishops-weed, *an herb.*
A Bisket.
A Sea-bisket.
A Bissextile, or *leap-year.*
Bistort, or *snake-weed.*
Bit (*from to bite*) *as he was bit by a Snake.*
A Bit *of bread*, &c.
The bit *of a Bridle.*
A Bitch, or *female Dog.*
A Bitch-fox.
To bite, or *gnaw.*
Bitten, or bit.
Bitter *of taste.*
Bitter-sweet, *an herb.*
Bitter-wort, *an herb.*
A Bittern, *a bird.*
Bitterness, (*from bitter.*)

Bit-

Bitumen, *a kind of clay, or ſlime.*
Bituminous.
Bixwort, *an herb.*

B L

A Blab, or *long-tongue.*
To blab, or *prate.*
Black, *dark, duſk,* &c.
Coal-black.
Lamp-black.
Shoomakers-black.
The black Art.
A Black-berry.
A Black-bird, or *Ouzel.*
A Black-cap, *a bird.*
A Black-moor.
The Uſher of the Black-rod.
A Black-ſmith.
A Black-tail, *a fiſh.*
The Black-vine, *an herb.*
Black-wheat, *an herb.*
To blacken, or *make black.*
Blackiſh, or *ſomewhat black.*
Blackneſs.
A Bladder.
The Gall-bladder.
The Bladder-nut.
A Blade (*in ſeveral ſenſes*)
The Shoulder-blade.
One-blade, } *herbs.*
Twy-blade, }
A pair of yarn-winding Blades.
A Blain, *boil,* or *ulcer.*
Blame, or *fault.*
To blame, *find fault,* or *cenſure.*
Blameable, or *blame-worthy.*
Blameleſs, or *faultleſs.*
A Blamer.
To blanch, or *whiten.*
To blanch, or *take off the hull of almonds, beans,* &c.
To blandiſh, or *ſooth up.*
Blandiſhment.
Blank, *pale, wan,* or *out of countenance.*
A Blank *in a Lottery,* or *at Dice.*
A Blanket *for a bed.*

A Blanquet-pear.
To blare, or *bellow;* or *to ſweal, as a candle does.*
To blaſpheme, or *ſpeak evil of.*
A Blaſphemer.
Blaſphemy.
A Blaſt, or *puff of wind.*
To blaſt, *as the wind,* or *lightning does.*
A Blay, *a fiſh.*
The Blaze *of fire.*
To blaze, or *flame up.*
To blaze abroad, or *divulge.*
A Blazer *of fame abroad.*
A Blazing-ſtar.
To blazon *a coat of arms.*
To blazon, or *ſet out.*
Blazonry, or *the Art of Heraldry.*
A Blea, or bleak, *a fiſh.*
To bleach, or *whiten in the Sun.*
A Bleacher *of cloths.*
Bleak, *cold,* or *pale.*
The Bleak-fiſh.
Bleakneſs.
Blearedneſs, *of eyes.*
Blear-eyed, *that has wateriſh eyes.*
To bleat, *like a Sheep,* or *Goat.*
To bleed, or *run with blood.*
A Blemiſh, or *ſpot.*
To blemiſh, or *ſtain one's reputation.*
Blemiſhes, *marks where the Deer has paſs'd in hunting.*
To bleſs, or *make happy.*
Bleſſedneſs.
Blew, (*from to blow*) *as the wind blew.*
Blew, or *azure colour.*
Blew-bottle, *a flower,*
Blew-mantle, *one of the Purſuivants at Arms.*
The Blew Shark, *a fiſh.*
Blewiſh, or *ſomewhat blew.*
A Blight, or *blaſt.*
Blighted, *blaſted,* or *decayed.*

Blind, or *void of ſight.*
To blind *one.*
Purblind, or *pore-blind.*
Sand-blind, or *moon-blind.*
Blindfold.
To blindfold, or *hood-wink.*
Blindmans-buff, *a play.*
Blindneſs.
Blind-nettle, *an herb.*
A Blind-worm.
To blink, or *twinkle with the eyes.*
A Blinkard.
Blinds, *boughs,* &c. *caſt in the Deers way.*
Bliſs, or *happineſs.*
Bliſsfull.
To bliſſom, or *tup, as a Ram does the Ewe,*
A Bliſter, *blane,* or *wheal.*
To bliſter, or *draw bliſters.*
A Bliſter-fly.
Blite, *a kind of flower.*
Blithe, *merry,* or *jocund.*
Blitheneſs, or blithſomneſs.
A bloach, or bloch.
Blob-cheeked.
A Block, or *ſtem of a Tree.*
To block up, or *beſiege.*
A Blockade,
A Block-head, or *ſtupid fellow.*
A Block-houſe, or *fort.*
Blockiſh, or *ſtupid.*
Blockiſhneſs.
Blood, or bloud.
A Bloom, *and to* bloom.
Bloomy, or *thick with bloſſoms.*
A Bloſſom, or *flower of a Tree.*
To bloſſom, or *put forth bloſſoms.*
A Blot, or *blur.*
To blot, or *blot out.*
A Blotch, or *wheel.*
To blote, *to ſwell;* or *to dry in the ſmoak.*
Bloted *Herrings.*
Bloud, *one of the Humours*

mours of the body.
To bloud, *to let bloud*, or *to fill with bloud.*
A Bloud-hound.
Bloud-shed, or *slaughter.*
Bloud-shot, *in the eyes.*
A Bloud-sucker, or *horse-leech.*
A Bloud-stripe.
A Bloud-stone.
Bloud-strange, *an herb.*
Bloud-thirsty.
Bloud-warm, or *luke-warm.*
Bloud-wort, *an herb.*
A Blouding, or *bloud-pudding.*
Bloudless.
Bloudy, *covered with bloud*, or *cruel.*
Bloudy-minded.
A Blow, or *stroke.*
To blow, (*in several senses.*)
A Blower.
Blown.
A Blubber, *a fish.*
Blubber, or *whale-fat.*
To blubber, *with weeping.*
To blunder, *dote, falter*, or *mistake.*
A Blunderbuss, *a sort of gun.*
Blunt, *dull*, or *rude.*
To blunt, or *make blunt.*
Bluntish.
Bluntness.
A Blur.
To blur, or *blot.*
To blurt *out a word.*
A Blush, *and* to blush.
To bluster, *as the Wind does.*

B O

A Boar, or *male Hog.*
A Boar-pig.
Boarish, or *boggish.*
A Board, or *plank.*
A Chess-board.
To board, (*in several senses.*)
A Boarder, *at another's table.*
To boast, *brag*, or *vaunt.*
A Boaster.
A Boat.
A Ferry-boat.
A Fly-boat.
A Passage-boat.
A Boatswain *of a Ship.*
A Bob, or *mock.*
To bob, *strike*, or *chouse.*
Bob-tailed.
A Bobbin, *to make lace with.*
To bode, or *presage.*
Bodied, *as* big-bodied, &c.
A pair of Bodies.
Bodiless, *without a body.*
Bodily, *belonging to the body.*
A Bodkin.
A Body (*in all senses.*)
A Bog, or *quagmire.*
A Bog-house.
To boggle, *falter*, or *scruple.*
Boggy, or *full of bogs.*
A Boil, bile, or *sore.*
To boil, or *seeth.*
A Boilary *of Salt.*
A Boiler, or *caldron.*
Boisterous, *stormy*, or *fierce.*
Boisterousness.
Bolbonach, or *saten-flower*
Bold, *hardy, stout*, or *saucy.*
Boldness.
A Boll *of Flax.*
A Bolster *for a bed.*
The Bolster *of a saddle.*
To bolster *up*, or *buoy up.*
A Bolt, *and to* bolt (*in several senses.*)
A Thunder-bolt.
Bolts, *an herb.*
The Bolt-sprit *mast of a Ship.*
A Bolus *of physick.*
A Bomb, *a sort of bullet shot out of a Mortar-piece.*
To bombard *a place*, or *shoot Bombs into it.*
Bombasine, *a kind of stuff*
Bumbast, *a sort of Cotton*, or *Fustian.*
Bombast, *trumpery*, or *affected Language.*
To bombast, or *stuff with* bombast, or *to hang out.*
A Bombastick *style.*
A Bond, band, or *tye.*
A Bond, or *obligatory writing.*
A Bond-man, or Bond-slave.
A Bond-woman.
Bondage, or *slavery.*
A Bone.
To bone, or *take out the bones.*
The Back-bone.
The Hip-bone, or *buckle-bone.*
The Jaw-bone, or *cheek-bone.*
The Shin-bone.
Boneless, or *without bones*,
A Bonefire.
A Bongrace, *to keep from sun-burning.*
A Bonito, *a kind of fish.*
A Bonnet, or *cap.*
The Bonnet, or *enlargement of a Sail.*
Bonny, *fine*, or *jolly.*
Bony, or *full of bones.*
A Booby, or *lubber.*
A Book.
A Day-book, or *journal.*
A News-book.
A Note-book.
A Pocket-book.
A Book-binder.
A Book-seller.
A Book-worm.
Bookish, or *given to Books.*
A Boon, *a request, gift*, or *good turn.*
A Boor, or *peasant.*
Boorish, or *rustical.*
A Boot, or *a pair of* boots
Boot, *profit*, or *advantage*; as *to* boot, *to no* boot.
What boots *it?*
Booted, or *having boots on.*
A Booth, *hut*, or *stall in a fair*, or *market.*
Booting, *a sort of rack, us'd in* Scotland, *by pegging on an iron-boot.*
Bootless, or *unprofitable.*
Boots, or *marsh-mary-golds.*

A

A Booty, or *prey.*
To play at bopeep.
Borage, *an herb.*
A Border, *of a country,* or *of a garment.*
To border.
A Borderer, *one that lives on the frontiers.*
I bore, or *did bear.*
The Bore *of a gun.*
To bore, or *pierce.*
The Bore-tree.
Borith, *an herb us'd by Fullers.*
Born, as, *a Child is.*
Base-born.
First-born.
Still-born, or *born dead.*
Born, or *carryed, as a burden.*
A Borough, or *Town incorporate.*
An Head-borough.
To borrow.
A Borrower.
A Bosom, *of a Person,* or *of the Sea.*
A Boss, or *stud.*
Bossed.
Botanical, *belonging to herbs.*
A Botanist, or *herbarist.*
A Botch, *patch,* or *bile,*
To botch, *piece and mend;* or *to bungle.*
A Botcher, or *mender of old cloths.*
Both, as *they are both alike.*
A Bottle.
To bottle, or *put into a bottle.*
A Glass-bottle.
A Stone-bottle.
A Sucking-bottle.
Bottle-nosed.
A Bottle *of hay.*
A Bottom, *and to* bottom *(in several senses.)*
Bottomless, *without a bottom.*
Bottomary or Bottomry, *borrowing mony upon the keel,* or *bottom of a Ship.*
The Bots, *in Horses.*
A Bough, or *branch.*
Bought *(from to buy)*

To boult, or *sift meal.*
A Boulter, or *meal-sieve.*
A Boulting-house.
A Bounce, *knock,* or *thump.*
To bounce, or *make a noise.*
Bound *(from to* bind.) *tyed,* or *obliged.*
A Bound, or *limit.*
To bound, *limit,* or *border upon.*
A Boundary, or *the bounds of a Country.*
Bounden, *as bounden duty.*
Boundless, *that has no bounds.*
To bound, or *rebound from the ground.*
A Bounding-stone.
Bountifull, *bounteous,* or *liberal.*
Bountifulness, *bounty,* or *liberality.*
A Bout, or *course.*
A Boutefeu, *incendiary,* or *make-bate.*
A Bow, *to shoot with.*
A Cross-bow.
An Ox-bow, *in a plough.*
A Rain-bow.
A Saddle-bow.
Bow-legg'd.
A Bow-bearer, *an under Officer in a Forest.*
A Bow-man, or *archer.*
A Bow-net.
A Bow-string.
The Bow *of a musical instument.*
A Bow, or *Congee.*
To bow, or *bend.*
The Bowels, or *entrails.*
To bowel, *embowel,* or *draw out the guts,* or *garbage.*
A Bower, or *arbour.*
Ladies-bower, *an herb.*
A Bowl, *to play with.*
To Bowl, or *throw a bowl.*
A Bowler.
A Bowling-alley.
A Bowling-green.
A Bowl *to drink out of.*
A Wash-bowl.
A Bowser, or *Treasurer of a College.*

A Bowyer, or *bow-maker.*
To bowse, or *drink hard.*
A Box.
A Dice-box.
A Dust-box.
A Spice-box.
A Box-maker.
The Box-tree.
A Box *on the ear.*
To box, or *cuff one.*
A Boy, or *lad.*
A School-boy.
Boyish, or *childish.*
Boyishness.

B R

To brabble, or *wrangle.*
A Brabbler.
A Brace *to fasten beams, in building;* or *to join words in Printing.*
A Brace, or *couple of Hares,* &c.
A Bracelet *for the arms.*
To brace, or *buckle.*
The Braces *of a coach,* or *Ship.*
An Archer's Bracer.
A Brack, or *flaw.*
A Bracket, *a kind of stay in timber-work.*
Brackish, or *somewhat salt.*
Brackishness.
To brag, or *boast.*
A Braggadochio, or *vain-glorious fellow.*
Bragget, or bracket, *a kind of drink.*
A Braid, or *curl.*
To braid, or *curl hair.*
A Brail, or *pannel of an Hawk.*
The Brain.
The Brain-pan.
To brain, or *dash out one's brains.*
Brain-sick.
Cock-brain'd.
Hare-brain'd.
Shittle-brain'd.
A Brake, *an instrument to dress Flax with.*
A Brake, or *snaffle for Horses.*
Brake, or *female-fern.*
To brake, *Hemp.*

A Bramble, or *brier.*
A Brambling, *a bird.*
A Branch, *of a tree,* or *candlestick.*
To branch *out,* or *spread into branches.*
A Vine-branch.
Branch-pease.
A Brancher, or *young bird that flyes from one branch to another.*
A Brand *of fire.*
A Brand, or *mark.*
To brand, or *set a mark on a malefactor.*
Brand-new, or *fire-new.*
A Brand-iron.
To brandish, or *shake a sword, &c. till it glitters.*
A Brandling, or *dew-worm.*
Brandy, *a strong liquor, distill'd from Wine-lees, &c.*
To brangle, or *brawl.*
A Brangler.
Brank, or *buck-wheat.*
Brank-ursin, or *bears-breech, an herb.*
Brann, *the refuse of meal.*
A Brant-goose, or *soland-goose.*
Brasil-wood.
Brass, *a metal.*
A Brass-pot.
Brass-work.
A Brat, or *beggerly child.*
A Bravado, *vain-glorious, daring,* or *boasting.*
Brave, *fine, gallant,* or *stout.*
A Brave, or *hector.*
To brave *it.*
Bravery, or *magnificence.*
A Brawl, or *strife in words.*
To brawl, *chide,* or *scold.*
A Brawler.
The Brawls, *a kind of dance.*
A collar of Brawn.
Brawn, or *hard flesh.*
Brawniness.
Brawny.
To bray, *bruise,* or *pound.*

To braze, or *do over with* brass.
Brazen, or *made of* brass.
To brazen *a thing out.*
Brazen-fac'd.
A Brazier.
A Breach, *rupture,* or *violation.*
Bread.
To bread *a porringer, for broth.*
Cake-bread.
Ginger-bread.
Manchet-bread.
Goats-bread, } *herbs.*
Sow-bread.
The Sweet-bread *of a breast of veal, &c.*
Bread-corn.
Breadth (*from* broad.)
A Break, *in the art of Printing.*
To break (*in all senses.*)
A Break-fast.
To break-fast, or *break one's fast.*
A Breaker.
A Bream, *a fish.*
A Sea-bream, or *gilt-head.*
A Breast.
A Breast-plate.
A Breast-work, *in fortification.*
Breath, *and to* breath.
Bred (*from to* breed.)
The Breech, or *fundament.*
Bears-breech *an herb.*
The Breech-pin *of a gun.*
A Boy newly breech'd.
Breeches, or *a pair of* breeches.
A Breed, or *race.*
To breed, or *engender;* or *to instruct.*
A Breeder.
A Breez, or *gale of wind.*
A Breez, or *Gad-fly.*
A Bret, or *burt-fish.*
Brethren, or *brothers.*
A Breviary, or *mass-book.*
A Breviate, or *short extract.*
Brevity, or *shortness.*

To brew *drink.*
A Brewer.
A Brew-house.
Brewis, or *sops in fat broth*
A Bribe.
To bribe, or *corrupt with gifts.*
A Briber.
Bribery.
A Brick.
A Brick-bat.
A Brick-kiln.
A Brick-layer.
A Brick-maker.
The Brick, or *sweet apple-tree.*
Bridal *of,* or *belonging to* *A* Bride, or *new married Woman.*
A Bride-groom.
A Bride-maid.
A Bride-man.
A Bridewell, or *house of correction.*
A Bridge.
A Draw-bridge.
A Bridge-master.
A Bridle, for a horse.
To bridle, or *curb.*
A Bridler.
Brief, or *short.*
A Brief, or *letters patent for a collection of money.*
Briefness, or *brevity.*
A Brier, or *bramble.*
Sweet-brier.
A Brigade, *three squadrons of Soldiers.*
A Brigadeer, or *Commander of a* brigade.
A Brigandine, *a coat of mail.*
A Brigantine, *a kind of Pinnace.*
Bright, or *clear.*
To brighten, or *make bright.*
Brightish.
Brightness, or *clearness.*
The Brim, or *edge of any thing.*
A Narrow-brimm'd hat.
To brim, *as a Sow does, that's ready to take Boar*
A Brimmer, or *full cup.*
Brimstone, or *sulphur.*

Brim-

Brimstone-wort, *an herb.*
Brine, *a salt pickle.*
To bring *(in all senses.)*
A Bringer.
Brinish, or *like* brine.
A Brink, or *brim.*
Briony, *an herb.*
Briony, *the white vine*; or *the wild vine.*
Brisk, *lively*, *vigorous*, or *sprightly.*
The Brisket, *of beef*, &c.
A Bristle.
To bristle, or *set up the bristles.*
Bristly, or *full of bristles.*
Bristol-ow, *nonesuch*, *a flower.*
A Bristow-stone.
Britannia, or *Great Britain*, *the Island of* England, Scotland, *and* Wales.
A Britain or *native of Great* Britain.
Britannica, *an herb.*
Brittle, or *apt to break.*
Brittleness.
A Broach, or *spit.*
To broach *(in several senses.)*
Broad, *large*, or *wide.*
Broad-awake.
Broad-brimmed.
Broad-faced.
Broad-footed.
Broad-leav'd.
Brocado, *or* broccado, *cloth of gold*, or *silver.*
A Brock, or *badger.*
A Brocket, or *buck of the second year.*
To broge, *for Eels.*
A Broil, *tumult*, or *quarrel.*
To broil *meat.*
A Broiler.
Brokage, *a broker's trade.*
Broke, or broken *(from to* break.)
Broken-bellied.
Broken-winded.
A Broker *(of all sorts.)*
A Pawn-broker.
To brome, or *bream a Ship.*

A Brooch, or *cu h of gold.*
A Brood, or *off spring.*
To brood, or *sit on* brood.
A Brood-hen.
A Brook, or *rivulet.*
Brook-lime, *an herb.*
Garden Brook-lime.
Long-leav'd brook-lime.
Broom, *a shrub.*
Butchers-broom, *an herb*
Thorny-broom, *a shrub.*
Broom-rape, *an herb.*
Broom-wort; *an herb.*
A Broom, or *besom.*
A Birch-broom.
A Flag-broom.
Broth, or *potage.*
Fish-broth.
A Brother.
A Brother-in-law.
A Foster-brother.
A Half-brother.
Twin-brothers.
A Brotherhood, or *fraternity.*
Brotherly *love.*
Brought *(from to* bring.)
The Brow *of an hill*, or *wall.*
An Eye-brow.
Beetle-brow'd.
To brow-beat *one.*
Brow-antler, *the start between the Stag's head and the beam-antler.*
Brown *of colour.*
Brown-bay.
Brownish, or *a little brown.*
Browse, or *browse-wood.*
To browse, or *feed upon shrubs*, *leaves*, &c.
A Bruise, *and to* bruise.
Bruise-wort, *an herb.*
A Bruit, or *report.*
To bruit, or *spread a report.*
A Brunt, or *onset.*
A Brush, *and to* brush.
A Brush-maker.
A Brusher.
A Brute, or *brute Beast.*
Brutish, *fierce*, or *stupid.*
Brutishness.

B U

A Bubble *of water.*
To bubble, *to rise up in bubbles*; or *to chouse.*
A Buccaneer, or *American pirate.*
A Buck, or *male deer.*
Buck-beans.
Bucks-horn, *an herb.*
Buck-mast, or *the Mast of beech.*
A Buck-rabbet, or *male-*rabbet.
Buck-thorn, *a shrub.*
Buck-weed.
Buck-wheat, or *french wheat.*
To buck *cloths.*
Buck-ashes.
Buck-lye.
A bucket *to hold water.*
A Well-bucket.
A Buckle, or *clasp.*
To buckle, *(in several senses.)*
A Shoo-buckle.
A Buckle-maker.
A Buckler, or *shield.*
Buckler-thorn, *an herb.*
Buckram, *a sort of cloth*
Buckrams, *an herb.*
Bucksome, *gamesome*, *brisk*, or *jovial.*
Bucksomeness.
A Bud, or *young sprout.*
To bud, or *bloom.*
A Rose-bud.
Budge, or *Lambs-fur.*
A Budge-bacheler.
To budge, or *stir.*
A Budget, or *pouch.*
Buff, or *buff-leather.*
A Buff-coat.
A Buffet, or *box on the ear.*
To buffet *one.*
A Buffle, or *wild Ox.*
A Buffle-head, or *dull sot*
A Buffoon, or *scurrilous jester.*
Buffoonry.
A Bug, *a noisome insect.*
A Bug, *bug-bear*, or *scare-crow.*

To

To bugger, or *commit* buggery.
A Buggerer.
Buggery, or *sodomy*.
Bugle, *a kind of glass; also a beast, and herb.*
A Bugle-horn.
Bugloss, *an herb.*
Vipers-bugloss.
Wild-bugloss.
To build, *an house*, &c.
A Builder.
A Master-builder.
Built, or *built up.*
Bulbous, *having a round head in the root.*
A Ship bulged, or *struck on a rock.*
Bulk (*in several senses.*)
To bulk out.
A Bulk-head, or *partition in a Ship.*
Bulky, or *big.*
A Bull, or *mandate of the Pope.*
A Bull, *a beast.*
A Bull-baiting.
A Bull-dog.
A Bull-finch, *a bird.*
A Bull-fly, or *Bull-bee.*
A Bull-head, *a fish.*
Bull-weed, *an herb.*
Bull-wort, *an herb.*
A Bullace, or *wild plum.*
A Bullet, or *ball for a gun.*
Bullion, *gold* or *silver uncoin'd.*
A Bullock, or *young* bull
A Bully, or Bully-rock, *a hectoring-fellow.*
A Bul-rush, or *mat-rush.*
A Bulwark, or *rampart.*
A Bumkin, or *Country-clown.*
A Bump, *swelling*, or *knock.*
To bump *out.*
A Butter-bump, or *bittern, a bird.*
A Bunch, *cluster, knob*, or *tuft.*
To bunch *out.*
Bunch-back'd.
A Bundle, or *packet.*
A Bung *of a vessel.*
To bung *up*, or *stop with* a bung.
A Bung-hole.
To bungle, *botch*, or *do a thing awkwardly.*
A Bungler.
A Bunn, or *little manchet*
The Bunt, or *hollowness of a Sail.*
A Bunt-line.
A Bunting, *a kind of lark.*
A Buoy, *a log of wood, laid to float over an anchor.*
To buoy *one up*, or *support him.*
A Burbot, or *river-weasel.*
A Burden, or *load.*
The Burden *of a song.*
To burden, or *impose a* burden.
A Burganet, *a kind of helmet.*
To burgeon, or *bud.*
A Burgess, *one that serves in Parliament for a Borough.*
A Burgher, or *Townsman.*
A Burgh-master, or Burgo-master; *a* Dutch *Magistrate.*
A Burglar, or *house-breaker.*
Burglary, or *the robbing of a house in the Night.*
A Burgomote, or *town-court.*
A Burial, or *funeral.*
A Burin, or *graving-tool*
To burl *cloth, as Fullers do.*
A Burler.
A Burling-iron.
Burlesk, *comical*, or *drolling.*
Burly, or *big.*
To burn (*in all senses.*)
Burnet, *an herb.*
Thorny-burnet, *a shrub.*
To burnish, *polish*, or *brighten; also to spread the horns, as an Hart does.*
A Burnisher.
Burnt (*from to* burn.)
Sun-burnt.
A Burr.
The Burr *of the ear.*
The Burr or *round knob of horn, next the Deer's head.*
Butter-burr, *an herb.*
Ditch-burr, or *clot-burr.*
The Burr-dock.
Burr-seed, or *burr-flag.*
A Burrel-fly.
A Burrow, or borough.
A Burrow, *covert*, or *den*
A Coney-burrow.
To burrow, or *run into the burrow.*
A Burser *of a College.*
Burst, *and to* burst, or *break.*
Burst-wort, *an herb.*
Bursten, or *broken-bellied.*
Burstenness.
A Burt, *a kind of Turbot.*
To bury *a Corps.*
A Bush *of brambles*, &c.
Silver-bush, *a shrub.*
A Tavern-bush.
A Bushel *of Corn*, &c.
Bushy, or *full of bushes.*
Business, *an affair*, or *employment.*
A Busk *for a Woman's breast.*
Buskins, or *hose coming up to the calf of the leg.*
A Buss, *and to* buss, or *kiss.*
A Bustard, *a bird.*
A Bustle, or *tumult.*
To bustle, or *make a bustle.*
But, but if, but yet.
A Butcher.
To butcher, or *murder one.*
A Butcher-bird.
Butchers-broom, *an herb*
Butchers-prick-tree.
A Butchery, or *great slaughter.*
A Butler, *an Officer that keeps the houshold-stores*
A Butt, *a vessel*, or *a mark to shoot at.*
The Butt-end *of a musket.*
To butt *at one.*

Bur-

Butter.
To butter, or *do over with* butter.
A Butter-bump, or *Bittern.*
A Butterfly, *an insect*, or *herb.*
Butter-milk.
Butter-wort, *an herb.*
Butters-bur, *an herb.*
A Buttery.
A Buttock, or *haunch.*
Great Buttock'd.
A Button *of coat*, or *of a plant.*
To button *a coat.*
Bachelors-button, *an herb*
A Button-fish.
A Buttress, *prop*, or *pillar to support a building.*
A Buttress, *a Farrier's tool, to pare horses hoofs*
A Butwin, *a bird.*
To buy, or *purchase.*
A Buyer, or *chapman.*
To buzz, or *hum*, *like Bees.*
To buzz *in one's ears.*
A Buzzard. *a fowl.*
A bald Buzzard.

BY

By, or *through.*
A By-blow, or *bastard.*
A By-end.
A By-path, or *by-way.*
A By-word.

CA

THE Cabal, of the *Jews*; *their Traditions*, or *secret Science of explaining Divine Mysteries.*
A Cabal, or *private consult.*
To cabal, or *plot privately.*
A Cabalist, *one well vers'd in the Jewish* Cabal.
Cabarick, or *barlewort, an herb.*
A Cabbage, *a plant.*
A Cole-cabbage.
The Cabbage *of a Deer's head, or that part where the horns grow.*
The Cabbage-worm.
A Cabbin, *a cottage*; or *a little room in a Ship.*
A Cabinet.
A Cabinet-maker.
A Cable-rope.
A Sheet-cable.
A Cacao-nut, *an* Indian *fruit, like a Chesnut, of which Chocolate is made.*
To cackle *like a hen.*
A Cackrel, *a fish*,
The Ox-ey'd cackrel.
The white cackrel,
The Cadbate-fly, or *Cadworm.*
A Cade *of herrings.*
A Cade-lamb, or *house-lamb, brought up by hand.*
A Cadence, or *fall of a period.*
A Cadet, or *younger brother.*
A Cadew, or *straw-worm.*
A Cag *of Sturgeon.*
A Cage, *for birds*, or *malefactors.*
To cajole, *sooth up*, *inveigle*, or *beguile.*
A Cajoler.
A Caitiff, *a miserable slave*, or *lewd wretch.*
A Cake.
To cake, *as coals do.*
A Bride-cake.
An Oat-cake.
A Spice-cake.
Cake-bread.
A Cake-seller.
A Calamary-fish,
The Calamin-stone.
Calamint, *an herb.*
Corn-calamint.
Bush, or *hoary* calamint.
Calamitous, *full of* Calamity, or *misery.*
To calcine, or *burn to a cinder.*
To calculate, or *reckon.*
A Calculation.
A Calender or *Almanack.*
A Calender *loose Trade* ...
To calender, or *set a gloss upon cloth*, &c.
A Calenture, or *burning feaver.*
A Calesh, or *little Chariot*
A Calf, *brought forth by a Cow.*
A Calf or *male Hart.*
A Sea-calf.
The Calf *of the leg.*
A Caliver, *a kind of Sea-gun.*
To calk *a Ship*, i. e. *to beat in Okum between every plank.*
A Calker.
A Call, *and to* call (*in all senses.*)
Callico-cloth, *that comes from* Calicut, *an* Indian *country.*
Callimanco, *a sort of stuff.*
A Calling, *Trade*, or *profession.*
Callous, or *brawny.*
Callow, *unfledg'd*, *not feather'd.*
Calm, or *still.*
A Calm, *at Sea.*
To calm, or *make* calm.
Calmness.
Caltrops, *irons with four spikes cast in the Enemies way, to stop their passage; also a flower.*
Land-caltrops.
Water-caltrops.
To calve, or *bring forth calves.*
Calves-foot, } *herbs.*
Calves-snout, }
Calvinism, *the Doctrine of* Calvin, *one of the first Reformers of the Church at* Geneva.
A Calvinist.
To Calumniate, *accuse falsly*, *slander*, or *detract.*
A Calumniator.
A Calumny, or *slander.*
A Camarade, or *companion.*
Cambrick, *fine linnen-cloth, made at* Cambray, *in*

in the low-Countries.
I came, or *did come.*
A Camel, *a beast.*
Cameline, } *herbs.*
Camels-hay.
A Cameleon, *a beast like a Lizard, that often changes colour; and is said to live by the air.*
A Camisado, *surprize*, or *sudden assault by Night.*
Camlet, *a kind of stuff.*
Hair-camlet.
Silk-camlet.
Worsted-camlet.
Cammock, or *rest-harrow, an herb.*
Camomil, *an herb.*
Bastard-camomil.
A Camp, or *station of an Army.*
To camp, or *pitch a Camp.*
A Campain, or Campagne, *a large plain; also the Summer expedition of an Army.*
A Campain-coat,
Camphire, *a sort of drug.*
Campions, *an herb.*
I can, or *am able.*
A Canal, or *artificial River.*
The Canaries, or *fortunate Islands, in the Atlantick Sea.*
A Canary-bird.
Canary-grass, *an herb.*
Canary-wine.
To cancel, *raze*, or *blot out.*
A Cancer, or *ulcer in a Woman's breast.*
Candid, *courteous*, or *sincere.*
A Candidate, *one that stands for an Office.*
A Candle.
A Tallow-candle.
A Watch-candle.
A Wax-candle.
Candlemass-day, *Feb.* 2. *the Purification of the Virgin* Mary.
A Candle-stick.
Candour, *integrity*, or *courteousness.*
To candy, or *crust over.*
Sugar-candy.
Candy-alexander } *herbs*
Candy-tufts.
A Cane, or Indian *reed.*
To cane, or *beat with a* cane.
A Sugar-cane.
The Canel-bone, *of the neck*, or *throat-bone.*
A Canibal, *or* Indian *maneater.*
A Canine, or *dog-like appetite.*
A Canker, or *corroding sore.*
The Canker, or *rust of iron, brass*, &c.
Cankered, *eaten with the canker*, or *rust.*
A Canker-worm.
A Cann, or *pot.*
Cannel, *an herb.*
A Cannon, or *piece of Ordinance.*
A Cannoneer, or *gunner.*
A Cannonade, or *Cannon-shot.*
To cannonade, or *batter with Cannon.*
I Cannot, or *am not able.*
A Canon, *rule*, or *Church-ordinance.*
A Canon, *a dignitary in a Cathedral*, or *collegiate Church.*
Canonical.
A Canonist, or *professor of the Canon-law.*
A Canonization.
To Canonize, or *make a Saint.*
A Canoo, *or* Indian *boat made of a tree.*
A Canopy, *a kind of curtain about beds.*
Can't, *for cannot.*
To cant, or *use an affected kind of speech.*
A Canter.
Canterbury-bells, *a flower.*
The Canticles, or *song of* Solomon.
To cantle out or *divide into parcels*
A Canto, *a song*, or *division in a Poem.*
A Canton, or *particular division of the Country of* Switzerland.
The Swiss-cantons.
To Cantonize, or *divide into Cantons.*
The Cantreds, or *Hundreds of a County in* England.
Canvas, *a kind of cloth.*
To Canvas, or *examine a business.*
A Cap, *and to* cap (*in several senses.*)
A Cap of maintenance, *usually carry'd before a Magistrate at great Solemnities.*
A Night-cap.
A Cap-case.
Capable, *fit to do*, or *suffer.*
Capacious, *large, vast*, or *spacious.*
To capacitate, or *put into a*
Capacity, *aptness to learn*, or *a natural disposition.*
Cap-a-pe, as *armed cap-a-pe*, i. e. *from head to foot.*
A Cape, *Promontory*, or *Tract of land running into the Sea.*
A Cape *of a coat.*
A Caper, or *jump.*
To caper, or *skip.*
A Cross-caper, *in dancing.*
A Caper, or *Pirate-ship.*
Capers, *a fruit.*
Capital, *belonging to the head*, or *chief.*
Capitation, or *pole-money.*
Capitation-stuff.
To capitulate, *treat upon terms*, or *make articles of agreement.*
A Capitulation.
A Capon, or *gelt Cock.*
Capons-tail, *an herb.*
A Capricio, *whimsey*, or *fantastical humour.*
Capricious, or *fantastical.*
A Capper, or *cap-maker.*
A Capstan, Capstand, or
Cap-

Capstern, *a kind of draw-beam in a Ship.*
A Captain, or *Head of a Company*, &c.
A Captain-lieutenant.
A Captainship.
Captious, *apt to take pet, quarrelsome*, or *censorious.*
Captiousness.
To captivate, *take prisoner*, or *subdue.*
A Captive, or *prisoner of War.*
Captivity, *bondage*, or *slavery.*
A Carat, *the weight of four grains.*
A Caravan, *a Company of merchants travelling together.*
Caraway, *an herb.*
A Carbine, *a kind of short Gun, us'd by horsemen.*
A Carbonado, or *meat broil'd upon the coals.*
A Carbuncle, *a precious stone, in colour like a burning coal; also a fiery botch*, or *plague-sore.*
A Carcass, or *dead body.*
Cardamum, *a spice.*
A pack of Cards.
A Coat-card.
A Trump-card.
A Card-maker.
A Card, *to card wooll with.*
A Carder *of Wooll.*
The four Cardinal, or *principal Vertues.*
A Cardinal, *a dignitary in the Church of* Rome.
A Cardinalship.
Cardinals flower, *or* American *bell-flower.*
A Cardoon, *a plant.*
The Cardoon-thistle.
Care, *heed, diligence*, or *regard.*
To care, or *take care.*
To careen, or *trim a Ship.*
A Career, *course*, or *full speed.*
Carefull, *heedfull, diligent*, or *pensive.*
Carefulness.
Careless, *negligent*, or *secure.*
Carelessness.
A Caress, or *treat.*
To caress, *treat*, or *make much of.*
Caresses, or *compliments.*
A Cargo, *a bill of lading*; or *the Goods in a Ship.*
To cark, *and care.*
A Carking, or *anxious care.*
A Carknet, or *chain of jewels for the neck.*
The Carline *thistle.*
The Carlings *of a Ship.*
A Carnage, or *great slaughter.*
Carnal, or *fleshly.*
Carnality, or *concupiscence.*
A Carnation, *a flower.*
Carnation, or *flesh-colour.*
Carnaval, or *Shrove-tide.*
Carneol, *an herb.*
Carney, *a Horse-disease.*
A Carob, *or* Carob-bean, *a fruit.*
A Carouse, or *drinking-bout.*
To carouse, *quaff*, or *drink large draughts.*
A Carp, *a fish.*
The prickly carp.
A Sea-carp.
To carp, *censure*, or *find fault with.*
A Carpenter.
A Ship-carpenter.
Carpenters-herb.
A Carper, or *censurer.*
A Carpet, *for a table*, &c.
A Turkey-carpet.
A Carr, *or* Cart.
A Carr-man.
A Carret, *or* Carrot; *a known root.*
White Carret, *or* skirwort
Carriage, or *behaviour.*
The Carriage *of goods.*
A Carrier *(in all senses.)*
A Carrion or *carcass of beasts,*
Carrion-lean,
A Carrousel, or *course of Chariots, Horses*, &c.
To carry *(in all senses.)*
A Cart, or *Carr.*
To cart *one.*
A Dung-cart.
A Go-cart, *for Children.*
A Cart-load.
A Cart-rut.
A Cart-wright, or *Cart-maker.*
A Carter, or *Carr-man.*
A Cartridge, Cartouch, or Cartoose, *to hold Gun-powder.*
A Carve *of Land, as much as may be till'd in a year by one plough.*
To carve, or *grave wood, stone*, &c.
To carve, or *cut up a fowl*, &c.
A Carver.
A Coach-carver.
A Case *(in all senses.)*
To case, or *put into a case.*
A Comb-case.
An Hat-case.
A Needle-case.
A Pin-case.
Case-shot, *for a piece of Ordinance.*
To case-harden *iron, steel*, &c.
The Casement *of a window*
Cash, or *ready money.*
A Cash-keeper.
To cashire, *disband*, or *turn out of service.*
A Cask, *a vessel*, or *head-piece.*
A Casket, or *little Cabinet.*
Cass-weed, *an herb.*
A Cassawary, *a great bird, with feathers like Camels hair.*
Cassia, *a shrub.*
Cassidony *vulg.* Cast me down, or *french lavender.*
A Cassock, *a kind of Gown.*
Cast, *hurl'd, thrown*, or *condemn'd by a Jury.*
A Cast, or *throw.*

A Ceremony, *rite, custom*, or *compliment*.
Certain, or *sure*.
Certainty.
A Certificate, or *testimonial, from a judge*, &c.
A Certifier.
To certify, or *acquaint*.
Ceruss, or *white lead*.
To cess, *assess, tax*, or *levy*.
A Cessation, or *giving over*.
A Cession, or *yielding up*.
A Cessionary *Bankrupt, that has given up his whole estate to his creditors*.
A Cessor, or *imposer of taxes*.

CH

A Chace, or *forest*.
A Chace, *at tennis-play*.
A Chace, or *pursuit*.
The Chad, *a fish*.
To chafe, or *warm*; *to fret*, or *fume*.
The Chafe-wax, *an Officer in Chancery that prepares the wax for Writs*, &c.
A Chafer, *a kind of beetle*.
A Goat-chafer.
A Green-chafer.
The Chafery, *that part of an iron-mill, where the iron is wrought into bars and perfected*.
Chaff, or *refuse of Corn*.
Chaff-weed.
Chaffer, *wares*, or *merchandize*.
To chaffer, *trade*, or *traffick*.
A Chaffern, *to heat water in*.
A Chaffinch, *a bird*.
Chaffy, or *full of chaff*.
A Chain (*of all sorts*.)
A Gold-chain.
To chain, or *tye with* chains.
Chain-shot, *bullets join'd with a chain*.
A Chair *to sit in*, or *a Sedan*.
A Privy-chair, or *close-stool*.
A Chair-man.
Chalcedony, *a precious stone*.
A Chaldron, or 36 *bushels of coals*.
A Calves-chaldron.
A Chalice, or *Communion-cup*.
Chalk, *a kind of earth*.
To chalk, or *mark with* chalk.
A Chalk-pit.
Chalky, or *full of* chalk.
A Challenge, *and to* challenge (*in several senses*.)
A Challenger.
A Chamber, or *room*.
A Bed-chamber.
A Bride-chamber.
A Chamber-maid.
Chamber-lye, or *urine*.
A Chamber-pot.
Chambering, and wantonness, (*a Scripture-phrase*.)
A Chamberlain.
The Lord high Chamberlain *of* England.
A Chamfer, *or* Chamfret, *a small gutter*, or *furrow upon a pillar*, &c.
To chamfer, *channel*, or *make hollow*.
To champ, or *chew*.
A Champain, or *large plain*,
A Champian, or *plain Country*.
A Champion, *to fight for one*.
The King's Champion.
A Chance, or *casual event*
To chance, or *happen*.
Chance-medley, or *casual murder*.
The Chancel *of a Church*.
A Chancellor.
The Lord high Chancellor *of* England.
Chancellorship.
The Chancery-court.
A Chandler, or *seller of necessary wares*.
A Corn-chandler.
A Tallow-chandler.
A Wax-chandler.
Change, *and to* change (*in several senses*.)
Changeable, *that may be changed, variable*, or *inconstant*.
A Changeling, *a Child put in the place of another*; or *a fool*.
A Changer, or *Money-changer*.
A Channel (*in different senses*.)
The Channel, or *narrow Seas about great* Britain.
Channelled, or *chamfred*.
To chant, or *sing*.
A Chanter, or *chief singer in a Cathedral*.
A Chantery, or *Chappel where the Service is sung*
A Chaos, *confused mass*, or *heap*.
A Chap, or *chink*.
To chap, *chink*, or *gape*.
The Chaps, or *jaws*.
A Chape *of a scabbard*.
The Chapiter, or *head of a pillar*.
A Chaplain, or *Minister of a Chappel*.
A Chaplet, or *garland*.
A Chapman, or *buyer*.
A Chappel.
A Chappelry, or *the jurisdiction of a* Chappel.
A Chapter, *the Clergymen of a Cathedral*, or *collegiate Church, assembled to choose a Bishop*, &c.
A Chapter-house.
A Chapter, or *division of a Book*.
A Character, *mark, manner of writing*, or *description*.
To characterize, or *give a a character of*.
Charcoal, *made of burnt wood, roots*, &c.
A Chare, *a fish peculiar to the lakes in* Lancashire.
A Chare, or *small business*.
A Chare-woman.
A Charge, *and to* charge (*in

(in all senses.)
Chargeable, *costly*, or *burdensome*.
A Charger, or *huge dish*.
The Charger *of a gun*.
A Charging-horse.
Chariock, *an herb*.
A Chariot, or *light coach*.
A Charioteer, or *Chariot-driver*.
Charitable, *bountifull, liberal*, or *pitifull*,
Charitableness, *a charitable disposition*.
Charity, *a Vertue*.
To chark, or *burn coals*.
Charles-wain, *a northern Constellation*.
A Charm, or *inchantment*.
To charm, or *bewitch*.
A Charmer.
A Charnel-house, *where sculls and bones of the dead are laid*.
A Charr, *a fish*.
To charr, or *chark coals*.
A Charter *of a Corporation*, &c.
The Charter-house, *or* Sutton's *Hospital in* London.
A Charter-party, *an indenture of Covenants between a Merchant and the Master of a Ship*.
A Chase, chace, or *forest*.
The Chase or *gutter of a cross-bow*.
To chase, *hunt*, *pursue*, or *drive away*.
To chase, as *Gold-smiths do*.
A Chaser.
Chaste, *continent*, *undefil'd*, or *modest*.
The Chaste-tree.
Chaste-wood, *an herb*.
To chasten (*a Scripture-word*) *for*
To chastise, *correct*, or *punish*.
Chastisement.
A Chastiser.
Chastity, *or* continency.
Chat, *or idle talk*.
To chat, or *prate*.
Chat-wood, *little sticks for the fire*.
Chattels, *all sorts of goods belonging to a personal estate*.
To chatter, as *birds do*; or *to prattle*.
A Chatter-pye, *a bird*.
A Chavender, *or* chevin, *a fish*.
Cheap, or *of low price*.
Dog-cheap.
To cheapen, or *beat down the price*.
A Cheapner *of wares*.
Cheapness.
Chear, *gladness*, or *good fare*.
To chear, *encourage*, or *hearten*.
Chearfull, *lively*, or *pleasant*.
Chearfulness.
Cheary, or *somewhat chearfull*.
A Cheat, or *impostor*.
A Cheat, or *cheating trick*.
To cheat, *cozen*, or *defraud*.
A Cheater.
A Check, *and to* check (*in several senses*.)
The Hawk checks, or *sports*.
Check-mate, *at chess*.
Checkered, *with colours*.
A Checker-board.
Checker-work.
A Cheek.
The Cheek-bone.
Blub-cheeked.
Cheese, *a known sort of food*.
Cheshire-cheese.
A Cream-cheese.
Cheese-bowls, *a flower*.
Cheese-cake.
Cheese-curds.
A Cheese-monger.
Cheese-running, or *Ladies bed-straw, an herb*.
A Cheeslip, *sow*, or *hog-louse*
To cherish, *nourish*, or *make much of*.
A Cherisher.
A Cherry, *a fruit*.
The Agriot-cherry.
Birds-cherry, *a shrub*.
A Black-cherry.
A Duke-cherry.
An Heart-cherry.
Winter-cherry, *an herb*.
A Cherry-pit, or *dimple in the chin*.
Cherry-wine.
Cherry-cheeks.
Cherub, *or* cherubin, *one of the Orders of Angels*.
Chervil, *an herb*.
Mock-chervil.
Wild-chervil.
A Cheslip, *a vermin, that lyes under stones and tiles*.
A Chesnut, *a fruit*.
A Chesnut-grove.
Chess, or *the play at chess*
A Chess-board.
A Chess-man.
A Chest, or *coffer*.
The Chest, or *breast of a Man*.
Hollow-chested.
A Chest-founder'd *Horse*.
Cheveril-leather *made of goats-skins*.
A Chevin, or *chub-fish*.
To chew *meat*, or *the cud*
A Chibbol, *a small kind of onion*.
A Chich, *or* chich-pease.
Chichlings, or *everlasting pease*.
A Chick, *or* chicken.
Chick-weed.
Berry-bearing chickweed.
Chickling, *an herb*.
Under-ground chickling.
Chid, *or* chidden, *from*
To chide, *rebuke*, or *brawl*
A Chider.
Chief, or *principal*.
A Chilblain.
A Child.
A Foster-child.
A God-child.
A Grand-child.
A Nurse-child.
Child-bearing.
Child-bed.

Child-

Child-birth.
Childermass-day, or *the festival of the H. Innocents.*
Child-hood.
Childish, *that acts like a Child.*
Childishness.
Childless, *that has no Children.*
Chill, chilly, or *sensible of cold.*
To chill, or *make cold.*
Chilness.
A Chime *of Bells.*
To chime *the bells*
A Chimera, *a feigned fire-belching Monster with a lion's head, a goat's belly and a dragon's tail. Also a whimsey,* or *idle fancy.*
Chimerical, or *imaginary*
A Chimney, *to convey smoke.*
A Chimney-piece, or *picture for a chimney.*
A Chimney-*sweeper.*
A Chin.
Long-chinn'd.
China, *a root us'd in drink*
China-ale.
China, or China-ware, *brought from* China, *a Country of* Asia.
A China-orange.
A Chinck, *an insect.*
The Chine, or *back-bone.*
To chine one, or *cut him quite through the back.*
A Chine *of beef,* or *of pork.*
The Chine-cough, *vulgo,* chin-cough.
A Chink, or *cleft.*
To chink, or *cleave,* as *the ground does.*
A Chip *of wood,* &c.
To chip, or *cut to chips.*
The Chip *of a plough.*
A Chip-ax.
The Chippings *of bread.*
A Chirographer; *an Officer in the Common-pleas, that records the fines,* &c.
Chiromancy, *palmestry,* or *divination by the hand-lines.*
To chirp, *like a bird.*
Chirurgery, or *Surgery.*
A Chirurgion, or *Surgeon.*
A Chisel, or *Chizzel.*
A Chit, or *young* chit.
A Chit-lark.
Chitterlings, *a sort of puddings.*
Chivalry, *Horsemanship, knight-hood,* or *tenure by Knights-service.*
Chocolate, *the composition and drink, made of Cacao-nuts.*
A Chocolate-mill, or *Chocolate-stick.*
Choice, *select,* or *excellent.*
Choice, or *variety.*
A Choice, or *election.*
A Choire, or *quire in a Church.*
To choke, *strangle,* or *stifle.*
A Choke-pear.
Choke-vetch, or choke-weed.
Choky, or *apt to* choke.
Choler, *a humour in the body; also wrath,* or *anger.*
Cholerick, *full of* choler, or *peevish.*
To choose, chuse, or *make choice of.*
A Chop *of mutton,* &c.
To chop, *mince,* or *cut small.*
A Chopping-block.
A Chopping-knife.
A Chorister, quirister, or *singer in a quire.*
Chorography, *the description of a Country.*
A Chorus, *the singing,* or *musick, in a stage-play; also a company of Choristers in a Church.*
Chose, or chosen *(from* to choose.*)*
A Chough, *a bird.*
A Chowse, or *foolish fellow.*
To chowse, or *cozen.*
To chowter, or *mutter.*
Chrism, *a kind of hallowed ointment us'd among Roman-catholicks, at Baptism, and the Coronation of Kings.*
A Chrisom, or Chrisom-cloth, *a cloth put upon a Child newly Christen'd.*
Chrisoms, *or* Crisoms; *infants that die within the month of birth,* or *wearing the Chrisom-cloth.*
A Chrisom-calf, *a Calf kill'd before it is a month old.*
CHRIST, *the anointed Saviour of the World.*
To christen, or *baptize.*
Christendom, *all the professors of Christianity throughout the World.*
A Christian, or *disciple of Christ.*
Christianity, or *the Christian Religion.*
The Christ-cross-row, or *alphabet of letters.*
Christmass, or *the festival of Christ's Nativity.*
Christmass-flower.
Christ-thorn, *a shrub.*
Christ-wort, *an herb.*
St. Christopher's *herb.*
Chronical Diseases, *that come at certain times.*
A Chronicle, *a sort of history.*
Chronicled, or *recorded in a Chronicle.*
A Chronicler, or *writer of* Chronicles.
The Books of Chronicles, *in the Old Testament.*
A Chronologer.
Chronological.
Chronology, *the Art of computing the times.*
A Chrysolite, *a kind of jasper.*
A Chrysoprasus, *another sort of precious stone.*
A Chub, *a clown,* or *jolt-head.*
The Chub-fish.
To chuckle, or *laugh by fits.*

A Chuff, or *Country-clown.*
Chuffy, or *clownish.*
A Church, *or* Parish-Church.
The Catholick, or *universal* Church.
To church *a Woman.*
A Church-man.
A Church-porch.
A Church-warden.
A Church-yard.
A Churl, *a country-bumkin,* or *covetous hunks.*
Churlish, *rustical,* or *morose.*
Churlishness.
A Churn, *a vessel to* Churn *butter in.*
A Churn-staff.
A Churr-worm, or *fen-cricket.*
To chuse, choose, or *make* choice of.
The Chyle, or *white juice of digested meat, ready to be turn'd into blood.*
Chymical.
A Chymist, *one well vers'd in*
Chymistry, or *the Art of dissolving metals, minerals, &c. and reducing them to their first principles.*

C I

A Cicatrice, or *scar.*
To cicatrize, or *close up a wound.*
Sweet Ciceley, *an herb.*
Wild-ciceley.
Cich, *or* cich-pease.
Cichlings, or *petty* ciches.
Cichory, *or* Succory, *an herb.*
Cider, *a drink made of apples.*
A Cieling *of a room.*
Cilery, or *drapery wrought on the heads of pillars,* &c.
A Cimeter, *a kind of broad back-sword, without a gard.*
Cinders *of coals.*
Cinnaber, *or* Cinoper, *a kind of red mineral stone for the vermilion colour.*
Cinnamon, *a spice.*
Cinque, or *five at dice.*
Cinque-foil, *an herb.*
The Cinque-ports, or *five remarkable havens of* England, *viz.* Dover, Hastings, Hith, Romney, *and* Sandwich.
The Warden of the Cinque-ports.
A Cion, or *graff.*
Ciperous, *a sort of bulrush.*
A Cipher *in Arithmetick.*
A Cipher, or *secret character.*
A Circle, or *round compass.*
A Circlet, or *roll for a dish at table.*
The Circuit, or *travelling of Judges to perform their Office in several Counties.*
Circular, or *round like a circle.*
To circulate, or *go round.*
The Circulation *of the blood.*
Circulatory Letters.
To Circumcise, or *cut off the fore-skin.*
Circumcision.
A Circumference, or *compass.*
A Circumlocution, as *when one word is expressed by many,*
Circumscribed, or *limited.*
Circumspect, or *wary.*
Circumspection.
A Circumstance, *a quality that accompanies a thing, as time, place,* &c.
Circumstanced.
Circumstantial.
The lines of Circumvallation *in a Siege.*
To circumvent, or *deceive.*
A Circumvention.
Circumvolution, or *rolling about.*
A pair of cisers, *or* sizzers
A Cistern *to hold water.*
A Cistern-cock.
Gum-cistus, *or* sweet-cistus, *an herb.*
A Citadel, or *fortress.*
A Citation, *from*
To cite, *warn in, summon,* or *quote.*
A Citizen, or *Free-man of a City.*
A Citron, *a kind of great Lemmon.*
A Citrull, *a Cucumber of a citron-colour.*
A Cittern, *a musical instrument.*
A City, or *great Town.*
A Mother-city, or *chief* City.
Civet, *a sort of perfume, like musk, being the excrement of certain beasts.*
A Civet-cat.
Civil, *political,* or *courteous.*
A Civilian, *a Doctor,* or *Student in the* Civil *law*
Civility, or *courtesy.*
To civilize, or *make* civil.

C L

To clack *wooll.*
To clack, or *make a noise.*
A Mill-clack.
A Clack-goose, or *barnacle.*
Clad, or *cloathed.*
A Claim, or *pretension.*
To claim, or *lay* claim *to,*
A Claimer, or *challenger.*
To Clamber, *or* clamber *up.*
Clamminess.
Clammy, or *gluish.*
Clamorous.
A Clamour, or *cry.*
To clamour, or *cry out against.*
Clancular, *or* Clandestine, i. e. *secret and close.*
A Clap, *and to* clap (*in several senses.*)

A Clapper, *one that claps his hands for joy.*
The Clapper *of a bell, mill,* or *door.*
Clarenceux; *the title of the second King at Arms.*
Claret-wine.
Claricords, *a musical instrument, so call'd.*
To clarify, or *make clear.*
A Clarion, *a kind of trumpet.*
A Clark, or Clerk.
Clary, *an herb.*
Wild-clary.
A Clash.
To clash, *to make a noise,* or *to disagree.*
A Clasp *for a book,* &c.
To clasp, *buckle,* or *embrace.*
A Class, or *form.*
A Classical *Author, an author of good credit.*
To clatter, *make a noise,* or *brangle.*
I clave, or *did* cleave.
Claver, *or* clover-grass.
A Clause, *period,* or *short sentence.*
A Claw, *of a beast, bird,* &c.
To claw, *to scratch,* or *flatter.*
A Claw-back, or *flatterer*
Clay, or *dirt.*
A Clay-pit.
Clean, *pure,* or *neat.*
Cleanliness.
Cleanly.
Cleanness.
To cleanse, or *make clean.*
A Cleanser.
Clear, *and to* clear (*in all senses.*)
Clear-sighted.
Clear-spirited.
Clearness.
To cleave, *cut,* or *divide;* or *to stick to.*
A Cleaver *of wood,* &c.
A Butcher's-cleaver.
Cleavers, *an herb.*
Cleft, *or* cleaved.
A Cleft, or *chink.*
Clemency, or *gentleness.*

The Clergy, or *Church-men*
A Clergy-man.
A Clerk (*of all sorts.*)
A Parish-clerk.
A Clerkship.
Clever, *or* cleverly, *neatly,* or *dexterously.*
A Clew *of thread.*
The Clew, or *corner of a Sail.*
A Clew-garnet, *a rope that tyes the sail-clew.*
To click, as *a watch does.*
A Clicker, or *knocker at a door.*
A *Lizard's* clicket.
A Client, *one that retains a lawyer to plead his cause.*
A Cliff, *or* clift, *the side of a hill.*
A Cliff, or *rock.*
A Cliff *in musick.*
A Clift, *or* cleft.
Climacterical, *ascending like a ladder,* or *dangerous;* as *some years of a man's life are, especially the* 81, *which is nine times nine, and the* 63, *which is seven times nine. Some hold that every seventh year is critical and hazardous.*
A Climate, *or* clime; *a part of the World.*
To climb, clime, *or get up.*
A Climber.
Climbers, or *climers, an herb.*
Climer *of* Virginia, or *Virginia ivy, a shrub.*
A Clinch, *a short and witty expression.*
To clinch *the fist,* or *a nail.*
A Clincher, or *witty person.*
To cling, or *stick to.*
Clingy, *apt to stick.*
To clink, as *metal does.*
To clip, *to shear;* or *to coll and embrace.*
A Clipper.
Clivers, *or* cleavers, *an herb.*
A Clock, or *beetle, an insect.*

A Clock (*to measure time.*)
A Clock-maker.
Clock-work.
A Clod, *or* clot.
To clod, or *break clods.*
Clodded, *gather'd together in* clods.
Cloddy, or *full of clods.*
A Clog, or *impediment.*
To clog, *hinder,* or *overload.*
Wooden clogs, or *pattens.*
A Cloister, or *convent.*
Cloistered up.
A Cloke, *a garment,* or *pretence.*
To cloke, *cover with a* cloke, *palliate,* or *disguise.*
A Riding-cloke.
A Cloke-bag.
Close, *thick, narrow, secret,* or *reserved.*
A Close-stool.
Close-fisted, or *covetous.*
Close-work'd.
A Close, or *conclusion.*
A Close, or *pasture.*
To close (*in several senses.*)
Closeness.
A Closet, *in a room.*
A Clot, *or* clod *of earth, bloud,* &c.
A Clot-bird,
A Clot-burr.
Cloth *of woollen,* or *linnen.*
Hair-cloth, or *sack-cloth.*
A Table-cloth.
A Cloth-rash.
A Cloth-worker.
To clothe, or *put on apparel.*
Clothes, as *a suit of* cloths.
Bed-clothes.
A Clothier.
To clotter, *like cream,* or *bloud.*
A Cloud, *in the sky.*
Cloud-berry.
Cloudiness *of weather.*
Cloudy.
A Clove *of cheese,* i. e. 8 *pounds.*

A Clove *of spice*, or *gar-lick.*
The Clove-gilliflower.
Clove-tongue, *an herb.*
Cloven, or *cleft.*
Cloven-footed.
Clover-grass.
Snail-clover, or *horned-clover.*
A Clout, or *rag.*
A Dish-clout.
A Shoo-clout.
Clouted cream.
Clouterly, or *bungler-like.*
A Clown, *or* country-fellow.
Clownish, *rustical*, or *rude.*
Clownishness.
To cloy, or *glut.*
A Club (*in several sen-ses.*)
To club, *to pay his* club, or *scot.*
Club-footed.
Club-law.
To cluck, as *a hen does.*
Clumsey, *thick and short*, or *awkward.*
Clung, or *stuck together*, (*from to* cling.)
To clung, as *wood will do when laid up after it is cut.*
A Cluster *of grapes, figs*, &c.
Clustery, or *full of clusters*
To clutch, clinch, or *hold a thing fast.*
A Clutch-fist, or *clutch-fisted miser.*
To keep out of one's clut-ches.
A Clutter, *bustle*, or *stirr.*
To clutter *together.*
A Clyster, or *glister.*

CO

A Coach, or *chariot.*
Coached, or *seated in a coach.*
A Coach-box.
Coach-hire.
A Coach-man.
A Coadjutor, or *fellow-helper.*
To coagulate, or *curdle.*
To coaks, *sooth up*, or *ca-jole.*
A Coakser.
A Coal.
Char-coal.
Pit-coal, or *Sea-coal.*
Scotch-coal.
Coal-black.
A Coal-pit, or *coal-mine.*
A Coal-mouse, *a bird.*
A Coast *of a Country.*
The Sea-coast.
To coast *along*, or *sail a-long the* coast.
A Coat, or *cottage.*
A Sheep-coat.
A Coat, *a garment.*
A Coat *of Arms.*
To coat *a Child.*
A Turn-coat.
A Waste-coat.
Coat-armour.
A Cob, *or* Sea-cob, *a bird.*
An Herring-cob, or *young herring.*
A rich Cob, or *miser.*
A Cob-iron, *on which a spit turns.*
A Cob-swan.
To cobble, or *mend shoos.*
A Cobbler.
A Cobweb.
Cobweb-*lawn.*
Cotcheneal, *a kind of grain us'd in dying scarlet.*
A Cock, *and to* cock (*in all senses.*)
A Game-cock.
An Heath-cock.
A Pea-cock.
A Sea-cock, *a kind of crab.*
A Turky-cock.
A Weather-cock.
A Cock-boat.
Cock-brain'd, or *giddy-brain'd.*
The Cock-crowing.
Cock-fighting.
A Cock-pit.
Cock-roches, *an insect.*
A Cock-sparrow, or *male sparrow.*
Cock-sure.
Cock-throwing *at shrove-tide.*
Cock-weed. } *herbs.*
Cocks-foot-grass, } *herbs.*
Cocks-head, or *sanfoin*, } *herbs.*
Cocks-tread, or cocks-treadle, *the sperm of an egg.*
Cockal, *a sort of play.*
A Cockatrice, or *basilisk.*
To cocker, or *be fond of.*
A Cocket, or *bill at the Custom-house.*
Cockish, or *lecherous.*
A Cockle, *a shell-fish.*
To cockle, or *wrinkle, as some woollen-cloth does.*
Cockle-weed, *that grows among corn.*
Hot-cockles, *a kind of sport.*
A Cockney, *one born within the sound of* Bow-*bell.*
A Cockrel, or *young cock.*
A Cockswain *of a ship.*
A Coco-nut, *a rare* Indi-an *fruit, that affords meat, drink, and cloth.*
The Cod, or *shell of pease, beans*, &c.
Codded, as *pease are.*
A Cod-fish.
The Cods *of a Man.*
A Cod-piece.
A Codicil, or *supplement to a Will.*
To coddle, or *stew.*
Codlins, *apples proper to stew.*
Co-equal, or *equal with another.*
Coercion, or *restraint.*
Coercive, or *capable of restraining.*
Coessential, *of the same essence*, or *substance.*
Coeternal, or *eternal with another.*
Coexistent, *that has a Be-ing, at the same time.*
Coffee, *the berry, and drink.*
A Coffee-house.
A Coffer, or *chest.*
A Cofferer *of the King's houshold.*

A

A Coffin for a dead body.
A Coffin-man, or coffin-maker.
A Cog in a mill-wheel.
To cog, or flatter.
Cogent, or enforcing.
A Cogger, or flatterer.
A Cognisance, or badge.
The Cognisance, or judicial hearing of a cause.
To cohabit, or dwell together.
Cohabitation.
A Co-heir, or joint-heir.
To cohere, or hang well together.
Coherence, or coherency.
Coherent.
A Coif, for the head.
A Night-coif.
Coifed, that wears a coif.
A Coil, or clutter.
To coil, or wind about a Rope.
Coin, or money.
To coin, or make money.
Coincident, or falling out together.
A Coiner, or minter.
Coins, little wedges us'd by Printers, to fasten the Letters in the Chace, or Frame.
A Coist, or queest, a bird.
A Coit, as to play at coits.
Cokers, or fishermens boats.
A Cokes, or fool.
Cold, or chill.
A Cold, as to catch cold.
Coldness.
A Cole-staff, or cowl-staff.
A Cole-wort, a plant.
The Colick, a disease.
The Stone-colick.
The Wind-colick.
To coll, as to clip and coll, or embrace.
Collapsed, or decayed.
A Collar (of all sorts.)
A Horse-collar.
A Collar-maker.
To collate, or bestow a benefice.
Collateral, or side-ways.
A Collation of a benefice; or comparing.
A Collation, or entertainment.
To collation a book, to examine the signatures, or letters of direction in every sheet, that none may be wanting.
A Colleague, or partner.
A Collect, or short prayer.
To collect, or gather.
A Collecter.
A Collection.
Collective.
A Collectour of Taxes.
A College.
A Colleger, or member of a College.
A Collegiate-Church.
A Collegue, or companion in an office.
A Collery, or store-house of coals.
A Collet, or bezil of a ring, or jewel.
A Collier, or carrier of coals.
The Hawk Collies, i. e. beaks.
A Collision, or dashing.
To collogue, or flatter.
A Collop, or slice of meat.
Scotch-collops.
A Collusion, or playing booty.
Collied, or smutted.
Colly, the black that sticks on the outside of a pot.
A Colly-flower, a plant.
A Colon, or middle point of distinction.
A Colonel of a Regiment.
A Colony, or plantation.
Coloquintida, a kind of gourd.
A Coloss, or colossus, a large statue; as that of the Sun at Rhodes, 70 cubits high, between whose feet the ships sail'd.
A Colour, and to colour (in several senses.)
Party-coloured.
The Colours of a Company of Soldiers.
A Colt of an horse, or ass.
Coltsfoot, an herb.
Mountain-coltsfoot.
A Colt-staff.
Coltish, or frolicksome.
Columbine, an herb.
A Column, or pillar.
A Comb, and to comb (in several senses.)
A Curry-comb, or horse-Comb.
An Honey-comb.
A Comb-brush.
A Comb-maker.
A Combatant, or champion.
A Combate, or fight.
A Combination, a joyning together; or a conspiracy.
To combine, or plot together.
Combustible, or apt to burn.
A Combustion, or hurly-burly.
To come (in all senses.)
A Come-off, shift, or pretence.
A Comedian, a writer, or actor of Comedies.
A Comedy, or comical play.
Comliness.
Comely, fair, beautifull, or decent.
A Comer.
A New-comer.
A Comet, or blazing-star.
Comfits, or sweet-meats.
A Comfit-maker.
Comfort, or consolation.
To comfort one.
Comfortable.
Comfortableness.
A Comforter.
Comfortless.
Comfrey, an herb.
Comical, belonging to a Comedy; merry, or jocose.
Comings in, incomes, or revenues.
The Comings in a ship, i. e. the planks that bear up the Hatches.
A Comma, a point of distinction.

A

A Command, or *injunction.*
To command, *enjoin, bid,* or *appoint.*
A Commander, *a bidder,* or *an Officer.*
A Commander, *a kind of beetle,* or *rammer.*
The ten Commandments.
To commemorate, or *solemnly remember.*
A Commemoration.
To commence, *to begin;* or *to take a degree.*
A Commencement, the *time when degrees are taken at* Cambridge; *the same with the* Act *at* Oxford.
To commend, *to praise;* or *to commit to one's trust.*
Commendable, or *praiseworthy.*
A Commendam, *a void benefice commended to an able Clerk, till it be otherwise dispos'd of.*
A Commendation.
Commendatory-letters.
A Commender.
Commensurate, or *proportionable.*
A Comment, *gloss,* or *exposition of a Text.*
To comment, or *write upon a thing.*
A Commentary.
A Commentator.
Commerce, or *traffick.*
A Commination, or *extreme threatning.*
To commiserate, or *take pity of.*
Commiseration, or *pity.*
A Commissary, *a Church-Officer that supplies the Bishop's place in the remote parts of his Diocess. Also one that has the distribution of provisions in an Army,* or *Garrison.*
A Commission, *delegation, warrant,* or *charge for the exercising of a an Office,* or *Jurisdiction*

A Commissioner.
To commit, *to act,* or *do; also to refer,* or *leave a business to one.*
A Committee *of Parliament.*
Commodious, *fit, convenient,* or *usefull.*
Commodities, *wares,* or *merchandizes.*
Common, *ordinary,* or *usual.*
The Court of Common-pleas.
Common-hunt, *the Lord Mayor of* London's *chief Huntsman.*
A Common, or *common pasture for cattel.*
The Commonalty, or *common people.*
A Commoner, or *member of the House of Commons.*
Commonness.
Commons, *the regular diet of a Society.*
The Commons, or *House of Commons.*
A Common-wealth, *the publick-weal,* or *a particular state.*
A Commonwealths-man
A Commotion, or *hurly-burly.*
To commune, or *talk together.*
Communicable, *that may be communicated.*
To communicate, *to impart to,* or *to receive the Sacrament of the Lord's Supper.*
Communication, or *converse.*
Communicative, or *free to impart.*
Communion, or *fellowship.*
The Communion, or *Lord's Supper.*
Community, *enjoying in common,* or *a body of Men united in civil society, for their mutual advantage.*

A Commutation, or *changing one thing for another.*
Commutative, *by way of change.*
Commutative Justice, *in buying, selling, borrowing, lending, and all manner of dealings.*
To commute, or *buy off a punishment.*
A Compact discourse, i. e. *that is brief and pithy.*
To compact, or *clap close together.*
A Compact, *bargain,* or *agreement.*
A Companion, or *fellow.*
A Companion of the Garter; *a member of that most Noble Order of Knighthood.*
A Company *(in several senses.)*
Comparable, or *to be compared*
Comparative.
To compare, *to liken,* or *examine one thing by another.*
A Comparison.
A Compartment, or Compartiment, *a proportionable division in building,* &c.
A Compass, or *circuit.*
To compass, or *surround.*
The Mariners Compass; *a round piece of pastboard, on which the* 32 *Winds are describ'd, & on which is fix'd a needle touch'd with the Load-stone, that continually points towards the North.*
A pair of Compasses *to draw circles,* &c.
Compassion, *fellow-feeling,* or *pity.*
Compassionate.
Compatibility.
Compatible, *that agrees,* or *suits with another thing.*
To compel, *force,* or *constrain.*

A

A Compellation, or *calling by name.*
Compendious, *brief,* or *short.*
Compendiousness.
A Compendium, *short abstract,* or *abbridgment.*
To compensate, or *make amends for.*
A Compensation, *recompense;* or *requital.*
A Competence, or competency, *a competent proportion;* or *allowance.*
Competent, or *sufficient.*
Competible, *that has relation to; suitable,* or *agreeable to.*
A Competition, or *Rivalship, when two sue for the same thing.*
A Competitor, or *rival.*
To compile, *make up,* or *gather together.*
A Compiler,
Complacency, *being well pleas'd,* or *delighting in a thing.*
To complain, *lament,* or *make moan.*
A Complainant, or *plaintiff at Law.*
A Complaint.
Complaisance, *a courteous compliance,* or *pleasing behaviour.*
Complaisant, *of a pleasing humour.*
A Complement, *a filling up what is wanting.*
Complete, compleat, *or perfect.*
Completeness.
A Completion, or *fulfilling.*
Complexly, or *jointly.*
Complexion, *the natural constitution,* or *temperature of the Body.*
A well complexioned *body.*
Compliance (*from to* comply.)
Compliant.
Complicated, or *wrapt up together.*
A Complication, *of diseases when many meet together.*
A Complice, or *an* accomplice, *a partner in an ill action.*
Complimental.
A Compliment, or *kind expression, in the most obliging terms.*
To compliment one.
A Complimenter.
To complot, or *plot together.*
To comply, *or* comply with; *to condescend,* or *submit to another's pleasure.*
To comport, or *demean himself.*
Comportment, or *behaviour.*
To compose, *to make a book, discourse, verses,* or *To quiet one's spirits, agree a difference,* &c.
A Composer.
A Composing-stick *us'd by Printers, to set the letters together.*
A Composition.
A Compositor, or *Printer's Composer.*
A Composure.
Compotation, or *drinking together.*
To compound, or *agree with Creditors, for debt.*
To comprehend, *contain, include,* or *lay hold on.*
Comprehensible.
Comprehension.
Comprehensive, *large,* or *containing much.*
Compression, *pressing,* or *thrusting close together.*
To comprise, *comprehend, take in,* or *contain.*
A Compromise, or *mutual promise of Parties at variance, to refer the business to arbitration.*
To compromise, or *stand to such arbitrement.*
To comptroll, *animadvert* or *over-look.*
A Comptroller *of the King's Houshold.*
Compulsion, *force,* or *constraint.*
Compunction, *remorse,* or *trouble of mind for an offence committed.*
A Compurgator, *one that by Oath justifies another's innocency.*
A Computation.
To compute, or *reckon.*
A Comrade, camarade, or *Companion.*
Concave, or *hollow, on the inside.*
Concavity.
To conceal, or *keep close.*
To concede, *yield,* or *grant.*
A Conceit, *fancy,* or *opinion.*
To conceit, or *imagine.*
Conceitedness, or *affectation.*
Conceivable.
To conceive *with young; to imagine,* or *understand.*
To concenter, or *meet in the same center.*
A Conception, or *conceiving with child; also a thought,* or *notion.*
A Concern, *business,* or *affair; also a matter of importance.*
To concern, *belong,* or *relate to;* or *to busy himself about.*
Concernment, or *concern.*
To concert, *contrive,* or *debate together about a matter.*
A Concession, *grant,* or *yielding.*
Concise, *short* or *brief.*
The Conclave, or *place where the Cardinals meet to choose a Pope.*
To conclude, *infer, determine, make an end,* or *resolve with himself.*
A Conclusion.
Conclusive.
To concoct, or *digest.*
Concoction.

Concomitant, *going together*, or *bearing company*.
Concord, or *agreement*.
To concord, or *agree together*.
A Concordance, or *general Index of all the words in the Bible*.
Concordant, or *agreeing together*.
A Concourse, or *meeting of people in one place*.
A Concubine, *a Woman that lies with a Man instead of an Husband*; *an harlot*, or *strumpet*.
Concubinage, *the keeping of a Concubine*.
Concupiscence, *lust*, or *vehement desire*.
The Concupiscible *appetite*, or *faculty*.
To concur, *to meet together*, or *to agree with one*.
Concurrence.
Concurrent, *agreeing together*.
A Concurrent, or *rival*.
A Concussion, or *shaking together*.
To cond *a ship*, i. e. *to give directions for the steering of it*.
To condemn, *censure*, *blame*, or *dislike*.
To condemn, or *sentence one to die*.
Condemnable, *that deserves*
Condemnation.
Conders, or *balkers*, *those that from a high place make signs to the Fishers which way the shole of herrings passes*.
To condescend, *stoop down*, or *yield to*,
Condescension.
Condign, or *deserved punishment*.
A Condition, *natural disposition*, *state*, *quality*, or *clause in a Covenant*.
Conditional, *upon certain conditions*.
Conditioned, or *naturally disposed*.
Fair-conditioned.
Ill-condition'd.
Condolence.
To condole *with one*, or *to express his sorrow for some misfortune of his*
To conduce, or *avail*.
Conducible, conducive, or *profitable*.
Conduct, *the direction*, or *manner of acting*, or *managing a business*.
To conduct, *guide*, or *lead one*.
A Conducter.
A Conductress.
A Conduit, *for water*.
A Conduit-pipe.
A Cone, *a geometrical figure like a Sugar-loaf*.
To confabulate, or *tell stories together*.
A Confabulation.
A Confection, or *mingling several things together*.
A Confectioner, or *comfit-maker*.
A Confederacy, or *alliance*.
To Confederate, *or* confederate *themselves*; *to joyn together in League*, or *Covenant*.
The Confederates, or *allies*
To confer, *bestow*, *compare*, or *discourse with*.
A Conference, *a parley*, or *discoursing together*.
To confess, or *acknowledge*.
Confession.
A Confessor, or Father-confessor, *a Priest*, *to whom Confession of sins is made by Roman Catholicks*.
To confide, or *rely upon*.
Confidence, *trust*, or *boldness*.
Confident, *bold*, *assured of*, or *resolute*.
A Confident, or *trusty bosom-friend*.
Configuration, *likeness of figures* or *mutual aspects of the stars*.
To confine, *limit*, *keep in*, or *imprison*.
A Confinement.
The Confines, or *borders of a Country*.
To confirm, *establish*, or *ratify*.
A Confirmation.
To confiscate *one's goods*, or *seize upon 'em as forfeited*.
A Confiscation.
A Conflagration, or *great burning*.
A Conflict, *bickering*, or *contention*.
A Confluence *of rivers*, or *of people*, i. e. *their flowing*, or *meeting together*.
To conform, *make fit*, or *suit himself to*.
Conformable.
A Conformation.
A Conformist, *one that conforms to the Church of* England.
Conformity.
To confound, *mix* or *jumble together*, &c.
To confront, *set face to face*, or *oppose*.
Confused, or *mingled together*.
A Confusion, *jumbling together*, *disorder*; or *disturbance*; *being abashed*, or *out of countenance*.
A Confutation.
To confute, *disprove*, *convince*, *overthrow*, or *baffle*.
To congeal, *thicken*, or *grow thick as ice does*.
Congealable.
A Congee, or *low bow*.
A Congelation, or *congealing*.
Congenial, *of the same kind*, or *disposition*.
A Conger, *a large sort of Eel*.
To Congratulate, or *rejoyce with one for his good fortune*.

A

A Congratulation.
A Congregation, or *assembly, more especially, for the performing of Divine Service.*
A Congress, or *meeting.*
Congregational, *belonging to such an assembly*
A Congress, *meeting*, or *rencounter.*
Congruence, *conformity*, or *suitableness.*
Congruent, or *agreeable.*
Congruity, or *fitness.*
Congruous, *proper, convenient*, or *fit.*
Conical, *belonging to the figure of a Cone.*
Conjectural.
A Conjecture, or *guess*; *and to* conjecture.
A Conjecturer.
To conjoyn, or *joyn together.*
Conjugal, *belonging to Marriage.*
A Conjunction, or *joyning together.*
Conjunctive.
A Conjuncture *of affairs.*
A Conjuration, *conspiracy*, or *plot.*
To conjure, *demand upon Oath, adjure*, or *earnestly entreat.*
To conjure, *or* conjer *up spirits.*
A Conjurer, or *Sorcerer.*
To conn, or *get without book.*
Connatural *born with*, or *springing together.*
A Connexion, *knitting*, or *joyning together.*
To connive, or *wink at a fault.*
Connivence *or* connivance
To conquer, or *subdue.*
A Conquerour.
A Conquest.

Consanguinity, or *kindred by bloud.*
Conscience, *the testimony or witness of one's own mind.*
Tender-conscienced.
Conscientiousness.
Conscionable, or *reasonable.*
Conscionableness.
Conscious, *knowing himself guilty*, or *privy to.*
To consecrate, *appoint*, or *set apart to an holy use.*
A Consecration.
A Consectary, or *inference, upon the demonstration of an argument.*
A Consent, *and to* consent, or *agree.*
A Consequence, or *conclusion*; *also matter of moment.*
Consequent, *following*, or *what follows upon some other thing.*
A Conservation, or *preserving,*
A Conserve *of roses*, &c.
To conserve, or *preserve and keep.*
A Conserver.
To consider, or *think upon.* &c.
Considerable, *that deserves to be considered.*
Considerate, or *discreet.*
Considerateness.
Consideration; *advising, taking heed*; or *a condition upon which a thing is done.*
To consign, *make over, assign*, or *deliver.*
To consist, or *be made up of.*
A Consistence, *essence*, or *being*; or *the thickness of liquid things.*
Consistent, *suitable*, or *agreeable.*
Consistorial, *belonging to.*
A Consistory, or *assembly of Ministers and Elders, of a Church.*
To consociate, or *unite together.*
Consolation, or *comfort.*
Consolatory, or *comfortable.*
To consolidate, *close*, or *make whole.*
A Consolidation, or *uniting of Benefices.*
Consonance, or *agreeableness*; *conformity*, or *suitableness.*
Consonant, or *agreeable.*
A Consonant, *a letter distinguished from a vowel.*
A Consort, or *companion.*
A Royal Consort.
A Consort *of musick.*
To consort, or *keep company.*
Consound, *or* comfry, *an herb.*
Conspicuous, *clear*, or *easy to be seen.*
A Conspiracy, or *plot.*
A Conspiratour.
To conspire, *complot*, or *plot together.*
A Constable *of a Hundred*, or *Parish.*
The Lord high Constable *of* England.
The Constable *of the Tower*, Dover-*Castle*, &c.
A Constableship, *such an Office.*
Constancy, or *stediness.*
Constant, or *stedfast*, &c.
A Constellation, or *company of stars.*
A Consternation, *a great fright*, or *amazement.*
To constitute, or *appoint.*
A Constitution, *Appointment, Law*, or *Ordinance*; *also the state and condition of a thing.*
Constitutive.
To constrain, *force*, or *compel.*
A Constraint, or *compulsion.*
A Construction, *a regular framing in building*; or *a due joining together of words*; *also an interpretation*, or *meaning.*
Constructive.
Constructiveness.
To construe, *or* conster *to expound*, or *interpret*
Consubstantial *of the same substance.*

Con-

Consubstantiation, *a Doctrine maintain'd by the Lutherans, who believe the body and blood of Christ to be substantially in the Eucharist, together with the substance of bread and wine.*

A Consul, *a soveraign Magistrate among the ancient Romans.*

A Consul, or *resident for Merchants at* Smyrna, *and other places.*

To consult, or *advise.*

A Consult, *or* consultation.

To consume *waste, spend, squander, spoil, destroy,* &c.

A Consumer.

Consummate, *perfect*, or *absolute.*

To consummate,*make perfect, accomplish,* or *finish.*

A Consummation.

A Consumption, *consuming*, or *wasting.*

The Consumption, *a disease.*

Consumptive, *that is in a consumption.*

A Contagion, or *infection.*

Contagious, or *apt to infect.*

Contagiousness.

To contain, *comprehend*, or *hold.*

To contemn, *despise, scorn*, or *slight.*

A Contemner.

To contemplate, *behold*, or *consider seriously*; *to muse upon*, or *meditate.*

A Contemplater.

A Contemplation.

Contemplative.

Contemporary, *of the same time*, or *standing.*

Contempt, or *scorn.*

Contemptible, *fit to be slighted, base*, or *mean.*

Contemptuous, *scornfull, reproachfull*, or *slighting*

To contend, or *strive.*

Content, or *satisfaction of mind.*

To content, or *give content*; *to pacify, humour,* or *recompence one for his pains.*

Contentation, *or* contentment.

Contentedness.

Contentfull, or *full of content.*

Contention, or *strife.*

Contentious, or *quarrelsome.*

Contentiousness.

The Contents *of a book, chapter,* &c.

A Contest, or *debate*; *and to* contest.

A Contestation.

A Context, or *portion of Scripture, preceding the* Text.

A Contexture, or *interweaving.*

Contiguous, *touching one another*, or *lying very near.*

Contiguousness, contiguity, or *nearness.*

Continency, or *chastity.*

Continent, or *chaste.*

A Continent, or *main land.*

Contingency, *a falling out by chance.*

Contingent, or *casual.*

Continual, *without intermission.*

Continuance, or *lastingness.*

A Continuation.

A Continuator *of an History.*

To continue, *hold on, abide*, &c.

A Contorsion, or *wresting.*

Contrabanded goods, *such as are forbidden to be exported.*

A Contract, or *bargain.*

To contract, or *make a* contract; *also to shorten*, or *to get an ill habit.*

A Contraction, or *shortning.*

To contradict, or *gainsay.*

A Contradiction.

Contradictory.

Contrariety.

A Contramure, or *outwall built about another wall.*

Contrariety.

Contrary, *repugnant*, or *one against another.*

A Contrast, or *little quarrel.*

A Contravention, or *acting contrary to an agreement.*

To contribute, or *give something with others.*

A Contributer.

A Contribution.

Contributary.

Contrite, or *penitent.*

Contrition, *remorse*, or *trouble of mind.*

A Contrivance.

To contrive, or *devise.*

A Contriver.

To control, *disprove, call to an account*, or *overlook.*

A Controller.

The Controller *of the Pipe in the Exchequer.*

A Controversy, or *dispute.*

To controvert, *to dispute*, or *argue pro and con.*

Contumacious, or *stubborn.*

Contumacy, or *stubbornness.*

Contumelious, or *affrontive.*

A Contumely, or *reproach.*

A Contusion, or *bruise.*

To convene, *assemble*, or *summon to appear.*

Convenience, conveniency, or *fitness.*

Convenient, or *fit and suitable.*

A Convent, *a monastery*, or *religious house.*

A Conventicle, or *private Assembly.*

A Convention, or *publick meeting of the States.*

A

A Conventioner, or *member of a Convention.*
Conventual, *belonging to a Convent.*
Conversant, *well-vers'd,* or *keeping company with.*
A Conversation.
To converse, or *be conversant with.*
A Conversion, or *turning.*
A Convert, *a Person turned, to the True Faith.*
To convert, or *turn after such a manner.*
A Converter.
Convertible Terms.
The Convex, or *outside of a globe.*
Convexity, or *hollowness on the outside.*
A Conveyance, or *carrying; also a deed whereby land is convey'd from one to another.*
A Conveyancer, or *maker of such writings.*
To convey, *carry,* or *make over.*
A Conveyer.
To convict, or *find guilty.*
A Conviction.
Convictive.
To convince one, or *thoroughly perswade him of.*
A Convocation, or *general assembly of the Clergy.*
The Convocation-house.
A Convoy, or *safe conduct of soldiers* or *ships.*
A Convulsion, or *violent pulling together of the sinews.*
Convulsion-fits.
A Cony, or *rabbet.*
A Cook *to dress victuals.*
A Master-cook.
A Cook-maid.
The Cook-room in a ship.
A Cook-fish.
Cookery, or *the Art of dressing meat.*
Cool, *and to* cool, or *make cold.*
A Cooler.
A Brewer's Cooler.
Coolness.
A Coop *for poultry.*
To coop up, *or* coop in.
A Cooper, *that hoops vessels.*
A Wine-cooper.
To Co-operate, or *work together.*
A Co-operation.
A Cooperator.
Co-ordinate, *of equal rank or degree.*
A Coot, or *Moor-hen.*
Copartners, *such as have equal shares in an estate by inheritance.*
A Copartner, *one that is joyn'd in partnership with another.*
A Cope, *a kind of Priest's vestment.*
To be able to cope, or *deal with one.*
The Coping, or *jutting out of a wall.*
Copious, or *plentifull.*
Copiousness.
A Cop, *or* tuft, *on the head of birds.*
Copped, or *sharp-topped.*
Copper, *a metal.*
A Copper, or *large vessel made of* Copper.
A Copper-smith.
Copperas, *a mineral.*
A Coppice, Coppis, *or* copse, *an Under-wood.*
Copulation, *a coupling,* or *joyning together.*
A Copy *(in several senses.)*
To copy out, or *write according to the* copy.
A Copy-hold, *a sort of Tenure by a* Copy *of the Rolls made by the Lord's Steward,*
A Copy-holder.
Coral, *a Sea-plant that grows on the rocks, and turns red when taken out of the water.*
Prickly, coral-tree, *a shrub.*
Coralline, or *sea-moss.*
Coral-wort, *or* tooth-wort, *an herb,*
A Cord, or *rope.*
To cord, or *tye with cords.*
Cordage, or *tackle.*
Cordial, *hearty,* or *sincere.*
A Cordial, *a kind of physical potion.*
Cordialness, or *sincerity;*
A Cordiner, *or* Cordwainer, *a shoomaker.*
Cordovan-leather, *made at* Cordoua *in* Spain.
The Core *of fruit, and of a boil.*
Coriander, *a kind of plant.*
A Cork-tree.
Cork-shooes.
To cork, or *stop with* cork.
A Cormorant, or *Sea-raven.*
Corn *for bread.*
A Corn *of salt.*
A Corn, or *excressence on the toe.*
To corn, or *powder with salt.*
Corn-flag, *an herb.*
Corn-rose, *or* Corn-poppey.
Corn-sallet, or *cornwall-sallet.*
Corn-violet.
A Cornel-tree, *and berry.*
Cornelian-berry, or *cherry.*
A Cornelian, *a kind of precious stone of a red colour.*
A Corner, or *nook.*
Corner'd, or *with corners.*
A Cornet, *a small shawm; also an Ensign in a troop of horse.*
A Cornet-*fish.*
A Cornet-*cucumber.*
A Cornice, or cornish, *a kind of ornament in building.*
To cornute, or *cuckold one.*
A Corollary, or *inference drawn from a proposition.*
The Coronation, or *crown-*

crowning of a King.
A Coroner, *an Officer, who with the assistance of a Jury of 12 Men: enquires on behalf of the Crown, into all untimely deaths.*
A Coronet, or *little crown; as a Duke's*, or *Earl's* coronet.
Corporal, corporeal, *or bodily,*
A Corporal, *a military Officer.*
A Corporation, *political body,* or *company established by a Royal Charter.*
A Corps, or *dead body.*
Corpulency, or *bigness of body.*
Corpulent, or *fat and gross.*
To correct, *amend, punish,* &c.
A Correcter.
A Correction.
A Corrective *medicine.*
A Corrector, or *Printer's* Correcter.
A Corrector *of the staple, a Clerk that records all bargains made there.*
Correlative, *mutually related to one another.*
To correspond, *answer,* or *agree.*
A Correspondence, *intercourse, intelligence, mutual commerce,* or *familiarity.*
Correspondency, *agreement,* or *proportion of one thing to another.*
Correspondent, or *suitable.*
A Correspondent, *one with whom correspondence is kept.*
Corrigible, *that may be corrected,* or *amended.*
A Corrival, *one that courts the same Mistress with another.*
To corroborate, or *strengthen.*
Corroborative.
To corrode, or *eat up; gnaw, fret,* or *gall.*
Corrosive.
Corrosiveness.
Corrupt, *naught, noisome,* or *full of faults.*
To corrupt, *spoil, destroy, putrefie, defile,* &c.
A Corrupter.
Corruptible, *that may be corrupted.*
Corruption.
Corruptive, or *apt to corrupt.*
A Corsair, courser, *rover,* or *pirate.*
A Corslet, *a kind of armour for back and breast.*
To cosen, cozen, or *cheat.*
Cosenage,
A Cosener, or *cheater.*
A Cosmographer.
Cosmographical, *belonging to.*
Cosmography; or *the description of the World.*
Cost, or *expence, and to* cost.
Cost-mary, *or* cost-weed.
Ale-cost, *an herb.*
A Costard apple.
A Costard-monger.
Costive, or *bound in body.*
Costiveness.
The Costive-tree.
Costly, or *expensive.*
A Cott, cottage, or *Hutt.*
A Sheep-cott.
A Cottager.
Cotton.
To cotton, or *agree.*
Lavender-cotton. } *herbs*
Cotton-grass. } *herbs*
Cotton-thistle. } *herbs*
Cotton-weed, *or* cud-weed. } *herbs*
A Couch, or *couch-bed.*
To couch *(in several senses.)*
Couch-weed, couch-grass, or *quitch-grass.*
Couchant *(in Heraldry) lying close to the ground.*
A Covenant, *bargain,* or *agreement.*
To covenant, or *make a* covenant.
A Covenanter, *one that took the* Scotch *Covenant.*
A Covent, convent, or *Monastery.*
Coventry-bells, *an herb.*
A Cover, *and to* cover *(in all senses.)*
A Coverlet, *for a bed.*
A Covert, *a shelter,* or *shady place for deer.*
Covertly, or *privately.*
To covet, or *desire eagerly.*
Covetous.
Covetousness.
A Cough, *and to* cough.
The Chin-cough.
I could *(from* can.)
A Coulter, or *Ploughshare.*
A Council, or *assembly of Counsellors.*
Counsel, or *advice.*
To counsel, or *advise one.*
A Counseller *at the Law.*
Counsellors, or *members of the privy Council.*
A Count, or *foreign Earl.*
To count, *tell over esteem of,* or *reckon.*
The Countenance, *visage,* or *Aspect.*
To countenance, *encourage,* or *shew favour to.*
A Counter, or *counting-board in a shop.*
The Counters, *two prisons in* London *so call'd.*
Counters *for Children to play with.*
*To run-*counter, or *act contrary to.*
A Counter-ballance, or *equal weight.*
To counter-ballance, or *make of a like,* or *even weight.*
Counterband, *or* contraband *goods.*
A Counter-battery, *a battery rais'd against another.*
A Counter-bond, or *bond*

to

to indemnify one that is bound for another.
A Counter-change, *or mutual exchange made between two Parties by compact.*
A Counter-charge, or *charge brought against an accuser.*
A Counter-charm, or *Charm us'd to spoil the force of another.*
A Counter-check.
To counter-check, or *censure a reprover.*
Counter-cunning, or *subtilty us'd by the adverse party,*
Counterfeit, or *false Coin.*
A Counterfeit, or *cheat.*
To counterfeit, *feign,* or *forge.*
A Counterfeiter.
A Countermand.
To countermand, or *recall a former command.*
A Counter-march, or *contrary march.*
A Countermine, or *mine digg'd against another mine.*
To countermine. or *make such mines.*
A Counterminer.
A Counter-mure, or *wall set against another.*
A Counterpain, or *coverlet, for a bed.*
The Counter-part, or *copy of a Writing,* or *Indenture.*
A Counter-plea, *contrary* or *cross plea.*
A Counter-plot, or *shamplot.*
A Counter-point *in Musick, by setting point,* or *note against note.*
A Counterpoise, *or* counter-ballance.
To counterpoise, or *weigh one thing against another.*
A Counter-poison, *an antidote,* or *contrary poison.*
A Counter-rail, or *rail set against another rail.*
A Counter-round *of Officers visiting the rounds.*
A Counterscarp, *a rampart rais'd opposite to a Town-Wall,* or *Fort.*
Counter-security, or *mutual security given to each party.*
A Counter-sophister, *one that holds an argument against another Sophister.*
A Counter-tally, *to confirm,* or *confute another tally.*
The Counter-tenor *in musick,*
To countervail; *to be of equal value,* or *make amends for.*
A Countess, *the Wife of a Count,* or *Earl.*
A Country.
A County, or *shire.*
A Couple, or *pair.*
To couple, or *joyn together.*
Courage, *valour,* or *boldness.*
Couragious, or *stout.*
Couragiousness.
A Courant, *a kind of dance,* or *a News-paper so call'd.*
A Courier, *a messenger that rides post.*
A Course *(in all senses.)*
To course, or *chase wild beasts.*
Course, *opposite to fine; as* course cloth.
Courseness.
A Courser, or *race-horse.*
A Horse-courser.
Coursers, or *disputants in Schools.*
A Court *(in several senses.)*
A Court-baron, *held by the Lord of a Mannour.*
The Court *of Chancery,* &c.
Court-days, *when Pleas are held.*
To court, or *woe a Mistress.*
Courteous, or *civil, kind,* &c.
A Courtesan, *or* courtezan; *a Court-Lady, a Lady of pleasure,* or *strumpet.*
To make a Courtesy, *or* cursy.
Courtesy, or *civility,* &c.
A Courtier, *one that attends at the Royal Court.*
A Courtlass, or *short sword.*
Courtliness, *or* courtship.
Courtly.
To Cousen, cozen, or *cheat.*
A Cousin, *a Relation.*
A Covy, or *flock of partridges.*
A Cow, *a beast.*
A Cow-herd.
To cow one; or *put him out of heart.*
Cow-quakes, Cows-parsnip, Cow-wheat, } *herbs.*
A Coward, *dastard,* or *faint-hearted fellow.*
Cowardise, *or* cowardliness.
A Cowcumber, *or* cucumber, *a fruit.*
A Cowl, or *Monk's hood.*
A Cowslip, *a flower.*
Our Lady's Cowslip.
A Coxcomb, or *silly fop*
To coxe, coaks, or *sooth up.*
Coy, or *shie.*
Coyness.

C R

A Crab, *wilding,* or *wild-apple.*
A Crab-fish.
A Crab-lowse.
Crabbed, *sower,* or *morose.*
Crabbedness.
A Crack, *and to* crack *(in several senses.)*
Crack-brain'd.
Crack-berry, *an herb.*
A Cracker, or *squib.*
A Nut-cracker.
To crackle, *as bays does in the fire.*

A

A Cracknel, or *simnel.*
Crackt, or *broken.*
A Cradle *for a Child.*
The Cradle *of a Lobster.*
Craft, or *skill.*
Craftiness, or *subtilty.*
An Handy-craft.
A Crafts-man.
Crafty, *sly*, or *subtil.*
A Crag, or *neck.*
A Crag, or *rock.*
Cragged, craggy, or *rough.*
To cram, *stuff*, or *thrust close.*
Crambling-rocket, *an herb*
The Cramp, or *stretching of the Sinews, a Disease.*
To cramp *one.*
The Cramp-fish.
A Crampern, *or* Cramp-iron, *an hook*, or *grapple of a Ship.*
Cranage, *a duty paid for the use of a Crane.*
A Crane, *an Engine, to* crane *up*, or *draw up wares.*
A Crane, *a Bird.*
Cranes-bill, *an herb.*
Crank, *lusty, brisk or jocund.*
The Crank *of a well.*
To crankle *in & out.*
Crannied, or *full of* crannies.
A Cranny, or *chink.*
Crape, *a sort of stuff.*
A Crash, *and to* crash.
Crasy, *or* crazy.
A Cratch, *crib*, or *rack.*
A Cravat, *a kind of neck-cloth, said to be first us'd by the* Croats *in the* German *Wars.*
A Lace-cravat.
A Point-cravat.
To crave, *desire*, or *beg.*
A Craver.
Cravingness.
The Craw, or *crop of a bird.*
To crawl, or *creep.*
A Crawler, or *crawling creature.*
The Cray, *a disease in Hawks that hinders their muting.*
A Cray-fish.
A Crayon, or *pastel, to draw*, or *design with, in dry colours.*
Crazed, or *crack-brain'd.*
Craziness, or *sickliness.*
Crazy, *weak, sickly*, or *distemper'd.*
The Cream *of milk*, &c.
Cream-cheese.
A Crease, or *pleat.*
To crease, or *fold.*
To create, *make, frame*, or *form.*
The Creation *of the World,*
A Creatour.
A Creature.
Credence, or *belief.*
Credentials, or *letters of* credence.
Credible, *to be believed.*
Credibleness, *or* credibility.
Credit, *reputation, esteem belief*, or *trust.*
To credit *one.*
Creditable, *of fair credit*, or *that brings credit.*
A Creditor, our, *one that lends*, or *trusts another with money*, or *goods.*
Credulity, or *aptness to believe.*
Credulous, *ready to believe.*
A Creed, or *Belief*; i. e. *a summary of the Christian Faith.*
The Apostles Creed.
The Nicene-Creed, *&c.*
A Creek, or *little Bay.*
To creek, *as a door does.*
To creep, or *crawl.*
A Creeper.
Creepers, or *andirons.*
A Creiance, *for a Hawk.*
A Crescent, i. e. *encreasing; the figure of a half Moon.*
Cresses, *an herb.*
Garden-cresses.
Sciatica-cresses.
Swines-cresses.
Water-cresses.
Winter-Cresses.
A Cresset-light, *or burning Beacon.*
A Crest, or *cop of a bird.*
The Crest, or *main of an horse.*
The Crest, or *upper part of an helmet*, or *scutcheon.*
Crest-faln, or *dejected.*
A Crevice, or *cray-fish.*
A Crevice, crevis, or *chink.*
A Crew, or *company*; as *a* crew *of rogues.*
The Boat's Crew.
Crewel, *a sort of worsted.*
A Crewet *or* crevet; *a little vial to hold Oil, Vinegar*, &c.
A Crib, cratch, or *manger.*
Cribbage, *a game at cards.*
A Cribble, or *sieve to purge Corn.*
A Crick, or *cramp in the neck.*
To crick, *or* creek.
A Cricket, or *low stool; also a kind of play with a ball.* &c.
A Cricket, *an insect.*
A Fen-cricket.
A Criketing-apple.
A Crier, or *publick* crier *of a Town, Court*, &c.
A Crime, or *high misdemeanour.*
Criminal, or *faulty.*
A Criminal, or *Malefector.*
Crimpling, as *to go* crimpling.
Crimson, *a sort of fine red colour.*
A Cringe, *congee* or *low bow.*
To cringe, or *bow.*
To crinkle, or *make in wrinkles*, or *folds.*
Full of Crinkles.
A Cripple, or *impotent person, that has lost the use of his limbs.*
To cripple, or *lame one.*
Cripplings, *in architecture, short spars on the side of a house.*

Crisp, *fried, or roasted brown.*
To crisp, or *curl.*
A Crisping-iron.
St. Crispin, *the shoo-makers Patron.*
A Critch, or *crib.*
Critical, *that judges,* or *that gives signs to judge by.*
Critical days, *wherein Physitians observe signs of life, or death, and judge of the distemper.*
A Criticism, or *nice judgment.*
To criticize, or *play*
The Critick, i. e. *a great scholar a judicious person;* or *an over-nice censurer.*
A Crock *a kind of earthen pot.*
A Crocodile, *a ravenous creature shap'd like a lizard, that lives both on land and water, and grows to a vast bigness, sometimes* 20, or 30 *foot long.*
A Croft, *a little field,* or *close, lying near a house.*
To croke, or *make a noise like a toad, frog,* or *raven.*
The Croking, or *rumbling of the guts.*
To croo *like a pigeon.*
A Crook, or *hook.*
By Hook, or *by* crook.
A Shepherds-crook.
Crook-back'd.
Crook-legg'd.
Crook-shoulder'd.
Crooked, *bended,* or *bowed.*
Crookedness.
To crookel *like a dove,* or *pigeon.*
A Crop *of Corn,* or *hay.*
The Crop, *or* craw, *of a bird.*
Crop-sick.
To Crop, *cut off,* or *gather.*
Crop-ear'd.

A Cropper, or *gatherer.*
A Crosier, or *Bishop's staff.*
A Croslet, or *forehead-cloth.*
Cross, *contrary,* or *peevish.*
Crossness.
A Cross, *and to* cross, *(in several senses.)*
A Cross-bill. *a bird.*
A Cross-bar-shot, *a round shot, with a long iron-spike.*
A Cross-bow.
A Cross-cloth *for an infant.*
Cross-grain'd, *stubborn,* or *peevish.*
Cross-legg'd, *with the legs a-cross.*
A Cross-path, *or* cross-way.
Cross-wort, *an herb.*
A Crotchet, *a kind of musical note; also a mark in Printing,* [ ]
A Crotchet, *whimsy,* or *conceit.*
Crotels, *the ordure of a hare.*
To crouch, or *bow down.*
A Crow, or *iron-bar.*
A Crow, *a bird.*
The Roiston-crow.
A Scare-crow.
To crow, *as a cock does;* or *to vapour.*
Crow-foot, *an herb.*
Crow-garlick.
Crow-toes, *a flower.*
A Crows-bill, *a Surgeon's instrument to draw out bullets, bones,* &c.
A Crowd, or *throng, and to* crowd.
A Crown, *a known coin, worth* 5 *s.*
A Crown, *a diadem, coronet,* or *garland.*
To crown *a King.*
The Crown *of the head.*
Crown-imperial, *an herb.*
The frier's crown-thistle.
To croyn, or *cry like a Deer.*

A Crucible, *a goldsmith's melting-pot;* or *a vessel us'd by Chymists.*
A Crucifix, or *the figure of Christ upon the* Cross.
A Crucifixion.
To crucify, or *nail to a* Cross.
Crude, *raw,* or *undigested.*
Crudity, *want of good digestion,* or *rawness of stomack.*
Cruel, *merciless,* or *fierce*
Cruelty.
A Cruet, *or* crewet, *a vial for vinegar, oil,* &c.
To cruise, or *rove up and down the Seas for prize,* &c.
A Crum *of bread,* &c.
To crum *a porrenger of broth, &c.*
To crumble, or *break small.*
Crump, or *bowed.*
Crump footed.
Crump-shoulder'd.
A Crumple, *and to* crumple.
A Crumpling-apple.
To crunk, or *cry like a Crane.*
A Crupper, or *rump.*
A Cruse, or *little vial.*
To crush, *squeez,* or *oppress.*
A Crust *of bread.*
Crusted, as *crusted with marble.*
Crusty, *that has an hard* crust; *also peevish,* or *fretfull.*
A Crutch, or *staff to lean upon.*
A Cry, *and to* cry.
A Cryer.
A Common-cryer *of a Court,* &c.
Crystal. *a sort of mineral stone, as transparent as the clearest glass.*
Crystaline, *like to crystal.*

CU

A Cub, or *whelp.*
A Cubbard, *or* cupboard.
A Cube, *a Geometrical figure like a die; being a solid square body, with six equal sides.*
Cubical, *or* cubick, *belonging to a* Cube.
Cubebs, *an* Indian *fruit.*
A Cubit, *a kind of measure from the elbow to the fingers ends.*
A Cucking-stool, *to duck Scolds*, &c.
A Cuckold, *a horned animal; one whose Wife has been debauch'd.*
To cuckold *one.*
A Cuckold-maker.
A Cuckoo, *a bird.*
The Cuckoo-fish.
The Cuckoo-flower.
The Cuckoo-gilliflower.
Cuckoo's-pintle, *an herb.*
A Cucumber, *a fruit.*
The Wild-cucumber.
The Cud *of beasts*; as *to chew the* cud.
Cudwort, *an herb.*
A Cudgel, *battoon*, or *stick.*
To cudgel one, or *beat him with a* cudgel.
A Cuff, or *fore-sleeve.*
A Cuff, or *box on the ear.*
To cuff, or *buffet.*
A Cuirass, *a kind of armour for the back and breast.*
A Cuirassier, or *horseman so armed.*
To cull, *to pick and choose*
A Cull-fish,
Cull me to you, *a flower.*
A Cullander, *a kitchen-vessel, to drain off liquors*, &c.
A Culler, *a sheep drawn out of a flock; not being good for meat.*
A Cullis, or *strained liquor us'd in ragoos.*
A Cully, or *foolish fellow.*
To cully one, or *make a fool of him.*
Culpable, or *blameworthy.*
Culrage, or *arse-smart, an herb.*
To cultivate, *manure*, or *till.*
Culture, *improvement*, or *polite education.*
A Culver-pigeon.
A Wood-culver.
A Culverin, *a piece of Ordinance so call'd.*
A Demi-culverin.
To cumber, *trouble*, or *hinder.*
Cumbersome.
Cummin, *a sort of plant.*
A Cunner, *a fish.*
Cunning, *skilfulness*, or *craftiness.*
A Cup *to drink out of.*
To cup *one with*
A Cupping-glass, *apply'd to the body with burning tow; to raise a blister on the part*, or *to draw blood by scarification.*
A Cup-bearer.
A Cupboard.
Cup-shot, or *drunken.*
A Cupolo, *a round louver*, or *arch in a building.*
Curable, *that may be cur'd.*
A Curacy, or curateship; *the Office of*
A Curate, or *vicar.*
The Curb *of a bridle.*
To curb, or *restrain.*
The Curd *of milk*, &c.
To curd, or *turn to* curds.
Cheese-curds.
Wild-curds.
To curdle *milk*
A curdled sky.
A Cure, *and to* cure, or *heal.*
The Cure *of Souls*, or *a Benefice.*
Curiosity, *affectedness*, or *neatness.*
Curious, *neat, nice*, &c.
Curiousness.
A Curl, or *curled lock.*
To curl *the hair.*
A Curlew, *a bird.*
The Curlings *of a Deer's head.*
A Curmudgeon, or *close-fisted fellow.*
A Curnock, i. e. 4 *bushels of Corn.*
A Curr, or *House-dog.*
Currish, or *dog-like.*
Currans, *a fruit.*
Current, or *passable*; as *current money.*
A Current, or *stream.*
The Currentness *of money*
A Currier, or *leather-dresser.*
To curry, *to rub down an Horse*; or *to dress leather.*
A Curry-comb.
A Curse, *and to* curse.
A Cursitor, or *Chancery-Clerk, that makes out original Writs. There are* 24 *of these Clerks, and they are a Corporation of themselves.*
Cursory, *slight*, or *hasty.*
Curst, *shrewd*, or *fierce.*
Curstness.
To make a Cursy.
A Curtail, or *drab.*
To curtail, or *cut off.*
A Curtain *for a bed, window*, &c.
A Curvet, *the prauncing of a Horse.*
To curvet, or *praunce.*
A Cushion, *for a Chair.*
Ladies-cushion, *a flower.*
A Custard, *made of milk, eggs*, &c.
Custody, *tuition, ward*, or *keeping.*
Custom, *use*, or *fashion*; *also a duty paid to the King, or State for goods exported and imported.*
A Custom-house.
Customable, *according to* custom.

Cu-

Customary, or *usual.*
A Customer, *he or she that uses to buy of one.*
A Cut, *and to* cut (*in all senses.*)
A Cutler, or *Sword-cutler.*
A Cut-purse,
A Cutted *Houswife.*
A Cut-throat.
A Cutter.
A Cuttle-fish.

C Y

A Cygnet, or *young swan*
A Cylinder, *a figure in form of a rolling-stone.*
A Cymbal, *a musical instrument.*
Cynical, *currish,* or *dogged,* from
The Cynicks, *a severe and crabbed Sect of Philosophers, the followers of* Antisthenes, *and* Diogenes.
Cypress, *a sort of fine curled linnen.*
A Cypress-tree.
Czar (*q*-Cæsar) *the title of the Emperor,* or *great Duke of* Muscovy.

D A

A Dab, or *blow on the chaps.*
A Dab-*chick,* or *didapper.*
A Dab-fish, or *sandling.*
To dabble, or *paddle in the water,* or *dirt.*
A Dace, *a fish.*
A Daffodell, *a flower.*
To dag *sheep*; *to cut off the skirts of the fleece.*
A Dagger, or *poniard.*
The Dagger-fish.
To daggle, dag, or *dawb one's cloths.*
A Daggle-tail.
Dag-locks, *Wooll cut off from the out-side of the fleece.*
Daily, or *every day.*
Dainties, or *dainty-dishes.*
Daintiness.
Dainty, or *delicate.*
A Dairy, or *milk-house.*
A Dairy-woman.
A Daisy, *a flower.*
The blew Daisy.
A Daker-hen.
A Dale, or *valley.*
Dalliance, or *wantonness.*
A Dallier.
To dally, *trifle,* or *play the fool.*
A Dam, *weer,* or *flood-gate in a river,* or *pond.*
A Mill-dam.
To dam *up waters,* &c.
Damask-prunes.
A Damask-rose.
Damask-silk, *or* linnen, *from* Damascus, *a City of* Syria.
To damask *Wine*, or *warm it a little, to give it a flavour.*
To damask, or *stamp rude marks on paper.*
A Damask-board, *for that use.*
A Dame, or *Mistress.*
Dames-violets, *an herb.*
Dammage, *loss, hurt, injury,* or *inconvenience.*
To damn; or *condemn to Hell-torments.*
Damnable.
Damnation.
To damnify, *or* endammage.
Damp, or *moist.*
A Damp, *and to* damp (*in several senses*)
Dampish, or *somewhat moist.*
Dampness.
A Damsin, *or* damson, *a kind of plum.*
A Dance, *and to* dance
A Dancer.
A Rope-dancer.
A Dancing-master.
A Dancing-school.
Dandelion, *an herb.*
To dandle, or *tend a Child.*
Dandriff, or *scurf, on the head.*
A Dandriff-comb.
Dane-wort, *an herb.*
Danger, or *peril.*
Dangerous.
To dangle, or *hang carelesly.*
A Dapper, or *spruce little fellow.*
A Dapple-grey *colour.*
To dare, *challenge, presume,* or *adventure.*
A Daring-glass, *to catch Larks.*
Dark, or *obscure.*
To darken, or *make* dark.
A Darling, or *beloved Child.*
To darn, or *mend linnen.*
Darnel, or *cockle-weed.*
Darnix, *a kind of cloth, made at* Dornick, or Tournay, *a Town in* Flanders,
A Dart, or *javelin.*
To dart, or *cast a* dart.
A Darter.
A Dash, *and to* dash, (*in several senses.*)
A Dastard, or *coward.*
A Date, *the fruit of the Palm-tree.*
The Date *of a Writing,* Coin, &c. i. e. *the time when made.*
To date *a letter,* &c.
A Daughter.
A God-daughter.
To daunt, *discourage,* or *frighten,*
Dauntless, or *fearless.*
A Daw, *or* jack-daw, *a bird.*
To dawb, *besmear, plaister, defile,* or *flatter.*
A Dawber.
To dawn, or *begin to grow light.*
The Dawn *of the* Day.
The Day-lilly, *a plant.*
A Days-man, or *umpire.*
To dazzle *the eyes*, or *one's reason.*

DE

A Deacon, (i. e. *Minister*) *a Church-officer.*
A Deaconess.
Deaconship.
Dead (*from to* die.)
Dead-nettles, or *arch-angel, an herb.*
To dead, deaden, or *make* Dead.
Deadly, or *causing death, &c.*
Deaf, *that cannot hear.*
To deafen, or *make* deaf.
To deal, *to distribute*; or *to trade.*
Deal, *or* deal-timber.
A great deal, or *very much.*
A Dealer, or *trader.*
A Dean, *of a Cathedral,* or *Collegiate Church, who presides over* 10 *Canons.*
A Rural Dean, *a Curate appointed by the Bishop to have jurisdiction over other Ministers, and Parishes in the Country.*
The Dean *of the King's Chappel, Arches,* &c.
Deanship, *the Office of a* Dean.
A Deanry, *the jurisdiction of a* Dean.
Dear, as *to price,* or *affection.*
To dearn, darn, or *stitch*
The Dearness *of provisions*
A Dearth, or *famine.*
Death.
A Death-watch, *an insect.*
To debar, *keep out,* or *hinder.*
To debase, *depress,* or *disparage.*
A Debate, *and to* debate (*in several senses.*)
To debauch, or *corrupt manners.*
Debauchery.
Debility, *weakness,* or *feebleness.*
A Deboshee, or *lewd wretch.*
A Debt, i. e. *somewhat due to another.*
A Debtor, *one that is in debt.*
A Decade, or *number of Ten.*
The Decalogue, or *Ten Commandments.*
To decamp, or *remove a Camp.*
A Decampment.
To decant, or *pour out of one vessel into another.*
A Decay, or *failure.*
To decay, or *fail, waste, grow worse,* &c.
Decease, or *death.*
Deceased, or *dead.*
Deceit, *fraud* or Guile.
Deceitfull.
Deceitfulness.
Deceivable, *that may be deceiv'd.*
To deceive, *beguile, cozen, gull,* or *trepan.*
A Deceiver.
December, i. e. *the tenth month from* March.
Decency, or *comliness.*
Decennial, *of ten years.*
Decent, *seemly, comely,* or *becoming.*
To decide, *determine,* or *put an end to Controversies.*
To decimate, or *punish every tenth soldier by lot.*
A Decimation, *such a punishment; also the sequestration of the tenth part of a Man's Estate.*
To decipher *a letter,* &c. i. e. *explain the contents of it, express'd in Ciphers,* or *secret characters.*
A Decipherer.
A Decision, or *ending of a Controversy.*
Decisive, *or* decisory, *apt for such a purpose.*
To deck, *garnish,* or *set out.*
The Decks *of a Ship.*
To declaim, or *exercise himself in making speeches.*
A Declaimer.
A Declamation, *an oration made upon a Subject.*
Declamatory, *that relates thereto.*
A Declaration, *manifestation,* or *shewing.*
Declarative, or declaratory.
To declare, *shew,* or *tell.*
A Declarer.
To decline, *avoid, decay,* &c.
The Declination *of an Empire.*
The Declivity, or *steepness of a hill.*
A Decoction, or *physick-broth, made of herbs, roots, seeds,* &c.
The Decorations, or *ornaments of the Stage.*
Decorum, *decency,* or *comeliness.*
A Decoy, *a place made fit to catch wild fowl.*
A Decoy-duck.
To decoy, *entice,* or *allure.*
The Decrease, *of the moon*
To decrease, *grow less,* or *decay.*
A Decree (*in several senses.*)
To decree, *determine,* or *resolve.*
Decrepit, *stooping with age; very old and crazy.*
The Decretals, or *Ordinances made by Popes, Bishops,* &c.
A Decretory, or *definitive sentence.*
To decry, *cry down,* or *speak ill of.*
To dedicate *a Church,* or *Book.*
A Dedication.
An Epistle dedicatory.
To deduce, or *gather one thing by Reason from another.*

Dedu-

Deducible, *that may be so inferr'd.*
To deduct, or *abate.*
A Deduction.
A Deed, *action*, or *writing.*
Deeds, *instruments*, or *writings of Contract between several parties.*
To deem, *judge*, or *think.*
Deemsters, *judges in the Isle of* Man, *who decide all Controversies without any process*, *writings*, or *charges.*
Deep (*in all senses.*)
Deepness, or *depth.*
A Deer, *a wild beast.*
A Fallow-deer.
A Red-deer.
A Rein-deer.
To deface, *disfigure*, *spoil*, or *blot out.*
A Defamation, or *slander.*
Defamatory.
To defame, *slander*, *discredit*, or *speak evil of.*
A Default, or *omission of what ought to be done.*
A Defeat, *and* to defeat (*in several senses.*)
A Defect, or *failing.*
A Defection, or *revolt.*
Defective.
A Defence (*in different senses.*)
To defend, *maintain*, or *protect.*
A Defendant, *in a* Law-*suit*; *he that is sued in a personal action, and joins issue with the Plaintiff.*
A Defender.
A Defendress.
A Defensative, or *antidote against poison.*
Defensible.
Defensive.
To defer, *put off*, or *delay.*
Deference, or *respect.*
A Defiance, *challenging*, or *out-braving.*
A Deficiency, *or defect*; *a want*, or *failing.*

Deficient, or *wanting.*
To defile, *daub*, *pollute*, or *corrupt.*
A Defile, or *narrow passage for an Army.*
A Defilement, or *pollution.*
A Defiler.
To define, *determine*, *declare*, or *explain.*
A Definition, or *short explication of the thing spoken of.*
Definitive, or *decisive.*
Definite, *certain*, or *limited.*
To deflour, or *ravish.*
A Deflourer *of Women.*
A Defluxion, or *flowing down of* rheum, or *humours.*
To deform, *disfigure*, or *make ugly.*
Deformity, *a being ugly*, or *mis-shapen.*
To defraud, *deceive*; *beguile*, *cheat*, or *cozen.*
To defray, *discharge one's expences*, or *pay his charges.*
To defy, or *challenge.*
A Degeneracy, or *depravation.*
Degenerate, *that is degenerated.*
To degenerate, *to fall from the better kind*; *to grow worse*, or *wild.*
To degrade, or *put from his degree*, *office*, or *dignity.*
A Degree, (*in several senses.*)
To dehort, or *disswade.*
A Dehortation.
To deject, or *cast down.*
Dejected.
Dejection *of mind.*
To deify, or *make a God of.*
A Deist; *that owns one God, without distinction of Persons.*
The Deity, or *Godhead.*
A Delay, *stay*, or *stop.*
To delay, *defer*, *put off*, or *prolong.*

Delayed-wine, i. e. *mingled with water.*
Delectable, or *pleasant.*
Delectableness.
Delectation or *delight.*
A Delegate, or *judge delegate.*
To delegate, or *appoint in another's stead.*
A Delegation, or *Commission.*
Deliberate, or *advised.*
To deliberate, *consider*, *debate*, or *advise.*
A Deliberation.
Deliberative.
Delicate, *dainty*, *neat*, or *nice.*
Delicateness, *or* delicacy.
Delicious, or *pleasant to the taste.*
Deliciousness.
Delight, *pleasure*, or *satisfaction.*
To delight, *to please*, or *to take delight.*
Delightfull.
Delightfulness.
To delineate, or *make the first draught of a Picture*; or *to describe.*
A Delineation.
Delinquency, or *offence.*
A Delinquent, or *offender.*
Delirious, *doting*, or *light-headed.*
To deliver, *free from*, *give in trust*, *utter in discourse*, &c.
A Deliverance;
The Delivery, *in speaking.*
To delude, *deceive*; *disappoint*, or *mock.*
To delve, or *dig.*
A Delver.
A Deluge, *a great flood*, or *inundation of waters.*
A Delusion, *deceit*, or *Cheat.*
A Demand.
To demand, *require*, *lay claim to*, or *ask.*
A Demandant *in a real action at Law*; *the same as Plaintiff in a personal.*
A Demander.

To demean, or *behave himself.*
A Demeanour, or *conduct.*
Demeans, *or* demesnes, *an Estate,* or *land held originally of one's self.*
The King's Demeans, or *Crown-revenues.*
Demerit; *an ill deserving*
Demi *in composition,* i. e. *half;* as
A Demi-cannon.
A Demi-god, &c.
A Demise, or *grant.*
To demise, *grant, farm,* or *let by lease.*
Democracy, or *popular Government; where the People have the rule.*
Democratical, *belonging to such a Government,*
To demolish, *pull down,* or *ruin any thing that is built.*
A Demolisher.
A Demon, or *evil spirit.*
A Demoniack, *one possess'd with a* Demon.
Demonstrable, *that may be demonstrated.*
To demonstrate, *prove,* or *shew plainly.*
A Demonstration.
Demonstrative, *belonging to* demonstration.
Demure, *seemingly grave* or *bashfull.*
Demureness, or *affected gravity.*
To demurr, or *put in exceptions.*
A Demurrer, *a pause,* or *stop upon a difficult point in any process.*
A Den, or *cave.*
A Denial, or *refusing to grant.*
Self-denial.
A Denison, *or* denizen, *a foreigner, infranchised,* or *made capable of bearing any Office, purchasing and enjoying all privileges, except inheriting lands by descent.*

To denominate, or *give name to.*
A Denomination.
To denote, *mark,* or *signify.*
To denounce, *declare,* or *proclaim.*
A Dent, or *notch.*
To dent, or *to make a* dent.
To deny, *disown, refuse,* or *abjure.*
To depaint, or *represent.*
To depart, *to go a-side;* or *to another place, to die,* &c.
A Departure.
To depend, *hang,* or *rely upon.*
A Dependance, *or* dependency.
Dependent.
Deplorable, or *to be lamented.*
To deplore, or *bewail.*
A Deponent, *one that gives information upon Oath before a Magistrate.*
To depopulate, *unpeople,* or *lay waste a Country.*
A Depopulation, or *laying waste.*
To deport, or *demean himself.*
Deportment, or *behaviour.*
To depose, or *lay down upon Oath; also to turn out of Office.*
A Depositary, or *Trustee.*
To deposite, *lay down,* or *trust a thing with one.*
A Deposition, or *information upon Oath.*
A Depravation, or *corruption.*
To deprave, *spoil,* or *corrupt.*
To deprecate, or *pray against judgments,* &c.
A Deprecation.
A Depredation, *preying upon, robbing,* or *spoiling.*
To depress, or *thrust down.*
A Depression.

A Deprivation.
To deprive, *bereave,* or *take away a thing from one.*
Depth, or *deepness.*
A Deputation, or *commission.*
To depute, or *appoint in the room of another.*
A Deputy, or *person so deputed.*
To deride, *mock,* or *laugh to scorn.*
A Derider.
Derision.
The Derivation *of words.*
Derivative.
To derive, *to draw,* or *proceed from the fountain,* or *original; also to convey to.*
To derogate, *take off from the worth of a thing, disparage,* or *diminish.*
A Derogation.
Derogatory, *that derogates.*
A Desart, or *wilderness.*
A Descant, or *division in Musick; also a comment* or *paraphrase.*
To descant *in musick,* or *discourse; to enlarge,* or *give his thoughts upon a thing.*
To descend, or *go down; also to come of a family.*
A Descent (*in several senses.*)
To describe, *write,* or *set down; to draw, pourtray,* or *depaint.*
A Describer.
A Description.
To descry, *discover,* or *spy out afar off.*
Desert, or *merit.*
A Desert, dessert, or *banquet of sweet-meats.*
To desert, or *forsake.*
A Deserter, *a soldier that runs away from his colours.*
A Desertion.
To deserve, or *merit well,* or *ill.*

A Design, *purpose*, or *intention.*
To design, *determine, resolve upon, contrive, plot*, &c.
A Designer *of draughts.*
Desireable, *to be wish'd for.*
Desire.
To desire, *covet, request, entreat*, or *sue for.*
Desirous.
To desist, or *leave off.*
A Desk *for books*, or *to write on.*
Desolate, *left alone, laid waste, ruin'd*, or *afflicted.*
A Desolation.
Despair, or *a being out of hope.*
To despair *of*, or *lose hopes*
A Desperado, or *desperate fellow.*
Desperate, *out of hope*; or *furious.*
Desperateness.
Desperation, *a despairing*, or *giving over.*
Despicable, *to be despised, base, sorry*, or *mean.*
To despise, or *slight.*
A Despiser.
Despite, *malice, scorn*, or *grudge*, &c.
In despite *of one.*
Despitefully, or *maliciously.*
To despoil, or *rob one of his substance.*
To despond, *despair*, or *be out of heart.*
Despondency, *a failing of courage*, or *being quite disheartned.*
Despondent, or *despairing.*
Despotical, or despotick, i. e. *absolute, and arbitrary.*
Destiny, or *fate.*
Destitute, *bereaved of*, or *forsaken.*
Destitution.
To destroy, *throw down, spoil, ruin*, or *deface.*
A Destroyer.
Destruction.
Destructive.
A Desultory, or *wavering judgment.*
To detach, or *set a-part a company of soldiers out of the main body of the Army, to make an attempt upon the enemy.*
A Detachment, *a party sent out upon such a design.*
To detain, *cause to stay, withold*, or *hinder.*
To detect, *lay open*, or *discover.*
A Detection.
A Detention, *detaining*, or *with-holding.*
Determinable, *that may be determined.*
Determinately, or *positively.*
A Determination.
To determine, *purpose*, or *appoint*; *to end a business*, &c.
To deterr, *affright*, or *discourage one.*
A Detersive, or *cleansing medicine.*
To detest, or *abhorr.*
Detestable.
Detestation.
To dethrone *a Prince, to depose*, or *put him from the Throne.*
To detract, *slander*, or *disparage.*
A Detracter.
Detraction, or *backbiting.*
Detractive.
Detriment, or *dammage.*
Detrimental, *that brings dammage.*
A Devastation, *laying waste*, or *spoiling.*
The Deuce, *at cards*, or *dice.*
To devest, *strip, dispossess*, or *deprive of.*
A Deviation, or *going a-stray.*
A Device, or *contrivance*; *also a motto*, or *emblem.*
The Devil, or *evil spirit.*
Devil's-bit, *an herb.*
Devil's-milk, *a kind of spurge.*
Devilish.
Devilishness.
To devise, *invent, contrive, imagine*, &c.
A Deviser.
Devoir, or *duty.*
To devolve, *roll down, fall*, or *come from one to another, as an Estate*, &c.
A Devolutary, *one that claims a Benefice fallen into lapse.*
A Devolution, or *devolving.*
To devote, *vow, consecrate*, or *give himself up to.*
Devotion, *being addicted to*, or *being devout and pious.*
To devour, *eat greedily, consume*, or *oppress.*
A Devourer.
Devout, or *godly.*
Devoutness.
Deuteronomy, i. e. *the second Law*, or *the repetition of it*; *one of the five books of* Moses, *so call'd.*
Dew, *a meteor.*
Mill-dew.
Dew-berries.
The Dew-claws, *of a bird*, or *deer.*
The Dew-lap, *of an Ox*; *the skin that hangs under the throat.*
Dew-grass, } *herbs.*
Sun-dew, }
The Dewing, or *falling of* dew.
Dewy, or *full of* dew.
Dexterity, or *activeness.*
Dextrous, *being handy, ready, nimble*, or *active*

D I

A Diabetes, or *continual pas-*

sage of the Urine, a disease, when one cannot hold his Water.

Diabolical, or *devilish.*

A Diadem, *an imperial or royal Crown; properly a white fillet or linnen-wreath with which Kings incircled their forehead.*

Diaeresis, *the division of a vowel; as an* [ë] *diaeresis mark'd with two tittles.*

A Diagram, *a geometrical figure drawn to demonstrate a Proposition; also a certain proportion of measures in musick.*

A Dial, *to shew the hour of the day.*

A Sun-dial.

The Dial-plate *of a watch,* &c.

A Dialect, *a particular idiom,* or *propriety of the same speech.*

Dialling, or *the art of making dials.*

A Dialogue, *a feigned discourse between several persons.*

A Diameter, *a right line which goes thro' the center of a circle, and touches the circumference in two points.*

Diametral, *or* diametrical, *belonging to a diameter.*

A Diamond, *a kind of precious stone.*

Diaper, *a sort of linnen, wrought with figures.*

The Diaphragm, i. e. *a fence, or partition; the Midriff or Apron that parts the breast from the stomack.*

A Diarrhea, *lask,* or *flux of the belly.*

A Diary, *journal,* or *day-book.*

Diascordium, *a sort of electuary.*

A Dibble, or *forked stick to set herbs in a garden.*

Dice, *as a game at dice.*

A Dicer, or *dice-player.*

A Dicing-house.

A Dickere *of leather,* i. e. *ten hides,* or *skins.*

To dictate, *endite,* or *tell one what he should write.*

The Dictates *of reason.*

A Dictator, or *soveraign Magistrate among the ancient* Romans, *chosen upon urgent occasions.*

A Dictionary, or *collection of words, digested and explain'd in alphabetical order.*

A Didapper, *dab-chick,* or *diver, a bird.*

A Die, *to play with.*

To Die, *(in several senses.)*

A Dier *of colours.*

Diers-weed.

Diet, or *food.*

To Diet *one, or prescribe his diet.*

The Diet, or *convention of the Estates in* Germany *and* Poland.

To differ, *to be unlike,* or *to disagree.*

Difference.

Different.

Difficult, *uneasie,* or *hard.*

A Difficulty.

Diffidence, *distrust,* or *doubting.*

Diffident, or *distrustful.*

To diffuse, *or spread abroad.*

Diffusive.

To dig, or *delve.*

A digger.

To digest, *to dispose or set in order;* or *to concoct.*

Digestible, *that may be digested.*

The Digestion, or *concocting of meat in the stomack.*

Digestive, *that helps the digestion;* or *prepares for cleansing.*

To dignifie, *or promote to dignity.*

A Dignitary, or *dignify'd Church-man, without cure of Souls; as a Prebend, Dean,* &c.

Dignity, or *honour and worth.*

A Digression, or *going from the subject in hand.*

A Dike, *ditch,* or *furrow.*

A Dilapidation, *a wastful destroying, or suffering a building to fall to ruin and decay for want of reparation.*

To dilate, or *widen;* or *to enlarge upon a thing.*

A Dilater, *or* dilatatory, *a Surgeon's widening instrument.*

Dilatory, or *full of delays.*

A Dilemma, *an argument that catches or convinces both ways;* or *a syllogism containing two propositions so fram'd, that neither can well be denied.*

Diligence, *carefulness,* or *industry.*

Diligent, or *industrious.*

Dill, *an herb.*

A Dilling, *darling,* or *beloved Child, born when the Parents are old.*

To dilute *wine,* or *allay it with water.*

Dim, *dark, obscure,* or *having a defect in the sight.*

To dim, or *make dim.*

Dimension, *the just measure,* or *proportion of a figure, as to length, breadth, and depth.*

To diminish, *abate, grow, or make less.*

A Diminution.

Dimissory Letters, *from one Bishop to another, about*

about the conferring of Orders, &c.
Dimitty, *a fine sort of fustian*.
Dimness, or *darkness of sight*, &c.
A Dimple, or *dent*.
Dimpled, *that has a dimple*.
A Din, or *noise*.
To dine, *or eat his dinner*.
To ding, *or throw a thing*.
A Dinner, or *meal at noon*.
By dint, or *edge of sword*.
A Diocesan, *a Bishop of or an inhabitant within*
A Diocess, or *the jurisdiction of a Bishop*.
To dip.
A Dipper, or *Anabaptist*.
A Diphthong, or *two vowels sounded together in one syllable*; *as* ai, ei, oi, ou, *&c*.
Direct, *straight*, or *upright*.
To direct, *rule*, *guide*, *give instructions*, &c.
A Direction.
The directness *of the sight*, &c.
A Directer, or *instructer*.
Directory, *apt to direct*.
The Directory, *a book of Rules for divine Service, sometime introduced instead of the Common-prayer Book*.
Direful, *dreadful*, *fierce*, or *cruel*.
A Dirge, or *popish office for the dead*; *or a lamentation sung at a funeral*.
Dirt, or *mire*.
Dirtiness.
Dirty, or *full of dirt*.
To dirty, or *make dirty*.
Disability, or *incapacity*.

To disable, *to make unable*, or *uncapable of*.
To disabuse, or *undeceive one*.
A Disadvantage, *loss*, or *hind'rance*.
Disadvantagious.
Disaffected *to*, *or dissatisfied with*.
To disagree, *dissent*, or *be at variance*.
Disagreeable.
A Disagreement, or *discord*.
To disallow, *dislike*, or *blame*.
To disannul, *make void*, or *abrogate*.
To disappear, *or vanish away*.
To disappoint, *deceive*, or *fail one*.
A Disappointment.
To disapprove, or *dislike*.
To disarm, or *take away his Arms*.
A Disaster, or *misfortune*.
Disastrous, or *unfortunate*.
To disavow, or *disown*.
To disband *an Army*.
To disbelieve, or *doubt of*.
To disburden, *unload*, or *ease*.
To disburse, or *lay out money*.
Disbursements, or *expences*.
To discard, or *turn out of service*.
To discern, *distinguish*, or *perceive*.
A Discharge, *and to* discharge (*in several senses*.)
A Disciple, *scholar*, or *learner*.
The Disciplinarians, or *Sectaries*.
Discipline, *strict order*, *instruction*, *or correction*.
To discipline, *to order*,
or *correct*; or *to scourge one another as the Friers do*.
To disclaim, or *renounce*.
To disclose, *discover*, or *reveal*.
Discoloured, *that has lost or chang'd its colour*.
A Discomfort, or *trouble*.
To discomfort, or *afflict himself*.
To discommend, or *dispraise*.
To discompose, or *disorder*.
Discomposure *of the mind*.
Disconsolate, or *comfortless*.
Discontent, *regret*, or *dissatisfaction*.
Discontented, or *dissatisfy'd*.
A Discontinuance, *breaking off*, or *interruption*.
To discontinue, *leave*, or *break off*.
Discord, or *disagreement*.
Discordant, *jarring*, or *untunable*.
To discover, *spy*, or *find out*.
A Discoverer.
A Discovery.
A Discount, or *abatement*.
To discount, *deduct*, *abate*, *or set off from the account*.
To discountenance, *discourage*, *put a stop*, or *give a check to*.
To discourage, or *dishearten*.
A Discouragement.
A Discourager.
A Discourse, *speech*, or *talk*.
To Discourse, *to hold a discourse*, or *debate*.
Discourteous, *unkind*, or *uncivil*.
A Discourtesy.

A Discredit, or *reproach.*
To discredit, *defame, disparage,* or *speak evil of.*
Discreet, or *prudent.*
Discretion, *a discerning judgment,* or *prudence.*
To discriminate, or *distinguish.*
A Discrimination, or *putting a difference between things.*
To discuss, *examine, search, sift,* or *inquire into.*
A Discussion.
A Discussive Medicine; *that dissolves humours.*
Disdain, or *scorn.*
To disdain, *scorn, set light by,* or *despise.*
Disdainful, *or* scornful.
Disdainfulness.
A Disease, or *distemper.*
Diseased, or *troubled with a disease.*
To disembogue, or *discharge it self, as a River does into the Sea.*
To disingage, or *free himself from.*
To disentangle *the hair, &c. or to get clear of a scurvy business.*
Disesteem, or *disrespect.*
To disesteem, *slight,* or *have no regard to.*
A Disfavour, or *discourtesie.*
To disfigure, *misshape, spoil,* or *deface.*
A Disfigurement.
To disfranchise, or *deprive of his freedom.*
A Disfranchisement.
To disgarnish, or *take away the garniture.*
To disgorge, *cast up,* or *vomit.*
Disgrace, or *discredit.*
To disgrace, *disparage,* or *shame.*
Disgraceful.
Disgracefulness.
A Disguise, *mask,* or *pretence.*
To disguise, *alter,* or *put into another guise,* or *fashion.*
Disgust, or *distaste.*
To disgust, *dislike,* or *be averse from.*
A Dish, or *platter.*
To dish *up meat.*
A Chafing-dish.
A Dish-clout.
A Dish-washer, or *wagtail, a bird.*
To dishearten, *put out of heart,* or *discourage.*
Dishonest, lewd, knavish, false, unjust; or *unhandsome.*
Dishonesty.
A Dishonour, or *reproach.*
To dishonour, or *disgrace.*
Dishonourable.
To disimbark, or *go off from on shipboard,* or *from an undertaking.*
To disingage, or *free himself from an ingagement.*
Disingenuous, unfair, or *uncivil.*
Disinhabited, void of Inhabitants, or *desolate.*
To disinherit, or *deprive one of his Inheritance.*
To disintangle, *disengage, unravel,* or *rid out.*
Disintersted, *void of self-interest.*
To disinvite, or *recal an invitation.*
To dis-join, or *separate.*
To dis-joint, or *dismember.*
A dis-kindness, or *ill turn.*
A dislike, or *aversion from.*
To dislike, or *disapprove.*
A Dislocation, i. e. *a displacing of Bones,* or *putting them out of joint.*
To dislodge, or *turn out of his lodging, raise,* or *rouse.*
Disloyal, *treacherous,* **or** *unfaithful.*
Disloyalty, or *unfaithfulness to a Prince,* or *Husband.*
Dismal, *dreadful, lamentable,* or *horrible.*
To dismantle, or *pull down the Walls, and Fortifications of a Town, Fort,* &c.
Dismayed, or *astonished.*
To dismember, *dis-joint* or *cut off a member,* or *joint.*
A dismembring-knife.
To dismiss, *send away,* or *discharge.*
A dismission.
To dismount, *unhorse,* or *take down.*
Disobedience.
Disobedient, *undutiful,* or *stubborn.*
To disobey, or *withdraw his obedience.*
A Disobligation *from.*
To disoblige, *offend,* or *affront.*
Disorder, or *confusion.*
To disorder, *put out of order,* or *confound.*
Disorderly, *confus'd,* or *unruly.*
Disordinate, *irregular,* or *extravagant.*
To disown, *disavow,* or *deny.*
To disparage, *discommend, slight,* or *speak ill of.*
A Disparagement, *an undervaluing;* or *an unequal match in marriage.*
A Disparager.
Disparity, *unlikeness,* or *unevenness.*
A Dispatch, or *riddance.*
To dispatch, *rid, make haste, send away,* or *kill one speedily.*
A Dispatcher *of business,* &c.
Dispatches, *Letters written about divers affairs.*

Dispensable, *that may be dispensed with.*
A Dispensation, *distributing*, or *dealing.*
A Dispensatory, or *book that shews how to make all sorts of physical Compositions.*
To dispense, *exempt*, or *free from the obligation of a Law; also to bestow or distribute.*
A Dispensation, or *indulgence.*
A Dispenser of *Alms.*
To dispeople, or *destroy the people.*
To disperse, *spread abroad*, or *scatter.*
Dispersedly, *here and there.*
A Disperser.
The Dispersion *of the Jews.*
To displace, *remove*, or *turn out of office.*
To displant, *pluck*, or *root up that which was planted.*
To display, *spread wide*, or *unfold.*
To displease, *discontent*, or *offend.*
Displeasant.
A Displeasure.
To disport, or *divert himself.*
A Disposal.
To dispose *of a thing*, or *to put it to some use.*
A Disposer.
A Disposition, *temper*, or *habit of mind*, or *body.*
To dispossess, or *put out of possession.*
A Disposure, *from to* dispose.
Dispraise, *censure*, or *blame.*
To dispraise, or *discommend.*
A Dispraiser.
Disprofit, *loss*, or *disadvantage.*
A Disproof, or *confutation.*
A Disproportion, or *inequality.*
Disproportionable, or disproportionate.
To disprove, *confute*, or *prove the contrary.*
Disputable, *that may be disputed.*
A Disputant, or *Logician.*
A Disputation *in any Science.*
A Dispute.
To dispute, *discourse*, *agree*, or *debate.*
A Disputer.
Disquiet, or *unquietness.*
To disquiet, *disturb*, or *trouble.*
A Disquieter.
A Disquisition, *strict*, *inquiry*, or *narrow search.*
To disrank, or *put out of rank or order.*
To disregard, *to have no regard to*, or *slight.*
To disrelish, *not to relish*, *to disapprove*, or *have aversion for.*
Disrepute, or *discredit.*
Disrespect, or *disregard.*
To disrespect, *slight*, or *be uncivil to.*
Disrespectful.
To disrobe, *pull of his robe*, or *strip.*
Dissatisfaction, or *discontent.*
Dissatisfactory.
Dissatisfied, *displeased*, or *troubled.*
To dissect, or *cut up a dead body.*
A Dissecter.
A Dissection.
To disseise, or *dispossess of his Land.*
A Disseisin.
A Disseisour.
To Dissemble, *pretend*, or *feign.*
A Dissembler,
Dissension, or *discord.*
To dissent, or *disagree in opinion.*
A Dissenter.
A Dissertation, *discourse*, or *debate upon a subject.*
To Disserve, *one*, or *do him an ill turn.*
A Disservice,
Disserviceable.
To dissever, or *separate.*
Dishevelled *hair*, i. e. *hanging loose.*
Dissimilitude, or *unlikeness.*
Dissimulation, or *dissembling.*
Dissoluble, *apt to be dissolv'd.*
To dissolve, *melt*, *undo*, or *put an end to.*
Dissolute, *loose*, *lewd*, or *debauched.*
Dissoluteness.
A Dissolution, or *dissolving*, *more especially by death.*
A Dissonance, or *disagreement in sound.*
Dissonant, or *jarring.*
To dissuade or disswade, *to perswade against*, or *advise the contrary.*
A Dissuader.
A Dissuasion.
Dissuasive.
A Dissyllable, *a word of two syllables.*
A Distaff, *for a spining-wheel.*
Distance *of place*, or *time.*
Distant, *being far asunder.*
Distaste, or *dislike.*
To distaste, or *give distaste.*
Distastful.
A Distemper, *disease*, or *indisposition*; *also a kind of size for painting.*
To distemper, or *put out of temper.*
Distemperature.
To distend, or *stretch out.*
A Distention.

A

A Distich, *a pair*, or *couple of verses that make a compleat sense.*
To distil, or *drop down by little and little*; or *to extract the essence of things by a still.*
A Distillation *of humours.*
A Distiller.
Distinct, *clear*, *plainly utter'd*; or *put a-part.*
A Distinction.
Distinctive.
To distinguish, *note*, *mark*, or *put a difference between.*
A Distorsion, *or* distortion.
To distort, *set awry*, or *wrest.*
To distract, *perplex*, *trouble*, or *make one mad.*
Distractedness.
A Distraction.
To distrain, or *seize upon one's goods for the payment of a debt*, or *duty.*
A Distrainer.
A Distress, or *destraining*; *also a great straight*, or *calamity.*
To distress, *one*, or *bring him into distress.*
To distribute, *bestow*, or *share among several persons.*
A Distributer.
A Distribution.
Distributive Justice, *that does right to all.*
A District, *a particular territory*, or *jurisdiction.*
A Distrust.
To distrust, *mistrust*, or *suspect.*
Distrustful.
To disturb, *trouble*, *hinder*, or *interrupt.*
A Disturbance.
A Disturber.
A Disunion.
To disunite, *separate*, or *divide.*
A Disuse, *or disusage.*
To disuse, or *leave off using.*
A Ditch, or *trench.*
To ditch, or *cast up a ditch.*
A Ditcher.
Dittany, *an herb.*
Bastard dittany.
Ditto, *the said*, or *the same.*
A Ditty, *a sort of song.*
The Divan, *the great Council*, *or High Court of Justice among the* Turks.
To dive *under water*, or *into a business.*
A Diver *under water.*
A Diver, or *didapper*, *a bird.*
The Dun-diver.
Divers, *sundry*, or *several.*
Diverse, *different*, or *unlike in circumstances.*
To diversify, *make diverse*, *vary*, or *alter.*
A Diversion, *going aside*, or *pastime.*
Diversity, *(or variety.)*
To divert, or *entertain one*; *or to take him off from a thing.*
To divertise, or *recreate.*
A Divertisement, *pastime*, or *recreation.*
To divide *into parts*, or *put asunder.*
A Dividend *in Arithmetick*, *the number to be divided*; *also a share of a stock.*
A Divider.
Divination, or *foretelling of things to come.*
Divine, *belonging to God.*
A Divine, or *professor of Divinity.*
To divine, *foretel*, or *guess.*
A Diviner, *soothsayer*, or *wizard.*
Divinity, *Deity*, or *Godhead*; *also the science*, *or knowledge of divine mysteries.*
Divisibility, *aptness to be divided.*
Divisible, *that may be divided.*
Division, *dividing*, or *being divided*; *a quarrel or faction.*
The Divisor, or *number by which another is divided.*
A Divorce, or *bill of* divorce.
To Divorce, or *put away his wife.*
A Divorcement, or *parting of Man and Wife.*
A Divorcer.
Diuretick, or *provoking urine.*
To divulge, or *publish abroad.*
A Divulger.
A Dizzard, or *dotard.*
A Dizziness, or *swimming in the head.*
Dizzy, *or giddy.*

D O

To do, or *act*, &c.
A Dob-chick, *a bird.*
Docible, *or* docile, *teachable*, or *apt to learn.*
Docility.
A Dock, *a place fit for the building*, or *laying up of Ships.*
A Dock, or *stump of a tail*; *also an herb.*
Dock-cresses.
Burr-dock.
To dock, or *cut off the tail.*
Strong-docked, *that has strong reins and sinews*, or *lusty.*
A Docket, or *little Bill*, *on Paper*, or *Parchment.*
The Clerk of the Dockets.
A Doctor, *a teacher*, or *professour of several faculties.*

Doctorship.
Doctrinal, or *instructive.*
Doctrine, *teaching, instruction*, or *knowledge.*
A Document, or *instruction.*
Dodder, *an herb.*
To dodge, or *be off and on.*
A Dodger.
A Doe, or *female buck.*
A Doe-rabbet.
A Doer, *from* to do.
A Dog, *a beast.*
A Lap-dog.
A Setting-dog.
A Bull-dog.
The Dog-berry-tree.
Dog-brier.
A Dog-kennel.
The Dog-days, or *time when the dog-star rules, for six weeks in* July *and* August.
A Dog-fish, or *sea-dog.*
A Dog-louse.
The Dog-rose.
The Dog-star. }
Dogs-bane. }
Dogs-grass, or *quick.* }
Dogs-mercury. } *herbs.*
Dogs-stones. }
Dogs-tongue. }
Dogs-tooth. }
A Dogs-ear, or *rumple of a book.*
To dog *one*, or *follow him up and down.*
A pair of Dogs, or *Andirons.*
The Doge, or *Duke of* Venice.
Dogged, *sullen*, or *morose.*
Doggedness.
A Dogger-boat.
Doggrel, *as rime* Doggrel, or *pitiful Poetry.*
Dogmatical, or *instructive; also positive*, or *wedded to his own opinion.*
A Dogmatist, or *broacher of strange opinions.*
To Dogmatize, i. e. *to speak positively*, or *peremptorily.*
A Doit, *a small coin in the* Low-Countries, *of less value than a farthing.*
A Dole, *a liberal gift*, or *distribution of alms.*
Doleful, *sad*, or *lamentable.*
A Dollar, *a* Dutch *coin.*
A Rix-dollar.
Dolorous, *grievous*, or *painful.*
A Dolphin, *a sea-fish.*
A Dole, *block-head*, or *sot.*
Doltish, *dull*, or *stupid.*
Doltishness.
A Dome, or *round cupolo of a building.*
Domestick, *belonging to the house* or *family.*
A Domestick Chaplain.
To domineer, *bear rule, vapour*, or *lord it.*
The Dominical-Letter, *that denotes the Lord's day throughout the whole year.*
Dominion, *rule*, or *jurisdiction.*
A Don, or *great* Spanish *Lord.*
A Donation, or *bestowing.*
A Donative, or *gift.*
Done, or *acted (from* to *do.)*
A Doner, or donour, *he that gives* Lands, *Tenements*, &c.
A Doom, *sentence*, or *judgment.*
A Dooms-man.
Dooms-day.
Dooms-day-book, or *King* William *the Conqueror's Tax-book, wherein all the Lands and Revenues of* England *were register'd.*
A Door *of a house*, or *room.*
A Folding-door, or *two leav'd door.*
A Door-keeper.
A Dor, or *drone.*
A Dorado, *a kind of fish.*
A Doree, or *St.* Peter's *fish.*
Dormant, i. e. *sleeping; as money that lies* dormant, *being put to no use.*
A Dormer, or dormer-window, *in the roof of a house.*
A Dormitory, *or* dorter; *a sleeping-room in a monastery.*
A Dormouse, *a little creature that sleeps all the winter in the hollow of a tree.*
A Dorter, *pannel*, or *pack-saddle.*
A Dose of *physick*, i. e. *as much as is given or taken at a time.*
To dose *one, or give him a dose.*
A Dot, or *small point.*
Dotage, or *doting.*
An old Dotard.
To dote, or *grow foolish.*
To dote *upon*, or *be extremely fond of.*
A Doter.
A Doting-tree, *a tree almost worn out with age.*
A Dotteril, *a silly bird that imitates the Fowler, 'till it be catch'd.*
Double, *twofold*, or *twice as much.*
To double, *make double*, or *fold up.*
Double-pellitory, *an herb.*
Doubles, or *folds of cloath.*
Double-edged.
Double-tongued.
A Doubler, or *large platter.*
A Doublet, *a sort of garment.*
The Doublets *of a bay wind-*

winding up and down, to deceive the Dogs.
Doublets *in throwing the dice.*
A Doubt, *scruple*, or *suspence.*
To doubt, or *be in suspence.*
Doubtful.
Doubtfulness.
Doubtless, *certainly*, or *without doubt.*
A Doucet, *a kind of custard.*
Doucets, *or* doulcets, i. e. *the stones of a Deer*, or *Stag.*
A Dove, or *Pigeon.*
A Ring-dove.
A Stock-dove.
A Turtle-dove.
Doves-foot, *an herb.*
The Doves-tail joint, *used by joyners.*
Dough, or *paste.*
Dough-baked.
The Down, or down *of feathers, flowers, moss*, &c.
A Down-bed.
A Dowager, or *endow'd Widow of a Prince*, or *Noble-man.*
A Dower, or *jointure upon marriage.*
Dowlas, *a sort of linnen-cloath.*
Down, or *downward.*
Down-hill.
A Down-look.
A Down-fall.
Down-right, or *absolute.*
The Downs, or *hilly plains; also the sand-banks on the coast of* Kent.
The Down-thistle.
A Dowry, or *marriage-portion.*
A Dowse, or *blow on the chops.*
To dowse *one*, or *give him a dowse.*
A Doxy, *trull*, or *dirty drab.*
To doze, or *stupifie.*

A Dozen, or *twelve*; *as a dozen of Eggs*, &c.

D R

A Drab, or *lewd Woman.*
Draff, or *wash for hoggs.*
A Drag, or *hook.*
To drag, or *draw.*
A Drag-net, *trammel*, or *sweep-net.*
Gum Dragant.
To draggle, or *draw in the dirt.*
A Draggle-tail.
A Dragon, *a kind of flying Serpent.*
The Sea-dragon, *a fish.*
Snap-dragon, *an herb.*
The Dragon-fly.
Dragon herb.
Dragon-wort.
A Dragoon, *or* dragooner, *an armed trooper, that fights both on foot and horse back.*
A Drain, or *sink.*
To drain, or *train waters by furrows, conduits*, &c.
A Drainer.
A Drake, *a male duck*; *also a kind of gun.*
A Fire-drake.
Drakes-root, *an herb.*
A Dram, *in weight, the 8th part of an ounce.*
Dramatick, *belonging to the stage.*
Drap de Berry, *a thick sort of woollen cloath made in* Berry, *a Province of* France.
A Draper, *a seller of linnen*, or *woollen cloath.*
Drapery, or *cloth-wares, also a representation of them in painting*, or *carving.*
A Draught (*in several senses.*)
A Draught-horse.
To play at Draughts.
To draw (*in all senses.*)
A Draw-bridge.
A Draw-net.

A Drawer.
A Cloth-drawer.
A Tooth-drawer.
A pair of Drawers.
Drawk, *an herb.*
To drawl *out his words*, *or speak dreamingly.*
Drawn (*from to draw.*)
A Dray, *to carry drink.*
A Dray-man.
Dread, or *great fear.*
To Dread, or *be afraid of*
Our dread *Soveraign.*
Dreadful.
Dreadfulness.
To dream *a dream in ones sleep.*
A Dream, or *idle fancy.*
A Dreamer.
Dreggy, or *full of*
Dregs, or *lees.*
A Drench, or *physical potion.*
To drench, or *give a* drench.
A Dress, or *garb.*
To dress, *trim*, *set out, prepare*, &c.
A Dresser *of meat*, &c.
A Dresser, or *dresser-board.*
A Vine-dresser.
To dribble, or *drip.*
A Driblet, or *small sum.*
A Drier (*from to dry.*)
A Drift, *driving*, *scope*, or *purpose.*
A Drift *of a Forest*; *a view of the cattel there.*
A Drill, or *baboon*; *also a boring-tool.*
To drill, *to bore holes*, or *to entice.*
Drink, *and to* drink.
A Drinker.
A Water-drinker.
A Drinking-match.
To drip, *as the fat of roast meat does.*
A Dripping-pan.
To drive, *a cart, coach, cattel*, &c. or *to force.*
Drivel, or *spittle.*
To Drivel, or *let the spittle fall on his beard.*
Driven, (*from to drive.*)

A Driver.
To drizzle; *as small rain does.*
Drizzly, or *full of dew.*
A Droll, or *merry companion; also a little stage-play.*
To droll; *jest,* or *joke.*
Drollery, or *joking.*
A Dromedary, *a kind of Camel, with a bunch on the back.*
A Drone, *a bee without its sting,* or *a slothful fellow.*
To droop, *languish,* or *grow dull and unactive.*
A Drop, and *to* drop.
Drop-wort. }
Snow-drops. } *herbs.*
Water-drops. }
Dropsical, or *hydropical, belonging to*
The Dropsie, *a Disease.*
Dross, *the scum of metals, dregs,* &c.
Drossy, or *full of dross.*
Drove, *(from to drive.)*
A Drove, or *heerd of beasts.*
A Drover.
Drought, *dryness,* or *thirst.*
Drousiness.
Drousie, *or* drowsie, *sleepy, or sluggish.*
To drown *(in several senses.)*
To drub, or *beat one on the soles of his Feet.*
A Drudge, *or slave.*
To drudge, or *do all mean offices; also to fish for oisters.*
A Drudger, or *oister-fisher.*
Drudgery, or *slavery.*
A Drug, or *dry simple us'd in physick; or a sorry commodity.*
Drugget, *a kind of stuff.*
A Druggist, *or* drugster, *a seller of drugs.*
A Drum.
To drum, or *beat the* drum.

A Kettle-drum.
A Drummer.
A Drum-major, or *chief of the Drummers.*
Drunk, or drunken, *oppressed with drink,* or *fuddled.*
A Drunkard.
Drunkenness.
Dry, *that has no moisture or juice; flat, parched, penurious,* &c.
To dry, or *make dry.*
A Dry-nurse, *that has lost her milk.*
To dry-shave, or *cheat notoriously.*

D U

To dub, or *make a Knight.*
Dubious, or *doubtful.*
Ducal, *belonging to a Duke.*
A Ducal coronet.
A Ducat, *or* ducket, *a Foreign gold-coin, worth about nine shillings.*
A Ducatoon, *a kind of coin, worth about* 5 s. 4 d.
A Duck, *a bird.*
To duck, *dive, bow,* or *congee.*
A Fen-duck, *or* moor-hen.
Duck-bill-wheat.
A Duckling, or *young duck.*
Ducks-meet, *or* duck-weed.
A ducker, or *diver.*
To take a thing in dudgeon, *or haintusly.*
Due, or *owing.*
A duel, or *single combat between two Persons.*
A Dueller, or duellist.
Duelling, or *fighting of duels.*
Dug, or *digged (from to* dig.*)*
A Dug, *of a beast.*
The Dug-tree.
A Duke.

A Dukedom, or *dutchy.*
A Dulcimer, *a kind of musical instrument.*
Dull, *heavy, lumpish,* or *slow.*
To dull, or *make* dull.
Dulness.
Dumb, or *speechless.*
Dumbness.
A Dump, or *sudden astonishment.*
A Dumpling, *a kind of pudding.*
Dun, or *brown colour.*
A Dun-neck, *a bird.*
To dun, or *press one for money.*
A Dunce, *block-head,* or *stupid fellow.*
Dunce-down, or *cats tail.*
Dung, or *ordure.*
To dung, or *manure ground.*
A Dung-farmer.
Cow-dung.
Horse-dung, *&c.*
A Dung-fly.
A Dung-hill.
A Dungeon, or *dark prison.*
A Dunner *(from to dun.)*
Dunny, or *deafish.*
A Duedecimo, *a book in* duodecimo, *having* 12 *leaves in every sheet.*
A Duplicate, or *counterpart of a writing.*
Durable, or *lasting.*
Durableness.
Durance, or *imprisonment.*
Duration, or *continuance.*
During or *whilst; as during that eclipse.*
Dusk, or *dark.*
The dusk *of the evening.*
Duskiness.
Duskish, *or* dusky.
Dust.
To dust, *cover with,* or *beat off the dust.*
Mill-dust.
Saw-dust.

A

A Dust-box, or *sand-box*.
A Dust-man, or *Scavenger*.
A Duster, or *clout to wipe off dust*.
Dustiness.
Dusty, or *full of* dust.
A Dutchess, or *Duke's Wife*.
A Dutchy, *or* Dukedom.
The Dutchy Court of *Lancaster*.
Dutiful, or *obedient*.
Dutifulness.
Duty (*from due*) *the part of, that which is owing to, or may be expected from*.

D W

A Dwarf.
Dwarf-bay.
Dwarf-cypress.
Dwarf-elder.
To dwell, or *continue in a place*.
A Dweller, or *inhabitant*.
To dwindle, *decay, waste*, or *consume away*.

D Y

A Dy, *or* die *to play with*.
To dye, or *give up the ghost*.
To dye *colours*.
A Dye-*house*.
Double-dyed.
Dyers-weed, *us'd for the yellow colour*.
The Dysentery, or *bloody flux*.

E A

Each, or *either of two*.
Eager, *sharp, earnest, tart, sower*, &c.
The eager, or *tide of a River*.
Eagerness.
An Eagle, *a bird of prey*.
An Eagle-stone.
An Eaglet, or *young Eagle*.
To ean, yean, or *bring forth Lambs*.

An Ear.
An Ear-picker.
An Ear-ring.
Ear-wax.
An Ear-witness.
To ear, or *shoot out* ears, *as corn does*.
Bears-ear, or *French cowslips*.
Hares-ear, or *scorpion-wort*.
Jews-ear, *an excrescence of the Elder-tree*.
Mouse-ear, *an herb*.
Eared, *that has ears*.
Lap-ear'd.
An Earl, *a noble-man*.
An Earldom.
Early, or *betimes*.
To earn, or *get*.
Earnest, *vehement*, or *diligent*.
Earnest, *or* earnest-money *given to bind a bargain*.
Earnestness.
The Earth, or *ground*.
To earth, or *go under ground, as a* Fox *does*.
Fullers-earth.
Potters-earth.
An Earth-apple.
An Earth-nutt.
An Earth-quake.
An Earth-worm.
Earthen, *made of earth*.
An Earthing *of Trees*, or *plants*.
Earthly, *belonging to the earth*.
Earthly-minded.
Earthly-mindedness.
An Earthy *smell*.
An Earwig, *an insect*.
Ease, *rest, leisure*, or *pleasure*.
To ease, or *give ease*.
Hearts-ease, *an herb*.
An Easel, or *painter's frame*.
Easement, or *easing*.
Easiness.
The East.
The East-wind.
North-east wind.
South-east wind.
Easter, or *the* Festival *of*

Easter; *the Christian Passover, wherein Christ's Resurrection is celebrated*.
Easterly, *or* eastern.
Eastward, or *towards the* east.
Easy *to be done*; *also gentle or good-natur'd*.
To eat.
Eatable, or *good to eat*.
An Eat-bee, *a bird*.
Eaten.
The Eaves *of an house*.
To Eaves-drop, or *hearken at the windows*, or *doors*.
An Eaves-dropper.
An Ew, or *female sheep*.

E B

An Ebb, *or* Ebbing, or *the lowest point of one's condition* or *fortune*.
To ebb, or *flow back, as the Sea does*.
Ebony, *the wood of a Tree in* India *and* Ethiopia, *that bears no leaves nor fruit*.
An Ebullition, or *boiling of the bloud*.

E C

An Eccho, *the reflection of a noise*, or *voice in a Wood, Valley*, &c.
To eccho *again*.
Ecclesiastes, i. e. *the Preacher*; *one of* Solomon's *Books so call'd*.
Ecclesiastical, or *belonging to the Church*.
Ecclesiasticus, *an apocryphal Book*.
An Eclipse, *a want or defect of the Sun*, or *Moon's light*.
Eclipsed, *under an eclipse*, or *darkned*.
An Ecstacy, exstasy, or *trance*.

E D

Edder, *a fish like a Mackarel*.

An

An Eddy, *or running back of water contrary to the tide.*
An Edge, *and to* edge (*in several senses.*)
An Edge-tool.
Edged, *that has an edge.*
A Two-edged *Sword.*
Edible, or *fit to be eaten.*
An Edict, *Proclamation, Ordinance,* or *Decree.*
Edification, or *improvement.*
An Edifice, or *building.*
To edify, *instruct*, or *advance in knowledge,* &c.
An Edition, or *putting forth of a book.*
To educate, or *bring up.*
Education, or *breeding.*

E E

To eek *out*, or *lengthen.*
An Eel, *a fish.*
A Sea-eel.
A Sand-eel.
An Eel-powt, or *young Eel.*
An Eel-spear.
E'en *for* even.

E F

An Effect, *consequence, end, issue,* or *chief point of a matter.*
To Effect, or *bring a thing to pass.*
Effective, or effectual.
Effectless, or *of no* effect.
Effects, or *Merchants goods.*
Effectual, *that can do much*, or *powerful.*
Effeminacy, or *softness.*
Effeminate, or *woman-like.*
To effeminate, or *soften; to make nice,* or *woman-like.*
Efficacious, or *effectual.*
Efficaciousness.
Efficacy, *great force virtue*, or *power.*
An Efficient, or *operating cause.*

An Effigie, *picture*, or *image.*
An Effort, or *endeavour.*
An Eft, Evet, or Newt; *a creature like a lizzard.*
An Effusion, or *spilling of blood.*

E G

An Egg, *of a bird.*
A wind-egg.
Egg-sauce.
An Egg-shell.
To egg, or *set one on.*
An Egger on.
Eglantine, *sweet-brier*, or *dog-brier.*
Egregious, *rare, excellent*, or *notorious.*
An Egress, or *going forth.*
An Egret, *a kind of heron.*

E I

An Ejaculation, or *short fervent prayer.*
Ejaculatory.
To eject, or *cast out.*
An Ejection.
Eight, *in number.*
Eighteen.
The Eighteenth.
The Eighth.
The Eightieth.
Eighty, or *fourscore.*
Either, or *one of the two.*

E L

Elaborate, or *done accurately, and with great pains.*
An Elbow.
To elbow, or *justle with the* elbow.
Elbow-grease, or *hard labour.*
Elbow-room.
Elder, or *more advanc'd in years.*
An Elder, *in Church-office.*
The Elder-rose.
Eldership, *in age.*
An Elder-tree.
Water-elder.
Elder-vinegar.

The Eldest brother.
Elecampane; *an herb.*
To Elect, or *choose.*
The Elect, or *elected Saints.*
An Election.
Elective.
An Elector, *one of those* German *Princes, who have a right to choose the Emperor.*
Electoral, as *his Electoral Highness.*
An Electorate, *the Office, Dignity*, or *Dominions of an* Elector.
An Electoress; *an* Elector's *Wife.*
An Electorship.
An Electuary, *a kind of medicinal composition.*
Elegancy, *fineness in speech, apparel,* &c.
Elegant, or *neat.*
An Elegy, *a Copy of Verses upon the death of any person.*
The four Elements, or *principles of which all mixt bodies are compos'd viz. Fire, Air, Earth and Water.*
The Elements, or *grounds of any Art*, or *Science; also the letters of the Alphabet.*
Elementary, or *belonging to an* Element.
An Elephant, *a beast.*
To elevate, or *lift up.*
An Elevatory; *an instrument to lift up broken pieces of the skull; also to draw bullets,* or *hail shot out of the flesh.*
The Elevation *of the Host among Roman-Catholicks.*
Eleven, *in number.*
The Eleventh.
An Elf, or *hobgoblin.*
Eligible, or *fit to be chosen.*
An Elixir, or *quintessence,* (*in Chymistry.*)
An Elk, *a wild beast like a stag; also a kind of ewe for bows.*

An Ell, *a measure.*
An Elm-tree.
Elocution, *a fit and proper order of speech*, or *good utterance.*
An Elegy, or *high commendation.*
To elope, as *when a Woman goes from her Husband, and lives with an adulterer.*
An Elopement.
Eloquence, or *good language.*
Eloquent, *well-spoken*, or *powerfull in speech.*
Else, as, *no man* else.
Elsewhere.
To elude, *wave*, or *shift off.*
An Elusion, or *fallacy.*
Elusory, or *deceitfull.*
The Elysian fields, or *paradise for the souls of the just, after their separation from the body, according to the notion of the ancient heathens.*

E M

'Em *for them*; as, *I love* 'em.
An Emanation, or *flowing out.*
To embale, or *make up into a* bale, or *pack.*
To embalm, *a dead body, to season it with spices and gums, wrapping it in cere-cloth*, &c *to keep it from putrifaction.*
An Embalmer.
An Embargo, or *arrest laid upon Ships.*
To embark, *to go on Shipboard*, or *enter upon a design.*
To embarras, *trouble*, or *perplex.*
An Embarrasment,
An Embassador, *or* Ambassador.
An Embassadress, *an Embassador's Wife.*
An Embassage, *or* Embassy.

To embellish, *adorn*, or *beautify.*
An Embellishment.
Embers, or *hot ashes.*
The Ember-weeks, *four quarterly seasons of devotion, of great antiquity in the Church; so call'd from the custom of eating nothing on those days till night, and then only a cake bak'd under the embers, which was term'd* Ember-bread.
The Ember-days *are, the* Wednesday, Friday *and* Saturday, *next after* Quadragesima - *Sunday*, *Whitsunday*, *Holy-rood day in* September, *and St.* Lucy's *day in* December.
To embezzil, *pilfer*, or *thievishly waste one's goods.*
An Emblem, *picture*, or *device, with a motto, by which some moral notion is express'd.*
An Emblematist, or *maker of* emblems.
Embodied, *united in the same body*, or *mingled together.*
To embolden, *make bold*, or *encourage.*
To emboss, or *chase plate.*
To embowel, or *take out the bowels.*
To embrace, *compass, hug*, or *fold in one's Arms.*
The Embraces.
To embrew, or *besprinkle*
To embroider, *a garment.*
An Embroiderer.
Embroidery, or *the Art of* embroidering.
To embroil, *disturb*, or *set at variance.*
An Embryo, *a Child not yet thoroughly shap'd in the womb; also any thing else before it comes to perfection.*
An Emendation, or *amendment.*

An Emerald, *a Precious stone of a green colour.*
An Emergency; *an appearing on a sudden*; or *a matter of great importance.*
An emergent *occasion.*
An Emeril-stone *us'd by Lapidaries*, to *cleanse, burnish and cut their precious stones.*
Eminence, *a rising ground* or *an high station.*
His Eminency; *the title of a Cardinal.*
Eminent, *appearing above others, excellent*, or *noted.*
An Emissary, *one sent abroad for intelligence.*
To emit or *send forth*; as *the Sun* emitted *his rays.*
An Emmet, or *pismire.*
Emmollient, *lenitive*, or *softning.*
Emolument, *gain properly by grist; profit gotten by labour and cost.*
An Emotion, or *trouble of mind.*
To impair, *diminish*, or *make worse.*
To empale, or *enclose a piece of ground within pales.*
To empannel *a Jury*, or *set down their Names in a Roll.*
To empeach, *see to* impeach.
An Emperor.
An Emphasis, or *strength of expression.*
Emphatical, or *very significant.*
An Empire, *the dominions of an Emperor.*
Empirical, *belonging to*
An Empirick, or *quack, that makes use of Receipts taken upon trust.*
To emplead, or *sue one.*
An Employ, *business*, or *trade.*
To employ, *or bestow his time and pains.*

An Employment.
To empoverish, or *make poor.*
An Empress, or *Emperor's Wife.*
To emprison, *see to* imprison.
Emptiness.
Empty, or *void.*
To empty, or *make* empty.
The Empyreal, or *highest Heaven.*
The Emrods, or *piles, a disease.*
An Emrose, *a flower.*
To emulate, or *vy with one.*
An Emulation, or *striving, to surpass others.*
An Emulator.
An Emulsion, or *medicinal potion.*

E N

To enable, or *make able.*
To enact, or *make a Law.*
Enamel, *a kind of composition us'd by Painters, Glaziers, Goldsmiths, Enamellers,* &c.
To enamel *a watch.*
An Enameller.
Enamoured, *in love.*
To encamp, or *pitch a camp.*
To enchant, *see to* inchant.
To enchase, or *set in gold.*
To encircle, or *encompass.*
To enclose, *shut in,* or *up.*
An Enclosure.
An Encomium, *a speech,* or *song in commendation of one.*
To encompass, or *surround.*
An Encounter.
To encounter, *to meet,* or *to engage in fight.*
To encourage, or *hearten.*
An Encouragement.
An Encourager.
An Encrease.
To encrease, *augment, enlarge,* or *grow more and more.*
An Encreaser.

To encroach, *usurp,* or *intrude, upon.*
An encroachment.
To encumber, *hinder,* or *trouble.*
An Encumbrance.
An End, *design,* or *conclusion.*
To End, *finish, bring to an end, put an end to,* or *leave off.*
Endless, *that has no end.*
To endammage, or *cause dammage, damnify,* or *hurt.*
To endanger, or *bring into danger.*
An Endeavour.
To endeavour, *essay,* or *attempt.*
To endew, or *digest, as a hawk does.*
To endite, or *pen a letter,* &c.
Endive, *an herb.*
To endorse, or *write on the back-side of a Deed.*
An Endorsement.
To endow, *to bestow a Dower,* or *to settle a maintenance upon a College, Hospital,* &c.
An Endowment.
To endue, *adorn,* or *supply one with.*
To endure, *suffer,* or *last.*
An Enemy, or *adversary.*
Energetical, *very forcible and strong.*
Energy, *efficacy, force,* or *powerfull working.*
To enervate, or *weaken very much.*
To enfeeble, or *make feeble and weak.*
To enfeoff, *to give in fee,* or *invest one with*
An Enfeoffment.
To enforce, *strengthen,* or *constrain.*
An Enforcement.
To enfranchise, or *make free.*
An Enfranchisement.
To engage, *promise,* or *pass his word;* or *to encounter.*

An Engagement.
To engender, or *breed.*
An Engine, or *machine.*
An Engineer.
English, as, *the* English *Tongue.*
To engraft *trees.*
To engrail, or *notch about (a term in* Heraldry.*)*
To engrave, or *cut upon Copper,* or *other metals.*
An Engraver.
To engross, or *write a Deed; also to buy up commodities.*
An Engrosser.
An Engrossment.
To enhance, or *raise the price of any thing.*
An Enhancer.
Enigmatical, *full of riddles,* or *obscure.*
To enjoy, *to have the use,* or *profit of.*
An Enjoyment.
To enjoyn, or *command.*
To enlarge, *amplify,* or *extend;* or *to set a prisoner at liberty.*
An Enlargement.
An Enlarger.
To enlighten, *give light to,* or *clear.*
Enmity, *variance, strife,* or *falling out.*
To ennoble, or *make noble.*
An Enodation, or *unknotting (in* Husbandry.*)*
Enormity, *irregularity, hainousness,* or *high misdemeanour.*
Enormous, *out of rule,* or *square; exceeding great,* or *hainous.*
Enough; *as* enough *and to spare.*
To enquire, *ask, search,* or *examine.*
An Enquirer.
An Enquiry.
To enrage, *make mad,* or *provoke.*
To enrich, or *make rich.*
To enroll, *register,* or *list.*

An

An Enrollment.
To enfaim, *or* enseam, *to purge a hawk of her fat.*
An Enseeled, *hawk, that has a thread drawn thro' the upper eye-lids, and made fast under the beak.*
An Ensign, or *standard-bearer; also the colours* or *standard it self.*
To enslave, or *make a slave.*
To ensnare, entrap, or *surprize.*
An Ensnarer.
To enstall, *see to* install.
To ensue, or *follow.*
An Entail, or *fee-tail, limiting the Heir to certain conditions.*
To entail *an Estate.*
To entangle, *embroil, perplex,* or *ensnare.*
An Entanglement.
An Entangler.
To enter, *go into, set down,* or *register.*
An Entermewer-hawk, *the colour of whose wings is diversify'd.*
The hawk enterpenneth, or *entangles her wings.*
An Enterprise, *attempt,* or *exploit.*
To Enterprise, or *undertake.*
An Enterpriser.
To entertain, *treat, lodge,* or *receive one kindly.*
An Entertainer.
An Entertainment.
To enthral, enslave, or *bring into thraldom.*
To enthrone, or *set upon the throne.*
Enthusiasm, or *fanaticism.*
An Enthusiast, *one that pretends to divine inspiration; a fanatick.*
Enthusiastical, ick, *belonging to such a frenzy.*
To entice, or *allure.*
An Enticement.
An Enticer.
Entire, *whole, uncorrupt,* or *sincere.*
Entireness.
To entitle, *to give a name, title,* or *right to.*
Entombed, or *put into a tomb.*
The Entrals, *bowels,* or *inward parts;* as *heart, liver, lights,* &c.
An Entrance, *going in, admittance,* or *beginning.*
Entrance-money.
To entrap, *ensnare,* or *cheat one.*
To entreat, *beseech,* or *court with fair words.*
An Entreater.
An Entreaty.
To entrench, or *ditch in.*
To entrust *one with a thing* or *commit it to his trust.*
An Entry, *passage,* or *taking possession.*
To envelop, *cover, infold,* or *wrap up.*
To envenom, or *poison.*
Envious, or *spiteful.*
To environ, *enclose,* or *surround.*
An Enumeration, or *reckoning up.*
An Envoy, i. e, *a Messenger,* or *foreign Minister of a lower degree than an Ambassador, sent from one Prince,* or *State to another.*
Envy, *hatred, ill-will,* or *spite.*
To envy *one's happiness,* &c.

E P

The Epact, i. e. *addition* or *intercalation; the difference of* 11 *days between the solar year of* 365, *and the lunar of* 354.
An Ephah; *an hebrew measure, of* 9 *gallons, about a bushel.*
An Ephemerides, or *journal of Astronomical Tables, ready calculated.*
An Ephemerist, or *maker of* Ephemerides, *Almanacks,* &c.
An Ephod, *a kind of linnen garment us'd by the* Jewish *Priests.*
An Epicure, *a voluptuous, sensual person,* or *glutton; so call'd from* Epicurus, *an* Athenian *Philosopher, who maintain'd, pleasure to be the chiefest good.*
Epicurism; *an* Epicure's *life,* or *opinion.*
To Epicurize, or *live like an* Epicure.
A Epidemical *disease, that is rife among the People.*
An Epigram, *a short witty kind of poem.*
An Epigrammatist, *a maker of* Epigrams.
An Epilogue, or *concluding speech at the end of a play.*
The Epiphany, *appearance,* i. e. *of a miraculous star to the wise Men* or *Christ's manifestation to the gentiles; a festival celebrated,* Jan. 6. *and commonly call'd Twelfth-day.*
Episcopacy, or *Church-government by Bishops.*
Episcopal, *of,* or *belonging to Bishops.*
Episcoparians, *of the* Episcopal *party.*
An Epistle, or *letter.*
An Epistle-dedicatory.
An Epistler, or *reader of the* Epistle *in a Cathedral.*
Epistolar, *of,* or *belongong to an* Epistle.
An Epithalamium, *a nuptial,* or *wedding song.*
An Epitaph, or *inscription on a tomb.*
An Epithet, *a word added to another to express some quality of it;* as *a noble person, an unbridled*

ri'd lust; *where the terms*, noble *and* unbridl'd *are the* Epithets, *expressing the qualities of the* person, *and* lust.

An Epitome, or *abbridgement*.

To epitomize, or *make an abbridgement*.

An Epoch, i. e. *stopping*, or *staying*, *a solemn date*, or *distinction of time*; as, *from the creation of the World*, Noah's *flood*, *the birth of our Lord*, &c.

E Q

Equal, or *alike*.

To Equal, or *make* equal.

An Equal, as, *he has not not his* equal.

Equality, or *likeness*.

To equalize, or *match*.

Equanimity, *evenness*, or *quietness*, *of mind*, or *temper*.

The Equator, *or* Equinoctial *line*; *an imaginary circle that divides the Heaven into two equal parts, North and South*.

Equiangular, *whose*, *angles*, or *corners are equal*

Equidistant, *of an equal distance*.

Equilateral, *whose sides are equal*.

An Equilibrium, or *equality of weight*.

The Equinoctial *line*, or Equator, *thro' which, whensoever the Sun passes, it makes*

The Equinoxs; or *Days and Nights of an equal length, which happens* March. 10, *and* September, 12.

To equip, *set*, or *fit out*; *to provide all things necessary*.

Equipage, *furniture*, *attire*, or *retinue*.

Equitable, or *just*.

Equity, *that which is just*, or *equitable*.

Equivalent *of equal worth*

An Equivalent, as *to give an* equivalent, i. e. *something of like value*.

Equivocal, *that has a doubtful*, or *double meaning when one word signifies several things*.

To equivocate, or *speak doubtfully*.

An Equivocation, or *doubtful expression*.

E R

E'er, *for* ever.

To eradicate, *pull up by the roots*, or *root out*.

An Eradication.

Ere, or *before that*.

Erect, or *upright*.

To erect, *set up*, or *build*.

An Erection.

An Erecter *of statues*, or *buildings*.

Eringo, *a sort of herb*.

Ermine, *a little northern weasel with its furr so call'd, which is very costly, and only fit for Princes and Noble-men to wear*.

An Ermin-tippet.

To err, *go out of the way*, or *mistake*.

An Errand, or *message*.

Errant, or *wandering*; *as* Knights errant, *who are feign'd to have rov'd all over the World, doing wonderful feats at arms*.

Errata, *the faults of a Book in Printing*.

Erroneous, *subject to errour* or *false*.

An Errour, *mistake*; or *over-sight*.

Ers, *bitter vetch*.

An Eruption, or *violent breaking out*.

E S

An Escape, *and to* escape, or *get away*.

An Escar, or *crust of a sore*.

An Escheat, or *forfeiture*, *to the Lord of the Mannour*.

Escheated *Lands*.

An Escheator, *an Officer who takes cognizance of* Escheats *due to the King*.

To eschew, *avoid* or *shun*.

An Escutcheon, or Scutcheon.

Especial, *particular* or *chief*.

An Espier (*from to* espy)

Espousals.

To espouse, *betroth*, *promise*, or *assure in wedlock*.

To espouse, or *maintain a cause*, *quarrel*, &c.

To espy, *to look about for*, or *discover*.

An Esquire, *a title of honour next below a Knight*.

An Essay, *tryal*, or *short Discourse upon any subject*.

The Essay *breast*, or *brisket of a Deer*.

To essay, or *try*.

The Essence, *substance*, *being*, or *nature of a thing*; *also a chymical extract*.

Essential.

To Establish, *make stable*, *settle*, or *decree*.

An Establisher.

An Establishment.

An Estate, *condition*, *rank*, *means*, or *revenues*.

The Estates *of a Kingdom*.

Esteem, or *reputation*.

To Esteem, *think*, *regard value*, or *judge of a thing*.

An Estimate, *and to* estimate, or *value*.

Estimation, *account*, or *repute*.

To estrange, *alienate*, or *divert from*

An Estrangement.

E T

To etch, or *grave with* Aqua fortis.

Eternal, *everlasting*, or *endless*.

Eternity.

Eternity.
To eternize, or *make eternal.*
Ethicks, *Morals*, or *Treatises of Moral Philosophy*
Etymological, *belonging to*
Etymology, or *the skill of deriving words from their true original.*

E V

To evacuate, *empty, make void, or void by stool, &c.*
An Evacuation *of humours.*
To evade, or *avoid the force of an argument.*
Evangelical, *of*, or *belonging to the Gospel.*
The four Evangelists, or *pen-men of the Gospel.*
To evaporate, or *dissolve into vapours.*
An Evaporation, *breathing or steeming out.*
An Evasion, *escape or shift.*
The Eucharist, i. e. *thanksgiving; the blessed Sacrament of the Lord's Supper.*
Eucharistical, *belonging thereto.*
An Eve, or *Vigil, the day before a holy-day.*
An Eve-churr, or *churr-worm.*
An Eveck, *a kind of wild goat.*
Even, *like, equal, smooth, plain*, &c.
To even, or *make even.*
Even, or *also.*
The Even, or *evening.*
Even-song, or *evening service.*
Evening-tide.
Evenness, *likeness*, or *smoothness.*
An Event, *chance, issue, or end of a thing.*
Ever, *at any time*, or *always.*
Everlasting, or *always continuing.*
Life-everlasting, *an herb.*

Everlastingness.
Every-one, *or* every body.
An Evet, or *eft.*
To evict, or *prove against one.*
An Eviction *against a prisoner.*
An Evidence, *proof*, or *testimony; also the person of a Witness.*
Evidenced, or *proved.*
Evidences, or *Deeds.*
Evident, clear, or *plain.*
Evil, or *bad; and an* evil.
The King's Evil, *a disease.*
To evince, *overcome*, or *prove by argument*, &c.
Evitable, *that may be shunn'd*, or *avoided.*
An Eunuch, or *guilded man.*
Europe, *one of the four parts of the World.*

E W

An Ew, *a female sheep.*
An Ewer, *to hold water.*
An Ew-lamb.
An Ew-tree.

E X

Exact, *accurate*, or *punctual.*
To exact, *demand*, or *oppress.*
An Exaction, or *extortion.*
An Exacter.
To exaggerate, *heap up, amplify*, or *aggravate.*
An Exaggeration.
To exalt, *lift up*, or *praise highly.*
An Exaltation.
An Examination.
To examine, *question, enquire into, search, or try.*
An Examiner.
An Example, *pattern*, or *Copy.*
To exasperate, i. e. *to make sharp, to provoke, vex*, or *anger.*
An Exasperation.
To exceed, *go beyond, surmount*, or *abound.*

To excell, *out-do*, or *surpass.*
Excellence, *or* excellency.
Excellent.
Except, *saving*, or *unless.*
To except, *take out, excuse from*, or *object against.*
An Exception.
Exceptionable, *that may be excepted against.*
Excerptions, or *notes pick'd out of books.*
An Excess, or *exceeding.*
Excessive, or *immoderate.*
Excessiveness.
An Exchange, or *changing.*
The Royal Exchange, *where Merchants meet.*
To Exchange, *truck*, or *barter.*
Bills or *Letters of* exchange.
An Exchanger *of Money*, &c.
The Exchequer, or *Royal Treasury; also the Court for all pleas relating to the Crown-revenues.*
The Chancellor and Barons of the Exchequer.
The Excise, *a Duty laid upon Beer, Ale, Cider*, &c.
An Excise-man, *a Collector of that Duty.*
The Excise-Office.
An Excision, *cutting off*, or *destroying.*
An Excitation.
To excite, *stir up*, or *egg on.*
An Excitement.
An Exciter.
To Exclaim, *bawl*, or *cry out against.*
An Exclaimer.
An Exclamation.
To exclude, *shut out, keep* or *debar from*
An Exclusion.
Exclusive.
To excommunicate, or *deprive of Church-Communion.*
An Excommunication.

An

One-eyed, *that has but one eye.*
Pink-eyed, *that has little eyes.*
Wall-eyed.
The Eye-sight.
An Ox-eye, *a bird, and herb.*
An Eyess, or *watery-eyed hawk, brought up under a kite.*
Eyre, *the Court of Justices itinerant, that take care of the King's forests.*
Justices in Eyre.

F A

A Fable, *feigned story,* or *devised tale.*
A Fabrick, or *building.*
Fabulous, or *full of fables.*
A Face, *and* to face *(in several senses.)*
Faceles, *a kind of pulse.*
A Fac-totum, *i. e.* do-all, *a printing-border, in the middle of which any letter may be put in,* or *taken out at pleasure.*
Facete, *or* fecetious, *pleasant and witty.*
Facetiousness.
Facil, or *easy to be done.*
To facilitate, or *make easy.*
Facilitation.
Facility, or *easiness.*
A Fact, *act,* or *deed.*
A Faction, or *division among people; a particular sect,* or *seditious party.*
Factious, or *given to faction.*
Factiousness.
A Factor, or *Merchant's Agent beyond Sea.*
A Factorship.
A Factory, or *company of* Factors.
A Faculty, or *natural power; also a license,* or *dispensation,* or *profession.*
The Faculties, or *Professions of Divinity, Physick,* &c.
The Faculty-Office.
To faddle, or *dandle a Child.*
To fade, *fall away; decay,* or *wither.*
Fag-end; as *the* fag-end *of cloth, stuff,* &c.
A Fagot, or *bavin.*
To Fagot *up,* or *make up into* fagots.
A Fagot-band.
A Fagot-man.
To fail, *disappoint, faint, miscarry,* &c.
A Failure, *or* failing.
Fain, or *forced to do a thing; also desirous;* as, *I would* fain *travel.*
Faint, *weak, feeble;* or *slack.*
To faint, faint away, or *fall into a swoon.*
Faint-hearted, or *cowardly*
Faint-heartedness.
Faintness, or *weakness.*
A Fair, or *mart.*
Fair, *beautiful, large, clear, equitable,* &c.
Fair-conditioned.
A Fair-dealer.
A Fairing, or *present given at a* fair.
Fairness.
A Fairy, or *hobgoblin.*
Faith, *belief,* or *trust.*
Faithfull.
Faithfulness.
Faithless, *not believing,* or *not to be trusted.*
Faithlesness.
A Falchion, *a kind of short hooked weapon.*
A Falcon, *a sort of hawk; also a piece of Ord'nance.*
A Falconer.
Falconry.
A Fall, *and to* fall *(in all senses.)*
A Down-fall.
A Pit-fall, *gin,* or *snare.*
A Water-fall.
Fallacious, or *deceitfull.*
A Fallacy, *deceit,* or *crafty device.*
Fallible, *that may fail,* or *err.*
The Falling-sickness, *a disease.*
A Fallow, or *reddish colour.*
A Fallow-deer.
A Fallow-field, *that lies untill'd.*
Faln, *or* fallen *(from to* fall.)
False, *untrue, wrong, counterfeit,* or *treacherous.*
False-hearted.
Falseness, *or* falshood.
A Falsifier.
To falsify, or *counterfeit a writing; also to break one's word.*
A Falsity, or *untruth.*
To falter, *stammer in speech,* or *to stumble.*
Fame, *report,* or *reputation.*
Familiar, *intimately acquainted with,* or *usual.*
A Familiar, *or* familiar *spirit.*
Familiarity, *a* familiar *way,* or *intimacy.*
A Family, *houshold,* or *lineage.*
A Famine, or *general want of provisions.*
To famish, *to starve one;* or *to perish with hunger.*
Famous, or *renowned.*
Famousness.
A Fan, *and to* fan, *(in different senses.)*
A Fanatick, *one that is frantick,* or *pretends to divine inspiration.*
Fancifull, or fantastical.
A Fancy, *and to* fancy, *(in several senses.)*
A Fane, or *weather-cock.*
A Fang, or *claw.*
The Fangs, or *fore-teeth.*
Fangled, or *new* fangled.
New Fangles, or *devices.*
A Fanner *of Corn.*
A Fantasm, fantome, or *apparition.*
Fantastical, fantastick, or *conceited.*

Fan-

Fantasticalness.
A Fantasy, *or* fancy.
Far, or *distant*, &c.
A Farce, *or* farced *meat*.
To Farce, or *stuff*.
A Farce, or *Mock-comedy*.
Farcy *or* fashions; *a horse-disease*.
A Fardel, or *bundle*.
A Lady's Fardingale, or *whalebone-circle*, *formerly worn about their hips*.
Fare, or *diet*, *and to* fare.
The Fare, or *hire of a Coach-man*, or *Waterman*.
Farewell, or *adieu*.
A Farm, *a house and land taken by lease*.
To farm out, or *let to* farm.
A Farmer.
The Farmers *of the Customs*.
A Farrier, *Horse-doctor*, or *shooer of horses*.
To farrow, or *bring forth pigs*.
A Sow with farrow.
A Fart.
To fart, or *let a* fart.
A Farter.
Farther.
The farthermost.
Farthest.
A Farthing, *the fourth part of a penny*.
A Fashion, *form*, *mode*, *custom*, &c.
To fashion, or *shape*.
Fashionable.
The King's fashioner, or *Tayler*.
The Fashions, *a horse-disease*.
A Fast, *and to* fast.
Lent-Fast.
The Ember-fast.
A Faster.
Fast, *firm*, *close*, or *swift*.
A Hold-fast *in a wall*, or *a niggard*.
To fasten, *make fast*, *bind*, or *tie*.

Fastness.
Fat, *gross*, or *plump*.
The fat *of meat*, &c.
Fatal, *belonging to* fate; or *deadly*.
Fatality, or *being liable to* fate.
Fate, or *destiny*.
Fated; as, *he is* fated *into ruin*.
A Father.
A Father-in-law, or *step-father*.
A Fore-father, or *progenitor*.
A Foster-father.
A Grand-father.
To father *a thing upon one*.
A Father-confessor.
A Father-lasher; *a fish*.
Fatherless, or *destitute of a* Father.
Fatherliness, or *fatherly affection*.
Fatherly, *belonging to a Father*.
A Fathom, or *measure of six feet*.
To Fathom, *measure by* Fathoms, or *to sound at Sea*.
A Fatigue, *toil*, or *weariness*.
Fatness, (*from* fat.)
The fatted *Calf*.
The fatting, or *feeding of Cattel*.
A Fatting-house.
To fatten, or *make fat*.
Fatty, or *full of fat*.
A Faucet, Fosset, or *tap*.
A Fauchion, *or* Falchion.
A Faulk'ner, *or* Falconer.
A Fault, *offence*, *error*, or *mistake*.
A Fault-finder.
To faulter, or falter *in speech*.
Faultless, or *free from* faults.
Faulty, *that is in* fault.
A Favour, *and to* favour. (*in several senses*.)
A Wedding-favour.
Favourableness.
Ill-favoured.

Well-favoured.
A Favourer.
A Favourite.
A Fausen; *a sort of large Eel*.
A Fautor, *favourer*, *abetter*, or *cherisher*.
A Fawn, or *young deer*.
To fawn *upon*, or *flatter one*.

F E

Fealty, q. d. fidelity; *the Tenant's Oath to be true to the Lord of whom he holds land*, &c.
Fear, *awe*, *dread*, or *fright*.
To fear, or *be afraid*.
Fearfull, *timorous*, or *to be* feared.
Fearfulness, or *timorousness*.
Fearless, or *void of* fear.
Fearlesness.
Feasible, *that may be done*.
Feasibleness.
A Feast, or *banquet*; *and to* feast.
A Smell-feast.
A Feaster.
Feat, *finical*, or *odd*.
A Feat, or *exploit*.
A Feather *of a bird*.
To feather *one's nest*.
A Feather-bed.
A Feather-seller.
Feather-footed.
Feather-top-grass.
Prince's-feather; *a flower*.
Feathered, or *covered with* feathers.
Featherless; *that has no* feathers.
Featness, (*from* feat.)
A Feature, or *lineament of the face*.
Well-featured.
A Feaver, or *ague*.
An Hectick-feaver.
Feaverish.
February; *the month so called from* februo, *an old*

old Latin word signifying to purify, or cleanse by Sacrifice.
Fed, *from to feed.*
A Fee, *reward, or pension.*
To fee one, or *give him a fee.*
A Fee, or *estate in fee.*
Fee-simple, *or* fee-absolute; *an estate made over in these words,* To us, and our heirs for ever.
Fee-tail, *or* fee-conditional; *that of which we are seized,* To us and our heirs, *with limitation,* i. e. *the heirs of our body,* &c.
Fee-farm, *Land held of another in fee,* i. e. *in perpetuity to himself and heirs; paying a yearly rent, to half, or a third part of the value.*
Feeble, or *weak.*
Feebleness.
To feed, *eat, nourish,* or *give food to.*
A Feeder.
To feel, *touch,* or *be sensible of.*
The sense of Feeling.
Fellow-feeling.
To feign, *devise,* or *pretend.*
A Feigner.
Felicity, or *happiness.*
A Fell, or *skin.*
A Sheep's fell.
A Fell-monger.
To fell, *cut,* or *strike down.*
A Feller *of wood.*
A Fellon, or *whitlow on the finger.*
A Fellow, or *companion.*
To fellow, or *match.*
A Fellow-servant.
A Fellow-soldier.
A Fellow-worker.
A Bed-fellow.
The Fellows, *or* fellies *of a wheel.*
Fellowship.
Fell-wort, *an herb.*
A Felon.
Felonious, *belonging to*
Felony, *any crime next to petty Treason,* as, *murder, theft, sodomy, rape,* &c.
Felt, (*from to feel.*)
A Felt, *or* felt-hat.
A Felt-maker.
A Feluca, *a kind of barge.*
A Female, *and the* female sex.
A Fen, or *marsh.*
Fen-berries.
A Fen-cricket; *an insect.*
A Fence, *or enclosure.*
To fence, or *enclose with hedges,* &c. *also to fortify,* or *to exercise with a sword.*
A Fencer.
A Fencing-master.
A Fencing-school.
A Fender, *belonging to a grate, to keep in the coals, cinders,* &c.
Fene-greek,
Fennel,
Giant-fennel,
Hogs-fennel, } *herbs*
Scorching-fennel,
Fennel-flower.
Fennish *of,* or *belonging to* fens.
A Feoffee, *he that receives a*
Feoffment, *any gift of Lands,* &c. *or grant in fee simple, by the delivery of seisin and giving possession, by word,* or *writing.*
A Feoffer, *a giver of a* feoffment.
A Ferment, or *leaven.*
To Ferment, or *work.*
A Fermentation, or *puffing up with leaven; the working of beer,* &c.
Fern, *a wild sort of plant.*
Finger-fern.
Oak-fern.
Ferny, or *full of* fern.
A Ferret, *a little beast, that drives rabbets out of the burrows.*
To ferret, or *search out,* or *to vex one.*
A Ferret-ribbon.
Ferriage, *money for the passage over a river.*
A Ferry, *and to* ferry *over the water.*
A Ferry-boat.
A Ferry-man.
Fertile, or *fruitful.*
Fertileness, *or* fertility.
Fervency, *or* fervour.
Fervent, *burning-hot, vehement,* or *zealous.*
A Ferular, *palmer,* or *hand-clapper, used in schools.*
The Ferule, *or* ferrule *of a cane,* or *walking-stick.*
A Fescue, *with which Children are taught to spell.*
A Fesse, or *girdle a-cross the middle of a scutcheon.*
To fester, or *putrefy.*
A Festival, or *feasting day.*
A Festoon, *garland of fruit,* or *flower-work in Architecture.*
A Fetch, or *subtil wile.*
To fetch (*in several senses.*)
A Fetcher *of water,* &c.
The Fetlock-joint *of an horse.*
A Fetter, or *shackle for the feet of malefactors.*
To fetter, or *bind with* fetters.
To fettle to, or *go about a business.*
A Feud, *deadly hatred,* or *quarrel.*
Feudal, *belonging to,* or *held in fee.*
A Fever, *or* feaver.
Feverfew, *an herb.*
The Feuille-mort, *or* fillemot *colour.*
Few; as *in few words.*
Fewel, *for the fire.*
Fewmets, *or* fewmishing, *the dung of a deer.*
Fewness, (*from* few.)

F I

Fiants; *the dung of a fox*, or *badger*.
A Fib, or *little lye*.
To fib, or *tell a* fib.
A Fibber.
Fibers, *the hair-like threads*, or *strings of muscles, veins*, and *roots*.
Fibrous, or *full of* fibres.
Fickle, *light*, or *inconstant*.
Fickleness.
A Fiction, *device, lye*, or *forgery*.
Fictitious, *feigned, fabulous*, or *counterfeit*.
A Fiddle, *a musical instrument*.
To fiddle, *to play upon a* fiddle, or *to trifle*.
A Fidler.
A Fiddle-stick.
Fidelity, or *faithfulness*.
To fidge about, or *stirr up and down continually*.
A Field, *for tillage, pasture*, &c.
A Corn-field.
A Field-battel.
A Field-fare, *a bird*.
A Field-mouse.
A Field-piece, *a sort of Cannon*.
A Fiend, *fury*, or *devil*.
Fierce, *cruel, wild*, or *boisterous*.
Fierceness.
Fiery, *full of* fire, *hasty*, or *passionate*.
To fiest, *or* fizzle.
A Fife, *a sort of pipe*.
Fifteen, (*in number*.)
The Fifteenth.
The fifth,
The Fiftieth.
Fifty.
A Fig, *a fruit*.
Not to care a fig *for one*.
A Figary, or *freak*.
A Fig-pecker, *a bird*.
Fig-wort, *an herb*.
A Fight, *and to* fight.
A Cock-fight.
A Sea-fight.
A Fighter.
A Figment, or *fiction*.
Figurative-expressions.
A Figure, *fashion*, or *shape*; *also an ornament in speech*.
To figure, or *draw* figures *upon*.
Figured-velvet.
A Filacer, *or* filer *of Writs; an Officer in the Common-pleas*.
The Filanders, *a disease in hawks, occasion'd by little worms*.
A Filberd, *the best sort of small nuts*.
To filch, or *steal privily*.
A Filcher.
A File, *a mechanical instrument*.
To file, or *polish with a* file.
File-dust.
A Filer.
A File, *to hang papers on*.
A File, or *rank of soldiers*.
A File-leader.
Filial, *belonging to a son*.
Filipendula, or *drop-wort*.
To fill, *or* fill up.
The Filler, *or* fill-horse.
Fillemot, *or* feuille-mort, *the colour of a dead leaf*.
A Fillet, *hair-lace*, or *band*.
Filletted. or *bound with a* fillet.
A Fillet *of veal*.
A Fillip, *and to* fillip *one*.
A Filly, filly foal; or *young mare*.
A Film, or *thin skin*.
Filosella, *a kind of course silk for tapistry-work*.
To filter, or *strain thro' a felt, bag*, or *woollen-cloth*.
Filth, or *ordure*,
Filthiness.
Filthy.
Filtration, or *filtering*.
A Fin *of a fish*.
Final, *belonging to*, or *brought to an end*.
A Final cause.
The Finary, *that part of an iron-mill, where the pigs are wrought into gross iron, and prepared for the Chafery*.
A Finch, *a bird*.
A Bull-finch.
A Chaff-finch.
A Gold-finch.
A Green-finch.
A Thistle-finch.
To find, (*in all senses*.)
A Finder.
Fine, *neat, spruce, smooth, soft, pure*, &c.
To fine, *refine*, or *clear Liquors, Metals*, &c.
A Fine, *amercement*, or *penalty*; *also money paid for the lease of a house*.
To fine, or *set a* fine *upon one*.
To fine-draw *Cloth*, &c.
A Fine-drawer.
Fine-drawn.
Fineness.
A Finer, or *refiner of metals*.
Finery, or *Gallantry*.
Finew, vinew, or *mouldiness*.
Finewed, or *grown mouldy*.
A Finger.
To finger, *or touch with the* finger.
The Ring-finger.
Finger-fern.
Lady's-finger, *an herb*.
Light-fingered
Finical, *spruce, nice*, or *conceited*.
Finicalness, or *affectedness*.
To finish, or *bring to an end* or *perfection*.
A Finisher.
Finite, *that has an end limited*, or *bounded*.
Finned, *having Fins*.
Fir, or *a Fir-tree*.
Fire, *or the element of* Fire.

To fire, *to set on fire*; *or to fire a Gun.*
St. Anthony's fire, *a kind of swelling full of heat and redness.*
A Bone-fire.
Wild fire *made with Gunpowder.*
A Fire-brand.
A Fire-drake, *a kind of fiery meteor.*
Fire-new, or *brand-new.*
The fire-pan *of a* Gun.
A Fire-shovel.
A Firer *of houses.*
A Fire-stone, or *marchasite.*
Fire-wood.
To firk, or *jerk.*
A Firkin, *the fourth part of a Barrel.*
A Firkin-man.
Firm, *fast and sure.*
The Firmament, or *starry skie.*
A Firmed Hawk, i. e. *well-feathered.*
Firmness.
First *(in number)*
The First-born.
The First-fruits, or *one year's profit of a spiritual living.*
The Firstlings *of a flock.*
A Fish.
To fish, or *catch* Fish.
A Shell-fish.
A Fisher, or *fisher man.*
The Kings-fisher, *a bird.*
A Fish-hook.
A Fish-market.
A Fish-monger.
A Fish-pond.
Fishy, *belonging to* fish.
To fisk, or *wag the tail.*
To fisk about, *to rove up and down madly.*
A Fissure, or *cleft.*
The Fist.
Fisted, as *club-fisted.*
A Fistick-nut.
A Fistula, *or deep running ulcer, like a pipe.*
To fight at Fisty-cuffs.
A Fisty-cuff-player.
Fit, or *meet, agreeable, or becoming.*
To fit, *prepare*, or *make* fit.
A Fit *of an Ague.*
Fitch, or *Pole-cat fur.*
A Fitch, or *vetch, a sort of pulse.*
A Fitchling.
A Fitchow, or *Pole-cat.*
Fitness *(from fit)*
Fitters; as *to cut to fitters*
Five *(in number)*
Fivefold.
The Five-foot, or *star-fish.*
To fix, or *fasten, settle*, &c.
A Fiz-gig, or *gadding Gossip.*
A Fizzle, or *silent fart.*
To Fizzle, or *foist.*

F L

Flabby, or *soft and moist.*
A Flag, *banner, ensign*, or *streamer.*
A Flag-ship.
Flags, or *sedge.*
Corn-flag.
Sweet Garden-flag.
Sword-flag.
Flag-flower.
A Flag-worm.
To flag, *wither, decay*, or *grow limber.*
A Flagelet, *a kind of pipe.*
Flaggy *(from to* flag *)*
Flagitious, *wicked, very lewd*, or *hainous.*
A Flagon, *a sort of pot.*
Flagrant, *burning-hot vehement*, or *notorious.*
A Flail, *to thresh corn with.*
A Flake *of fire, snow*, or *ice.*
A Flam, *idle story*, or *put off.*
To flam, or *sham one.*
A Flamboy, *a sort of link*
A Flame, *and to* flame.
The Flank, or *side of the body; also of an army*, or *rampart.*
To Flank, or *strengthen with flanks.*
A Flanker.
Flannel, *a kind of stuff.*
A Flap, *and to* flap, *(in several senses)*
A Fly-flap.
To flare, or *sweal as a Candle does with the wind.*
A Flash, *and to* flash *(in different senses)*
A Flasher *of water.*
Flashy, *waterish*, or *fresh-tasted.*
A Flask, or *box for gunpowder*; or *a bottle of* Florence-*wine.*
A Flasket, *a great sort of basket.*
Flat *(in all senses)*
To flat, or *make* flat.
Flat-footed.
Flat-nosed.
Flatness, or *evenness.*
Flats, or *shallows in the Sea.*
To flatter, *sooth up*, or *speak fair.*
A Flatterer.
Flattery.
Flatulent, or *windy.*
A flavour, *a pleasant relish in wine*, &c.
To flaunt it.
A Flaw, *chink, chop*, or *small defect.*
A Flawn, *a kind of custard.*
Flawy, or *full of* flaws.
Flax.
A Flax-man, or *dealer in* flax.
Toads-flax, or *flax-weed an herb.*
Flaxen, *made of* flax.
A Flea, *an insect.*
To flea, flay, or *pull off the skin.*
A Water-flea.
Flea-bane, } *herbs.*
Flea-wort, }
Flea-bit, *or* flea-bitten.
A Fleaer, *that pulls off the skin.*
A Fleam, *an instrument to let a horse blood.*
Fled *(from to fly)*
Fledge, *fit to fly out of the nest.*

A Fleece *of Wooll.*
To fleece *one.*
To fleer, or *cast a saucy look.*
A Fleerer, or *scorner.*
Fleet, or *swift.*
A Fleet *of Ships.*
The Fleet, *a noted prison, in* London.
To fleet, or *skim milk.*
A Fleeting-dish.
Fleeting, or *fading away.*
Flegm, *an humour of the body.*
Flegmatick, *belonging to flegm,* or *full of it.*
The Flesh *of living creatures.*
To flesh, or *encourage one.*
Flesh-colour.
A Flesh-hook.
Fleshiness (*from* fleshy)
Fleshless.
Fleshly, or *carnal.*
Fleshy, or *full of flesh.*
A Fletcher, or *arrow-maker.*
A Flew, or *fish-net.*
I Flew, or *did fly.*
Flexibility, or *aptness to bend.*
Flexible, or *pliant.*
Flexibleness.
To Flicker, or *laugh scornfully.*
The Flier *of a jack.*
A Flight, or *escape,* or *a company of birds.*
A Flight-shot.
Flimsy, or *limber,* &c.
To Flinch, *start,* or *give out.*
A Flincher.
Flinders, as *all to* flinders.
A Fling.
To Fling, *throw,* or *kick.*
A Flinger.
A Flint, *or* Flint-stone.
A Flint-glass.
Flippant, *brisk,* or *nimble of tongue.*
A Flirt, or *jeer, and to* flirt.
A Flirt, or jill-flirt, *a sorry baggage.*
To flit, or *remove from one place to another.*
Flitting, or *uncertain.*
A Flitch, or *side of bacon.*
A Flitter, or *rag;* as *all to flitters.*
A Flitter-mouse, or *bat*
Flitting, as *a staked horse that eats up all the grass within his reach.*
Flix-weed, *an herb.*
A Float *of timber.*
To Float, *or swim upon the water.*
Float-grass.
A Flock, or *company of people, birds,* &c.
To flock *together.*
A Flock *of Wooll.*
A Flock-bed.
The Flook, or flouk *of an anchor, that part which takes hold of the ground.*
The Floor *of a house,* &c.
Floored.
A Flooring *with boards.*
Floramour, or *flower gentle.*
Florences, *a kind of cloth brought from* Florence *in* Italy.
A Florentine, *a kind of tart,* or *pudding.*
Floret-silk.
Florid, or *full of Rhetorical flowers.*
Floridness *of style.*
A Florin, *a kind of coin worth about* 1 s. 6 d.
A Florist, *one that has skill in flowers.*
Flotes, *pieces of timber joyn'd to* convey goods *down a river.*
Flotten, or *skim-milk.*
A Floud, or *over-flowing of waters.*
A Land-floud.
A Floud-gate.
To Flounce, *plunge in the water,* or *be in a toss with anger.*
A Flounder, *a Sea-fish.*
A Flourish, *and to* flourish (*in all senses*)
A Flout, or *jeer, and to* flout.
A Flouter.
To flow, *as the tide,* &c.
Flower *of meal.*
A Flower.
To flower, or *blossom* or *to mantle as drink does.*
Flower gentle.
A Flower-de-luce.
The Yellow flower-de-luce.
The Flower of the sun.
The little Sun-flower.
Flower velour, or *velvet-flower.*
Bristol-flower.
The Cuckoo-flower.
Helmet-flower.
Our Lady's flower.
Penny-flower.
Satten-flower.
Wall-flower.
A Flower-pot.
Flower-work, *in masonry.*
Flower'd, as *flower'd-silk.*
Flowk-wort.
Flown, (*from to* fly)
Flowry, or *full of flower.*
The Flowry reed *of* India.
The Flue, or *down of a* Rabbet.
Fluellin, *an herb.*
Fluency, *or* fluentness *of discourse.*
Fluent, *easy,* or *eloquent in speech.*
Fluid, or *apt to run as water does.*
Fluidity, or fluidness.
A Fluke, *a sort of insect.*
Flummery, *a jelly of oatmeal.*
Flung, (*from to* fling)
To be flush *of money.*
A Flush *at Cards, when all are of a suit.*
Flushed, fleshed, or *animated with success.*
A Flushing *in the Face.*
Fluster'd *in drink,* or *fuddled.*
A Flute, or *recorder, a kind of pipe.*
Fluted, or *channelled.*
Fluting *in Architecture.*
To flutter, or *try to fly.*
A Flux, flix, or *looseness.*
The Flux *and* Reflux, or *ebbing and flowing of the Tides.*

To flux *one for the pox.*
To fly *as a bird does; to run away,* or *escape by flight.*
A Fly, *an insect.*
A Blitter-fly.
Catch-fly, *or* fly-bane, *an herb.*
A Dog-fly.
A Dung-fly.
A Fire-fly.
A Flesh-fly.
A Gad-fly, or *Ox-fly.*
A Spanish-fly.
A Water-fly.
A Fly-boat.
A Fly-flap.
A Fly-blow.
To fly-blow *meat,* or *to defame one.*

FO

A Fob, or *little pocket.*
To fob *one off.*
A Fob-action *at law.*
The Focel-bones *of the arms and legs.*
Fodder, *any kind of provender for cattel.*
A Fodder, or 2000 *pounds weight of lead.*
To fodder, or *forage.*
A Fodderer.
A Foe, or *enemy.*
A Fog, or *mist.*
Fogginess.
Foggy.
Foh! *or* fy!
A Foil, *and to* foil (*in several senses.*)
A Foin, *a kind of weasel,* or *polecat; also the furr of that creature.*
A Foin, or *pass in fencing.*
To foin, or *make a* foin.
A Foist, or *little pinnace.*
A Galley-foist.
To foist, *stuff in,* or *forge; also to fizzle,* or *let a silent* fart.
A Foisting-hound.
Foisty, or *musty.*
A Fold, or *pleat;* or *an enclosure for Cattel.*
A Sheep-fold.
To fold (*in all senses.*)
Two-fold.
A Hundred-fold.
A Folder.
A Folding-stick, *to fold Books, Letters,* &c.
A Fole, or *Colt.*
To Fole, or *bring forth a* Fole.
Fole-bit, Fole-foot, } *herbs.*
Foliage, *a kind of branched-work.*
A Folio-book, or *a book in* folio; *having two leaves to the sheet.*
Folks, or *people.*
To follow (*in all senses*)
A Follower.
Folly, or *foolishness.*
Fome, or *froth, and to* fome,
To foment, *warm, comfort, cherish,* or *encourage.*
A Fomentation, or *cherishing, more especially by applying warm cloths dipt in some liquor to the body.*
A Fomenter.
A Fond, fund, or *stock.*
Fond, *indulgent,* or *kind.*
A Font *for baptism; also a compleat set of printing-letters.*
Food, *victualls,* or *sustenance.*
A Fool, *dolt,* or *sot.*
To fool, or *make a* fool *of one.*
Foolery.
Fool-hardiness.
Fool-hardy, or *foolishly rash.*
Foolish, or *simple.*
Foolishness.
A Foot (*in several senses*)
To foot *it, go on* foot, or *trip it in dancing.*
To foot *stockings.*
Bears-foot, Calves-foot, Crow-foot, Doves-foot, Fole-foot. } *herbs.*
Hares-foot, *an herb.*
A Foot-ball.
A Foot-boy.
A Foot-man.
A Foot-pace.
A Foot-step.
A Foot-stall *of a pillar.*
A Foot-stool.
Footed, *as broad footed*
Cloven-footed.
Hunch-footed.
Splay-footed, &c.
A Fop, *antastical,* or *impertinent fellow.*
Foppery.
Foppish.
Foppishness.
For; *as for that reason.*
Forage, *provision for cattel in war-time.*
To forage, or *go a foraging.*
A Forger.
To forbear, *to leave off; to spare,* or *suffer one.*
Forbearance.
To forbid, *to command a thing not to be done,* or *suffer'd.*
Forbidden.
A Forbidder.
Forborn, (*from to* forbear.)
Force, *strength, endeavour, violence,* &c.
To force, or *compel,* &c.
Forceless, *that has no force.*
Forces, or *military* forces; *an Army,* or *body of soldiers.*
Forcible.
A Ford, or *shallow place in a River.*
To ford, or *pass over a* ford.
Fordable, *that may be* forded.
Fore-armed, or *armed, before-hand.*
To fore-bode, or *presage.*
Forecast.
To Forecast, *consider before,* or *foresee.*
The Forecastle, *of a ship, i. e. the fore-part above deck.*

A

A Fore-door.
Fore-fathers, or *ancestors.*
The Fore-feet *of a beast.*
The Fore-finger.
The Fore-flap *of a shirt.*
The Fore-front *of a house.*
To forego, *let a thing go, quit,* or *part with.*
Fore-goers, *Purveyors, going before the King and Queen in progress to provide for them.*
Foregoing; as, *the* foregoing *Chapter.*
A-fore-hand, or *before-hand.*
A Fore-head.
Foreign, *strange, outlandish,* or *disagreeable to the purpose.*
A Foreigner, or *stranger*
A Fore-horse, *the horse that goes first.*
Fore-judged, or *expell'd the Court.*
To fore-know, or *know before-hand.*
Fore-knowledge.
Fore-known.
A Foreland, *cape,* or *promontory.*
The Fore-locks *of a horse.*
Fore-loin, or fore-loyn, *when a hound meets a chace, and goes away with it before the rest.*
The Fore-man *of a Jury.* or *inquest.*
The Fore-mast *of a ship*
Foremost.
Fore-ordained.
The Fore-part *of a thing.*
A Fore-runner.
A Fore-sail.
To Fore-see.
A Fore-seer.
A Fore-sight.
To Fore-shew.
The Fore-skin.
To fore-speak.
A Forest, *a great wood,* or *harbour for wild beasts.*
Forest-work, *a sort of tapistry work.*
To forestall *the Market,* i. e. *to buy goods before they are brought thither.*
A Forestaller.
A Forester, or *keeper of a forest.*
A Fore-taste.
A Fore-taster.
The Fore-teeth.
To foretell, *tell aforehand,* or *prophesy.*
A Fore-teller.
To Fore-think, or *think before-hand.*
A Fore-thought.
Fore-told *(from to* foretell.*)*
A Fore-top *of hair.* &c.
To fore-warn.
A Fore-wind.
A Forfeit, *default, fine,* or *penalty.*
To forfeit, or *make a* forfeit *of.*
Forfeitable, or *liable to be* forfeited.
A Forfeiture.
A Forge, *for a smith.*
To forge; *as a smith does; to devise, counterfeit,* &c.
A Forger.
A Forgery, or *a* forging *of false stories.*
To forget, *not to remember,* or *mind.*
Forgetful, or *apt to* forget.
Forgetfulness.
Forget me not, *an herb.*
To forgive, or *pardon.*
Forgiven.
Forgiveness.
A Fork *(of all sorts.)*
To fork, or *take up with a* fork.
A Dung-fork.
A Fire-fork.
An Oven-fork.
A Pitch-fork.
Forked, or *made like a* fork.
Forkedness.
A Forket, or *little* fork.
A Fork-fish.
Forlorn, *forsaken, dejected,* or *lost.*
The Forlorn-hope *of an Army, a party put upon the most desperate service.*
A Form, or *bench.*
A Form, *shew,* or *appearance.*
To form, or *fashion.*
Formal, *in* form, *punctual, precise,* or *affected.*
A Formalist, or *follower of* forms.
Formality.
To formalize, or *play the* formalist.
Former *(from* fore.*)*
Formidable, *to be feared,* or *dreadful.*
Formidableness.
A Formulary, *a president for doing a thing;* or *a book of* forms.
Fornication, or *whoredom between unmarried persons.*
A Fornicator, or *whoremaster.*
To forsake, *leave,* or *quit.*
Forsaken.
A Forsaker.
Forsooth, i. e. *in truth;* as, *yes* forsooth.
To forswear; *to swear falsly,* or *to renounce.*
A Forswearer, or *perjurer.*
Forsworn.
A Fort, or *sconce.*
Forth, or *out of doors.*
Forth-coming, or *ready to appear.*
Forthwith, or *incontinently.*
The Fortieth *(from* forty.*)*
Fortifiable, *that may be* fortified.
A Fortification.
To fortifie, *make strong,* or *fence.*
A Fortifier.
Fortitude, *stoutness of mind, courage,* or *valour.*

A

A Fortlet, *or* little fort.
A Fortnight, *the space of fourteen nights, or days,* i. e. *two weeks.*
A Fortress, or *strong-hold.*
Fortuitous, *casual*, or *what happens by chance.*
Fortunate, or *lucky.*
Fortunateness.
Fortune, *hazard*, *hap*, *chance*, *luck*, *condition*, or *estate.*
A Fortune-teller.
Forty (*in number*)
Forward, *or* forwards.
To forward, *help*, or *promote.*
Forwardness.
A Foss, or *ditch.*
The Foss-way, *one of the grand high-ways of* England, *made by the* Romans; *so call'd from being ditched on both sides.*
A Fosset, *or* faucet, *that part of the tap thro' which the liquor runs.*
To foster, *nourish*, *cherish*, or *bring up.*
A Foster-brother.
A Foster-child.
A Foster-father.
A Fosterer.
A Fother, *or* fodder *of Lead.*
A Fougade, *a kind of fire-work*, *or mine.*
Fought (*from to fight*)
Foul, *filthy*, *nasty*, *base*, *ill-favour'd*, &c.
To foul, *or make foul.*
Foulness.
Found (*from to find*)
To found; *to cause to be built*, or *to cast metal.*
A Foundation.
A Founder.
A Bell-founder.
A Letter-founder, *for Printers.*
To founder, or *spoil the legs of a horse.*
To founder, *leak*, or *take in water; as a ship does.*
A Foundling, *an exposed child.*

A Fountain, *a place where the water breaks out, and springs forth in drops from the earth.*
Four (*in number*)
Fourfold.
Four-footed, *having four feet.*
Fourscore.
A Four-square *figure.*
Fourteen.
The Fourteenth.
The Fourth.
A Foul, or *great bird.*
A Water-fowl.
A Fowler.
To go a fowling; or *to catch* fowls.
A Fowling-piece.
A Fox, *a beast.*
To fox, or *fuddle one.*
Fox-glove, } *herbs.*
Fox-tail, }
Foy, as *to give*, or *pay one's* foy; i. e. *to treat his friends upon his departure.*

FR

A Fraction, *breaking*, or *disunion*; *also a broken number in* Arithmetick.
A Fracture, or *breaking of a bone.*
Fragile, *apt to break*, *brittle*, or *frail.*
Fragility.
A Fragment, or *broken piece of a thing.*
Fragrancy, *a being.*
Fragant, or *smelling sweet.*
Fraight, *the burden of a ship*; or *money paid for goods carried therein.*
To fraight, or *load a ship.*
A Frail *of raisins, containing about* 70 *pounds.*
Frail, *brittle*, *weak*, or *infirme.*
Frailty.
The Frame *of a Table, Picture, Piece of Ordinance,* &c.
To Frame, *fashion*, *build*, *devise*, or *forge.*
A Framer.

A Franc, *or* French *silver worth* 1 *s.* 6 *d.*
A Franchise, *freedom*, *exemption*, or *privilege.*
Frank, *free*, *liberal*, or *sincere.*
Frank-chace, *a liberty of* free chace *in a forest.*
A Frank *to feed a boar in.*
Frankincense, *a sweet-scented* Arabian *Gum, from a tree that has bark and leaves like a laurel.*
Frankness, *freeness*, or *sincerity.*
Frantick, or *mad.*
Franticknefs.
Fraternal, or *brotherly.*
A Fraternity, or *brotherhood.*
Fraud, *deceit*, or *guile.*
Fradulent, or *deceitful.*
Fraught, or *well stored.*
A Fray, *scuffle*, or *quarrel.*
To fray, or *fret*; as *cloth does by rubbing.*
A Freak, *whimsy*, or *conceit.*
Freakish, *full of* freaks.
Freakishness.
A Freckle *in the face.*
Freckled, or *full of freckles.*
Free, *and to* free (*in all senses*)
A Free-booter, *a soldier, that serves for plunder without pay*; *a pirate*, or *rover at sea.*
A Free-born Cityzen.
Freedom.
A Free-hold, or *free tenure for term of life.*
A Free-holder.
Freeness in giving, or *liberality.*
A Free-man, *one that is free of a company*, *or corporation.*
A Free-mason.
Free-stone.
To escape scot-free.
A Freez *in Architecture.*
Freez-cloth.

To freez, or *congeal*, as *water does.*
French, *belonging to* France.
To speak French, i. e. *the language of that Country*
French-beans, or *kidney-beans.*
A French-man.
French-marygold, *a flower.*
The French pox.
French-wheat.
Frenchify'd, or *brought over to the* French *interest.*
A Frensy, or frenzy.
Frentick, frantick, or *mad.*
Frequency, or *oftenness.*
Frequent, *often*, or *common.*
To frequent, *haunt*, or *resort to.*
Fresco; as, *to walk in* fresco., i. e. *in the fresh Air*; *to drink* in fresco, i. e. *cool liquors.*
To paint in fresco, i. e. *on walls newly plaistered that the colours may sink in.*
Fresh, *new*, or *unsalted.*
A Fresh-man, or *novice in an University, College*, &c.
To freshen, *make* fresh, or *unsalt.*
Freshness.
Fresh-shot, *fresh water discharg'd from a great river for a mile or two into the Sea.*
A Fresh-water-fish.
A Fresh-water soldier, *a raw soldier*; *also an herb so call'd.*
A Fret, *and to* fret (*in several senses.*)
Fretful, or *peevish.*
Fret-work.
A Fricassy, *a dish of fried meat.*
Friday, *the sixth day of the week, on which the hermaphrodite goddess*, Friga *was worshipped by our* Saxon *fore-fathers.*
Good Friday, *kept holy, in commemoration of Christ's passion.*
To fridge, *or* frig *about*
A Friend, *lover*, or *intimate acquaintance.*
Friendless, or *destitute of* friends.
Friendliness.
Friendly, *loving like a* friend.
To be friends *with one, after a falling out.*
Friendship.
A Frier, or *monk.*
Friers-cowl; *an herb.*
Friers-piss, or *urine-wort*
A Frigat, or *light Man of War, usually having but two decks.*
A Fright.
To fright, frighten one, or *make him afraid.*
Frightfull.
Frightfulness.
Frigid, *cold*, *impotent*, or *slight.*
Frigidity.
The hawk frills, or *trembles.*
A Fringe, *for a bed, garment*, &c.
To fringe, or *set off with* fringes.
A Fringe-maker.
A Fripperer, or *broker, that sells old cloths new vamp'd*
The Frippery, *trade, shop*, or *street where such stuff is sold.*
A Frisk, or *caper.*
To frisk, or *leap up and down.*
The Frisket *of a printing-press.*
Frit, *salt*, or *ashes fried*, or *bak'd with sand.*
A Frith, or *arm of the Sea.*
A Fritter, *a kind of pancake.*
Frivolous, *vain, sorry, slight*, or *trifling.*
The Frize, or *cornice of a pillar.*

Frize, or freez, *a sort of cloth.*
To frizzle, or *curl.*
A Frizzler.
Fro; as, *to go to and* fro.
A Frock *for a child, groom labourer*, &c.
A Frog, *a living creature.*
The Frog, or frush *of a horse's foot.*
Frog-bit; *an herb.*
The Frog-fish.
Frog-grass, or *toad-grass.*
Frog-lettuce.
A Froise, or *pancake with bacon.*
Frolick, *merry and jocund.*
A Frolick, or *merry prank.*
Frolicksome, or *full of* frolicks.
Frolicksomness.
From; as, *from time to time.*
The Front, or *fore-part of a thing.*
A Frontire, *the borders of a Country.*
The Frontispeice, or *fore-front of a building*; *also the title-page of a book, engrav'd on a copper-plate.*
A Frontlet, or *fore-head cloth.*
The Front-stall, or *fore-part of a horse's bridle.*
Frost.
A Hore-frost, or *White frost.*
Frosted; as, *frosted buttons.*
Frost-bitten.
A Frost-nail, *and to* frost-nail, *a horse.*
Frosty; as *frosty weather.*
Froth, *and to* froth.
Frothy, *full of* froth, *light*, or *trifling.*
The Frounce, *a disease in hawks.*
Froward, *surly, peevish*, or *stubborn.*

Frowardness.
A Frown.
To frown, or *look sourly upon one.*
Frozen (*from to* freez.)
To fructify, *bear fruit*, or *make fruitful.*
Frugal, *thrifty*, or *sparing.*
Frugality, *thriftiness*, or *good husbandry.*
Fruit *of trees*, or *of the earth*; *also profit, benefit*, &c.
The First-fruits *of a spiritual living.*
A Fruiterer, or *seller of fruit.*
A Fruitery, *fruit-house*, or *fruit-loft.*
Fruitfull.
Fruitfulness.
Fruition, or *enjoyment.*
Fruitless, *barren*, or *unprofitable.*
Frumenty, or *potage made of wheat and milk.*
A Frump, or *jeer.*
To frump, *flout*, or *taunt.*
A Frumper.
The Frush *of a horse's foot.*
To frustrate, *deceive, disappoint*, or *make void.*
A Frustration.
A Fry, or *spawn of fishes.*
To fry *meat.*
A Frying-pan.

F U

A Fub, or *little child.*
To fuddle, or *drink hard.*
A Fuddle-cap, *or* drunkard.
A Fugitive, *that flies out of his Country*, *a vagabond.*
A Fugue, or *chace in musick.*
Full, *perfect, whole, abounding*, &c.
To full *cloth.*
A Hand-full.
A Mouth-full.
Fullage, *money paid for fulling.*
Full-bodied.
Fullers-earth.
A Fuller *of cloth.*
Fullers-teasel, *an herb.*
Fulness.
To fulfill, *accomplish*, or *perform.*
A Fulmart, *a sort of polecat.*
Fulsome, *nauseous*, or *nasty.*
Fulsomeness.
To fumble, *handle*, or *go about a thing untowardly.*
A Fumbler.
A Fume, or *vapour.*
To fume up.
To fume, or *fret.*
Fumets, *the dung of hares*, or *rabbets.*
A Fumigation, *smoaking*, or *perfuming with smoak*
Fumitory, or *earth-smoak an herb.*
A Fummer, fulmart, or *polecat.*
Fumous, or *apt to* fume *up.*
A Function, *calling*, or *performance of any office*, or *duty.*
A Fund, or *bank of money.*
The Fundament, or *breech*
Fundamental, *chief*, or *principal.*
A Funeral, or *burial.*
A Funeral-song.
Fungous, *spungy*, or *full of holes like a mushroom.*
A Funnel, or tunnel, *to convey liquors into a vessel*
The Funnel, or *upper part of a chimney.*
To furbish, *brighten*, or *polish.*
A Furbisher.
Furious, *enraged, mad*, or *transported with fury.*
To furl *the sails*, i. e. *to wrap*, or *fold them up.*
A Furlong, *the eighth part of a mile*, or *of an acre.*
A Furlough, or *license granted by a superior to an inferior military Officer, to be absent for a while from his charge.*
Furmety, or frumenty.
A Furnace, or *kiln.*
To furnish, *provide, supply*, or *set out.*
Furniture.
Furr, *the skin of certain wild beasts.*
To furr, or *line with* furr.
A Furrier.
A Furrow, or *trench.*
Further.
To further, *aid*, or *promote.*
Furtherance.
A Furtherer.
Fury, or *rage.*
A Fury, or *hellish fiend.*
Furz, *a prickly shrub.*
The fuse, or *footsteps of a buck.*
The Fusee *of a watch.*
A Fusee, or fusil, *a kind of fire-lock gun.*
A Fusileer, *a soldier that bears such arms.*
The Fust, *trunk*, or *body of a pillar.*
Fustian, *a sort of stuff.*
Fustick-wood, *used by diers.*
Fustiness.
Fusty, or *musty.*
Future, *to be*, or *to come*
Futurity, *future time*, or *state.*
To fuzz; as, *stuff that fuzzes.*
A Fuzz-ball, or *puckfist.*

F Y

Fy; as, fy *upon't*, fy *for shame!*
To fyst, foist, or *fizzle.*
A Fysting-hound.

G A

Gabardine, *a kind of* Irish *mantle*, or *course Cassock.*
To Gabble, or *babble.*

A Gabbler.
Gabel, or *excise upon salt in* France.
A Gabion, *a kind of basket filled with earth, and us'd for a defence in sieges.*
The Gabel-end, or *top-front of a house.*
A Gad *of steel.*
To gad, or *ramble up and down.*
A Gad-fly, *or* Gad-bee.
A Gadder *abroad.*
The Gaffle *of a cross-bow.*
A Gag.
To gag, or *stop one's mouth.*
Gag-toothed.
A Gage, *and to* gage (*in several senses.*)
A Gager, or *measurer of vessels.*
A Gaging-rod.
To gaggle *like a goose.*
Gain, or *profit.*
To gain, or *get.*
A Gainer.
Gainfull.
To gainsay, *withstand in words*, or *deny.*
A Gainsayer.
Galades, *a kind of shell-fish.*
Galbanum, *a sort of gum.*
A Galbula, *a bird.*
A Gale, or *blast of wind; and an herb so call'd.*
Galingale, *a sort of water flag.*
The Gall, *a humour of the body.*
The Gall-bladder.
A Gall, or *fret.*
To gall, *vex, fret*, or *annoy.*
A Gall-nut, *the fruit of an oak.*
Gallant, *gay, spruce*, or *neat.*
A Gallant, *a spark*, or *suiter to a Lady; also an herb.*
To gallant, or *court a woman, in the way of a* gallant.
Gallantness, or gallantry.
A Galleass, or *huge double* Galley.
A Gallery *to walk in.*
A Galley, *a kind of ship with oars, much us'd in the mediterranean Sea.*
The Admiral-galley.
A Galley-foist.
A Galley-slave.
A Galley-pot.
A Galliard, *a kind of merry-dance.*
Gallicane; as, *the* Gallicane *Church*. i. e. *that of* France.
A Gallicism, or *Idiom of the* French *tongue.*
Galligaskins, *a sort of wide breeches, so call'd from the* Gascons, *who first brought 'em in use.*
A Gallimawfry, or *hotch potch of several sorts of minced meats.*
A Gallion, *a kind of ship of a large size.*
A Galliot, *a small* galley.
A Gallon, *a liquid measure, containing four quarts.*
Galloon-lace.
A Gallop.
To gallop, or *ride with speed.*
A Hand-gallop.
Galloshes, *cases to wear over the shoos in dirty weather.*
A Gallows, or *gibbet.*
Galls, *a kind of shrub.*
A Gally-worm.
Gantlop, or gantlope, *an usual military punishment, so called from* Gaunt, *a town in* Flanders; *the offender being forc'd to run half naked thro' the whole regiment, and to receive a lash, or slap with a switch from every soldier.*
A Gambado, *a kind of spatter-dash*, or *leathern leg-case, fix'd to the saddle, instead of stirrups.*
Gambol; as, *to play*, or *show* gambols, i. e. *odd gestures*, or *tumbling tricks.*
A Gamboling, or *throwing up the legs.*
A Game, or *sport.*
To game, or *use* games *and pastimes.*
Game, *prey got by hunting*, or *fowling.*
A Game-cock.
Gamesome, *frolicksome*, or *wanton.*
Gamesomeness.
A Gamester.
A Gaming-house.
A Gammon *of bacon.*
The Gam-ut, or *scale of musick; also the first, or lowest note of it.*
To ganch, or *throw one upon hooks*, or *iron-spikes; a* Turkish *way of execution.*
A Gander, or *male goose.*
Gander-gosses; *an herb.*
A Gane-fish.
A Ganer, *a bird.*
A Gang, *company*, or *crew.*
Gang-flower.
Gang-week, *procession*, or rogation-*week.*
A Gangreen, or *mortified eating ulcer.*
To gangreen, or *fall into a* gangreen.
A Gantlet, or *iron-glove.*
A Gaol, jail, or *prison.*
A Goal-bird, or *lewd wretch.*
A Gaoler.
A Gap, or *breach in a hedge, wall*, &c.
To gape, *yawn, bawl, cleave*, or *chink as the ground does.*
A Garb, *the manner of dress*, or *carriage.*
Garbage, *entrals*, or *refuse.*
To garbage, or *take out the* garbage.
To garble, or *cleanse from dross and dirt; as Grocers do their spices.*
Garbles, *the dust and dross so separated.*

A Garbler *of spices, a City-officer.*
A Gard, *and* to gard *(in several senses)*
A Gard-House.
A Garden, *for flowers, herbs,* &c.
A Kitchen-garden.
A Gardener, *or* gardiner.
Gardening, or *the art of ordering Gardens.*
A Gardian, *Tutor,* or *Warden.*
Gardian of the Spiritualities; *one that has jurisdiction in a vacant Diocess.*
Gardianship, *the office of* a gardian.
Gare, *a course sort of Wooll.*
A Gargarism, *a medicinal liquor to wash* or *cleanse the mouth and throat.*
To gargarize, or *gargle the mouth.*
The Gargle, or *gullet of the throat.*
Garish, *gay,* or *gawdy.*
A Garland, or *coronet of flowers,* &c.
Sea-garland, *an herb.*
Garlick, *a plant.*
Bears-garlick.
Snakes-garlick.
Wild, *or* crow-garlick.
A Garment, *of woollen, linnen, silk,* &c.
A Mourning-garment.
A Garner, or *granary for corn.*
Garnish-money, *a fee given by a prisoner, to his fellows and keepers, at his first admittance.*
To garnish, or *set out a dish.*
A Garnisher.
A Garret, or *uppermost room in a house.*
A Garrison, or *strong place supplied with soldiers and provisions for its defence.*
To garrison, *a place,* or *put a* garrison *into it.*
A Garrison-town.
Garrulity, *babling,* or *talkativeness.*
A Garter; *for the leg.*
To garter up.
A *Knight of the* garter
Garter, *principal King at Arms.*
Gascoyns, *the hinder thighs of a horse.*
A Gase, or gast-*hound.*
A Gash, *and to* gash, or *cut.*
A Gasp, or *the last* gasp.
To gasp, *or gape for breath.*
Gastliness.
Gastly, or *dreadful.*
A Gate, *of a town, house, field,* &c.
A Postern-gate.
A Gate, or *manner of going.*
A Gate-keeper.
A Calve's gather, or *pluck.*
To gather *(in all senses.)*
A Gatherer.
Gaudies, or *double commons,* on gaudy, or *festival days in Colleges,* or *Inns of Court.*
Gaudiness.
Gaudy, or *gay.*
Gave *(from to* give.)
Gavel, *tribute,* or *toll.*
Gavelkind, *q. d.* give all kin, *an equal division of the father's Lands at his death, among all his Sons;* or *those of a brother, dying without issue, among all his brethren: This custom is still in force in* Kent, Herefordshire, *and elsewhere.*
A Gauger, *or* gager *of vessels.*
A Gavot, *a sort of dance.*
Gawz, *a thin sort of silk-stuff.*
A Gawz-hood.
Gay, *gallant, fine,* or *brisk.*
Gayety, or *gallantry.*
Gayter-tree, or *prick-wood.*
To gaze, or *stare.*
A Gazing-stock.
A Gaze-hound, *that hunts by sight.*
A Gazel; *an Arabian deer.*
A Gazette, or *news-book.*

G E

Gear, *or* geer, *stuff,* or *furniture.*
To be in his geers.
Geese, *the plural number* of goose.
To geld, or *cut out the genitals.*
A Gelder.
A Gelding, or *gelt horse.*
Gelt *(from to* geld.)
The Gelder-rose.
A Gem, or *jewel.*
A Gemmary, or *jewel-house.*
A Gemmow, or *double ring.*
A Genealogist, *a writer of*
A Genealogy, or *description of pedegrees.*
General, or *universal.*
A General, or *commander of an Army.*
A Generalissimo, or *chief Commander.*
The Generality *of the people.*
Generalship, *the office of* a General.
Generation, *engendring,* or *begetting; also an age of Men.*
The Generative *faculty.*
Generousity, *or generousness.*
Generous, *noble, magnificent,* or *liberal.*
Genesis, *i. e.* generation, *the first book of* Moses; *so called, because it declares the creation of all things.*
Genet, *a* Spanish *horse; also a kind of martin,* or *weasel.*
Genial, *festival,* or *belonging to* generation.

The

The Genitals, or *privy parts.*
A Genius, *a good, or evil spirit, (as is thought) attending upon particular persons, or places; also one's natural temper,* or *disposition.*
A Gennit, *or* genniting, *a sort of apple.*
Gent, *in a good garb, fine,* or *neat.*
Genteel, *spruce, neat,* or *gentleman-like.*
Genteelness.
Gentian, or *fell-wort.*
Dwarf-gentian.
A Gentil, *a kind of maggot.*
A Gentile, or *heathen.*
Gentilism, *heathenism, the opinion* or *practice of heathens.*
Gentility, *a gentleman's degree,* or *a genteel air.*
Gentle, *mild, courteous,* or *tame.*
A Tercel-gentle, *a kind of falcon.*
A Gentleman, *a person of honourable extraction.*
Gentleness (*from* gentle.)
A Gentlewoman.
Gentry; *the rank of Gentlemen*; as, *the* nobility *and* gentry.
Genuine, *natural,* or *proper.*
A Geographer.
Geographical, *belonging to*
Geography, or *the description of the countries and parts of the earth.*
Geometrical.
A Geometrician, or *professor of*
Geometry; *the Art of measuring all sorts of solid bodies,* or *plain figures, distances,* &c.
A Ger-falcon, *a bird of prey, between a vulture and a falcon.*
Germane; as, *a cousin* germane.

Germander, *an herb.*
Tree-germander.
Water-germander.
The Gesses *of a hawk.*
A Gesture, or *action of the body.*
To get, *beget, gain, procure catch,* &c.
A Getter.
Gewgaws, *trifles,* or *bawbles for children to play with.*

GH

A Gherkin, or *pickled cucumber.*
To ghess, guess, or *conjecture.*
A Ghizzard *of a fowl.*
A Ghost, or *spirit.*
The Holy Ghost.
Holy-ghost root.
Ghostly, or *spiritual.*

GI

A Giant, *a person of a prodigious stature.*
Gib; as, *a* gib-cat, or *boar-cat.*
Gibberish, *jargon,* or *nonsensical talk.*
A Gibbet, or *gallows.*
Gibble-gabble, or *tittle-tattle.*
Gibblets, or goose-giblets.
A Gibe, or *scoff.*
To Gibe, *mock,* or *jeer.*
A Giber.
Giddiness.
Giddy, *dizzy, conceited, light,* or *wanton.*
Giddy-headed, *or* Giddy-brain'd.
A Gift, or *present.*
A New-years-gift.
A Gifted person, *one of admirable parts.*
A Gig, or *top.*
Gigantick, or *giant-like.*
To giggle, or *laugh wantonly.*
A Gigot, *a loin and a leg of mutton together; also a kind of hash,* or *minced meat.*

Gill creep-by-the-ground *an herb.*
To gild, or *do over with gold.*
A Gilder.
A Leather-gilder.
A Gilliflower.
A Glove-gilliflower.
A Stock-gilliflower.
The Gills *of fish.*
Gilt (*from* to gild.)
A Gilt-head, *a fish.*
A Gimmal, gimbal, or *gimmow-ring.*
A Gimlet, or *piercer.*
Gimp-lace.
A Gin, or *snare.*
Ginger, *a spice.*
Ginger-bread.
A Ginger-bread-baker.
Gingerly, *softly,* or *gently.*
To gingle; as, *little bells do.*
A Gipsy, or *rambling fortune-teller.*
A Girasol, *a sort of precious stone, of an eye-like lustre; and of a sparkling gold-colour when plac'd towards the Sun.*
A Gird, or *taunt.*
To gird, *surround, bind,* or *twine.*
Slack-girded.
The Girder-beam *of a house.*
A Girdle.
A Sword-girdle.
A Girdler, or *girdle-maker.*
A Girl, or *wench.*
A Girle, *a roe-buck of two years old.*
Girlish.
Girt (*from* to gird.)
A Girth, *or* girdle *for a horse.*
To girth, or *bind on the* girth.
Gith, or *nigella; an herb.*
Bastard-gith.
Citron-gith.
A Gittern, *or* Cittern, *a musical instrument.*

To give (*in all senses.*)
Given.
A Giver.
Gives, *shackles*, or *fetters*.
A Gizzard, *or* ghizzard.

GL

Glad, or *joyfull*.
To glad, or *make* glad.
Gladdon, gladdin, or gladwin; *an herb*.
A Glade; *an open place in a wood*.
Gladness, or joy.
A Glaive, *a weapon like a halbard*.
A Glance, *and to* glance (*in different senses.*)
The Glanders, *a disease in horses*.
To glare, or *dazzle*.
Glass.
A Glass *to drink out of*.
A Flint-glass.
A Daring-glass, *to catch larks*.
A Looking-glass.
A Glass-house.
A Glass-maker.
Glass-wort; *an herb*.
Glassy, or *belonging to* glass.
To glaver, or *fawn*.
To glaze, *work with glass*, *polish*, *set a gloss upon*, &c.
A Glazier.
A Glead, *or* glede, *a sort of kite*.
A Gleam, or *ray of light*.
To glean, or *lease corn*.
A Gleaner.
The Glear, glair, or *white of an egg*.
To glear, *or do over with* glear.
Glebe, *or* glebe-land, *the land belonging to a parsonage besides the tithes*.
Gleek, *a game at cards*.
Glib, *smooth*, or *slippery*.
Glibness.
To glide, or *slide along*.
To glimmer, or *begin to appear; as, the light does*.
A Glimpse, or *flash of light*.
Glitt, or *gleet, the matter of a sore*.
A Glister, or *clyster*.
A Glister-pipe.
To glister, glisten, glitter, or *shine*.
Gloar; *as* gloar-fat.
A Globe, or *round body like a ball*.
The Celestial and Terrestial Globes.
A Globe-daizy.
The Globe-fish.
The Globe-thistle.
Globous, *or* globular, *round like a* globe.
Gloominess.
Glomy, *dark*, *or cloudy*.
Glorification.
To glorify, or *give* glory *to*.
Glorious, *full of* glory; *excellent*, or *honourable*
Glory, *renown*, *fame*, *honour*, &c.
To glory, or *boast*.
Vain-glorious.
Vain-glory.
A Gloss, *a short comment*, or *exposition of a text*.
A Gloss, or *lustre*; *as*, *of cloth*, &c.
To gloss, or *comment upon*.
A Glossary, or *dictionary*, *explaining divers languages*.
A Glosser, or *polisher*.
A Glove *for the hands*.
Fox-glove, *or* our Lady's glove, *an herb*.
A Glover.
To glow, or *burn like a coal*.
A Glow-worm, *an insect*.
To glowr, or *look doggedly*.
To gloze, *sooth*, or *flatter*.
A Glozer.
Glue, *and to* glue.
Stone-glue.
Gluish, or *gluey*.
A Glut.
To glut, or *gorge himself*.
A Glutton, *a greedy eater*.
Gluttonous.
Gluttony.

GN

A Gnar, gnur, or *knot in wood*.
To gnash *with the teeth*.
A Gnat, *an insect*.
A Gnat-snapper, *a bird*.
To gnaw, or *bite*.
Gnawn, or *gnawed*.
A Gnawer.
A Gnomon, *needle*, or *pin of a dial*.

GO

To go (*in all senses.*)
A Go-cart *for Children to learn to go*.
Go-to-bed-at-noon, *an herb*.
A Goad, *a pointed stick to prick Oxen forward*.
A Goal, *at foot-ball*, or *running*.
The Goar *of a garment*.
A Goat, *a beast*.
A Goat-chafer, *an insect*.
A Goat-herd, or *keeper of Goats*.
Goatish, *stinking like a* Goat, or *lecherous*.
A Goat-sucker, *a kind of owl*.
Goats-beard, *an herb*.
Goats-bread, *a kind of eatable root*.
Goats-marjoram. } *herbs*
Goats-rue, }
Goats-thorn, *a shrub*.
A Gob, *or* gobbet *of meat*.
To gobble, *eat great* gobs, *or swallow down greedily*
A Goblet, or *standing cup*.
To give one the go-by.
God, *a Being supreme*, *infinite*, *almighty*, &c.
A Goddess.
A God-child.
A God-daughter.
A God-father.
The Godhead.
Godless, or *atheistical*.
Godliness.
Godly, or *pious*.
A God-mother.
A God-son.
A Godwit, *a sort of bird*.
Goff, *a kind of play at ball*

A Goff stick.
Gog; *as, to be a-gog for, or bent upon a thing.*
Goggle-eyed.
Gold, *the most precious of all metals.*
Gold of pleasure; *an herb*
Leaf-gold,
A Gold-beater.
Gold-cups, *a flower.*
A Gold-finch, *a bird.*
A Gold-finer.
The Gold-flower.
A Gold-hammer, *a bird.*
Golden, *or belonging to* gold.
The Golden-number (*in* Chronology) *so call'd because writ in golden, or red letters; or for its great use in finding out the changes of the moon. It yearly encreases from* 1 *to* 19, *and then begins again with* 1; *because the sun and moon are said to compleat their mutual aspects in* 19 *years.*
A Goldeny, *a fish.*
Golden-rod; *an herb.*
Goldilocks, *or* golden-tufts; *an herb.*
A Golding-apple.
The Devil's Gold-ring; *an insect.*
A Goldsmith.
Gome, *a sort of black grease.*
A Gomer, *an* Hebrew *measure somewhat exceeding our gallon.*
A Gondola, *a* Venetian *wherry* or *boat.*
Gone (*from to go.*)
Good, *benefit,* or *advantage.*
Good, *honest, just, profitable, convenient, fair, kind, pleasant,* &c.
Good-conditioned.
Good-humoured.
Good-natured, *&c.*
A Good-fellow, *or merry companion.*
Good-friday, *on which Christ's passion is commemorated.*
Goodliness.
Goodly, *fair, or fine.*
Good-man, *the usual title of a country house-keeper.*
Good-wife, *or* goody, *a title commonly given to a country woman.*
Goodness.
Goods, or *substance, in furniture, commodities,* &c.
A Googe, *a joyner's tool.*
A Goose, *a bird*; or *a taylor's pressing-iron.*
A Green-goose.
A Soland-goose.
A Stubble-goose.
A Winchester-goose, *a swelling in the groin.*
A Goose-cap, *fool,* or *coxcomb.*
A Goose-berry, *a fruit.*
Goose-foot, } *herbs.*
Goose-grass, }
Goose-gibblets.
Gor-bellied, *or* gore-bellied, *that has a great paunch,* or *belly.*
A Gor-belly, *a great belly,* or *a glutton.*
Gore, *clotted,* or *corrupt bloud.*
To gore, *prick,* or *push with a horn.*
The Gorge, or *crop of a hawk.*
To Gorge, *fill,* or *glut.*
Gorgeous, *gallant, fine,* or *costly.*
Gorgeousness, or *costliness, especially of apparel.*
A Gorget, or *whisk for a Woman; also a piece of plate that military Officers usually wear about their neck.*
To gormandize, *devour greedily,* or *be given to gluttony.*
A Gormandizer.
Gors, *goss,* or *furz, a shrub.*
A Gosling, or *young goose.*
The Gospel, i. e. *God's Word,* or *good Tidings.*
A Gospeller, *he that reads the* Gospel *in a Cathedral.*
A Goss-hawk, *a large sort of hawk.*
A Gossip, *q.* God-sib, *of kin before* God; *a* God-father, *or* God-mother.
A Drinking-gossip.
A Gossipping, or *merry meeting of* Gossips.
Got, *or* gotten (*from to* get.)
Governable, or *tractable.*
To govern, *rule, guide,* or *manage.*
A Governante, *or* Governess *in a family.*
Government.
A Governour, or *ruler.*
A Gourd, *a kind of plant.*
Bitter-gourd, or *coloquintida.*
A Gourd-pear.
A Gournet, *a bird.*
A Red-gournet.
A Grey-gournet.
The Gout, *a disease.*
The Joint-gout.
Goutiness.
Gouty, *that has the* gout.
Gout-wort; *an herb.*
A Gown, *a sort of garment.*
A Night-gown.
Gowned, *that wears a* Gown.

G R

To grabble, or *handle untowardly.*
Grace (*in several senses.*)
To grace, *set off,* or *adorn*
A Bon-grace *for a Child.*
Graceful, or *comely.*
Gracefulness.
Graceless, *void of* grace, or *comeliness.*
Gracious, *full of* grace, *courteous,* &c.
Graciousness.
Gradual, *from one degree to another;* or *by degrees.*

A Graduate, *one that has taken a degree in an University.*

A graff, *or* graft.

To graft *trees.*

A Grafter.

A Grain *(in several senses.)*

Grain of paradise, *a sort of fruit.*

Grain-colour.

Grained, *that has* grains, or *kernels.*

Gramercy, or *I thank you.*

Grammar, or *the Art of right reading, writing, and speaking.*

A Grammarian, or *professor of that Art.*

Grammatical, *of* or *belonging to* grammar.

A Grample, or *sea-fish.*

A Grampus, *a sort of whale.*

A Granado, *or* grenado.

A Granary, or *store-house for Corn.*

A Grenate, *a precious stone resembling that of the pomegranate-fruit.*

Grand, *or* great.

A Grand-child.

A Grandame, *or* Grand-mother.

A Grand-daughter.

A Grandee, *a noble-man of* Spain, *or* Portugal.

Grandeur, *greatness of mind,* or *estate.*

A Grand-father, *or* grand-sire.

Grand Signior, *i. e.* Great Lord, *a title commonly given to the Emperour of the* Turks.

A Grange, or *farm-house.*

Granite, *a kind of speckled* Italian *marble.*

A Grant, or *gift.*

To grant, *give, make over to,* or *yield.*

A Grape, *the fruit of the vine.*

Grape-flower.

Sea-grape, *a shrub.*

Be[illegible]-grapes.

Muscadel, *or* muscadine grapes.

Graphical, *curiously described, express,* or *accurate.*

A Grapple, grapnel, *or* grappling-iron *of a ship.*

To grapple, or *grasp, and lay hold of.*

To grase, or *feed.*

A Grasier, or *feeder of Cattel.*

A Grasp, or *handful; and to* grasp.

The Grass *of a field,* &c.

Arrow-headed-grass.

Cotton-grass.

Clover-grass.

Crested-grass.

Dogs-grass.

Feather-grass.

Finger-grass.

Goose-grass.

Hairy-grass.

Haver-grass *or* Oat-grass.

Knot-grass.

Meadow-grass.

Pearl-grass, *or* quaking-grass.

Reed-grass.

Rush-grass.

Scorpion-grass.

Scurvy-grass.

Vipers-grass.

A Grasshopper; *an insect.*

Grassy, or *full of* grass.

A Grate, *and to* grate *(in several senses.)*

Grateful, *thankful,* or *kindly taken.*

Gratefulness.

A Grater *to* grate *bread, spice,* &c.

A Gratification.

To gratify, *pleasure,* or *requite one.*

Gratis, *i. e.* for thanks, *freely,* or *without any cost.*

Gratitude, or *thankfulness.*

Gratuitous, or *freely done.*

A Gratuity, or *free gift.*

Gratulatory, *full of thanks,* or *rejoycing with another.*

Grave, *sober,* or *serious.*

A Grave, *to bury the dead.*

A Grave-maker.

To grave *or* engrave.

To grave *a ship, to* i. e. *burn off the old stuff, and to lay on new.*

Gravel, or *sand.*

To gravel, or *cover with* gravel; *also to put one to a* Non-plus.

Gravelly, or *full of* gravel.

A Gravel-pit.

Graven, as *a graven-image.*

A Graver, *or* engraver; *also the tool us'd in* graving.

Gravity, *soberness,* or *seriousness.*

Gravy, *the juice of meat.*

A Gray, or *badger.*

The Gray colour.

Dapple-gray.

Gray-eyed.

A Gray-hound.

Grayish, or *somewhat* gray.

A Grayling, *a fish.*

Grayness.

To graze, or *pass lightly on the ground;* as *a bullet does.*

Grease, or *fat.*

To grease, or *dawb with* grease.

Greasiness.

Greasy.

Great, *big, large, huge, mighty, powerfull,* &c.

To greaten, or *make* great.

Greatness.

Greaves; *an armour for the legs.*

A Grecian, *a native of* Greece, or *one skill'd in the* Greek tongue.

A Grecism, *a propriety of that language.*

Greediness.

Greedy, *ravenous,* or *covetous.*

A Greedy-gut, *one that eats* greedily.

Greek,

Greek, or *the* Greek tongue.
Green *of colour*, or *fresh*.
A Green, or *green-plot*.
A Bowling-green.
Winter-green, *an herb*.
A Green-finch, *a bird*.
A Green-fish.
A Green-goose.
Greenness.
Greenish, or *somewhat* green.
Green-weed.
A Greeting, or *salutation*.
Greml, *a sort of herb*.
A Grenadeer, or *soldier that throws* Grenados.
A Foot-grenadeer.
A Horse-grenadeer.
A Grenado, *a hollow bullet filled with fine powder, and shot out of a mortar-piece*.
A Hand-grenado.
I Grew (*from to* grow.)
A Grice, or *young wild boar*.
A Grid-iron.
Grief, *sorrow*, or *trouble*.
A Grievance.
To grieve, *make sad*, or *be sorrowfull*.
Grievous, *full of grief*, or *trouble*.
Grievousness.
A Griffin, *a fabulous creature, having the head wings and feet of an eagle, and the other parts like a lion*.
A Grig, *a little sort of Eel*.
A merry Grig, or *jovial companion*.
A Grillade, *a dish of broiled meat*.
Grim, *stern*, or *austere in countenance*.
A Grimace, *a wry mouth*, or *crabbed look*.
Grimness.
To grime, *smut*, or *dawb*.
To grin, or *wry the mouth*
To grind (*in several senses*.)
A Grinder.
A Grind-stone.

A Gripe, *and to* gripe (*in different senses*.)
Grisly, or *hideous*.
Grist; as, *to bring* grist *to the mill*.
A Gristle, or *tendrel*.
Gristly, or *full of* gristles.
Grit, *dust of stones*, or *metals*.
Gritty, or *full of* grit.
Grizled, or *hoary*.
A Groan, or *sigh*.
To groan, or *fetch* groans.
A Groat, i. e. *four pence*.
Groats, *or* oatmeal-groats.
A Grocer, *whole-sale dealer* or *seller of spice*, &c.
Grocery-ware.
Grogram, *a sort of stuff*.
The groin, *the parts about the privities*.
Gromel, *an herb*.
A Groom, *of the King's bed-chamber*, or *of the stables*.
The Groom-porter.
A Groop *in stables, for horses*.
A Grove, or *mine*.
To grope, or *feel softly*.
A Groper.
A Gross, or *twelve dozen*.
Gross, *thick, fat, dull, blockish*, &c.
Grossness.
A Grot, grotto, or *cave*.
Groteck, or *antick work*; *rude figures that represent things after an odd and confused manner*.
A Grove, or *little wood*.
Groveling, *lying with one's face*, or *belly on the ground*.
To grouse, or *mutter*.
Ground (*from to* grind.)
The Ground, or *earth*.
To ground, or *establish*.
The Ground, groundwork, or *foundation of a thing*.
Ground-ivy; *an herb*.
Groundless, *uncertain*, or *feigned*.
A Groundling, *a fish*.

Ground-pine, *a plant*.
Stinking ground-pine.
The Grounds, or *principles of an Art*; or *the dreggs of drink*, &c.
The Groundsil *of an house*; *also an herb so call'd*.
Ground-worms.
Groupage, *a lofty kind of Curvet, in horse-manage*.
Grout, or *gruel*.
A Grout-head, or *logger-head*.
To grow, *spring, rise, prove, become*, &c.
Grown.
Growth.
A Grub, *a maggot*, or *a dwarf*.
To grub up, or *root out*.
A Grubbing-ax.
A Grudge, or *hatred*.
To grudge, or *bear a* grudge; *to envy*, or *repine at*.
Grudgingly, or *with an ill-will*.
Gruel, or water-gruel, *potage made of oatmeal*.
Barley-gruel.
Gruff, *or* grum, i. e. *dogged*, or *surly*.
To grumble, or *murmur*.
A Grumbler.
Grumous, *full of lumps, and clots*.
To grunt *like a hog*.
To gruntle, or *complain*.

GU

A Guarantee, or *maintainer of a Treaty*.
To guard, *or* gard.
Gubbins, *the parings of haberdine*, &c.
A Gudgeon, *a fish*.
The Guelder-rose, or *elder-rose*.
Guerkins, *a sort of Cucumbers proper for pickling*.
A Guess, *and*
To guess, or *divine*.
A Guesser.
A Guest, or *person entertain'd*.

stuff'd at a feast.
Gugaws, *trifles*, or *toys for Children.*
To guggle, or *make a noise*; *as a bottle that is emptying.*
Guidance, or, *conduct.*
A Guide, or *leader.*
To guide, or *conduct.*
A Guidon, or *banner (in* Heraldry.)
A Guild, *tribute*, or *amercement*; *also a brotherhood*, or *company incorporated by the Prince.*
A Guilder, *a* Dutch *coin.*
A Guild-hall; *the chief Hall of a City.*
Guile, *fraud*, or *deceit.*
Guilefull.
Guilefulness,
A Guillam, *a bird.*
Guilt, *the being conscious of a fault*, or *crime.*
A Guilt-head, or *sea-breem.*
Guiltiness.
Guiltless, *free from* guilt, or *innocent.*
A Guimad, *a fish peculiar to the River* Dee *and the Lake* Pemble-meer.
Guimp, *or* gimp-lace.
A Guiney, *or* guinea, *a Gold coin worth* 1 *l.* 1 *s.* 6 *d.*
A Guise, or *fashion.*
A Guitar, *a musical instrument.*
A Gulchin, or *little glutton.*
Gules, *red*, or *vermilion colour (in* Heraldry.)
A Gulf, *or* gulph, *a part of Sea running between two lands, which embrace and almost encompass it.*
A Gull, or *breach in the bank of a River.*
A Gull, *or* sea-gull, *a bird.*
To gull, or *deceive.*
A Guller, or *wezand.*
To gully, or *make a noise in drinking.*
A Gully-gut, or *glutton.*
A Gulp.
To gulp down, or *swallow at once.*
The Gum *of trees.*
Gum-cistus; *an herb.*
Gummed, or *stiffen'd with* gum.
Gummy, or *full of* gum.
The Gums, or *jaws in which the teeth are set.*
A Gun, *to shoot with.*
A Pot-gun.
A Gunner,
The Art of Gunnery.
Gun-shot.
A Gun-smith.
A Gurnny, *or* gurnard, *a fish.*
To gush out, or *run out violently.*
A Gusset *of a shirt.*
A Gust, *taste*, *or relish.*
A Gust, or *sudden blast of wind.*
A Gut,
To gut, or *draw out the* guts *of a fish*, &c.
Gut-wort; *an herb.*
A Guttling, or *greedy-gut.*
A Gutter *to convey water.*
Guttural, *as* guttural *letters pronounced thro' the throat.*
To guzzle, or *tipple.*
A Guzzler,

GY

Gymnosophist, *a sect of* Indian *Philosophers*, *so call'd from their custom of going naked.*
A Gyr-falcon, *a bird of prey.*
A Gyronnee (*a term in* Heraldry) *half a square in a scutcheon cut off by a crooked line.*

HA

A Haak, or *poor John*, *a fish.*
A Habardasher, *hatter*, or *seller of hats.*
Haberdine, *a sort of salt-fish.*
A Habergeon, *or* harbergion, *a little coat of mail.*
Habiliments, *apparel*, *attire*, or *armour.*
An Habit, or *state of the mind*, or *body*; or *a garb of clothes.*
Habitable, *that may be inhabited.*
An Habitation, or *dwelling.*
Well-habited, or *well-cloth'd.*
Habitual, or *grown customary.*
Habituated, *that has got an* habit *of a thing.*
Habitude, habit, or *custom.*
Hab-nab; *at a venture, whether it happen*, or *not.*
To hack, *hew* or *cut.*
To hackle, or *cut small.*
A Hackney-horse, or *coach.*
To hackney out, or *let out horses to hire.*
Had (*from* have.)
A Haddock, *a kind of cod-fish.*
A Haft, hilt, or *handle*,
To haft, or *set into a* haft.
An Hag, old hag, or *witch.*
Haggs, *a fiery meteor*, *appearing on mens hair*, or *horses mains.*
A Hagard hawk, or *wild hawk*, *that has sometime preyed for herself.*
A Haggess, *or* haggis, *a kind of pudding made of livers*, *lights*, &c.
To haggle, or *stand hard in buying*, &c.
A Haggler.
Hail, or *sound and whole.*
Hail, *a meteor*, *and To* hail.
To hail, *or* hale *a ship.*
A Hail-stone.

Hainous,

Hainous, *detestable, odious*, or *outragious*.
Hainousness
Hair; as, *the* hair *of the head, &c.*
An Hair-lace.
Maiden-hair, *an herb*.
An Hair-cloth.
Hair-brained.
Haired; as, *red-haired, rough-haired*, &c.
Hairiness (*from* hairy.)
Hairless, or *without* hairs.
Hairy, or *full of* hairs.
Hairy-river-weed.
An Hake, or *pot-hook*.
An Halbard, *or* halberd, *a sort of weapon*.
An Halbardeer, *a soldier that bears a* halbard.
The Halcyon, or *King's-fisher, which in calm weather builds, and breeds on the Sea-shore*.
Halcyon days, i. e. *quiet and peaceable times*.
To hale, or *pull*; *also to call to a ship, demanding, whence she comes, and whether bound?*
The Half, or *moiety of any thing*.
A Half-moon.
An Hallibut, *a fish*.
A Hall, or *court in a nobleman's house*.
A Town-Hall.
Westminster-Hall.
Hallage, *a fee for cloths brought for sale to* Blackwel-Hall.
Hallelujah, i. e. *praise the Lord*.
To hallow, *consecrate*, or *sanctify*,
The Halm, haulm, or *stem of corn*.
An Halser, *or* hawser, *the cord that hales a ship*, or *barge along the river*.
An Halsier, halster, or haler *of a ship, barge*, &c.
A Halt, *or* alt, *a stop upon a march*.
To halt, *to make an* halt; or *to go lame*.
An Halter, or *rope to tye about the neck*.
Haltered, *that has a halter on*.
Halves (*from* half) *as to divide into* halves.
Ham, *the part behind the knee*.
The Hame *of an horse-collar*.
A Hamkin, *a pudding made in a shoulder of mutton*.
A Hamlet, *a little home*, or *village*.
To hammel, or *hamstring a dog*.
A Hammer.
To hammer, or *beat with a* hammer.
Hammer-hard, *harden'd with hammering*.
A Hammock, *a little Sea-bed*
A Hamper, or hanaper, *a sort of large basket*.
To hamper *entangle*, or *perplex one*.
A Clerk of the Hanaper.
To Ham-string, or *hough a dog*, &c.
Hamstrung.
Hanch; as, *an* hanch *of Venison*.
A Hand.
To hand *a thing*, or *convey it from* hand *to* hand.
Right-handed.
Left-handed.
A Handfull.
A Hand-gun.
A Handkercher, *or* handkerchief.
A Neck-handkerchief.
A Hand-maid.
A Hand-mill,
A Hand-saw.
A Handspeek, or *leaver*.
A Handle.
The Handle *of a cup*, &c.
To handle, *feel, manage, treat of*, &c.
Handsel, or *the first sale of Goods*.
To handsel, or *give* handsel.
Handsome, *neat, fair, beautifull*, or *genteel*.
Handsomness.
Handy, *dexterous*, or *skilful*.
Handy-dandy, *a kind of play*.
A Handy-craft.
A Handy-crafts-man.
A Handy-work.
To hang (*in several senses*.)
A Hanger, *a short crooked sword*.
A Hanger on, or *spunger*.
A Pot-hanger.
A Suit of Hangings, *for a room*.
A Hangman, or *common executioner*.
A Hank, or *skean of thread*, or *silk*.
To have one upon the hank.
To hanker *after a thing*.
The Hanse-towns, *the free imperial Towns in* Germany, *associated for commerce*; *being about 72 in number*.
Han't, *for have not*.
Hap, or chance, & *to* hap.
To happen, or *fall out*.
Happiness.
Happy, *blessed, lucky*, or *fortunate*.
A Hapse, or *catch*.
To hapse, or *fasten with a* hapse.
A Haque, *a sort of hand-gun about three quarters of a yard long*.
An Harangue, *oration*, or *speech*.
To Harangue, or *make a speech*.
To Harass, *tire, weary out, vex*, or *trouble*.
A Harbinger, *an officer that goes before to provide lodgings*.
An Harbour, or *haven for ships*.
To harbour, *lodge*, or *entertain*.
An Harbourer.
Harbourless.

Hard (in all senses.)
Hard-beam, or horn-beam, a tree.
Hard-hearted, or cruel.
Hard-heartedness.
A Hard-mouthed-horse.
Hard-skinned.
To harden, or make hard.
Hardiness, valour, or boldness.
Hardness.
A Hard-rowed-fish.
Hards of flax, or tow.
Hardship, fatigue, or toil.
Hardy, valiant, that can endure hardship.
Fool-hardy.
A Hare, a wild beast.
To hare, hurry, or perplex one.
Hare-brained, or rash.
A Hare-foot, a bird, and plant.
Hare-hearted, or timorous.
A Hare-lip.
A Hare-pipe, or snare.
Hares-bells, a flower.
Hares-ear, Hares-lettice, Hare-strong, herbs.
Haricots, or french-beans.
A Harier, a kind of hunting dog.
Hark; as, hark sirrah!
A Harlot, or whore, so call'd from Arlotta the Concubine of Robert II. Duke of Normandy and Mother of K. William I. Sirnam'd the Conqueror.
Harm, or hurt.
To harm, or do one harm.
Harmful.
Harmlesness.
Harmless, that does, or takes no harm.
Harmonious, full of Harmony, melody, musical consent, or agreement.
Harness, armour, or furniture for a team.
To harness, or put on such harness.
[illegible]tting-harness, the bearer of which has but single allowance.
Horse-harness.
Leg-harness.
A Harness-maker.
A Harp, a musical instrument.
To harp, or play on the harp.
The Jews-harp.
An Harper.
Harping-irons, us'd in whale-fishing.
An Harpsecord, or harpsecol, a musical instrument.
Harpies, three fabulous filthy birds with virgins faces, bears ears, vultures bodies, hooked hands, and sharp talons: The emblems of covetous persons, griping usurers, extortioners, &c.
A Harquebuss, a kind of hand-gun.
A Harrow, or drag with teeth to break clods of earth.
To harrow a field.
A Harrower.
A Harrower-hawk.
To harry, or tire out.
Harsh, rough, or uncouth
Harshness.
Harslet; as a hogs-harslet, or entrals.
A Hart, or stag five years old.
A Hart-Royal, that has been hunted by the King or Queen.
A Goat-hart, or stone-buck.
Hearts-ease, a flower.
Harts-root, Harts-tongue, Harts-trefoil, Hart-wort, herbs.
A Harvest, or crop of corn.
Hay-harvest.
A Harvest-man.
A Hash, or dish of cold meat sliced and heated with spice, &c.
To hash, or dress meat after that manner.
Hask-wort; an herb.
A Hasel, or hasle-nut.
Hasle-wort; an herb.
A Hasp, and to hasp, or bolt.
A Hassock, or bass to kneel upon.
Hast (from to have.)
Haste, or speed, and To haste.
To hasten, or cause one to make haste.
Hastiness (from hasty.)
Hastings, fruit early ripe.
Green-hastings, or hasty peas.
Hasty, sudden, or testy.
A Hasty-pudding.
A Hat.
A Beaver-hat.
A Hat-band.
A Hat-maker.
A Hatch, or brood of young.
The Hatch of a door.
To hatch (in several senses.)
A Hatchel, a tool to hatchel or card flax with.
The Hatches, or trap-door, of a ship, to let goods down into the hold.
An Hatchet, or ax.
Hatchet-fac'd.
Hatchet-vetch.
To hate, abominate, or have an aversion to.
Hateful, full of hatred, or odious.
Hatefulness.
A Hater.
Hatred.
A Hatter, or hat-maker.
Have; as, I have loved.
To have, possess, obtain, &c.
A Haven, or harbour.
Haughtiness.
Haughty, proud, or arrogant.
To hauk, or spit.
A Hauker.
Haulm, halm, or stubble.
A Haunt.
To haunt, or frequent.
A Haunter of taverns, &c.
A Hauriant (in Heraldry)

cry) *a fish represented, set upright.*
Havock, *slaughter*, or *spoil.*
A Haut-boy, *or* hoboy *a musical instrument.*
A Haw, *the fruit of a* Haw-thorn.
Cumberland haw-thorn.
A Haw *in the eye.*
To hum and haw.
A Hawk, *a bird of prey.*
To hawk, *or go a fowling with a* hawk.
A Brancher, or *young* hawk.
An Eyess-hawk.
A Goss-hawk.
A Haggard, *or wild* hawk
A Harrower-hawk.
A Hobby-hawk.
A Sore-hawk.
A Sparrow-hawk.
A Hawked, or *hooked nose*
Hawk-weed.
Hawkers, or *pedlers, particularly, those that sell News-books about the streets.*
A Hawser, *or* halser *to hale a barge*, &c.
Hay, *for cattel.*
A Hay, or *net to take conies.*
Rowing-hay, or *latter-math.*
To dance the Hay.
A Hay-cock.
A Hay-loft, or *hay-mow.*
A Hay-maker.
A Hay-rick, *or* hay-stack
A Hayward, *or* haward, *the common field-keeper of a Town.*
A Hazard, or *chance; also a game at dice*, &c.
To hazard, or *venture.* &c.
Hazardous or *dangerous.*
A Haze, *rime*, or *thick fog.*
To haze, hawze, or *scare one with a noise.*
A Hazle-hen, *a bird.*
A Hazle, *or* hasle-nut.
Hazy, *rimy*, or *foggy.*

HE

He; as, *'tis he whom I love.*
A Head, *and to* head *(in all senses.)*
A Block-head.
The Head-ach, *or* head-ake.
A Head-band *for a book.*
A Head-borough, or *constable.*
A Head-land, *that lies a-cross the plough'd lands*
The Head-men *of a city.*
A Head-piece *(in several senses.)*
The Head-stall *of a bridle.*
Headiness, or *rashness.*
Headless, or *without a* head.
Head-long, with *the* head *foremost.*
A Headsman or *executioner that beheads a malefactor.*
Headstrong, *unruly*, or *refractory.*
Heady, *obstinate*; or *apt to fly up into the* head.
To heal, or *cure.*
Heal-dog; *an herb.*
Health, *a good disposition of body.*
Healthfull, or *wholsome.*
Healthfulness.
Healthy, *or* healthfull, *that enjoys* health.
A Heap, *and to* heap up.
A Heaper, or *hoarder up of any thing.*
To hear *(in all senses.)*
Heard.
A Heard, herd, or *company of cattel.*
A Hearer.
To hearken, listen, or *give ear to.*
Harkners *after news, and tales.*
A Hearsay, *bruit*, or *report.*
A Hearse, or *litter to carry a corpse.*
A Hearse-cloth.
The Heart.
The Heart-strings.
A Sweet-heart.
Heart-burning, *a disease*, or *a grudge.*

Hearted; as,
Faint-hearted, or *cowardly.*
False-hearted, or *deceitfull.*
Hard-hearted, or *cruel.*
Light-hearted, or *cheerfull.*
Stout-hearted, or *couragious.*
To hearten up, *animate*, or *encourage.*
An Hearth *to keep fire.*
Hearth-money.
Heartiness, or *sincerity.*
Heartlesness, *being out of* heart.
Hearts-ease, or *content; also an herb.*
Heartless, *cowardly*, or *formal.*
Hearty, *cordial and sincere*, or *lusty.*
Heat, or *hotness.*
To heat, *make*, or *grow hot.*
A Heater *to iron cloths with.*
Heath, *a shrub.*
An Heath, or *common.*
A Heath-cock.
The Heath-rose, *or* heath of Jericho.
A Heathen, *Gentile*, or *infidel.*
Heathenish.
Heathenism.
To heave, *lift up*, or *swell, as dough does.*
A Heave-offering.
Heaven, *the firmament*; or *mansion of blessed spirits.*
Heavenly.
Heaviness.
Heavy, *weighty, sad*, or *dull.*
An Hebraism, or *propriety of.*
The Hebrew *tongue.*
An Hecatomb, or *sacrifice of a hundred beasts.*
A Heck; *an engine to take fish in the river* Owse, *by* York.
Hectick, or *habitual*:

a:

as, *an hectick feaver, that preys by degrees upon the solid and noble parts of the body.*
A Hector, *bully*, or *bragadochio.*
To hector, *vapour*, or *insult.*
A Hedge, *fence*, or *mound.*
To hedge in, *or encompass with a* hedge.
A Quick-set-hedge.
A Hedge-creeper, or *begger.*
A Hedger, *that makes* hedges.
Hedge-fumitory; *an herb*
An Hedge-hog, *a little beast.*
Hedge-hog-liquorice.
Hedge-hog trefoil, Hedge-hyssop, Hedge-nettle, } *herbs*
A Hedge-sparrow.
Heed, *and to* heed, or *mind.*
Heedfull, or heedy; *wary cautious, diligent,* &c.
Heedfulness.
Heedlesness.
Heedless, *negligent*, or *careless.*
The Heel *of the foot*; or *of a shoe, boot,* &c.
Larks-heel, *an herb.*
Yellow-larks-heel.
A Heel-maker.
Hegira; *an account of time, among the* Turks *and* Arabians, *reckon'd from* July, 16, 662, or (*according to others*) 627, *when* Mahomet *fled away from* Mecca.
An Hegler, or *seller of provisions by retail.*
A Heifer, or *young cow.*
Height (*from* high.)
To heighten, *advance*, or *increase.*
Heinous, *or* hainous.
An Heir, or *successor to an estate, by right of blood.*
A Joint-heir, or co-heir.
An Heiress, or *female* heir.
He'll, *for he will.*
Held (*from to* hold.)
A Heliotrope, *the herb turnsole; also a precious stone.*
Hell, *the residence of the damned.*
A Hell-hound, or *fiend.*
Hellebore, *white*, or *black; an herb.*
Hellish, *belonging to* hell.
The Helm *of a ship, the handle that guides the rudder.*
A Helmet, or *head-piece.*
Helmet-flower.
Help, or *aid.*
To help, or *assist.*
A Helper.
Helpfull.
Helpless, or *destitute of* help.
Helter-skelter, or *confusedly.*
A Helve, or *handle of an ax.*
To helve, or *put on a* helve
The Hem *of a* garment.
To hem (*in several senses.*)
An Hemisphere, i. e. *half the compass of the visible Heavens.*
Hemlock, *a poisonous plant.*
The Hemorhoids, *emrods*, or *piles; a disease*
Hemp, *a plant.*
Hempen, or *made of* hemp.
The Hemp-tree.
A Hen, *a fowl.*
A Guiney-hen.
A More-hen.
A Pea-hen.
A Sea-hen, *a fish.*
A Turkey-hen.
Henbane, *a venomous herb.*
Hen-bit, or *chick-weed.*
Hen-hearted, or *cowardly.*
To hen-peck; as, *when a Woman masters her Husband.*
A Hen roost.
Hens-bill, Hens-feet, } *herbs.*
Hence, or *from* hence
Henceforth.
Henceforward.
A Hep, *the fruit of an* hep-tree.
An Heptagone, *a figure that has seven angles*, or *corners.*
The Heptarchy, or *former state of* England, *under seven petty Kingdoms, under the* Saxons.
Her, *and* herself.
An Herald, *an officer at Arms.*
The College of Heralds.
Heraldry, *the Art of blazoning*, or *setting out Coats of Arms.*
An Heraldship, *the office of an* Herald.
An Herb.
A Pot-herb.
Herbage, or *pasture, also a liberty to feed cattel in a forest.*
An Herbal, or *book treating of* herbs.
An Herbalist; *one that has skill in* herbs.
Herb-bane.
Herb-bennet.
Herb-christopher.
Herb-frankincence.
Herb-gerard.
Herb of grace.
Herb-robert.
Herb-truelove.
Herb-twopence.
Herb-william.
Herb-willow.
A Herb-seller.
A Herd, or *company of cattel.*
To herd, or *flock together.*
A Cow-herd, or *neatherd.*
A Hog-herd.
A Shepherd.
A Swine-herd.
An Herdsman.

Here,

Here, or *in this place.*
Hereabouts.
Hereafter.
Hereat.
Hereby.
Hereditary, *that comes by inheritance.*
Herein.
Hereof.
An Heresy, or *erroneous opinion in matters of Faith.*
Heretical, *belonging to,* or *infected with* heresy.
An Heretick.
Hereto (*from* here.)
Heretofore.
Hereupon.
An Heriot, *a Tenant's best chattel, due at his death to the Lord of the mannor, by custom;* as, *an horse, ox, &c.*
An Heritage, or *inheritance.*
An Hermaphrodite, (i. e. *Mercury-Venus,*) *a person of both Sexes.*
An Hermit, or *solitary monk.*
A Hermit-fish.
An Hermitage, *the place where an* hermit *lives.*
A Hern-shaw, *or* hernery, *a place where* herons *breed.*
A Heroe, *a man of great worth, and renown, excelling in valour, and other vertues.*
Heroical, *or* heroick.
An Heroine, or *female Heroe.*
A Heron, *a bird.*
Herons-bill; *an herb.*
A Herring, *a fish.*
A Herring-woman.
Heterodox, *of another,* or *different judgement from what is generally received in the Catholick Church.*
Heterogeneous, *of a different kind.*
Heteroscians, (*in Geography*) *these that live in either of the temperate Zones, and have their shadows cast on a contrary side.*
To hew, or *cut.*
A Hewer of *wood,* or *stone.*
Rough-hewn, or *unpolish'd.*
A Hexagon, or *figure with six angles,* or *corners.*
Hey-day!
Hey-ho!
A Hey-hold, or *hick wall, a bird.*
An Hey-net.
An Hey-thorn-tree.

H I

The Hicket, hickup, *or* hick-cough; *a convulsive motion of the stomack.*
A Hickwall, *or* hickway; *a bird.*
Hid, *or* hidden.
To Hide, *keep close,* or *conceal.*
A Hide, or *skin of a beast.*
A Hide of Land, *as much as can be till'd by one plough; about* 100 *acres.*
Hide-bound.
Hideous, *frightful,* or *horrible.*
Hideousness.
A Hider, (*from* to hide.)
Hierarchy, or *Church-government.*
Hieroglyphicks, *certain sacred,* or *mystical characters by pictures of creatures, in use among the ancient* Egyptians.
Hig-taper, *an herb.*
High (*in all senses.*)
A High born Prince.
A High-crowned hat.
A High-flown style.
The High-landers *in* Scotland.
A High-metall'd *horse.*
To be high-minded, or *proud.*
A High-mounted *nose.*
A High-spirited dame.
The High-way.
An High-way-man, or *robber.*
Highness; *as, his Royal Highness.*
A Hill, or *rising ground.*
A Mole-hill.
A Hillock, or *little* hill.
Hilly, or *full of* hills.
The Hilt, or *handle of a sword.*
Him, *and* himself.
A Hin, *a liquid measure among the ancient* Jews.
A Hind, *the female of a stag.*
Hind-berries.
The Hind, *or* hinder *part of any thing.*
The Hind-feet *of a beast.*
To hinder, *keep from, disturb,* or *stop.*
An Hinderance.
A Hinderer.
The Hindermost, or *last of all.*
The Hinge *of a door.*
A Hint, or *intimation.*
To hint, or *give an* hint.
A Hip, or hep, *a sort of berry.*
The Hip, or *upper part of the thigh.*
The Hip-gout.
Hipped; *as* high-hipped.
Hip-wort, *an herb.*
Hippocras, *a kind of spiced compound wine.*
An Hire, or *wages.*
To hire, or *take,* or *let to* hire.
An Hireling.
A Hirer *of land, and rents.*
Hirse, or *millet, a grain.*
His, *and* his own.
To hiss, or *make a noise like a serpent,* or *goose.*
Hist! *a note of silence.*
An Historian.
Historical.
An Historiographer, or *writer of* histories.
An History, or *relation of matters of fact.*
A Hit, *and to* hit, or *strike.*

To Hitch, or *riggle farther.*

Hitch-buttock, or *level-coil a game.*

A Hithe, *a wharf to load or unload wares; as* Queen-hithe *in* London.

Hither.

The Hithermost.

Hitherto.

Hitherward.

A Hive, or *Bee-hive.*

Hive-dross, or *bee-glew.*

H O

Ho, Ho! *in calling one.*

A Hoar-frost.

Hoariness (*from* hoary)

Hoarse.

Hoarseness.

Hoary, *having gray heirs frosty*, or *mouldy.*

To hobble along, or *go lamely.*

A Hobby, or *Irish horse; also a kind of haw*

A Hobgoblin, or *Phantome.*

A Hob-nail.

A Hoboy, or haut-boy, *a Musical Instrument.*

Hock, *a sort of* German *wine.*

A Hock, *or little gammon of bacon.*

Hock-tide, *i. e. a* high-day, or *Festival, formerly kept the second Tuesday after* Easter-week, *in memory of the* Danes *being turn'd out.*

A Hocus-pocus, or *juggler; also the term commonly us'd by those that shew tricks by slight of hand.*

A Hod, *to carry morter in.*

A Hod-man, *one that carries morter; also a stranger admitted into Christ's-Church College in* Oxford.

A Hodg-podg, or Hotch-potch.

A Hog, *a Beast.*

A Bacon-Hog.

A Barrow Hog, or *gelt hog.*

A Hedge-hog.

A Sea-Hog.

A Hog-badger.

A Hog-fish.

A Hogget, hogrel, or *young Sheep.*

A Hog-heard.

Hoggish.

A Hog-grubber, *a hoggish niggardly fellow.*

A Hog-louse, *an Insect.*

Hogs-beans. }
Hogs-bread. } herbs
Hogs-fennel. }

A Hogs-head, *a liquid measure containing 63 gallons; or the fourth part of a Tun.*

A Hog-steer, *a wild Boar three years old.*

A Hog-sty.

A Hogoe, *an high taste; or relish.*

A Hoiden, or *clownish, rustical woman.*

To Hoise, hoist *up*, or *heave up.*

Hola! ho! *do you hear?*

A Hold, *and to* hold (*in all senses.*)

The Hold *of a Ship.*

Holden.

A Holder *forth*, or *Fanatical preacher.*

A Free-holder.

A Holdfast, or *Iron-hook in a Wall; also a griping Miser.*

A Hole, or *hollow place.*

The Arm-hole.

A Lurking hole.

A Pock-hole.

The Sight-hole *in a Crossbow*

The Touch-hole *of a Gun.*

Holiness (*from* holy)

Holland, or Holland-cloath, *a sort of Linnen made in that Country.*

A Holland-shirt.

Hollow, or *having holes; as a Reed, Pipe, Spunge &c.*

To hollow, or *make* hollow

To Hollow, or *cry out as Hunters do.*

Hollow-cheeked.

Hollow-eyed.

Hollow-hearted

Hollow-root, *an herb.*

The Holly, or *holly Oak.*

Sea-holly.

Rose-holly.

The Holm, Holm-oak, or *Holly-tree.*

Holp up (*from* to help) as *I am finely* holp up.

A Holster *for a Pistol.*

A Holt, or *small wood.*

Holy, *Sacred, Godly*, or *Devout.*

An Holy-day.

The Holy Elm-tree.

The Holy Ghost, or *Holy-Spirit, the second Person of the ever blessed Trinity.*

Holy-herb. }
Holy-hocks. }
Holy-rose. } herbs.
Holy-seed. }
Holy-thistle. }

Holy Thursday, *on which Christ's Ascension is celebrated, 10 days before* Whitsunday.

Holy-water, *us'd by* Roman *Catholicks in their Devotions.*

Court Holy-water; *fair words and nothing else.*

Homage, *a duty owing from a vassal to his Lord.*

A Homager, *one that is oblig'd to do* homage.

A Home, *house*, or *habitation.*

To keep at home.

A Home-blow.

Home-bred, as Home-*bred wars.*

A Home-spun *Cloth.*

Home-news.

A Home-thrust *in fencing.*

A Home-stall, or *Country house.*

Homeliness.

Homely, *mean, course; or not very agreeable.*

Homewards, or *towards home.*

Homicide, or *man-slaughter.*

A Homilist, or *writer of* homilies.

A Homily, *Sermon*, or *Discourse.*

Ho-

Homogeneal, *of the same kind.*
A Hone, *a fine kind of Whet-stone for Razors*, &c.
Honest, *just and upright, chaste, vertuous*, &c.
Honesty, *uprightness*, or *chastity*; *also a Flower so call'd.*
Honey, *made by Bees.*
Virgin-Honey.
A Honey-Apple.
A Honey-comb.
Honey-comb'd, *as a Cannon that is ill cast, and rugged on the inside.*
Honey-dew.
Honey-moon, *the first sweet Month after marriage.*
Honey-Suckle, *a shrub and flower.*
French honey-suckle.
Trefoil Honey-suckle.
Honey-wort.
Honied, or *sweeten'd with* Honey.
Honour, *glory, credit, reputation*, or *respect.*
To honour, *do honour, shew respect*, or *have in reverence.*
Honourable.
Honourary, *titular, belonging to, or done as a mark of honour.*
An Honourer.
Honours, *the most noble sort of Seignories, on which other inferiour Lordships and Mannors have their dependance: As the* Honours *of* Windsor, Hampton-court, Greenwich, *&c.*
Honour-Courts, *held in such places.*
A Hood, *of several sorts*
A Livery-Hood.
A Riding-hood.
Monk-shood, *an herb.*
Hooded *and* Scarfed.
Hood-man-blind, or *blind-mans-buff, a sport.*
To Hood-wink, or *blind-fold one.*
The Hoof *of a Beast.*
A Hook.

Hose, or *Stockings.*
To Hook *in*, or *draw in with a* hook.
A Flesh-hook.
A pair of Pot-hooks.
A Sheep-hook.
A Tenter-hook.
A Weeding-hook.
A Well-hook, or *drag.*
Hooked, or *made like a* hook.
A Hoop, *a bird.*
A Hoop *to* hoop *a tub with.*
To Hoop, or whoop *and hollow.*
A Hooper, or *wild Swan.*
To hoot, or *cry out.*
A Hop, *and to* hop, or *jump.*
Hop, *or* hops, *a Plant.*
A Hop-yard.
Hope, *trust, affiance, looking for any thing*, &c.
To Hope, or *have* hope.
The forlorn hope *of an army.*
Hopeful.
Hopefulness, or *towardly disposition.*
Hopeless, or *without hope.*
A Hopper, *one that hops.*
A Mill-hopper.
Scotch-hoppers, *a play.*
Hopper-arst.
A Hord, *heap*, or *treasure.*
To Hord *up money*, &c.
A Horder.
Hore-hound, *an herb.*
Base-hore-hound.
Horizon, (*i. e.* bounding:) *that great Circle which determins the sight of any person, plac'd in a plain, or in the midst of the Sea, by which the Heaven seems to be joyn'd to the Earth, with a kind of closure, dividing the half Sphere of the Firmament which we see, from the other half that is not visible to us.*
Horizontal, *conformable to the* Horizon.
A Horn *of a beast* &c.

A Bugle-horn.
An Ink-horn.
A Shoe-horn.
The Horn-beam *Tree.*
A Horn-beak, *a Fish.*
A Horn-book *to teach Children to spell.*
Horned, or *having* horns.
A Horn-owl, *or* horn-coot
A Horn-work, *a kind of fortification.*
A Hornet, or *great Wasp*
An Horoscope, (*i. e.* marking of hours) *the ascendent of one's Nativity; that part of the Firmament which rises up from the East, at the hour of one's Birth.*
Horrible, *terrible*, or *heinous.*
Horribleness.
Horrid, or *dreadful.*
Horrour, *a trembling for fear or cold; extreme fright*, or *astonishment.*
A Horse, *a labouring Beast.*
To Horse *one*, or *take him on his back.*
A Cart-horse.
A Sea-horse.
A Sumpture-horse.
A Horse-breaker.
A Horse-courser.
Horse-foot, or horse-hoof, *an herb.*
Horse-flower.
A Horse-fly, *an Insect.*
Horse-heal, *an herb.*
A Horse-keeper.
A Horse-Litter.
A Horse-leech.
A Horse-man.
Horsemanship, *the art of managing a Horse.*
Horse-mint. }
Horse-radish. } herbs.
Horse-shoe-vetch. }
Horse-tail }
Horse-tongue
Horse-trappings.
Hosanna, *a Hebrew word, signifying*, save I beseech thee O Lord.
The Hose *of a Printing-Press.*

A Hosier, *one that sells Stockings.*
Hospitable, *that uses* hospitality.
An Hospital, or *house built for the relief of poor, sick, decrepit,* or *impotent persons.*
Hospitalers, *an order of religious Knights.*
Hospitality, *a readiness to entertain and relieve strangers.*
An Host, or *Army; also the consecrated bread in the Communion.*
An Host, or *Landlord that receives Guests.*
An Hostage, or *pledge.*
An Hostess, *the good Wife of an Inn.*
Hostile, *belonging to,* or *like an enemy.*
Hostility, as *an act of* hostility.
An Hostler, or *Horse-groom in an Inn.*
Hot (*from* heat.)
Hot-cokles, *a sport.*
Hot-headed.
A Hot-house.
Hot-spurred.
A Hotch-pot, Hotchpotch, *or* hodge-podge, *a dish of slic'd-meat boil'd with herbs, roots,* &c. *or any kind of odd mixture of things.*
A Hovel, or *shelter for Beasts.*
The Hough, *the joint of the hinder Leg of Beasts.*
To hough, or *hamstring;* or *to break the clods of Earth.*
A Hound, or *hunting-dog.*
A Blood-hound, or *drawing hound*
A Pointing-hound.
A Gase, or Gast-hound.
A Grey-hound.
The Hound-fish.
The spotted hound-fish.
Hounds-tongue, *an herb.*
The Hound-tree.
An Hour, *the 24 part of a day.*
An Hour Glass.
A House (*in several senses.*)
To House, or *receive into the house.*
An Ale-house.
A Brew-house.
A Coffee-house.
A Market-house.
A Store-house.
A Town-house.
A Work-house
To be Housed, *as beasts are.*
A House-keeper.
House-leek, *an herb.*
House-room.
A House-warming.
A Household.
A House-holder.
Household-Stuff.
A House wife.
Housewifry.
To Hout, or *cry out.*
How as, *how do ye* do?
However.
To Howl, *or cry as a Dog,* or *Wolf does.*
An Howlet, *a night-bird,*
Howsoever.
A Hoy *a kind of Ship.*

H U.

The Huckle-bone.
Huck-shoulder'd.
A Huckster, *that sells things by retail.*
A Huddle, or *bustle.*
To Huddle, or *confound things together.*
A Hue, or *colour.*
A Hue *and cry,* or *pursuit after a Malefactor.*
A Huff, *or swaggering Fellow.*
To Huff, *blow,* or *vapour.*
Huffish, *given to* huffing.
To Hug, or *embrace.*
Huge, or *great.*
To do a thing in hugger-mugger.
A Hull, or *husk.*
To Hull, or *clear from the* hulls.
The Hull, *body,* or *bulk of a Ship.*
To Hull, or *lye a hull, as a Ship does, when all her Sails are taken in.*
A Hulk, *a kind of great Ship.*
The Hulver-tree.
To Hum *or buzz like Bees.*
Humane, *belonging to Man; also courteous, civil, obliging* &c.
A Humanist, *one that is vers'd in* humane *learning.*
Humanity, Humane *nature; liberal; knowledge learning,* or *courtesie.*
Humble, *lowly,* or *submissive.*
To humble, or *make* humble.
Humbleness.
An Humble-bee, *an Insect, an herb.*
The Humbles *of a Deer.*
Humid, *damp,* or *moist.*
Humidity, or *moistness.*
A state of Humiliation.
Humility, or *humbleness.*
An Humorist, *one that is full of conceits and* humours.
Humour, *moisture, juice,* or *sap; also a fancy, disposition of the mind,* or *body,* &c.
To humour, or *please one.*
Humoursome, *or* humorous, *fantastick,* or *obstinate in his own* humour.
A Hunch.
To hunch, or *thrust one with the Elbows.*
Hunch-back'd, or *crook-shoulder'd.*
A hundred (*in number*) or *the division of a County in* England.
A hundredfold.
The hundredth.
Hung (*from* to hang.)
Hunger, *the appetite,* or *desire of eating.*
Hunger-starv'd.
Hungry.

A Hunks, *a meer* hunks, or *sordid fellow*.
To hunt, *to pursue wild beasts*, or *to search after a thing*.
A Hunter.
A hunting-staff.
A Huntsman, *one that manages the hunting-dogs*.
A Hurdle, *of rods watled together*.
Hurdled, *enclos'd with* hurdles.
Hurds, or *hards of flax*, &c.
To hurl, *cast*, or *throw*.
A Hurler.
A Hurlbat, or whorlbat, *a kind of weapon us'd by the Ancients in their solemn Games, for exercise*.
A hurly-burly, *confusion* or *tumult*.
A Hurricane, *a most tempestuous wind*.
A Hurry, or *bustle*, *and To* hurry.
A Hurt, *wound*, or *sore*; *also mischief*, *dammage*, *injury*, &c.
To Hurt, or *do one* hurt.
Hurtful, or *mischievous*.
Hurtfulness.
A Hurtle-berry.
Hurtless, or *harmless*.
Hurt-sickle, *an herb*.
A Husband (q. d. *house-band*) *a married man*, or *master of a family*.
To husband, or *manage a thing*; or *to till the ground*.
A Husbandman.
Husbandry.
Hush! *make no noise*.
To hush, or *keep silence*.
A Husk, or *hull of Peas*, *Beans*, &c.
Husked, *that has a husk*.
Husky, or *full of* husks.
Hustings, (*i. e. the house of Causes*) *a principal and ancient Court in* London, *held before the Lord Mayor and Aldermen*; *as also in some other Cities*, *as* Lincoln, Winchester, York, *&c*.
A Hutwife, *or* housewife.
A Hut, *or little* Cottage.
A Hutch, or *coop*.
To huzz, or *keep a noise*.
An Huzza, or *joyful acclamation*.

HY

To hy, or *make haste*.
Hyacinth, or *crow-toes*, *a flower*; *also a kind of precious stone*.
An Hydrographer, *one skill'd in* Hydrography, *the description of the water*, or *art of making Sea-charts*.
Hydropical, *belonging*, or *subject to the Dropsy*.
A Hyena, *a very subtil ravenous Beast*, *like a Wolf*, *with a main*, *and long hairs all over the body*; *which counterfeits man's voice to destroy the living*, *and routs up graves to prey upon the dead*.
A Hymn, or *spiritual song*.
An Hyperbole, *a rhetorical Figure*, *which consists in speaking a great deal more*, *or less than is precisely true*.
Hyperbolical, *belonging to*, *or utter'd after such a manner of expression*.
Hypochondriack *distempers proceeding from a windy melancholy*; *so call'd from their seat in the* Hypochondria. *i. e. the upper part of the belly*, *about the short ribs*.
Hypocrisy, *dissimulation*, or *knavery cloak'd with a shew of Religion*.
An Hypocrite.
Hypocritical.

JA

T*O* Jabber, *speak fast prattle*, *or chat*.
A Jacinth, *or* hyacinth, *a precious stone*.
A Jack (*in several senses*.)
The Jack-*fish*.
A Jackall, *a beast said to be the Lion's Harbinger*.
A Jack-an-apes, or Monkey.
Jack, by the hedge, *an herb*.
A Jack-daw, *a bird*.
A Jack Hawk, or *male* Hawk.
A Jack-pudding, or *buffoon*.
Jack-with-a-lanthorn, *a meteor*.
The Jacks *in Virginals*.
A Jacket, *a sort of Garment*.
A Jacob's-staff, *a Mathematical instrument*.
A Jacobus, *a broad piece of Gold coyn'd by* James *the* I. *King of Great* Britain.
A Jade, *a sorry horse*, or *mare*; *a whore*.
To Jade, or *tire one*.
A Jadish *trick*.
A Jag, or *notch*, *and To* jag.
A Jail, *goal*, or *prison*.
A Jailer, or *prison-keeper*
A Jakes, or *house of Office*.
A Jakes-farmer.
The Jambs, or *side-posts of a door*.
St. James's wort, *an herb*.
To Jangle, or *quarrel*.
A Jangler.
A Janizary, *a* Turkish *foot-soldier*.
January *the first month in the year*, *which had its name from the God* Janus, *or from* Janua *i. e. a Gate*; *because it gives entrance*, *as it were*, *to the rest of the months*.

A Jar.

A Jar, or *earthen pot for Oil containing* 20 *gallons.*
T Jar, *disagree, or quarrel.*
A Jargon, or *gibberish.*
Jasmin *or* jessamin.
A Jasper, *or* jasper-stone, *a green sort of marble, with red veins.*
A Jass-hawk, *or* eyess-hawk.
A Javelin, *a kind of dart.*
The Jaundice, *a disease.*
The black Jaundice.
The yellow-Jaundice.
A Jaunt.
To Jaunt, or *trudge up and down.*
The Jaunts *of a wheel.*
The Jaw, or Gum *in which the Teeth are set.*
The Jaw-bone.
The Jaw-teeth.
A Jay, *a bird.*

I B

Ibis, *a tall strong bird in* Ægypt, *with a long bill which kills the Serpents that infest the country.*
Ice, or *water congeal'd by frost.*
To ice, or ice *over a cake, fruit* &c. *with sugar.*
Ice-bound, *as a ship* ice-bound *in the harbour.*
An Ice-house.
An Ichneumon, *a kind of rat that kills Crocodiles, by creeping unawares into their mouths and devouring their entrals.*
Ichnography, *the draught of a building.*
An Icicle.
Icing-glass, *a sort of mineral.*
Icy, *or full of* ice.

I D

I'd, *for I would.*
An Idea, *the form of any thing conceiv'd in the mind.*
An Ideom, *propriety,* or *peculiar phrase of any language.*
An Idiot, or *natural fool.*
Idiotism, or *simplicity.*
Idle, *slothful,* or *trifling.*
Idleness, or *sluggishness.*
An Idol, *image,* or *representation of a false Deity.*
An Idolater.
An Idolatress.
Idolatrous, *given to*
Idolatry, or *worshipping of* Idols.
To Idolize *one,* or *make an* Idol *of him.*

J E

Jealous, *suspicious,* or *mistrustful.*
Jealousy.
Jeat, *a sort of stone.*
A Jeer, *and*
To jeer, or *scoff.*
A Jeerer.
Jehovah, *the sacred name of God, denoting his essence, i. e.* who was, is, and is to come.
Jejune, *hungry, dry, empty or barren.*
A Jelly *of meat,* or *fruit.*
Jelly-broth.
To Jeopard, *hazzard,* or *endanger.*
Jeopardy, *danger,* or *peril.*
A Jerk, *and to* jerk *(in several senses.)*
A Jerkin, *or* Jacket.
Jessamin, *or* jasmin *a sweet shrub.*
Yellow-jessamin.
Jessamin-butter, *made of the flowers of that Tree, with other Ingredients.*
A Jest, *and to* jest, or *joke.*
A Jester.
Jesuitical, *of or belonging to The Order,* or *Society of* Jesuits, *instituted by* Ignatius Loyola, *a* Spanish *Soldier, and confirm'd by Pope* Paul, III. *Sept.* 27. 1540
Jesus, *the same with* Joshua, *i. e. a* Saviour; *a name given to our ever blessed Lord and Redeemer, and solemnly declared by an Angel, before his birth.*
Jesus-College *in* Oxford, *founded by* Hugh Price, *Doctor of Laws*, A. D. 1571.
To Jet, *or run up and down.*
A Jewel, *gem,* or *precious stone.*
A Jewel-house.
A Jeweller.
Jewish *belonging to the nation of the* Jews, *or people of* Judæa, *so call'd from the largest Tribe of* Judah.
Jews-ear, *a spungy substance growing about the Elder-tree root.*
A Jews-trump, *a kind of musical instrument.*

I F I G

If, *as if it be possible.*
If *so be.*
Without ifs, or ands
Ignoble, *mean,* or *base in birth,* or *disposition.*
Ignominious, *full of*
Ignominy, *disgrace, infamy, slander,* &c.
Ignoramus, (*i. e.* we are ignorant;) *a term usually writ by the grand Inquest, upon a bill of information, when they find it too weak to make good the presentment.*
An Ignoramus, *an ignorant,* or *foolish person.*
Ignorance.
Ignorant, *not knowing, unskilful,* or *illiterate.*

J I

A Jig, *a kind of dance.*
A Jill, *a small sort of wine measure.*
A Jill, or Jill-flirt, *an idle slut.*

To Jilt,

To Jilt, *or play the* jilt.

I L

The Iliack *passion*, or *twisting of the guts.*
I'll, *for* I will; as *I'll do it.*
Ill, evil, *bad*, *naught*, or *sick*.
Ill-conditioned.
Ill-contrived.
Ill-favoured.
Ill-gotten.
Ill-grounded.
Ill-look't.
Ill-natured.
Ill-principled.
Ill-shaped.
Ill-spoken *of.*
An Illation, or *inference.*
Illegal, *contrary to* Law.
Illegality, or *unlawfulness.*
Illegitimate, *unlawfully begotten*, or *base-born.*
Illiberal, or *niggardly.*
Illiberality.
Illiterate, or *unlearned.*
Illogical, *not agreeable to the rules of* Logick.
To Illuminate, or *enlighten.*
An Illumination.
An Illusion, *deceit*, *sham*, or *false representation.*
Illusory, *mocking* or *deceitful.*
To Illustrate, *make clear*, or *explain a thing.*
An Illustration.
Illustrious, or *renowned.*
Illness, or *indisposition.*
Ill-will, or *envy.*

I M

A Image, *representation*, or *statue.*
Imagery, *carved*, or *painted* image-work.
Imaginable, *that may be* imagined.
Imaginary, *that has no being at all, but in one's fancy.*
An Imagination, *thought*, or *fancy.*
The Imaginative *faculty.*
To Imagine, *devise*, *fancy*, *think*, or *suppose.*
To Imbalm, *a dead body*, *with spicies*, *gums*, &c. *to keep it from putrefaction.*
An Imbalmer.
An Imbargo, *an arrest laid upon ships*, or *merchandizes by publick authority.*
To imbargo, or *put a stop to all traffick by Sea.*
To imbark, *take ship*, or *go a-board.*
To Imbase, *gold*, or *silver*; *to mix it with baser metal, than it ought to be.*
Imbecillity, *weakness* or *feebleness.*
To imbellish, *set out*, *adorn* or *beautify.*
An Imbellishment.
To imbezel, *waste spoil*, *purloin*, or *pilfer.*
To imbibe, *drink in*, or *receive eagerly.*
To imbitter, *to make bitter*, or *to exasperate.*
Imbodied, or *made into one* body.
To imbolden, *make* bold, or *encourage.*
Imbossed work, *raised with* bosses, or *bunches.*
An Imbosser *of plate.*
To imbrace, *or* embrace.
To imbroider, or *work curiously with a Needle*, &c.
An Imbroiderer.
Imbroidery.
To imbroil, *to cause* broils, *disturbances*, or *divisions.*
To imbrue, or *defile one's hands with blood.*
To imbue, or *season the mind with principles.*
Imitable, *that may be* imitated.
To imitate or *follow another's example.*
An imitation.
A imitator.
Immaculate, or *unspotted.*
Immanity, *hugeness*, *outoutragious cruelty*, or *barbarity.*
Immanuel, *i. e.* God with us; *a name attributed by the Prophet* Isaiah, *to our Lord and Saviour Jesus Christ.*
Immarcessible, *incorruptible*, *that never withers* or *fades.*
Immaterial, *without matter.*
Immaturity, *unripe*, or *not come to perfection.*
Immediate, *that which follows*, or *happens presently.*
Immemorable, *not worth remembance*, or *not remarkable.*
Immense, *vast*, *exceeding large*, or *unmeasurable.*
The Immensity *of* God.
To immerse, *plunge*, or *dip in.*
An immersion, or *plunging in baptism.*
Immethodical, *without a due method.*
Imminent, *hanging over one's head*, *ready to fall*, or *at hand.*
Immoderate, *without the bounds of* moderation.
Immobility, or *unmoveableness.*
Immoderation.
Immodest, *that wants* modesty.
Immodesty.
Immoral, *of corrupted* morals.
Immorality.
Immortal, *that never dyes.*
Immortality.
To immortalize, or *make* immortal.
Immoveable, *that cannot be moved*, or *stedfast.*
An Immunity, *freedom*, or

or, *privilege.*

To immure, or *shut up within walls.*

Immutability.

Immutable, or *unchangeable.*

An Imp, *a familiar Spirit that attends upon Witches.*

To imp *a feather in a Hawk's wing*; i. e. *to put a new piece on an old broken stump.*

To impair, *diminish*, or *make worse.*

To impale, or *set* pales *about a place.*

To impale, or *drive a stake through the body of a malefactor*; *a punishment in* Turkey.

To impannel, or *constitute a Jury*; *to enter their names in a roll call'd the* Pannel.

Imparity, *unevenness*, or *inequality.*

To impark, or *inclose a piece of ground for a* Park.

To impart, or *communicate to.*

Impartial, *not inclin'd to favour either party*; *just and equitable.*

Impartiality.

Impassable, *not to be pass'd through.*

The impassibility *of the Divine nature, being*

Impassible, or *incapable of suffering.*

Impatience.

Impatient, *that has no* patience; or *hasty.*

The impatronization, or *full enjoyment of a benefice.*

To impeach, or *accuse another as guilty of the same crime with one's self.*

An impeacher.

An impeachment.

Impeccability.

Impeccable, *uncapable of offending, sinning*, or *doing amiss.*

To impede, or *hinder the execution of a design*, &c.

An Impediment.

To impell, *drive*, or *force on.*

To impend, or *hang over, as dangers*, or *judgments do.*

Impendent.

Impenetrability.

Impenetrable, *that cannot be pierc'd.*

Impenitence, or impenitency.

Impenitent, *that does not repent of his crimes*; or *unrelenting.*

Imperceptible, or *not to be perceived.*

Imperceptibleness.

Imperfect, *or not perfect.*

An imperfection.

Imperial, *belonging to the Emperour*, or *Empire.*

The Imperial Lilly, *a flower.*

The Imperialists, or *the Emperor's forces.*

Imperious, *insulting*, or *domineering.*

Imperiousness.

Impertinence.

Impertinent, *not belonging to the matter in hand, idle, absurd* or *silly.*

Impervious, *or impassable.*

Impetuous, *violent, boisterous*, or *furious.*

Impetuousness, or impetuosity.

Impiety.

Impious, *ungodly*, or *wicked.*

Implacable, *not to be appeas'd*, or *reconcil'd.*

Implacableness, or implacability.

To Implant, *ingraft*, or *fasten into.*

To implead, or *sue one at* Law.

Implements, *tools*; or *furniture for a house*, or *trade.*

Implicit, *involv'd with another, intricate*, or *obscure.*

To implore, *beseech*, or *beg as it were with tears.*

To imploy, *or* employ.

An imploy, imployment, or *business.*

To imply, *signifie*, or *infer.*

Impolite *unpolished, rude*, or *rough.*

Impolitick, *not conformable to the rules of* policy.

The import, *sense*, or *meaning of a thing.*

To import, *to carry in, to signifie*, or *to advantage.*

Importance, or *consequence.*

Important, or *considerable.*

The Importation *of commodities.*

Importunate, *very urgent*, or *troublesome.*

To importune, or *request earnestly.*

Importunity.

To impose, *to set upon, enjoyn, cheat* &c.

To impose (*in* Printing) i. e. *to place the pages in the* Form, or *Chace, and make 'em ready for the Press.*

An imposition.

An impossibility.

Impossible *that cannot be done.*

An impost, *duty*, or *custom, for goods* imported.

A impostor, or *cheat.*

To impostumate, or *grow into an* impostume.

An impostume, *an unnatural swelling of humours*, or *corrupt matter in any part of the body.*

An Imposture, or *cozenage.*

Impotency, or *want of strength.*

Impotent, *unable*, or *weak.*

To im-

To impoverish, or *make poor.*
An impoverishment.
To impower, or *give power to.*
Impracticable, *that cannot be put in practice.*
To imprecate, *wish evil to*, or *curse.*
An imprecation.
Impregnable, *not to be taken by force.*
Impregnate, or *with child.*
To impregnate, *get with child*, or *make fruitful.*
An Impregnation.
An Imprese, *Emblem*, or *device with a motto.*
An Impression, *stamp*, or *mark; also a certain number of Printed books.*
To imprest, or *compell Soldiers to enter into the publick service.*
Imprest-money, or *advance-money given them upon that account.*
Imprimed, *so the hunters call the Deer, when it forsakes the herd.*
To imprint, or *fix a thing in one's mind.*
To imprison, or *cast into* prison.
An imprisonment.
Improbability *a being*
Improbable, *that cannot be prov'd*, or *unlikely.*
Improbity, or *dishonesty.*
Improper, *not proper.*
To impropriate *a Church-Living.*
An Impropriation, *a parsonage passing by inheritance.*
An Impropriator, *a Layman that gets possession of a spiritual living.*
An impropriety *of speech.*
Improveable, *that may be improved.*
To improve, *make better, encrease, advance or thrive.*
An improvement.
An Improver.
An improvidence.
Improvidence, *that neglects to provide*, or *has no forecast.*
Imprudence.
Imprudent, *unwise*, or *indiscreet.*
Impudence.
Impudent, or *shameless.*
To impugn, *oppose, withstand*, or *contradict.*
An Impugner.
An impulse, *motion*, or *incitement to.*
An impulsion, *pushing on*, or *instigation.*
Impulsive.
Impunity, or *freedom from punishment.*
Impure, *unclean*, or *filthy.*
Impurity.
An imputation, or *laying to one's charge.*
Imputative righteousness.
To impute, *attribute*, or *ascribe.*
An imputer.

IN

In, *as in times pass'd.*
Inability, or *incapacity.*
Inaccessible, *not to be come to.*
Inadvertency, *heedlesness*, or *inconsiderateness.*
Inamour'd, or enamoured *a being in love.*
Inanimate, *without life* or *soul.*
Inarticulate, *not articulate* or *indistinct.*
To inaugurate, *consecrate, install*, or *investe with an office*, or *dignity.*
An Inauguration.
Inauspicious, or *unlucky.*
Inbred, or *unnatural.*
To incamp, , encamp, or *pitch a* camp.
An Incampment.
An Incantation, *inchanting*, or *charming.*
Incapable, *unable*, or *unfit.*
To incapacitate, or *make incapable.*
Incapacity, or *inability.*
Incarnate, or *flesh-colour.*
An Incarnation, or *assuming of flesh.*
An incarnative, *a Medicine that causes flesh to grow.*
An Incendiary, *a burner of houses*, or *a sower of dissensions.*
Incence, *a perfume with* frankincense,
Incence-wort, *an herb.*
To incense, *inflame, provoke*, or *urge.*
An incentive, *provocation, motive*, or *incitement.*
An inceptor, (*i. e.* beginner) *one that is about to take a degree in the University.*
Incessant, *without ceasing, continual*, or *uninterrupted.*
Incest, or *carnal copulation with one that is too near of kin.*
Incestuous, *or guilty of* incest.
An Inch, *a measure.*
To inch out, or *make the most of a thing.*
By inch-meal.
To inchain, or *put in* chains.
To inchant, or *bewitch.*
An Inchanter.
An inchantment, or *charm.*
An Inchantress.
To inchase, or *set in Golds*
An Inchipin, *the lower gut of a Deer.*
Incident, *that happens commonly.*
Incidently, or incidentally *by the way.*
To incircle, or encircle.
An incision, *a cutting*, or *lancing.*
To incite, or *stir up.*
An incitement.
An Inciter.
Incivil, or *unmannerly.*
Incivility.

Incle, or

Incle, or *tape.*
Inclemency, *severity, rigour,* or *unkindness.*
Inclinable; *that has*
An inclination, or *disposition.*
To incline, *bend,* or *lean towards.*
Incloistered, *put into a Cloister,* or *Monastery.*
To inclose, *or* enclose.
An inclosure.
To include, *shut* or *take in;* or *comprehend.*
Inclusive.
Incogitancy, or *heedlesness, inconsiderateness,* or *unadvisedness.*
Incognito, *unknown* or *in private.*
Incombustible, *that cannot take fire.*
An Income, or *revenue.*
Incommensurable, *that has not an equal measure* or *proportion.*
To incommode, or *trouble one.*
Incommodious, *inconvenient, unprofitable,* or *unfit.*
An Incommodity.
Incommunicable, *that cannot be* communicated, or *imparted to another.*
Incompact, *not well join'd,* or *jointed.*
Incomparable, *without compare, that has not its like.*
To incompass, or *surround.*
Incompassionate, *that has no* compassion.
Incompatible, *that cannot stand, agree together,* or *endure one another.*
An incompetency, or *insufficiency.*
Incompetent, *improper, incapable,* or *unfit.*
Incompetibility.
Incompetible, *unsuitable,* or *not agreeable.*
Incomplete, *that is not complete.*
Incomposed, *uncouth,* or *ill favour'd.*
An Incomposure, or *disorder.*
Incomprehensible, *not to be* comprehended, or *conceived.*
Incomprehensibleness, *or* incomprehensibility.
Inconceivable, *not to be* conceived.
An incongruity, or *disagreeableness.*
Incongruous, or *improper.*
An Inconsquency, or *weakness in arguing.*
Inconsequent.
Inconsiderable, *not worth* considering, or *taking notice of.*
Inconsiderate, *rash, giddy,* or *indiscreet.*
Inconsiderateness.
Inconsistence.
Inconsistent, *or incompatible that cannot consist,* or *stand together.*
Inconsolable, *that will admit no comfort.*
Inconstancy.
Inconstant, *fickle,* or *unstable.*
Incontinency, or *lewdness.*
Incontinent, *unchaste,* or *immediate.*
An inconvenience, *or* inconveniency.
Inconvenient, *not convenient,* or *unfit.*
Inconversible, or *unsociable.*
Inconvertible Terms.
Incorporate, or *imbodied.*
To incorporate, *to mix,* or *to unite in a* corporation.
Incorporeal, or *bodiless.*
Incorrect, or *full of faults.*
Incorrigible, *that cannot be corrected, reclaimed past correction,* or *head strong.*
Incorrupt, *or* incorrupted.
Incorruptible, *free from corruption,* or *never decaying.*
Incorruptibleness.
An incounter.
To incounter, *to meet,* or *to engage in fight.*
To incourage, *animate,* or *promote.*
An incouragement.
An incourager.
An increase.
To increase, or *augment.*
An increaser.
Incredible, *past all belief.*
Incredibleness, *or* incredibility.
Incredulity.
Incredulous, or *hard of belief.*
To incroach, *or* encroach; *to usurp,* or *intrude upon.*
An incroacher.
An incroachment.
An incrustation, *rough-casting,* or *pargeting.*
An incubus, or *night-mare, a disease;* also *a Devil that has carnal knowledge of women.*
To inculcate, or *beat into one's head, by frequent repetition.*
Inculpable, *unreprovable,* or *blameless.*
A business incumbent *upon one.*
An Incumbent, *one that is in present possession of a spiritual living.*
To incumber, *perplex,* or *trouble.*
An incumbrance.
To incur, or *run into.*
Incurable, or *not to be cured.*
Incurableness.
An incursion *running upon,* or *inrode.*
To indammage, *hurt,* or *prejudice.*
To indanger, or *expose to* danger.
To indear, or *render one beloved.*
An indearment, or *great cause of affection.*
An indeavour.

To indeavour, or *attempt*.
Indebted, *in debt*, or *obliged to*.
Indecency.
Indecent, or *unseemly*.
Indecimable, *not tithable*, *that ought not to pay tithes*.
Indeed, or *really*.
Indefatigable, *unwearied*, *that cannot be tir'd*.
Indefeasible, *that cannot be defeated*, or *made void*.
Indefinite, *not defined*, or *bounded*.
Indelible, *not to be razed*, or *blotted out*.
To indemnify, or *save harmless*.
Indemnity.
To indent, or *notch*.
An Indenture, or indented writing, *comprising a contract between several parties*.
Independency, *a being*
Independent, *that has no dependency upon another*.
Independents, or Congregationalists, *a Sect which first appear'd in* England *about An.* 1643, *holding that Churches should not be subordinate; as Parish-Churches to those of a Province, and Provincial to National; but all coordinate and equal, without superiority*.
Indevotion, *a want of devotion*.
An Index, (i.e. shewer) *the hand of a clock*; or *a Table that shews the principal matters contain'd in a Book*.
Indian Cresses, *an herb*.
Indian Flow'ry-reed.
An Indication, *shewing*, *sign*, or *proof*.
To indict, *impeach*, or *accuse in due form of Law*.
An Indictment.
An indicter.
An Indiction (*in* Chronology) *a term of fifteen years, which was appointed by the Emperour* Constantine *the Great*, *instead of the heathenish way of reckoning by* Olympiads, *and began at the dissolution of the* Nicene *Council*.
Indifferency.
Indifferent, *equal*, or *that inclines to neither side*; also *mean* or *ordinary*.
Indigence, *want*, or *penury*.
Indigent, or *needy*.
Indigested, undigested, *raw*, *confused*, or *disordered*.
Indigestible, *that cannot be digested*.
Indigestion, or *want of digestion*.
Indignation, *great anger*, *wrath*, or *disdain*.
An indignity, *an unworthy dealing*, or *affront*.
Indigo, *a kind of stone us'd in dying blew*.
Indirect, *not direct*, *unfair*, *unhandsome*, or *base*.
Indiscernable, *not to be discern'd*, or *perceiv'd*.
Indiscreet, *imprudent*, or *unadvised*.
Indiscretion.
To indispose, or *make unfit*.
Indisposed, *sick*, or *out of order*.
An indisposedness, or *aversion*.
Indisposition, or *illness*.
Indisputable, or *not to be disputed*.
Indissolvable, *not to be dissolved*.
Indissoluble, *that cannot be loosed*, *untied*, or *undone*.
Indistinct *not distinguish'd one from another*, or *confused*.
Indistinguishable, or *not to be distinguished*.
To indite, endite, or *pen a letter*, &c.
An inditer.
Individual, *not to be divided*, or *separated*.
An individual, or individuum, *an individual*, *singular*, or *particular person*, or *thing*.
Indivisible, *that cannot be divided*.
Indivisibleness.
Indocible, or indocile, *unapt to be taught*, or *to learn*.
Indocility, or indocibility.
Indolence, or indolency.
Indolent, *insensible of grief or pain*.
To indorse, or *write upon the back-side of a Deed*, *Indenture*, &c.
An Indorsement.
To indow, endow, or *settle revenues upon an Hospital*, *College*, &c.
An Indowment, or *natural gift*.
Indubitable, or *not to be doubted*.
Indubitate, or *undoubted*.
To induce, *lead to*, *draw on* or *perswade*.
An Inducement, or *motive*.
An Inducer.
Inducted, *that has receiv'd*
An Induction, or *admittance to a spiritual living*.
To indue, *adorn*, or *supply with*.
To indulge, *make much of*, or *gratify*.
Indulgence, *pardon*, *favour*, *toleration*, *kindness*, &c.
Indulgent, *kind*, *mild*, or *gentle*.
Indurable, *that may be indured*, or *born*.
To indurate, *harden*, or *make hard*.
An Induration.
To indure, *bear*, or *suffer*, *to last*, or *continue*.
Industrious, *full of*
Industry, *pains-taking*, or *diligence*.

To inebriate, *fuddle*, or *make drunk*.

Ineffable, *unspeakable*, *not to be utter'd*, or *express'd*.

Ineffectual, or *unsuccessful*.

Inequality, *unevenness*, *unlikeness*, or *disproportion*.

Inestimable, *that cannot be sufficiently valued*.

Inevitable, or *unavoidable*, *that cannot be avoided*, or *shunn'd*.

Inexcusable, *not to be excused*.

Inexhaustible, *that cannot be exhausted*, *drawn dry*, or *emptied*.

Inexorable, or *not to be prevail'd upon*, *with entreaties*.

Inexpedient, *that is not expedient*, *convenient*, or *fit*.

Inexperience, *want of experience*, or *skill*.

Inexperienced, *that has no experience*.

Inexpiable, *not to be expiated*, *atoned*, or *appeased*.

Inexplicable, *that cannot be explained*; or *unfolded*.

Inexpressible, or *not to be* expressed.

Inextinguishable, *not to be quenched*, or *put out*.

Inextricable, *which one cannot rid himself*, or *get out of*.

Infallibility, *a faculty of never erring*.

Infallible, *that cannot err*, or *be deceived*.

Infamous, *base*, *villainous*, *shameful*, *scandalous*, &c.

Infamy, or *disgrace*.

Infancy, *the first period of humane life*.

An Infant, *babe*, or *young child*, *that has not attain'd to the use of speech*.

An Infanta, *a daughter of* Spain, *or* Portugal.

The Infantry, or *foot of an army*.

Indefatigable, or indefatigable.

To infatuate, *make foolish*, or *besot*.

An Infatuation.

To infect, *stain*, *corrupt*, or *poison*.

An infection.

Infectious, *poisonous*, or *noisome*.

To infeeble, *make* feeble, or *weaken*.

Infelicity, or *unhappiness*.

To infeoff, or *give land in fee*.

An infeoffment.

To infer, *bring in*, *gather*, or *conclude from the premises*.

An inference.

Inferiority, *a being*

Inferiour, or *of a lower degree*.

Inferiours, *those that are below others*.

Infernal, or *hellish*.

Infertile, *unfruitful*, or *barren*.

Infertileness, *or* infertility.

To infest, *annoy*, or *trouble*.

An Infidel, or *unbeliever*.

Infidelity, *the state of an unbeliever*, *unfaithfulness* or *disloyalty*.

Infinite, or *endless*.

Infiniteness, *or* infinity.

Infirm, *weak*, *feeble*, or *faint*.

An Infirmary, or *place for sick persons in an Hospital*, *or Monastery*.

An infirmity, or *weakness*.

To infix, *fix*, or *fasten in*.

To inflame, or *set on fire*.

An Inflammation, *an unnatural burning*, or *swelling of any part of the body with heat*.

An inflation, *windy swelling*, or *puffing up*.

Inflexibility.

Inflexible, *not to be bent*, *bowed* or *prevail'd upon*.

To inflict, or *lay a punishment upon*.

An Infliction.

An Influence, *a sending forth virtue*, or *operation*.

To influence, *have power over*, *cause*, or *produce*.

An Influx, *a flowing*, or *running into*.

To infold, or *fold in*.

To inforce, force *upon*, *oblige*, or *constrain*.

An inforcement.

To inform, *to give notice*; *to teach*, or *instruct*.

An Information.

An informer, *one that accuses another of any offence against the Laws*.

Infortunate, or *unlucky*.

To infranchise, *a Law-Term*, *signifying to make free*.

An Infranchisement.

Infrequent, *uncommon* or *rare*.

To infringe, *break*, or *violate a Law*, *custom*, *privilege*, &c.

An infringement.

An Infringer.

To infuse, *to steep*, or *to indue with*.

An infusion.

To ingage, *or* engage.

An Ingagement, or *promise*; also *a battel*, or *encounter*.

To ingeminate, *redouble*, or *repeat often*.

To ingender, or *breed*.

An ingenio, *a sugar-house*, or *Mill in* Barbadoes.

Ingenious, *quick-witted*, *shrewd*, or *cunning*.

Ingenite, or *inbred*.

Ingenuity,

Ingenuity, *or* ingeniousness.
Ingenuous, *free-born, well-bred*, *Gentleman-like*, *sincere*, &c.
To ingest, or *put into the mouth*, or *stomack*.
Ingestion.
Inglorious, *dishonourable*, *obscure*, *base*, or *mean*. *i. e.*
An Ingot, or *wedge of Gold*.
To ingraft, *let in a graft*, or *implant*.
To ingrail, *or notch about about* (*a term in* Heraldry.)
To ingratiate himself, or *curry favour*.
Ingratitude, or *ungratefulness*.
To ingrave, *or* engrave.
An Ingraver.
An ingredient, (*i. e. going in*) *one of the parts of a compound medicine*.
Ingress, or *entrance into*.
To ingross, *or* engross *Writings*, or *Merchandizes*.
An ingrosser.
The ingrossment *of wares into one*, or *few hands*.
To inhabit, *live*, or *dwell in*.
Inhabitable, *not* habitable, or *not to be dwelt in*.
An Inhabitant, *inhabiter*, or *dweller in a place*.
To inhaunce, *or* enhaunce; *to raise the price of a thing*.
An Inhancer.
Inherent, *cleaving to, sticking*, or *abiding in*.
To inherit, *possess*, or *enjoy for himself and heirs*.
An inheritance, *heritage*, or *estate by succession*.
An Inheriter.
To inhibit, or *forbid*.
An Inhibition, or *prohibition*.
Inhospitable, *not given to hospitality, not affording entertainment*, or *barbarous*.
Inhumane, *void of humanity*, *rude*, *savage*, or *cruel*.
Inhumanity.
To inject, *cast*, or *squirt in*.
An injection.
Inimitable, or *not to be imitated*.
To injoy, or *enjoy, to have the use*, or *profit of*.
An Injoyment.
To injoyn, enjoyn, or *command*.
Iniquity, *want of equity*, *injustice*, or *wickedness*.
An initial *letter that begins a word*.
To initiate, *to enter upon*, or *instruct in the first grounds of any art*, or *science*.
An Initiation.
Injudicious, *void of* judgment, or *discretion*.
An Injunction, *strict charge*, or *command*.
To injure, *wrong*, or *prejudice*.
An Injurer.
Injurious, *against right*, *wrongful*, or *unjust*.
An injury.
Injustice, *an action contrary to the rules of justice*, *unfair dealing*, or *ill usage*.
Ink, *to write*, or *print with*.
An Ink-horn.
An Ink-maker.
To inkindle, *inflame*, or *provoke*; *as his zeal is inkindled*.
Inkle *or* incle, *a sort of tape*.
An Inkling, or *hint of a business*; also *a small* or *uncertain report*.
An Inland Country, *i. e. situated far in the main land*.
To inlarge, *or* enlarge.
An Inlargement.
To inlay, *or work in wood, gold*, or *silver*, *with several pieces curiously set together*.
An Inlet, *entrance*, or *passage into*.
To inlighten, enlighten, *or* give light *to*.
An Inmate, or *lodger admitted to dwell jointly with another*.
Inmost, *most within*, or *most secret*.
An Inn, or *publick house for the entertainment, of Travellers*, or *strangers*.
To inn, or *lodge at an* Inn.
To inn, or *lay up Corn*.
An Inn-holder, or *innkeeper*.
The Inns of Court, *certain Colleges for Counsellers*, *and Students at Law*; *such as the* Inner *and* middle Temple, Lincolns-Inn, Grays-Inn, *&c*.
Serjeants-Inns, *two higher houses set a-part for the Judges, and Serjeants at Law*.
The Inns of Chancery, *for* Attorneys *and Students in that Court*; *beeng eight in number*, viz. Bernard's, Clement's, Clifford's, Davie's, Furnival's, Lion's, New-inn, *and* Staple's.
Innate, *inbred*, or *natural*.
Innavigable, *that cannot be sailed on*.
Inner, *or more within*.
Innermost.
Innocence, *or* innocency.
Innocent, *that does no hurt*, or *free from guilt*.
An Innocent, *natural fool*, or *ninney*.
The Innocents-day, or *Childermass-day*, December the 28. *a festival celebrated in memory of those* innocent *Children, whom* Herod *kill'd*, *as*

at our Lord and Saviour's Nativity.

To innovate, or *bring up new customs instead of old ones; to change,* or *alter.*

An Innovation.

An Innovator.

Innoxious, or *harmless Beasts,* &c.

Innumerable, *not to be numbred.*

Innumerableness.

To Inoculate, or *ingraft a bud.*

An Inoculation.

Inoffensive, *that gives no* offence.

Inoffensiveness.

Inofficious, *backward in doing one any good office;* or *discourteous.*

Inofficiousness, *a disobligeing humour.*

Inordinate, *disorderly,* or *unruly.*

Inordinateness.

An Inquest, or *inquiry made by a Jury,* as the Coroner's inquest.

The Court of inquest, at Guild-hall, *that takes cognizance of all complaints preferr'd for debt, under the sum of* 40 *s.*

To inquire, or enquire; *to demand,* or *search into.*

An Inquirer.

An Inquiry.

An Inquisition, or *strict enquiry according to Law.*

The Spanish Inquisition, *first erected, A. D.* 1478. *against the* Jews *and* Moors, *and since turn'd against Protestants,* or *rather against all that are not rampant* Roman Catholicks; *a most bloody and execrable Tribunal, where none is permitted to know his Accusers, and the least suspicion of Heresy,* or *commerce with reputed Hereticks, is a sufficient Crime, to be expiated only by death, a strange way of propagating the Christian Religion.*

Inquisitive, *desirous to pry into,* or *to know every thing.*

An inquisitour, *a Sheriff, Coroner,* &c. *having power to enquire into certain cases.*

To inrage, *incense,* or *exasperate.*

To inrich, or *make rich.*

An inrode, *incursion,* or *hostile invasion of a Country.*

To inroll, *record,* or *register.*

An Inrollment.

Insatiable, *that cannot be satisfied,* or *ever have enough.*

Insatiableness.

An Inscription, or *title writ* or *engrav'd.*

Inscrutable, or *unsearchable.*

Insects, *(i. e. cut* creatures) *any small creatures (according to* Scaliger) *whose parts being cut off retain life; as* Flyes, *Worms, Pismires,* &c.

Insensate, *void of common* sense, *stupid,* &c.

Insensible, *that has no* sense *of feeling;* or *that is not to be perceiv'd.*

Insensibleness.

Inseperable, or *not to be parted.*

Inseparableness.

To Insert, *put in,* or *add.*

An insertion.

The inside *of a thing.*

Insight, *skill,* or *knowledge of a business.*

Insignificancy.

Insignificant, *that* signifies *nothing,* or *unprofitable.*

To insinuate, *intimate,* or *give a hint of;* also *to wind,* or *creep into one's favour by degrees.*

An Insinuation.

Insinuative, or *apt to insinuate.*

Insipid, *unsavoury, without taste,* or *relish.*

To insist, *stay upon, press for,* or *urge.*

To inslave, or *make a slave of.*

An Inslaver.

To insnare, *draw into a* snare, or *surprize.*

Insociable, *not* sociable, *not dispos'd for society,* or *company.*

Insociableness.

Insolence, *or* insolency.

Insolent, *proud, haughty, presumptuous,* or *sawcy.*

Insoluble, *or* indissoluble, *that cannot be dissolved.*

Insolvency, *the state of one who is not able to pay his debts.*

Insolvent, or *not capable of paying.*

Insomuch, or *so that.*

To inspect, *look narrowly into,* or *oversee.*

An Inspection.

An Inspectour.

An Inspersion, *a sprinkling on.*

Inspiration, *a being mov'd with the divine spirit.*

To inspire, or *suggest, incline to,* or *put a notion into one's head.*

To inspirit or *put life, and* Spirit *into one.*

Instability, *unsteadiness, unconstancy,* or *fickleness.*

Instable, or *unsteady.*

To install, or *put into possession of an office, properly in a Cathedral Church, where every one has a particular stall,* or *seat.*

An installation, *or* installment.

An instance, *a particular example;* also *a solicitation,* or *pursuit of a thing.*

To instance, *to give an* instance, or *example.*

Instant, *eager, earnest, urgent*

gent, or *near at hand*.
An instant, or *short moment of time*.
An Instauration, *repairing, renewing*, or *restoring to the former state*
Instead, *in the room*, or *place of*.
The instep, or *upper part of the foot*.
To instigate, *prick forward, provoke to*, or *egg on*.
An instigation.
An instigatour.
To instill, *drop in*, or *let fall by little and little*.
An Instillation.
An Instinct, *an inward motion, natural bent*, or *inclination*.
To institute, *appoint*, *ordain*, or *found*.
Institutes, *principles of Religion*, or *Law-Ordinances*.
An institution, *foundation, order*, or *appointment*.
Institution, or *the Bishop's investing a Clerk with the spirituality of a Rectory*, or *Parsonage*; *as induction intitles him to the temporality of it*.
To instruct, *teach*, or *prepare one for*.
An instructer.
An instruction.
Instructive, *full of instruction*.
Instructiveness.
An instrument (*in several senses*.)
Instrumental, *belonging to an instrument*, or *serviceable as a means*
A Mathematical, or *Musical*
Instrument-maker.
Instruments, or *tools of all sorts*.
To issue, ensue, or *follow*.
Insufficiency.
Insufficient, *not* sufficient, *unable*, or *ineffectual*.
Insular, *of*, or *belonging to an Island*.
An insult, *assault, onset*, or *affront*.
To insult, or *domineer over*.
Insuperable, *that cannot be overcome*.
Insuperableness.
Insupportable, *not to be born*, or *endured*.
An Insurance, or *security given for goods*, &c *in consideration of a sum of money*.
The Insurance-Office.
To insure *Merchandizes*, *Ships*, or *Houses*.
An insurer.
An Insurrection, *rising against*, or *seditious uprore of the people*.
An Intail, *or* fee-tail, *the conveying of an estate to a person, with limitation to the heirs of his body*.
To intail *an estate*, or *make it over in such a manner*.
An intailer.
To intangle, *to twist*, or *perplex*, or *to engage himself in*.
An intanglement.
An intangler.
Integrity, *honesty, sincerity*, or *uprightness*.
The intellect, or *faculty of understanding*.
The intellectual *parts*.
Intelligence, *advice, news*, or *correspondence*.
An intelligencer.
Intelligent, *understanding, perceiving*, or *knowing well*.
Intelligible, *plain*, or *easy to be understood*.
Intemperance, *a being*
Intemperate, *that is not master of his own appetites and affections*; or *disorderly*.
Intemperateness.
The intemperature *of the air*.
To intend, *mean*, or *purpose*.
An Intendant, *the chief governour of a French Province*.
An Intendment, *purpose*, or *meaning*.
Intense, *very great*, or *excessive*, as *an intense heat*.
Intenseness.
Intensively, or *in the highest degree*.
To be intent, or *close bent upon a thing*.
An intent, or *purpose*.
An intention, *design*, or *proposed end*.
Intentional.
Intentive, or *earnestly applying himself to*.
The intercalarday, *the odd day of leap-year*.
Intercalation, *the putting* between, or *adding of a in* February *every fourth year*.
To intercede, (*i. e. to pass between*) *to do the office of a mediator*, or *intreat in one's behalf*.
An Interceder.
To intercept, *take up by the way, prevent*, or *surprize*.
An intercession, *mediation* or *praying for another*.
An intercessour, or *mediatour*.
To interchange, *or* exchange *writings from one to another*.
Interchangeably, *mutually*, or *by turns*.
An intercourse, *mutual correspondence*, or *commerce*.
To interdict, *to forbid*, or *to suspend a Church from divine service*.
An Interdiction.
To interess, or *concern himself*.
Interest, *right, advantage profit*, or *title*; *also use-money*.
To interfere, *rub*, or *knock one heel against the other in going, as a horse does*.
Interjacent, or *lying between*.

In the interim, or *in the mean while.*

Interiour, or *more inward.*

To interlard, *or* lard *lean meat with fat.*

An interlocutory order *made in a Court of Judicature, for the present till the Cause be heard.*

To Interleave, or *put blank* leaves *of paper between the pages of a Book.*

To interline, or *insert between two* lines.

To interlope, or *intercept the traffick of a company, without lawful authority.*

An interloper.

An interlude, *that which is done between the acts of a Stage-play.*

To intermeddle, or *concern himself with another's business.*

An intermeddler.

Intermesses *in* (Cookery) *certain dishes serv'd up to table between the Courses.*

Intermediate, *that is,* or *lyes between.*

To intermingle, *or* intermix.

An intermission, or *discontinuance.*

To intermit, *cease*, or *leave off, for a while.*

An Intermittent, *pulse,* &c.

To intermix, *mingle between,* or *amongst.*

An Intermixture.

Internal, or *inward.*

To interplead, *try,* or *discuss a point, that falls out accidentally, before the main Cause can be determin'd.*

An Interpleader.

To interpolate *bring to a new form, falsify,* or *alter an Original.*

An Interpolation.

An interpolator.

To interpose, *put,* or *set between.*

An Interposition.

To interpret, *explain, expound,* or *translate out of one Language into another.*

An Interpretation.

An Interpreter.

An Interpunction, *a pointing, or distinguishing by points.*

To interr, *bury,* or *lay in the ground.*

An Interrment, or *burial.*

An interreign, *the space of time, between the death of one King and the Succession of another.*

To interrogate, *demand,* or *ask a question.*

An Interrogation.

The interrogation-point *express'd thus* (?) *in* Latin, English, &c. *and thus* (;) *in* Greek.

Interrogative, *us'd in the asking of questions.*

Interrogatory, or *belonging to questioning.*

An Interrogatory, or *examination of parties in a Law-suit.*

To interrupt, *disturb,* or *hinder.*

An Interrupter.

An Interruption.

Intersperfed, or *sprinkled here and there.*

To intertain, *or* entertain, *to treat* or *receive one.*

An Intertainment.

An Interval, *any space,* or *distance of time,* or *place.*

To intervene, or *come between.*

An Interview, or *meeting between Princes,* or *Persons of Quality.*

Interwoven, *or* work'd between, *with Silk, Silver,* &c.

Intestate, *that dyes without making a Will.*

An intestine, or *Civil War as it were in the bowels of a State.*

The intestins, or *entrals.*

To inthrall, *to bring into* thralldom, or *bondage.*

To inthrone, or *set upon the* throne.

To intice, *allure,* or *draw in cunningly.*

An Inticement.

An Inticer.

Intimacy, or *great familiarity.*

An intimate, or *bosom friend.*

To intimate, *shew, signify, hint,* or *give to understand*

An Intimation.

To intimidate, *make fearful,* or *affright.*

Intire, *or* entire, *whole, sound,* or *sincere.*

Intireness.

To intitle, *to give a* title, or *right to.*

Into, *as he went* into *the Town.*

Intolerable, or *unsufferable, that cannot be endured,* or *born.*

Intolerableness.

To intomb, or *put into a* tomb.

To intoxicate, *invenom, bewitch,* or *make drunk.*

An Intoxication.

Intractable, *that cannot be managed,* or *unruly.*

Intractableness.

To intrap, *catch in a* trap, or *ensnare.*

To intreat, or *beseech.*

An Intreaty.

To intrench, *to fortify with a* trench; also *to usurp,* or *encroach upon*

An Intrenchment.

Intricacy, *a being.*

Intricate, *entangled, perplexed,* or *difficult.*

An intrigue, *cunning design,* or *contrivance.*

Intrinsical, intrinsick *inward,* or *secret.*

To introduce, *bring,* or *lead in.*

An introduction.

Introductory.

To intrude, or *thrust himself*

ſelf rudely into a buſineſs, company, &c.
An intruder.
An intruſion.
To intruſt, or *put in* truſt *with*.
An intuition, *beholding*, or *looking upon*.
The intuitive *faculty*.
To invade, *ſet upon*, *attack*, or *uſurp*.
An invader.
Invalid, *of little force*, or *ſtrength*.
To invalidate, *weaken*, *annul*, or *make void*.
Invalidity.
An invaſion, or *inrode into a Country*, *made by an Enemy*.
Invective, *reproaching*, or *railing*.
An invective, *vehement ſpeaking againſt*, or *outrage in words*.
To inveigh, *declaim*, *rail*, or *ſpeak bitterly againſt*.
To inveigle, *entice*, or *deceive by fair words*.
An inveigler.
To invelop, *cover*, or *wrap up*.
To invenom, or *poiſon*.
To invent, *find out*, *deviſe*, or *contrive*.
An inventer.
An invention.
Inventive, *ingenious*, or *apt to invent*.
An inventory, or *liſt of a deceaſed Perſon's goods and chattels*.
Inventory'd *of which an* inventory *is made*.
An inverſion.
To invert, or *turn the wrong way*, or *upſide-down*.
To inveſt, *to put in poſſeſſion of a thing*; or *to ſet down before a place*, *in order to beſiege it*.
An inveſtigation, *tracing as it were by the footſteps*, *ſtrict ſearch*, or *diligent enquiry*.

An inveſtiture, or inveſture, *a livery of ſeiſin*, or *putting in poſſeſſion of an eſtate*, &c.
Inveterate, *rooted in*, or *ſettled by long continuance*.
Invidious, *that cauſes envy*.
Invigilancy, *a want of* vigilancy, or *watchfulneſs*.
To invigorate, *to give vigour*, *courage*, or *life to*.
Invincible, *that cannot be overcome*.
Invincibleneſs.
Inviolable, *not to be* violated, or *broken*.
Inviolate, *not* violated, or *entire*.
To inviron, *or* environ, *to ſurround*, or *compaſs about*.
Inviſible, *not to be ſeen*.
Inviſibleneſs.
An invitation.
To invite, *bid*, *call*, or *deſire one to come*.
An inviter.
An inundation, *flood*, or *overflowing of waters*.
To invocate, invoke, or *call upon*.
An invocation.
An invoice, or *particular account of goods*, *with their value*; *cuſtom*, &c. *ſent by a Merchant to his Factor*, or *Correſpondent*.
To involve, *entangle*, or *engage in*.
Involuntary, *contrary to one's own will*.
To inure, or *accuſtom*.
Invulnerable, *that cannot be wounded*.
Inward, *on the inſide*.
The inward, or *entrals of a Beaſts*.

J O

Job's *tears*, *an herb*.
A Jobb, or *ſmall piece of work*.
A Jobber.

A Stock-Jobber.
A Jobbernoll, or *loggerhead*.
A Jockey, or *horſe-rider*.
Jocoſe, *full of jokes*, or *jeſts*.
Jocular, or *ſportful*.
Jocund, or *merry*.
Jocundneſs.
A Jog, *and to* jog, or *jolt*.
To joggle, or *move*.
A John-apple.
Poor-John *a fiſh*.
Sweet-John, *a flower*.
St. John's-bread, *a tree*.
St. John's-wort, *an herb*.
A joice, or joiſt, *a piece of Timber us'd in building*.
To joiſt *a floor*.
A Joll, or *head of Salmon*.
A Cock's jollop.
Jollineſs, *or* jollity.
Jolly, or *brave and briſk*.
A Jolt, *and to* jolt, or *jog as a Coach does*.
A Jolt-head, or *great head*.
Jonquil, *a ſort of flower*.
Joſeph's flowers.
A Jot, *tittle* or *point*.
Jovial, *pleaſant* or *merry*.
The Hawk, jouks, or *falls a-ſleep*.
A Journal, *Day-book*, *Regiſter*, or *account of what paſs'd daily*.
A Journey, or *travelling by land*.
A Journey-man, *one that works by the day*.
Journey-work.
Jowler, *i. e. great-head*, *a Dog's name*.
Joy, or *gladneſs*.
To joy, *to rejoice*, or *to give joy*.
Joyful, *or* joyous.
Joyfulneſs.
To joyn, *couple*, *ſet*, or *faſten to*, or *unite*, &c.
A Joyner.
Joynery, or *joyners-work*.
A Joynt (*in ſeveral ſenſes*)
To joynt *a piece of meat*, or

or *part it by cutting the joynts.*

A long-joynted *horse.*

A Joynt-heir, or *coheir.*

Joynt-Tenants *that hold lands,* or *tenements by one title.*

A Joynter, *a kind of plane to smooth boards.*

A Joynture, or Dowry *settled upon a Wife; in respect of marriage.*

A Joyst, or joist *in building.*

I R

Iris, *a kind of* Flower *de-luce.*

Irksome, *troublesome,* or *tedious.*

Iron.

An Iron-bar.

A Cramp-iron.

An Iron-monger.

Iron-sick *as a ship is; when the spikes and nails are so worn out,* or *eaten away with rust, that they stand hollow and let in water through the Planks*

Iron-wort, *an herb.*

An Ironical *expression.*

An Irony, *a figure of* Rhetorick, *when one speaks contrary to what he means, with a design to mock another.*

To Irradiate, or *dart its beams upon.*

An irradiation.

Irrational, or *void of reason.*

Irreconcilable, *not to be* reconciled

Irrecoverable, *not to be* recovered.

Irrefragable, *undeniable, that cannot be baffled,* or *withstood.*

Irregular, *not* regular, *out of rule,* or *disorderly.*

Irregularity, or *going out of rule; more especially such as hinders a man from taking Holy Orders*

as being base born, maimed, much deformed, guilty of any crime, &c.

Irreligion.

Irreligious, *ungodly,* or *profane.*

Irremediable, *that cannot be* remedied, or *helped.*

Irremissible, *not to be remitted,* or *forgiven.*

Irreparable, *that cannot be repaired,* or *restored to its first state.*

Irreprehensible, *unreprovable,* or *blameless.*

Irresistible, *not to be resisted,* or *withstood.*

Irresolute, *unresolved, doubting,* or *wavering.*

Irresolution, or *want of* resolution.

Irreverence, or *want of respect.*

Irreverent, *that yields no reverence,* or *respect; profane,* or *rude.*

Irrevocable, *not to be revoked,* or *called back.*

Irrision, *laughing to scorn,* or *mocking.*

To irritate, *provoke,* or *stir up.*

An irritation *of humours.*

An irruption, *violent breaking in; an inrode,* or *forcible entrance.*

I S

An Isabella *colour.*

An Ising-pudding.

An Island, *a land encompass'd on all sides with the Sea,* or *fresh water rivers.*

An Islander, or *inhabitant of an* Island.

An Isle, or Island.

An Isle *of a Church.*

An Issue, *offspring; effect, end of a business, matter depending in suit,* &c.

An Issue, (or *running sore.*)

An Issue *in the Arm,* &c.

To Issue, *stream, spring,* or *sally forth.*

Issueless, *that has no issue* or *children.*

An Isthmus, or *narrow neck of land between two seas, adjoyning to the continent.*

The Corinthian Isthmus.

It, as it *is I.*

The Italick *letter,* or *character.*

The Itch, *a disease, and* to itch.

Itchy, or *troubled with the* itch.

An Item, or *caution.*

To iterate, *do over again* or *repeat.*

An iteration.

An Itinerant, *travelling,* or *taking a journey.*

An Itinerary, *a book that describes the roads to several places.*

Its (*from it*) *as to put a sword into its scabbard.*

It's *for* it is, *as* it's *well done.*

J U

Jubarb, or *house-leek, an herb.*

A Jubilation, *shouting for joy,* or *solemn rejoycing.*

The year of Jubile,lee,(*i. e.* rejoycing, or releasing) *celebrated by the ancient* Jews *every* 50th *year, when bond-men were made free, possessions return'd to the first owners,* &c.

Among Christians a Jubilee *year was ordain'd by Pope* Boniface VIII. *A.D.* 1300. *to be kept every hundredth year; afterwards appointed every fiftieth year by* Clement VI. *and lastly in* 1475. *every twenty fifth year by* Sixtus IV. *which custom is still continued.*

Judaical,

Judaical *or* judaick, *of*, or *belonging to the* Jews.
Judaism, *the religion* cu*stoms*, or *rites of the* Jews.
To Judaize, or *follow the Doctrine of the* Jews.
A Judge *in civil*, or *criminal causes*.
A Judge Lateral.
To judge, *suppose, deem, determine, hear causes*, &c.
Judgement (*in several senses*.)
Judicature, as *a Court of Judicature*.
Judicial, ary, *relating to a Judge*, or *judgement*.
Judicious, *full of judgment, rational*, or *discreet*.
A Jug, *a sort of drinking-pot*.
A Juggle, or *trick*.
To juggle, or *play legerde-main*.
A Juggler.
The jugular, or *throat-vein*.
The juice *of meat*, or *fruit*.
Juiceless, *that has no* juice.
Juiciness, *a being*
Juicy, or *full of* juice.
A Jujube, *a sort of* Italian *Plum like an Olive*.
To Juke, *or* jug *as birds do when ready to go to roost*.
A Julep, *a kind of physical drink*.
July, *the month so call'd in honour of* Julius Cæsar *the first* Roman *Emperour, who likewise established the* Julian *year, consisting of* 365 *days, and* 6 *hours; which account of time is still us'd in* England.
A Jumble, *and*
To jumble, *mingle together*, or *confound*
A Jumbler.
A Jump, or *short coat*.
A Jump, or *leap*, *and to* jump.
A Jumper.
A Juncto, *cabal, private faction*, or *combination*.
A Juncture, *an instant of time*, or *state of affairs*
June, *one of the* 12 *months of the year, so call'd* (*according to* Festus) *as it were* Juno's *month*, or *from* Juniores, *i. e.* the *younger sort of people*.
A Juneting-Apple.
Junior, *younger*, or *of later standing*; *as he is my* Junior.
A Juniper tree.
A Junk, *a sort of ship*.
To Junket, *go a* junketting, or *to hunt after*.
Junkets, or *dainty dishes*.
Ivory, *workt from the teeth of Elephants*, or *sea-horses*.
An Ivory-comb.
Jupiter's distaff, *an herb*.
A Jurat, or *sworn assistant for the Government of a corporation*; as
The Mayor and jurats *of* Rye, *&c*.
A Juridical day, or *Court-day*.
Jurisdiction, *power and authority to administer justice*, &c.
A Juror, or jurour, *one of the*
Jury, *a company of men sworn to deliver the truth, according to the evidence given before them about the matter in question*.
The Grand Jury, *consisting of* 24 *grave and substantial persons, who take cognizance of all bills of inditement, which they either approve by writing upon them* Billa vera, or *disallow by indorsing* Ignoramus.
The Petty-jury, *of twelve men at least, are impanell'd upon all sorts of Causes, both criminal and civil, and upon due examination, bring in their verdict*.
Just now, just so, just then &c.
Just, *right, lawful, equitable*, &c.
Justice, or *equity*.
A Justice, *a* Judge *that administers justice*.
A Justice of peace.
The Lord chief justice *of the King's Bench*, &c.
Justifiable, *that may be justified*.
To justifie, *to maintain, to clear himself, make good, prove by Evidence*, &c.
To Justle, or *push*.
To justle, just, or *run a tilt*.
A Justler.
Justs, or *Turnaments, tiltings on horse-back with lances*, or *spears*.
To jut out, *as a wall does*.
A Jutty, or *building that* juts *out*.
Juvenile, or *youthful*.
Ivy, *an herb*.
Ground-Ivy.
Virginian-Ivy.

KA

A Kalender, Calendar, or *Almanack*.
Karle-hemp.
A Katharine-pear.
To kaw, *as a Jack-daw does*.
A Kay, key, or *wharf*.

KE

To keck, *as one does when something sticks to the throat*.
Kecks, *hollow stalks*, or *kicks*.
A Kedger, *or* kedge, *the least sort of Anchor*.
A Keel, *a kind of vessel to cool drink in*.
The Keel, or *bottom of a ship*.

A

A Keeling-fish.
Keen, *sharp*, or *eager*.
Keennels.
A Keep, or *Fort in a Castle.*
To Keep (*in all senses.*)
A Keeper.
An Under-Keeper.
The Lord Keeper of the great Seal of England, *whose office is the same in effect with that of the Lord High Chancellour, the difference only lying in the Title. Thro' his hands pass all Charters, Commissions, and Grants of the King under the great Seal.*
The Lord Keeper of the Privy-Seal, *through whose hands are convey'd all Charters,* &c. *sig ed by the King, before they come to the great Seal, and some Instruments that do not pass the great Seal at all.*
A Keg, *of Sturgeon.*
To set one's arms a-kembo.
A Ken, *and* to ken, or *spy out.*
A Kennel *in a street,* &c.
A Dog-kennel.
Kennets, *a sort of course* Welsh *Cloth*
Kept, (*from to keep*)
A Kerchief, *a linnen-cloth worn by some women on their heads.*
An Hand-kerchief.
A Kern, or *Country-bumpkin.*
A Kernel *of fruit,* or *of the body.*
Kernelly, or *full of* kernels.
Kernel-wort, *an herb.*
Kersey, *a course sort of woollen cloth.*
A Kestrel, *a kind of hawk.*
A Ketch, *a small ship.*
A Kettle, or *Caldron.*
A Kettle-Drum.
A Kettle-Drummer.
A Kew, or *humour.*

A Key *for a lock.*
A Key-bearer.
A Key-hole.
A Key, or *wharf for landing*, or *shipping off goods.*
A Key, or *cliff in musick.*
Ashen-keys.
The Keys *of an Organ.*

K I

A Kibe, *on the heel.*
A kick, *and to* kick.
A Kick-shaw, *or* French *ragoo.*
A Kid, or *young goat.*
To Kid, or *bring forth* kids.
A Kidder, *badger*, or *engrosser of Corn.*
A Kidnapper, *stealer*, or *enticer of Children,*&c. *to sell them in order to be transported.*
A Kidney.
Kidney-beans, or *french-beans.*
Kidney-vetch.
Kidney-wort, *an herb.*
A Kilderkin, *half a barrel,* or *the eighth part of a hogshead.*
To Kill, or *slay.*
Kill-buck, *a dog's name.*
A killer.
A Kiln, or *furnace.*
A Brick-kiln.
A Lime-kiln.
Kin *by blood*, or *marriage.*
Kind, *gentle, loving*, or *obliging.*
A Kind, *sort, sex*, or *manner.*
A Kinder, or *company of Cats.*
To kindle *a fire.*
To kindle, or *bring forth young, as a hare does.*
Kindness, or *courtesy.*
Kindred, or *relations.*
A King, or *soveraign Prince.*
A King at Arms, or *chief of the Heralds.*

The Kings-evil, *a disease.*
King-cob, *an herb.*
A King's-fisher, *a bird.*
King's-spear, *an herb.*
A Kingdom, *a country*, or *several countries subject to a King.*
Kinsfolks, *persons related one to another.*
A Kinsman.
A Kinswoman.
A Kintal, *about a hundred pound weight.*
Kipper-nuts.
The Kirk, or *Church of* Scotland.
A Kirtle, *a short kind of jacket.*
A Kiss, *and to* kiss.
A Kit, or *pocket-Violin.*
Kit-keys, or *ashen keys.*
A Kitchen, *where meat is dress'd,* &c.
A Kitchen-boy.
A Kitchen-maid.
Kitchen-stuff.
Kitchen-tackle.
A Kite, *a bird of prey.*
A Paper-kite.
The Kite-fish.
Kite's-foot, *an herb.*
A Kitling, or kitten, *a little cat.*
To Kitten, or kittle; *to bring forth* kittens.

K N

A Knack, or *toy*; also *a peculiar skill.*
Knags, *that grow out of the hart's horns near the forehead.*
A Knap, or *top of a hil*
To knap, *snap*, or *break.*
Knap-bottle, *an herb.*
A Knap-sack, or *snap-sack.*
Knap-weed.
Silver-knap-weed.
A Knave, *a* Saxon *word properly denoting a servant, but now commonly taken for a paltry dishonest fellow, cheat*, or *shark.*
Knavery.

Knavish,

Knavish.
Knavishness, *or a knavish disposition.*
To kneed *dough.*
A Kneeder.
A Kneeding-trough.
A Knee.
Knee-grass.
Knee-holm, *a shrub.*
The Knee-pan.
A pair of knee-strings.
To kneel, kneel down, or *bow the* knee.
A Knell, or *passing-bell.*
Knew, *(from to* know)
A Knick *of the fingers.*
A Knick-knack, or *childrens-toy.*
A Knife *to cut victuals with.*
A Chopping-knife.
A Cutting-knife *for shoomakers.*
A Pen-knife.
A Pruning-knife.
A Knight *in* Saxon, *one that serves*, or *bears arms on horse-back; now a title of honour, next above an Esquire.*
A Knight, *(a sea-term) a piece of timber carv'd in the shape of some head, of which there are chiefly two in a ship, viz. the* main-knight *and the* fore-knight, *having four sheevers for the halliards, and one for the top-ropes to run in.*
To Knight one, or *make him a* knight.
The Knight-Marshal, *an Officer in the King's house who takes cognizance of offences committed within the verge of the Court*, &c.
A Knight of the Post, *a profligate wretch hir'd to swear falsely.*
Knighthood, *the order*, or *dignity of a* Knight.
Knight-service, *a tenure that oblig'd a man to bear arms in war, for the defence of his country and was abolish'd by* 12 Car. 2.
Knights Bachelors, or *simple* Knights *of the lowest order, but most ancient institution.*
Knights Banneret *made in the field, by cutting off the point of their Standard, and turning it as it were into a* Banner. *They may display their arms in the King's army*, as Barons do; *and such as are created under the standard, by the King personally present, take place of* Baronets.
Knights Baronet, *an order establish'd by King* James I. *A. D.* 1611.; *who are next to* Barons *in dignity, taking place of* Knights Bachelors , *and ordinary* Bannerets.
Knights of the Bath, *so call'd because they usually bath'd themselves and observ'd several religious ceremonies the night before their creation. They take place of* Knights Bachelors; *but come after* Baronets.
Knights-errant, or wandring fabulous Knights, *celebrated in Romances for their wonderful exploits.*
Knights of the Garter, *or* of St. George, *the most noble order, consisting of* 25 *Companions, of whom the Sovereign is chief instituted by K.* Edward III. *An.* 1350. *The ornaments of this Order are a blew Garter, deck'd with precious Stones, and a gold Buckle worn on the left Leg; a* Chaperon *Collar of St.* George; *Crown, Cloke, Kirtle*, &c. *To these K.* Charles I. *added the Cross of* England, *encircled with the Garter and Motto, as also with Silver-beams resembling those of the Sun in full lustre; to be worn by all the companions on the left side of their upper Garment.*
Knights of St. John of Jerusalem, *a Religious Order erected by K.* Baldwin, I *about* 1104. *They remov'd from* Jerusalem *to* Rhodes, *and were thence call'd* Knights of Rhodes, *till expell'd by the* Turks *in* 1523. *Their chief seat is now in the Isle of* Maltha, *and they are well known by the name of* Knights of Maltha. *This Order had large possessions in* England, *and their Prior the first in dignity, sat in the House of Lords, but they were suppress'd by K.* Henry VIII. *for adhering to the Pope.*
Knights of the shire, *two eminent Gentlemen chosen by the free-holders in every County, to serve in Parliament:* Esquires *are also admitted to this Office, provided they are resident in the respective Counties, for which they are return'd.*
Knights of the Temple, *or* Knights Templars, *instituted by Pope* Gelasius, or *(as others say) by* Baldwin II. *K. of* Jerusalem, *A. D.* 1119, *to defend the* Temple, *H. Sepulchre and Christian strangers, against the assaults of Infidels: They usually wore a blew Cloke, with a red Cross. This Order flourish'd* 200 *years, and was spread far in Christendom; but at last growing vicious and too powerful, they were suppress'd by Pope* Clement V.

Clement V. 1309, *as also by the Council of Vienna, in 1312. Their revenues were given to other religious houses, and more especially to the Knights of St. John of* Jerusalem, *of whom the Lawyers purchas'd the* Temple-inn *founded by them in* Fleet-street.

Knight-fee, *an inheritance sufficient to maintain a* Knight. *Such as had* 20. *l.* per. an. *in* fee, or *for life*, by 1 Ed. 2. *might be compell'd to be made Knights: which Statute was repeal'd* 17 Car. 1.

Knights-spur, *an herb.*

To knit (*in several senses*)

Knit-back, *an herb.*

A Knitter *of Stockings.*

A Knitting-needle.

A knob, or *bunch.*

To Knob, *bunch out*, or *grow into* knobs.

Knobby, or *full of knobs.*

A Knock, *and to* knock (*in all senses.*)

The Knocker *of a door.*

A Knoll, or *little hill.*

A Knop, or *top of a flower.*

Gold-knops, *a flower.*

A Knot, *and to* knot (*in several senses*)

The Knot-berry bush.

Knot-grass.

Knottiness.

Knotty, or *full of* knots.

Knots, *a delicious sort of small Fowl, well known in some parts of* England *and formerly much esteemed by the* Danish *King* Canutus.

To know, *be acquainted with, have skill, or be well vers'd in.*

To knowl, or *ring a* knell.

Knowledge, *understanding, or skill.*

Known.

A Knuckle, or *joint in a bone.*

Knuckle-deep.

A Knur, knurl, or *knot in wood.*

L A

A Label, or *ribbon of a* Mitre, or Garland; *a slip of Parchment hanging at an Indenture*, &c. *Also the three lines that hang down from the file of a Scutcheon, and denote the elder brother.*

A Laboratory, or *Chymist's Work-house.*

Laborious, *painful toilsome*, or *that takes great pains.*

Laboriousness.

Labour, *and to* labour, or *take pains.*

A Labourer.

A Ship that labours, *i. e. rolls, and tumbles.*

A Labyrinth, or *maze with so many windings and turnings, that one cannot get out, without a guide, or a clew of thread for direction.*

Lacca, or lake, *a kind of gum.*

Lace.

To Lace; *to tie with*, or *to set on a* lace.

Bone-lace.

A Hair-lace.

A Neck-lace.

A Lace-maker.

Laced-time, *an herb.*

Lack, *want*, or *defect.*

To lack, *want*, or *stand in need of.*

Lacker, *a sort of varnish us'd in imitation of gilding.*

A Lackey, or *foot-man.*

A Laconick-style, *i. e. close and pithy, so call'd from the* Lacedemonians, *a people of* Greece, *who affected a short way of expression.*

A Lad, *a young stripling.*

A Ladder.

Ladder-to-heaven, *an herb.*

To lade, *to load*, or *to scoop out.*

Laden, as *laden with rich commodities.*

A Bill of lading.

A Ladle *for a pot.*

The Ladles *of the water-mill-wheel.*

A Lady, *a woman of quality.*

The Lady-cow, *a kind of Beetle.*

Lady-laces, *a striped grass.*

Lady-ship, *the dignity of a* Lady.

Ladies-bed-straw.
Ladies-bower.
Ladies-comb.
Ladies-glove.
Ladies-hair.
Ladies-Looking-glass
Ladies-mantle.
Ladies-milk.
Ladies-seal.
Ladies-slipper.
Ladies-smock.
Ladies- thistle, or *white-thistle.*
Lady-traces.
} *herbs.*

Lag, *or* last.

To lag, or *stay behind.*

Lag-wort, *an herb.*

Laick, *belonging to the* Laity.

Laid (*from to* lay.)

Lain, (*from to* lye)

Lair *a place where Deer harbour by day.*

The Laity, or *people not in Orders, in opposition to the* Clergy.

A Lake, *a place of a large extent, deep and full of water, having no communication with the Sea, unless it be through some great River.*

A Lamb, or *sheep under a year old.*

Lamb, or *Lambs-flesh.*

A Lambkin, *a young*, or *little Lamb.*

Lambs-lettice.
Lambs-tongue.
} *herbs.*

Lame, *depriv'd of the use of one's Limbs*, or *imperfect*.
To lame, or *make* lame.
Lameness.
To lament, *mourn*, or *bewail*.
Lamentable, *to be lamented*.
A Lamentation.
A Lamenter.
To Lamm, or *baste one's sides*.
Lammas, or lammas-day, (q. *lamb-mas*, or *loaf-mas*) *the first day of* August.
A Lamp *to burn with oil*.
The Lampas, or lampers, *a disease in horses, when their gums swell*, &c.
A Lampern, or lampril, *a little lamprey*.
A Lampoon, or *libel in verse*.
To Lampoon *the Court*.
A Lamprey, *a fish*.
A Sea-Lamprey.
A Lanar-hawk.
A Lanaret, or *male* lanar.
A Lance, *a kind of weapon*.
To lance, *cut*, or *scarify*.
A Lancepesado, *that commands ten Soldiers, the lowest Officer in a foot-company*.
A Lancer, or *lance-man*.
A Lancet, *us'd by Surgeons, in letting blood*, &c.
To lanch *a ship*, or *set it a float*.
Land, or *ground*.
To land, *to come to*, or *to set on shore*.
A Landedman, *one that has large possessions in* land.
A Land-flood.
A Landgrave, *a Count*, or *Earl of a Country in* Germany.
A Land-lady.
Land-leapers-spurge.
Land-lock'd, or *shut in between the* lands, (*a Sea-term*.)
A Land-loper, or *vagabond*.
A Land-lord, or *proprietary of Land, Houses*, &c.
A Land-mark, or *boundary*.
A Land-pirate, or *high-way-man*.
A Landress, or *washer-woman*.
A Landry, *the place where cloths are wash'd*, &c.
A Landskip, *a picture representing land, hills, woods, trees, rivers*, &c.
A Land-spaniel.
A Lane, or *narrow passage*.
A By-lane.
A Language, or *speech*.
Langued (*in* Heraldry) *tongued*, or *having a tongue*.
Languid, *faint*, or *weak*.
To languish, *lye drooping, pine* or *consume away*.
Languishment.
Lank, *slender*, or *limber*.
Lankness.
A Lanner, or lanar *hawk*.
A Lantern, or Lanthorn *to give light in the dark*.
A Lantern-maker.
A Lap, or *bosome*; also *the plait, or fold of a garment*.
To lap, or *lick up, as dogs do*; or *to fold up*.
A Lap-dog.
Lap-eared; *that has hanging ears*.
A Lapidary, or *jeweller*.
The lappet *of a gown*.
Lap-piece, *the opening of a hound at his game*.
A Lapse, or *slip*; also *the forfeiture of a presentation to a benefice, when neglected by the Patron for six months*.
Lapsed, or *fallen*; as *the lapsed condition of mankind*.
A Lap-wing, *a bird*.
Larboard, (*a Sea-Term*) *the left side of the Ship*.
Larceny, *a Law-word that signifies theft, properly of personal goods, or chattels in the owner's absence*.
Petty-Larceny, *when the things stolen do not exceed the value of* 12 d.
The Larch-tree, or *Turpentine tree*.
Lard, *the fat of pork beaten*.
To lard *meat, to stuff it with* lard or *fat*.
A Larder, *an office in a nobleman's house where the Victuals are kept*.
A Yeoman of the Larder.
A Larding-pin.
A Lare, or *turner's lath*.
Large, *great*, or *ample*.
A Large *in Musick, consisting of eight sembriefs*.
Largeness.
Largess, *bounty*, or *a great gift*.
A Larinch, or *larch-tree*.
A Lark, *a bird*.
The Capped-Lark.
A Sea-lark.
A Sky-lark.
A Tit-lark.
A Wood-lark.
Lark-heel, or Larks-spurr, *an herb*.
Yellow larks-heel.
Lascivious, *wanton*, or *frolicksome*.
Lasciviousness.
Laser-wort, or lazer-wort, *an herb*.
A Lash, *and* to lash, *or whip*, &c.
A Lasher.
A Lask, or *looseness of the belly*.
A Lass, or *young wench*.
The last, or *latest*.
A Last, *a sort of measure*, as *a* Last *of* Cod-fish, i.e. 12 *barrels*: *Of* Corn, *or* Rapeseed 10 *quarters*: *Of* Hides 12 *dozen*: *Of* Leather 20 *dickers*: *Of* Pitch, Tar, *or* Ashes, 14 *barrels*: *Of* Wood 12 *sacks*, &c.
A Shoomaker's last.
To last, *continue*, or *endure*.

Lastage

Lastage, *a custom*, or *duty paid for wares sold by the* Last.
A Latch, *of a door.*
A Latchet *of a shoo.*
Late, *as* late *in the year.*
Lateness.
Latent, or *lying hid.*
The Later-math, or *after-pasture.*
Lateral, *as a* judge-lateral, or *Assessour.*
A Lath *such as are used in building.*
To lath, or *cover with laths.*
A Turner's lath.
A Lathe, or *large division of a County, containing* 3 *or* 4 *hundreds*, as *in* Kent, Sussex, *&c.*
A Lather, or *froth of sope.*
To lather, or *rise up in a* lather.
Latine, as *the* Latine *tongue.*
A Latinism, or *latine expression.*
A Latinist, *one well vers'd in the* latine *tongue.*
Latitude, or *breadth.*
The Latitude *of a place (in* Geography *) is its distance North* or *South from the Equinoctial line.*
A Latitudinarian, *one that takes too much liberty in point of Religion.*
Latten, *in, Iron tinned over.*
Latter; *as to think of his* latter *end.*
A lattice-window, *made with cross-bars of wood, iron*, &c.
Lattised *done in form of a* Lattice.
Laud, *and*
To laud, or *praise.*
Laudable, *commendable*, or *praise-worthy.*
Laudanum, *a sort of gum, from the leaves of the shrub* Cistus ledon.
Lavender, *an herb.*
French lavender.
Sea-lavender.
Lavender-Cotton.
A Laver, or *Vessel to wash in.*
A Laverock, *a kind of bird.*
To laugh (*in several senses.*)
A Laugher.
A Laughing-stock.
Laughter.
Lavish, or *prodigal.*
To lavish, *lash out*, or *squander away.*
Lavishness.
A Laund, *or* lawn *in a Park.*
Lawreate, *crowned with laurel; as a Poet* Laureate.
A Laurel-tree.
Spurge-laurel.
A Law, *statute*, or *ordinance*; as *the* Law *of Nature.*
A Law-giver, *or* Law-maker.
A Law-suit, or *process in* Law.
To law *a dog*, or *cut out the ball of his foot.*
Lawful.
Lawfulness.
Lawless.
Lawn, *a sort of fine cloth.*
A Lawn, or *plain in a Park.*
A Lawyer, or *practiser in the* law.
Laxative, or *loosening.*
I lay, or *did lye.*
A Lay *and to* lay (*in all senses.*)
A Layer, or *young sprout.*
A Layer, *bed*, or *channel of a Sea-creek, where Oisters are thrown in, to breed.*
Lay-land, or *fallow ground that lies untilled.*
A Lay-man, or *secular Person, as oppos'd to a Clergy-man.*
A Lay-stall, or *dunghill.*
A Lazar; *one full of sores and scabs, a leper.*
A Lazaretto, or Lazar-house, *an hospital for lepers*, &c.
A Lazarole-tree.
Laziness.
Lazy, or *slothfull.*
The Lazule, *or azure stone, a blewish kind of marble.*

L E

Leacherous, *given to*
Leachery, or *lustfulness.*
Lead, *a Metal.*
To lead, or *do over with lead.*
Black-lead.
White-lead.
Red-lead.
A Lead-plummet.
Lead-wort, *an herb.*
Leaden, or *made of* lead.
The Leads *of a house.*
To lead, or *conduct.*
A Leader.
A Ring-leader, or *head of a party.*
A Leaf *of a tree, plant*, &c.
Leaf-gold.
A League, *Covenant*, or *agreement*; also *a measure of way, containing the space of three miles.*
A Leaguer, or *siege.*
A Leak, *and*
To leak, or *spring a* leak, i. e. *to take in water as a Ship does.*
Leaky, or *full of* leaks.
A Leam, or leash, *a line to hold a dog*, or *hawk in*
Lean, or *lean meat.*
Lean, *opposite to fat, slender, scraggy, barren*, &c.
To lean, *incline*, or *bend.*
A Leaning-stock.
Leanness (*from* lean.)
A Leap, *and to* leap, *or jump.*
A Leap, or *weel to take fish in.*
A Leaper.
The Leap-year, *in which are* 366 *days.*

To

To learn, or *attain to the knowledge of a thing.*
A Learned man.
A Learner.
Learnt.
A Lease, *a letting*, or *demising of Lands*, or *Tenements to another for term of years*, or *Life, for a rent reserved.*
A Lease Parole, or *Lease made by word of mouth.*
A Leassee, *the person to whom a Lease is granted.*
A Leassor, *he that lets it.*
To lease, or *glean corn.*
A Leaser, or *gleaner.*
A Leash, or *thong to tye beasts with.*
A Leash of *hounds, hares*, &c. *i. e. three.*
Least (*from* little) *as not in the* least.
Leasure, or *time to spare.*
Leasurely, *or* leasurably.
Leather, *made of the skin of beasts.*
A Leather-bottle.
A Leather-dresser.
A Leather-gilder.
A Leather-seller.
Leathern, or *made of leather.*
Leave, *licence*, or *permission.*
To leave, *let alone*, *forsake, give over*, &c.
Leaved, *that has leaves*, as
Broad-leaved.
Narrow-leaved.
Leaven, *to mingle with Dough.*
To leaven, or *put in leaven.*
A Leaver, *a bar to lift*, or *bear timber.*
Leaves (*from* leaf) *as the* leaves *of a Tree*, &c.
A Lecture, *reading*, or *lesson.*
A Lecturer, *a publick reader professor*, or *preacher.*
Led (*from* to lead)
A Ledge.
A Ledger-book *in Merchants accounts.*
The Lee (*a sea-term*) *that part which is opposite to the wind.*
A Lee-shore, *upon which the wind blows.*
A Leech-worm.
A Horse-leech, *an insect.*
A Leek, *a plant.*
House-leek, *an herb.*
The Leer, or lair *of a Deer, the place where he lies to dry himself from the dew.*
To leer, *to cast a cunning*, or *wishly look.*
The Lees, or *dregs, of wine*, &c.
A Leet, or Court-leet, *held in every mannour to enquire of all offences under high Treason.*
The Leetch, or *middle of a sail.*
A Leeward *ship*, i. e. *a ship that does not sail so near the wind as she might.*
A Leeward-Tide, *when the wind and tide go both one way.*
Left, (*from* to leave) *forsaken*, or *not medled with.*
Left, *as the* left hand.
Left-handed.
The Leg, *from the knee to the ankle.*
Leg-harness
Legged, *as*
Baker-legg'd.
Bow-legg'd.
Crooked-legg'd.
Crump-legg'd.
A Legacy, or *gift made over by a last will and testament.*
Legal, *according to*, or *proper to the Law.*
Legality
A Legatary, or legatee, *he or she to whom any thing is bequeathed.*
A Legate, *the Pope's Ambassadour.*
A Legateship, *the office and function of a Legate.*
A Legend, or *fabulous relation*; also *the words that are stampt about the edge of a piece of Coin.*
The Golden-Legend *a book of the lives of Saints.*
Legendary stories.
Legerdemain, or *slight of hand.*
Legible, or *that may be easily read.*
A Legion, *a* Roman *body of Soldiers containing an uncertain number of men, from 3 to 6 thousand.*
Legionary, *belonging to a* legion.
Legislative, *that has power of making Laws.*
A Legislatour, or *Law-giver.*
Legitimate, *according to Law, lawful and right*
To legitimate, *a bastard.*
Legitimation.
A Lemmon, *a fruit.*
A Lempet, or *limpin-fish.*
To lend, *or* lend *out.*
A Lender.
Length *of time, place*, &c.
To lengthen, or *make long.*
Lenitive, *that eases*, or *asswages pain.*
A Lenitive, or *Medicine proper for that purpose.*
Lenity, or *gentleness.*
Lent, (*from to* lend,) *as money*, lent.
Lent, or *the season of* lent *the time of fasting forty days before Easter.*
Lenten *belonging to* lent.
A Lentil, *a kind of pulse.*
The Lentisck, or *mastick-tree.*
A Leonard-hawk.
A Leopard, *a wild beast.*
Leopard's-bane, *an herb.*
A Leper, *a leprous man*, or *woman.*
Lepid, *witty and pleasant.*

The Leprosy, *a Disease causing a scurf all over the body.*

Leprous, *afflicted with* leprosy.

Leprousness.

A Lerry, or *curtain-lecture.*

Less, *or* lesser.

To lessen, or *make* less.

Lesses, *the dung of wild beasts.*

A Lesson, *reading*, or *instruction.*

Lest, *or* lest that.

A Let, or *hind'rance.*

To let (*in all senses.*)

Lethargick, *belonging to*, or *sick of*

The Lethargy, or *drowsy disease.*

A Letter *of the Alphabet*, as *A. B. C.* &c.

A Letter *writ and sent to an absent person.*

The Italick Letter, or *Character.*

The Roman-Letter.

A Letter of Attorney, *authorizing an* Attorney, or *assign, to do a lawful act in one's stead*; as *to give seisin of lands, to receive debts, to sue a third person*, &c.

Letters *of* Mark, *or* Mart, *impowering one to take by force of arms, such goods as are due by the law of* Mark, or *reprisals.*

Letters Patent, *i. e. open writings sealed with the great Seal of* England; *by which a man is authoriz'd to do*, or *enjoy, what otherwise of himself he could not.*

A Letter-founder, *that casts Letters for Printers.*

Lettered, or *well learned.*

Lettice, *a sallet herb.*

Cabbage-lettice.

Headed-Lettice.

Sea-lettice, or *milk-thistle.*

Wild lettice.

A Lettice, or lattice-window.

The Levant, *the east*, or *eastern countries, especially those near the mediterranean Sea.*

The Levant-fleet.

The Levantines, or *People that live in the* levant.

Level, *even or plain.*

To Level, or *make* level.

A Carpenter's Level.

Level-coil, or *hitch-buttock, a term us'd in gaming, when three play by turns, two only playing at a time, and the loser sitting out.*

A Levellier.

A Leveret, or *young hare.*

Leviathan, *a* Hebrew *word, signifying a sea-dragon*, or *whale.*

The Levites, *those of the tribe of* Levi, *who took their name from* Levi, *one of* Jacob's *sons, and had the Priesthood for their inheritance.*

Levitical, *of*, or *belonging to the* Levites.

Leviticus, *one of* Moses's *five books, shewing the functions of the Levitical order.*

Levity, or *fickleness.*

A Levy *a raising of Taxes*, or *soldiers.*

To levy *raise, collect*, or *exact.*

Lewd *wicked, wanton*, or *riotous.*

Lewdness.

L I.

Liable, or *expos'd to.*

To Libb, or *geld.*

A Libbard, or *Leopard.*

Libbard's-bane, *an herb.*

A Libel, or *scandalous pamphlet*; also *a term in the Civil Law, denoting the original declaration of any action.*

To libel, or *defame one.*

Liberal, *free and bountiful.*

The Liberal Sciences.

Liberality, or *bountifulness.*

Liberdine, *a poisonous herb.*

A Libertine, or *lewd, dissolute liver.*

Libertinism, or *licentiousness.*

Liberty, *freedom*, or *leave.*

Libidinous, or *lustful.*

Liblong, or *live long, an herb.*

A Library, or *collection of Books*; also *a study*, or *place where they are kept.*

A Library-keeper.

Lice, (*from* louse) *a sort of vermin.*

Lice-bane, *an herb.*

Licence, or *leave.*

To licence, *authorize*, or *give leave.*

A Licencer of *books.*

A Licentiate, *one that has* licence *to practise in any faculty*, or *art.*

Licentious, *lewd, dissolute*, or *disorderly.*

Licentiousness.

A Lich-owl, *a bird.*

Lichwale, *an herb.*

A Lick, or *gentle stroke.*

To lick, or *lick up with the tongue.*

A Lick-dish.

Lickerish, *that has a nice palate*, or *dainty tooth.*

Lickerishness.

Licorish, *a root.*

Wild-licorish.

A Lid, or, *cover.*

An Eye-lid.

A Pot-lid.

Lie *made of ashes.*

A Lie, or *untruth.*

To Lie, or *tell a lie.*

A Lier.

Lief, as *I had as* lief.

A Liege Lord, or *Soveraign that owns no superior.*

A Leige-man, *that owes allegiance to his* liege Lord.

Liege-

Liege-people, or *subjects of a King.*
The Lientery, *a kind of flux*, or looseness.
In Lieu, *instead*, or *in the place of.*
The Lieutenancy *of London*; or *council of the Militia Officers.*
A Lieutenant *one that holds the place*, or *does the Office of another.*
A Lieutenant *of a foot-company, of a Troop of horse, of a ship*, &c.
A Lieutenant General *of an army.*
A Lieutenant Colonel *of a Reigment.*
The Lord Lieutenant *of a County.*
A Lieutenantship, *the Office of a* Lieutenant.
Life, *a manner of living spirit*, or *sprightliness.*
Life-everlasting, *an herb.*
A Life-gard, or *gard of the King's person.*
Lifeless, *that has no life*, or *spirit.*
Life-time.
A Lift *and*
To lift, *or* lift *up.*
A Shop-lift, *that steals goods out of a shop.*
A Litter *up.*
A Ligament (*in* Anatomy) *a string* or *band, with which the joynts of bones and gristles are bound together.*
A Ligature, *a binding, made by a Surgeon in any part of the body.*
Light, *and to* light (*in all senses*)
A Light; *a candle, torch*, or *window of a house.*
Light-arm'd.
Light-finger'd.
Light-footed; or *light-heel'd.*
Light-headed.
Light-hearted.
Light horsemen.
Lightless, or *void of light.*
Lightness.
The Lights, or *lungs of a beast.*
Lightsom; *clear, bright*, or *chearful.*
Lightsomness.
To lighten (*in several senses.*
A Lighter, *a kind of boat to carry coals in*, &c.
A Lighter-man.
Like *in quality*, or *quantity*
To like, *love*, or *approve.*
Likeliness, *or* likelihood.
To liken, or *compare to.*
Likeness.
Likewise.
The Lilach, or *pipe-tree.*
A Lilly, *a flower.*
The Day-lilly.
The Lilly *of the valley.*
The Water-lilly.
A Limb, or *member.*
To limb, or *tear limb-meal.*
A Limbeck, *alembick*, or *still.*
Limber, or *supple.*
Limberness.
The Limbers, *or* Limber-holes *in a ship; through which the water is conveyed to the well of the Pump.*
Lime *to make morter with*
A Lime kiln.
A Lime-stone.
To lime, *or* line, *as a Dog does a bitch.*
Bird-lime
A Lime-twig.
A Lime-hound, or *blood-hound a great Dog to hunt the wild boar.*
A Lime-tree.
Lime-wort, *an herb.*
A Limit, or *bound.*
To limit, or *set limits.*
A Limitation.
A Limmer, *a Dog engender'd between an hound and a mastiff.*
To Limn, or *paint in water-colours.*
A Limner.
A Limon, *or* lemmon.
Limp, or *limber.*
To limp, or *halt.*
A Limpet, *a shell-fish.*
A Limpin *a fish.*
Limpness, or *limberness.*
A Linch-pin, *the pin that keeps on the wheel to the axle-tree.*
The Linden *tree.*
Line, or *Flax.*
A Line, (*in several senses.*)
To line *a Coat*, &c. or *to strengthen with a fortification.*
A Clothes-line.
A Jack-line.
A Fishing-line.
A Plumb-line, *us'd by Masons*, or *Carpenters.*
A Lineage, *race*, or *stock.*
Lineal, *as a lineal descent.*
A Lineament, *feature*, or *proportion drawn out in* lines.
Ling, *a sort of salt-fish.*
Ling, or *furze.*
Ling-wort, *an herb.*
To linger, or *delay.*
A Lingerer.
A Linger, *or* linget, *a bird.*
A Linguist, *one skill'd in several Languages.*
A Liniment, or *thin ointment.*
The Lining *of a garment.*
A Link *of a chain.*
To link, or *tie together.*
A Link, or *Torch.*
A Link-boy.
A Link, or *Sausage.*
A Linnen-cloth.
A Linnen-draper.
A Linnen-weaver.
A Linnet, *a singing bird.*
Linseed, *or* line-seed.
Linsy-woolsy, *stuff mix'd with linnen and woollen.*
Lint, *to dress a wound with*
A Lintstock, *a carved staff about half a yard long, with a cock at one end to hold the Gunner's match, and a sharp point at the other, to stick in the ground.*

The Lintel, *head-piece, or upper post of a door.*
A Lion, *a wild beast.*
A Lionel, or *little Lion (in* Heraldry)
A Lioness, or *she-lion.*
Lions-paw, *or* Lions-foot, Lions-mouth, Lions-tooth, } *herbs.*
The Lion-tawny, *colour.*
A Lip.
A Hare-lip.
Lip-salve.
Lipped, as *blubber-lipp'd.*
Liquid, *moist* or *melted.*
Liquids, or *liquid letters,* viz. l, m, n, rs ; *so call'd, because they are pronounced soft and as it were, melt in the mouth.*
To liquify, or *become liquid.*
Liquorish, or licorish.
Liquour, *any thing, that's liquid.*
To liquour *boots.*
Liriconfancy, *a flower.*
To lisp, or *falter in speech.*
A Lisper.
A List, *and to* list *(in several senses.*)
To listen, or *hearken.*
A Listener.
Listless, or *careless.*
The Litany, or *general supplication, a particular prayer in the* English *Common-prayer book to be us'd on certain days.*
Literal, *according to the* Letter ; as *a literal sense.*
Literature, *skill in* Letters, or *learning.*
Litharge, *the scum* or *froth of lead, silver,* or *gold.*
Lithe, *limber,* or *supple.*
Litheness.
Lither, or *lazy.*
Litherness.
Litigious, *quarrelsome, that promotes Law-suits.*
Litigiousness, *a contentious humour.*

Litter, or *straw for cattel to lye on.*
A Litter *of pigs, puppies,* &c. i. e. *all that are brought forth at the same time.*
A Litter, *a kind of chariot.*
A Horse litter.
Little, *small,* or *short in stature.*
Littleness.
A Liturgy, *form of Common Prayer,* or *publick Church-Service.*
Live, or alive ; as *live cattel, live hair,* &c.
To live, or *lead a life.*
Long-lived.
Liveliness.
Lively, *lusty, brisk,* or *sprightful.*
A livelyhood, or *maintenance for life.*
Living-idly, or live in idleness, *a flower.*
Live-long, *an herb.*
A Liver, as *a good,* or *bad liver.*
The Liver, *one of the noble parts of the body.*
Liver-grown.
Livered, as *a white* liver'd *fellow.*
A livering-pudding.
Liver-wort, *an herb.*
A Liver, *a* French *coin, worth about* 1 s. 6 d.
A Livery, or *suit of clothes of different colours and trimming, given by the Nobility and Gentry, to be worn by their Servants, either with,* or *without a cognizance,* or *badge.*
Livery-lace.
The Livery, *or* Livery-men *of a Company,* or *Corporation, that have a right to wear*
A Livery-gown.
Livery of Seisin, or *a delivery of possession of Lands, Tenements,* &c. *to one that has a real,* or *probable right to 'em.*

Livery-stables, *where horses are kept and let out to hire.*
A Livery-writ, *which lies for the heir to obtain the Seisin, or possession of his lands at the King's hands.*
Lives, (*from life*) *as during their natural lives.*
Living, or *substance.*
A Living, spiritual living, or *benefice.*
A Lizard, *a little greenish beast, like our evet but bigger and without poison, breeding in* Italy *and other hot Countries.*
A Sea-Lizard.

LO

Lo, or *behold!*
A Loach, *a small fish.*
A Load, or *burden, and*
To Load, or *put on a* load.
A Cart-load.
Loaden.
A Loader.
The Load-star, or *north star, that guides Mariners.*
The Load-stone, *that has a peculiar virtue to draw iron to it self, and its great use in Navigation is well known.*
A Loaf *of bread.*
A Sugar-loaf.
Loam, or *clay.*
A Loan, or *thing lent.*
To loath, *not to relish, to have an aversion to,* or *disdain.*
Loathsom.
Loathsomness.
A Lob, *or* lobbe, *a great kind of North sea-fish.*
A Lob, *or* lobcock, *a Country-Clown.*
A Lobby, *a gallery,* or *kind of passage-room.*
Lob-lolly, *grout or gruel.*
A Lobster, *a Sea-fish.*
A Lob-worm, *to fish with for Trouts.*
Local, *of or belonging to a place.*

A Lock, *and to* lock *(in several senses.)*
A Pad-lock.
A Lock-smith.
A Locket *of Diamonds.*
Lockram, *a course sort of linnen-cloth.*
Lockron, *or* locker-gowlons, *a flower.*
A Locust, *a sort of grashopper.*
The Locust-tree.
Lodemanage, *the hire*, or *fee of*
A Lodes-man, *steers-man*, or *Pilot.*
Lode-works, *certain works belonging to the stannaries*, or *tin-mines in* Cornwall.
A Lodge, *and to* lodge *(in several senses)*
A Lodgment *in a siege.*
A Lodger, or *one that* lodges *in a house.*
The lodges, *where a buck lies at rest.*
A Loft, *garret*, or *upper room.*
An Apple-loft.
A Corn-loft.
A Hay-loft.
Loftiness, *a being*
Lofty, *high*, or *haughty.*
A Log, or *stump of wood.*
A Log-line, *or* minute-line *to find out the course of a Ship.*
Log-wood, or *block-wood much used by Dyers.*
Logarithms, *certain artificial numbers in Arithmetick, which are made according to a set proportion, and always retain equal differences.*
A Logger-head, or *blockhead.*
Logical, *of* or *belonging to* Logick.
A Logician, *one well skill'd in*
Logick, i. e. *the Art of reasoning*, or *discoursing.*
To loiter, *make delays*, or *spend time idly.*

A Loiterer.
To loll, or *lean upon.*
To loll *out one's tongue.*
Lome, *or* loam.
London's pride, *or* London-tufts, *a flower.*
Lonely, lonesome, or *solitary.*
Lonesomness.
Long, *that has length, continues a great while*, or *is tedious.*
A Long *in Musick.*
To long for, or *be very desirous of.*
Long-joynted.
Long-legged.
Long-lived.
Long-necked.
Long-winded.
Longanimity, or *long-suffering.*
Longevity, or *long life.*
Longitude (*in* Geography) *shews the distance of one place from another Eastward; to be reckon'd from some certain and fixed* Meridian, *or line drawn from the North to the South Pole.*
Long-sufferance, or *long-suffering.*
A Looby, or *loggerhead.*
The Loof *of a Ship.*
To loof *up*, or *keep close to the wind in sailing.*
A Look, *and to* look *(in all senses)*
A Looker on, *or spectateur.*
A Looking-glass.
Venus Looking-glass, *an herb.*
A Weaver's Loom.
To loom, or *appear (a* Sea *Term) as that Ship* looms *a great sail*, i. e. *seems to be a large ship.*
A Loom-gale, *a fresh*, or *stiff gale.*
A Loop, *at each end of a button-hole.*
A Loop-hole.
Loop-lace.
Loose, *and to* loose *(in different senses)*

To loosen, or *make* loose.
A Looseness.
Loose-strife, *an herb.*
A Loover, *or* louver, *an open place, on the top of a roof, for air, smoak*, &c.
A Loover-hole.
To lop, or *cut away boughs.*
A Lopper *of trees.*
Lopper'd; or *curdled. Milk.*
A Lord, *a Noble-man*, or *the proprietor of a Mannour.*
To lord it, or *domineer.*
A Lordain, *or* lordant; *a lazy lubber, dunce*, or *blockhead.*
Lordly, or *stately.*
A Lordship, *the title, jurisdiction*, or *Mannour of a* Lord.
A Loriner, *or* Lorimer *that makes bits for bridles, and such sort of small iron-ware.*
A Loriot, *a bird.*
To lose *his estate, money*, &c.
A Loser.
Loss, or *dammage.*
Lost, as *all is lost.*
A Lot, as *the lot is cast.*
The Lote-tree.
Loth, or *unwilling.*
A Lottery, or *place where lots are cast.*
Lovage, *an herb.*
Loud, as *a loud voice.*
Loudness.
Love, *amity, affection*, or *kindness.*
To Love, *have* love, or *inclination for.*
Love, *a flower.*
Love-apple, *a spanish roat.*
A Love-knot.
A Love-letter.
Love-sick.
Love-toys, or *tricks of* love.
Self-love.
Loveliness.
Lovely, *charming*, or *amiable.*
A Lover.

A Lough, *an* Irish *word for a Lake.*
A Louse, *a vermin.*
To louse, *look,* or *pick lice.*
A Crab-louse.
A Hog-louse.
A Wood-louse.
Louse-wort.
Lousiness.
Lousy, or *full of lice.*
A Lout, or *clownish fellow.*
Low, *not tall not deep, mean, humble,* &c.
To low, or *bellow.*
A Low-built *ship.*
A Low-bell, *a light and a bell, to amuse and catch birds.*
A Low-beller, *that fowls with a* low-bell.
The Lowings, or *thongs of an hawk.*
Lowliness, or *humbleness.*
Lowly, or *lowly-minded.*
A Low-masted, or *under-masted ship.*
To lowr, *frown,* or *look sour.*
Lowry, or *spurge-laurel.*
Loyal, or *faithful.*
Loyalty, or *fidelity.*
A Loyn *of Veal,* Mutton, &c.
The Loyns, or *reins.*
A Lozel, *a lazy body.*
A Lozenge, or *physical composition for a cough; made up in little square* cakes; also *a figure (in* Heraldry) *of the same shape.*

LU

A Lubber, or *drudge, that does all mean services in a house.*
A Lubber, or *lazy drone.*
A Flower-de-luce.
A Lucern, *a sort of* Russian *wild beast almost as big as a Wolf, yielding a very rich Furr.*
Lucid, *bright,* or *shining.*
Luck, or *chance.*
Luckiness.
Lucky, or *fortunate.*
Lucre, *profit,* or *gain.*
A Lucubration, or *night-study, a waking, or studying by Candle-light.*
Ludicrous, or *sportive.*
The Lug *of the ear.*
To lug, or *hale.*
Lug-wort, *an herb.*
A Luggage, or *burden.*
Lukewarm, *between hot and cold.*
Lukewarmness.
To lull a-sleep, *as a nurse does her Child.*
A Lullaby-song.
Lumber, *the worst sort of house-hold stuff.*
A Luminary, *a light body; as of the Sun and Moon.*
Luminous, *bright,* or *full of light.*
A Lump, or *mass.*
The Lump-fish.
Lumpish, or *heavy.*
Lumpishness.
Lunacy, *frenzy,* or *madness.*
Lunar, *of or belonging to the Moon.*
Lunary, or *Moon-wort.*
A Lunatick, *one that is mad or distracted, at certain seasons, according to the course of the Moon.*
A Lunch *of bread.*
An Afternoon's luncheon.
Lunes, *leashes,* or *long lines to call in hawks.*
The Lungs.
Lung-wort, *an herb.*
Lupines, *a flat sort of pulse like small beans of a bitter and harsh taste.*
A Lurch, *at Cards, Tables,* &c.
To lurch *one.*
A Lurcher, *that lies upon the* lurch; also *a sort of dog.*
A Lure, or *device of leather, with wings and a bait of flesh us'd by a faulconer,*
To lure, or *call back the hawk.*
To lurk, or *lye hid.*
A Lurker, *in corners*
A Lurking-hole.
A Lurry, or *bustle.*
Lushious, or *over-sweet, so as to cloy.*
Lushiousness.
Lust, or *concupiscence.*
To lust, or *lust after.*
Lust-wort, *an herb.*
Luster, lustre, or *brightness.*
Lustfull.
Lustfulness.
Lustiness.
Lusty, *lively, strong,* or *sturdy.*
A Lutanist, or *lute-player.*
A Lute, *a Musical instrument.*
To lute, or *cover with loam (a* Chymical *Term.)*
Lute-string, *a sort of silk.*
Lutheranism, *the Doctrine of* Martin Luther, *who being at first an* Augustine *Monk, inveigh'd against the errors of the Church of* Rome, *and began the Reformation,* A. D. 1515.
The Lutherans *or, followers of* Luther.
A Luxation, or *putting out of joint (a Term in* Surgery.)
Luxuriant, or *growing rank, as luxuriant plants.*
Luxurious, *that lives in* luxury.
Luxuriousness.
Luxury, *excess,* or *superfluity in carnal pleasures, sensuality,* or *riotousness.*

LY

To ly, ly along, ly down, &c.
To ly, or *tell a* lie.
Lye, *to wash clothes with.*
A Lynx, *a wild beast, of the nature of a Wolf, that has spots like a deer, and is very quick-sighted.*
A Lyra-viol, *a musical instrument.*

A

A Lyre, or harp.
Lyrick, belonging to a harp; as lyrick Verſes, that were ſung to that inſtrument.

M A

A MAcaroon, a ſort of ſweet-meat.
Maccabees, two apocryphal Books, containing the Hiſtory of Judas Maccabæus and others of that family.
Mace, a ſpice.
Reed-mace, an herb.
A Mace, carried before certain Magiſtrates and ſtate-Officers.
A Mace-bearer.
To macerate, infuſe, or ſoak; or to make lean.
To Machinate, plot, or contrive.
A Machination, or device.
A Machine, or engine.
A Mackerel, a ſea-fiſh.
Mad, furious, out of his wits, or diſtracted.
To mad, or make mad.
Mad-apples.
A Mad-cap, or frantick perſon.
Mad-wort, an herb.
Madame, the title of a Lady.
Madder, an herb uſed in dying Wooll, &c.
Baſtard-madder.
Maddiſh, or ſomewhat mad
Made (from to make.)
Madge-howlet, a ſort of owl.
Mad-nep, an herb.
Madneſs, fury, or diſtractedneſs.
A Madrigal, an Italian amorous ſonnet.
To maffle, or falter in ſpeech.
A Maffler, or ſtammerer.
A Magazine, or ſtore-houſe of Arms, and war-like ammunition.
A Magget, or Maggot, a ſort of worm.
Magget-headed, or maggot-pated.

Maggotty or full o maggots.
Magical, of, or belonging to Magick.
A Magician, conjurer, or ſorcerer.
Magick, the black Art, dealing with familiar ſpirits.
Natural Magick, or natural Philoſophy, a lawful, and uſeful Science.
Magiſterial, dogmatical, or imperious.
Magiſtracy, the dignity, or office of a
Magiſtrate, judge, or civil Governour.
Magna Charta, or the great Charter, the moſt ancient written Law of England, granted by K. Henry III. confirm'd by Edward I. and other ſucceeding Kings.
Magnanimity, or greatneſs of Spirit.
Magnanimous, couragious of a ſtout heart, or generous ſpirit.
A Magnet, or load-ſtone.
Magnetick, belonging to the load-ſtone.
The Magnificat, or ſong of the bleſſed Virgin Mary.
Magnificence, or grandeur.
Magnificent, noble, or ſtately.
A Magnifico, or nobleman of Venice.
To Magnifie, make great, extoll, or amplify.
The Magnitude, or bigneſs of a Star.
A Mag-py, a bird.
Magydare, an herb.
A Mahometan, a follower of Mahomet.
Mahometiſm the religion contriv'd by that impoſtor
A Maid, or Maiden.
A Maid, a fiſh ſo call'd.
A Maid-ſervant.
A Maid-marrion, a boy dreſt up in girl's cloths in a morrice dance.

A Chamber-maid.
A Nurſery-maid.
Maiden-hair, an herb.
Engliſh black Maiden-hair.
A Maiden-head, or virginity.
Maiden-lips, an herb.
Majeſtical, or majeſtick, belonging to, or full of
Majeſty, the authority ſtate and grandeur of a King.
A Coat of mail.
A Mail, budget, or coffer to travel with.
A Mail-horſe that carries the mail.
Mailed, or ſpeckled, as a hawk's feathers are.
Maim, curtailed of any member.
To maim, or mangle.
Main, chief, or principal.
The main of a Horſe.
Main-prize, i. e. taking a perſon into one's hands, or cuſtody, upon ſecurity for his appearance in a court of judicature.
To main-prize, or give ſuch ſecurity.
To maintain, uphold, ſupport, or defend.
Maintainable, that may be maintain'd.
A Maintainer.
Maintenance.
A Maior, or mayor of a Town.
The major, or greater part.
A Major of a Riegment, an officer next to the Lieutenant General.
A Major General, next the the Lieutenant General.
The majority, the major, or greater part.
A Major-Domo, or Steward.
Majorſhip, the office of a Major.
Maiz, a ſort of Weſt-Indian Corn.
To make (in all ſenſes)
A Make-bate, one that cauſes quarrels; alſo an herb ſo call'd.

A make-

A Make-hawk, *an old stanch flying* hawk, *to* make, or *teach a young one.*
A maker.
A Lace-maker.
A Malachite, *a kind of precious stone, of a mallow-green colour.*
A Malady, or *distemper.*
The Malanders, *a horse-disease.*
Malapert, *saucy*, or *impudent.*
Malapertness.
Male, as *the male and female.*
Male-administration, or *the ill management of an affair.*
The Male-contents, or *discontented party.*
A Malediction, *evil speaking*, or *curse.*
A Malefactor, or *evil doer, offender*, or *criminal.*
Malevolence, *ill will*, or *spight.*
Malevolent, *ill-natur'd, spightful, of an ill aspect*, or *influence.*
Malice, *envy*, or *hatred.*
Malicious.
Maliciousness.
Malign, or *bent upon Mischief.*
To Malign, *envy*, or *bear malice.*
Malignancy, or *malignant nature.*
Malignant, as *a malignant Disease.*
A Malignant, or *ill-affected person.*
Malignity, *ill-will, the obstinacy of a Disease*, &c.
A Malkin, maukin, or *oven-mop.*
A Mall, *a place where they play at*
Mall, *a sort of game.*
A Mall-stick.
A Mallard, or *male wild duck.*
Malleable, *that may be work'd with the hammer.*
A Mallet, or *wooden hammer.*
Mallows *an herb.*
Marsh-mallows.
Malmsey, *a sort of luscious wine so call'd from* Malvasia *a Town of the Isle* Chios, *where the best is made.*
A Malocotoon, *a kind of peach.*
Malt, *to make drink.*
A Malt-kiln.
A Malt-long, or *malt-worm.*
A Maltster, or *malt-man.*
A Mammock, or *fragment.*
A Man.
To Man a ship, Town, &c. *to store it with a competent number of* men.
A Man of war, or *armed ship.*
A Man-child, or *male-child.*
A Man-slayer, *one that commits*
Manslaughter, i. e. *the unlawful killing of a man upon a suddain quarrel without premeditated malice. To felony, but admitted to the benefit of the Clergy.*
A Chess-man, *at Chess-play.*
A Foot-man.
A Horse-man.
A Marks-man, or *expert archer.*
A Merchant-man, or *ship that conveys Merchandizes.*
To manacle, or *bind a Malefactor with*
Manacles, or *hand-fetters.*
A Manage, or *place to ride the great horse in.*
To manage, or *carry on a business.*
Management, *or* managery
A Manager.
A Manchet, *or* manchet-bread, *the finest sort.*
A Manciple, *Steward*, or *Caterer in a Colledge*, or *Hospital.*
A Mandamus, *a sort of writ*; also *a letter from the King to the heads of a College, Corporation*, &c. *requiring the admission of some person into their Society.*
A Mandatary, *one that obtains a degree*, or *benefice by virtue of a Mandamus.*
A Mandate, *a particular command*, or *Order by the King*, or *Bishop.*
A Mandilion, *a kind of loose Cassock for Soldiers.*
A Man-drake, *a strange plant, bearing yellow apples, with a large white root like a radish, sometimes us'd by Surgeons to cast their patients into a deep sleep.*
Manful, *full of manhood, stout* or *couragious.*
Manfulness.
The Mange, or *scab, on dogs, cats*, &c.
A Manger *for Cattel.*
Manginess.
To mangle, *tear in pieces, cut* or *slash.*
A Mangler.
Mango, *a kind of East Indian fruit, of the bigness of an apple, usually pickled and eaten as a sallet.*
Mangy, or *full o the mange*
Manhood, *man's estate*, or *valour.*
Manifest, *plain, clear*, or *apparent.*
To manifest, or *make manifest.*
A Manifestation.
A Manifesto, or *publick declaration of a Prince*, or *State.*
Manifold (*from many*) *various*, or *of divers sorts and ways.*
A Maniple, or *bandful.*
Mankind, or *the race of men.*

Manlineſs.
Manly, or manlike, *valiant, couragious,* &c.
Manna, or *honey-dew.*
A manned, or *tamed hawk.*
A Manner, *faſhion, guiſe,* or *cuſtom.*
Ill-mannered.
Mannerlineſs.
Mannerly, *civil, courteous,* or *obliging.*
Manners, *good,* or *ill conditions, inſtitutions, rules of life, behaviour,* &c.
A Manour, *Lordſhip,* or *juriſdiction of a Lord.*
The Manour-houſe.
A Manſion, or *dwelling-place.*
A Mantle, *a ſort of long robe,* alſo (*in* Heraldry) *the flouriſh on each ſide of a Scutcheon.*
To mantle, or *flower as drink does.*
The Hawk mantles, or *ſpreads her wings along after her legs.*
A Mantlet, *a kind of pent-houſe for* Soldiers *in a Siege.*
The Mantle-tree *of a Chimney.*
A Mantoe, *a ſort of womens-gown.*
A Mantoe-maker.
Manual, *as a ſign manual,* or *ſigning under hand and Seal.*
A Manual, or *pocket-book.*
A Manuduction, or *leading by the hand.*
A Manufacture, *handy-work,* or *workmanſhip.*
A Manufacturer, *one that has undertaken a* Manufacture.
Manumiſſion, *the enfranchiſing,* or *freeing of a Vaſſal,* or *Slave.*
To Manumit, or *ſet free.*
Manure, *any thing that is uſ'd for fattening the Soil,* as *dung, marl,* &c.
To manure, or *till the ground.*
A Manurer.
A Manuſcript, *a book,* or *Copy written with the hand, in oppoſition to a printed Copy.*
Many a good many, a great many, &c.
Many-feet, or *pourcontrel, a ſort of fiſh.*
A Map, or *repreſentation of the whole globe of the Earth,* or *of ſome particular Country upon a plan,* or *plain ſuperficies.*
A Maple-tree.
Marble, *a hard ſort of ſhining ſtone.*
To marble, or *paint paper marble-wiſe.*
A Marble-cutter.
Marble-flower.
March, *the month ſo call'd* (*according to* Varro) *from it's being dedicated to the God* Mars.
A March *of an army.*
To march, or *go as ſoldiers do.*
A Marchaſite, or *fire-ſtone.*
The Marches, *frontiers,* or *borders of a Country.*
Lords-marchers, *Noblemen that formerly liv'd and excercis'd a kind of abſolute power on the* Marches *of* Wales *and* Scotland.
A Marchioneſs, or *Marqueſs's Lady.*
A March-pane, *a ſort of macaroon.*
A Mare, or *female horſe.*
A Mare-colt, or *filly.*
The night-mare, *a diſeaſe.*
A Mare-faced *horſe.*
Margarites, *an herb.*
The Margin *of a book.*
Marginal, *belonging to the* margin, *as marginal notes.*
Maries-feal, *an herb.*
Mariets *a flower*

A Marigold *a flower.*
African-marigold.
Corn-marigold.
French-marigold.
Marſh-marigold.
To marinate, or *pickle.*
Marine, or *ſerving at ſea;* as *a marine regiment.*
A Trumpet-marine, *a kind of muſical inſtrument.*
A Mariner, or *ſea-man.*
Marjoram, *or* marjorom, *an herb.*
Sweet-marjoram.
Wild-marjoram.
Maritime, or *bordering,* on *the ſea.*
A Mark, *and to* mark (*in ſeveral ſenſes.*)
A Mark *of ſilver,* i.e. 13 *s,* 4 *d.*
A Marker *at tennis-play.*
A Fiſh-market.
A Fruit-market.
A Hay-Market
A Meal-market.
A Market, or *market-place.*
A Market-houſe.
A Market-woman.
Marketable, *fit to be ſold in the market.*
Marl, *a kind of chalky clay.*
To marl *ground,* or *fatten it with* marl.
A Marl-pit.
Marmalet, *or* marmelade *of quinces,* &c.
A Marmoſet, *a kind of black monkey with a ſhaggy neck.*
A Marmotto, or *mountain-rat.*
A Marqueſs, *or* Marquis, (*q.* Lord Marcher) *the title of a Nobleman, between a Duke and Earl.*
Marquetry, or *curious inlaid work, with wood of divers ſorts and colours.*
A Marquiſate, *or* marquiſedom; *the territories of a* Marqueſs.
Marquiſhip, *the title,* or

or dignity of a Marquess.
To marr, or *spoil.*
Marriage, or *wedlock.*
Marriageable, *of age to marry.*
Marriageableness.
A Marriage-song.
The Marrow *of a bone.*
To marry, *or* be married; *to take, or give a wife.*
A Marsh, *Fen*, or *bog.*
A Salt-marsh.
A Marshal, (*i. e. master of the horse*) *a name appropriated to several Officers.*
To marshal, or *put in order.*
The Earl Marshal *of* England.
The Marshal of *the* King's house, or *Knight-Marshal.*
The Marshal of the King's-bench, *that has the custody of the* King's-bench *prison in* Southwark.
A Marshal of a Regiment, *whose office is to execute all orders of the council of war.*
A Camp-marshal.
A Provost-marshal, *that searches for, and punishes robbers.*
The Marshalsey, i. e. *the Marshal's seat, Court,* or *prison in* Southwark.
Marshalship, *the office of a* Marshal.
Marshy, *fenny*, or *moorish.*
A Mart, or *great fair.*
A Mart-Town, *a large one, where People of several nations, come, upon account of trade, and commerce.*
A Marten or martern, *a kind of ferret.*
Martial, or *warlike.*
A Martin, or martinet, *a bird.*
A Sand-martin.
A Martingale, *a sort of rein for a Horse.*
Martlemas, *or* martinmas *the festival of St.* Martin, *Nov.* 11
Martlemas-beef.
A Martlet, *or* martin *a bird.*
A Martyr, (*i. e.* witness,) *one that has seal'd the truth of Christianity with his blood.*
Martyred, *that has suffer'd* Martyrdom.
A Martyrology, or *book of Martyrs.*
A Marvel, *and*
To marvel, or *wonder.*
Marvel of Peru, *an* American *plant, with admirable flowers.*
Marvellous, or *wonderful.*
A Mascarade, or *company of* masked *people dancing with their vizards on.*
A Mascle (*in* Heraldry) or *a short lozenge with a square hole in the middle; the Symbol of prudence, constancy and justice.*
Masculine, *of the male kind*, or *manly.*
A Mash, or *mixture*; or *a drench for a horse.*
To mash, or *mingle.*
The Mashes *of a net.*
A Mask, or *vizard.*
Masked, *that has a* mask *on.*
A Masker.
Maslin-corn, *or* Maslin bread, *wheat and rye mingled together.*
A Mason, or *worker in stone.*
Masonry, or *masons work.*
A Masquerade, *or* mascarade.
A Mass, or *lump.*
The Popish Mass, or *solemn Church-service.*
A Mass-book.
A Massacre, or *great slaughter.*
To Massacre, or *murder; properly to kill with a* Mace, or *Club.*
Massiness *a being*
Massy, or massive, *solid and weighty.*
The Mast *of a ship.*
The Fore-mast.
The Missen, *or* mizzen *mast.*
The Top-mast.
The Mast of a Forest, *i. e. the fruit of Oak, Beech, Chesnut,* &c.
The Mast-tree.
A Master, *Governour*, or *Teacher.*
The Master of the Armory, *an Officer that takes care of the King's Armour.*
A Master of Arts, *in an University.*
A Master of the Ceremonies, *who introduces Ambassadours into the King's presence.*
Masters of the Chancery, *assistants to the Lord Chancellour*, or *Lord Keeper of the great Seal, in matters of judgment.*
A Master of the horse, *that has the oversight of the Stables of a Prince*, or *Noble-man.*
The Master, of the King's household, *under the grand Master*, or *Lord Steward.*
The Master of the Jewel-*house, that has charge of all the plate for the King* or *Queen's table*; as also, *of all Plate in the Tower of* London, *loose Jewels, Chains*, &c
The Master, or Warden *of the Mint, whose office is to receive the Gold, Silver and Bullion to be coined,* &c.
The Master of the Ordinance, *who has the care of all the King's Ord'nance, artillery,* &c.
The Master of the Rolls, *formerly call'd* Clerk of the Rolls, *is an assistant to the Lord Chancellour, hearing causes and giving orders in his absence. His office takes name from the safe keeping of the*

the Rolls of all Patents and Grants, to pass the great Seal, and of all Records of the Court of Chancery.
A Master of a ship.
The Master of the Wardrobe, an Officer whose business it is to take care of the King and Queen's Royal Robes; as also of all Hangings, Bedding, &c. for the King's houses. This Office was once kept near Paddle-wharf, in London.
To master, get the better of, subdue, or keep under.
A Master-piece, or most accurate workmanship.
Master-wort, an herb.
A Dancing-master.
A Fencing-master.
A Musick-master.
A School-master.
A Writing-master.
Masterless, that has no master, headstrong, or refractary.
Masterly, or master like.
To get the mastery of a thing.
Mastick, a kind of gum.
Herb-mastick.
Masticot, a fine yellow powder us'd by painters.
A Mastiff-dog.
A Mat for a room, &c.
To mat, or cover with mats.
A Bed-mat.
A Door-mat.
A Mat-maker.
Mat-fellon. } herbs.
Mat-weed. }
A Marachin-dance, a kind of morris-dance.
A match, and to match (in all senses.)
A match-maker, or procurer of marriages.
Matchable, that may be match'd, or equaliz'd.
Matchless, that has not his match; incomparable.
Match-wood.
A Mate, companion, or partner.
To mate, scare, or terrifie one.
Check-mate, at Chess, when the King is close shut up so that there is no way left for his escape, which puts an end to the game.
Material, consisting of matter; also important, or weighty.
Materials for workmanship.
Maternal, of, or belonging to a mother.
Math, as the Letter math, or latter crop of hay.
Mathematical.
A Mathematician, or professour of the Mathematicks, certain noble Sciences taught by demonstration, as Arithmetick, Geometry, Astronomy, &c.
Mathe, an herb.
The Matrice, matrix, or womb.
Matrices, or moulds to found Printers Letter in.
A Matricular (q. motherly) book at the University, where young Students are put as it were under the tuition of their common mother.
To matriculate, or register a Scholar in such a book.
Matrimonial, of, or belonging to
Matrimony, or wedlock.
A Matron, a grave and motherly woman.
Matter, and to matter (in all senses)
Mattins, or morning-prayers.
A Mattock, a kind of pick-ax us'd in husbandry.
A Mattress, or flock-bed.
Maturation, or ripening.
Mature, or ripe.
Maturity, ripeness or perfection.
Maudlin, or half drunk.
Swet-maudlin, an herb.
Maugre, or in spite of.
A Mavis, a kind of Thrush.
To maul, or beat one soundly.
A Maulkin, or malkin for an Oven.
A Maul-stick us'd by Painters.
A Maund, a great open basket with handles to carry victuals, &c.
Maundy-Thursday, the day before Good-Friday, when the King, or his Almoner washes the feet of several poor men, and gives them a certain dole of money, cloth, &c.
The maw of a Calf.
Mawkish, or squeamish.
A great Mawks, or flattern.
A Maxim, general ground rule, or unquestionable principle of any art.
May the most pleasant month of the year, anciently consecrated to Maia Mercury's mother.
A May-bug, an insect.
May-bush, an herb.
A May-fly, an insect.
May-games.
A May-pole.
May-lilly, or liriconfancy.
May-weed, an herb.
To may, or can; as if you will you may.
To mayl hawks, or pinion their wings.
A Mayor, or chief Magistrate of a City, Corporation, or Town.
Mayoralty, a Mayor's office and dignity.
A Maze in a Garden; a place full of turnings and windings.
To be in a maze, i. e. perplexed not knowing whereabouts one is.
A Mazer, a broad drinking cup.

ME

ME, as *what is it to me?*

A Meacock, or *uxorious man that is over fond of his wife.*

Mead, *a kind of drink made of honey*, &c.

Mead *us'd by poets for*,

A Meadow, *meadow-ground*, or *rich pasture ground.*

Meadow-parsnep.

Meadow-Saffron.

Mead-sweet, *or* meadow-sweet, *an herb.*

Meager, or *lean.*

Meagerness.

A Meal, or *repast.*

Meal, or *flower.*

Bean-meal.

A Meal-man, or *seller of meal.*

A meal-sieve.

A Meal-tub.

A Meal-worm.

Mealy, *like* meal, or *full of* meal.

Mealy-mouthed, or *over-bashful, that is afraid to declare his mind.*

Mealy-tree, *a plant.*

Mean, *low*, or *poor.*

A Mean *the middle between two extremes.*

The mean-part, or *tenor in Musick, between bass and treble.*

To mean, *to purpose, to understand*, or *to signify.*

In the mean time.

Meanness *of birth*, &c.

Means, *a method*, or *way*; or *an Estate.*

Meant, (*from to mean*)

A Mear, or *balk in a field, that parts one man's land from another.*

A Mear-stone, *set up for a boundary.*

A Mease *of* 500 *herrings.*

A Measure, *proportion*, or *quantity of things measured.*

To measure, or *mete.*

A Measurer.

Measures, *purposes*, or *designs.*

Meat, or *food.*

A Meat-pye.

Sweet-meats.

White-meats.

Meazeled, a. or *meazel'd hog.*

The Meazels, *or* meazles, *a disease.*

Mechanical, *or* mechanick.

A Mechanick, *handycrafts man*; or *tradesman.*

The Mechanicks, or *art of handycrafts.*

Mechoacan, *an* Indian *root of good use in Physick.*

A Medal, *a sort of Coin, with a device made upon some solemn occasion.*

To meddle *with*, or *be concern'd in a business.*

A Meddler.

To mediate, (*i. e.* come between) *to intercede*, or *entreat for another.*

A Mediation.

A Mediator.

A Mediatrix, or *female mediator.*

Medicable, *that may be heal'd*, or *curable.*

A Medicament, or *medicinal composition.*

Medicated meats, i. e. *mingled with physical ingredients.*

Medicinable, medicinal, or *Physical.*

A Medicine, or *physical remedy.*

Medick-fodder, or *spanish trefoil, an herb.*

A Mediocrity, or *mean.*

To meditate, *think, muse*, or *reflect upon.*

A Meditation.

A Meditative *posture.*

The Mediterranean, or *midland Sea, so call'd because it runs between the three great continents of* Europe, Africa, *and* Asia.

A medium, or *mean.*

A Medlar, *a fruit.*

A medley, or *mixture of odd things.*

Meek, mild, or *gentle.*

Meekness.

A mean, *carriage, demeanour, presence*, or *air of one's countenance.*

Meer, *very arrant*, &c. as *a meer knave.*

A Meer, *lake*, or *standing water that cannot be drawn dry.*

Winder-meer lake, *in* Westmorland.

Meet, *fit*, or *convenient.*

To meet, meet with, *come together*, &c.

Meeter, or *rhime.*

The Megrim, *a disease in the head.*

Melancholick, *subject to*

Melancholy, *a distemper proceeding from abundance of black choler.*

Melancholy, or *sad.*

A Melicet, or *keeling a fish.*

A Melicotony, *or* Melocotoon, *a sort of peach.*

Melilot, *an herb.*

Mellow, *ripe and tender.*

Mellowness.

Melodious, or *harmonious.*

Melody, *a sweet Consort in Musick.*

A Melon, *a fruit*,

A Musk-melon.

To melt, or *dissolve.*

A melter *of* metals.

A melting-house.

Melwel, *a sort of Cod-fish.*

A Member, or *limb.*

A Membrane, *the uppermost thin skin in any part of the body.*

Memoirs, or *plain, historical relations, of remarkable things.*

Memorable, *worthy to be remember'd*, or *remarkable.*

A Memorandum, or *short note of something to be remembred.*

9

A Memorial, or *Monument, that causes a thing to be remember'd.*
An Ambassador's Memorial, or *writing presented for an answer.*
Memory *the faculty of remembring*, or *calling to mind.*
Men, (*from* man) as *most men believe.*
To menace, or *threaten.*
Menaces, or *threats.*
To mend, or amend; *to refit*, or *correct.*
A mender *of old cloths.*
A Mendicant, or *begging Frier.*
A Menial, or *household-servant.*
A Menow, *a small fish.*
The Menstruous, or *monthly courses in women.*
Mental, *of*, or *belonging to the mind.*
Mention, or *speaking of.*
To mention, or *make* mention *of.*
A Menuet, *a sort of dance.*
Mercenary, *greedy of gain*, or *that is hired for reward*, or *wages.*
A Mercer, or *Silk-man.*
Mercery, or *mercery-ware.*
Merchandize, or *commodities to trade with.*
Merchandizing, or *traffick.*
A Merchant, *one that buys* or *trades in any thing.*
A Merchant-man, or *ship for a trading voyage.*
Merciful, or *full of mercy.*
Mercifulness.
Merciless, *that has no compassion*, or *cruel.*
Mercurial, *ingenious, lively*, or *brisk.*
Mercury, or *quick-silver*; also *a plant so called.*

Childing Mercury, Dogs-Mercury, English Mercury, Mercury's finger } *herbs*

A Mercury, or *News-book.*
A Mercury-woman, *that sells news-papers.*
Mercy, *pity*, or *compassion.*
The Meridian (*in* Geography) *an imaginary circle which passes thro' the* Poles *of the world and* Zenith *of every place; being always the same, when we go from North to South; but changes in passing from East to West.* '*Tis so call'd, because when the sun comes to it, in its daily course, noon is made to those that are under it.*
Merit, or *desert.*
To merit, or *deserve.*
Meritorious, *that deserves a reward.*
A Merlin, *a sort of hawk.*
A Merlin-fish.
A Mermaid, *a Sea-monster, like a woman in the upper parts, and a fish below.*
A Merriment.
Merry, *joyful*, or *jocund.*
The merry thought *of a Capon.*
The Mesentery, *a thick fat skin that fastens the bowels to the bak and to each other.*
Meslin, or maslin-corn.
A Mess *of meat*, or *pottage.*
A Mess-mate.
A Message, or *errand.*
A Messenger.
Messengers of the Exchequer, *four Pursuivants attending the Lord Treasurer.*
Messiah, *an* Hebrew *word signifying* Christ, or *anointed.*
A Messuage, or *tenement*; i. e. *a dwelling house, with some adjacent land belonging to it.*
Met, (*from to meet.*)
A Metal, *digg'd out of the earth, as gold, silver*, &c. also *the breech of a great gun*
A Gun under-metall'd, *whose mouth is lower than the breech.*
Metallick, *of*, or *belonging to* metals.
To Metamorphize, *transform*, or *change the form*, or *shape.*
A Metamorphosis, or *transformation of shape.*
A Metaphor, (*i. e.* translation,) *a Rhetorical figure, when a word is translated from its proper signification, to another.*
Metaphorical, *belonging to such a figure.*
Metaphysical, *of*, or *belonging to*
Metaphysicks, *a science which treats of* Beings, *that are above corporeal things, & abstracted from individuals*; as God, *Angels*, *the souls of men*, &c.
To mete, or *measure.*
A Mete-wand.
A Meter.
A Coal-meter.
A Meteors, (i. e. Apparitions on high, in the air) as *rain, snow, hail, thunder, lightning*, &c.
Metheglin, *a drink made of wort, herbs, honey, and spice boil'd together.*
Methinks, *it seems to me*, as, *methinks, he is innocent.*
A Method, or *ready way to teach*, or *do any thing.*
Methodical, *belonging*, or *agreeable to some* method
A Methodist, *that affects to be methodical*, or *treats of* methods.
To methodize, or *put into a* method.
Methought (*from* methinks)
Metonymical, *belonging to*
A Metonymy (*i. e. changing of names*) *a figure in Rhetorick, when the cause is put for the effect,*
the

the subject for the adjunct, and on the contrary
A Metropolis, *mother-city, capital,* or *chief town.*
A Metropolitan, or *Archbishop.*
Mettle, *vigour,* or *sprightliness.*
Mettled, or *mettlesome.*
Meter, or *verse.*
A Hawk's mew, *a place where hawks are kept.*
A Sea mew, *a bird.*
To mew, or *cry like a Cat.*
To mew, or *shed the horns as a stag does.*
To mew up, or *shut up.*
The Mews, or *Kings stables in* London, *where his hawks were formerly kept.*
Mezzo-tinto, *a particular way of engraving.*

M I

Mice, *the plural of* mouse.
Mickle, or *much;* as *many a little makes a mickle.*
Michaelmas, or *the festival of St.* Michael. September 29.
A Microscope. *a kind of magnifying glass, to discern small bodies,*
Middle, as *the* middle *region of the air.*
The Middle, *or* midst *of a thing.*
Mid-day, or *noon.*
Mid-lent, or *the middle of* Lent.
Mid-lent Sunday.
Mid-summer.
Mid-summer-day, or *the Festival of St.* John *Baptist. June* 24.
The Mid-way.
Mid-winter.
Middle-aged.
Middle-sized.
Middling, as *pins o a middling sort.*
A Midland *Province.*
Midnight.
The Midriff, *a membrane, or thin skin that divides the heart and Lungs from the lower entrals.*
The midst, as *in the very* midst *of the crowd.*
A Midwal, or *Martinet, a bird.*
A Midwife, *to deliver Women in labour.*
A Man-midwife.
The Art of Midwifry.
Might, as *I might (from* to may.)
Might, *power,* or *force.*
Mightiness, *a being*
Mighty, *powerfull,* or *of great power.*
Milch, *as a* milch-cow, *that yields milk.*
Mild, or *gentle.*
Mildernix, *a kind of Canvas, for sail-clothes,* &c.
Mildew, *a sort of dew, that falls on trees, plants,* or *corn.*
Mildewed, or *blasted.*
Mildness, or *gentleness.*
A Mile, *the distance of a thousand paces,* or 1760 *yards.*
Milfoil, *an herb.*
Militant, or *combating,* as *the Church Militant.*
Military, or *warlike.*
The Militia, or *trained bands.*
Milk, *and*
To milk *a Cow,* &c.
Butter-milk.
A Milk-house.
A Milk-maid, or *milk-woman.*
A Milk-pail.
Milk-porridge.
A Milk-sop, *sot* or *fool.*
The Milk-stone.
Milk-thistle, } *herbs.*
Milk-trefoil, } *herbs.*
Milk-vetch, } *herbs.*
Milk-weed, *or* Wolves-milk, } *herbs.*
Milk-wort. } *herbs.*
Milky, *of,* or *like milk, milk-white.*
The Milky-way, *a broad white circle encompassing the heavens, sometimes with a double path, but for the most part with a single one; found to be an heap of fixed stars only discern'd by the* Telescope.
A Mill.
To mill, or *thicken in a* mill.
A Hand-mill.
A Griest-mill.
An Horse-mill, or *ass-mill.*
An Oil-mill.
A Paper-mill.
A Water-mill.
A Wind-mill.
A Mill-clack, or *mill-clapper.*
A Mill-dam.
Mill-dust.
A Mill-eat, *a trench to convey water to, or from the Mill.*
A Mill-hopper.
Mill-mountain, *an herb.*
The upper and neither Mill-stones.
A Millenarian, *or* millenary, *a fifth Monarchy-man, that holds* Christ's *reign upon earth for* 1000 *years.*
A Millener *that sells ribbons, gloves,* &c.
A Miller *that manages a* mill.
Millers-thumb, *a fish.*
Millet, or *hirse, a kind of small grain.*
Indian-millet.
Millet-grass.
A Million, or *Ten hundred thousand.*
The Milt, or *spleen;* also *the soft roe of fishes.*
A Milter, or *male fish.*
Milt-waste, *an herb.*
Milt-wort, or *spleen-wort.*
Mimical, *apish,* or *belonging to*
A Mimick, or *buffoon, that imitates the gestures of others.*
To mince, or *cut very small.*
A minc'd-pye.

Mincing,

Mincing, or *affected, as a mincing gate speech,* &c.
Mind, *and to* mind, (*in all senses.*)
High-minded, or *haughty.*
Ill-minded.
Well-minded.
Mindful, or *careful.*
Mindt lnels.
Mine, or *belonging to me, as this book is* mine.
A Mine, *in the earth, out of which metals and minerals, as Gold, Silver, Copper, &c. are digg'd.*
A Mine *in sieges, a hole, or trench digg'd under ground and fill'd with gun-powder to blow up those that come on it.*
A Miner, *one that works in such a* mine.
Mineral, as *mineral waters.*
A Mineralist, *one well skill'd in*
Minerals, *certain metallick substances found in mines,* as *Antimony, Oaker, talk* &c.
A Minever, *a sort of furr.*
A Minew, *or* menow, *a small fish.*
To mingle *or* mix.
A Mingle-mangle, or *hotch-potch.*
Miniature, *the drawing of Pictures, in little with* minium, or *red lead.*
A Minim, *a musical note;* also *a sort of printing-letter.*
A Minion, *darling*, or *favourite;* also *a piece of Ord'nance so call'd.*
A Minister, or *pastor of a Church.*
A Minister, *Agent*, or *Ambassador.*
To Minister, or *officiate.*
A Ministery, or *management of affairs.*
The Ministry, *the office*, or *function of a Minister*, or *Divine.*

Ministers of State, or *chief Counsellours.*
A Minks, *or* minnekin; *a nice Dame.*
Minnekins, *the smallest sort of Pins;* also *a kind of gut-strings for musical instruments.*
A Minnow, *a fish.*
Minor, or *under age.*
Minority, or *nonage.*
A Minster, or *Church,* as York-*minster.*
Westminster-abbey, &c.
A Minstrel, *fiddler* or *Piper.*
Mint, *a sweet-scented herb.*
Cat-mint.
Coloured mint.
Garden-mint.
Horse-mint, or *wild mint.*
Spear-mint.
Water-mint.
The Mint, *the place where the King's Coyn is made,* as *in the Tower of* London.
To mint, or *coin money.*
The Master, or Warden of the Mint.
The Provost of the Mint, *an Officer who provides for all the* moneyers *and oversees them.*
A minter, or *coiner.*
Minute, or *very small.*
Minute tythes, *certain small tythes belonging to the Vicar.*
A Minute, *the* 60th. *part of an hour.*
A Minute-line, or *log-line, used at sea.*
A Minute-watch.
The Minutes, or *rough draughts of Instruments.*
A Miracle, *a wonderful*, or *preternatural thing.*
Miraculous, or *wonderful.*
Miraculousness.
Mire, *dirt*, or *mud.*
A Quag-mire.
Mired, or *daubed with* mire.
A Mirobolan *plum.*
A Mirrour *looking-glass,* *pattern*, or *model.*
Mirth, *pleasure*, or *jollity.*
Miry, *full of mire.*
Mis, *a particle which in composition denotes some errour*, or *deceit*, as
A misadventure, or *mischance. In* Law *the word signifies the killing of a man, partly by negligence and partly by chance; as by carelesly throwing a stone, shooting*, &c. *for which the offender has pardon for life, but forfeits his goods.*
Misadvice, or *bad counsel.*
To misadvise *one.*
To misapply *one thing to another.*
To misapprehend, or *not to apprehend rightly.*
A misapprehension.
To misbecome.
To misbehave *himself.*
Misbehaviour.
Misbelief.
To misbelieve, or *have a wrong belief.*
A Misbeliever.
To miscall *one*, or *give him a wrong name.*
A Miscarriage, *and*
To miscarry (*in several senses.*)
Miscellaneous, or *mixt together without order.*
Miscellanies, *books upon several subjects;* or *collections of various matters.*
A mischance, or *ill accident.*
Mischief, *dammage, hurt; an ill turn*, or *Villany.*
To mischief *one*, or *do him a mischief.*
Mischievous, *unlucky hurtful*, or *villanous.*
Mischievousness.
A Misconceived *prejudice.*
A misconjecture, *and*
To Misconjecture, or *guess wrong.*
A Misconstruction.
To misconstrue, or *make*

an ill construction *of.*
To miscount, or *misreckon.*
Miscreancy, *the state of*
A Miscreant, *infidel*, or *unbeliever.*
A Misdeed, or *trespass.*
To misdemean, or *behave himself ill.*
A Misdemeanour.
High Misdemeanour, *a crime next to high treason.*
A Misdoing, or *misdeed.*
To misdoubt, or *doubt wrongfully.*
To misemploy, or *employ to ill purpose.*
A Miser, or *covetous wretch.*
Miserable, *calamitous*, or *niggardly.*
Miserableness.
Misery, or *calamity.*
Mis-fashioned, or *mis-shapen.*
A misfortune, or *disaster.*
To misgive, or *forebode ill*; as *my mind* misgives *me.*
To misgovern, or *rule amiss.*
Misgovernment.
A Mishap, or *mischance.*
To mishappen, or *fall out ill.*
A Mish-mash, or *hotchpotch.*
To misimploy, or misemploy.
To Misinform, or *give a false account of.*
A Misinformation.
To misinterpret, or *give a wrong sense of.*
A Misinterpretation.
To misjudge, or *pass a wrong judgment.*
To mislead, or *seduce.*
A Misleader.
Misled.
To mislike, *dislike*, or *disallow.*
To mismanage, or *manage untowardly.*
A Mismanagement.

To misname, or *nickname.*
To misplace, or *put out of its due place.*
A Misplacement.
A Misprision, *mistake, neglect*, or *contempt.*
Misprison committed by Clerks, *their neglect in engrossing*, or *keeping Records.*
Misprision of Felony, *a being privy to it, which is finable by the Justices before whom the party is convicted.*
Misprision of Treason, *the concealment*, or *not disclosing of known Treason; for which the offender is to be imprison'd as long as the King thinks fit, and lose his goods, with the profits of his Lands during his life.*
Misproportioned.
A Misquotation, or *false citation.*
To misquote, or *cite wrong*
To misreckon, or *mistake in* reckoning.
To misremember, or *call to mind amiss.*
To misrepresent, or *give a wrong character of.*
A misrepresentation.
A Misrepresenter.
Misrule, *disorder*, or *tumult.*
The Lord of Misrule, *the ringleader in a disturbance*, or *the chief among the revellers.*
Miss, *for young* mistress.
A Miss, or *Lady of pleasure.*
A miss, *want*, or *lack of a thing.*
To miss, *omit*, *mistake*, *fail*, *want*, &c.
A Missal, or *Mass-book.*
Misseltoe, or mistletoe, *a shrub.*
To mis-shape, or *disfigure.*
Mis-shapen.
A Mission, or *sending*; as *the* mission *of the Apostles.*

A Missionary, *a popish Priest sent to preach, in foreign Countries.*
A Missive, or *letter sent to one.*
To mis-spell *a word.*
Mis-spelt, or *wrong spelt.*
To mis-spend, or *lavish.*
Mis-spent.
A Mist, or *fog.*
A mistake, *errour*, or *oversight.*
To Mistake, *take one for another*, *misunderstand*, or *commit an errour.*
Mistaken, or *deceived.*
To mis-time *a thing*, or *do it out of season.*
A Mistle-bird, *a kind of Thrush that feeds on*
Mistletoe, *or* Misseldine, *a shrub growing on Oak-trees.*
I mistook or *did* mistake.
A Mistress *of a house*, or *a sweet-heart.*
A School-mistress.
A mistrust, or *suspicion.*
To mistrust, *distrust*, or *suspect.*
Mistrustful.
Misty, or *foggy.*
To misunderstand, or *have a wrong notion of.*
A misunderstanding, *breach of friendship*, or *coldness between parties.*
Misunderstood.
Misusage, or *ill treatment.*
To misuse, or *abuse.*
A Mite, *an ancient small Coin.*
A Mite, or *little worm in Cheese, Meat, Corn*, &c.
A Miter, *or* mitre *in joynery.*
A Bishop's miter, or *cap.*
Mithridate, *a strong treacle, or preservative against poison, first invented by* Mithridates *King of* Pontus.
To mitigate, *allay, asswage*

or *pacify.*
A Mitigation.
Mitred, or *wearing a* miter.
Mittens, *a kind of woollen gloves, usually worn in the winter.*
Mittimus, (*i. e.* we send) *a warrant to send an offender to prison.*
To mix, or *mingle.*
A mixen, or *dunghill.*
Mixt (*from to mix*)
A Mixture.
The Mizzen *mast and sail in a ship.*
To mizzle, or *rain small drops.*

M O

A Moan, or *plaint.*
To moan, *or make* moan.
Moanfull.
A Moat *in the sun-beams.*
Mobby, *a drink in the West*-Indies *made of Potatoes.*
The Mobile, *or* mob; *the giddy multitude.*
A Mock, or *scoff.*
To mock, *scorn, scoff*, or *laugh at.*
Mockadoes, *a kind of stuff.*
A Mocker.
Mockery.
A Mocking-stock.
A Mock-poem.
Mock-privet, *an herb.*
Mock-willow.
A Mode, or *fashion.*
A Model, or *pattern.*
To model, *frame, or make a draught of.*
Moderate, *that does not exceed.*
To moderate, *govern, regulate,* or *set bounds to.*
Moderation.
A Moderatour, *that determines disputes.*
Modern, *in opposition to* ancient, *late,* or *of this time.*
Modest, *discreet in behaviour,* or *bashful.*
Modesty.
A Modicum, or *small pittance.*
A Modification *restriction,* or *limitation.*
To modify, *moderate, qualifie,* or *limit.*
Modish, *according to the* mode, or *fashion.*
A Modilion *in Architecture.*
Modulation, *tuning*, or *warbling in musick.*
A Modwall, *a bird.*
Mohair, *a sort of stuff.*
A Moiety, or *half share* (*a* Law-*term.*)
To moil, or *drudge*, or *to dawb with dirt.*
Moist, *wet*, or *damp.*
To moisten, or *make* moist.
Moistness, *or* moisture.
The Mokes, or *mashes of a net.*
A Mole, *a spot*, or *mark in the body;* also *a rampart* or *peer in a harbour, to break the force of the waves.*
A Mole, *or* mole-warp, *a little creature that lives under ground.*
A Mole-but, *a fish.*
A Mole-hill.
A Mole-trap.
To molest, *disturb*, *vex,* or *trouble.*
A Molestation.
A Cross moline *in Heraldry.*
To mollify or *soften.*
Moloch, *a brazen idol worshipped by the* Israelites, *having the body of a man and the head of a calf.*
Molosses, *the dregs of syrup made in the boiling of sugar.*
To molt, or *shed the feathers as birds do.*
Molten, or *cast*, *as the molten calf.*
A Mome, *a very* mome, or *stupid person that has neither life nor soul in him.*
Moment, or *importance.*
A Moment, or *instant of time.*
Momentany, *that lasts, as it were, but a* moment, or *of a short continuance.*
A Monarch, or *Prince that rules alone.*
Monarchical, *belonging to*
Monarchy, or *the government of a Monarch.*
A Monastery, *Convent*, or *College of Monks.*
Monastical, *or* monastick, *belonging thereto.*
Monday, *the* 2d. *day of the week; so call'd from the* Moon, *which was worshipped on that day, by our* Saxon *ancestors.*
Money, or *Coin.*
Earnest-money.
Entrance-money, *for a scholar's admission.*
Press-money, *given to impressed Soldiers* or *Seamen.*
A Money-bag.
Moneyed, or *well stor'd with money.*
Moneyers, or *Mint-men, employ'd to shear, forge, beat round and stamp,* or *coin the money.*
Moneyless, or *destitute of* money.
Money-wort, or *herb two-pence.*
A Monger, *a small vessel for fishing.*
Monger, *an ancient name for a Merchant, now us'd only in certain compound words;* as
A Cheese-monger.
A Costard-monger.
A Fell-monger.
A Fish-monger.
An Iron-monger.
A News-monger.
A Pelt-monger.
A Wood-monger.
A Whore-monger, *&c.*

A Mongrel, *a creature got by two kinds.*
A monition, *admonishing, warning*, or *exhortation.*
Monitory, or *admonishing.*
A Monitour, *admonisher*, or *remembrancer.*
A Monk, *a religious person*; or *a blot in printing.*
Monkery, or *the profession of a* Monk.
A Monkey, or *Ape.*
Monkish, *belonging to*, or *like a* Monk.
Monkly, as *a monkly habit.*
Monks-hood, *an herb.*
The Counter-poison Monks hood.
Round-leav'd Monks-hood.
Monks-rhubarb, *an herb.*
A Monocord, *a sort of musical instrument with one string.*
A Monopolist, *or* monopolizer, *one that makes it his business*
To monopolize, (*i. e.* to sell alone) or *engross commodities into his own hands, so that none can gain by 'em but himself.*
A Monopoly, *such an engrossing commodities.*
A Monosyllable, or *word of one syllable.*
A Monster, *prodigy*, or *living Creature shap'd, contrary to nature.*
A Sea-monster.
Monstrous, *being like a* monster, *beside the course of nature*, or *prodigious.*
Monstrousness.
A Montero-cap, *a kind of Cap us'd by hunters, horsemen*, &c.
A Month, *so call'd from the course of the Moon; properly, the time from the new-moon, to its change again.*
A Twelve-month, *the space of a year according to the Calendar, allowing 30 and 31 days to the month; altho' a month by the week contains but 28 days; at which rate there are 13 months in a year.*
Monthly, *that happens*, or *is done every month.*
A Monument, or *tomb*, &c.
A mood, or *humour.*
Moody, or *humoursome.*
The Moon.
An Half-moon.
A Moon-calf, or *false conception.*
Moon-eyed, or *owl-eyed, that sees better at night than by day.*
Moon-fern, *a shrub.*
Moon-shine.
A Moon-shiny night.
A Moon-stone.
Moon-wort, *an herb.*
A Moor, marsh, or *fen.*
A Moor-hen, *a fowl.*
A Moor, *or* black-moor.
To moor *a ship*, or *lay out her Anchor to the best advantage for her safety.*
Moorish, or *boggy.*
A Moot, *and to* moot, or *dispute, as Lawyers doe.*
A Moot-case.
A Moot-hall.
Moot-men, *Students at Law that argue readers Cases.*
A Mooter, *or moot-man.*
To blow a moot *at the fall of a Deer.*
Mooped, *up*, or *pull'd up by the roots (a term in Heraldry)*
A Mop *to wash a room with*
A Mope, *or* mome.
To mope, *to become stupid*, or *sottish.*
Mope eyed, or *dim-sighted.*
A Moppet, or *little moppe*, *a young infant.*
Moral, *of or belonging to manners.*
The Moral *of a fable*, or *application of it to the manners of men.*
Morality.
To moralize, *a story*, or *explain the moral sense of it.*
A Morass, or *moorish ground.*
Morals, *manners*, or *conditions.*
More; as *a little more.*
Morel, *a sort of plant.*
A Morel-berry, or *morel cherry.*
Moreover.
Moresk-work, *a course and antick sort of painting*, or *carving.*
A Morisco, or *morris-dance.*
A Morkin, *or* morking *a beast that dies by mischance*, or *sickness.*
Morling, *or* mortling, *the wool taken from the skin of a dead sheep.*
The Morning.
The Morning-Star.
A Mornings-draught.
Morose, *sullen, churlish, froward*, or *peevish.*
Moroseness.
A Morice-dance, *a kind of antick dance, usually perform'd by five Men and a Boy in Girls habit.*
A Morris-dancer.
To morrow, or *the next day.*
A Morse, or *Sea-horse.*
A Morsel, or *bit of bread*, &c.
All-a-mort, *very sad*, or *dejected.*
Mortal, *subject to death*, or *deadly.*
Mortality.
A Mortar *to pound in.*
A Stone-mortar.
A Morter-piece, *to discharge bombs, carcasses, stones*, &c.
Mortar, *of Lime and Sand.*
A Morter-maker, or *dawber.*
Mortgage, (*i. e.* dead-pledge) *a pawn of Lands, Tenements, &c. for money borrow'd, to be the Creditor's*

Creditor's for ever, if the money be not repaid at the time agreed upon.

To mortgage *an estate*, or *pawn it in such a manner.*

A Mortgagee, *the party to whom any thing is* mortgaged.

The Mortgager, *he* or *she that has* mortgag'd.

Mortification.

To mortify, *to make sad; to subdue one's affections,* &c.

A Mortise, *(in Carpenter's work) an opening of a piece of Timber, to let in a tenon.*

Mortised, or *made with a mortise.*

A Mortling, or morling, *the wool of a dead sheep.*

A Morquary, *a duty paid upon a* man's *death to his parish Church, viz. 3 s. 4 d. if his goods are above the value of 20 Nobles; 6 s. 8 d. if between 30 and 40 pounds; and 10 s. if above forty pounds.*

Mosaical, *belonging to* Moses; as *the Mosaical* Law.

Mosaick-work, *curious inlaid work, wrought with Stones, Metals,*&c. *in the shape of knots, flowers and other devices.*

A Moschetto, *a kind of stinging Gnat, very troublesome in several Countries.*

A Mosche, or Mosque; *a Turkish Temple.*

Moss, *a downy herb growing upon Trees, Springs, Stones,* &c. also *a kind of sugar-work made by Confectioners, in imitation of it.*

A Moss-trooper, or Scotch-robber, *like the* Irish-Tories, *and* Italian *Banditi.*

Mossiness, *a being*

Mossy, or *full of moss.*

Most, a *for the* most *part.*

A Mote, or *atom, a thing so small as seems not divisible.*

A Mote, or *ditch.*

Moted *about*, or *surrounded with a ditch.*

A Mote, *an old word for a meeting.*

A Ward-mote, or *assembly of the inhabitants of a ward.*

A Moth, *a worm*, or *flye that eats cloths.*

Moth-eaten.

Moth-mullein, *an herb.*

Moth-wort, *or mug-wort.*

A Mother.

A Mother-in-law.

A God-mother.

A Grand-mother.

A Step-mother.

A Mother-city, or *chief City.*

A Mother-tongue.

Mother of Pearl, *a shell-fish.*

Mother of time *an herb.*

The Mother, or *dregs of Oil, Wine,* &c.

The Mother, or *womb; also a disease in that part.*

Fits of the Mother.

Mother-wort, *an herb.*

Mother-hood, *the quality* or *functions of a* mother.

Motherless, *bereft of a* mother.

A Motion, *moving, march, instance, impulse, inclination,* &c.

To motion, or *propose a thing.*

Motionless, or *void of motion.*

A Motive, or *inducing argument.*

A Motley, or *mixt colour.*

A Motto, *word*, or *short sentence, applied to an emblem* or *device.*

To move, *stir, provoke, incite, propose,* &c.

Movable, *that may be* moved.

Moveable Feasts, *that are kept on the same day of the week, but vary in the day of the month,* as Advent-sunday, Shrove-tuesday, Easter-day, &c.

Moveableness.

Moveables, or *moveable goods.*

A Movement; or *motion in dancing,* &c.

A Mover.

A Mould *and to* mould *(in several senses)*

Mould, *earth*, or *dust.*

To moulder, *or* moulder away, *to fall to dust*, or *waste.*

Mouldy; as *mouldy-bread*

To moult, or *fall off as feathers do.*

A Moulter, or *young duck.*

To moulter, or *shed the feathers.*

A Mound, *fence*, or *hedge.*

To Mound, or *secure with a mound.*

A Mount, or *hill.*

To mount, or *get up on horse-back,* &c.

Well-mounted, *that has a good horse under him.*

A Mountain, or *part of the earth rais'd to a great height above that which lies round about it.*

A Mountaineer, or *inhabitant of the* mountains.

Mountainous, or *hilly.*

A Mountebank, *quack*, or *juggling pretender to Physick.*

To mourn, *lament*, or *wear mourning apparel.*

A Mourner.

A Mourning-Cloke.

Mournful.

The mourning *of the chine, a horse-disease.*

A Mouse, *a little creature.*

To mouse, or *catch mice*

Mouse-ear

Mouse-ear } herbs.
Mouse-tail. } herbs.

A Mouse-trap.
A Dormouse.
A Field-mouse.
A Flitter-mouse, *rere-mouse*, or *bat*.
A shrew-mouse.
Mouse-colour, or *mouse-dun*.
A Mouser, as *a Cat that is a good* mouser.
A Mouth *of living creatures*, &c.
The Mouth of a River, or *the place where it empties it self into the Sea*.
A mouthing-fellow.
To mouth *bawl*, or *to mock with the mouth*.
Lions-mouth *an herb*.
Mouthed, as
Foul-mouth'd, *that uses scurrilous language*.
Meal-mouthed, or *backward in speaking*.
Wide-mouthed.
Wry-mouthed.
A Mouthfull.
A Mow, *pile*, or *stack of Corn, hay*, &c.
To mow, or *cut down Corn hay*, &c.
A Mower.
To mount *a Cannon*, i. e. *set it on the carriage*, or *lay its mouth higher*.

MU

Much, very much, too much, &c.
Much-good, *an herb*.
Muck, *dung*, or *pelf*.
Mucked, or *dunged*.
A Muck-hill, or *dung-hill*.
To be in a muck sweat.
To be muck-wet, or *dropping-wet*.
A Muck-worm, or *rich covetous worldling*.
To mucker, or *heard up*.
A Muckender, or *handkerchief, for a child*.
Mud, *slime*, or *slimy dirt*.
A Mud-wall.
Muddiness.
To Muddle, as *Geese do in the brooks*.
Muddy, or *full of* mud.
To muddy, or *make* muddy.
A Mue, or mew *for a hawk*.
A muff, or *case for the hands*.
An Ermin-muff.
A Sable-muff.
To muffle up.
A Muffler, *a cloth tied about the chin*.
A Mufti, (*i. e.* resolves of doubts) *a name given to the chief Priest among the Turks*.
A Mug, *a kind of drinking-pot*, or *cup*.
Mug-wet } *herbs*.
Mug-wort. } *herbs*.
A Mulatto, *the son of a Negro*, or Indian *Woman, and of a man of another Nation*; or *of a Negro man and a woman of another country*.
A mulberry, *a fruit*.
A Mulct, *fine, amerciament*, or *penalty*.
A Mule, *a beast engender'd of a Horse and an Ass*.
Mule-fern.
A Muleteer, or *mule-driver*.
To mull *white-wine, Sack* &c. *i. e. to burn and season it with sugar, spice*, &c.
Mullein, *an herb*.
Moth-mullein.
Petty-mullein.
Sage-mullein.
A Muller-stone, *to grind colours on*.
A Mullet, *a fish*.
The English mullet.
Mulse, *wine and honey boil'd together*.
Multipliable, or *multiplicable, that may be tiplied*.
The Multiplicand, *an Arithmetical term, signifying the number that is to be multiplied*.
Multiplication, or *multiplying*; also *a rule in Arithmetick*.
A Multiplicity, or *great variety of business*.
A Multiplier *in* (Arithmetick) *that number by which another is multiplied*.
To multiply, *encrease*; or *propagate*.
A Multitude, or *great number of people*.
Mum, *a sort of drink first made at* Brunswick *in* Germany.
Mum-chance, *a term commonly us'd when not so much as one word is spoken in a company*.
To mumble, or *mutter*.
A Mumbler.
A Mummer, or *mute person, in mascarade*.
Mummery, or *buffoonry*.
Mummy *a medicinal composition made of dead bodies imbalmed in* Egypt, Arabia, *&c*.
To beat to mummy, *i. e. to bang one so as to bruise him all over*.
To mump, *to bite the lip; like a rabbet*, or *to disappoint*.
A Mumper, *a canting term for a begger*, or *spunger*.
To go a mumping.
The Mumps, *a sort of squinsey*, or *swelling of the chaps*.
To munch, or *chew*.
A muncher.
Mundane, or *worldly*, as *mundane pleasures*.
Munday, or monday.
Municipal, *belonging to the*

the state, or community of a free Town, or Corporation.
The Municipal Laws.
Munificence, or *liberality.*
Munificent, *free of gifts, bountiful, or liberal*
The Muniment-house, *in Cathedrals, Collegiate Churches, Castles, &c. a room purposely made for the keeping of their Seal, Charters, evidences, &c.*
Muniments, *such sort of authentick Deeds, and Writings, so call'd from the* Latin *word* munio *to defend; because by these a man secures his title to his estate.*
Murder, *a wilful felonious killing of another; upon premeditated malice.*
To murder, or *kill one in such a manner.*
A Murderer.
A Murdering-piece, or *great gun so call'd.*
A Murdering-shot, *to clear the decks of a ship, when boarded.*
Murderous, *ready to commit murder, cruel,* or *bloody.*
To mure up *a door,* or *window,* i. e. *to stop it up with bricks, stones, &c.*
Murengers, *two Officers in the City of* Chester, *yearly chosen to see the walls kept in good repair.*
A Murmur, *and*
To murmur, *grumble*, or *repine.*
A Murmurer.
A Murnival, *at Cards, when four are of the same sort.*
A Murr-bird.
A Murrain, or *rot among Cattel.*
Murrain-grass *an herb.*
Murrey, *a dark brown colour.*
A Murrion, *a kind of steel head-piece.*

Muscadine, *or* muscadel *wine,* or *grapes.*
The Muscat pear.
A Muscle (*in* Anatomy) *a part of the body made of fibres, flesh,* &c. *the instrument of voluntary motion.*
A Muscle, *a kind of shell-fish.*
Musculous, or *full of* muscles.
Muse, *or* muset, *the place thro' which a hare goes to relief.*
To be in a muse, or *brown study.*
To muse *meditate,* or *think upon.*
The nine Muses, *taken by the ancients for the Goddesses of* Musick, *and* Poetry *and the patronesses of Learning. Their names are* Calliope, Clio, Erato, Thalia, Melpomene, Terpsichore, Euterpe, Polyhymnia, *and* Urania.
The musing, or *passing of hare through a hedge.*
A Mushroom, or *toadstool.*
Musical, *of,* or *belonging to* Musick.
A Musician, *one well skill'd in*
Musick, or *the art of singing and playing upon musical instruments.*
A Musick-house.
A Musick-school.
Musk, *a kind of perfume, that grows in a little bag,* or *bladder within certain* Indian *beasts;* also *an herb so call'd.*
A Musk-apple.
A Musk-ball.
A Musk-cat.
A Musk-deer.
A Musk-pear.
The great winter musk-pear.
The Musk-rose.
Musk-scabious, *an herb.*
Musked, or *perfumed with* musk.

A Musket, or *male Sparrow-hawk.*
A Musket, *a sort of gun.*
A Musketeer, or *soldier arm'd with a* musket.
Musket-proof.
Musket-shot.
A Muskin, or *tit-mouse, a little bird.*
Musky, *full of,* or *having the scent of* musk.
A Musrol, *the nose-band of a horse-bridle.*
Muslin, *a fine sort of linnen-cloth.*
A Muslin-cravat.
A Muss, or *scramble.*
A Musselman, i. e. *a true believer* (*among the* Turks.)
Must, or *mould.*
Must, as *wine in the* must, i. e. *new and sweet.*
Must, as *it must be done.*
Mustaches, or *whiskers.*
Mustard, or *mustard-seed.*
A Mustard-pot.
Tower-mustard, *an herb.*
Treacle-mustard.
Yellow *Arabian* mustard.
A muster, or *flock of Peacocks.*
A Muster, or *review of military forces.*
To muster, or *make such a review.*
A Muster-master.
The Muster-master *general of the King's forces.*
A Muster-roll.
Mustiness.
Musty, *fusty,* or *mouldy.*
Mutable, or *changeable.*
A Mutation, or, *change.*
Mute, or *dumb*, as *to stand* mute, i. e. *refuse to plead to an Indictment.*
The mute *Letters,* viz. *b. c. d. g. h. k. p. q. t. so call'd because they have no sound, without the help of vowels.*
Mutes, or *dumb persons, among the Turks, who are usually employ'd in the executing of Criminals.* Mute

Mute, or dung.
To mute, or make dung as a hawk does.
To mutilate, maim, or curtail.
A Mutilation.
Mutinous, or factious.
A Mutiny, or Sedition, especially among soldiers.
To mutiny, or raise a mutiny.
To mutter, or speak between the teeth.
A Mutterer.
Mutton, or sheep-flesh.
Mutual, reciprocal; or alike on both sides.
The Muzzle, or snout o certain beasts.
A Muzzle, or halter for an horse.
The Muzzle, or mouth of a musket.
The Muzzle-ring of a great Gun.
To Muzzle, or tie up the Muzzle of a beast.
My, as this is my book.
A Myriad, (in number) i.e. ten thousand.
Myrrh, a sweet gum of an Arabian tree.
Myrtle, or the myrtle-tree.
A Myrtle-grove.
Myrtle-wine.
Mysterious, full of mystery.
A Mystery, or great Secret, especially in Religion and Trade.
Mystical, mysterious, hidden, or secret.
A Mythologist, one skill'd in
Mythology, the explaining of fables, or poetical fictions.

N A

To nab one, or catch him napping.
Nacker, or naker; mother of pearl, the shell of the pearl-fish.
Nadir (in Astronomy) that point of the heavens which is directly under our feet, opposite to the Zenith.
A Naff, a kind of bird.
A Nag, or young horse.
A Nait, or genuine stone, among Jewellers.
A Nail, and to nail (in different senses.)
A Tack-nail or broad-headed nail.
A Nailer, nail-maker, or nail-smith.
The nailing of Cannon, the driving of a nail into the touch-hole of a great gun.
Nail-wort, an herb.
Naked, uncovered, or bare.
Stark naked.
Nakedness.
A Name, and to name (in several senses.)
A Christian-name.
A Nick-name.
A Surname,
Nameless, that has no name.
Namely, by name, or to wit.
The Nap, hair or shag of cloth, &c.
To nap, or raise the nap of cloth.
A Nap, or short Sleep.
The Nape, or hinder part of the neck.
A Naphew, or French turnep.
A Napkin for a Table, &c.
Napless, or thread-bare.
To take one napping, or to surprize him.
Nappy, or full of nap.
Nard, a plant and ointment.
Spikenard.
A Narration, narrative, or relation of some matter of fact.
Narrow, or straight.
To narrow, or make narrow (in knitting.)
Narrowness.
Nastiness a being
Nasty, or filthy.
A Nation, the people of a countrey.
National, or belonging to, a Nation.
Native, as one's native Countrey.
A Native, one born in a certain place; as a native of London.
Nativity, or birth.
The Festival of Christ's Nativity, or Christmasday.
Natural, that proceeds from nature, or inbred.
A Natural, or fool.
A Naturalist, or one skill'd in natural Philosophy.
Naturalization.
To naturalize a foreigner, to make him as a natural Subject.
Naturalness, or natural affection.
Nature, the original dispositions, properties, or qualities of things.
Natured, as
Good-natur'd, good condition'd
Ill-natured.
Naval, belonging to ships, or to a Navy.
The Nave, or body of a Church.
The Nave, or stock of a wheel that part wherein the spokes are set.
The Navel of the belly.
Navel-burst.
Navel-gall, a Horse disease.
A Navel-string.
The Navel-timbers, ribs, or futtocks of a ship.
Navel-wort, an herb.
Sea-navel-wort.
Naught, or bad.
Naughtiness.
Naughty, vicious, or lewd.
A Naughty-pack, or vicious person.
Navigable, over which one may sail.
To navigate, or sail.
Navigation, or the Art of sailing

sailing.
A Navigator, or *sailer.*
Naulage, *money for fraight or passage.*
To nauseate, *loath*, or *be ready to vomit.*
Nauseous, or *loathsome.*
Nauseousness.
A Navy, or *fleet of ships.*
The Navy-office.
Nay, as *to say nay.*
A Nay, or *denial.*

NE

To neal, or *harden glass.*
A Neap-tide, *in opposition to a Spring-tide.*
Dead-neap, *the lowest Tide which happens, four days before the full* or *change of the Moon.*
Near, *near at hand*, &c.
A near Man, saving or *frugal.*
Nearness.
Neat, *spruce, cleanly, comly*, &c.
Neat-handed.
Neat-handedness.
Neatness.
A Neat, *an Ox, a Cow*, or *a Steer.*
A Neat-herd.
A Neat-house.
Neats-leather.
Neats-feet.
A Neats-tongue.
A Neb, nib, or beak.
The Neb, *or nib of a Pen.*
Necessaries *for life, things that are*
Necessary, or *needful.*
To necessitate, *compel*, or *force out of* Necessity.
Necessitous, or needy.
Necessity, *constraint*, or *Want.*
A Neck, (*in several senses.*)
A Neck-band.
A Neck-cloth, or *neck-kerchief.*
A Neck-lace.
A Necromancer, or *Conjurer.*
Necromancy, *a kind of divination, by calling up the Spirits of the dead.*
Necromantick, *belonging to the black Art.*
Nectar, *the feigned drink of the Gods.*
A Nectarine, *a kind of peach.*
Need, *necessity*, or *want.*
To need, or *stand in* need *of.*
Needful, or *necessary.*
Neediness, or *extreme poverty.*
A Needle, *to sew with.*
The Needle *of a Dial, Watch*, &c.
A Pack-needle.
Shepherds-needle, *an herb.*
A Needle-case.
The Needle-fish.
A Needle-full, *of thread, silk*, &c.
A Needle-maker.
Needless, *unnecessary unprofitable*, or *superfluous.*
Needs, *as it must* needs *be so.*
Needy, *necessitous*, or *poor.*
Ne'er, for *never.*
To neez, or *sneez.*
Neez-wort, *an herb.*
A Negation, or *Denying*
Negative, or *belonging to Denial.*
A Negative, or *negative expression*, as *the criminal stands upon the* Negative, i.e. *denies the Fact he is charged with.*
A Neglect, *omission*, or *disregard.*
To neglect, *omit, have little regard, to slight*, or *take no notice of.*
A Neglecter.
Negligence, *ill looking to a thing, carelesness*, or *heedlesness.*
Negligent, or *careless.*
To negotiate, *manage*, or *transact.*
A Negotiation.
A Negotiator.
A Negro, or *black-moor.*
A neif, *a law-word, for a bond-woman, born in one's house.*
To neigh, or *cry, as a horse does.*
A neighing-bird.
A Neighbour, *one that lives near another.*
Neighbourhood.
Neighbouring, *bordering*, or *adjoining.*
Neither, as *neither more nor less.*
Nep, nip, or *cat-mint, an herb.*
A Nephew, *the son of a brother*, or *Sister.*
A Nerve, or *sinew.*
Nervous, *that has firm sinews strong*, or *lusty.*
Ness, *a word formerly us'd for a Point of land, running into the Sea, and still retain'd in some compounds*; as
Holderness, *in Yorkshire.*
Sheerness-fort, &c.
A Nest, or *birds-nest.*
A Nest, or *company of rabbets.*
A Nest-cock, or *fondling always kept at home.*
A Nest-egg.
To nestle, *make a nest*, or *settle any where.*
To nestle about, *tumble up and down*, or *be restless.*
A Nestler.
A Nestling, or *young bird not fledg'd.*
A Net, *to catch birds* or *fish.*
A Cabbage-net.
A Draught-net.
A Casting-net.
A Net-maker.
Net-work,
Nether, or *lower*, as *the nether milstone*,
The Netherlands, or *low Countries.*
Nethermost.
A Nettle, *an herb.*

To nettle, *sting, vex* or *teaze*.
The blind Nettle.
The dead Nettle, *that has no sting*.
The Sea-Nettle, *a fish*.
A Nettle tree,
Never, never at all, never so, &c.
Nevertheless.
Neuter; or Neutral, *that takes part with neither side*.
Neutrality.
New, *that has not been before, fresh*, or *of late time*.
A New beginner.
New coin'd.
A New comer.
To new dress, or *dress anew*.
New fangled, or *affecting novelty*.
New-fangles, or *new devices*.
A Newgate-bird, or *arrant rogue, belonging to the College of Newgate*.
A New-laid egg.
New *married*.
The New-moon.
To New-mould, or *cast anew*.
New-vamped, or *newly refitted.*,
New-years-day, *Jan.* 1.
A New-years-gift, or *present usually made on that day*.
Newness.
News, or *new intelligence of affairs*.
The News-book, or *paper containing publick news*.
A News-monger.
A Newt, or eft, *a sort of lizzard*.
Next, next after, next to, &c.

N I

A Nias-hawk; *a young hawk that has not yet prey'd for it self*.
A Nib, or *bill of a bird*.
The Nib *of a pen*.
Nibbed, as *a hard-nibbed pen*.
To nibble, *to bite a little and often*.
Nice, *curious, effeminate, dainty, scrupulous, shy*, &c.
A Niceness, or *curiousness*.
Nicety, *a nice way*, or *punctilio*.
A Niche, or *hollow place in a wall, for a Statue*.
A Nick, *and* to nick or *notch*.
In the Nick, or *very instant of time*.
To nick a business, or *Compass it in due time*.
A Nick-name, or *burlesque name given to a person, in derision*.
To nick-name, *one*.
A Nide, or *flock of pheasants*.
A Nidget, ninny or *meer fool*.
Nigella, or *gith, a plant*.
Citron-Nigella.
Field, *or* bastard nigella.
Garden-nigella.
A Niggard, or *covetous miser*.
Niggardliness.
Nigh, or *near*.
Nighness.
A Night, *opposed to day, that space of time, during which the Sun is absent*.
Midnight.
A Night-cap.
A Night-gown.
A Night-hawk, *a bird*.
The Night-mare, *a disease*.
A Night-rail, *a kind of linnen-gorget, worn by women about their necks*.
A Muslin-night-rail.
A Night-raven.
Night-revellings,
Night-shade, *an herb*.
Night-studies.
Inchanters-night-shade.
A Night-walker.
A Nightingale, *a bird*.
Nill, *the sparkles, or ashes, that come from brass tried in the furnace*.
To nim, *filch*, or *steal*.
Nimble, *active*, or *quick*,
Nimbleness
A Nincumpoop, or nickumpoop, *a stupid sot*, or *dull-witted fellow*.
Nine, or *the number of nine*.
Ninefold.
Nine-pins, *to play wit* .
Nineteen.
The Nineteenth.
The Ninetieth.
Ninety, or *fourscore and ten*.
A Ninny, or *sillyfellow apt to be made a fool of*.
The Ninth, *(from nine.)*
A Nip, *and*
To nip or *pinch*.
A Nipper, or *pincer*.
Nippers, *certain small ropes, that hold off the cable from the capstan*.
The Nipple *of a breast*.
Nipple-wort; *an herb*.
Nisi prius, *a writ so call'd from the two first* Latine *words of it; injoining the Sheriff to bring an inquest before the Justices as a certain day*.
The Justice of *Nisi prius*.
A Nit, *in the hair*.
Nitre, *a kind of salt-peter*.
Nitrous, or *abounding with* nitre.
Nitty, or *full* of nitts.
A Nizy, or *fool*.
No, as *no I will not*.
No body.
Nobility, *the rank or degree of noble-men*.
Noble, *of high birth, illustrious, magnificent, generous*, &c.
A Noble, *an ancient coin, worth* 6 s. 8 d.
A Noble-man.
Nobleness, as *the nobleness of a family*.
The Noblets, or *nobility*.

A Nock *of an arrow.*
To nock, or *notch.*
Nocturnal, or *nightly*; as *a nocturnal meeting.*
A Nod, or *beck.*
To nod *with the head,* or *to take a nap.*
A Noddle, *a burlesque word for the head.*
A Noddy, or *ninny.*
A Node, *a hard knob,* or *swelling,*
The Nog *of a mill.*
A Noggin, or *mug.*
A Noise, *a sound,* or *a report.*
To noise abroad, *set abroad,* or *publish.*
Noisome, *loathsome, nasty,* or *stinking.*
Noisomness.
Noisy, *that makes a* noise.
A Nombril, *the lower part of a scutcheon.*
Nominal, as *a nominal* or *titular King.*
To nominate, *to mention, to name,* or *propose one,* as *fit to be chosen*; or *to appoint.*
A Nomination *to a Benefice,* &c.
Nomparel, *or* Numpearl, (*i. e.* incomparable) *one of the least sort of printing Letters.*
Nonage, *the state of Persons under age.*
Non-appearance, or *default of appearing in a court of Judicature.*
For the Nonce, or *on purpose.*
A Non-conformist, or *Dissenter, that refuses to conform to the Church of* England.
Non-conformity.
None, or *no body.*
None-such, or *bristol-flower.*
Non-performance, or *not performing.*
A Non-plus, (*i. e.* no farther) *an extremity beyond which one cannot pass.*
To be non-plus'd, or *put to a* non-plus; *to be balked* or *puzzled.*
Non-residence, *the unlawful absence, of a Clerk from the place of his spiritual Charge.*
Non-resident, *that does not reside in his Cure.*
Non-sense, *impertinence, that is contrary to common sense.*
Nonsensical, or *absurd.*
A Non-suit, or *letting the* Suit *fall.*
To non-suit *one.*
A Nook, or *corner.*
Noon, or *mid-day.*
Nooning, noon-rest, or *taking a nap after dinner.*
A Noose, or *snare.*
To noose *one,* or *get him into a* noose.
A Nope, *a bird.*
Nor; as *neither one* nor *the other.*
Norroy, (*q.* Northroy) *the northern King at arms,* or *third Herald of* England, *whose office is the same on the north side of* Trent *riv. that* Clarencieux *has on the south-side.*
The North.
The North-pole.
The North-star.
The North-wind.
North-east,
North-west.
Northerly, or *northern.*
Northward, or *toward the* North.
The Nose, or *extreme part of the face.*
To nose *one,* or *affront him to the face.*
A hawk-nose.
The Nose-band *of a bridle.*
Nose-bleed, *an herb.*
A Nose-gay *of flowers.*
A Nosel, or *nozel of a candlestick.*
The Nostrils, (*q. d.* nose-thrils) or *holes of the* nose.
Not, not at all, not yet.
Notable, *remarkable,* or *considerable.*
A Notary, or *Scrivener that takes Notes* or *draughts of contracts,* &c.
A publick Notary, *that attests deeds,* or *writings to make 'em authentick in foreign Countries; especially such as relate to Merchants affairs.*
A Notch, or *mark,* as *the notch of an arrow, tally,* &c.
To notch, or *make a notch.*
To notch *hair,* or *cut it unevenly.*
Notch-weed.
A Note, *and to* note (*in all senses.*)
A Note-book.
Nothing, nothing at all.
Notice, or *knowledge.*
A Notification, or *information.*
To notify, signify, or *declare,* or *give to understand.*
A Notion, *conception,* or *imagination.*
Notional, *belonging thereto.*
Notorious, *manifest, clear,* or *evident.*
Notoriety, or *notoriousness.*
Notwithstanding.
Novel, or *new-fangled.*
A Novel, *short Romance,* or *relation of a pleasant intrigue.*
Novelty, *newness,* or *change.*
November, *i. e. the ninth month, in reckoning from* March.
Nought, or *nothing.*
A Novice, *a* Monk, or *nun newly enter'd into the Order*; or *a young beginner, in any art, faculty,* or *profession.*
Noviciate, *the state of a Novice.*
To nourish, *nurse up, cherish.*

rish, feed, keep, or *maintain.*
A Nourisher.
Nourishment.
Now, even now, just now.
Noxious, or *hurtful.*
The Nozel, or nozzle *of a candlestick.*

N U

A Nude *contract (in* law*) a bare promise o a thing without any consideration given on that account.*
A Nudity, or *naked picture*
The Nuel, or *spindle of a winding stair-case.*
Null, *void,* or *of no force.*
Nulled, *abolish'd,* or *made void.*
To nullify, or *make null.*
The Nullity, or *invalidity of an Act.*
A Nullo, or *cypher, that stands for nothing.*
Num, or *stiff.*
To num, or *stupify.*
A Number.
The Golden Number, (*in* Chronology) *see* golden.
To number, *tell,* or *count.*
Numberless, *that can't be numbred.*
Numbers, *the fourth book of* Moses, *so called from the numbering of the* Israelites.
The Numbles, nombles or *entrals of a deer.*
Numeration, (*i. e.* numbring) *that part of* Arithmetick, *which shews the value of the figures, in their respective places.*
A Numerical difference, *(in* Logick*) by which one individual thing is distinguished from another.*
Numerous, or *great in number.*
Numness. (*from* num)
A Nun, or *religious Woman.*
A Nun, or *titmouse, a bird*

A Nuncheon, luncheon, or *afternoon's repast.*
A Nuncio, as *the Pope's nuncio,* or *envoy.*
A Nuncupative Will, or *Will made by word of mouth.*
A Nunnery, or *cloister of* Nuns.
Nuptial, *of,* or *belonging to a Wedding.*
A Nurse, *and* to nurse.
A Nurse-child.
A Nurse-keeper, *a woman that attends a sick Person,* or *one that lies in.*
A Nursery, or *nursing-room.*
A Nursery *of young trees, plants, &c.*
Nurture, *education,* or *bringing up in good manners.*
A Nusance, or *annoyance.*
The Nut *of a cross-bow, musical instrument, Printing-press,* &c.
A Nut, *a fruit.*
The Bladder-nut, *a plant.*
A Chesnut.
An Earth-nut, *pig-nut,* or *ground-nut.*
An Hasel-nut, or *filberd.*
An Indian nut.
A Pistachoe-nut.
The Vomitive-nut.
A Wall-nut.
The Water-nut.
A Nut cracker.
A Nutmeg *a sort of spice.*
A Nut-shel.
Nutriment, or nourishment.
The nutritious juice, (*in* Anatomy) *that affords nourishment to the several parts of the body.*
Nutritive, or *nourishing.*
To nuzzle, or *nestle as a child does in his mother's bosom.*
A Nye, or *great flock of pheasants.*

A Nymph, or *fairy.*
Nymphal, *belonging to Nymphs,* as *a nymphal dress.*
Nymphs, *among the ancient heathens, were certain Virgin-Goddesses; some belonging to Rivers and Springs, and others to Woods and Hills.*

O A

An Oaf, *Idiot,* or *fool.*
An Oak, or *oak tree.*
Ever-green-Oak, *a plant.*
The Holm-oak.
A Mast-oak.
The Scarlet-oak.
A Stone-oak.
An Oak-apple.
Oak of *Cappadocia* } *herbs*
Oak of *Jerusalem* }
Oak-fern, *an herb.*
Oaken, or *made of Oak.*
Oaker, *a mineral.*
An Oar, *of a ship,* or *boat*
The Oar, or *veins of metal unrefined, as it comes from the mine.*
Brass-oar.
Gold-oar.
A pair of Oars, i. e. *a boat row'd by two watermen.*
Oaten, or *made of oats.*
An Oath.
The Oath of *Allegiance and Supremacy.*
Oats, *a kind of grain.*
Wild-oats.
An Oat-cake.
Oat-meal, or *flower of* oats; also *an herb.*
Oat-thistle, or *oat-land thistle.*

O B

Obdurate, or *harden'd;* as *an obdurate sinner.*
Obedience, *obeying,* or *submission.*

Obedient

Obedient, or *dutiful.*
To do one Obeisance; or *shew him a great deal of respect and reverence.*
An Obelisk, *a great square stone all of one entire piece, broad beneath and growing smaller towards the top; usually set up for a monument;* also *a kind of mark in printing* (÷)
To Obey, *be obedient,* or *submit.*
An Object, as *colour is the object of sight.*
To object, or *object against*
An objecter.
An Objection.
An Obit, *dirge,* or *Office said for the dead.*
An Objurgation, *chiding, rebuking,* or *reproving.*
An Oblation, or *offering.*
An Obligation, *tye, bond,* or *bill under one's hand* &c.
Obligatory, *that* obliges, or *binds.*
To oblige, *endear, engage,* or *constrain.*
Oblique, *crooked,* or *awry.*
Obliquity, or *wryness.*
To Obliterate, or *blot out.*
Oblivion, or *forgetfulness.*
An Act of oblivion, *to forget and forgive all that is past.*
Oblivious, or *forgetful.*
Oblong, *longish,* or *of a figure inclining to long*
Obloquy, *speaking ill of slander,* or *reproach.*
Obnoxious, *subject,* or *liable to*
Obnoxiousness.
An Obole, *half pennyweight,* or 12 *grains among Apothecaries.*
Obscene, *unclean, filthy,* or *unchaste.*
Obscenity, *ribaldry,* or *bawdery.*
Obscure, *dark, not clearly express'd,* or *mystical.*
Obscured, or *darken'd with clouds.*
Obscurity.
An Obsecration, *an earnest begging,* or *beseeching.*
Obsequies, *funeral rites,* or *solemnities.*
Obsequious, *dutiful,* or *submissive.*
Obsequiousness.
Observable, *fit to be observ'd.*
Observance.
Observant, *that has regard to,* or *respectful.*
An Observation, *observing, noting,* or *marking.*
An Observator, or *monitor in a School,* &c.
An Observatory, *a place where Astronomical observations are made.*
The Royal-observatory *at* Greenwich.
To observe, *to watch, note, mark, shew respect,* &c.
An Observer.
Obsolete, *grown out of use,* or *disus'd.*
An Obstacle, or *hindrance,*
Obstinacy, or *stubborness.*
Obstinate, *wilfull, self-will'd,* or *stubborn.*
Obstreperous, *full of noise* or *that makes a great noise.*
To obstruct, *stop up,* or *hinder.*
An obstruction.
Obstructive.
To obtain, *get,* or *bring to pass.*
An Obtestation, or *injunction in earnest and solemn words, as it were calling God to witness.*
To obtrude, *thrust,* or *force upon.*
An Obtruder.
Obtuse, or *blunt.*
Obventions *Church-fees,* or *spiritual revenues.*
To obviate, *withstand,* or *prevent.*
Obvious, *i.e. in the way one is going in, plain,* or *easy to be understood.*

OC

An Occasion, *a proper season, fit and convenient to do any thing; a cause, matter,* &c.
To occasion, or *cause.*
Occult, *secret,* or *hidden.*
An Occupant, *one that takes first possession of a thing.*
An Occupier *of land,* &c.
To occupy, *employ, possess,* or *use.*
An Occupation.
To occur, *come in the way,* or *offer it self.*
An Occurrence, *casual adventure, rencounter,* or *conjuncture of affairs.*
The Ocean, or *main sea that surrounds the whole globe of the earth. 'Tis so call'd in* Greek *from its* swiftness, *and is chiefly divided into four great parts,* viz.
The Atlantick Ocean, *that lyes between the west of* Europe *and* Africa, *and the east side of* America.
The Hyperborean Ocean, or North sea, *which environs the land, towards the North Pole.*
The Pacifick Ocean, *so nam'd from its continual calmness; lying between the west side of* America *and* Asia.
The Southern Ocean; *or* South sea, *which encompasses* Magellanica *and the continent under the South pole.*
Ockam, or Okam, *old ropes untwisted and pull'd out as it were into new flax.*
White Ockam, *flax,* or *tow, to be beat into the seams of a ship.*
Ockamy, *Latten,* or *Copper-metal.*
Ockamy-spoons.

Octangular, *that has eight angles*, or *corners*.
An Octave, *the eighth note in Musick*; *also eight days successively following some great festival*.
An Octavo, or *a book in* octavo; *of which eight leaves make a sheet*.
October, *the eighth month after* March.
An Octogon; or *figure of eight angles*.
Ocular, *belonging to the eyes*; as *an* ocular witness, or *eye-witness*.
An Oculist, *a Physitian skill'd in the distempers of the eyes*.

O D

Odd, *not even*.
Oddness.
Odds, or *difference*.
To be at odds, or *at variance*.
An Ode, *a Poem that is sung to the harp*, *or a copy of* Lyrick *verses*; as Horace's Odes.
Odious, or *hateful*.
Odiousness.
Odium, *the censure*, or *blame that is incident to a fault*.
Odoriferous, or *sweet smelling*.
An Odour, or *scent*.

O E

Oeconomical, *of*, or *belonging to*
Oeconomy, *the government of a house*, or *family*.
An Oecumenical, or *general Council*.
O'er, *for* over.

O F

Of *concerning*, or *about*
Off, or *afar off*.
Off-ward, *i. e. towards the sea* (*among mariners*)
Offal, *refuse*, or *dross*.
Offals, *garbage*, or *fragments of meat*.
An offence, *fault*, or *transgression*.
To offend, *transgress*, *hurt*, or *displease*.
An Offender.
Offensive.
An Offer, *and to* offer (*in all senses*.)
An Offering, or *sacrifice*.
A Burnt-offering.
A Heave-offering.
A Meat-offering.
A Sin-offering,
A Trespass-offering.
An Offertory, or *place where* Offerings *are kept*.
An Office, (*in several senses*.)
The Faculty-office, *near* Doctors Commons *in* London, *where marriage-licences*, &c. *are taken out*.
An Insurance-office, *for the insuring of merchants goods at Sea*, or *of houses from fire*.
The Post-office, *where letters are taken in*, *and convey'd to all Parts*.
An House of Office.
An Officer.
An Official, *the Chancellour of a Bishop's Court*, or *an Arch-deacon's substitute*.
To officiate, *to perform an Office*, or *the divine Service*.
Officious, *ready to do one a good office*, *serviceable*, or *very obliging*.
Officiousness.
An Off-spring, *those that spring from*, or *are descended from others*.
Oft, often, or oftentimes.

OG OH. OI OK

An Ogee, or *ogive*, (*in Architecture*) *a member of a moulding*, *consisting of a round and a hollow*.
Ogresses, *in* (Heraldry) *certain round figures*, *resembling bullets*.
Oh! Ohoe!
Oil, *made of olives*, &c.
To oil, or *do over with* oil.
Linseed-oil.
Sallet-oil.
Train-oil.
An Oilet-hole.
Oiliness.
An Oil-man, *a maker*, or *seller of* oil.
An Oil-mill, or *oil-press*.
An Oil-stone *for painters*.
Oily, *belonging to* oil, *fatty*, or *smooth like* oil.
An Ointment.
An Oister, *a shell-fish*.
An Oister-man, *that deals in* oisters.
Oister-green } *herbs*.
Oister-loit. }
Oker, *a mineral of which several colours are made*.
Red-oker.
Yellow-oker.

O L

Old, *aged*, or *ancient*.
Oldish, or *somewhat* old.
Oldness, or *antiquity*.
Oligarchical, *belonging to*
An Oligarchy, *a government in the hands of a few principal men*.
An Olitory, or *kitchen-garden*.
An Olive, *a fruit*.
A Wild-Olive.
Spurge-olive, *an herb*.
An Olive-bit, *a kind of bit for horses*.
An Olympiad, *the space of four compleat years*; *a famous account of time in use among the antient* Grecians. *The first Olympiad happen'd*, A. M. 3174, *and this way of reckon-*

reckoning was brought in by Iphitus, *taking its rise from* *The* Olympick Games, *which were first instituted by* Pelops, *then renew'd by* Atreus *and* Hercules, *and celebrated every fifth year, in honour of* Jupiter Olympius, *in the plains of* Elis, *a City of* Peloponnesus, *near the Town of* Olympia. *These Games were continu'd with great solemnity, for five days, in five kinds of exercises, viz. leaping, running, wrestling, quoiting and whorlbats. The names of the Conquerours were set down on publick record, but the prize they won, was only a garland of olive-branches.*

Omber, *a game at Cards.*

An Omelet, *a pancake of eggs.*

An Omen, *a token of good, or bad luck.*

An Omer, *a* Hebrew *measure containing three pints and a half.*

To Ominate, *give* omen *of presage*, or *forebode.*

Ominous, *ill-boading*, or *portending ill-luck.*

An Omission, or *neglect.*

To omit, *leave out*, *let pass*, or *neglect.*

Omnipotence, *a being*

Omnipotent, or *almighty.*

Omnipresence.

Omnipresent, *that is every where present.*

Omniscience, or *infinite knowledge.*

Omniscient, *that knows all*

ON

On, *or* upon

Once, at once, but once, *&c.*

One *in number.*

One-berry } *herbs.*
One-blade }

One-ey'd.

Onely.

Onely-begotten.

An Onion, *a plant.*

An Onset, *attack*, or *assault.*

On't, *for* on it.

Onward, *or* onwards.

An Onyx, *a precious stone of the colour of one's nail.*

Ooziness, *a being*

Oozy *moist*, *wet*, or *plashy.*

An Opal, *a kind of precious stone.*

Open, *and* to open (*in several senses*)

Open-handed, or *liberal.*

Open-hearted, *free-hearted*, *cordial*, or *sincere.*

Open-heartedness.

Open-mouthed, or *apt to talk.*

Openness, or *freedom.*

An Opera, *a kind of play, with variety of songs and musick.*

To operate, or *work* as *physick does.*

A Operation.

Operative, or *apt to work.*

An Operatour *for the teeth, one skill'd in cleansing 'em and making artificial ones.*

An Opiate, *a kind of medicinal composition.*

To opine, or *give his* Opinion, *sentiment*, or *judgment.*

Opinionate, opinionated; *or* opinionative, *wedded to*, or *stiffly persisting in his own* opinion.

Opinionativeness.

Opium, *the juice of black poppey.*

The Ople, or *water-elder.*

An Oppilation, (*in* Physick) *an obstruction*, or *stoppage.*

An Opponent, or *adversary in a disputation.*

Opportune, *seasonable*, or *convenient.*

An Opportunity, *occasion* or *fitness of time and place.*

To oppose, *withstand*, *resist*, or *object against.*

An Opposer.

Opposite, *contrary*, or *over against.*

An Opposition.

To oppress, *overthrow*, *crush*, *trouble*, or *vex.*

An Oppression.

An Oppressour.

Opprobrious, or *reproachful.*

To oppugn, or *oppose an opinion.*

An oppugner.

Optick, *belonging to the sight.*

Opticks, *a science, which explains the nature and proprieties of the sight.*

Option, or *choice.*

Opulency, or *wealth.*

Opulent, *rich*, or *wealthy.*

OR

Or; as *friend*, or *foe.*

Or, *the gold-colour* (*in* Heraldry.)

Orache, *or* orage, *an herb.*

An Oracle, *a divine answer*, or *counsel.*

Oracular, *or* oraculous, *belonging to*, or *that has the authority of an* Oracle.

Oral, *deliver'd by word of mouth.*

An Orange, *a fruit.*

A China-Orange.

A Sevil-Orange.

Orange-chips.

Orange-coloured.

An Orange-house.

Orange-peel.

An Oration, or *speech.*

An Orator.

Oratory, *belonging to an Orator.*

The Art of Oratory, *the Science of* Rhetorick, or *eloquence.*

An Oratory, or *private* *Chappel*

Chappel to pray in.
An Orb, *circular compass, or sphere; as the Planets move in their several orbs.*
Orbicular, or *round like a circle.*
Orchal, or orchel, *a kind of colour, to die with.*
An Orchard, or *place full of fruit-trees.*
Orchis, *an herb.*
Ordael, or ordeal, (i.e. *Judgment in* Saxon) *certain particular ways of tryal, by which persons accused of crimes, were oblig'd to clear themselves; as by camp-fight, duelling, &c.*
Fire-ordael, *when the party accused, undertook to prove his innocence, by walking blind-fold and bare-foot, over red-hot plough-shares.*
Water-Ordael, *a purgation by putting one's arms into boiling water,* or *by being plunged in cold water. These Tryals were instituted long before the conquest, and continued in force till the reign of K.* John, *when they were abrogated and utterly condemn'd by Pope* Stephen, II.
To ordain, *appoint,* or *enact, to put into holy orders &c.*
An Ordainer.
An Order, *and to* order (*in all senses*)
An Orderer, or *disposer.*
An Ordinance, *law,* or *Statute.*
The Master of the Ord'nance, or *Artillery.*
Ordinary, *common,* or *usual.*
An Ordinary, *an eating-house,* or *set meal; also a Diocesan Bishop,* or *his Suffragan.*
The Ordinary *of Newgate.*

An Ordination, *appointing,* or *admitting into Holy Orders.*
Ordination-days *in the Church of* England, *are the 2d.* Sunday *in* Lent; Trinity Sunday; *the Sunday following; the* Wednesday *after* September 14; *and* Decemb. 13.
Ordure *excrements,* or *filth.*
Organ, or organy, *an herb.*
Orgal, *dried lees of wine, us'd by Dyers.*
An Organ, or *instrument.*
Organ-ling, *a sort of fish.*
Organical, *having proper* organs, *instrumental, us'd as a means,* &c
An Organist, *a player on*
A pair of Organs, *a most melodious musical instrument.*
The Organ-keys.
The Organ-pipes.
Oriel College in *Oxford, founded by* Adam de Brom *Almoner to* K. Edward II. April 20. 1324, *under the name of S.* Mary's house; *to which K.* Edward III. *gave a Tenement call'd* Le Oriele, *on which ground the College now stands.*
Orient, as *an orient Pearl,* i.e. *of great lustre,* or *brightness.*
Oriental, or *eastern.*
An Orifice, *the hole,* or *mouth of a wound,* &c.
Original, or *belonging to*
An Original, *first draught,* or *pattern.*
An Origine, *first rise,* or *source of a thing.*
An Ork, *a kind of sea-monster.*
An Ornament, *embellishment,* or *set off.*
An Orphan, or *fatherless child.*
Orphanism, *the state of an orphan.*

Orpiment, *a yellow kind of Arsenick.*
Orpin, or orpine, *an herb.*
Orrice, Iris, or *flower-de-luce, a plant.*
Orthodox, *that holds a right belief.*
Orthodoxy, or *such a state.*
Orthography, *the right,* or *true way of writing,* or *spelling.*
Orts, *scraps,* or *mammocks.*
An Osier-*tree.*
Osmund the waterman, or osmund-royal, *an herb.*
An Osprey, *a ravenous bird.*
An Ossifrage, (*i.e.* bone-breaker) *a kind of Eagle.*
Ostentation, or *vain-glorious boasting.*
An Ostler, or hostler *in an Inn.*
An Ostlery.
An Ostrich, or estridge, *a great* African *fowl.*

O T

The other, *one of two.*
Otherwise.
An Otter, *an amphibious creature.*

O V OU

Oval, *round like an Egg.*
An Oubut, *an Insect.*
An Ouch, *a kind of Collar of Gold worn by women; also a Bosse,* or *Button of Gold in which some rich stone,* or *Jewel is set.*
An Oven *to bake in.*
Over, as *over head and ears.*
To over-act, or *do a thing with to much affectation.*
To over-aw, *brow-beat,* or *keep in awe.*
To over-bear, or *surpass one*

It **over-blows**, *(a sea-term)* i.e, *the wind blows so hard, that the ship can bear no sail.*
To over-bid, or *bid too much.*
Over-bold, *too hardy,* or *rash.*
Over-born, from *to over-bear.*
To over-boil, *or* boil *too much.*
To over-burden, or *over-load.*
Over-cast, and
To over-cast, *cover over work over; case, line,* &c. or *to throw beyond the Jack in bowling.*
An over-cast, *at bowls.*
Over-cautious, *too wary* or *too circumspect.*
To over-charge, *over-load,* or *oppress.*
An over-clouded *Judgment, cover'd as it were with clouds,* or *darken'd.*
Overcome, *and*
To overcome, *conquer,* or *subdue.*
An Overcomer.
Over-curious, or *too nice.*
Over-curiousness.
To over-do, or *do beyond what is needful.*
Over-done.
To over-drink *himself,* or drink *more than his head can bear.*
Over-earnest, *too* earnest, or *eager.*
Over-earnestness.
To over-eat *himself,* or *get a surfeit by eating to excess.*
Over-fierce, *too fierce,* or *cruel.*
To over-fill, or *fill beyond measure.*
Over-fine, or *that exceeds in fineness.*
To overflow, or *run over, as water does.*
To over-fly, or *fly beyond the mark.*
Over-fond, or *too indulgent.*
Over-forward, or *too eager.*
Over-fraighted, *or* over-loaded, *as a ship is, that has taken in too much fraight.*
Over-gallantly, or *with too great a shew of* gallantry.
To over-go, or *go beyond the bounds.*
Over-gone.
Over-great, or *too great.*
To over-grow, *to grow too fast,* or *in too great abundance.*
Over-grown.
A Over-grown Sea *(according to the mariners phrase) when the waves swell excessively.*
Over-happy, *extremely happy* or *fortunate.*
To over-hasten, or *make too much* haste,
Over-hastiness.
Over-hasty, *too rash,* or *that is ripe too soon.*
To over-hear, *or* hear *as it were, by the by.*
Over-heard.
To over-heat, or *make too hot.*
Over-heavy, *heavy* or *weighty.*
Over-joy'd, or *transported with* joy.
Over-kind, or *over-fond.*
Over-laden, or *over-loaded.*
Over-laid, *as an Infant by its Nurse.*
To over-lay, or *stifle a Nurse-child.*
To over-live *himself, to live too dissolutely.*
To over-load, or *surcharge.*
Over-long, *too long* or *too tedious.*
To over-look, *to inspect,* or *review; to connive at; to look scornfully upon,* &c.
An Over-looker, *or inspector; that looks after the workmen,* &c.
An over-masted *ship, whose masts are too big for its bulk.*
To over match, *or* match *unequally.*
Over-measure, *that which is given above the* measure.
Over-much, *too* much, *too great,* or *superfluous.*
Over-paid, *(from to over-pay.)*
Over past, as *the time is* over-past, or *slipt away.*
To over-pay, or *pay more than is due.*
To over-perswade, *or* perswade, *contrary to one's inclination.*
An over-plus, or *surplusage, that which is over and above.*
To over-poise, or *outweigh.*
To over-power, or *prevail over by force.*
To over-prize, or *overrate.*
Over-prodigal, *too prodigal,* or *profuse.*
An Over-rate, or *excessive rate.*
To over-rate, *to set too great a* rate or *price upon;* also *to assess,* or *tax one too high.*
An over-reach, or *strain, a Horse-disease.*
To over-reach, *to do himself hurt with* reacing; *to surprize, cheat,* or *cozen.*
To over-read *himself,* or *crack his brains with study.*
To over-reckon, or *reckon too much.*
Over-rid, *or* over-ridden.
To over-ride, or *tire a horse, with excessive* riding.
Over-rigid, *too* rigid, *or too severe.*

Over-rigidness.
Over-ripe, or *too ripe.*
To over-roast, *or* roast *too much.*
To over-rule, *to govern with absolute power master*, or *prevail over.*
An over-ruling Providence, *that governs the whole world.*
Over-run.
To over-run, *make an incursion into,or invade a Countrey.*
To over-run *a page (in* Printing *)* or *run it over again.*
Over-scrupulous,*too scrupulous*, or *nice.*
To oversee, *over-look, inspect*, or *let slip.*
Overseen, *that is under one's inspection*; or *mistaken.*
An Over-seer, *that has the management or tuition of.*
To over-sell, or sell *for too great a price.*
Over-set, *overturn'd*, or *overthrown.*
To over-set *a Coach, Ship*, &c.
To over-shadow, or *cover with his* shadow.
To over-shoot *the mark, to shoot beyond it*; or *to go too far in a Business.*
An Over-sight, *an inspection* or *a mistake.*
To over-sleep *himself*, or sleep *beyond the usual hour.*
An Over-slip, or *omission.*
To over-spread, or *cover all over.*
To over-stock *himself*, or *lay up too great a* stock *of commodities*, &c.
To over-strain *himself*, or *do beyond his strength.*
To over-stretch, *to stretch a thing too much*, or *to carry on a matter too far.*
Overt, *open*, or *manifest* as
An Overt-act (*in law*) i. e. *some plain matter of fact that serves to prove the design that was in hand.*
To overtake, *catch*, or *surprize.*
Overtaken.
An Overtaker.
To over-talk *himself*, or *spend his spirits with too much talking.*
To over-tax, or *burden with* taxes.
An Overthrow, *and*
To overthrow, *turn topsy turvy, cast down, defeat*, or *destroy.*
An Overthrower.
Overthrown.
Over-thwart, *a-cross, from side to side.*
To over-thwart, *cross*, or *frustrate.*
To over-tire, or *weary one too much.*
To over-top, *come to a greater height, surmount*, or *surpass.*
To over-trade *himself*, or *carry on a greater trade, than he can well manage.*
An Overture, *an opening*, or *disclosing of a matter*; or *a proposal*; also *a flourish of musick before the opening of the Scenes in a stage-play.*
To over-turn, *overthrow*, or *subvert.*
To over-value, or *set too great a value upon.*
Over-violent, *too* violent, or *too* boisterous.
To over-vote, or *have the plurality of votes*, or *voices.*
Over-wening, *presuming too far*, or *having too great an opinion of himself.*
To over-weigh, or *weigh more than needs.*
Over-weight.
Over-well, or *too well.*
To overwhelm, *to cover over, to plunge*, or *oppress.*
Over-worn, or *quite worn out.*
Ought, or any thing, as *if I had* ought *to do with him.*
Ought, or *should*, as *it* ought *to be so.*
An Ounce, *the sixteenth part of a pound* Averdupois, or the *twelfth part of a pound* Troy-weight.
An Ounce, or *lynx, a wild beast.*
Our, as *he is* our *friend.*
Ours, as *this is* ours.
An Ousel, *a sort of black bird.*
Out, out *of*, &c.
To out-bid, or bid *more than another.*
An Out-bidder.
To out-brave, or *dare one*
An Outcast, or *despicable person.*
An Out-cry, or *exclamation.*
An Out-cry, or *sale of goods by auction.*
To out-do, or *surpass another.*
Outdone.
Outed, *turned out*, or *dispossess'd.*
Outer-darkness, i. e. *that which is without.*
To out-face *one*, or *bear him down to his very face.*
To out-fast, *or* fast *longer than another.*
An Out-gard, or *advanced gard of an army.*
To out-go, or go *faster than another.*
Outgone.
An Out-house, *that depends on a larger building.*
To out-jeer *one*, or *surpass another in* jeering *or* raillery.
An out-jutting *wall, that has a* projecture *beyond the*

the main work.
Outiandish, or *foreign.*
An Out-law, *one depriv-ed of the benefit of the* law.
To out-law *one*, or *pro-secute him to an*
Outlawry, i. e. *the state of those that lose the King's protection, and all the benefits of a subject.*
The Clerk *of the* Outlawries, or *Deputy to the King's Attorney general for making out the writs of* Capias utlagatum *after* outlawries.
To out-learn, or *outstrip another in learning.*
An Out-line, or *line drawn on the outside.*
To outlive, *live longer than another*, or *survive.*
An Out-liver.
The Out-most.
An Out-parish, or *parish without the walls of a City.*
Out-parters, *a kind of thieves in* Scotland, *that make matches for the robbing of men and houses.*
To out-pass, or *out-go.*
An Outrage, *a grievous Injury, violent assault*, or *affront.*
Outragious, *violent, furious, cruel, fierce*, &c.
Outragiousness.
To out-ride, or ride *beyond another.*
Out-riders, *bailiffs errant, employ'd by the Sheriffs, to summon persons to the County*, or *Hundred-courts.*
Out-right, *altogether*, or *absolutely.*
To out-run, or *run beyond another.*
To out-shine, or *surpass in splendour.*
To out-shoot, or shoot *farther than another.*
The Out-side of a thing.
An Out-standing, or *jutting out* (*in* Architecture.)
An Out-street, or *street in the Suburbs of a City.*
To out-strip, or *out-run.*
To out-vy *one at wagering.*
To out-walk, or *Walk beyond another.*
An Out-wall, or *wall on the outside.*
Outward.
To out-weigh, or *exceed in weight.*
To out-wit *one*, *to surpass one in wit and subtilty*, or *to circumvent him.*
The Out-works *of a place*, or *ramparts on the outside*
Ouze, or *miry sedge.*
An Ouzel, or ousel, *a bird.*
Ouzy, *or* oozy, *moist, wet*, or *plashy.*

O W

To ow, or *be indebted.*
An Owl, *a night-bird.*
The great Owl.
A Horn-owl,
A Scrich-owl.
Owl-eyed.
Own, *as written with his* own *hand.*
To own, *to acknowledge, to claim, to possess*, &c.
An Owner, or *proprietary.*
The powder of oak-bark, *used by* Tanners Owse, *in tanning leather*, &c.

O X

An Ox, or *gelt bullock.*
A Sea-o .
Ox-bane, *a herb.*
Ox-heal, or *bellebore-root.*
An O -eye, *a bird and and root so call'd.*
An Ox-fly.
An Ox-gang *of land*, i. e *so much as may be plow'd b, one* ox *commonly taken for* 15 *acres.*
Ox-lip, *an herb.*
An Ox-stall, or *stable for* oxen.
Ox-tongue, *an herb.*
Oxycrat (*in* Surgery) *an easy remedy, made of water and vinegar, to allay the heat of inflammations*, &c.
Oxymel, *a Syrup made of honey, vinegar and water.*

O Y O Z

Oyer and terminer, *a special commission granted to certain Judges to hear and* determine *criminal* causes.
Oyes, (*i. e.* hear ye) *a word us'd by publick criers, when they make proclamation.*
Oyl, *or* oil *made of olives*, &c.
An Oze, or *oozy ground.*
An Ozier-tree, osier-tree, or *sallow.*

P A

A Pace, or common pace, *the measure of two feet, and a half; and in some places three and a half.*
The Geometrical pace *of five foot, by which miles are usually measur'd.*
A Pace, or *herd of Asses.*
A Pace, *gate*, or *manner of going*; also *a certain measure in dancing*, &c.
To pace *an horse*; *to* pace, or *amble as a horse does*, &c.
A Pacer, or *pacing horse*
A pacing-saddle.
An Edict of Pacification, *to pacifie all parties.*
The Pacifick, or *south sea*,

so nam'd because always peaceable and calm.

A Pacifier, or *peace-maker.*

To pacify, *quiet* or *appease.*

A pack, or *bundle.*

To pack, pack *up*, or *make up into a* Pack.

A Pack, or *horse-load of wool*, i. e. *seventeen stone, and two pound.*

A pack *of Cards, Dogs, Knaves*, &c.

To pack *the Cards*, or *put 'em together.*

Pack-cloath, to pack *merchandizes in*

A pack-fork, *such as Pedlers use in carrying their* packs.

A Pack-horse.

A Pack-needle, *to sow up* packs.

A Pack-saddle.

Pack-thread.

A Wool-pack.

A Packer *of Merchants goods*, &c.

A Packet, or *little bundle.*

A Packet-boat.

A Pad *for a horse to carry a port-mantle.*

To pad, or *rob on the road.*

A Pad-nag, *a nag that goes easy.*

A Padder, *or* foot-pad, *that robs on the high-way on* foot.

To paddle, or *dabble in the water.*

A Paddle-staff.

A Paddock, or *great toad.*

A Paddock-stool, or *toad-stool.*

A Paddock, or *enclosure in a park, to exercise the dogs.*

Paddow-pype } *herbs*
Padelion. }

A Padlock, *a sort of lock.*

To padlock, or *shut with a* padlock.

A Pagan or *heathen.*

Paganism, *the principles and practices of* Pagans.

A Page, or *young lad attending upon a person of quality.*

A Page, or *side of a leaf, in a book.*

A Pageant, or *triumphal Chariot.*

Pageantry, *pomp, shew,* or *ostentation.*

A Pagod, (q. d. *the Pagan's God*) *an Idol, worshipped by the heathens in* India, China, *&c.*

Paid, (*from to* pay.)

A Paigle, or *cow-slip.*

A Pail *to carry water in*

A Milk-pail.

Pain, *punishment, torment, trouble*, or *grief.*

To pain, or *put to* pain.

Painful, *that causes*, or *takes pains.*

Painfulness.

A Pains-taker.

Paint, *and*

To paint *pictures*, &c.

A Painter.

A Painter-stainer, *that designs and paints coats of arms.*

A House-painter.

A Pair or *Couple.*

A Palanquin, *a sort of portable chair, us'd in the* Indies.

Paired, or *matchtd.*

The pairing-time *for birds.*

A Palace, *King's Court*, or *Prince's mansion.*

Palatable, or *pleasant to the taste.*

The Palate, or *roof of the mouth.*

A Count Palatine, or *chief Officer in the* Palace, or *Court of an Emperor*, or *Soveraign Prince.*

The Count, *or* Prince Palatine *of the* Rhine, *one of the Electoral Princes of the* German *Empire.*

A County Palatine, *a principal* County, or *shire; enjoying large immunities and privileges;* as *power to exercise a kind of regal authority in determining causes criminal and civil, executing malefactors; making grants*, &c. *within its jurisdiction.*

The Counties Palatine *in* England, are *those of* Chester, Durham, Ely, *and* Lancaster; *but their power was limited by* 27, *Hen.* VIII.

The Palatinate or *County* Palatine *of the* Rhine; *the territories of the* Elector Palatine *in* Germany.

Pale, as *a pale colour.*

A Pale, (*in* Heraldry) *two direct lines drawn from the top to the bottom of a Scutcheon.*

A Pale, or *stake.*

To pale, in, or *enclose with* pales.

Paleness.

A Palfrey, *a horse for state, deck'd with rich trappings*, &c.

Palish, or *somewhat pale.*

A Pallisado, *in* (Fortification) *a fence of pales,* or *wooden stakes, from five to seven foot high, arm'd with two or three iron-points, which are fix'd before fortresses, ramparts*, &c.

To palisado, or *fortify in such a manner.*

A Pall, *a kind of robe* also *a covering usually laid over a Corps at funerals.*

A Velvet-pall.

To pall, *die*, or *grow flat, as wine and other liquors* do.

A Pallet-bed.

To palliate, *cloke*, or *disguise.*

A Palliative, or *imperfect Cure.*

Pall-mall *a kind of sport*,

by *striking a bowl with a mallet thro' an iron-arch at each end of a long alley made smooth for that purpose*; as
The Pal-mall *in* St. James's *park*.
The Palm *of the hand*, or *the measure of a hand's breadth*.
A Palm, or *palm-tree*.
To palm, or *cog a die*.
Palm-Sunday, *the next before* Easter, *in commemoration of Christ's being met by the people, with palm and olive-branches in their hands when he solemnly enter'd* Jerusalem *riding on an Ass*.
A Palmer, or *Pilgrim that carries a bough*, or *staff of* palm, *in going to visit the Holy Places*.
A Palmer, or *ferula, with which boys in Schools are struck on the palms of their hands*,
A Palmer-worm.
Palmestry, or *the skill of telling fortunes, by certain lines* or *marks on the* palms *of one's hand*.
A Palour, *a sort of fish*.
Palpable, *that may be easily felt* or *perceiv'd*.
The Palpitation, or *panting of the heart*.
A Palsgrave, or German *Count Palatine*.
The Palsy, *a disease*.
To palter, *prevaricate*, or *deal indirectly*.
A Palterer,
Paltry, or *sorry*.
To pamper, or *indulge*.
A Pamphlet, *a stitch'd book*, or *a libel*.
A Pamphleteer, *one that writes*, or *deals in* Pamphlets.
A Pan, *a kind of dish of earth* or *metal*,
A Baking-pan.
The Brain-pan.
A Dripping-pan.
The Fire-pan *of a gun*.
A Frying-pan.
The Knee-pan.
A Warming-pan.
A. Pan-pudding, or *pudding made in a pan*.
Panado, *a kind of gruel made of bread-crum and currans*.
A Pancake, or *cake bak'd in a frying-pan*.
A Pander, *pimp*, or *male bawd*.
A Pane, or *square of glass, wainscot*. &c.
A Panegyrick, or *speech deliver'd before a solemn assembly of people*; or *an oration of thanks and praise to an Emperor, Prince*, &c.
A Panegyrist, or *maker of such orations*.
The Pangs or *agonies of death*, or *the throws of a woman in labour*.
A Panick *sudden and distracting fear without known cause, anciently said to be inflicted by the* God Pan.
Panick, *a grain like millet*.
Outlandish panick.
Panick-grass.
Pannage, *the feeding of swine upon mast in the woods*; or *money paid for such a licence*.
Pannage, *a tax upon cloth*.
A Pannel or pane *of wainscot*, &c.
A Pannel or *roll of the Jurors names, return'd to pass their verdict in any tryal*.
The Pomel, or *gorge of a hawk*.
A Pannier, *a basket* or *dorser to carry bread in*.
A Pannier-man, *an under officer, in the Inns of Court, that winds the horn for dinner and supper; providing mustard pepper, and vinegar, for the Hall*.
Pansy, or *hearts-ease a flower*.
To pant, or *beat as the heart*, or *brain does*.
The Pantais, or Pantass, *a hawk's bird fetching of wind*.
Pantaloons, or *pantaloon-breeches*.
A Panther, *a fierce wild beast, thought to be the female leopard*.
A Pantler, or pantrer, *he that keeps the bread, in a noble-man's house*.
A Pantofle, or *slipper*.
To stand upon his Pantofles, or *carry it high*.
The Pantry, or *room where the bread*, &c. *is kept*.
The Yeoman of the Pantry, *at the King's Court*.
Pap *for children*.
A Pap, *teat*, or *dug*.
The Papacy, *papal dignity*, or *popedom*.
Papal, *of*, or *belonging to the* Pope.
Paper *to write on*.
Blotting-Paper.
Cap-paper, or *brown paper, to wrap up wares in*.
A Paper-book, or *book of blank paper*.
Paper-buildings, i. e. *made only of timber*.
A Paper-mill,
A Paper-maker.
Papers, or *writings*.
A Paper-skull'd fellow.
A Papist, *one that professes the popish Religion*.
Pappy, or *soft like* Pap.
Papistry, or *Popery*.
A Parable, *similitude*, or *dark saying*.
Parabolical, *belonging to*, or *express'd in Parables*; also *obscure*.
The Paraclete, *Advocate* or *comforter, an epithet attributed to the H. Ghost*.

A Pa-

A Parade, or *great shew, especially of military Officers in a rich garb.*

Paradise, or *the garden of* Eden.

The bird of Paradise.

A paradox, *a sentiment contrary to the vulgar opinion.*

A Paragon, *a compleat* or *perfect model.*

A Paragraph, *the smaller section of a book where the line breaks off.*

Parallel, *every where alike*, or *equally distant asunder.*

A Parallel, or *comparison of one person with another*; as *the parallel of* Alexander *and* Cæsar.

A Parallel (*in* Geography) *a space of the terrestrial* Globe, *compris'd between two circles, parallel to the Æquinoctial line; between which in the longest day of Summer, there is a variation of a quarter of an hour.*

To parallel or *compare.*

Paralytical, *belonging to the palsy.*

Paralytick, or *sick of the palsy.*

Paramount, *as* Lord paramount; *the chief Lord of the fee.*

A Paramour *an he*, or *she lover*; *a sweet-heart.*

A Parapet, or *breast-work* (*in* Fortification) *an elevation of earth upon the rampart, behind which the soldiers stand, and where the cannon is planted, for the defence of the place.*

A Paraphrase, or *exposition of a thing by other words.*

To Paraphrase, or *make a paraphrase.*

A Paraphraser, *or* Paraphrast.

Paraphrastical, or *belonging to such expositions.*

A Paraquetto, *one of the lesser sort of parrets.*

A Parasite, *a flatterer, smell-feast*, or *spunger.*

A Parasitical plant, *that lives upon the stock of others*; as *Misletoe, Moss*, &c.

A Parathesis, (*in Printing*) *the matter contain'd within two Crotchets.* [ ]

To parboil, or *boil but in part.*

A Parbuncle, (*a sea-term*) *a rope doubled about a cask to hoise it up.*

A Parcel *a small portion*, or *bundle.*

Parcel-makers, *two Officers in the* Exchequer, *that make the* parcels *of the escheators accounts.*

To parcel, or *divide into parcels.*

To parch, or *dry up.*

Parchment, or *vellum*

A Parchment-maker.

Pardon, *and*

To pardon, or *forgive.*

Pardonable, or *to be pardoned.*

To pare, *clip, chip*, or *cut.*

A Pareil, *a kind of Printing Letter.*

A Paring, *that which is par'd off.*

A Paring-knife.

A Paring-shovel.

A Parent, *Father*, or *Mother.*

Parentage, or *kindred.*

A Parenthesis, *thus markt* ( ) *a Clause put into the midst of a Sentence, which being left out, the Sense remains entire.*

To Parget, or *plaister.*

A Pargeter.

A Paricide, or *Murderer of Parents*; or *such a murder.*

Herb-Paris.

Plaister of Paris.

A Parish, or *Parish-Church*

A Parish-Clerk.

The Parish-duties.

A Parish-Priest.

A Parishioner, or *Inhabitant of a Parish.*

Parity, or *equality.*

A Park, *a piece of Ground enclosed and stor'd with wild Beasts, for chace*; as Hide-Park.

St. Jame's Park, *&c.*

A Parker, or *Park-keeper.*

Park-leaves, *an herb.*

A Parley, or *Conference, in order to surrender a Place upon Terms.*

To Parley, or *come to a parley.*

A Parliament, or *general Assembly of the Estates of a Kingdom*; *in* England *of the three Estates*, viz. *King, Lords Spiritual and Temporal, and Commons.*

The Parliament-house.

Parliamentary, *conformable to the method of* Parliaments.

A Parlour, or *Room to receive Company in.*

Parmacity, *a kind of drug.*

Poor-Mans's Parmascity, *an herb.*

Parmesan, *a sort of Cheese brought from* Parma *in* Italy.

A pretty Parnel, or *young Female-Lover.*

Prattling-parnel, *an herb.*

Parochial, *of*, or *belonging to a Parish.*

A Parole, *a word*, or *promise to return, as a Prisoner set at liberty, upon his* Parole.

A Lease-parole, *and*

A Will-parole, *i. e. made by word of mouth.*

A Paroxysm, or *fit of a Disease.*

A Parret, *a Bird.*

To parse, or *expound a Lesson, as School-boys do*

Parsimonious, *saving, frugal*, or *thrifty.*

Parsimony, or *thriftiness.*

Parsley, *a pot-herb.*
Bastard-parsley.
Garden-parsley.
Milky-parsley.
Stone-parsley.
Wild-parsley.
Parsley-hedge. } *herbs.*
Parsley-pert.
A Parsnep, *or* Parsnip, *a known Root.*
Cow-parsnep.
Water-parsnep.
A Parson, or *Minister of a Parish-Church.*
A Parsonage, or *a Parson's Cure.*
A Part, *and to* part *(in all senses)*
To partake, or *take part of.*
A Partaker.
A Parter, or *finer of Gold and Silver.*
Partial, *that sides too much with a Party.*
Partiality.
To participate, or *partake of*
A Participation.
Particular, *singular*, or *special.*
A Particular, or *Inventory of an Estate.*
To particularize, *to insist on the* particulars, *or to produce particular Instances.*
A Partition, or *Division.*
A Partition-Wall.
A Partizan, *a Weapon like an Halbard.*
A Partner, *one that joyns with another in some Concern.*
Partnership.
A Partridge, *a bird.*
A Party, *a certain Person, a Faction,* or *a body of Soldiers.*
Party-coloured.
A Party-Jury, or *Half-Tongue,* i. e. *a Jury of half English-men and half Foreigners, impanell'd for the Tryal of a Criminal of a Foreign Nation.*

To pary, *put by,* or *keep off a blow.*
The Pasch-flower.
Paschal, *of,* or *belonging to the Passeover.*
To pash, or *dash together.*
A Pasquil, *a Libel pasted up for publick view.*
A Pass, *and to* pass *(in all senses.)*
Passable, *that may be passed,* also *tolerable* or *indifferent.*
A Passage, *passing, entry, clause in a Book, chance, play at dice,* &c.
A Passage-boat.
A Passenger, *one that passes,* or *travels by land* or *water.*
The Jews Passeover, *wherein they commemorated the destroying Angel's passing by their Houses, and their going out of Egypt, by eating the Paschal Lamb,* &c.
The Christian Passeover, *or* Easter; *a Festival, in which we celebrate the Resurrection of our Lord and Saviour Jesus Christ.*
A Passenger.
Passibility, or *aptness to suffer.*
Passible, or *capable of suffering.*
Passion, *suffering,* or *anger.*
The Passions, or *affections of the mind.*
Passion-flower.
The Passion-Week, or *the Week before Easter, when Christ's* Passion *is commemorated.*
Passionate, *hasty,* or *inclined to anger.*
Passive, or *ready to suffer.*
A Pass-port, or *safe Conduct.*
Pass-rose. }
Pass-velour. } *flowers.*
Pass-worts. }

Past, or *passed.*
Paste, or *dough.*
Book-binders Paste.
To paste, or *do over with* Paste.
Paste-boards.
A Paste-bowl.
Pastel, *an herb us'd by Dyers.*
The Pastern, *the Ankle,* or *Huckle-bone of a Beast's Foot.*
A Pastil, *a kind of Comfit made up in little Rolls.*
A Pastime, *sport,* or *recreation.*
A Pastor, or *Minister of a Church.*
Pastoral, *belonging to a Shepherd,* or *to a Curate.*
A Pastoral, *a kind of Poem.*
Pastry, or *Pastry-work.*
A Pastry-Cook.
Pasturable, *serving for* Pasturage, pasture, *or* Pasture-ground, *for the feeding of Cattel.*
To pasture *Cattel,* or *put them into* Pasture.
A Pasty, *a sort of Pye.*
An Apple-pasty.
A Lamb-pasty.
A Venison-pasty.
Pat, *convenient,* or *pertinent.*

A Pat, or *little stroke.*
To pat, or *hit one a* pat.
A Patacoon, *a* Spanish *Coin, worth about* 4 *s.* 8 *d.*
A Patch, *and*
To patch, *piece,* or *mend.*
A Patcher.
A Pate, or *head.*
A Long-pated, or *sharp-witted fellow.*
A Patent, or *royal grant, the same with*
Letters-Patent.
A Patentee, *he to whom the King has granted a*
Pa-

Patent.
Paternal, or *fatherly*.
The Pater-Noster, or *Lord's Prayer.*
A Path, or *way to walk in.*
A Foot-path.
Pathetical, or pathetick, *that stirs up the Affections.*
Patheticalness.
Patience, *a Vertue enabling to bear Afflictions, &c. with Courage and Resolution.*
Patience, or Monk's *Rhubarb, an herb.*
Patient, or *that suffers long.*
A Patient, *sick* or *wounded Person under cure.*
A Patriarch, (*i. e.* chief Father) *the Head of a Family*; also *a Church-Dignitary, above an Archbishop.*
Patriarchal, *of*, or *belonging to a* Patriarch.
A Patriarchate, *the Jurisdiction of a* Patriarch.
Patrimonial, *belonging to*
A Patrimony, *Inheritance* or *Estate left by a Father.*
A Patriot, *a Father of his Country*, or *publick Benefactor.*
The Patroll, or *nightly rounds made by the Gards, in a Garrison,&c.*
A Patron, *a great Master, powerful Friend, Protector*, or *Advocate*; also *one that has the right of presenting to a Benefice.*
Patronage, *the Office of a Patron.*
A Patroness, *a female Patron.*
To patronize, *to be a Patron, to protect, or defend.*
A Patten, or *wooden Shooe.*
A Pattern, *model*, or *sample.*
A Pavan, *a kind of dance.*
To pave, *as to pave a street*, or *set it with stones.*
A Pavement, or *paved floor.*
A Paver.
Paviage, *Money paid for paving the streets*, or *high-ways.*
A Paving-beetle.
A Pavilion, or *Tent of War.*
The Paunch, or *nethermost part of the Belly.*
To paunch, or *gore one on the Belly.*
A Paunch-belly, or *gorbelly.*
A Pause, or *stop*
To pause, *rest*, or *muse upon a Thing.*
The Paw, or *foot of some beasts, as of a Bear, Wolf, Cat, &c.*
To paw, as *a Dog does.*
Sharp-pawed.
A Pawn, or *pledge.*
To pawn, or *give in* pawn.
A Pawn-broker.
A Pawner.
Pay, *and* to pay (*in several senses.*)
A Pay-master.
Payable, *to be paid.*
A Payer.
A Payment.

PE

A Pea, *a kind of pulse.*
A Pea-cock, *a fowl.*
A Pea-hen.
Peace, *concord, rest, quietness, silence, &c.*
A Clerk of the Peace.
A Justice of Peace.
A Peace-maker.
Peaceable, or *quiet.*
Peaceableness.
A Peach, *a fruit.*
The Nut-peach.
A Quince-peach, or *yellow* peach.
A Peak, *a sharp point*, or *the top of a hill.*
The Peak *of a coif, &c.*
A Peaking-fellow, *i. e. one that has a sorry look.*
A Peal, or *noise of Bells*, &c.
A Pear, *a fruit.*
A Bell, or *gourd-pear.*
A Breast-pear.
A Butter-pear.
A Bon-chretien-pear.
A Catharine-pear.
A Choak-pear, or *wild pear.*
A St. James's Pear.
A King-pear.
A long-tail'd, or *long-stalk'd* pear.
A Musk-pear.
An Orange-pear.
A Pound-pear.
A Quince-pear.
A Russet-pear.
A Sand-pear.
A Tankard-pear.
A St. Thomas's-tide Pear, or *winter-pear.*
A Venus-pear.
A Warden-pear.
A Water-pear.
A Pear-bit, *a kind of* bit *for Horses.*
A Pear-main, *a sort of Apple.*
A Pearch, *a fresh-water fish.*
A Pearch, *rod*, or *pole, a Land-measure, commonly of* 16 *Foot and a half, of which* 40 *in length, and* 4 *in breadth make an Acre of Ground.*
To pearch, or *light upon, as a bird does.*
A Pearching-stick, *for a Cage.*
A Pearl, *a Jewel bred in certain shell-fish.*
A Pearl, or *white in the Eye.*
Mother of Pearl, *the shell in which the Pearls are found.*
Pearl-grass.
The Pearl-letter, *one of the smaller sorts of Printing Letters.*
Pearl-plant. } *herbs.*
Pearl-wort. }

A

A Peasant, or *Country-man.*
Peas, *a sort of pulse.*
Chich-pease.
Gray-pease.
Green-pease.
Heath-pease, *an herb.*
Long-pease.
Winged wild pease.
A Pease-cod.
A Pebble, *a round and hard stone.*
A Peccadillo, or *small fault.*
Peccant (*in* Physick) as *a peccant* or *malignant humour.*
A Peck, *a dry measure, the fourth part of a bushel.*
To peck, *with the bill, as a bird does.*
Peculiar, *particular,* or *singular.*
A Peculiar, *a Parish,* or *Church exempt from the Ordinary, and the Bishop's Courts.*
The Court of Peculiars.
A Pecuniary Mulct, or *fine paid in Money.*
The Pedals, or *low Keys of some Organs, to be touch'd with the* Foot.
A Pedant, *a paltry Schoolmaster,* or *unpolite Scholar, that has a great Opinion of his own Learning.*
Pedantick, or *imitating a Pedant.*
Pedantry, *a* pedantick *way* or *humour.*
A Pederero, *a sort of ship-gun.*
The Pedestal, or *foot-stall of a Pillar.*
A Pedigree, *genealogy,* or *descent from Ancestors.*
A Pediment, *an ornament in Architecture.*
A Pedler, *that sells small wares.*
Pedling, as *to go pedling about.*
A Peek, or *grudge.*

A Peal, or *rind, and*
To peal, or *pull off the* peal.
Orange-peal.
An Oven-peel, *to set pies* &c. *into the oven.*
A Printer's-peel, *with which they hang up the printed sheets to dry.*
A Salmon-peel, or *young* Salmon.
To peep, or *look thro' a hole;* or *to cry as a bird does.*
A Peer, *a mole in a harbour* or *rampart, rais'd against the force of the sea;* as *the peer of* Dover.
A Peer *of the Realm;* or *lord.*
Peerage, *a* Peer's *dignity;* or *a Tax for the maintenance of a* Sea-peer.
Peerless, *matchless,* or *incomparable.*
To *be tried by his* Peers, i. e. *equals.*
Peevish, *fretful,* or *froward.*
Peevishness.
A Peg, *and*
To peg, or *fasten with* pegs.
Pelf, *paltry stuff,* or *ill-gotten riches.*
A Pelican, *a bird.*
Pellamountain, *an herb.*
A Pellet of *lead, paste,*&c.
Pellitory *of the wall.* }
Pellitory *of* Spain. } *herbs.*
Double-pellitory. }
Pell-mell, *helter-skelter,* or *confusedly;* as *they enter'd the Town* pell-mell.
A Pelt or *skin.*
Pelt, (*in* Falconry) *the torn parts of a dead fowl.*
A Pelt-monger, or *skinner.*
Pelt-wool, *wool pull'd off from the skin of dead sheep.*
To pelt, *chafe,* or *be in fume.*
To pelt *one with stones,*&c.
A Pen *to write with.*

To pen, or *commit to writing.*
A Pen-case.
A Pen-knife.
A Pen-man, *one skill'd in fair writing, inditing,* or *composing of books.*
The Pen-men *of the Holy Scriptures.*
A Pen, or *fold for cattel.*
To pen *up,* or *shut up in such a* pen.
A Sheep-pen.
Penal, *that inflicts punishment;* as *the* penal laws *against Papists,* &c.
A Penalty, or *fine impos'd as a punishment.*
Penance, *a sort of mortification practis'd among* Roman Catholicks.
Pence, (*from* penny) as *two pence, three pence.* &c.
A Pencil, *to draw,* or *paint with.*
A Pencil-case.
A Pendant, or *ear-jewel.*
The Pendants, or *streamers of a ship.*
Pendulum, (*i e.* hanging *down*) *the iron-rod in a clock that swings with an equal poise, and exactly regulates its motion.*
A Pendulum-watch.
Penetrable, or *that may be* penetrated.
To penetrate, *to pierce thro'* or *to dive into.*
Penetrative, or *apt to* penetrate.
A Penguin, *a sort of bird.*
A Peninsula, *a tract of land surrounded with water except in one place, where it is join'd to the Continent, by a small neck of land.*
Penitence, or *repentance.*
Penitent, *repenting,* or *being sorrowful, for committing sin,* &c.
A Penitent, or *penitent person.*

Pe-

Penitential, or *belonging to repentance.*

A Penitentiary, *a Priest that enjoyns* penance.

A Pennant, *a cable to hoise up heavy goods into a ship.*

Penned (*from to* pen) as *a letter well* penned.

A Penny, *of English coin.*

A Half-penny.

An Earnest-penny.

A Penny-father, or *old miser.*

The Penny-post.

Penny-flower.

Penny-grass. } *herbs.*
Penny-rot.
Penny-royal.

A Penny-weight, or 24 *grains.*

Penny-wort of the wall, *an herb.*

A Penny-worth.

A Pension, *Salary,* or *yearly allowance.*

Pensions, *in the Inns of Court, certain yearly payments, made by every member to the house.*

A Pensioner, *one that receives a pension*; *at* Cambridge, *a scholar that pays for his Commons.*

Gentlemen Pensioners, *the noblest sort of Royal Gard, all of honourable birth, who gard the King's person, in his palace with Partisans, and have a salary of* 80 l. per ann.

Pensive, *thoughtful,* or *sad.*

Pensiveness.

Pent *up,* or *shut up close.*

A Pentagon, *a figure of five angles,* or *Corners.*

The Pentateuch, or *five Books of* Moses.

Pentecost, or *Whitsuntide so call'd in* Greek, *from its being the* 50th *day after* Easter.

A Pent-house, *to keep off Rain.*

Penurious, or *niggardly*

Penuriousness.

Penury, or *extreme want of necessaries.*

Peony, *a plant.*

The People, or *common* people.

To people *a Country,* or *fill it with* people.

Pepper, *a spice.*

To pepper, or *season with* pepper.

Guinny-pepper.

Jamaica-pepper.

A Pepper-box,

Pepper-proof.

The Pepper-plant.

Pepper-wort, *an herb.*

Peradventure, or *perchance.*

A Perambulation, *a walking* or *travelling about*; or *a surveying.*

To parceive, *to understand, to spye,* or *to find out.*

Perceivable, or perceptible *that may be perceived.*

A Perception, or *perceiving.*

Perchance, or *perhaps.*

Perdition, *ruin,* or *destruction.*

A Perdrigon, *a sort of plum.*

Perdu. as *to lye* perdu.

Perdues, (i. e. *lost*) *the forlorn hope of a Camp, so call'd, because given over for lost men, by reason of the danger of their service.*

A Peregrination, or *travelling in foreign Countries.*

A Peregrine *hawk.*

Peremptorily, or *absolutely.*

Peremptory, *express, final,* or *determinate.*

Perfect, *complete,* or *entire.*

To perfect, *make* perfect, or *finish.*

Perfectness, or perfection.

Perfidious, *false,* or *treacherous.*

Perfidiousness.

To perform, *bring to pass,* or *accomplish.*

A Performance.

A Performer.

A Perfume, or *sweet scent, and*

To perfume.

A Perfumer, or *seller of* perfumes.

Perfunctory, *slight,* or *careless.*

Perhaps, as *perhaps you don't know him.*

A Peridot, *a greenish sort of precious stone.*

Peril, or *danger.*

Perillous, or *full of* peril.

A Period, *perfect sentence, close,* or *conclusion*: *In* Astronomy, *the space of time, during which a star makes its full course.*

Periodical, *that returns at certain seasons.*

Periœci, (*in* Geography) &c. *those that live under the same Parallel, but opposite Meridians*; *having the same seasons of the year and length of days*; *but when 'tis noon with one, 'tis midnight with the other.*

Periscians, *the inhabitants of the frigid Zones, whose shadows turn round in the space of* 24 *hours.*

To perish, *to be quite spent, gone* or *lost*: *to die, be kill'd,* or *cut off.*

Perishable, *apt to perish,* or *come to ruin.*

Perjured, *that has forsworn himself.*

A Perjurer.

Perjury, or *taking a false Oath.*

A Periwig, *an artificial head of hair.*

A Periwig-maker.

Periwinkle, *a sea-snail, also an herb.*

To perk up, *lift up the head,*

head, or appear lively.
Permanent, *durable, or constant.*
Permission, *leave, or allowance.*
To permit, *suffer, or give leave.*
The Permutation, *or changing of a spiritual living.*
To permute, *or change Benefices.*
Pernicious, *destructive, mischievous, or hurtful.*
Perniciousness.
A Perpender, *or* perpend-stone, *(in Architecture) a stone made just of the breadth of a Wall; shewing its smoothed ends on each side.*
Perpendicular, *that is directly down-right.*
A Perpendicular, *or perpendicular line.*
To perpetrate, *or commit a Crime.*
Perpetual, *that does not cease, continual, everlasting, or endless.*
To perpetuate, *or make perpetual.*
Perpetuity.
Perplex, *intricate, difficult, or doubtful.*
To perplex, *entangle, confound, or disquiet.*
Perplexity.
A Perquisite, *a casual profit, or gain, that arises by an Office, &c.*
Perry, *a drink made of pears.*
To persecute, *(i. e. follow hard after) to vex, trouble, or oppress.*
Persecution.
A Persecuter.
Perseverance, *or constancy in well-doing.*
Perseverant, *apt*
To persevere, *continue constantly, or be stedfast to the end.*
To persist, *abide, hold on, or continue.*
A Persistance *in an opinion.*
A Person, *a Man, or Woman; as a publick or private Person.*
Personable, *or comely.*
A Personage, *or honourable Person.*
Personal *of, or belonging to a* person.
To personate, *act, or represent a* person.
Perspective, *a Science that gives an account of the Sight and its Objects.*
A Perspective, *or Landskip.*
A Perspective-glass.
Perspicacious, *quick-sighted, or of a ready apprehension.*
Perspicacity.
Perspicuity, *clearness, or plainness in speaking or writing.*
Perspicuous *clear, or evident.*
A Perspiration, *or breathing thro' the Pores.*
To persuade, *or* perswade, *to make one believe, advise, induce, or prevail with one.*
A Persuader.
A Persuasion.
Persuasive, *or persuasory, that is apt to persuade.*
Pert, *brisk, or lively.*
To pertain, *appertain, belong to, or concern.*
Pertinacious, *(i. e. that holds fast) obstinate, stubborn, or stiff in Opinion.*
Pertinacity *or* pertinacy.
Pertinence, *fitness, or suitableness.*
Pertinent, *fit, or pat.*
Pertness, *or briskness.*
A Perturbation, *disorder or trouble of mind.*
Perverse, *froward, untoward, or cross-grain'd.*
Perverseness, *or perversity.*
A Perversion, *or seducing.*
To pervert, *turn up side down, debauch, or seduce.*
A Perverter.
Pervicacy, *stubbornness, frowardness, or wilfulness.*
A Perusal *of a Book, &c.*
To peruse, *look, or read over.*
A Peruser.
Periwincle, *an herb.*
Pest, *or plague, as he is the* pest *of Mankind.*
A Pest-house, *an Hospital for Persons sick of the Plague.*
To pester, *embarass, or trouble.*
Pestiferous, *that brings, or causes the Plague.*
The Pestilence, *or* plague, *a Disease caus'd by the infection of the Air.*
Pestilence-wort, *an herb.*
Pestilent, *pleguy, or destructive; as a* pestilent *heresie.*
Pestilential, *that partakes of the Plague; as pestilential fevers, vapours, &c.*
A Pestle, *for a Mortar.*
A Pestle *of Pork,* i. e. *the end of the Leg.*
To take Pet, *or to be in a* pet; *to fret or fume.*
A Petard, *a hollow engine made of metal, in form of a Cap, from 7 to 8 Inches deep, and 5 Diameter in the Muzzle. 'Tis charg'd with Powder beaten very small, and fix'd to a thick Plank, called the* Madrier, *in order to break open Gates, &c.*
A Petardeer, *he that manages the* petard.
Peter-pence, *a tribute of a penny for every house, heretofore given to the Pope, by* Inas *King of the* West-Saxons.
St. Peter's-*corn, an herb.*
St. Peter's-*fish.*

St. Peter's wort, *an herb.*
A Petition, or *request to a superiour.*
To Petition, or *present a* petition.
A Petitioner.
To petrify, or *turn into stone.*
A petronel, *a kind of gun, for a horseman, hanged at the breast.*
A Petticoat, *a woman's garment.*
A Pettifogger, or *ignorant practitioner in the Law.*
Pettish, *apt to take* pet, *peevish,* or *froward.*
Pettitoes, or *Pigs-feet.*
Petty, or *little*; as *a petty King.*
Petty-cotty, *an herb.*
Petty-larceny, or *small theft, when it does not exceed the value of* 12d.
Petty-treason. *See* Treason.
Petulancy, *a being.*
Petulant, *sawcy, malapert,* or *wanton.*
A Pew, *to sit in, at Church.*
A Pewet, *a bird.*
Pewter, *a metal.*
A Pewter-dish.
A Pewterer.

P H

The Phancy, *or* Fancy.
A Phantasie, or *vision.*
Phantastry, or *fantasticalness.*
A Phantome, *apparition,* or *ghost.*
Pharisaical, *belonging to the* pharisees.
Pharisaism, *the profession of the*
Pharisees, *a* Jewish *Sect that pretended to extraordinary Holiness; so called from the* Hebrew *word* Pharas, *to separate; because they were set a-part from the common People, and addicted to the study of the Divine Law.*
Pharmacy, *the Art of preparing Medicines,* or *Physical Remedies.*
A Pheasant, *a delicate fowl.*
A Pheasant-pout, or *young pheasant.*
A Pheon, *(in* Heraldry*) the head of a dart.*
Philological, *belonging to*
Philology, (i. e. *the love of discourse,* or *learning) the study of Humanity,* or *of the liberal Sciences.*
A Philosopher, *one skill'd in* philosophy.
Philosophical, *belonging to that Science.*
To philosophize, or *play the* philosopher.
Philosophy, (i. e. *the love,* or *study of wisdom) the knowledge of divine and humane things; being chiefly of two sorts,* viz. *Moral and Natural.*
A Philter, or *love-potion.*
Phlebotomy, *the Art of opening a vein,* or *of letting Blood.*
A Phœnix, *a fabulous bird, said to be of the bigness of an Eagle, and to live* 660 *Years; then having made her Nest of hot Spices which are set on fire by the sun-beams, she burns, and a worm rises out of her ashes, which grows to be a new* Phœnix.
Phlegm, *one of the four humours of the Body.*
Phlegmatick, or *full of* phlegm.
Phrantick, or *mad.*
A Phrase, *expression,* or *manner of Speech.*
To phrase it; or *express a thing in a peculiar manner.*
A Phraseology, *or* phrase-book.
Phrensie, or *madness.*
The Phthisick, or *tisick, the consumption of the Lungs.*
A Phylactery; *a Parchment-scroll, in which the ten Commandments,* or *some Passage of the Scripture were writ; worn by the* Pharisees, *on their fore-heads, arms, and hem of their Garments.*
Phyllyrea, or *mock-privet, an herb.*
Physical, *belonging to* physick.
A Physician, *one skill'd in* Physick, *the Art of curing diseases;* or *medicines made for that purpose.*
To physick, or *use* physick.
A Physiognomer, *or* physiognomist, *one well vers'd in*
Physiognomy, *the skill of guessing at the Natures, Conditions, and Fortunes, of persons by a view of their Face, Body,* &c.
Physiology, or *natural Philosophy, treating of the nature of things, by their causes, effects,* &c.

P I

A Piaster, *an* Italian Coin, *about the value of our Crown.*
A Piazza, *a porch,* or *walking-place with Pillars; as the Piazza of* Covent-Garden.
Pica, *a Printing-letter, of which there are three sorts,* viz. *small, great, and double.*
A Pibble, or *pebble-stone.*
A Pick, *a sort of tool.*
To pick, *(in all senses.)*
A Pick-ax.
A Pick-lock.
A Pick-pocket.

Pick-purse, *an herb.*
A Pick-thank, *a flattering tale-bearer.*
Pickage, *money paid at Fairs for breaking the Ground, to set up Booths,* or *Stalls.*
A Pickaroon, *a sort of Pirate-ship.*
To pickeer, or *skirmish.*
A Picker, *of bones, quarrels,* &c.
An Ear-picker.
A Horse-picker.
A Lock-picker.
A Tooth-picker.
Picket, *a game at Cards.*
Pickle, *a sort of seasoning.*
To pickle, *fish,* or *flesh.*
A pickled *rogue, one full of all manner of mischief.*
A Pickrel, or *young pike-fish.*
A Picture, *painting, image,* or *representation.*
Pictured, or *represented.*
A Picture-drawer, or *maker of Pictures.*
To piddle, to *trifle,* or *to eat here and there a bit.*
A Piddler.
A Pie, or *pasty.*
An Apple-pie.
An Eel-pie.
A Minc'd-pie.
A Mutton-pie.
A Pudding-pie.
A Stake-pie.
A Veal-pie, *&c.*
A Pie, or Mag-pie, *a bird.*
A Sea-pie.
A Piece, *portion, slice, chop,* &c.
A Chimney-piece.
A Piece-broker.
A Piece of Ord'nance.
A Field-piece.
A Fowling-piece.
Piece-meal, *in pieces,* or *peice by piece.*
To piece, or *patch.*

A Piecer *of old Clothes.*
Pied, or *spotted;* as *a pied Horse.*
To piep, or *cry like a chick.*
Pie-powder-Court, (i. e. *the dusty-foot Court) held in Fairs, to yield Justice to buyers and sellers, and redress disorders,* &c. *so call'd from the expedition in the hearing of causes, before the dust goes off from their Feet.*
To pierce, *to bore thro',* or *to broach.*
A Piercer, *to pierce with.*
Piety, or *godliness.*
A Pig, *or* sucking-pig.
To pig, or *bring forth* pigs.
A Barrow-pig.
A Guinea-pig.
A pig *of Lead.*
Pig-ey'd, *that has little eyes.*
A Pigeon, *a bird.*
A Rock-pigeon.
A Rough-footed-pigeon.
A Wild-pigeon.
A Wood-pigeon.
A Pigeon-hole.
A Pigeon-house.
Pigeons-foot, *an herb.*
Pigeons-herb.
A Pike, or *spear.*
A Pike-man.
A Pike-staff.
A Pike, *a fish.*
Piked, *picked,* or *sharp-pointed*
A Pilaster, *a square Pillar set in a Wall.*
A Pilch, or *covering for a saddle.*
A Pilch, or *flannel-clout for a young Child.*
A Pilchard, *a sea-fish.*
A Pile, or *heap of wood, a post, a mass of Building,* &c.
To pile *up,* or *heap up in* a pile.
To play at Cross *and* Pile.
The Piles, *a disease in the Fundament.*

Pile-wort, *an herb.*
Great pile-wort.
Small pile-wort.
To pilfer, or *steal little things.*
A Pilferer.
A Pilgrim, or *traveller upon account of* Religion.
A Pilgrimage.
A Pill, or *medicinal Composition, made up round like a little ball.*
To pill *off,* or *peel.*
To pill *and* poll, *to use extortion, to pillage* or *plunder.*
Pillage, or *plunder.*
To pillage *a Town,* &c.
A Pillager.
A Pillar, *of wood,* or *stone to support a building.*
Pilled, or *bare of hair.*
A pilled *Ewe.*
A Pillion, *for a woman to ride on.*
A Pillory, *a well known wooden engine to punish several sorts of offenders.*
A Pillory-knight.
A Pillow, *to lay the head upon.*
A Pillow-bear, or *linnen bag to cover a* pillow.
A Pilot, or *chief Steersman of a Ship.*
A Pimp, *a procurer of,* or *attendant upon whores.*
To pimp, or *play the* pimp.
Pimpernel, *an herb.*
Pimping, pitiful, or *sorry;* as *a pimping business.*
A Pimple, or *push.*
A Pin, *and to* pin (*in all senses.*)
An Axle-pin, *or* linch-pin, *the iron-pin that keeps the wheel in.*
A Crisping-pin, *to curl hair with.*
A Larding-pin, *to* lard *meat with.*

A

A Rolling-pin, *to roll out paste.*
A Pin-case, *to put pins in.*
Pin-dust.
A Pinner, or *Pin-maker; also a pounder of cattel.*
A Pincer, or *pair of* pincers.
A Pinch, *and to* pinch *(in several senses.)*
A Pinch-fist, *or* pinch-penny; *a scraping miser.*
A Pinch-gut, or *pinch-belly.*
A Pincher.
A Pine, or *pine-tree.*
A Wild-pine.
Ground-pine, *an herb.*
A Pine-apple.
To pine, pine *away*, or *languish.*
A Pinfold, *to* pin *up cattel.*
A Pink, *a little ship*; or *a flower so call'd.*
A double-pink.
To pink, or *cut and figure silk, taffety,* &c.
A Pinker.
Pink-eyed, *that has small eyes.*
A Pinnace, *a small sea-vessel.*
A Pinnacle, or *battlement of a building.*
A Pinner, *a kind of coif for a woman's head.*
The Pinnion *of a fowl, clock,* &c.
To pinnion, or *bind the arms of a malefactor.*
A Pinnock, *a bird.*
A Pint, *a liquid measure.*
A Pintel, (*in* gunnery) *an iron-pin that keeps the gun from recoiling.*
A Pioneer, or *labourer in an army, employ'd in levelling rough ways, casting up trenches,* &c.
A Piony, *or* peony, *an herb and flower.*
Pious, or *godly.*
The Pip, *a disease in poultry, being a white thin scale on the tip of the tongue.*
To pip, or *take away the* pip.
A Pipe, *reed, channel, a sort of musical instrument,* &c.
To pipe, or *play upon the* pipe.
A Bag-pipe.
A Conduit-pipe, or *water-pipe.*
A Tobacco-pipe.
The Wind-pipe, or *pipe of the lungs.*
A Pipe, or *half a tun of wine, containing* 126 *gallons.*
The Pipe, or *great roll in the exchequer, so call'd.*
The Clerk of the Pipe.
The Pipe-office
A Piper, or *player on the pipe*; also *a kind of fish.*
A Pipe-tree.
The Piperridge-tree.
A Dinner piping-hot.
A Pipkin, *a little earthen pot.*
A Pippin, *a sort of apple.*
Piquant, *quick,* or *sharp.*
A Pique, *peek,* or *grudge.*
Piracy, *the practice of*
A Pirate, *sea-robber, Rover,* or *Corsair.*
Piratical, *of,* or *belonging to a* pirate.
Pish! or *fy!*
A Pismire, or *ant, an insect.*
Piss, or *stale.*
To piss, or *make water.*
Piss-a-bed, or *the herb sow-thistle.*
A Piss-pot, or *chamber-pot.*
A Pisser.
Pist *upon.*
A Pistachoe, *or* pistake-nut, *a kind of small nut that grows in the eastern Countries.*
A Pistol, *a little sort of gun.*
A Pistol-case.
A Pistole, *a foreign gold Coin, worth* 17 s. sterl.
A French Pistole, *or* Louis d'or.
A Spanish Pistole.
A Pit, *deep hole;* or *cave,* &c.
The Arm-pit, or *arm-hole.*
A Coal-pit, or *Coal-mine.*
A Clay-pit.
A Gravel-pit.
A Sand-pit.
A Pitfall, or *gin to catch birds.*
A Pittance, or *small portion, properly a monk's mess,* or *allowance for a meal.*
Pitch, *and* to pitch (*in all senses.*)
Pitch, *an herb.*
Stone-pitch.
A Pitch-fork.
A Pitcher, *an earthen water-pot.*
A true Pitcher-man, or *great drinker.*
Pitching-pence, *a duty paid for* pitching or *setting down every Sack of Corn* &c. *in a market* or *fair.*
Pitchy, or *made of* pitch.
Piteous, or *wretched.*
Pith, or *marrow.*
Pithy, or *full of* pith.
Pitiful, *sad, sorry, wretched*; or *compassionate.*
Pitifulness.
Pitiless, *not to be mov'd with pity; unmerciful.*
Pity or *compassion.*
To pity, or *take* pity *of.*
A Pivot, or *tampin, a round piece of iron like a top, which being fix'd at the bottom of a gate, serves to turn and bear it up.*
The Pizzle *of a bull,* &c.

P L

Placable, or *easily appeas'd.*

A

A Placaert, *a* Dutch *ordinance*, or *proclamation*.
A Placard, *a* French *edict*, *order*, or *bill posted up*: *In our law*, *a licence to maintain unlawful games*.
A Place, *and to* place (*in several senses*.)
A Place of arms, (*in* Fortification) *a piece of ground sufficient to draw up the men to be sent from thence as occasion requires*.
A Market-place.
A Placket, *the fore-part of a woman's petticoat*.
A Plad, *a kind of mantle worn by the* Scotch *highlanders*, *about their shoulders*.
A Plagiary, or *book-thief that sets forth other mens works*, *under his own name*; *properly a man-stealer* or *kid-napper*.
The Plague, or *pestilence*.
To plague, or *vex one*.
A Plague-sore, or *plague-token*,
Plaguy, *pestilent*, *pernicious*, or *mischievous*.
A Plaice, *a sea-fish*.
Plain, *even and smooth*, *clear and manifest*; *sincere*, *homely*, &c.
A Plain, *a plain field*, or *a plain surface*.
Plainness, *smoothness*, *clearness*, *&c*.
A Plaint, or complaint (*in law*) *the exhibiting of any Action personal* or *real in writing*.
A Plaintiff, *one at whose suit such* plaint *is made*.
A Plaister *for a sore*.
A Plaister-box.
Plaister, or *fine morter*.
To plaister, or *do over with* plaister.

A plaisterer.
A Plait, *and*
To plait, or *fold*.
A Plan, *Platform*, or *draught of a thing*.
A Plane, *a tool us'd by carpenters and joyners*.
To plane, or *make smooth with a* plane.
A Planer *of boards*, &c.
A Plane-tree.
A Bastard-plane-tree.
A Planet, or *wandring star*. *The seven* planets *according to their order*, *are* Saturn, Jupiter, Mars, *the* Sun, Venus, Mercury *and the* Moon.
Planet-struck, *blasted*, *stunned*, or *amazed*.
Planetary, *of*, or *belonging to the* planets.
Planimetry, *a branch of* Geometry; *the Art of measuring plains and solids*.
A Planisphere, *a sphere* or *globe describ'd upon a plain surface*.
A Plank or *board*.
To plank, or *cover with* planks.
A Plant *of an herb* or *tree*.
To plant, *set trees*, &c; *to settle a Colony*; or *to level a piece of ordnance*.
Plantain, *an herb*.
Broad-leav'd plantain.
Ribwort-plantain,
The Plantain-tree.
A Planter, (*from to* plant.)
A Plantation, *colony*, or *settlement of people in a foreign Countrey*.
The American plantations.
A Planting-stick, or *dibble to set* plants *with*.
A Plash, *a puddle of standing water*.
To plash, or *dash with water*.
To plash, or *spread the boughs of a tree*.

Plashy, or *full of puddles*.
Plat, or *flat*; *as the plat-veins of a horse*.
A Platform, or *draught of a building*, &c.
To plat, or *wreath*.
Plate, *utensils made of gold*, or *silver*.
A Plate, or *thin flat piece of metal*; as
A Copper-plate, *to engrave upon*.
To plate, or *cover with* plates *of metal*.
A Plate, *to eat victuals upon*.
An Earthen plate.
A Silver-plate.
A Platter, or *wooden dish*.
A Platter-face, or *broad face*.
Plats, (*a sea-term*) *certain flat ropes to keep a cable from galling*.
Plausible, *that seems fair*, *so as to be well accepted*, or *received favourably*.
Plausibleness.
A Play, *and to* play (*in all senses*.)
A Stage-play.
A Player.
A Dice-player.
A Stage-player.
A Sword-player.
A Play-house.
Play-days, *for children at school*.
A Plea, *an allegation in law*, or *an excuse*.
Common-pleas, *such as are held between* common *persons*.
The Court of Common-pleas.
A foreign Plea, *when* matter *is alledg'd*, *that must be try'd in another Court*.
Pleas of the Crown, *all suits in the King's name*, *for offences against his Crown and dignity*.

To plead, *&c.*
To plead *a Cause*, or *alledge an excuse.*
A Pleader.
Pleasant, *delightful, merry*, or *witty.*
Pleasantness.
To please, *to give content, to delight*, or *humour one*, &c.
Pleasurable, *pleasant*, or *agreeable.*
Pleasure, *delight, content, satisfaction, a good turn*, &c.
To pleasure, *do one a pleasure*, or *gratify him.*
A Plebeian *one of the Commonalty*, or *vulgar sort.*
A Pledge, or *pawn.*
To pledge, or *leave for a* pledge.
To pledge *one in drinking.*
A Pledget, *(in* Surgery) *a piece of linnen-cloth dipt in water*, &c. *and laid to a sore.*
Plenarty, *oppos'd to a vacation; the filling up of a vacant benefice.*
Plenary, or *full*, as *a plenary indulgence.*
A Plenipotentiary, *a Commissioner that has full power and authority from his Prince, to treat with other Princes* or *States about a Peace*; &c. as
The Plenipotentiaries, *at the treaty of* Reswick.
Plenteous, *or* plentiful, *copious, abounding, fruitful*, &c.
Plenteousness, *or* plentifulness.
Plenty, *abundance*, or *great store.*
Plethorick, *full of humours*, or *pursy.*
A Plethory, *(in* Physick) *a fulness* or *abounding of humours.*
The Pleurisy, or *stitch in the side, a disease.*
Pliable, *easy to be handled.*
Pliableness.
Pliant, *flexible*, or *supple.*
Pliantness.
The Plight, or *state of the body.*
To plight, or *engage*; as *to* plight *one's faith* or *troth*, i. e. *solemnly to give his word*, or *promise.*
A Plinth (*in* Architecture) *the square foot of a pillar.*
To plod upon a business, i. e. *to have his head full of it.*
A Plot, or *spot of ground.*
The Ground-plot *of a building.*
A Plot, *device, design*, or *conspiracy.*
To plot, *conspire*, or *contrive.*
A Plotter.
A Plover, *a bird.*
A Plough, *or* plow, *to till the ground with.*
Plough-alms, *a penny anciently paid to the Church, for every plough-land.*
A Plough-man, or *plow-jobber.*
Plough-man's *spikenard*, *an herb.*
A Plough-land, or *a hide of land, containing about* 100 *acres.*
Plow-oxen, *oxen us'd in plowing.*
The Plough-share, or *coulter.*
The Plough-staff.
The Plough-tail, or *plow-handle.*
A Plough-wright, or *maker of* plows.
To plough, plow or *till a field.*
The Pluck, or *entrals of a calf* or *sheep*, i. e. *the heart, lights, liver*, &c. *usually sold together.*
To pluck, *pull, gather*, or *crop.*
Pluckt, pluckt up, *&c.*
A Plug, or *great peg, to stop the bottom of a cask*, &c.
A Plum, *a fruit.*
An Amber-plum.
An Horse-plum.
An Orange-plum.
A Sugar-plum.
A Wheat-plum.
A Plum-cake.
Plum-porridge.
A Plum-pudding.
To fall down plum, or *downright.*
Plumage, *feathers*, or *a bunch of feathers.*
A Plumb, plumb-rule, or plummet *us'd by carpenters, masons, bricklayers*, &c.
A Plume *of feathers.*
To plume, *pick*, or *pull off the feathers.*
A Plummer, *a worker in lead.*
A Plummet and line, *to sound the depth of the Sea.*
Plump, *fat*, or *juicy.*
To plump.
To plump, or *grow* plump.
Plump-faced.
Plumpness.
Plunder, *booty*, or *pillage by soldiers*;
To plunder, or *get* plunder.
A Plunderer.
A Plunge, *toss*, or *trouble*; as *to be in a great* plunge.
To plunge, or *dip over head and ears.*
A Plungeon, or *ducker*; *a water-fowl.*
A Plunket-colour; *a kind of blew.*
The plural number, *(in* Grammar) *when mention is made of more than one thing*; as *two horses; three dogs*; &c.
A Plurality, or *greater number*, as *of voices, livings*, &c.
Plush, *a kind of silk-manufacture.*

To ply, or *be intent upon*; as *to ply his work, book, oars,* &c.
To ply *at a place, as watermen and porters do.*

P O

To poach, poche, or *boil an egg.*
A Pocard, *a water-fowl.*
To poche, or *destroy game by unlawful means*; as *ginns, snares,* &c.
A Pocher.
A Pock, or *scab of the small pox.*
A Pock-hole.
A Pocket, *in a suit of clothes.*
A Pocket, or *half a sack of wool.*
A Coat-pocket.
A Pocket-book.
A Pocket-dagger.
A Pocket-handkerchief.
Pocket-money.
A Pick-pocket.
Pockified, *or* pocky, *that has got the* French *pox.*
Pock-wood.
The Pod, or *husk of pease,* &c.
Podders, or *pease-cod gatherers.*
A Poem, *a composition in verse,* or *copy of verses.*
Poesy, *Poetry,* or a *Poet's work; properly, a contexture of Poems,* or *poetical pieces.*
A Poet, *one that writes* or *makes verses.*
A Poetess, or *female Poet.*
Poetical, *or* poetick, *that has the air and character of* poesy.
Poetry, *or* Poesy, *the Art of making verses.*
A Point, *mark of distinction, sharp top of any thing, head of a matter,* &c.
A Point *in the tables,* or *at dice, cards,* &c.
The Ace-point.
The dewce-point.
The tray-point.
The cater-point.
The cinque-point.
The sise-point.
A Point, or *tag to tie with.*
A Point of land, *the extremity of a* Cape, or *head-land at Sea.*
The Points *of* the Compass; or *the 32 divisions of the wind.*
Point, or *point-lace.*
Point-blank, *positively,* or *directly.*
A Point-maker, *a woman that makes* point-lace.
Point-wise, or *in form of a* point.
To point, *distinguish by* points, *shew with the finger, make sharp at the end,* &c.
To point, or *level a cannon against a place.*
Pointless, *without a* point; as *a pointless sword.*
A Poise, or *weight.*
A Counter-poise.
To poise, *weigh,* or *try by the hand which is heaviest.*
A Well-poised *body.*
Poison, *and*
To Poison, *give* poison, *infect, corrupt,* or *spoil.*
Counter-poison, *an herb.*
A Poisoner.
Poisonous, *full of poison,* or *destructive.*
A Poitral, *a breast-plate*; or *a horse's breast-leather.*
A Poke, or *bag.*
To poke, or *thrust in a finger, stick,* &c.
The Polar Circles, *two Circles parallel to the* Æquator, *and equidistant from the* Poles *of the world and the* Tropicks. *One of 'em is call'd,* the Arctick polar Circle, *and the other, the* Antarctick.
The Poles (*in* Astronomy) *two ends of the imaginary axle-tree, whereon the heavens are turned. One is termed the* North *or* Arctick Pole, *from the constellation nam'd in* Greek Arctos, *i. e.* the bear; *and the other, the* South, *or* Antarctick, *as being opposite to the former.*
A Pole, or *long staff.*
A Pole, or *pearch to measure land,* &c.
A Pole-ax.
A Pole-cat.
Poledavies, *a kind of course canvas, us'd by Salesmen, in making up their wares.*
Poley, *an herb.*
Polemical, *belonging to* Polemicks, or *Disputations in Divinity.*
Policy, *craft, subtilty*; or *a prudent managing of affairs.*
A Policy of assurance, *a writing drawn up between a merchant-adventurer and an* Insurer, *who undertakes to secure his ship,* or *goods.*
To polish, *smooth,* or *adorn.*
Polishable, *that may be polish'd.*
A Polisher.
Polite, *neat, accurate, genteel,* or *well-bred.*
Politeness.
A Politician or *statesman.*
Politick, *crafty, prudent*; or *belonging to civil government.*
Politicks, *the Art of government*; or *a Book containing politick Precepts.*
Polity, *the governance,* or

rule of a Town, Commonwealth, &c.
Ecclesiastical Polity, or *Church-government*.
A Poll, or *head*; also *the setting down of the names of every Person, at an Election*.
A Poll, *of ling-fish*.
To Poll, or *shave the head*; or *to compute the number of Persons concern'd in an Election*.
Poll-money, *paid upon*
A Poll-tax, *a personal tax, by which every subject is assess'd by the* Poll, or *head according to his degree*.
A Pollard, *a sea-fish*; also *a Stag that has cast his head*.
A Pollard, *or* Pollenger; *a tree that has been often cropp'd*.
To pollute, *defile, make filthy, corrupt, stain*, &c.
Pollution, or *uncleanness*.
Polygamy, *a marriage contracted by one Man, with several Wives together*.
A Polygone, *a figure that has many angles*, or *corners*.
Polygony, or *knot-grass*, *an herb*.
A Polyphon, *a musical Instrument, that has many things and a great variety of sounds*.
A Pomander, *musk-ball*, or *roll of Perfume*.
Pomatum, *a sweet kind of ointment*.
To pome, *(in gardening)* i. e. *to grow into a head*.
A Pome-citron. } *Fruits*.
A Pomegranate }
The Pommel *of a Sword*, or *Saddle*.
To Pommel, or *bang one soundly*.
Pomp, *state*, or *grandeur, such as is us'd in solemn shews*.
Pompets, or *Printer's ink-balls*.
A Pompion, *or pumpkin, a kind of Melon*.
Pompous, *stately*, or *sumptuous*.
A Pond, or *standing Pool*.
A Fish-pond.
To ponder, *consider*, or *weigh in mind*
Ponderous, *weighty*, or *heavy*.
A Poniard, or *dagger*.
To poniard *one*, or *stab him with a* Poniard.
Pontage, *a Contribution for the repairing of Bridges*; also *a Bridge-toll*.
A Pontifical habit; *such as is fit for an high-priest, Pope*, or *great Prelate*.
A Pontoon, or *Bridge of Boats*.
A Pool, or *pond*.
The Pool-evil, *a kind of swelling incident to horses*.
The Poop, or *stern of a ship*.
To poop, or *foist*.
Poor, *needy, mean, barren, lean*, &c.
Poorish, or *somewhat poor*.
Poorness, or *poverty*.
To pop, *in*, or *out*, *to enter*, or *depart suddenly*, or *unexpectedly*.
To pop *out a word*, or *let it fall unawares*.
The Pope, or *Bishop of* Rome.
The Popedom, or *Pope's dignity*.
Popery, *the popish* or *Roman Catholick Religion*.
A Popinjay, *a sort of green Parret*.
Popish, *belonging to the Person*, or *Doctrine of the* Pope.
A Poplar-tree.
The White-poplar.
Poppy, *a Plant*.
Garden-poppy.
Sparling-poppy.
Wild-poppy.
The Populacy, *the common*, or *meanest sort of People*.
Popular, *belonging to*, or *in request among the People*.
Popularity, *the affecting of popular applause*.
Populous, or *full of People*.
Populousness.
Porcelain, or *China-ware*.
A Porch, or *entry to an house*.
A Church-porch.
A Porcupine, *a kind of hedge-hog, said to shoot its prickles like Arrows, when provok'd to anger*.
To pore, or *look close*.
Pore-blind.
The Pores of the Body, *the small and invisible holes in the Skin, thro' which the hair grows, and sweat humours*, &c. *pass out insensibly*.
Pork, or *swines-flesh*.
A Porket, or *young hog*.
Porous, or *full of Pores*.
Prophyry, *a kind of reddish Marble, finely streaked with white Veins*.
A Porpoise, *a sea-hog*.
A Porrenger, *to eat spoon-meats in*.
Porridge, or *potage*.
A Porridge-dish.
Milk-porridge.
Port, *fashion, credit*, or *behaviour*.
A Port, or *haven*.
The Port, or *Court of the Grand Seignior*.
The Ports, or *port-holes of a Ship*; *the square holes thro' which the great Guns are thrust out*.
Portable, *that may be carry'd*.

Portage,

Portage, *money paid for carriage.*
A Portal, *a lesser gate.*
A Portcullis, *a falling gate, let down to keep out the Enemies*; also *the name of one of the Marshals,*or *Pursuivants at Arms.*
To portend, *forbode, foreshew,* or *betoken.*
Portentous, *monstrous, betokening some future mischance.*
A Porter, *that carries burdens,* &c.
The Groom-porter.
Porters of the Verge; *certain Officers that bear white Wands before the Judges.*
A Portgreve, *or* portreve, *the chief Magistrate, in some Sea-port Town, and anciently of the City of* London.
A Porticoe, or *porch.*
A Portion, *part, share,* or *inheritance.*
A Portioner; as *when two,* or *three Ministers serve a cure by turns, and share the Tithes.*
Portliness, *a being*
Portly, *majestick,* or *comely.*
A Portmantle, *to carry necessaries on horse-back.*
The Port-men, *the inhabitants of the Cinque-ports*; or *the* 12 *Burgesses of* Ipswich.
A Portmote, *a Court kept in Sea-Port Towns.*
A Portraiture, *picture,* or *draught.*
To portray, *to draw the form,* or *proportion of a thing.*
A Port-sale, or *publick sale by out-cry, in a Haven.*
A Pose, or *rheum in the head.*
To Pose, or *puzzle.*
A Position, *the state of a question,* or *an argument to be debated.*
Positive, *absolute,* or *peremptory.*
A Posnet, or *skillet.*
To possess, *get, obtain, enjoy,* &c.
Possession.
A Possessour.
A Posset, or *posset-drink.*
Possibility, or *likelihood.*
Possible, *that may be done,* or *may happen.*
A Post, *and to* post *(in all senses.)*
A Foot-post.
The Penny-post.
In Post-haste.
A Post-house.
A Post-horse.
A Post-master.
The Post-office.
The Brow-post, or *transom over the threshold.*
A Shore-post.
Postage, *money paid for the carriage of Letters.*
The Post-communion, or *Church-service after the communion.*
A Post-date, *and*
To postdate *a Writing*, i. e. *to date it some time after the real* date.
Posterity, or *offspring.*
A Postern, or *back-door*; also (*in* Fortification) *a false door at the bottom of the* curtain *for private sallies.*
A Postil, *a short Note* or *exposition.*
A Postillion, *that leads the fore-horses of a coach,*&c.
To postpone, *set behind,* or *make less account of.*
Posthumous, *that is born* or *publish'd, after the death of the father,* or *Author.*
A Post-script *of a letter, something added at the bottom, after the writing of it.*
A Posture, *motion and carriage of the body*; or *the state of affairs.*
A Posy, or *nosegay.*
The Posy, or *motto of a ring.*
A Pot, *a sort of vessel to hold liquor.*
To pot *butter, venison,* &c. i. e. *to put it into a* pot, *after it has been well season'd.*
A Chamber-pot.
A drinking-pot.
A Gally-pot.
A Porridge-pot.
A watering-pot *for a garden.*
Pot-ashes.
A Pot-companion, or *continual toper.*
Pot-belly'd, *that has a great belly.*
A Pot-gun.
A Pot-hanger.
A Pot-herb.
A Pot-hook.
A Pot-lid.
A Pot-shard.
Potable, *that may be drunk.*
Potage, or *broth.*
Plum-potage.
A Potatoe, *a kind of root.*
Potencee (*in* Heraldry) *made like the top of a crutch.*
Potent, or *powerful.*
A Potentate, *a soveraign Prince*; or *a person of great power and authority.*
A Potion, or *physical drink.*
A Love-potion.
A Potter, *a maker,* or *seller of earthen ware.*
A Pottle, *two quarts* or *half a gallon.*
A Pouch, or *bag.*
Shepherds-pouch, *an herb.*
To pouch *out,* or *thrust out the lips.*
Pouch-mouthed.
Poverty, *a poor* or *mean condition.*
A Poulterer or *seller of poultry.*

A Poultice, *or* Poultis, *a kind of physical decoction, apply'd outwardly to a part, to asswage swellings, inflammations,* &c.
A Pounce, or *talon of a bird of prey.*
To pounce, or *grasp with the* pounces.
A Pound, *or* pound-weight, 16 *ounces* Averdupois, *and* 12 Troy-*weight*; also 10 *s. sterling in money.*
A Pound, or *enclosure for cattel detain'd for some trespass.*
To pound, or *beat in a mortar.*
To pound, or *shut up in a* pound.
A Pounder *of cattel.*
Poundage, *the* pounder's *fee*; also *an allowance of twelve pence in the* pound *upon the receipt of money.*
To pour, pour *in*, pour *down*, &c.
A Pourcuttle *a fish.*
Powder, *and to* powder *(in several senses.)*
Gun-powder.
Sneezing-powder.
A Powder-monkey, *in a Ship, a boy that brings the* powder *to the gunners.*
A Powdering-tub.
Power, *ability, force, authority,* &c.
Powerful.
A Powt, or *sea-lamprey a fish.*
An Eel-powt.
A Salmon-powt,
To powt, or *look surly.*
The Pox or French-pox, *a loathsom disease.*
The Chicken-pox.
The Small-pox.
A Poy, or *Pole, that rope-dancers stay themselves with.*
Practicable, *that may be* *done* or *practised.*
Practical, *or* practick, *belonging to*
Practice, *custom, use*; or *the exercise of any faculty.*
To practise, or *put into* practice.
A Practitioner, or *one that* practises *in the law.*
Pragmatical, *over-busy in other mens affairs, saucy,* or *arrogant.*
Pragmaticalness.
Praise, *and*
To praise, *or* commend.
To praise, or *set a value upon goods.*
A Praiser.
Praise-worthy.
To prance, or *throw up the fore-legs, as a horse does.*
A Prancer, *or prancing-horse.*
A Prank, or *trick.*
To prank *up, trim, deck,* or *set out.*
To prate, or *talk saucily.*
Practick, *(among merchants) a licence to traffick in the Ports of* Italy *and the straights.*
To prattle, or babble.
Prittle-prattle.
A Prattler,
Pravity, or *corruption of manners.*
A Prawn, *a sea-fish.*
To pray, *to entreat, beseech, invoke, implore,* &c.
A Prayer.
A Morning-prayer.
An Evening-prayer.
The Common-prayer, or *publick Service of the Church of* England.
The Lord's prayer.
To preach, *make sermons,* or *discourses in publick.*
A Preacher.
A Preamble, *prologue,* or *preface.*
A Prebend, *a sort of benefice belonging to a Cathedral,* or *collegiate Church.*
A Prebend, *or* prebendary, *he that has a* prebend.
Precarious, *got by favour*; or *held only at another's will and pleasure.*
A Precaution, *a* caution *given* or *taken beforehand.*
To precede, *to go before,* or *to excell.*
Precedency.
Precedent, or *fore-going.*
A Precedent, *or* president.
A Precept, or *instruction.*
A Precinct, or *particular Jurisdiction comprehending several parishes.*
Precious, *of great price,* or *value.*
Preciousness.
A Precipice, *steep place, downright pitch,* or *fall.*
Precipitate, or *over-hasty.*
To precipitate, or *throw one head-long down a* precipice.
To precipitate *a business,* or *to hurry it away.*
Precipitation, *over-hastiness* or *rashness.*
Precise, *exact, particular,* or *scrupulous.*
Preciseness.
A Precisian, *one that is over-scrupulous in point of Religion.*
A preconceived opinion, i. e. *taken up before-hand.*
A Precontract, *a* Contract *made before another*; or *a former bargain.*
Predatory, *of*, or *belonging to robbing.*
A Predecessour, *he that was in Place* or *Office before one.*
A Predestinarian, *one that believes* predestination.
To predestinate, or *appoint before-hand.*
Predestination.
To predetermine, or *to* *deter-*

determine before-hand.

Predial Tithes, i. e. *Tithes of things arising from the ground only*; as *corn, hay, fruit.* &c.

In the same Predicament, *state* or *condition.*

A Prediction, or *foretelling.*

To predispose, or *dispose before hand.*

Predominancy, *a being*

Predominant or *over-ruling.*

To predominate, or *over-power.*

Pre-elected, or *elected before.*

Pre-election.

Pre-eminence, or preheminence, *great honour, prerogative,* or *rule.*

Pre-eminent, or *eminent above the rest.*

Pre-emption, *first buying,* or *buying before others.*

To pre-engage, or *engage before-hand.*

A Pre-engagement.

To pre-exist, *to exist,* or *have a being before.*

Pre-existence.

A Preface, or *discourse, declaring the design of a book,* &c.

To preface, or *tell before-hand.*

Prefatory, *in form of a* preface.

A Prefect, *a* Roman *governour* or *ruler.*

Prefecture, *the Office of a prefect.*

To prefer, *to set more by, to advance,* or *to propose.*

Preference, or *pre-eminence.*

Preferment, *advancement,* or *promotion.*

Preferrable, *to be preferr'd.*

The Preferrer *of an Indictment,* &c.

To prefigure, or *represent by figure afore-hand.*

To prefix, or *appoint before-hand.*

Pregnancy, *a being* pregnant, or *great with child*; also *subtil, refined, substantial,* &c.

Prejudicate, opinions *proceeding from*

Prejudice, *properly a rash judgment, before the matter be heard*; *a being prepossessed*; also *an injury,* or *dammage.*

To prejudice, or *do prejudice.*

Prejudicial, *disadvantageous,* or *hurtful.*

A Preke *a fish.*

Prelacy, *the state of*

A Prelate, or *dignify'd clergy-man*; as *an Arch-bishop,* or *bishop.*

Preliminary, *prefatory,* or *set at the entrance*; as *a preliminary Discourse.*

The Preliminaries *of a Treaty of peace.*

A Prelude, *a flourish of musick, before the playing of a tune*; or *an entrance into a business.*

Premature, or *untimely.*

To premeditate, or *think of before-hand.*

Premeditation.

To premise, or *speak of before, by way of preface.*

The Premises, or *things before specified.*

To premonish, or *fore-warn.*

A Premonition.

A Premunire, as *to run himself into a* premunire, *to involve himself in trouble.*

A Prentice, or apprentice.

Pre-occupation, or *pre-possession.*

To pre-ordain, or *ordain before hand.*

A Preparation, or *preparing.*

Preparatory, or *in order to.*

A Preparative, *that serves,*

To prepare, *provide,* or *make ready.*

Preparedness, *a being prepared.*

Prepensed, or *premeditated*; as *prepensed malice.*

To Preponderate, *outweigh,* or *be of greater importance.*

To preponderate, *a business, to weigh it well before one undertakes it.*

To prepossess *one's mind,* or *take it up before hand.*

Prepossession, or *prejudice.*

Preposterous, *the order of which is perverted, topsy-turvy*; or *having the wrong end forward.*

A Prerogative, *a peculiar preheminence* or *authority above others,* or *a special privilege.*

The Prerogative-Court, *where all wills are prov'd and all administrations taken, that belong to the Arch Bp. of* Canterbury's *prerogative.*

A Presage, *omen* or *token.*

To presage, *apprehend before hand, divine, foretell,* or *betoken.*

A Presbyter, or *lay-elder.*

The Presbyterians, *a Sect that admit lay-elders into their Church-government.*

Presbytery, *the Church-government,* or *principles of the* Presbyterians.

Prescience, or *fore-knowledge.*

To prescribe, *order,* or *appoint.*

A Prescript, or *Ordinance.*

Prescription, *appointment,* or *limitation*; also *a claim upon account of long possession.*

Presence, *a being present.*

Presence *of mind,* or *readiness.*

A Presence-chamber.

Present, *opposite, to* absent.

A Present, or *gift.*

To present, *to make a present; to offer; to bring an information against.* &c.

A Presentation; *the act of a Patron offering a clerk to the Bishop, to be instituted in a benefice of his gift.*

A Presentee, *the clerk so presented.*

The Presentment *of an Offence in Court.*

Preservation, or *preserving.*

A Preservative, or *preserving remedy.*

To preserve, *conserve,* or *keep safe and sound.*

A Preserver.

To preside, or *be chief in an assembly,* &c.

Presidency, *the Office* or *dignity of*

A President, *governour,* or *overseer.*

The Lord President *of the King's privy council.*

A President, *example,* or *instance.*

A Press, *and* to press (*in all senses.*)

An Oil-press.

A Printing-press.

A Wine-press.

A Press-bed.

A Press-man *that works at the printing-press.*

A Press-pin, *us'd by bookbinders to wring their* press.

A Pressure, *calamity,* or *affliction.*

Prest, *pressed,* or *imprested.*

Prestation-money, *paid yearly by the Arch-deacons, to their Bishops.*

Prest-money, or *earnest-money given to an imprested souldier* or *seaman.*

To presume, *to imagine, suppose,* or *hope; to take too much upon him,* &c.

Presumption.

A Presumptive-heir.

Presumptuous, *proud;* or *self-conceited.*

Presumptuousness.

To presuppose, or *suppose before.*

A Presupposition.

A Pretence, *colour,* or *shew.*

To pretend, *to make shew of,* or *lay claim to.*

A Pretender.

A Pretension, or *laying claim.*

To pretermit, *omit; let pass,* or *neglect.*

Preternatural, *contrary to the course of nature; extraordinary.*

A Pretext, or pretence.

Prettiness, *beauty, neatness,* or *elegancy.*

Pretty, or *handsom.*

To prevail, *get the better of, overcome,* or *obtain by persuasion.*

Prevalent, or *powerful.*

To prevaricate, or *betray one's cause to the adversary; to play fast and loose; to be jack on both sides; to shuffle and cut,* &c.

A Prevarication.

A Prevaricator.

To prevent, *get before, hinder before-hand,* or *do a thing before another.*

A Prevention.

Previous, *that goes before.*

A Prey, or *booty.*

To Prey, or *make a* prey.

A Price, *rate,* or *value set upon a thing.*

A Prick, *and* to prick (*in all senses.*)

Prick-wood, or *spindle-tree, a shrub.*

A Pricker, *a huntsman on horseback;* also *a joyner's tool.*

Pricket, *an herb.*

A Pricket or *young buck a year old.*

A Prickle, or *sharp point.*

Prickly, or *full of prickles.*

Prickly coral-tree.

Pride, *arrogancy,* or *haughtiness.*

To pride *himself in a thing, to take a* pride *in it.*

A Prier, (*from* to pry) *one that searches into other mens business.*

A Priest, *one that is set a-part to offer sacrifices and perform other sacred rites. Among christians, a clergy-man next in dignity to a Bishop.*

A Chief priest, or *high priest.*

A Priestess, or female priest, *among the ancient heathens.*

Priesthood, *the order* or *office of a* priest.

Priest-ridden, *that is govern'd altogether by* Priests.

Priests-pintle, *an herb.*

A Prigging, or *pilfering fellow.*

Primacy, *the office and dignity of a* Primate.

Primage, *a duty paid to the mariners for the loading of a ship, at the setting forth from any haven.*

Primary, *the first in order of the first rank* or *quality.*

A Primate, or Metropolitan, *the first* or *chief Archbishop.*

Prime, *chief, excellent,* or *singular.*

The Prime, or *flower of one's age; of the nobility,* &c.

Prime, *and* to prime *a gun,* or *put powder into the touch-hole.*

To Prime, or *lay the first colour in painting.*
Prime-print, or *privet a shrub.*
A Primer, *or* primmer, *a little book to teach children to read.*
Long-primmer, *a sort of printing-letter.*
Primitive, *of* or *belonging to the first age.*
Primogeniture, or *birthright.*
A Primrose, *a flower.*
A Prince, *the chief governour of a state;* or *one that holds the first rank.*
The Prince of Wales, *a Title peculiar to the King of* England's *eldest son.*
A Princess, or *female* Prince.
Princes-feather, *an herb.*
Principal, or *chief.*
A Principal, or *head of a College.*
The Principal, or *principal sum of money, distinguish'd from the interest of it.*
A Principality, *the dominions of a* Prince.
A Principle, *source, cause, maxim, opinion,* &c.
The Principles, or *grounds of an Art.*
Principled, or *endu'd with principles;* as *a person* well-principled.
A Print, *mark, character,* or *printed picture.*
To print *books, pictures, callicoe,* &c.
A Printer.
A Master-printer.
A Journey-man printer.
The Art of PRINTING, *first invented by* Lawrence Coster *of* Haerlem, or (*as others say*) *by* John Guttemburg *of* Strasburg, *was brought very early into* England *by* Caxton *and* Tourner, *whom* K. Henry VI. *sent on purpose to learn it. One of the first printed Books now extant, is* Tully's *Offices* 1465. *kept in the* Bodleian *Library at* Oxford; *where is also to be seen S.* Jerom *upon the Creed, printed in the same City* Dec. 17. 1468.
A Printing-house.
A Prior, *the head of a priory.*
A Prioress, *a Nun next in order to an Abbess.*
Priority, or *precedency.*
A Priorship, *the office and quality of a* Prior.
A Priory, *a sort of benefice;* also *a monastery.*
A Prism, (*in* Geometry) *a solid body that has two bases, equal and parallel each to the other.*
A Prison or *jail.*
A Prisoner.
Pristine, *ancient, accustomed, wonted,* or *former.*
Prithee, *for I pray thee.*
Prittle-prattle, or *idle talk.*
Privacy, *familiarity,* or *secrecy.*
A Privado, *a private friend,* or *favourite.*
Private, *particular,* or *secret.*
A Privateer, or *pirate-ship.*
Privation, *a being deprived of lack,* or *want.*
Privet, or *prime-print, a shrub.*
Ever-green privet.
Mock-privet.
A Privilege, (*i. e. a* private or particular *law*) *a special prerogative,* or *preheminence.*
Privileged, *that has some privilege.*
Privity *as without one's* privity, or *knowledge.*
The Privities, or *privy parts.*
Privy, *secret, particular, conscious of,* or *accessory to.*
The King's *privy council.*
A Privy Councellor.
The Privy purse, or *Keeper of the privy purse, an Officer that defrays the King's private expences.*
The privy Seal, *us'd to such grants as pass the great Seal, and sometimes in things of less moment, that never come to the great Seal.*
The Lord Keeper of the *privy Seal.*
A Privy, or *house of Office.*
A Prize, *reward, booty, tryal of skill at sword-playing,* &c.
To prize, or *set a value on.*
To argue pro *&* con, *i. e. for and against.*
Probability, or *likelihood.*
Probable, or *likely.*
The Probate, or *proving of a Will.*
A Probation, or *tryal of skill by such as are a out to take their degrees in an University.*
A Probationer, *a Scholar, that undergoes such a* probation.
Probationership.
A Probe, *a Surgeon's instrument to search a wound.*
Probity, *uprightness, honesty,* or *integrity.*
A Problem, or *proposition, with a question annex'd to it.*
Problematical, *belonging thereto.*
To proceed, *to go forward.* or *to come of a thing.*
The Proceedings *at law.*
A Process, or *continued Order of things;* or *a law-suit.*
A Procession, or *solemn*

march

march of the Clergy and people in the Romish Church. Also the visitation of the bounds of a parish, in Rogation-week, perform'd by the minister, some of the principal inhabitants and children.
Procession-week.
Processional, of or belonging to a procession.
To proclaim, publish, or declare solemnly.
A Proclaimer.
A Proclamation.
Proclivity, inclination or disposition.
A Proconsul, a Roman magistrate, sent to govern a Province with consular power.
Proconsulship, the Office of a Proconsul.
To procrastinate, put off from day to day, delay or defer.
Procrastination.
To procreate, or beget children.
Procreation.
A Proctor, one that undertakes to manage a Cause in an Ecclesiastical Court.
Proctors of the Clergy, Deputies chosen by the Clergy of every Diocess, to sit in the lower Convocation-house.
A Procurator, he that gathers the fruits of a Benefice, for the Parson.
To procure, or get for another.
A Procurer.
Prodigal, lavish, wasteful, riotous, &c.
Prodigality.
Prodigious, contrary to the common course of nature, monstrous or excessive.
Prodigiousness.
A Prodigy, a wonderful monstrous and unnatural thing.
To produce, or bring forth.
A Product of one's wit, fancy, &c.
The Product of two numbers, (in Arithmetick) or the result of two numbers multiplied one by another.
The Productions, or products of the earth.
Productive, or apt to bring forth.
A Proem, preface, or beginning of a matter.
A Profanation, or profaning.
Profane, ungodly, wicked, irreligious, &c.
To profane, turn holy things to a common use, unhollow, or pollute.
Profaneness.
To profess, to declare openly, protest, acknowledge, own, &c.
A Profession.
A Professor, or publick reader in an University.
A Professorship, the office of a professor.
A Proffer, and
To proffer, offer, or assay.
Proficiency the quality of
A Proficient, one that has made good progress in learning.
The Profil, or draught of a building or work in Fortification. Also (in painting) the design of a place drawn sideway.
Profit, or gain.
To profit, or get profit.
Profitable, useful, or advantageous.
Profitableness.
Profligate, debauched or lewd.
Profligateness.
Profound, or deep.
Profoundness, or depth; as profoundness of learning.
Profuse, lavish, wasteful, riotous, or dissolute.
Profuseness.
A Profusion, or squandering away of money.
To prog, or use all endeavours to get.
A Progenitor, or ancestor.
A Progeny, offspring, or issue.
To prognosticate, or foretell.
A Prognostication.
A Prognosticator.
A Prognostick, sign, or token of something to come.
A Progress, proceeding, or going forward.
Numbers in Arithmetical Progression; as 2, 4, 6, &c.
Progressive, that goes on.
To prohibit, or forbid.
A Prohibition.
Prohibitory, that prohibits.
A Project, or contrivance.
To project, design, or contrive.
A Projecter.
A Projecture, or jutting out in building.
Prolifick, fit for generation, or fruitful.
Prolix, large, or tedious.
The Prolixity, or length of a discourse.
A Prolocutor, or Speaker of the Convocation-house.
A Prologue, or speech before a play.
To prolong, delay, defer, lengthen, or spin out.
Prominent, hanging over, jutting or standing out.
Promiscuous, mingled together, or confused.
A Promise, and
To promise, engage, or give one's word.
A Promiser.
A Promontory, or high hill, lying out a great way into the Sea.

To

To promote, carry on, advance, or prefer.
A Promoter.
Promotion, or *preferment.*
Prompt, *ready,* or *quick in doing a thing.*
To prompt, *put in mind,* or *suggest.*
A Prompter.
Promptness, or *readiness.*
Prone, or *inclin'd to.*
Proneness.
A Prong, or *pitch-fork.*
To pronounce, *speak forth, utter,* or *declare.*
A Pronunciation.
A Proof, *proving, tryal,* or *token.*
A Prop, *and to* prop.
A Vine-prop.
To propagate, *spread abroad,* or *encrease.*
A Propagation.
Propense, *prone,* or *inclined.*
Propension, *or* Propensity.
Proper, *peculiar, fit, convenient, tall,* &c.
Properness, or *tallness.*
Property, *a natural disposition; right* or *rightful use of a thing.*
Prophane, or profane.
A Prophecy, or *revelation.*
To prophesy, *to tell of things to come* or *to expound divine mysteries.*
A Prophet.
A Prophetess, or *female Prophet.*
Prophetical, *or* prophetick, *belonging to prophecy.*
To propitiate, *atone, pacify,* or *appease.*
A Propitiation.
A Propitiatory *sacrifice.*
The Propitiatory, or *mercy-seat, a place of atonement.*
Propitious, *favourable, kind, merciful,* &c.
Proportion, or *just measure, the relation of one thing to another.*
To proportion, *to make* proportionable, or *conformable to the rules of* proportion.
A Proposal.
To propose, *set before one, offer,* or *present.*
A Proposer.
A Proposition.
To propound, or *propose.*
A Proprietary, or proprietor, *an owner,* or *one that has a property in a thing.*
A Propriety *of speech,* or *peculiar manner of expression.*
To prorogue, or *put off till another time.*
The Prorogation *of a parliament.*
To proscribe, or *banish.*
A Proscription, *a banishment, outlawry;* or *publick sale of confiscated goods.*
Prose, *in opposition to verse.*
To prosecute, *to carry on a design;* or *to sue one at law.*
A Prosecution.
A Prosecutor.
A Proselyte, *a stranger converted to our Religion.*
A Prospect, or *view.*
A Prospective-glass, *to see things afar off.*
To prosper, *to make,* or *to prove* prosperous.
Prosperity, or *happiness.*
Prosperous, *happy, fortunate, successful,* or *favourable.*
A Prostitute, or *common strumpet.*
To prostitute, *expose,* or *set open to every one that comes.*
Prostitution, or *prostituting.*
Prostrate, or *laid flat along.*
To prostrate *himself.*
Prostration.
To protect, or *defend.*
Protection.
A Protector.
The lord Protector *of* England, *a title assum'd by the usurper* O. Cromwell.
A Protest, or *declaration against a Party, for non-payment of a Bill of Exchange.*
To protest, protest *against,* or *declare against.*
Protestancy, or Protestantism, *the protestant,* or *reformed Religion.*
Protestants, *the professors of that Religion, so call'd from their publick protestation, to appeal from the Emperor* Charles V's *decrees, to a general Council; which was made at* Spires *in* Germany, *A. D.* 1529.
A Protestation, or *free declaration of one's mind.*
A Protomartyr, or *first martyr,* as Abel *in the Old Testament, and S.* Stephen *in the new.*
A Protonotary, *or* Prothonotary, (*i.e.* a chief Scribe, *or* Secretary) *an Officer of the King's Bench and Common-pleas: The former records all civil actions sued in that Court; as those of the Common pleas (who are three in number) enter and enroll all declarations pleadings, assizes, recognizances,* &c. *in the same Court, and make out all judicial Writs.*
A Prototype, *an original* type, or *first pattern.*
To protract, *delay,* or *prolong.*
Protuberant, or *bunching out.*
Proud, *haughty,* or *insolent.*
To prove, *to make good, to try,* or *to become.*

Pro-

Provender, or *food for cattel.*
A Proverb, *a common saying.*
Proverbial, *belonging to a proverb.*
To provide, *prepare*, or *take care of.*
Providence, or the divine Providence, *which rules over the world.*
Provident, *careful*, or *that has fore-cast.*
A Provider, or *purveyor.*
A Province, *a considerable part of a Country*; also *the jurisdiction of an Archbishop.*
The united Provinces *in the low Countries.*
A Province-rose.
Provincial, or *belonging to a* province.
A Provincial, *a superiour of all the Monasteries in a* province.
Provining, *the setting of vine branches in the ground for encrease.*
Provision, *any thing that is provided.*
House-shold-provisions.
Provisional, *done by way of proviso.*
A Proviso, or *condition annex'd to a contract.*
A Provocation, or *provoking.*
A Provocative *medicine.*
To provoke, *incense, urge, stir up*, or *excite.*
A Provoker.
A Provost, or *governour of a College.*
A Provost-Marshal, *an Officer in the King's Navy, who has charge of the prisoners taken at sea.*
The Provost *of the* Mint, *who is to provide for all the* Moneyers *and to oversee them.*
A Provostship, *a Provost's Office*, or *dignity.*
The Prow, *fore-castle*, or *fore-part of a ship.*

To prowl, or *gape after gain.*
A prowling-fellow, *one that is upon the catch.*
Proximity, or *nearness*; as *proximity of blood.*
A Proxy, *one that does the part of another*, or *acts for him, in his absence.*
Prudence, or *Wisdom.*
Prudent, *wise*, *sage*, or *discreet.*
Prudential, *partaking of prudence*; as
Prudential motives.
A Prune, or *dried plum.*
A Damask-prune.
To prune, or *lop trees.*
The hawk prunes, or *picks her self.*
A prunello, *a sort of plum and silk.*
To pry into, or *make an over-curious search.*

P S P T

A Psalm, *hymn*, or *divine song*, as David's *Psalms.*
A Psalmist, or *writer of* psalms.
The Psalter, or *book of* Psalms.
A Psaltery, *a kind of musical instrument like a harp, but more pleasant.*
Ptisane, or *barley-broth.*

P U

A Publican, *a farmer of publick revenues*, *customs* or *rents.*
Publick (*i. e. belonging to the* people) *open*, *manifest*, &c.
To publish, *to make* publick, or *to proclaim.*
A Publisher.
To pucker, *shrink up*, or *lye uneven.*
A Puck-fist, or *fuzz-ball.*
A Pudder, or *bustle*; as *to make*, or *keep a* pudder *about trifles.*

A Pudding, (*a dish well known in* England.)
A Bag-pudding.
A Black-pudding.
A Bloud-pudding.
A Gut-pudding.
A Hasty-pudding.
A Hogs-pudding.
A Livering-pudding.
A Pan-pudding.
A Tansey-pudding.
A White-pudding.
Pudding-grass.
Pudding-pipe, *a reed.*
A Pudding-pie.
To come in pudding-time, *i. e. very opportunely, in the nick of time.*
A Puddle *of water, and to* puddle.
A Puet, *a bird.*
A Puff *of wind.*
To puff, *to blow*, or *to swell.*
An Earth-puff.
A Puff-ball, or *puckfist.*
Puff-paste.
A Puffen, *a fish.*
A Puffin, *a sea-fowl.*
Puffins, *a sort of apples.*
A Pug, or *little monkey.*
Puissant, *powerful*, or *mighty.*
To puke, or *be ready to vomit.*
The Puke-colour.
A puking, or *queasy stomack.*
A puling, or *sickly constitution.*
Pulick-mountain. } *herbs*
Puliol-mountain. }
Puliol-royal. }
A Pull, *and to* pull (*in all senses.*)
A Pull-back, or *hinderance.*
A Pullet, or *young hen.*
A Pulley, *with a cord to draw up wares*, &c.
A Pulley-piece, *an armour for the knee.*
The Pulp, *fleshy*, or *substantial part of fruit*, &c.
A Pulpit, *to preach in.*
Pulse, *as beans, pease*, &c.

Tue

The Pulse, or *beating of the arteries.*
To pulverize, or *reduce to powder.*
A Pumice-stone.
The Pump-dale *in a ship thro' which the water runs to the scupper-holes.*
A Pump, *to draw water.*
To pump, or pump *out.*
A Pumpkin, *a kind of melon.*
Pumps, *a sort of shoes.*
A Pun, or *quibble, and to* pun.
A Punch, *to* punch *a hole with.*
Punch, *the Seaman's nectar; made of Brandy, water, lime-juice, and sugar.*
Rum-punch.
A Punchion, *a kind of chizel.*
A Punchion *of Wine, containing eighty gallons.*
A Punchinello, or *stage-puppet.*
A Punctilio, *nice point,* or *insignificant trifle.*
Punctual, or *exact.*
The Punctuation, or *pointing of a sentence.*
Pungent, *sharp,* or *pricking;* as *a pungent sauce.*
A Punger, *a sort of sea-fish.*
To punish, or *chastize.*
Punishable, *fit to be punished.*
A Punisher.
A Punishment.
A Punk, *an ugly whore.*
A Puny, *a younger brother* or *novice.*
A Puny, or *junior judge.*
A Pupil, or *orphan under age;* or *the disciple of a College-tutor.*
A Puppet, or *poppet.*
A Puppet-play.
A Puppet-player.
A Puppy, or *whelp.*
Purblind, or *near-sighted.*
A Purchase, *and*
To purchase, or *buy an estate.*
A Purchaser.
Pure, *clean, clear, without mixture,* &c.
Pureness.
A Purfle, *a trimming of tinsel,* or *gold-thread, formerly us'd for womens gowns;* also *a kind of ornament about the edges of some musical instruments,* as *Viols, Violins,* &c.
To Purfle or *adorn with a* purfle.
A Purgation, or *clearing one's self of a crime.*
Purgative, *of a purging quality.*
Purgatory, *an imaginary place of purgation for the souls of the faithful; according to the* Roman-catholick *Creed.*
A Purge, or *purging potion.*
Purification, or *purifying.*
The Purification *of the Virgin* Mary; or *Candlemas day,* Feb. 2.
To purify, *make pure, cleanse,* or *refine.*
The Puritans, *a nick-name impos'd on the dissenters from the Church of* England.
Purity, or *pureness.*
Purl, or *wormwood-ale.*
Purl-royal, *wormwood and sack.*
A Purl, *set on at the end of lace.*
To purl, *as a spring does.*
To purloin, *pilfer,* or *steal.*
A Purloiner.
Purple-colour.
The Purple, *a shell-fish.*
Purple-grass, *an herb.*
The Purples, or *spotted-feaver.*
Purport, or *true meaning.*
The Purport, or *tenour of a writing.*
A Purpose, or *design.*
To purpose, *intend,* or *design.*
A Purr, *a sort of bird.*
A Purse, *to keep money in.*
A Purse-bearer, or *cash keeper.*
A Purse-maker.
A Purse-net.
Purse-proud.
A Cut-purse.
Shepherds-purse, *an herb*
The Purser of a ship, *that has the charge of the provisions,* &c.
A Purser, or *bowser of a College.*
A Pursevant, *or* Pursuivant (*i. e.* a follower) *a King's messenger upon special occasions.*
The Pursevants, *or* Marshals at arms, *four in number,* viz. Blew-mantle, Rouge-cross, Rouge-dragon, *and* Portcullis; *who commonly succeed in the place of* Heralds, *when they die,* or *are preferr'd.*
Pursiness, *a being short-winded.*
Purslain, *an herb.*
Garden-purslain.
Wild purslain.
Pursuance, as *in pursuance of the Orders receiv'd from Court.*
Pursuant, *according to.*
To pursue, or *run after.*
A Pursuer.
A Pursuit.
A Pursuivant, *or* Pursevant.
Pursy, *over-fat,* or *short-winded.*
To purvey or *provide necessaries.*
Purveyance; *the providing corn, fuel, victuals,* &c. *for the King's house.*
A Purveyor.
A Push, or *blister.*
A Push, *and*
To push, or *thrust.*
A Pusher on.

Pu-

Pusillanimity, or *cowardize.*
Pusillanimous, *faint-hearted, mean-spirited,* or *cowardly.*
A Puss, or *cat.*
A Pustule, *a little wheal,* or *bladder on the skin.*
Put, *a game at cards.*
A Put off, or *delay.*
To put (*in all its senses.*)
Putrefaction, or *rottenness.*
To putrefy, *corrupt*, or *rot.*
Putrid, or *corrupt*; *as a putrid feaver.*
A Puttock, *a bird.*
Puttocks (*a sea-term*) *small shrowds, from the main to the top-mast shrowds, for the easy getting up to the top.*
Putty, *a sort of composition us'd by painters to stop up holes in wood,* &c.
A Puzzle, or *dirty slut*; also *difficulty,* or non-plus.
To puzzle, or *confound.*

PY

A Pye, or *pasty.*
A Pye, or *mag-pye, a bird.*
A Pygarg, *a wild beast like a fallow deer, mention'd* Deut. 14. 5.
A Pygmy, or *dwarf, so call'd from*
The Pygmies, *certain fabulous people, said to be but from one to three cubits high, and to be continually at war with the Cranes. Their women have children at 5 years of age, and are counted old at eight.*
A Pyramid, *a body bounded by several Triangles that make a* basis, *from the extremity of which it rises smaller and smaller to the top, till all meet in one point.*
Pyramidal, *belonging* to, or *in form of a* pyramid.
The Pyramids *of* Egypt, *vast piles of building rais'd up spire-wise and design'd for monuments for the King's of that Country. They are still to be seen and one of 'em is said to be 600 foot high.*
A Pyx, *a vessel wherein the host is kept in the* Roman *Church.*

QUA

A Quack, *Mountebank,* or *ignorant pretender to the Art of Physick.*
Quadragesima-Sunday, *the first Sunday in lent; so call'd, as being about 40 days from Easter.*
A Quadrangle, *a figure having four* angles, or *corners.*
Quadrangular, *in form of a* quadrangle.
A Quadrant, *a Mathematical instrument; being the quarter of a circle.*
Quadrate, or *four-square.*
To quadrate, or *agree.*
Quadrats, *certain square pieces of metal, used by Printers to fill up the blanks* or *void spaces in composing.*
Quadrilateral, *having four sides.*
Quadripartite, *divided into four parts.*
Quadruple, or *four-fold.*
To quaff, *tipple,* or *drink hard.*
A Quaffer.
A Quagmire, or *bog.*
A Quail, *a bird.*
To quail, or *curdle,* as *milk does.*
Quaint, *polite, elegant,* or *neat.*
Quaintness.
Quakerism, *the Religion* or *tenets of the*
Quakers, *a modern Sect, not much differing from the old Enthusiasts, and so nam'd from their* quaking or *trembling, when in their raptures they vainly pretend to be mov'd by the spirit of* God.
A Qualification, *particular faculty,* or *endowment.*
To qualify, *give one a qualification,* or *make him fit*; also *to appease* or *pacify.*
A Quality, *manner, condition, rank,* &c.
A Qualm, or *fainting-fit.*
Qualmish, or *subject to* qualms.
A Quandary, *doubt,* or *suspense.*
Quantity, *bigness, extent,* or *number.*
Quarantain, or quarantine, *the space of forty days, during which admittance is denied to persons coming* or *suppos'd to come, from an infected place.*
A Quarrel, or *brangle.*
A Quarrel, or *pain of glass.*
To quarrel, or *fall out.*
A Quarreller.
Quarrelsom.
Quarrelsomness.
A Quarry, *a place where stones are digged for building.*
A Quarry-man, *one that works in a* quarry.
The Quarry, or *reward given to hounds, after hunting.*
To quarry, or *feed upon the* quarry.
A Quart, *a known liquid measure.*
A Quart-Bottle.
A Quart-pot.
A Quartan ague, *that comes every third day.*
A Quarter, *and to* quarter (*in several senses.*)
A Quarter of wheat, i. e. *eight striked bushels.*
A Quarter, (*among Carpen-*

penters) a piece of timber generally four-square, and four inches thick.

Quarter-days, *four in number, viz. the annunciation of the Virgin* Mary *commonly call'd* Lady-day, March 25; *the festival of S.* John Baptist, or *Midsummer-day* June 24; *the festival of S.* Michael *the Archangel*, or Michaelmass-*day* Septemb. 29; *and the Nativity of our Lord God, or* Christmass-*day* Decemb. 25.

The Quarter-deck of a ship, *all that part which ranges over the steeridge, as far as the master's cabbin.*

A Quarter-master *in an army.*

The Quarter-sessions, *a Court held quarterly by the Justices of the peace, in every County.*

A Quarter-staff, *a kind of weapon us'd by Park-keepers*, &c.

The two Quarter-pieces *of a shooe.*

A Quarter-wind.

Quarteridge, or *money paid quarterly.*

A Quartern, *the fourth part of a pint; as a quartern of brandy.*

Quarters, or *lodgings for soldiers.*

Winter-quarters.

A Quarto-book, or *a book in* quarto; *every sheet of which makes four leaves.*

A Quash or *pompion.*

To quash, *spoil, frustrate,* or *defeat.*

A Quaternion, *a file of four soldiers.*

A Quaver, or *half a crotchet in musick.*

A Semi-quaver.

A Quaver, or *shake in singing.*

To quaver, or *run a division.*

A Quaviver, or *sea-dragon, a fish.*

QUE

A Queach, *quick-set*, or *thick bushy plot of ground.*

A Quean, or *drab.*

Queasiness, or *weakness of the stomack.*

Queasy, or *apt to vomit.*

A Queen, or *soveraign Princess.*

A Queen Consort, *that is married to a King.*

A Queen dowager, *a Queens widow, that lives upon her* dowry.

Queen-gold, *a revenue that belongs to every Queen Consort of* England *arising from certain fines for divers grants of the King upon pardons, contracts*, &c.

Queen's College, *in* Oxford; *which owes its name to Queen* Philippa *Wife of K.* Edward III. *but its foundation to her Chaplain* Robert de Eglesfield *Rector of* Burgh *under* Stanmore *in* Westmorland, *A. D.* 1340.

To quench, *extinguish, put out*, or *allay.*

A Quencher.

A Querister, or *quirister.*

A Quern, or *hand-mill.*

A Querry, or *stable.*

A Gentleman of the querry, *one of those, whose office it is, to hold the King's stirrup when he mounts on horseback.*

Querulous, *apt to complain, full of complaints* or *doleful.*

A Query, *question*, or *doubt.*

Quest, as *to go in* quest *of one, to seek after him.*

The Quest, or quest-men, *certain persons, chosen yearly in every Parish, to enquire into abuses and misdemeanours, especially such as relate to weights and measures.*

To quest, or *vent as a spaniel does.*

A Question, *demand, doubt*, or *matter in debate.*

To question, *to doubt, examine*, or *call in* question.

Questionable, or *to be questioned.*

A Questionist *in* Cambridge, *one that stands for the degree of bacheler of Arts.*

Questionless, or *doubtless.*

Questions *and* commands *a sport.*

To quetch, *stir, budg*, or *make the least noise.*

A Quibble, *and*

To quibble, or *pun.*

A Quibbler.

Quick, *alive, sprightly, smart, nimble*, &c.

A Quick-sand.

A Quick-set-hedge.

Quick-sighted.

Quick-silver.

Quick-witted.

To quicken, *enliven, hasten*, &c.

A Quicken-tree.

Quickness, *nimbleness, readiness*, or *subtilty.*

To give one quid *for* quo.

Quiddany, *or* quiddeny; *a conserve of* quinces.

A Quiddity, or *quirk.*

Quiet, *calm*, or *peaceable.*

Quiet, or *rest.*

To quiet, or *make* quiet.

A Quieter.

Quietness or *repose.*

The Quill *of a pen.*

The Quill-turn *of a wheel.*

A Quillet, as *the* quirks *and* quillets *of the law.*

A Quilt *for a bed.*

A Hair-Quilt.

A Quilt-maker.

To quilt *a petticoat.*

A Quince, *a fruit.*

Quinquagesima Sunday, or

Shrove-sunday, so nam'd from its being the fiftieth day before Easter.

Quinquennial, *of five years continuance.*

The Quinsy, or *squincy, a disease in the throat.*

Quintain, *a kind of tilting on horse-back with poles, still in use at marriages in* Shropshire *and elsewhere. He wins the garland, that breaks most poles, and shews most activity.*

A Quintal, *or* kintal; *an hundred pound weight.*

A Quintessence, *a certain subtil and spirituous substance extracted out of minerals,* &c. *by chymical operations.*

A Quip, or *jeer.*

A Quire *of paper.*

A Quire, *or* choir, *the company, and the place in a Church where the divine service is sung.*

A Quirister, or *singer in a quire.*

A Quirk, *shift,* or *fetch.*

A Quirry, or *groom of a stable.*

Quit, *free,* or *secure.*

To quit, *renounce, leave, abandon,* &c.

Quit-rent; *a certain small rent paid yearly by most tenants to the lord of the mannour.*

Quitch-grass, or *couch-grass.*

Quite, and clean.

Quits, or *even*; as *I shall be quits with you.*

A Quiver *for arrows.*

To quiver, *shiver,* or *quake.*

QUO

A Quodlibet, *quiddity,* or *quirk.*

Quodlibets, *or* quodlibetical *questions, disputed* pro *&* con *in schools, where a man may hold what part of the controversy he pleases.*

A Quoil, or *wedge.*

To quoil, *or* coil *a cable.*

A Quoit, *or* coit *to throw.*

A Quoit-caster.

Quorum, *as justices of the* quorum, *so call'd, because some matters of importance cannot be transacted without their presence,* or *assent.*

A Quota, or *share of contribution.*

A Quotation, *or* citation.

To quote, or *cite an Author.*

A Quotidian *ague, that comes daily.*

RA

THE *hawk* rabates, i. e. *leaves the game, and recovers the beater's fist.*

A Rabbet, or *coney.*

To rabbet, or *channel boards, a Term used among carpenters and joyners.*

A Rabbin, *or* rabby, *a* Jewish *Doctor.*

The Rabble, or *dregs of the people.*

A Race, *stock,* or *lineage*

A Race, or *course.*

A Horse-race, or *course of horses.*

A Race-horse.

A Rack, *and to* rack *(in several senses.)*

A Cheese-rack.

A Rack, or *neck of mutton,* or *veal.*

Rack-vintage, *the second voyage to* France, *&c. for racked wines.*

A Racket, *to play with at tennis.*

To keep a racket, or *to make a great noise and bustle.*

The radical, or *natural moisture.*

A Radish, *a root.*

A Horse-radish.

Raffling, *a kind of game with three dice.*

A Raft, *a float-boat of timber.*

A Rafter, or *beam.*

The Raftering *of an house.*

A Rag, or *tatter.*

A Rag, *rake,* or *company of colts.*

Rag-wort, *an herb.*

Rage, or *fury.*

To rage, or *be in a* rage.

Ragged, *beset with rags.*

Raggedness.

A Ragoo, *a high-season'd* French *dish.*

A Rail, *and*

To rail *in a place.*

A Rail, *a bird.*

To rail, *taunt,* or *reproach.*

A Railer.

Raiment, or *clothing.*

Rain, *and to* rain.

The Rain-bow.

A Rain-deer.

Rain-water.

Rainy, or *full of* rain.

To raise, *make to* rise, *lift up, promote,* &c.

A Raiser.

Raisins, or *dried grapes.*

Raisins *of the sun.*

Malaga-raisins.

A Rake, *and to* rake *(in several senses.)*

An Oven-rake.

A Raker.

A Rake-hell, or *wicked wretch.*

A Rake-shame, *a base rascally fellow.*

Rallery, *or* jesting.

To rally *troops,* or *get them together again.*

To rally, *play upon one,* or *jeer him.*

A Ram, or *male sheep.*

To ram, *beat in,* or *drive in.*

Ramage, *boughs, branches,* &c.

A Ramage-hawk, or *wild hawk.*

A Ramble, *and*

To ramble, or *rove up and down.*

A Rambler.

Rambooz, *a sort of drink made*

made at Cambridge, *o. eggs, ale, sugar,* &c.
A Rammer, *to ram in stones*; or *a gun-stick.*
Rammish, *stinking like a ram,* or *goat.*
Rammishness.
A Ramp, *or* ramp-scuttle, *a ramping girl.*
To ramp, or *rove about.*
Rampant (*in* Heraldry) *when a beast is painted rearing up the right foot as it were ready to combat*; as *a lion rampant.*
A Rampart, *a heap of earth rais'd about a place to set the soldiers thereon, and plant the cannon for its defence.*
Rampion, or *wild rape, an herb.*
Ramsons, or *buck-rams, an herb.*
Mountain-ramsons.
I Ran, or *did run.*
Rancour, *malice,* or *inveterate hatred.*
A Rand *of beef,* or *sturgeon.*
The Rand *of a shoe.*
At random, *without aim, rashly,* or *inconsiderately.*
Rang, (*from to* ring) as *they rang the bells.*
A Range, or *row.*
The Range-Beam *of a coach.*
To range, (*in several senses.*)
A Ranger, *in a forest.*
Rank, *growing up apace, over-fruitful, of a stinking smell,* &c.
A Rank, or *row.*
To rank, or *set in order.*
To rankle, or *fester.*
Rankness, *a being* rank.
To ransack, or *rifle.*
A Ransom, and
To ransom, or *redeem.*
To rant, *rave,* or *swagger,*
A Ranter.
A Rap, *and*
To rap, or *strike.*
Rapacious, or *ravenous.*
A Rape, *a division of a County, particularly in* Sussex, *divided into six rapes.*
A Rape, or *ravishing.*
A Rape, or *wild turnep.*
Rape-seed.
Rape-wine.
Rapid, or *swift, as the stream of a river is.*
Rapidity.
A Rapier, *a long sort of sword.*
Rapine, *violent robbery,* or *pillage.*
Rapt, *ravished,* or *transported*; as *rapt up with joy.*
A Rapture, or *ecstacy.*
Rare, *thin, seldom, excellent,* &c.
Rarefaction.
To rarefy, *make* or *grow thin.*
Rareness, or *scarcity.*
A Rarity, *a rare,* or *choice thing.*
A Rasberry, *a fruit.*
A Rascal, *a sorry vain fellow.*
A Rascal-deer, or *a lean deer.*
The Rascality, or *dregs of the people.*
Rash, *heady,* or *unadvised.*
A Rasher, or *slice of bacon.*
Rashness, (*from* rash.)
A Rasor, *to shave with.*
The Rasor-fish.
A Rasp, *a kind of file.*
To rasp *bread.*
A Raspis-berry, *or* rasberry.
A Rat, or *great mouse.*
A Water-rat.
A Rat-catcher.
A Rat-trap.
Rats-bane.
A Rate, *and to* rate (*in several senses.*)
Rateen, *a sort of woollen stuff.*
A Rater, *valuer,* or *assessor.*
Rathe, or *early,* as *rathe fruit.*
A rathe egg.
Rather, nay rather, *&c.*
The Ratification *of a treaty of peace.*
To ratify, or *confirm.*
Ratiocination, or *reasoning.*
Rational, or *reasonable.*
A Rattle *for children.*
To rattle, *clatter, make a noise,* or *chide.*
The Rattle-snake.
The Rattles, or *waddles of a cock.*
The Ratlings, or *steps of ship-shrowds.*
Ravage, *and*
To ravage, *spoil,* or *make havock.*
A Ravager.
To rave, *to be light-headed,* or *mad.*
To ravel, ravel *out,* or *run into threads*; as *cloth* or *stuff does that is not close wove.*
A Ravelin (*in* Fortification) *a small triangular work, without flanks that has but two faces and is generally rais'd before the curtains.*
A Raven, *a bird.*
A Night-raven,
A Sea-raven.
Ravening, *or* rapine, *a word us'd* Luke 11. 39.
Ravenous, or *greedy.*
To ravin, or *eat greedily.*
To ravish, *deflowr,* or *commit a rape.*
A Ravisher.
Ravishment.
Raw, *crude, undigested, unripe, rude, unskilful,* &c.
Raw-boned.
Rawness, *a being raw.*
A Ray, or *thorn-back a fish.*
The Rays, or *Sun-beams.*

To

To raze, *demolish*, or *lay even with the ground.*

A Razor, or rasor.

RE

A Reach, *and to reach (in several senses.)*

A Reach, or *winding of a a River*, as Chelsea reach *in the* Thames.

Read, as *a read-man*, or *a well-read man.*

To read *a lesson.*

A Reader.

Readiness, *a being ready.*

To re-adjourn, or *adjourn again.*

Re-admission.

To re-admit, or *admit again.*

Ready, or ready at hand; *a being prepar'd*, *present*, or *willing.*

Real, *true*, *which is indeed.*

A Real, *a* Spanish *coin*, *worth six pence.*

Reality, *truth*, or *sincerity.*

A Realm, or *Kingdom.*

A Ream *of Paper*, *containing* 20 *quires.*

To reap, *mow*, or *cut down Corn.*

A Reaper.

The Rear, or *hindermost part of an Army.*

A Rear-admiral.

To rear, or *set on end.*

To rear, or *bring up a Child.*

Reason, *the reasoning faculty*; *a cause* or *proof*, *moderation*, &c.

To reason, *discourse*, *dispute*, or *argue.*

Reasonable, *conformable to the rules of reason just*, *equitable*, or *indifferent.*

Reasonableness.

A Reasoner, or *arguer.*

To re-assemble, *summon again*, or *meet together again.*

To re-assume, or *take upon himself again.*

To re baptize, or *baptize again.*

A Rebate, *and*

To rebate, or *chamfer.*

A Rebatement, or *abatement in accounts.*

A Rebeck, *a kind of musical instrument.*

A Rebel, or *traytor.*

To rebell, or *take up arms against his Soveraign.*

Rebellion.

Rebellious, *disobedient*, or *stubborn.*

Rebelliousness.

A Rebound, *and*

To rebound, or *bounce up again.*

A Rebuff, *a notable repulse* or *opposition.*

To rebuild, or *build again.*

Rebuilt.

A Rebuke, *and*

To rebuke, *check*, or *reprove.*

Rebukeful.

A Rebuker.

A Rebus, *a kind of symbol*, or *device with a Motto*; *more especially of a name*; as one Choppington *had for his Sign*, *an ax chopping a Tun.*

To recall, or *call back.*

To recant, *unsay*, or *retract what one has spoken*, or *written.*

A Recantation.

To re-capitulate, *to rehearse briefly the heads of a former discourse at large.*

A Recapitulation.

To recede, *go back*, or *retire.*

A Receipt, or *receiving*; *an acquittance for money receiv'd*; or *a prescrib'd remedy.*

Receivable, *that may be received.*

To receive, *to take*, *admit*, *entertain*, &c.

A Receiver.

Recent, or *new.*

A Receptacle, or *place to receive or keep things in.*

A Reception, or *entertainment.*

Receptive, *apt*, or *fit to receive*, or *hold.*

A Recess, *a withdrawing*, or *retirement.*

A Recheat, *a hunter's lesson when they lose the game.*

Rechless, or retchless.

Reciprocal, *mutual*, or *interchanging.*

Reciprocation; *as a reciprocation*, or *mutual return of love.*

A Recital, or *rehearsal.*

To recite, *rehearse*, or *say without book.*

To reckon, *to count*, or *compute*; *to judge* or *esteem.*

A Reckoner.

To reclaim, *to reduce one to reason*, or *to tame a hawk.*

The Partridge reclaims, i.e. *calls back her young ones.*

A Recluse, *a Monk that is always confin'd to his Monastery.*

A Recognizance, *a bond*, or *obligation acknowledged in some Court of Record*, or *before some Judge*, *Master of Chancery*, *Justice of Peace*, &c.

The Recoil or *running back of a Cannon.*

To recoil or *give back.*

To recollect, *to call to mind*, or *to reflect upon himself.*

To recommence, or *begin again.*

To recommend, *to commit to one's favour*, or *care.*

Recommendable, or *praise worthy.*

A Recommendation.

A Recommendatory *letter.*

A Recompence, or *requital.*

To recompence, *requite*, or *reward.*

A

A Recompencer.

Reconcilable, *that may be reconcil'd.*

To reconcile, *make those friends that are at variance, or to bring in favour again.*

A Reconcilement, *or* reconciliation.

A Reconciler.

To reconduct, or *conduct back again.*

A Record, or *testimony. In* Law, *an authentick and uncontrollable written testimony, contain'd in parchment-rolls, and preserv'd in* Courts of Record.

The Records of the Tower.

A Recorder, or *keeper of* Records: Also *a judicious person for the most part well vers'd in the Law, whom the Mayor or other Magistrate of any City or Town Corporate, having a Court of record, associates to himself for his better direction in the execution of justice and Proceedings according to Law.*

To recover, *get again, regain,* or *come to himself again.*

Recoverable, *that may be recover'd.*

A Recovery.

To recount, or *recite.*

To have recourse to, or *make application to.*

To recreate, (q. d. *to* create *anew) to refresh, divert,* or *delight.*

Recreation, *refreshment,* or *sport.*

Recreative, *pleasant,* or *diverting.*

Recredentials, *an answer to the* credential *letters of an Ambassador.*

To recriminate, or *charge one's accuser.*

A Recrimination.

A Recruit, or *new supply.*

To recruit, *fill up,* or *reinforce.*

A Rectangle, (*in* Geometry) *a figure having four sides, the four angles of which, are all right* or *straight.*

A Rectifier.

To rectifie, *set to rights, correct,* or *amend.*

The Rectitude, or *straightness of a line.*

A Rector, (i. e. *governour) the Parson of a Parish-Church,*or *the principal of a College.*

A Rectorship, *the Office, and dignity of a* rector.

A Rectory, *a Parish-Church, with all its rights, glebes, tithes,* &c.

A Recumbency, or *relying upon a promise,* &c.

Recusancy, or *nonconformity.*

A Recusant, *one that refuses communion with the Church of* England.

The red *colour.*

Red-faced.

Red-gowm, *a disease in young children.*

Red-haired.

Red-hot, as *a red-hot iron.*

The red-letter tribe, *a name impos'd on the Roman Catholicks, from their keeping so many holy days mark'd in the almanacks with red letters.*

A Robin-red-breast, *A* Red-shank. *A* Red-start. *A* Red-wing.	*birds.*

A Bloud-red *Colour.*

Reddish, or *somewhat red.*

To redeem, *ransom, recover, rescue,* &c.

Redeemable, *that may be redeem'd.*

A Redeemer.

A Redemption.

To redeliver, or *deliver again.*

To re-demand, *demand,* or *ask again.*

A Reintegration, or *renewing of kindness,* &c.

Redness, (*from* red.)

To redouble, or *encrease much.*

A Redoubt, (*in* Fortification) *a small square fort, that has no defence but in front.*

To redound, *to turn to,* or *light on.*

Redressess, *that cannot be redressed.*

A Redress *of grievances.*

To redress, or *reform.*

A Redresser.

To reduce, *to bring back,* or *bring into subjection.*

Reducible.

A Reduction.

Reductive, *that helps to reduce.*

Redundancy, *a being*

Redundant, *over-flowing, abounding, very plentiful* or *superfluous.*

A Reed, or *cane.*

A Reed-bank.

Reed-mace, or *cats-tail, an herb.*

Burr-reed.

The Indian flow'ring-reed.

The sweet-smelling reed.

To re-edify, or *rebuild.*

A Reek, *and*

To reek or *steam.*

A Reek, or *stack of hay.*

A Reel, *to wind thread,* or *yarn on.*

To reel, or *wind on a reel.*

To reel, or *stagger.*

To re-enter, *enter upon,* or *take possession of again.*

A Re-entry.

To re-establish, *to establish,* or *settle again.*

A Re-establishment.

A Reeve, reve, or greve, *in*

(*in Saxon, a governour*) *the bailiff of a franchise or mannor.*

A Portreve, *a governour of a port, or haven.*

To reeve *a rope* (*among sailers*) *to draw it thro' the block.*

A Re-examination.

To re-examine, *or* examine *again.*

A Refection, or *repast.*

A Refectory, *the room where Friers* or *Nuns eat together.*

To refel, *prove false, disprove,* or *confute.*

To refer, or *leave a matter to one.*

A Referee, or *arbitrator to whom a law-business is referr'd.*

A Reference.

To refine, *to make finer, purge,* or *purify.*

A Refiner.

To refit, or *fit out again.*

To reflect, *turn,* or *cast back; to consider again;* or *to censure.*

A Reflection.

Reflexive, or *apt to reflect.*

To reflow, or *flow back.*

A Reflux, *ebb,* or *ebbing of water.*

A Reform, *the disbanding of some part of an army.*

To reform, *correct, amend, cashire,* &c.

A Reformado, *or* reformed Captain, *one that having lost part of his men, has the rest taken from him and otherwise disposed of; he himself being either cashir'd* or *serving, as an inferiour Officer; or common soldier with double pay.*

A Reformado, or *volunteer in a man of war.*

A Reformation.

A Reformer.

Refractariness, *a being*

Refractary, *wilful, obstinate, stubborn,* or *unruly.*

To refrain, or *forbear.*

A Refrane, *or* Spanish *Proverb.*

To refresh, *renew,* or *recruit.*

A Refreshment

Refrigerative, or *cooling, a physical term.*

A Refuge, or *place of safety, to fly to.*

Refulgency, or *brightness, as of precious stones.*

Refulgent, *bright,* or *glittering.*

To refund, or *pay back.*

A Refusal, or *denial.*

The Refuse, or *dress of any thing.*

To refuse, or *deny.*

A Refutation.

To refute, *confute disprove,* or *convince by reason.*

To regain, *get again,* or *recover.*

Regal, *royal,* or *belonging to the King.*

Regal Fishes, *which the King claims by his prerogative, as whales, sturgeons,* &c.

To regal, or *treat one nobly.*

The Regalia, or *Royalties of a Prince.*

A Regalio, or *sumptuous entertainment.*

A Regard, *and*

To regard, *consider,* or *respect.*

A Regardant, (*in* Heraldry) *a beast painted looking back at one.*

A Regarder, *a forest-officer, appointed to make the regard of the forest and over-look all the other Officers.*

Regardless, *negligent,* or *that has no regard to.*

Regenerate, or *born anew.*

Regenerated, or *brought to*

Regeneration, *a new and spiritual birth.*

Regency, *the state of*

A Regent, *one that governs a Kingdom, during the minority,* or *incapacity of a King.*

A Queen regent.

A Regent Master, *at* Cambridge.

The Regent-house.

A Regicide, *the murder* or *murderer of a King.*

The Regiment, or *government of the Church.*

A Regiment of soldiers, *under the command of a Colonel; if it be of horse, it contains 5, 6, 7, or 8 troops; if of foot, it has from 8 to 12 companies.*

A Region, or *Country;* also *a particular extent of the air.*

A Register, or *book of records;* or *the person that keeps it.*

A Register *in printing, a rule for the equal distribution of the lines and pages.*

To regorge, *cast up,* or *vomit.*

A Regrater, or *Huckster.*

A Regress, or *coming back.*

Regret, *grief, sorrow,* or *discontent.*

Regretted, or *lamented.*

Regular, *conformable to rule.*

Regularity.

To regulate, *set in order, govern, discipline,* &c.

A Regulation.

A Rehearsal.

To rehearse, *tell, relate,* or *repeat.*

A Rehearser.

To reject, *cast off,* or *slight.*

A Rejection.

A Reign, *and*

To reign, or *govern in qua-*

quality of a King.
To re-imbark, or re-embark, *to take shipping again.*
To re-imburse, or *pay back again.*
A Re-imbursement.
A Rein *of a bridle.*
To re-inforce, *strengthen again, to add more strength,* or *recruit.*
A Re-inforcement.
To re-ingage, or re-engage, *to engage again.*
To re-ingratiate, or *get into favour again.*
The Reins or *kidneys.*
To re-instate, or *restore to the same* state.
To rejoice, *to cause*, or *to have joy.*
A Rejoynder, *an answer* or *exception to a replication.*
To re-iterate, or *repeat.*
A Re-iteration.
A Relapse, *the returning of a fit of sickness.*
To relapse, *to fall sick again,* or *to commit the same fault.*
To relate, *to tell* or *rehearse*; *to belong to*; *to bear proportion*; or *to be of kin.*
A Relater.
A Relation.
Relatively, or *that has relation to a thing.*
A Relaxation, *respit,* or *breathing-time.*
A Relay, (*in hunt-ing*) *the setting of fresh dogs upon a wild beast.*
A Release, or *discharge.*
To release, *discharge*, or *set at liberty.*
A Releasement.
To relent, *to abate as heat and cold do*; *to repent, yield,* or *give way.*
The Relicks, or *remains of Saints.*
A Relict, *a law word for a widow.*
Relief, *comfort, aid,* or *supplies.*
To relieve, *succour, help,* or *assist.*
A Reliever.
Relievo, *a particular way of imbossing in mason's work*; as *a piece done in* alto *or* basso relievo.
Religion, *the worship of* God; *piety*; or *devotion.*
Religious, *godly, devout,* or *conscientious.*
Religiousness.
To relinquish, *forsake*, or *part with.*
A Relish, or *taste.*
To relish, *to give*, or *have a good savour*; *to approve of*, or *be agreeable.*
Relishable, *that relishes well.*
Reluctancy, *averseness*, or *unwillingness.*
To rely, *confide*, or *depend upon.*
To remain, *to continue, to be behind,* or *over and above.*
A Remainder.
The Remains, *all that is left of a thing.*
To remand, or *send back again.*
A Remark, *and*
To remark, *note*, or *observe.*
Remarkable, *worthy remark, notable,* or *considerable.*
Remediless, *that is past remedy.*
A Remedy, *and*
To remedy, *cure*, or help.
To remember, *call to mind,* or *be mindful.*
A Remembrance.
A Remembrancer.
To remind, or *put in mind.*
Remissness, *a being*
Remiss, *slack*, or *careless.*
Remissible, or *pardonable.*
Remission, or *forgiveness.*
To remit, *send back, slacken, forgive,* &c.
A Remitment, or *consignation.*
A Remnant, *remainder,* or *fragment.*
A Remonstrance, or *expostulatory declaration.*
Remonstrants, *those that make remonstrances.*
To remonstrate, *to declare in such a manner.*
Remorse, *the check* or *sting of conscience.*
Remorseless, *that feels no remorse.*
Remote, or *far distant.*
Remoteness.
Removable, *that may be removed.*
A Removal, or *change of abode.*
A Remove, *and*
To remove, *put* or *set away, move from one place to another,* &c.
A Rencounter, *a meeting by chance, adventure* or *accidental scuffle.*
To rencounter, or *meet with.*
To rend, or *tear.*
To render, *return, yield up, translate,* &c.
A Rendevous, or rendezvous, *a place appointed for meeting*; or *a meeting place for an army.*
To rendez-vous, or *appear at the place appointed.*
A Renegade, or renegado, *one that has denied,* or *apostatized from the Christian religion.*
To renew, *to begin* a-new, or *to revive.*
A Renewer.
A Renewal.
Rennet, *a calves-maw, commonly us'd to curdle milk with for cheese-curds,* &c.
A Rennet-bag.
A Renovation, or *renewing.*
To renounce, *forsake,* or *abjure.*
Renown, *fame*, or *great re-*

reputation.
Renowned, or *famous.*
Rent, or *torn.*
A Rent, *in a petticoat,* &c.
Rent, *a sum of money issuing yearly out of lands and tenements.*
To rent, or *take by* rent.
House-rent.
A Renter-Warden *that receives the* rents *of a company* or *corporation.*
To renter, or *fine-draw.*
Re-obtained, or *obtained again.*
To repair, *to mend,* or *to betake one's self to.*
The Repairs *of Houses Ships,* &c. also (*in hunting*) *the haunt of a hare.*
A Repairer.
Reparation, or *satisfaction for dammage.*
A Repartee, or *quick answer.*
A Repast, or *meal.*
To repay, or *pay again.*
The Repeal *of a Statute.*
To repeal, *abrogate,* or *disannul.*
To repeat, *rehearse,* or *do the same thing over again.*
To repel, *beat* or *drive back.*
A Repeller.
To repent, or *be sorry for any thing done amiss.*
Repentance.
To repeople, or *people again.*
A Repetition, or *repeating.*
To repine, *grieve,* or *grudge.*
A Repiner.
To re-plant, or *plant again.*
To replenish, or *fill* (*a Term in* Divinity.)
A Replevin, or replevy, *the releasing of cattel,* or *other goods distrain'd by virtue of a Writ call'd* replegiari facias, *upon surety to answer the distrainer's suit.*
To replevy *a distress,* or *recover goods distrain'd.*
A Replication, or *the Plantiff's reply to the Defendant's answer.*
A Reply, or *answer.*
To reply, or *make a reply.*
A Report, or *relation.*
The Report, or *noise of a gun.*
To report, *tell, relate, declare,* or *give an account of.*
A Reporter.
Repose, or *rest.*
To repose, or *rest himself;* or *to put trust in one.*
A Repository, *a storehouse,* or *place where things are laid up and kept.*
To reprehend, *find fault with,* or *reprove.*
A Reprehender.
Reprehensible, or *reprovable.*
A Reprehension.
To represent, shew, *lay before one, make it appear, resemble,* &c.
A Representation.
A Representative, *one that represents another's person.*
To repress, *restrain,* or *keep in subjection.*
A Reprieve, or *respit of a malefactor from execution.*
To reprieve, or *grant a reprieve.*
A Reprimand, or *check.*
To reprimand, *check, rebuke,* or *reprove.*
To reprint, or *print again.*
Reprisal, *the right of reprisal, or law of marque, by which he that has justice done him in another Country, redresses himself by the goods belonging to persons of that Country, taken within his own bounds.*
A Reproach, or *infamy.*
To reproach, *twit, charge with,* or *upbraid.*
Reproachable, *that deserves reproach.*
Reproachful, *shameful,* or *injurious.*
A Reprobate (*in* Divinity) *a person whom God has not chosen to be saved;* also *a lewd,* or *profligate wretch.*
To reprobate, or *cast off.*
Reprobation.
A Reproof, or *rebuke.*
Reprovable, *worthy to be reprov'd.*
To reprove, *blame, check,* or *rebuke.*
A Reprover.
A Reptile, or *creeping insect.*
A Republican, or *Common-wealths man.*
A Republick, or *Common-wealth.*
To repudiate, *divorce,* or *put away.*
A Repudiation.
Repugnancy, or *averseness.*
Repugnant, or *contrary to.*
A Repulse, or *denial.*
To repulse, *deny,* or *reject.*
Reputation, *or* repute, *credit,* or *esteem.*
Reputed, *counted,* or *look'd upon.*
A Request, or *petition.*
A Master of requests.
To request, or *entreat.*
To be in request, *to be much sought after,* or *highly esteem'd.*
To require, *demand,* or *exact.*
Requisite, or *necessary.*
A Requital.
To requite, *reward,* or *make amends for.*
A Reremouse, or *bat.*

To

To resalute, or *salute again.*
A Resalutation.
To rescind, *repeal*, or *disannul.*
A Rescript, *an answer to a petition*; or *the return of a Writ.*
A Rescue, *and*
To rescue, *save*, or *deliver.*
A Research, or *strict enquiry.*
Resemblance, or *likeness.*
To resemble, or *be like.*
To resent, *to be sensible of*, or *to take it ill.*
A Resentment.
A Reservation.
A Reserve, as *a reserve of Soldiers, Affection*, &c.
To reserve, *keep*, or *save.*
Reserved, *grave, close*, or *wary.*
Reservedness.
Re-settled, or *re-established.*
To reside, *abide*, or *continue in a place.*
A Residence.
Resident, or *residing.*
A Resident, *a foreign Minister of State, that* resides *in the dominions of another Prince*, &c.
A Residentiary, *one that resides in his benefice.*
The Residue, *the rest, remainder*, or *what is left in arrearage.*
To resign, *give up*, or *surrender.*
A Resignation.
A Resigner.
A Resignment.
To resist, or *withstand.*
Resistance, or *opposition.*
A Resister.
A Resolve, or *purpose.*
To Resolve, *to determine*, or *to explain.*
The Resolves, or *Debates of the House of Commons*
A Resolvedness, or *firm resolution.*
Resolute, *fully resolved, stout, bold*, or *hardy.*
Resoluteness.
A Resolution, *purpose*, or *design*; also *assurance, boldness*, or *courage.*
A Resort, or *Concourse.*
To resort, or *repair to a place.*
To resound, or *ring again.*
Respect, *esteem, regard, deference*, or *relation.*
To respect, or *honour.*
Respectful.
Respectfulness.
Respective, or *peculiar.*
Respiration, *breathing*, or *fetching breath.*
A respit, *a breathing time*; *or a further time allow'd to pay money in.*
To respit, or *give respit.*
Resplendency, *a being*
Resplendent, *bright*, or *glittering.*
Responsals, *or* responses, *the answers made by the Clerk and People in the Church-Service.*
Responsible, *liable to answer*, or *account for*; or *that is capable of making good payments.*
Rest, *and to* rest, (*in all senses*)
Rest-harrow, *an herb.*
Restauration, *a restoring*, or *re-establishment.*
Restful, or *that is at rest.*
A Resting-place.
Restitution, *a restoring, yielding up again*, or *making good.*
Restive, *stubborn*, or *headstrong.*
Restiveness.
Restlesness, *a being*
Restless, *that has no rest*, or *quiet, busy, impatient*, &c.
A Restorative, *a medicine to restore strength.*
To restore, *give back, return*, or *make good.*
A Restorer.
To restrain, *keep in*, or *curb.*
A Restraint.
A Restriction, or *limitation.*
Restrictive, *or* restringent, (*in* Physick) *of a binding quality.*
Resty, *idle, slothful*, or *obstinate.*
The Result, or *up-shot of a business.*
To result; as *what results* (*what follows*) *from that?*
To resume, or *take up a discourse again* &c.
A Resumption, *the taking again into the King's hands, what he had granted upon surprise.*
A Resurrection, or *rising up again to life.*
Retail, *and*
To retail, or *sell by parcells.*
The Retail-trade.
A Retailer, or *seller by retail.*
To retain, *hold back, keep in mind*, or *to himself.*
A Retaining-fee *given to a Counsellor at Law, to keep him from pleading for the adverse party.*
A Retainer, *a client*, or *servant, belonging to the* retinue, *that attends only upon special occasions.*
To retaliate, or *return like for like.*
A Retaliation.
To retard, *stop, hinder*, or *delay.*
To retch, or *stretch.*
To retch himself, or *to* retch *out, as one does that comes from sleeping.*
To retch, reach, or *be ready to vomit.*
Retchlesness, or *laziness.*
Retchless, *idle*, or *careless.*
A Retention, or *stoppage of*

of urine.
The retentive *faculty.*
A Retinue, or *train of attendants.*
To retire, *go back*, or *withdraw.*
Retiredness.
A Retirement.
A Retort, *a kind of chymical vessel, us'd in distilling.*
To retort, or *return an argument*, &c.
To retract, or *recant*; *to revoke what one has said or written.*
A Retractation.
A Retreat, *and*
To retreat, or *retire from a place.*
To retrench, *cut off, lessen*, or *impair.*
To retrench, or *fortify with*
A Retrenchment, *a work made of part of a rampart, when the enemy is so far advanc'd, that he is no longer to be resisted or beaten from the old rampart.*
A Retribution, *recompence*, or *compensation.*
To retrieve, *get again*, or *recover.*
A Return, *and to* return (*in all senses.*)
Returnable, *that may be* return'd.
To reveal, *disclose*, or *discover.*
A Revealer.
A Revelation.
St. John's Revelation.
To revel, or *riot.*
A Reveller.
A Revel-rout, or *riotous concourse of people.*
Revels, *sports of dancing, masking, dice-playing*, &c. *in the Inns of Court.*
The Master of the revels, *an officer that has the ordering of these pastimes.*
Revenge, or *vengeance*, *and*
To revenge, or *take revenge.*
Revengefull.
A Revenger.
A Revenue, *rent*, or *income.*
To revere, or *honour, with awful respect.*
Reverence, *such respect.*
To reverence, *honour*, or *shew respect.*
Reverend, *to be rever'd*, or *reverenced.*
Reverent, reverential, or *respectful.*
The Reverse, or *back-side of a Medal, Coin*, &c.
To reverse, *repeal*, or *abrogate.*
The Reversion *of an estate*, or *office.*
To revert, or *return, as an estate, or honour does.*
A Review, or *overlooking*; *especially a muster of military forces.*
To review, *view again*, or *overlook.*
To revile, *taunt, reproach*, or *rail at.*
A Reviler.
A Revisal, or *re-examining.*
A Revise, or *second proof* (*in Printing.*)
To revise *a piece of work, to look over it again, in order to correct or amend it.*
A Reviser.
To revive, *to enliven, to come to life again, to renew*, &c.
A Reviver.
A Re-union.
To re-unite, *to unite again*, or *to reconcile.*
Revocable, *that may be revok'd.*
A Revocation.
To revoke, *recall, repeal, renounce*, or *abjure.*
A Revolt, or *defection.*
To revolt, *rebell*, or *apostatize.*
A Revolter.
To revolve, *ruminate*, or *cast in one's mind.*
A revolution (*i.e.* whirling about) *a certain course of the planets, time*, &c.) or *a change of government.*
A Revulsion (*in* Physick) *a drawing back, or forcing of humours from any part of the body.*
To revy, or *see again, at cards.*
A Reward, or *recompence.*
To reward, or *requite.*
A Rewarder.

R H

A Rhapsody, *a confused collection of Poems*, &c. *as* Homer's Rhapsody.
Rhenish *Wine, that comes from the parts about the river* Rhine.
Rhetorical, *of or belonging to* Rhetorick.
A Rhetorician, *orator*, or *professor of*
Rhetorick, *the art of speaking well*, or *eloquently.*
A Rheum, or *defluxion of humours.*
Rheumatick, *that is troubled with* rheum.
The Rheumatism, or *running gout, a disease.*
A Rhinoceros, *a wild beast; so nam'd from a horn bending upon its snout.*
A Rhomb, (*in* Geometry) *a body bounded by six equilateral oblique-angled squares.*
The Rhombs, or *points of the mariners compass.*
Rhubarb, *a physical root.*
Monks-rhubarb, *an herb.*
Rhyme, rime, *meter*, or *verse.*

R I

A Rib, *a part of the body.*

dy; or *the side-timber of a ship.*
To rib-roast, or *cudgel one.*
Ribaldry, *debauchery,* or *obscene talk.*
A Riband, or *ribbon.*
A Ribbon-weaver.
Rice, *a sort of grain.*
Rich, *full of*
Riches, or *wealth.*
A Riches, *a company of marterns,* or *sables.*
Richness, *a being* rich.
A Rick, *of corn,* or *hay.*
The Rickets, *a disease in children.*
Rid, as *to get rid.*
To rid, *discharge, free, deliver from,* &c.
A Riddance.
Ridden (*from to* ride) *as* Jesuit-ridden,
Priest-ridden, *said of those that suffer themselves to be govern'd absolutely by such* Jesuits *or* Priests.
A Riddle, or *dark saying.*
A Riddle, or *coal-sieve.*
To riddle, or *sift.*
To ride, *to travel on horse-back, in a coach, waggon,* &c.
The ship rides, i. e. *is held fast with the anchors.*
A Rider.
A Riding, or *division in* Yorkshire.
A Riding-cap.
A Riding-hood.
A Ridge, *the top of a hill,* or *house.*
A Ridge, or *balk of land between two furrows.*
A Ridge-band *of a horse harness.*
The Ridge-bone *of the back.*
A Ridge-tile.
Ridged, *that has many* ridges.
A Ridgeling, or ridgil, *the male of any beast that has been but half gelt.*
Ridicule, as *to turn a thing to* ridicule.
To ridicule, or *make*
Ridiculous, *fit to be laughed at.*
Ridiculousness.
Rie, or rye, *a sort of corn.*
Rife, *common,* or *frequent.*
Riff-raff, or *refuse.*
To rifle, *pillage,* or *rob.*
A Rifler.
A Rift, *cleft,* or *chink.*
A Rig, *a horse that has been cut and yet got a colt.*
A Rig, or tom-rig, *a wanton girl.*
To rig *a ship, to furnish her with tackling,* as *cordage, ropes,* &c.
Right, straight, *true, genuine, just, honest,* &c.
Out-right, or *altogether.*
A Right, or *privilege;* also *power, justice, equity,* &c.
To right *one,* or *do him justice.*
Righteous, *just,* or *equitable.*
Righteousness.
Rightful, or *lawful.*
Rights; as *to set things to right.*
Rigid, *stiff, strict, stern,* or *austere.*
Rigols, *a sort of musical instrument, us'd in* Flanders.
Rigour, *extremity,* or *severity.*
Rigourous, or *full of* rigour.
The Rim, *or bottom of the belly.*
A Rime, *a kind of mist that dissolves by degrees.*
A Rime, or *cadence of words.*
To rime, or *make rimes.*
Rime-doggrel, *a paltry rime.*
A Rimer, *versifier,* or *riming poet.*
A Rind, *bark,* or *peel.*
A Ring, *and to* ring (*in all senses.*)
An Ear-ring.
The Devil's gold-ring, *an herb.*
A Seal-ring.
A Stone-ring.
A Wedding-ring.
Ring-bolts, *for pieces of ordinance.*
A Ring-dove, *a bird.*
The Ring-finger.
A Ring-head, *an engine to stretch woollen.*
A Ring-leader, or *head of a party.*
Ring-straked, or *marked, a word us'd* Gen. 30. 39.
A Ring-tail, *a kind of kite with a white tail.*
A Ring-walk, *a hunter's round walk.*
A Ring-worm, or *tetter.*
To rinse, *or wash lightly.*
Riot, *excess, luxury,* or *debauchery.*
A Riot, *rout, rabble,* or *tumult: In* Law, *it denotes the forcible doing of an unlawful act, by three or more persons met together for that purpose.*
To riot, or *make a* riot.
Riotous.
Riotousness.
To rip, or *unsow.*
Ripe, *mellow, perfect,* or *come to maturity.*
To ripen, *to make* ripe, or *to grow* ripe.
Ripeness.
A Ripier, *one that brings fish from the Sea-coasts to sell in the inland parts.*
A Rise, *and to* rise (*in several senses.*)
A Rising, *insurrection,* or *popular tumult.*
A Risk, *hazard,* or *venture.*
A Rite, or *Church-ceremony.*
Funeral Rites, or *solemnity*

nities at burials.
A Ritual, or *mass-book, containing the rites and ceremonies of the* Romish *Church.*
A Rival, *properly one that has water from the same* river, *with another; a competitor, especially in love-affairs.*
To rival one, or *to court the same mistress.*
To rive, or *cleave asunder.*
Riven, or *cleft.*
A River, *a great quantity of water, continually running in a channel from its spring-head, which is either a fountain* or *a lake, till it falls into the Sea.*
A Rivet, *and*
To rivet, or *clinch.*
A Rivulet, *a small current of water, arising for the most part from springs, but its course is but short, and its bed straight and shallow.*
A Rix-doller, a German *coin, worth about* 4 s. 4 d.

RO

A Roach, *a fish.*
A Road, or *high-way; also a station for ships.*
A Roader, *a ship that rides at anchor in a road.*
To roam *about*, or *rove up and down.*
A Roamer.
A Roan horse, *which being of a bay, black*, or *sorrel colour, has the body set all over very thick, with gray* or *white hairs.*
To roar, *to cry out; to cry like a* Lion; *or to make a noise, as the Sea does.*
A Roaring-boy, or *debo-shee.*
Roast, or *roasted.*
To roast *meat before the fire.*
To rob, *spoil, pillage, deprive of*, &c.
A Robber.
A Church-robber.
A Robbery.
A Robe, *a sort of garment worn by Magistrates*, &c.
A Parliament-robe.
A Yeoman *or* Master of *the* robes.
Herb-Robert, *a plant.*
A Robin-red-breast, *a bird.*
Ruffling-robin, } *herbs.*
Wake-robin, }
Robins, *or* robbins, *the small ropes that make fast the sails to the yards.*
Robust, *strong, lusty, hardy*, or *sturdy.*
A Rocambole, *a sort of garlick.*
Roche-allum.
A Rochet, *a kind of surplice worn by Bishops.*
A Rock *of stone.*
Rock-crystal.
A Rock-pigeon.
To rock *a cradle.*
Rocket, *an herb.*
Baserocket.
Doublerocket.
A Rocket, *a sort of fire-work.*
Rockiness, *a being*
Rocky, or *full of rocks.*
A Rod, or *wand; a measure of* 16 *foot and a half*, &c.
An Angling-rod.
A Curtain-rod.
Golden-rod, *an herb.*
The Usher of the black rod, *an officer that attends the house of Lords.*
A Rod-net, *to catch black birds, wood-cocks*, &c.
I rode, or *did ride.*
A Rodomontado, *a vain-glorious bravado, from* Rodomonte, *the vapouring hector in* Orlando furioso.
A Roe, *a she wild goat.*
The Roe or *milt of a fish.*
A Roe-buck.
Rogation-week, *the next week but one before* Whitsunday; *so called from the* Latin *word* Rogatio, *i. e.* an humble request; *because the Church was wont in this week to make Prayers and Supplications for the divine blessing on the Fruits of the Earth*, &c.
A Rogue, *rascal*, or *villain.*
To rogue, or *stroll about.*
Roguery, *villany*, or *rallery.*
Roguish, *wicked*, or *malicious*; also *facetious*, or *wanton.*
Roguishness.
To roist, or *swagger.*
A Roister.
A Roll, *and to* roll (*in all senses*)
A Court-roll.
A Muster-roll.
Roll-butter, or *butter made up in* rolls.
A Roller, or *swathing-band for Children.*
A Roller, *to move great stones* or *timber with a leaver.*
A Rolling-pin.
A Rolling-press, *to print pictures, callicoes*, &c.
A Rolling-stone.
The Rolls, *the office where the Chancery-Records are kept.*
The Master of the rolls.
Roman, *belonging to* Rome; as *the* Roman Church.
Roman-Catholicks, or *Papists that embrace the Doctrines of the* Church of Rome; *so called from their boasting themselves to be the only true Members of the* Catholick, or

Uni-

Universal Church.
The Roman *Character in writing* or *printing.*
English-Roman, *a sort of large printing-letter.*
A Romance, or *feigned story about amorous adventures and intrigues.*
To romance, or *tell a magnificent lye.*
A Romancer.
A Romanist, Roman Catholick, or *Papist that adheres to the Church of* Rome.
Romantick, *belonging to a* Romance,or *fictitious.*
Romish, *belonging to the Church of* Rome.
A Rondel, (*in* Fortification) *a round Tower rais'd at the foot of the* Bastions.
A Rood,*the fourth part of an acre*; also *an old English word for the* Cross; as
The Holy-rood days.
A Rood-loft, *a shrine, in which the* Rood *or Image of* Christ *on the Cross, generally made of wood was plac'd just over the passage out of the body of the Church into the Chancel.*
The Roof, or *palate of the mouth.*
A Roof, or *top of a house.*
Roof-trees,*certain rafters in a Ship, reaching from the half deck to the forecastle.*
A Rook, *a bird.*
A Rook, or *notorious cheat.*
To rook, *cheat, gull,* or *deceive.*
Room, *place*, or *space.*
A Room, or *chamber in a house.*
A Club-room, *where a particular* Club, or *Society meet together.*
A Dining-room.
A Lodging-room.
A Withdrawing-room.
A Roost, or *peach for Poultry*
To go to roost on.
A Hen-roost.
A Root, *of a tree, herb,* &c.
To root, or rout, *as a Hog does.*
To root *out*, or root *up.*
The Holy Ghost's root.
The Hollow root.
A Rope, or *cord.*
A Rope *of onions,* &c.
A Rope-dancer.
A Roper, or *rope-maker.*
Rope-weed, or *Bindweed, an herb.*
A Rope-yard, or *place where* ropes *are made.*
To rope, or *run thick, as some liquors do.*
Rope-yarns, (*among Mariners*) *the tow of untwisted* ropes.
Ropy, *clammy*, or *slimy.*
The Rosary, or *our Lady's Psalter, said with Beads containing* 15 Paternosters, *and* 150 Avemaries; *and much in use among the Confraternity of the* Rosary, *instituted by St.* Dominick.
A Rose, *a flower.*
A Canker-rose.
A Damask-rose.
The Elder-rose, or *guelder-rose.*
The Holy-rose, or *sagerose.*
The Rose of Jerusalem, or *our Lady's rose.*
A Musk-rose.
The white Musk-rose.
A Province-rose.
The double red rose.
The Sweet-brier-rose.
A Velvet-rose.
The Wild rose.
A Rose-bud.
A Rose-cake.
A Rose-noble, *a sort of Coin.*
Rose-vinegar.
Rose-water.
Rose-wood, *a shrub.*
Rose-wort, *an herb.*
I rose, or *did rise.*
Rosemary, *a plant.*
Wild-rosemary.
Rosin, *an oily juice that runs out of some trees.*
Rosined, or *rubb'd with rosin.*
To rost. or roast *meat.*
Rosy, *of the colour of roses.*
A Rot, or *murrain among Cattel,* &c.
To rot, *perish with the rot*, or *grow rotten.*
Rote; as *to speak by* rote, or *without book.*
Rotten, *rotted*,or *corrupt.*
Rottenness, or *corruption.*
Rotten-ripe.
To rove, or *ramble about.*
A Rover.
A Rover, *at sea*, or *pirate.*
At Rovers, or *at random.*
Rouge-cross, *and*
Rouge-dragon; *two of the Marshals* or *pursevants at arms.*
Rough, *rugged*, *eneven, harsh, grim,* &c.
Rough-cast, *and*
To rough-cast *a wall*, &c. *to lay it with lime and course sand.*
A Rough-footed *pigeon.*
To rough-hew *a piece of timber.*
Rough-hewn.
A rough Mason.
Roughness.
The Rounce *of a Printer's press.*
Rouncevals, *a great sort of pease.*
Round, *a* round *and to* round (*in several senses.*)
To round one *in the ear.*
A Roundelay, *a kind of catch*, or *song.*
A Round-head, *opposed to a* Cavalier *in the late civil war*; *one of the parliament.*

liament-party, who usually were short hair.

A Round-house, or *prison*; or *the Master's cabin in a ship.*

Roundness.

The Rounds, (*a military term*) *a turn which an Officer takes with a few soldiers; in a garrison,* &c, *to see that the Centries do their duty.*

To rouse, *raise*, or *stir up.*

The hank routes, i. e. *shakes her self.*

To rouse *in the cable* (*a sea term*) i. e. *to hale in so much of it, as lyes slack.*

A rousing, or *whisking lye.*

A Rousselet, *a kind of pear.*

A Rout, *and to* rout (*in several senses.*

A Rout, or *herd of wolves.*

A Row, or *rank.*

To row *with oars.*

A Row-barge.

A Rower.

The Rowel *of a spur.*

A Rowel, (*in surgery*) *a skain of thread* or *silk drawn thro' the nape of the neck.*

To rowel *a horse.*

Rowen hay, or *latter hay.*

Royal, *kingly*, or *belonging to the King.*

The Royal Exchange.

The Royal Society, *a Company of noble and learned persons, skill'd in the most useful Sciences; incorporated by K.* Charles II. *under the name of the President, Council, and Fellows of the* Royal Society *of* London, *for the improving of natural Knowledge.*

Royalty, or *the Royal dignity*, as

The Ensigns of Royalty, *which in* England *are the Crown; the* Scepter and Cross; *the Scepter and dove; the Globe; the Orb and Cross; S.* Edward's *staff; four several Swords, and other ornaments us'd at the Coronation.*

The Royalties, or Royal Rights, (*as the Civilians say*) *fix in number*, viz. *The power of Judicature; Power of life and death; Power of war and peace; Goods that have no owners, as waysts estrays,* &c. *coining of money; and levying taxes.*

R U

A Rub, *and to* rub (*in several senses.*)

A Rubber, or *rubbing-cloth,*

To *play* rubbers, or *a double game at any sport.*

A Rubbing-brush.

A Rubbing-house, *for race-horses.*

Rubbish, *or* rubble *of old houses,* &c.

A Rubrick, *a* Canon, *rule* or *sentence printed in red letters.*

A Ruby, *a precious stone of a red colour.*

A Rudder *of a ship.*

The Rudder-bands.

Ruddle, *a sort of red chalk.*

A Ruddock, *a bird.*

A Ruddock, or *land-toad.*

Ruddy, or *reddish.*

Rude, *uncivil, unhandsom, unskilful.* &c.

Rudeness.

A Rudiment, *principle,* or *first ground of an Art.*

Rue, *an herb.*

Goats-rue.

To rue, *to have cause to repent*, or *to suffer great dammage,*

Rueful, *sad*, or *pitiful*

A Ruff, *to wear about the neck.*

A Ruff, *a bird, and fish so call'd.*

A Ruff, at *cards.*

A Ruffian, *assassin, bravo*, or *desperate villain.*

Ruffingly, *boisterous*, or *ill-bred.*

A Ruffle, *fold*, or *wrinkle.*

A *pair of* ruffles, or *ruffled cuffs.*

To ruffle, *frizzle*, or *wrinkle; to disorder, anger, make one chafe,* &c.

Ruffling-robin *an herb.*

A Rug *for a bed.*

Rugged, *rough*, or *uneven.*

Ruggedness.

Ruin, or *destruction.*

To ruin, *destroy, undo, lay waste*, or *spoil.*

Ruinous, *ready to fall to* ruin.

A Rule, *and to* rule (*in all senses.*)

A Ruler, or *governour.*

A Ruler, *to rule paper,* or *parchment.*

Rum, *a drink us'd in* Barbadoes, *much stronger than Brandy.*

Rum-punch.

A Rumb, *or* Rhomb, *a point of the mariners compass.*

To rumble, or *make a noise.*

To ruminate, *to chew the cud;* or *to think upon a thing.*

To rummage, or *remove lumber out of one place into another; properly to clear the ship's hold that goods may be conveniently stowed.*

A Rumer, *a kind of drinking-glass.*

A Rumour, or *report.*

The Rump *of a fowl.*

A Rumple, or *fold made by tumbling* or *touzing.*

To rumple *a garment.*

Ru-

Run, *and to* run(*in all senses.*)
A Runagate, *a vagabond* or *rambling fellow.*
A Runaway, *one that has run from his master, colours*, &c.
A Rundlet, *a little barrel of wine, oil*, &c. *containing* 18 *gallons and a half.*
Rung, (*from to* ring.)
A Runner, *in a race.*
The Runner,or *upper stone of a mill.*
A Runt, *a* Scotch, *or* Welsh *neat.*
An old Runt, or *old trot*; *a decrepit old woman.*
A Rupture, *a breaking of friendship*, or *of the peace.*
A Rupture, or *burstenness.*
Rupture-wort, *an herb.*
Rural, *of* or *belonging to the Country.*
A Rural Dean, *an Officer under the Arch-deacon.*
A Rush, or *bulrush.*
The Sea-rush.
The sweet rush.
To rush *in*, or *enter by force.*
A Russet-colour.
The Rust *of iron*, &c.
To rust, or *grow rusty.*
Rustical,*or* rustick,*clownish, unmannerly*, &c
Rusticity, or *clownishness.*
Rustiness, *a being rusty.*
To rustle, or *make a noise.*
Rusty, or *full of rust.*
The Rut, or *tract of a wheel.*
The Rut, or *copulation of deer, wild boars*, &c.
To rut, or *go to* rut.
The rutting-time.

R Y

Rye, *a kind of corn.*
Rye-bread.

S A

A Sabbatarian, *an observer of the seventh day* sabbath.
The Sabbath, or *sabbath-day.*
Sable, or *black* (*in* Heraldry.)
A Sable, *a kind of black martern, that yields a rich furr.*
A Sable-muff.
A Sable, or *scimetar, a kind of broad sword.*
Sacerdotal, or *priestly.*
A Sack, or *bag.*
To sack *up*, or *put up in* sacks.
Sack-cloth.
A Sack of wooll, *containing* 26 *stone* 14 *pound to the stone*: *In* Scotland 24 *stone, and each stone* 16 *pound.*
Sack, or *canary-wine.*
To sack, *pillage*, or *lay waste.*
A Sack-but,*a kind of musical instrument.*
A Sacrament, (*in* Divinity) *a visible sign of an invisible grace.*
The Sacrament of the Lord's Supper.
Sacramental, *of* or *belonging to a* Sacrament.
Sacred, *holy*, or *inviolable.*
Sacredness.
A Sacrifice, or *sacred offering.*
To sacrifice; or *offer sacrifice.*
A Sacrificer.
Sacrilege, *the stealing of things out of a holy place*, or *Church-robbing.*
Sacrilegious, *belonging thereto.*
Sad, *sorrowful, mean*, or *pitifull.*

A Saddle, *for a horse.*
To saddle,or *set on a saddle.*
Saddle-back'd, *that has a very broad back.*
A Saddle-bow.
A Saddle-cloth.
A Pack-saddle.
A Saddler, or *saddle-maker.*
The Sadduces, *an heretical Sect among the ancient* Jews, *who deny'd the resurrection*, as also *the being of angels and spirits*: *They took their name from* Sadoc *their first founder*, or *from the* Hebrew *word* Sadoc, *i. e.* justice, *by reason of their pretensions exactly to follow the rules of justice and equity.*
Sadducism, *the principles and doctrine of the* Sadduces.
Sadness, or *sorrowfulness.*
Safe, *sound*, *secure*, or *out of danger.*
A Safe, *a kind of cupboard to keep victuals in.*
A Safe-conduct, or *passport, a protection granted for a stranger's coming in and going out of a Country.*
Safegard, or *protection.*
A Woman's Safegard, or *dust-gown.*
Safety, *soundness*, or *security.*
Saffron, *a plant.*
Bastard-saffron.
Meadow-saffron.
To sag, or *hang on one side.*
Sagacious, *subtil, shrewd, apprehensive*, &c.
Sagacity.
Sage, or *wise.*
Sage, *an herb.*
Sage *of* Jerusalem.
Wood-sage.
Sage-rose, or *holly-rose.*
Sageness, *gravity*, or *prudence.*

The Sages, or *wise men of* Greece.
Said, (*from to say*)
To saignor a moat, *to empty the water by conveyances under ground, that it may be more easily pass'd after having cast hurdles upon the mudthat remains.*
A Sail *for a ship* or *boat.*
To sail, or *set sail.*
The main Sail.
The mizzen-Sail.
The sprit-sail.
The Top-sail.
The Trinket-sail.
The Sail-yard.
A Sailer.
The Sailer-fish.
Sainfoin, *a kind of grass.*
A Saint, or *sanctified person.*
Saint Anthony's fire, *a painful swelling with great heat and redness.*
To saint, or *make a saint.*
All-saints day Novemb. 1.
Sake, as *for thy sake.*
A Names-sake, *one of the same name.*
A Saker-gun.
A Saker-hawk.
A Salamander, *a spotted creature like a lizard, that will for a while endure the flames of fire.*
A Salary, or *allowance of wages.*
The Sale, or *selling of goods.*
Saleable, or *fit for sale.*
Saligot, *an herb.*
To salivate, or *flux.*
A Salivation.
A Sallet *of herbs.*
Sallet-oil.
A Sallow-tree, or *goats-willow.*
A Sally, or *rushing out of forces in a besieged place, to attack the besiegers and ruin their works.*
To sally, or *sally forth.*
A Sally-port, *a door thro' which a sally is made.*
Sally, *and to* sally a bell; *a particular way of ringing it.*
A Salmon, *a fish.*
A Salmon-peel, or *young salmon.*
A Salmon-pipe, *an engine to catch* salmon.
A Salmon-trout.
Salt, *and to* salt, or *season with salt.*
Bay-salt.
Rock-salt.
A Salt, or *salt-seller.*
A Silver-salt.
A Salt-box.
A Salt-house, *a place where* Salt *is made.*
A Salt-man, *one that cryes salt about the streets.*
A Salt-marsh.
A Salt-pit.
A Salt-seller, *to hold* salt.
A Salt-spring.
A Salter or *dealer in salt.*
A Salter, *or* Sautoir (*in* Heraldry) *S.* Andrew's *cross.*
Salt-peter, *a mineral.*
A Salt-peter house *where it is prepar'd.*
Salvation, (*i.e.* saving, *in* Divinity) *a being rescu'd from damnation and attaining to everlasting happiness.*
A Salve *for sores,* &c.
Eye-salve.
Lip-salve.
Salvage-money, *a recompence allow'd by the civil Law to a ship that has*
Salved, *sav'd* or *rescu'd another from enemies* or *pirates.*
A Salver, *a piece of plate with a foot, to hold a glass* or *cup of wine,* &c. *so as to save the carpet,* or *cloths from drops.*
A Salvo, *caution,* or *reserve,* as *he came off with a* salvo.
A Salutation, or *greeting.*
To Salute, or *shew one respect by some mark of civility.*
A Saluter.
A Samarr, *a sort of gown for a woman.*
Same, the very same; *alike* or *all one.*
Sameness.
Samphire, *a sea-plant.*
Golden-flower'd samphire.
A Samplar, *pattern,* or *model.*
A Sample *of any Commodity, a little given as a pattern to shew the quality of it.*
Sanctification.
A Sanctifier.
To sanctify, or *make holy.*
Sanctimony, or *devoutness.*
A Sanction, or *decree.*
Sanctity, or *holiness.*
The Sanctuary, *the most holy place of the* Jewish *Tabernacle.*
A Sanctuary, or *place of refuge.*
Sand, or *gravel.*
A Sand-bag, *for a graver to turn his plate on.*
A Sand-bank, or *shelf in the Sea.*
Sand-blind, or *purblind.*
A Sand-box, or *dust-box.*
A Sand-pit.
A Sandal, *a kind of shoe, open on top, and fasten'd with latchets.*
Sandarack, or *red arsenick, a mineral us'd by painters.*
Sanders, *an* Indian *wood of three sorts;* viz. *red, white and yellow, and of great use in Physick.*
Sandever, *the dross of glass.*
A Sandling, *a sea-fish like a plaice.*
Sandy, *full of* sand, or *like* sand.
A Sangiack, *a* Turkish *Governour next in dignity to a* Beglerbeg.

San-

Sanguinary, *bloody, bloud-thirsty*, or *cruel*.
A Sanguine, or *ruddy complexion*.
Sanicle, or *self-heal*, *an herb*.
Bears-ear sanicle.
Spotted sanicle.
Yorkshire sanicle.
The Sap *of a tree*.
To sap, or *undermine a wall*.
Sapless, *that has no* sap.
A Sapphire, *a precious stone, of a deep sky-colour*.
Sappy, or *full of sap*.
A Saraband, *a kind of dance*.
A Sarcasm, *a bitter biting taunt when one is jeer'd as it were out of his skin*.
Sarcastical, *belonging thereto*.
The Sarcel, or *pinion of a hawk's wing*.
Sarcling-time, *the season when the husbandman weeds his corn*.
A Sardin, or *pilchard a sea-fish*.
A Sardonyx, *a precious stone, partly of the colour of a man's nail, and partly of a cornelian colour*.
A Sarplar, or *pocket of wooll; half a sack containing* 13 *stone*.
A Sarplier, or *packing-cloth*.
A Sarce or searce, *a kind of hair-sieve*.
Sarsenet, *a slight sort of silk*.
A Sash, or *silk-girdle*.
A Sash-window, *a corruption of the* French *word* chassis.
Sassafras, *an* Indian *tree, the rind of which has a sweet smell like cinnamon*.
A Sasse, *sluce*, or *lock of a river, with floud-gates, to shut up and let out water*.
I sat, or *did sit*.
Satan, (*in* Hebrew) *the adversary of mankind or the Devil*.
Satanical, or *devilish*.
A Satchel, *a little sack* or *bag*.
To satiate, *satisfy, cloy*, or *glut*.
Satiety, *fulness*, or *glutting*.
Satisfaction.
Satisfactory, *that is sufficient*
To satisfy, *content, make good, pay*, or *discharge a debt*, &c.
Sattin, *a sort of silk*.
Sattin-flower.
Saturday, *the last day of the week, on which the God* Saturn *was anciently worshipped*.
Saturn, *the most ancient of the heathen Gods, the father of* Jupiter *and* Juno; also *the uppermost of the seven stars call'd Planets*.
A Saturnine, or *melancholy complexion*.
A Satyr, *or* Satire, *a kind of Poetry sharply inveighing against vice and vicious persons*.
Satyrical, *belonging to a satyr*.
Satyrion, or *rag-wort, an herb*.
Satyrs, *certain paltry Demi-gods said to dwell in woods and desarts, and represented like men upwards, with horned heads whisking tails and goats feet; the emblems of insolence and lasciviousness*.
Savage, or *wild*.
Savageness.
The Savage, or *wild people in the* Indies.
Sauce, *for meat*.
Sauce-alone, *an herb*.
A Sauce-box, or *insolent fellow*.
A Sauce-pan.
Sauced, or *season'd with* sauce.
A Saucer *for vinegar*, &c.
Sauciness, or *arrogance*.
Saucy, *insolent*, or *malapert*.
A Saucidge, *or* sausage.
Save, save that, save only, *&c*.
To save, *deliver, preserve, keep, spare*, &c.
A Save-all, *for a candle*.
Savin, *a sort of shrub*.
Savingness, *frugality*, or *sparingness*.
A Saviour, *one that saves rescues* or *redeems*, as Our Lord and Saviour Jesus Christ.
To saunter *about*, *to go idling up and down*.
A Savonet, *a kind of wash-ball*.
A Savour, *taste*, or *smell*.
To savour or *relish*.
Savoury, *that tastes* or *relishes well*.
Savoury, *or* winter-savoury, *a pot-herb*.
Savoys, *a sort of cabbage, first brought from the Dutchy of* Savoy.
A Sausage, *a kind of pudding made of pork, veal*, &c.
Bolonia-sausages, *thick and short made at* Bolonia *a City in* Italy.
A Sausage, *or* warlike sausage, *a long piece of cloth, sow'd up like a gut; dipt in pitch; and fill'd with gun-powder; to set fire to mines, fougades, bomb-chests*, &c.
A Saw, *a tool*
To saw *timber with*.
A Hand-saw.
A Whip-saw.
Saw-dust.
The Saw-fish.
Saw-wort, *an herb*.
A Sawyer.
I saw, or *did see*.

Saxa-

Saxifrage, (*i. e.* stone-break) *an herb that breaks the stone in the body.*
Red Saxifrage.
The Saxons, *a warlike people, who having got footing in great* Britain *about A. C.* 450. *subdu'd most part of the Island and divided it into seven petty Kingdoms, which were united under K.* Egbert *in* 819. *and call'd* England, *i. e.* the land of the Angles. *These* Saxons *with the* Angles *and* Jutes *their neighbours came hither from* Jutland *a Province of* Denmark, *and are said to have taken name from their crooked swords termed* Seaxes, *in their language.*
Say, *a thin sort of silk stuff.*
To say, or *speak.*
An Hear-say, or *uncertain report.*

S C

A Scab, *gall,* or *fret.*
The Scabbard, or *sheath of a sword.*
A Scabbard-maker.
Scabbed, or scabby, *full of scabs.*
Scabious, *an herb.*
A Scaffold, *for building,* &c.
A Scalado, *the* scaling or *mounting of a Town-wall with ladders.*
To scald *with boiling water.*
Scalding-hot.
A Scale; *and to* scale (*in several senses.*)
The Scale of Musick, *in which the figure, order and names of the musical notes are set down.*
A pair of Scales *to weigh with.*
A Scall, or *scurf on the head.*
A scalled head.

Scall'd-pated.
A Scallion, *a kind of shalot.*
A Scallop, *a shell-fish.*
The Scalp, or hairy scalp *the skin that covers the scull.*
A Scalping-iron, *a Surgeon's instrument, to scrape off corrupt flesh from the bones.*
Scaly, or *full of scales.*
To scamble away, or *squander.*
To scamble, or *rove up and down.*
A scambling Town, *the houses of which stand at a great distance one from another.*
Scammony, *an herb.*
To scan, *canvas,* or *narrowly examine a business.*
A Scandal, *offence,* or *stumbling-block.*
To scandalize, *offend, slander,* or *give occasion of* scandal.
Scandalous, *that gives offence.*
Scandalum magnatum, *a Writ to recover dammage for wrong done to a Peer,* or *any great officer of the realm by scandalous reports,* &c.
Scant, *less than is requisite* or *scarce.*
Scantiness.
A Scantling, *model,* or *measure.*
Scanty, or *too straight.*
A Scape, *and*
To scape, or *escape.*
A Scar, or *seam of a wound.*
To scar, or *turn to a* scar.
Scaramouch, *the name of a famous* Italian *buffoon who acted in* London *An.* 1673.
Scarce, *or* scarcely.
Scarce, *rare, dear,* or *hard to come by.*

Scarceness, *or* scarcity.

A Scare, *a fish.*
To scare, or *fright.*
A Scare-crow, *a figure made of straw* or *clout, and set up in the field to scare away the birds.*
A Scarf, *worn by women, military Officers,* &c.
The Scarf-skin, or *outmost skin, which serves to defend the body, and being full of pores, evacuates sweat,* &c.
Scarfed, as *hooded and scarfed.*
A Scarification.
To scarify, *lance,* or *make incisions in the flesh.*
The Scarlet-colour.
Scarlet, or *scarlet-cloth.*
Scarlet-beans, *a plant.*
The Scarlet-oak, *a tree.*
A Scarlet-robe.
A Scarp, (*in* Fortification) *the sloping of a wall.*
A Scatch, *a kind of horse-bit.*
Scatches, or *stilts.*
A Scate, *a sea-fish.*
To scate, or *slide with* scates, *a kind of pattens to go upon the ice.*
To scatter, *disperse,* or *spread abroad.*
A Scavenger, *a parish-Officer, that takes care of cleansing the streets.*
The Scenes, in a Play-house; *the pictures representing landskips, buildings,* &c, *round about the stage.*
Scenography, *the draught of a building, with its front, sides, dimensions,* &c. *according to the rules of Perspective.*
A Scent, or *smell.*
To scent, *as a dog does.*
Sweet-scented, or *perfumed.*
A Scepter, *a King's commanding staff; one of the badges of the royal dignity.*

A

A Scepter-bearer.
Scepticism, *the doctrine, or opinion of*
The Scepticks, *a Sect of Philosophers that doubted of every thing, and would not admit of any determination.*
A Scedule, *a scroll of paper,* or *parchment.*
A Scheme, *draught,* or *figure.*
Schism, *a rent* or *division in the Church.*
Schismatical, *belonging thereto.*
A Schismatick, or *separatist.*
A Scholar, *a learner that goes to* School; or *a learned man.*
Scholastick, *of* or *belonging to a Scholar,* or *School.*
Scholastick Divinity, *relating to controverted points, such as are usually disputed in Schools.*
A Scholiast, *the writer of*
A Scholion, *a gloss, brief exposition,* or *short comment.*
A School, *a place where any Art* or *Science is taught.*
To school, *tutor,* or *chide one sharply.*
A Boarding-school.
A Dancing-school.
A Fencing-school.
A Grammar-school.
A Writing-school.
A School-boy.
A School-fellow.
A School-man, or *School-divine.*
A School-master.
A School-mistress.
Sciagraphy, *the first rude draught of a building,* &c.
The Sciatica, or *hip-gout.*
A Science, *knowledge,* or *skill.*
The seven liberal Sciences, *viz.* Grammar, Logick, Rhetorick, Arithmetick, Geometry, Astronomy, *and* Musick.
A Sciolist, *a smatterer in any kind of knowledge.*
A Scion, *a young sprig,* or *graft.*
A pair of Scissors.
A Scoff, *and*
To scoff, *mock,* or *flout.*
A Scoffer.
A Scold, or *scolding Woman.*
To scold, *brawl,* or *wrangle.*
A Scollop, *a sea-fish;* also *a kind of indenting in embroidery.*
Scolopendra, *a venomous worm, having eight feet and a piked tail.*
A Sconce, *fort,* or *block-house.*
A Sconce, or *candlestick.*
To Sconce, or *fine one.*
A Scoop, *for corn.*
A Scoop, *a kind of shovel to throw up water.*
To scoop *away,* or *throw away with a* scoop.
A Scope, *design,* or *aim.*
Scorbutick, *troubled with,* or *subject to the Scurvey.*
To scorch, or *parch.*
Scordion, or *water-germander, an herb.*
A Score, *an account,* or *reckoning.*
A Score, *for twenty,* as *threescore, fourscore,* &c.
To score, *or* score *up.*
Scorn, *contempt,* or *disdain.*
To scorn, or *despise.*
A Scorner.
Scornful.
Scornfulness.
A Scorpion, *a venomous insect, of a blackish colour, that has seven feet and stings with the tail.*
The Scorpion-fish.
A Scorpion-stone.
Scorpion-wort, or *scorpion-grass.*
A Scot, shot, or *club.*
To pay scot *and* lot, *i. e. all sorts of duties that belong to the subject.*
Scot-free, *exempted from paying his* scot, or *free from punishment.*
A Scovel, or *maulkin, to clean an oven.*
To scoul, *powt,* or *frown.*
A Scoundrel, or *pitiful sorry fellow.*
To scour, *cleanse,* or *purge;* also *to scamper,* or *run away.*
To scour *the Seas,* or *clear them from Pirates.*
A Scourer.
A Scouring, or *great looseness.*
A Scourge, or *whip made of thongs,* &c.
To scourge, *whip, punish,* or *chastise.*
A Scourger.
A Scout, or *spye, sent to bring tidings of the enemies forces.*
To scout, *or* scout *about.*
Scout-watches.
A Scrag, *or* lean scrag; *a body that has nothing but skin and bones.*
The scrag-end *of a neck of mutton.*
Scraggy, or *very lean.*
To scrall, *or* scrawl.
A Scramble, *and*
To scramble, or *strive to snatch.*
To scramble, or *climb up.*
A Scrambler.
To scranch, or *bite a thing that is hard.*
A Scrap, *bit,* or *fragment.*
To scrape, *grate, shave, gather up,* &c.
A Scraper.
A Scrach, *and*
To scrach, *claw,* or *scrape.*
A Scratcher.
The Scratches, *a horse-disease.*
To scrawl, *scribble,* or *write*

write a very bad hand.
A Scrawler.
A Scray, *a sort of sea-swallow.*
To screak, *or* creek, as *a door does.*
To scream, scream *out*, or *cry out.*
To screech, *howl*, or *hoot.*
A Screech-owl.
To screek, or *shreek out.*
A Screen *to keep off the heat of the fire*, &c.
A Screen-fan.
To screen, *defend*, or *protect.*
The Screw *of a vice, press*, &c.
A Screw-tap.
To screw *the barrel of a gun*, &c.
To screw into, or *insinuate himself into one's favour.*
Scribble, *and*
To scribble, *write pitifully*, or *dash with the pen.*
A Scribbler, *a sorry writer*, or *a very bad Author.*
A good Scribe, or *able pen-man.*
The Scribes, *a powerful Sect among the ancient* Jews, *who expounded the Law to the People; upon which account they were call'd Doctors of the Law, and Lawyers, in* St. Luke.
A Scrip, *bag*, or *pouch.*
Scriptural, *of*, or *belonging to*
The Holy Scripture, or *Sacred Writings of the Old and New Testament.*
Scripturists, *those that ground their* Faith *upon* Scripture *only.*
A Scritory, *a cabinet, with a Table to write upon.*
A Scrivener, *that engrosses, Writings, as Bonds, Bills, Indentures*, &c.
A Money-Scrivener.
A Scroll *of Parchment.*
A Scrub, or *old broom.*
A Scrub, *or* grub, *a pitiful mean fellow.*
To scrub, or *rub hard.*
Scruff, *a kind of fewel gather'd by poor people.*
A Scruple *of weight, the third part of a dram.*
A Scruple, or *doubt.*
To scruple, or *make a scruple.*
Scrupulous, or *full of Scruples.*
Scrupulousness.
To scruse, *thrust hard*, or *press.*
A Scrutiny, *a strict search* or *enquiry.*
A Scry, or *great flock of fowls.*
A Scud, or *sudden shower of rain.*
To scud *away*, or *start away of a sudden.*
A Scuffle, *fray*, or *tumult.*
To scuffle, or *contend with one.*
A Sculk, or *company of* Foxes.
To sculk, or *lye hid.*
The Scull, or *scull-bone of the head.*
A Scull-cap.
A Scull, *a sort of oar.*
A Sculler, *a boat row'd with little* Sculls.
The Scullery, *a place to wash and scour in.*
A Scullion, or *drudge, that does the meanest services in a kitchen.*
A Scullion-wench.
Sculpture, *the art of graving* or *carving*; also *a* print, or *engraved picture.*
Scum, *froth*, or *dross.*
To scum or *skim a pot*, &c.
The Scuppers, *or* scupper-holes *in a ship, through which the water runs off from the deck.*
A Scurf, or *scab.*
Scurfy, or *full of scurf.*
Scurrility, *buffoonry*, or *saucy scoffing.*
Scurrilous, *railing*, or *saucily abusive.*
Scurviness, *a being*
Scurvy, *untoward, ill-natur'd*, or *paltry.*
The Scurvy, *a disease.*
Scurvy-grass, *an herb.*
The Scut, or *tail of a rabbet.*
A Scutcheon, *or* Escutcheon *on which a coat of arms is blazon'd.*
The Scutcheon *of a lock.*
A Scuttle, or *dust-basket.*
The Scuttle *of a mast.*
The Scuttles, or *hatches in a ship.*

S E

The Sea, *that general collection of waters which encompasses the Earth, and has different names, according to the different Countries it washes*, as
The British *Sea.*
The Irish *Sea.*
The Mediterranean or *inland Sea, that runs between the Continents of* Europe, Africa, *and part of* Asia, &c.
Sea-bind-weed, *an herb.*
A Sea-calf.
A Sea-captain.
A Sea-chart, sea-card, or *sea-map.*
Sea-coal, or *pit-coal.*
The Sea-coast, or *sea-side.*
A Sea-devil, *a kind of monstrous fish.*
A Sea-drag, *whatever hinders a ship's course when under sail*; or *any thing hung up over the ship, as shirts, gowns*, &c.
A Sea-duck, *a bird.*
Sea-faring, *that uses the sea.*

A Sea-fight.
Sea-foal-foot, } *herbs.*
Sea-grass,
Sea-gates, (*among Mariners*) *the waves* or *billows of the Sea.*
A Sea-hog, or *porpoise.*
A Sea-lamprey, *a fish.*
Sea-leak, } *herbs.*
Sea-lettice,
Sea-longs, *the froth of the Sea.*
A Sea-mew, *a bird.*
Sea-navel-wort, } *herbs.*
A Sea-onion,
A Sea-port *Town.*
Sea-sick.
Sea-ward, *in the main Sea.*
A Seal, or *signet.*
To seal, or *set a seal to a writing.*
A Sealer.
A Seal-ring.
A Seal, or *sea-calf.*
Seam, *the tried fat of a hog*
A Seam, or *stitch.*
A Seaman, or *Mariner.*
Seamed, *that has seams.*
The Seams *in a horse, when the hoofs grow soft and rugged.*
Seam-rent, or *ript.*
A Seamster, *a man that sows* or *sells linnen.*
A Seamstress.
A Sean, *a sort of fish-net.*
To sear *with a hot iron.*
A Searing-iron.
Sear-leaves, or *withered leaves.*
A Searce, or *fine sieve.*
To search, or *sift through such a sieve.*
A Search, or *enquiry.*
To search, search *into*, search *out*, &c.
A Searcher.
A Season, or *proper time.*
To season *meat, to powder, corn*, or *pickle it.*
Seasonable, *opportune*, or *convenient.*
Seasonableness.
A Seasoner of *meat.*
The Seasonings, *a distemper incident to Strangers in the* West-Indies.
A Seat, *to sit on*; or *a mansion-house.*
To Seat, or *place in a* seat.
A Judgment-seat.
The Mercy-seat.
A Secession, or *going aside*; as *the secession of a Parliament.*
To seclude, or *shut out from any share in the Government.*
The Second *in number.*
A Second *in a duel.*
A Second, *the sixtieth part of a minute.*
To second, or *back one.*
A Second-hand suit.
The Secondary *causes* (*a Philosophical Term.*)
A Secondary, *an Officer, who is* second, *or next to the chief Officer.*
The Secondary of the Counters, *the next Officer to the Sheriffs of* London.
Secresy, or *privacy.*
Secret, or *kept close.*
A Secret, *a thing to be conceal'd*, or *a mystery.*
A Secretary, *one that is employ'd in writing Letters, Dispatches*, &c, *relating to publick* or *private affairs.*
The Principal Secretary of State.
The King's Secretaries, *Officers that sign the dispatches of the Seal.*
The Secretaries, or *Clerks of the King's Chamber and Closet.*
Secretaryship, *the office and station of a* Secretary.
Secretness, *or* secresy.
A Sect, *faction*, or *party.*
A Sectary, *one that adheres to any sect.*
Secular, or *temporal, belonging to the Age* or *World*; as *the Secular Power.*
A Secular Priest, *in opposition to a* regular; *one that takes upon him the cure of Souls, and does not live under any rules of religious orders.*
To secularize a Monk, *to make him a secular Priest.*
Secure, *safe*, or *careless.*
To secure, *save, put into a place of safety*, or *protect*; also *to clap in prison.*
Security, *safety, surety for the payment of money*, &c. also *carelesness, a being without any fear of danger.*
A Sedan, or *chair, in which persons of quality are usually carry'd.*
Sedate, *composed*, or *undisturbed.*
Sedateness.
Sedentary, *that sits much*, or *works siting.*
Sedge, *a kind of weed.*
Sediment, *the settlement* or *dregs of any thing.*
A Sedition, *mutiny*, or *popular tumult.*
Seditious, *given* or *tending thereto.*
To seduce, *mislead, abuse*, or *deceive.*
A Seducement, or *reduction.*
A Seducer.
Sedulity, *a being*
Sedulous, *diligent, carefull*, or *industrious.*
A Sée, or *Bishop's seat.*
To see, *look, behold, discern, perceive*, &c.
The Seed *of herbs*, or *living creatures.*
To seed, or *run to* seed.
Seed-pearl.
A Seed-plot.
Seed-time, or *sowing-time.*
A Seeds-man, *a sower*, or *seller of* seed.
Seedy, or *full of seed.*

To seek, *look for*, or *search*.
A Seeker.
To seel *a room, to make the* Sceling, *or* cieling.
A Seel, *or* seeling *of a ship, a violent rolling of it from one side to another*.
A Seem *of Glass*, i. e. 120 *pound weight. Of Corn, eight bushels.*
To seem, *appear*, or *pretend to be*.
Seemliness, *a being*
Seemly, *decent*, or *convenient*.
Seen (*from to* see.)
A Seer, *one that sees, a Prophet in the Old Testament*.
To seeth, or *boil*.
Seething-hot.
Seggrum, *an herb*.
A Seignior, (*in* Law) *a Lord of the Fee*, or *of a Mannor*.
The Grand Seignior, (*i. e.* Great Lord) *a title given to the* Turkish *Emperor*.
A Seigniory, *a lordship* or *the jurisdiction of a Lord*.
Seisin, *a* Law *term for possession*.
Seizable, *that may be seized*.
To seize, *to apprehend*, or *to take possession of*.
A Seizure *of goods*, &c.
Seldom, or *rarely*.
Seldomness.
Select, or *choice*.
To select, or *pick out*.
Self; as *my self, thy self*, &c.
Self-conceit, or *admiration of* one's self.
Self-conceited.
Self-conceitedness.
Self-denial.
Self-dependent.
Self-ended, or *selfish*.
Self-evident.
Self-heal, *an herb*.
Self-interest.
Self-love.
Self-murder.
The Self-same.
Self-will.
Self-willed.
Selfish, *that only minds his own interest*.
Selfishness.
A Sellander, *a dry scab on the bent of a Horse's, hinder ham*.
To sell, *utter*, or *put off Commodities*.
A Seller.
A Book-seller.
A Selvage, *the edge of linnen cloth*.
Selves, (*from self*) as *themselves*.
Semblance, or *appearance*.
A Sem-brief, *a musical note, containing two minims, four crotchets*, &c.
A Seme, *or* seem *of corn*.
A Semi-circle, *the half of an entire circle*.
Semi-circular, *belonging thereto*.
A Semi-colon, *a point of destinction, thus marked* (;)
A Seminary, *seed-plot*, or *nursery of plants*, &c. or *a college of young Students*.
A Seminary-Priest, *a Priest taken out of such a College*.
A Semi-quaver, *a note in Musick*.
A Semi-tone, or *half tone*.
The Senate, *properly the supreme Council among the ancient* Romans; or *the place where they assembled; a Parliament*, or *the bench of Aldermen in a City*.
The Senate-house.
A Senator, *a Member of the* Senate, *an Alderman*, &c.
The Senatorian *dignity*.
To send, or *dispatch a messenger*, &c.
The Ship sends much, (*a Sea-phrase*) *when she falls deep a-stern*, or *a-head into the hollow between two waves*.
Sena, *a physical plant*.
The Seneschal, or *Steward of a Court*.
Sengreen, or *house-leek, an herb*.
A Senior, or *elder*.
Seniority, or *eldership*.
A Sennight, *or* seven nights, *the space of a week*.
Sensation, (*in* Philosophy) *the power*, or *faculty of the senses*.
Sense, *feeling, meaning, judgment*, or *opinion*.
The Five Senses, as *Hearing, Seeing, Feeling, Tasting, and Smelling*.
Senselesness, *a being*
Senseless, *void of* sense or *understanding*.
Sensible, *that feels*, or *perceives; may be felt* or *perceiv'd*.
Sensibleness, or sensibility.
Sensitive, *that has the faculty of feeling*.
The Sensitive Plant, *that closes up when touch'd: 'Tis of a fine green colour, and bears yellow flowers*.
Sensual, *voluptuous*, or *carnal*,
Sensuality.
Sent, (*from to* send.)
A Sentence, *a certain number of words, a wise saying*; or *the decision of a Judge*.
To sentence, or *pass sentence upon, as a Judge does*.
Sententious, or *full of Sentences*.
A Sentiment, or *opinion*.
A Sentinel, *or* Sentry, *a stationary Soldier*, or *one that is upon guard*.

The

The Sentry, or *gard.*
Senvy, *a plant.*
Senvy-seed, or *Mustard-seed.*
Separable, *that may be separated.*
Separate, *distinct*, or *particular.*
To separate, *part, divide*, or *put asunder.*
Separateness.
A Separation.
A Separatist, or *Schismatick, one that separates himself from the Church.*
September, *the seventh month, reckoning from* March.
Septuagesima-sunday, *the third Sunday before Lent, so call'd, because it is about the 70th. day from* Easter.
The Septuagint, or *Greek Translation of the Bible, by the 72 Interpreters, or* Jewish *Elders, appointed for that prupose by* Ptolemey Philadelphus *King of* Egypt.
A Sepulchre, or *grave.*
A Sequence, or *following of things in order as*
A Sequenoe *of King, Queen and Knave (at Cards)*
To Sequester, *or* Sequestrate (*in the* Civil Law) *as a Widow does that disclaims to have any thing to do with her deceased Husband's Estate. In the* Common Law, *it signifies to separate a thing in dispute from the possession of the contending parties.*
A Sequestration.
A Sequestrator, *the third person to whose custody the thing in controversy is committed.*
The Seraglio, or *Palace of the Grand Seignior.*
Seraphical, *or* seraphick, *belonging to*
Seraphim (*i. e.* shining *or* flaming) *the highest order of Angels.*
A Seraskuier, *a Generalissimo*, or *Commander in chief of the* Turkish *Forces.*
A Serenade, or *night-musick, play'd by a lover to charm his mistress.*
To serenade one, or *play love-musick at her door*, or *under her window.*
Serene, *clear, fair, bright, without clouds*, or *rain*; also *cheerful, quiet, calm.*
Most Serene, *a Title given to Soveraign Princes.*
Sereneness, *or* serenity.
Serge, *a kind of woollen stuff*
A Serge-suit.
A Series, *order, course*, or *succession of things.*
Serious, *sober, grave*, or *earnest.*
Seriousness.
A Sermon, or *discourse made in a Pulpit, upon some text of Scripture.*
Sermountain, *an herb.*
A Serpent, or *creeping creature; as a Snake, Adder*, &c.
A Water-serpent.
Serpentary, or *viper-grass*, Serpents-tongue, } *herbs*
Serpentine, *of* or *belonging to a Serpent.*
To serve (*in all senses*)
A Servant.
An Houshold-servant.
A Maid-servant.
Service, *the state of one that* serves, also *attendance, a good turn*, &c.
A Service-tree.
Serviceable, *fit for Service*, or *useful.*
Serviceableness.
Servile, *slavish, mean*, or *base.*
Servileness, *or* servility.
A Servitor, or *serving-man; a poor University Scholar, that attends upon others.*
Servitude, or *slavery.*
Sesame, *a sort of* Indian *corn.*
Seseli, or *hart-wort an herb.*
To sess, *assess*, or *tax.*
Session, or *sitting; as a session of parliament.*
The Quarter, *or* general Sessions; *the assizes that are held four times a year in all the Counties of* England, *to determine civil and criminal Causes.*
The Sessions-house, or *place where the sessions are held.*
Set, *put, placed, fixed, appointed*, &c.
A Set, *and to* set (*in all senses.*)
Sharp-set, or *very hungry.*
Sun-set.
Well-set, *compact*, or *strong-joynted.*
A Set-off, or *ornament.*
Set-foil, or *tormentil an herb.*
Set-wort, or setter-wort *an herb.*
A Setter, or *Bailiff's setter.*
A Setter, or *setting-dog.*
A Bone-setter.
A Settle, or *settle-bed.*
To settle, *fix, establish, adjust, abide*, &c.
Settledness, or *firmness.*
A Settlement.
Setwall, *an herb.*
Seven, *in number.*
Seven-fold.
A Sevennight, *or* sennight.
Seventeen.
The Seventeenth.
The Seventh.
The Seventieth.
Seventy, or *three score and ten.*
To sever, or *part.*
Several, or *sundry.*
Severe, *rigorous, harsh, stern*, or *crabbed.*
Severity, or *rigour.*

To

To ſew, or *ſow with a needle.*

Sewel, (*a Term us'd by hunters*) *any thing hang'd up to keep a deer from entring a place.*

A Sewer, *an Officer that uſhers in the meat of a King* or *noble-man.*

The Sewer *of the kitchen,* or *of the hall.*

A Sewer, *drain,* or *common ſhore.*

The Commiſſioners of Sewers, *perſons authoriz'd by the great ſeal of* England *for the clearing and maintaining of ſewers.*

The Sewet, or *fat of meat as*

Beef-ſewet.

Mutton-ſewet.

Veal-ſewet.

A Sex, or *mark of diſtinction between male and female.*

Sexageſima-Sunday, *the next before Shrove-ſunday and about the* 60th *day before* Eaſter.

A Sexton, *an under officer in a Church.*

S H

A Shab, or *ſhabby fellow.*

Shabbineſs, *a being*

Shabby, *pitiful, baſe, mean,* or *worn out.*

A Shack-bolt, *ſhackle,* or *fetter.*

To ſhackle, or *put in ſhackles.*

A Hand-ſhackle.

The Shackles *in a ſhip, a kind of rings, that ſerve to ſhut up the ports.*

A Shad, *a ſea-fiſh.*

The Shade *of a tree,* &c.

To ſhade, or *cover with a ſhade.*

Night-ſhade, *an herb.*

Shadineſs.

A Shadow, or *ſhade.*

The Shadows *of a picture.*

To ſhadow, *to caſt a ſhadow,* or *to draw a ſhadow in painting.*

Shadow-graſs.

Shady, or *full of ſhades.*

A Shaft (*in ſeveral ſenſes.*)

Shag, *a ſort of hairy ſtuff*

Shag-breeches.

A Shag-haired *dog.*

A Shag, *a ſea-fowl.*

Shagged, or *rough with hair.*

A Shake, *and to* ſhake (*in ſeveral ſenſes.*)

Shaken.

Shall, *the ſign of the future Tenſe*; as *I* ſhall *live.*

A Shallop, *a light ſhip,* or *bark.*

Shallow water, *of little depth.*

A Shallow, or *ford in a river.*

The Shallows *of the ſea.*

Shallowneſs, *want of depth* or *of wit.*

A Shalm, *or* ſhawm, *a muſical inſtrument.*

Shaloon, *a ſort of woollen ſtuff.*

A Shalot; *a kind of onion.*

A Sham, or *flam.*

To ſham, *mock,* or *cheat one.*

A Sham-plot.

The Shambles, *a place where meat is ſold.*

A Shamade, *a beat of drum for a parley.*

Shame, *and*

To ſhame, *put to* ſhame or *diſgrace.*

Shame-faced, or *baſhfull.*

Shame-facedneſs.

Shamefull, *infamous,* or *diſgracefull.*

Shamefulneſs.

Shameleſneſs, *a being*

Shameleſs, *void of* ſhame or *impudent.*

A Shamoy, *a kind of wild goat.*

Shamoy-gloves, *made of the skin of that beaſt.*

The Shank, or *ſhin-bone.*

Small ſpindle-ſhanks.

The Shank *of a key, pillar, anchor,* &c.

The Shank, or *tunnel of a chimney.*

A Shanker, *a ſore* or *botch in the groin.*

A Shape, *form, figure,* or *proportion.*

A Point-ſhape.

To ſhape, or *give a ſhape to*

Shapeleſs, *that has no ſhape.*

Shapen.

A Shard, or *broken piece of a ſtone, tile,* &c.

A Pot-ſhard.

A Share, *part,* or *portion.*

To ſhare, ſhare *out,* or *divide into* ſhares.

A Plough-ſhare.

The Share-bone.

Share-wort, *an herb.*

A Sharer.

A Shark, *a greedy ſea-fiſh.*

A Shark, or *ſharking fellow.*

To ſhark *up and down, to live upon the catch.*

Sharp, *keen, rough, ſmart, ſower, harſh,* &c.

A Sharp *in muſick.*

To ſharp *upon one,* or *over-reach him.*

Sharp-ſet, or *very hungry.*

Sharp-ſighted.

Sharp-witted.

To ſharpen, *make* ſharp, or *whet.*

A Sharper, *a ſubtil fellow, that lives by his wits.*

To ſhatter, *ſhake,* or *break to pieces.*

A Shatter-pate, or *ſhatter-pated fellow.*

To ſhave, *ſhear,* or *cut off the hair with a raſor.*

Shave-graſs.

Shaven.

A Shaver.

The Shavings *of planed boards,*

boards, &c.
A Shaving-tub, *to hold book-binders paper-shavings.*
She, as *she is a woman.*
A She-cousin.
A She-friend.
A Sheaf, *a bundle of corn,* or *arrows.*
To sheaf *corn,* or *bind it up into sheaves.*
To shear, or *clip.*
Shear-grass.
A Shearer, or *sheep-shearer.*
A Shear-man, or *cloth-shearer.*
A pair of Shears; or *great sizzers.*
A Sheat, or *young pig.*
A Sheat-fish.
The Sheat-anchor, *an anchor of the largest size.*
The Sheat-cable, or *master-cable.*
A Sheath, *for a knife* or *sword.*
To sheath a sword *to put it up in the* sheath or *scabbard.*
To sheath a ship, i. e. *to case the parts under water with thin boards, having hair and furr laid between the casing and the old sides; to keep the worms from eating thro' the planks.*
A Sheath-maker.
Sheats, *or* sheat-ropes, *which are fasten'd to the clew of all sails.*
Sheaves, *(from* sheaf*)* as *to make up the* sheaves *of corn.*
A Shed, *hut,* or *shelter made of boards.*
Shed, *and to* shed or *spill,* as *to shed bloud,* or *tears.*
Bloud-shed.
To shed, or *cast the teeth, horns,* &c.
A Sheep, *and a flock of* sheep.
A Sheep-coat.
A Sheep-fold
A Sheep-hook.
Sheep-rot.
A Sheeps-head, *a meer blockhead,* or *stupid fellow.*
A Sheeps-pluck.
Sheepish, *shame-faced, soft-headed,* or *silly.*
Sheepishness.
Sheer, *quite, altogether;* as *this fancy is sheer new.*
To sheer, or *wave to and again, as a ship does, that is not steer'd steddily.*
Sheer-hooks, *irons fix'd in the yard-arms, to cut the enemies shrowds,* &c.
A Sheet, or *linnen-sheet.*
A Sheet *of paper,* or *lead.*
The Sheevers *that run round in the pullies and blocks of a ship.*
A Shekle, a Jewish *silver-coin worth about* 2 s 6 d; also *another of gold,* 15 s. *value.*
A Sheldrake, *a fowl.*
A Shelf, *for books,* &c.
A Hanging-shelf.
A Shelf, or *heap of sand in the sea.*
The Shelf, or *till of a printer's press.*
A Shell *of several sorts;* as
An Egg-shell.
A Nut-shell.
A Sword-shell.
A Tortois-shell.
Shell-fish.
Shell-work.
To shell, or *slip off the* shells *of pease, beans,* &c.
A Shelter, or *place to secure one from foul weather; a sanctuary* or *place of refuge.*
To shelter, *defend,* or *protect.*
Shelterless, *that has no shelter.*
Shelves, *from* shelf.
Shelving, *that leans on one side.*
A Shepherd, or *keeper of sheep.*
A Shepherdess.
Shepherds-bodkin }
Shepherds-needle. } *herbs.*
Shepherds-purse. }
Sherbet, *a pleasant drink made of lemmon.juice, sugar, amber,* &c. *in great vogue among the* Turks *and* Persians.
A Sheriff of a County, *from the* Saxon shire-reve, *i. e.* governour of the shire; *a chief magistrate in every County, nominated by the King: But there are two Sheriffs for* Middlesex, *chosen by the Citizens of* London, *under the name of* Sheriffs of London and *Middlesex.*
An Under-sheriff.
A Sheriffalty, *or* Sheriff-ship, *the Office of a sheriff* or *the time during which that Office is held.*
Sherry, *or* sherry-sack, *brought from* Xeres *a Town in* Spain.
A Shew, *and to* shew *(in all senses.)*
A Shewer, as *a shewer of tricks.*
Shewn, or *shewed.*
A Shield-bearer.
A Shield, or *buckler.*
A Shield *of brawn.*
To shield, or *defend.*
A Shift, *and to* shift *(in several senses.)*
A Shifter, as *a notable shifter,* or *cunning Sophister, that knows all shifts* or *evasions.*
A shifting-fellow, or *shark.*
A Shilling, *a known coin.*
A Shilling-worth.
The Shin, or *fore part of the leg.*
The Shin-bone.
Shine, or *shining.*
The Moon-shine.
The Sun-shine.

To

To ſhine, *to give light* or *to gliſter.*
Shineſs, or *reſerved neſs.*
A Shingle, *a lath,* or *wooden tile.*
A Shingler, or *ſhingle-maker.*
The Shingles, *a Diſeaſe; a kind of heat breaking out about the waſte, which kills the patient, if gets quite round.*
A Ship, or *ſea-veſſel.*
To ſhip, or *ſhip off goods to put 'em on ſhip-board.*
An Admiral-ſhip.
A Fire-ſhip.
A Flag-ſhip.
A Pirate-ſhip.
A Shore-ſhip, or *bilander.*
A Spial-ſhip.
A Tranſport-ſhip.
To go on Ship-board.
A Ship-boat.
A Ship-boy.
A Ship-carpenter, or *ſhip-wright.*
A Ship-ladder.
A Ship-man, or *mariner.*
A Ship-maſter.
Ship-timber.
Ship-wrack, *the wrack* or *ruin of a ſhip by a ſtorm.*
To ſhip-wrack, or *ſuffer ſhipwrack.*
A Shire, or *County*; as Oxford-ſhire.
Gloceſter-ſhire, *&c.*
A Shirt, or *ſhift.*
A Shirt of mail.
To ſhit, *ſhite*, or *cack.*
A Shit-a-bed.
A Shit-breech.
Shitten, or *beſhit.*
A ſhitten, or *pitiful ſorry fellow.*
A Shittle, or ſhuttle *us'd by weavers.*
A Shittle-brain'd, or ſhittle-headed ſellow, *one that is always unconſtant and wavering.*
A Shittle-cock, *to play with.*
A Shiver, or *piece of cleſt wood.*
To ſhiver, or *quake for cold* or *fear.*
To ſhiver, or *break in pieces.*
A Shock, or *ſix sheaves of corn.*
A Shock, *encounter*, or *fight.*
To ſhock, *oppoſe*, or *be contrary to.*
Shod, *having shoes on.*
A Shog, *and*
To ſhog, or *ſhake.*
A Shole, or *company of fiſh.*
Sholes, or *flats in the water.*
A Shoo, or *ſhoe, and*
To ſhoo, or *put on shoes.*
An Horſe-ſhoo.
A Shoo-clout.
A Shooing-horn.
A Shoo-maker.
A Shoomaker-row, or *ſhoomaker-ſtreet.*
Shoock, (*from to ſhake*)
A Shoot, or *young ſpring.* alſo *a shot with an arrow.*
A Shoot, or *great pig that has done ſucking.*
To ſhoot, (*in ſeveral ſenſes.*)
A Shooter.
A Printer's Shooting-ſtick.
A Shop, *to ſell wares in.*
A Shop-board.
A Shop-keeper.
A Shop-lift, or *thief that ſteals goods out of a ſhop.*
Shorage, *money paid for goods brought on* ſhore.
A Shore, or *bank of the ſea.*
A Shore-bird.
A Shore, *common shore* or *drain.*
A Shore, or *prop.*
To ſhore, or *prop up.*
A Shorling, *the fell of a* ſhorn *sheep.*
Shorn, (*from to* ſhear.)
Short, *brief, ſuccinct, of little continuance,* &c.
Short-hand.
A Short-ſhank, *or* ſhort-ſtart, *a ſort of apple.*
Short-ſighted.
Short-winded.
To ſhorten, *make* ſhort, *abbreviate*, or *diminish.*
Shortneſs.
Shot, (*from to* ſhoot.)
A Shot, or *barrow-pig.*
Shot, *to charge a gun with.*
Cannon-ſhot.
Musket-ſhot.
Shot-free, *that cannot be wounded*, or *hurt by* ſhot.
A Shot, Scot, or *reckoning.*
Shot-free, *or* ſcot-free, *that pays nothing.*
Shotten, as *a ſhotten herring, that has no roe.*
A Shove, *and*
To ſhove, or *thruſt.*
A Shove-net.
A Shovel, or *ſpade.*
To ſhovel, or *throw up with a* Shovel.
A Fire-ſhovel.
A Paring-ſhovel.
Shovel-board, *a ſort of game.*
A Shoveler, *a bird.*
It ſhould, or *ought.*
A Shoulder.
To ſhoulder, or *put on the ſhoulder.*
The ſhoulder-blade, or *ſhoulder-bone.*
A Shoulder-piece, or *armour for the ſhoulder.*
Shoulder'd, as
Big-ſhouldered.
Broad-ſhouldered.
High-ſhouldered.
A Shouldering-piece (*in* Architecture.)
A Shout, *loud cry*, or *out-cry.*
To ſhout, or *make a ſhout.*
A Shower *of rain.*

To

To ſhower, *or* ſhower *down.*
Show'ry, or *rainy weather.*
A Shred *of cloth*, *ſtuff*, &c.
To ſhred, or *cut ſmall.*
A Shrew, *or* ſhrew-mouſe, *a kind of field-mouſe, very miſchievous to cattel; for the going of it over a beaſt's back will lame it in the chine, and the bite of it, cauſes the beaſt to ſwell to the heart and die.*
A Shrew, *ſcold*, or *curſt woman.*
Shrewd, *ſubtil*, *ſmart*, or *ingenious.*
Shrewdneſs.
A Shriek, *and*
To ſhriek, or *cry out*, as *upon a ſudden fright.*
A ſhrill, or *ſharp voice.*
Shrilneſs.
A Shrimp, *a little ſea-fiſh.*
A River-ſhrimp.
A Shrine, *a kind of coffer* or *box*, *to keep relicks in.*
To ſhrink, as *the ſinews do.*
The ſhrinking-ſhrub.
Shrivalty, *for* ſheriffalty, *the time during which one holds the office of ſheriff.*
To ſhrivel, or *wrinkle.*
Shrove-tide, *or* Shrove-tueſday 7 *weeks before* Eaſter, *taking name from the old* Saxon *word to* ſhrive, i. e. *to* confeſs; *becauſe at that time confeſſion of ſins was uſually made, in order to a more religious obſervation of lent-ſeaſon immediately enſuing.*
A Shrowd, or *covering to wrap up a dead body.*
To ſhroud himſelf, or *get shelter.*
The Shrowds *of a ſhip, the ropes, that come from both ſides of the maſts.*
A Shrub, *a dwarf-tree*, or *a ſorry fellow.*
To ſhrub, or *cudgel one.*
Shrubby, or *full of ſhrubs.*
To ſhrug, or *ſhake the ſhoulders.*
Shrunk, (*from to* ſhrink.)
To ſhudder, or *ſhiver with cold.*
To ſhufle, *baffle*, or *prevaricate.*
To ſhuffle, or *mingle the cards.*
A Shuffler.
To ſhun, *avoid*, *wave*, or *decline.*
To ſhut, or *shut up.*
The Shutters *of a window.*
A Weaver's Shuttle.
Shy, *reſerved*, *wary*, or *nice.*
Shyneſs.

S I

A Sice, *ſice-point*, or *caſt of* ſix, *at dice.*
Sick, or *indiſpoſed.*
Heart-ſick.
To ſicken, or *fall ſick.*
Sickiſh, *a little indiſpos'd.*
A Sickle, or *reaping-hook.*
Sickineſs, *a being*
Sickly, or *apt to be ſick.*
Sickneſs.
The falling-ſickneſs.
The green-ſickneſs.
A Side (*in ſeveral ſenſes.*)
The Bed-ſide.
The Sea-ſide.
The Side-bars, *of a ſaddle.*
The Side-beams *of a Printer's preſs.*
A Side-blow.
A Side-board *table.*
Side-long, or *on one ſide.*
A Side-ſaddle.
A Sides-man, *a Pariſh Officer, that aſſiſts the Church-warden.*
The Sideſmen *of a fowl.*
Sideways, as *he went ſideways.*
A Side-wind.
To ſide, or *take part with one.*
Sidelays (*in* hunting) *when dogs are laid in the way, to be let ſlip at a deer, as he paſſes by.*
Sider, *or* cider, *a drink made of apples.*
A Siege, *laid to a Town.*
A Siege, or *purging ſtool.*
A Sieve, *to ſift corn*, &c.
A Bolting-ſieve, or *ranging-ſieve.*
A Sieve-maker.
To ſift, or *paſs thro' a ſieve*,
To ſift, or *pump one.*
A Sigh, or *groan.*
To ſigh, or *fetch ſighs.*
A Sight, *look*, *shew*, &c.
The Sight *of a gun* or *croſs-bow, a little mark at the end, to direct the ſight in taking aim.*
Sighted, as
Dim-ſighted.
Quick-ſighted.
Short-ſighted.
Sightleſs, *depriv'd of ſight* or *blind.*
Sightly, *fair to the ſight*, *ſpecious*, *handſom*, or *neat.*
A Sign, *and to* ſign (*in ſeveral ſenſes.*)
A Sign manual, or *the ſetting of hand and ſeal to a Writing.*
The Signs of the Zodiack, *certain conſtellations, that are ſuppos'd to reſemble living creatures, and are* 12 *in number*, viz. Aries, or *the ram*; Taurus, *the Bull*; Gemini *the twins*; Cancer *the crab-fiſh*; Leo *the lion*; Virgo *the Virgin*; Libra *the ballance*; Scorpio *the*

the Scorpion; Sagittarius, *the Archer*; Capricornus, *the horned goat*; Aquarius, *the water-bearer*; *and* Pisces *the two fishes*.

Signal, *notable*, or *remarkable*.

A Signal, or *token given in War*.

To signalize himself, or *make himself famous*, *by some signal action*.

A Signature, *the setting of one's hand to an instrument*, or *writing*: Also (*in* Printing) *the particular letter of the Alphabet, set at the bottom of every sheet, to keep them in order*.

A Signet, or *seal in a ring*.

The King's privy Signet, *that serves to seal his Majesty's letters; and is also us'd for grants*, &c. *which afterwards pass the great seal*.

Significancy, *a being*

Significant, *expressive*, or *emphatical*.

Signification, or *meaning*.

To signify, *to import*, *to give notice*, *to presage*, &c.

Silence, *a being silent*.

To silence, or *impose silence*.

Silent, *that says nothing*, *quiet* or *still*.

Silk, (*raw*, or *wrought*.)

Sowing-silk.

Stitching-silk.

A Silk-dier,

Silk-grass, *a plant*.

A Silk-man, or *seller of silk*.

A Silk-throwster, *that throws*, i. e. *winds*, *twists and spins silk*.

A Silk-weaver.

A Silk-worm.

Silken, or *of silk*.

A Sill, or *threshold*.

A Sillibub, *a sort of drink made of stale beer* or *wine sweeten'd with sugar*, *milk milked into it from the cow*, &c.

Silliness, *a being*

Silly, *sottish*, *foolish*, or *simple*.

Silver, *a metal*.

Quick-silver.

A Silver-hilted sword.

A Silver-mine.

Silver-lace.

The Silver-sickness, or Silver-squincey, *when a Pleader being bribed by the adverse party*, *feigns himself sick*, or *not able to speak*.

A Silver-smith, *one that makes silver-plate*.

Silver-tougued, or *eloquent*.

Silvered over, or *cover'd with silver*.

A Simile, *similitude*, or *comparison*.

A Simetar, or Cimeter, *a kind of broad Sword much us'd in* Turkey *and* Persia.

A Simnel, *a sort of cake* or *bun made of fine flower*.

Simonical, *done by Simony*.

A Simoniack, or simonist, *one guilty of*

Simony, *a trade of spiritual things, so call'd from* Simon Magus *a* Samaritan *Sorcerer, who offer'd money to the Apostles to be endu'd with the power of giving the* Holy *Ghost*.

To simper, *to smile*; or *to begin to boil*.

Simple, *single*, *plain*, *downright*, *sincere*; also *mean unskilful*, &c.

Simpleness, or *silliness*.

Simples, *physical herbs*, or *drugs*.

A Simpleton, or *silly person*.

Simplicity, *plain dealing*, or *downright honesty*; also *indiscretion* or *foolishness*.

Simpling; as *to go a simpling*, or *gathering of* Simples.

Sin, or *Transgression, the violating of Divine* or *Humane Laws*.

To Sin, or *commit sin*.

A Sin-offering.

Since; as *not long since*.

Sincere, *pure*, *without mixture*, *honest*, *cordial*, *ingenuous*, &c.

Sincerity, or *integrity*.

To Sindge, or *burn lightly*.

A Sinew, *or nerve is a fibrous*, *round*, *long*, *white*, *porous substance*, *which conveys the animal Spirits*, *to make the parts of the Body moveable and sensible*.

Sinful, *vicious*, *wicked*, *lewd*, *criminal*, &c.

Sinfulness.

To sing, or *make melody with the voice*.

A Singer.

A Singing-master.

Single, *simple*, *alone*, &c.

Single-hearted, *sincere*, or *honest*.

A Single-soled shoo.

A Single, or *tail of a deer*.

To single out, *pick out*, or *set a-part from the rest*.

Singleness of heart, or *sincerity*.

Singular, *particular*, *special*, or *extraordinary*.

Singularity.

Sinister, *unlucky*; *untoward*, *indirect*, *unjust*, *unlawful*, &c.

A Sink, or *drain to convey foul water*.

A Kitchen-sink.

A Sink-hole.

To sink, *to drive* or *settle to the bottom*; *to fail*, or *faint*, &c.

A Sinner, *one that commits sin*.

Sinoper, *ruddle*, or *red lead*.

lead.

A Sip, *and*

To sip, or *drink but a little at a time.*

A Sipper.

A Sippet, *a small slice of bread soak'd in broth, soop, sauce,* &c.

Sir, *a Title of honour, usually prefix'd to the Christian Names of Knights* ; as

Sir William Temple, *&c.*

A Sirname, *or* surname, *the name of one's Family.*

Sirrah! (*an injurious term) denoting a rascal* or *vain fellow.*

A Siskin, or *green finch.*

A Sister.

A Sister-in-law.

Twin-sisters.

Sisterhood, *the quality of a sister*; or *a society of spiritual sisters* or *nuns.*

To sit, *at table, at work*, &c.

A Site, *or* situation.

A Sithe *to mow with.*

A Sitter (*from to sit*)

Situate, situated, or *seated.*

A Situation, *the seat of a Town, Fort,* &c.

Six (*in number*)

Sixfold.

Sixteen.

The Sixteenth.

The Sixth.

The Sixtieth.

Sixty, or *threescore.*

A Size, *proportion*, or *measure.*

Size, *for whiting.*

To size a wall, *&c. to wash it first with* size, *in order to white it.*

To size, as *Taylers do seams.*

To size, *a term us'd in* Cambridge, *when a Scholar scores for his diet*; as *in* Oxford *he is said to battel in the buttery-book.*

A Sizer, *a* Cambridge-*scholar of the lowest rank the same with a* Servitor at Oxford.

Sizzers, *or* a pair of sizzers *to cut out cloth, stuff,* &c.

S K

A Skain, *or* skean *of thread.*

To skatch *a wheel, to stop or stay it with a piece of wood put underneath.*

Skatches, or *stilts.*

A Skegger-trout.

A Skeleton, *an artificial connexion of dryed bones, by the help of their ligaments, or else wires, in their natural order and position.*

A Skep, *a kind of vessel to put corn in.*

Skew, as *to look* skew, *or* a-skew; *to leer*, or *look shy.*

A Skewer.

To skewer *up meat*, or *fasten it with a* skewer.

A Skeyn, *a kind of* Irish *short sword.*

A Skiff, or *ship-boat.*

Skilful, or *expert.*

Skill, *knowledge, capacity*, or *experience.*

Skilled, *that has* skill, or *is well versed in.*

A Skillet, *a kitchen-vessel.*

To skim, or *scum.*

The Skin *of Men*, or *Beasts.*

The Fore-skin, *that covers the head of a man's yard.*

The Scarf-skin (*in* Anatomy) *the thin upper skin of a humane body.*

To skin, or *skin over*; as *the wound begins to skin.*

To skin, or *take off the skin.*

Skink, Scotch *potage made of knuckles and sinews of Beef long boiled.*

A Skink, *a kind of land-Crocodile.*

Skinned, as *thick-skinned.*

A Skinner, or *seller of skins.*

A Skip, *and*

To skip, or *jump.*

A Skip-jack, or *pitiful fellow, that scampers up and down.*

A Skipper, or *jumper.*

A Skipper, *the Master of a* Dutch *ship*; also *a common Sea-man.*

A Skirmish, *and*

To skirmish, or *fight confusedly in small parties.*

A Skirmisher.

A Skirret, *a sort of root.*

A Skirt, *the border of a Garment*, or *of a Country.*

Skittish, *wanton, frisking*, or *capricious.*

Skittishness.

A Skreen, *or* screen.

To skulk, *lye hid*, *or* lurk *here and there.*

A Skulker, *one that plays least in fight.*

A Skute, or *skiff.*

The Sky, or *Firmament.*

Sky-colour *a sort of blew.*

A Sky-light, or *window on the top of a building that receives light from the sky.*

S L

A Slab, or *puddle.*

A Slab, *the outmost board of a sawn piece of Timber.*

To slabber, *to dawb with foul water*, or *to drivel.*

Slabbiness.

Slabby.

Slack, *slow, careless*, or *negligent.*

To slack, or slacken, *to abate*, or *grow less vehement.*

Slackness, or *remisness.*

Slain (*from to slay*)

To

To slake, *temper*, or *allay*.
To slam, or *worst one at Cards.*
A Slander, *and*
To slander, *back-bite*, or *speak evil of.*
A Slanderer.
Slanderous.
Slank, or *thin.*
Slank, *a Sea-weed.*
Slant, *or* slanting, *lying side-long*, or *a-cross.*
A Slap or *blow.*
To slap, or *give one a* slap.
To slap up, or *lick up.*
A Slap-sauce, or *lick-dish.*
A Slash, *and*
To slash, *cut*, or *whip.*
A Slate, *a sort of stone.*
To slate, or *cover with slates.*
A Slater.
To slatter, *to mind nothing, to leave all at random.*
A Slattern, or *slattering woman.*
A Slave, or *bond-servant.*
To slave, or *toil and moil like a* slave.
Slaver, or *drivel.*
To slaver, slabber, or *drivel.*
Slavery, or *bondage.*
Slavish, *belonging to slavery.*
Slavishness.
Slaughter, *carnage, murder*, or *havock.*
To slaughter, or *massacre.*
Man-slaughter.
A Slaughter-house.
A Slaughter-man, or *butcher.*
A Slay, *an instrument of a weaver's loom, having teeth like a comb.*
To slay, or *kill.*
A Slayer.
A Man-slayer.
A Sleave, *a fish.*
Sleaved *silk*, i.e. *work'd fit for use.*

Sleazy, *slight*, or *ill-wrought*, as *some sorts of linnen-cloth are.*
A Sled, *or* sledge, *a kind of carriage, without wheels.*
A Smith's sledge, or *great hammer.*
Sleek, or *smooth.*
To sleek, or *make sleek.*
A Sleek-stone, *to smooth linnen, lace*, &c.
Sleep, *and to* sleep.
A Sleeper.
Sleepiness, or *drowsiness.*
Sleepless, *that has had no sleep.*
Sleepy, *inclined* or *apt to sleep.*
To sleer, or *look a-skew.*
Sleet, *rain and snow together, and*
To sleet, *or* fall as sleet does.
The Sleeve *of a garment.*
Sleeveless, *that has no sleeves.*
A Sleight, or *trick.*
Sleight of hand.
Slender, *small, thin*, or *mean.*
Slenderness.
I slept, or *did sleep.*
I slew, or *did slay.*
A Slice, *and to* slice (*in several senses.*)
A Printer's ink-slice.
Slick, *sleek*, or *smooth.*
Slid, (*from to* slide.)
A Slide, *a frozen place* slid *upon.*
To slide, *to glide along* or *to move a thing up and down.*
Slight, *thin wrought, trivial*, or *careless.*
A Slight, or *contempt.*
To slight, *to despise*, or *make no account of; to demolish*, &c.
A Slighter.
The Slightness *of a piece of work.*
Sliness, (*from* sly.)
Slim, or *slender.*
Slime, *mud*, or *a gross humour.*

Sliminess.
Slimy, or *full of slime.*
A Sling, *and*
To sling, or *throw stones with a sling.*
A Brewer's Sling.
A Slinger.
A Slink, *a cast calf.*
To slink, or *steal away.*
A Slip, *and to* slip (*in several senses.*)
Slip-shoos.
A Slipper, or *pantofle.*
Slipperiness, *a being*
Slippery, *apt to slip, that causes to slip, variable* or *uncertain.*
A Slit, *and to* slit.
A Sliver, or *slice.*
To sliver, or *cut into slivers.*
A Sloe, or *wild plum.*
A Sloe-worm.
To slope, or *lye slanting.*
Slopeness.
Slops, *wide breeches for seamen.*
A Slop-seller.
Slot, *the view*, or *print of a stagg's foot in the ground.*
Sloth, *laziness*, or *sluggishness.*
Slothful.
Slothfulness.
A Slouch, or *country-bumpkin.*
A Sloven, *a nasty ill-bred fellow.*
Slovenliness.
Slovenly, *that acts like a sloven.*
A Slough, *a deep and muddy place*, or *a damp in a coal-pit.*
The Slough, or *cast skin of a snake.*
A Slouth, or *herd of bears.*
Slow, *slack, dull, heavy, ling'ring*, &c.
Slowness.
To slubber *over a business*, or *do it carelesly.*
A Sluce *to let in*, or *keep out water.*

A

A Slug, *a kind of shot for a gun.*
A Slug-snail.
A Sluggard, or *slug-a-bed.*
Sluggish, *drowsy*, *lazy*, or *lumpish.*
Sluggishness.
A Slumber, *and*
To slumber, or *sleep lightly.*
Slung (*from to* fling.)
Slunk (*from to* slink.)
A Slur, *scurvy trick*, *blot*, or *disgrace.*
To slur, *soil*, or *dawb.*
A Slut, or *dirty wench.*
Sluttish, *like a slut*, *filthy*, *nasty*, &c.
Sluttishness.
Sly, *cunning*, or *subtil.*

S M

A Smack, *and to* smack (*in several senses.*)
A Smack-sail.
Small, or *little.*
The Small *of one's back.*
Smallage, *an herb.*
Smalness.
Smalt, or *blew enamel.*
Smart, *sharp*, *brisk*, *witty*, *ingenious*, &c.
Smartness.
Smart, or *pain.*
To smart, as *a sore does.*
A Smatch, or *relish.*
A Smatterer, *one that has some tincture*, or smatch *of learning.*
A Smattering, *tincture*, or *slight knowledge.*
To smear, *besmear*, or *dawb.*
A Smell, *and to* smell.
A Smeller.
A Smell-feast, *trencher-friend*, or *hanger on.*
A Smell-smock, or *effeminate fop, that spends most of his time among women.*
Smelt, (*from to* smell.)
A Smelt, *a fish.*
A River-smelt.

To smelt, or *melt metal in the oar.*
A Smelting-furnace.
To smicker, or *look wantonly.*
A Smile, *and*
To smile, or *simper.*
To smirk, *smile*, or *look pleasant.*
To smite, *strike*, or *hit.*
A Smiter.
A Smith, or *black smith.*
A Copper-smith.
A Gold-smith.
A Gun-smith.
A Lock-smith.
A Silver-smith.
A Smithy, or *smith's shop.*
A Smock, or *woman's shift.*
Smoke, *and to* smoke.
Smokiness.
Smoky, or *full of smoke.*
Smooth, *even*, *level*, or *polite.*
To smooth, or *make smooth.*
Smooth-tongued.
Smoothness.
To smother, *suffocate*, or *strangle.*
A Smotherer.
Smug, *neat*, or *spruce.*
To smug up, or *set himself off to the best advantage.*
To smuggle *goods*, *to bring them in by stealth*, *without paying custom.*
A Smuggler.
Smugness, (*from smug.*)
Smut, or *soot.*
To smut, or *dawb with smut.*
Smuttiness.
Smutty, *full of smut*; also *obscene* or *full of ribaldry.*

S N

A Snack, or *share.*
A Snacket, *a kind of hasp for a casement.*
A Snacot-fish.
A Snaffle, or *bit for an horse.*

A Snag, or *lump.*
A Snagged tooth, *that does not stand even.*
A Snail, *or* shell-snail *an insect.*
A Dew-snail.
A Sea-snail.
A Snail-stone.
Snail claver. } *herbs.*
Snail-trefoil. } *herbs.*
A Snake, *a serpent.*
A Water-snake.
Snake-weed, *an herb.*
Snake-wood.
A Snap, *and to* snap (*in different senses.*)
Snap-dragon, *an herb.*
A Snap-haunce, or *fire-lock.*
A Snap-sack, *for a soldier.*
A Snap-short, *one that is*
Snappish, *rude*, *captious*, *morose*, &c.
A Snare, or *gin.*
Snared, or *catch'd in the* snare.
A Snarl *of thread*, *silk*, &c.
To snarl or *be entangled*, as *a skain of thread*, &c.
To snarl, or *grin like a dog.*
A Snatch, *a little bit* or *morsel.*
To snatch, *or* snatch away *to pull or take hastily*, or *by force.*
A Snatcher.
To sneak *along*, or *creep up and down pitifully.*
Sneakingness, or *meanness of spirit.*
A Sneaks, or sneaksby, *a pitiful fellow, that scarce dares shew his head.*
The Sneath *of a sithe.*
The Sneck, *or* snecket *of a door.*
To sneer, *to laugh ridiculously*, or *scornfully.*
To sneez.
Sneezing-powder.
Sneezing-wort, *an herb.*
To snicker, or *laugh wantonly.*

A Snip, or *little bit.*
To snip *off*, or *cut off with a jerk.*
A Snipe, *or* snite *a bird.*
To snitt, or *snuff up.*
The hawk snites, or *wipes her bill.*
Snivel, *the filth of the nose.*
Snivelling, or *full of snivel.*
To snook, or *lye lurking for a thing.*
To snore, or *rout in sleeping.*
A Snorer.
To snort, or *snore.*
Snot, or *snivel.*
Snotty, or *full of snot.*
The Snout *of a beast.*
Calves-snout, *an herb.*
Snouted, *that has a snout.*
Fair-snouted.
Snow, *a meteor, and*
To snow.
A Snow-ball.
Snow-drops, *a flower.*
Snow-water.
Snowy, *abounding with snow.*
To snub, *to check one severely, without suffering him to speak*; or *to keep in subjection.*
A Snudge, or *old curmudgeon.*
To snudge *along*, or *go like an old* snudge.
The Snuff *of a candle*, or *lamp.*
A Snuff-dish.
Snuff, snush, or *sneezing-powder.*
To snuff, *to take snush*; also *to take pet*, or *be angry.*
Snuffers, or *a pair of* snuffers *to snuff a candle.*
To snuffle, or *speak thro' the nose.*
A Snuffler.
Snug, *close*, or *compact.*
To snug, or *lye close in bed.*
To snuggle, *or* snuggle *together.*
A Snurl, or *rheum in the head.*
Snush, *or* snuff.
A Snush-box.
Snut-nosed, or *flat-nosed.*

SO

So, as *is it so ?*
Soap, *or* sope.
To soar, or *fly high.*
A soar-hawk.
To sob, *and sigh.*
Sober, *serious, grave*, or *temperate.*
Soberness.
Sobriety, *a vertue that moderates the appetite in eating and drinking.*
Socage, *a* Law-*term from the* French soc i. e. *a plough-share*; *denoting a tenture of lands, by certain inferiour services in Husbandry, performed to the lord of the fee.*
A Socager, *or* sock-man, *one that holds lands by such a tenure.*
Sociable, *that delights in*, or *is fit for* society.
Sociableness, or *a sociable temper.*
A Society, *company* or *fellowship.*
Socinianism, *the tenets of The* Socinians *an heretical Sect, that deny the Divinity of our Lord and Saviour Jesus Christ, according to the execrable opinion, of their Ringleader* Faustus Socinus *of* Sienna, *who flourish'd A. D.* 1555.
The Socket *of a candlestick.*
Socks, or *a pair of* socks *to wear next the feet.*
A Sod, or *turf.*
Sod, *or* sodden (*from to seeth.*)
Sodder, or solder.
A Sodomite, *one that commits*
Sodomy, or *Buggery, the sin of* Sodom, *the chief of the five Cities in* Palestine *that were destroy'd by fire from heaven*; *the territory where they stood being swallow'd up in the brimstone-lake, commonly call'd the dead-sea.*
Sodom-apples, *certain apples growing in those parts which appear very fair to the eye, but crumble away upon the least touch, being full of soot and smoke.*
Soft, *tender, gentle*, or *delicate.*
Soft-footed.
Soft-headed, or *soft-brained.*
Soft-hearted, or *pitiful.*
To soften, *to make*, or *grow* soft.
Softish, or *somewhat soft.*
Softness.
So ho!
Soil, or *ground fit to bring forth fruit.*
The Soil, *slough*, or *mire of a wild boar.*
To soil, *to manure the soil*; to *slur, dawb*, or *defile.*
To take soil, *as a deer does.*
To sojourn, or *stay in a place.*
A Sojourner.
A Soke, *and*
To soke, or *steep.*
An old Soker, *sound tippler* or *hard-drinker.*
Solace, or *comfort.*
To solace, or *recreate himself.*
The Solanders, *a horse-disease.*
Solar, *of* or *belonging to the Sun.*
Sold, (*from to sell.*)
Solder, *us'd in the working and binding of metals.*
To Solder, *to joyn*, or *fasten with* solder.
Gold-solder.
A Soldier, or foot-soldier; *one that serves in the Wars*;

Wars; from the French *word* Solde, *which signifies the pay that is given for such service.*
The Soldiery, *the militia*, or *body of soldiers.*
Sole, *only*, or *alone.*
The Sole *of the foot*, or *of a shoo.*
To sole, or *clap* soles *on a pair of shoos.*
The Dog soles, or *fastens on the pigs ears.*
A Sole, *a kind of fish.*
The Spotted sole-fish.
A Solecism, or *incongruity of speech, contrary to* Grammar-*rules. The word is deriv'd from the* Soli, *a People of* Cilicia, *in* Greece, *who being transplanted into the lesser* Asia, *lost the purity of their mother-tongue, and were noted for their rude and barbarous expressions.*
Solemn, *that which is celebrated*, or *done in due order at some certain time.*
A Solemnity, or solemn pomp, *anciently, an anniversary*, or *yearly feast*
A Solemnization, or *solemnizing.*
To solemnize, or *celebrate.*
To solicit, or sollicit.
Solid, *firm, hard, sound, substantial, massy*, &c.
Solidity, *a being solid; in* Geometry *it is magnitude, with breadth, length and thickness.*
Solids, *or* solid bodies, *certain regular figures*, as *a cube cylinder, pyramid*, &c.
A Soliloquy, or *meditating alone with one's self.*
A Solifidian (*in* Divinity) *one that holds faith only without works, necessary to salvation.*
Solitariness, *a being*
Solitary, *lonely*, or *without company.*
Solitude, *a solitary place*, or *a retired life.*
Solomon's seat, *an herb.*
To sollicit *entreat earnestly, importune*, or *press*; also *to manage a* law-suit.
A Sollicitation, or *sollliciting.*
A Sollicitor at Law, *a Person employ'd to take care of, and follow suits in Courts of* Law, or Equity; as
The King's Sollicitor General.
Sollicitous, *full of care and fear; troubled*, or *much concerned about a business.*
Sollicitude, *carking care, anguish of mind*, or *great trouble.*
Solstice (i. e. *the standing of the sun*) *when the sun seems as it were to stand still, and proceeds no farther in its course, but begins to go back, which happens twice in a year*, viz.
The Summer-solstice, *when the sun being come to the* Tropick *of* Cancer, *makes the longest summer-day, about* June 12.
The Winter-solstice, *when upon the sun's arrival at the* Tropick *of* Capricorn, *we have the shortest day of winter, about* December 12.
Solsticial, *belonging to the* Solstices.
Solvable, *that may be* solved; or *that is able to pay.*
Soluble, *loose*, or *apt to go to stool.*
To solve, *or* resolve *a question, argument*, or *objection.*
Solvent, or *able to pay.*
A Solution, or *resolving of a doubt, question*, &c
A Solutive, or *loosening Medicine.*
Some, or *some persons*, &c.
Something, *or* somewhat.
Somewhere.
A Son.
A God-son.
A Grand-son.
A Son-in-law.
A Song (*from to sing*)
A Songster, or *singer.*
A Sonnet, *a sort of song* or *poem, consisting of* 14 *verses.*
Sonship, *the quality of a* Son.
Soon, or *quickly.*
Soop, or *potage, after the* French *way.*
To soop, or *sup up.*
The Soot *of a chimney.*
To sooth up, or *flatter.*
A Soothsayer, or *Diviner.*
Soothsaying.
A Sop, *a slice of bread dipt in sauce*, &c.
A Wine-sop.
To sop, as *to sop bread*, &c.
Sugar-sops.
Sope, *to wash*, or *scour with.*
Castle-sope.
To sope, or *rub over with* sope.
A Sope-boiler.
A Sope-house.
Sope-wort, *an herb.*
A Sophism, or *cavil*; *a subtil, but false and deceitful argument.*
A Sophister, *a cunning and cavilling disputer*; *a prating cavilier.*
Sophistical, *captious*, or *deceitful.*
To sophisticate, *corrupt, adulterate*, or *falsify.*
A Sophisticator.
Spohistry, *the art of deceiving by false arguments.*
Sophy, *a Title usually given to the King of* Persia.
A Sorb-apple, or *service-*

vice-berry.
A Sorcerer a wizzard, magician, or, inchanter.
A Sorceress, or witch.
Sorcery, witch-craft, or the black art.
Sordid, foul, base, mean, niggardly, pitiful, shameful, infamous, &c.
Sordidness, a sordid humour.
A Sordine, or little pipe put into the mouth of a Trumpet, to make it sound low.
Sore, sharp, raw, tender, cruel, &c.
A Sore, or ulcer.
A Plague-sore.
A Sore, a male deer four years old.
Sore-age, the first year of a hawk.
A Sore-hawk.
A Sorel, a fallow deer of three years.
Soreness (from sore)
Sorrance, a horse-disease.
Sorrel, an herb.
French-sorrel.
Wood-sorrel.
The Sorrel-colour among horses; a redlish colour intermixt with red or white hairs.
Sorrow, grief, or trouble.
Sorrowful, sad, or woful.
Sorry, troubled; also paltry, or of little value.
A Sort, kind, or manner.
To sort, match, or suit according to the sorts.
Sortable, or suitable.
A Sot, a fool void of sense, or one that has lost his senses by drinking.
To sot one's time away, or spend it sottishly.
Sottish, stupid, or senseless.
Sottishness.
Souce, a sort of pickle.
To souce Pork, or steep it in the souce.

Soveraign, or sovereign, independent, supreme, chief, or excellent.
A Soveraign, an absolute Prince, or Monarch.
Sovereignty, or supreme power.
Sought (from to seek)
The Soul, the principle of life.
Soul-saving.
All-souls-day, Novemb. 2.
A Souldier, or soldier.
Sound, whole, safe, honest, solid, healthful, &c.
Sound, the object of hearing, as the sound of a Bell, Glass, Musical Instrument, &c.
The Sound-board of an Organ.
The Sound-hole, and sound-post of a musical instrument.
A Sound, any great inlet of Sea, between two head-lands, as Plimouth-sound, &c.
The Sound, or straights of the Baltick Sea, between Denmark and Sweden; so called by way of excellency, as being the largest and most noted of all others.
A Sound, or sounder, a herd, or great company of Swine.
To sound, to make or yield a sound; to try the depth of the Sea, to pump or sift one, &c.
Soundness, a being sound entire, solid, &c.
Sour, sharp, tart, crabbed, &c.
To sour, to turn, or to make sour.
Sourness.
A Source, or spring-head of a river, the place from whence it takes its rise and flows.
The Source, original, cause, or occasion of any thing.
A Sous, a French penny.

The South, or south-quarter of the World.
The South-wind.
South-east.
South-west.
Southerly, or southern.
Southern-wood, an herb.
Southwards, or towards the south.
A Sow, a female hog; also an insect so call'd.
A Sow of lead.
A Sow-pig.
A Sow-gelder.
Sow-bread, an herb.
Sow-thistle.
To sow seeds or grain, to raise strife, dissensions, &c.
To sow, or sew needle-work.
A Sower.
Sown, or sowed.
Sowr, or sour.
A Sowse, or great noise.
To sowse, or dowse one; to buffet him soundly.

SP

A Space, or distance of time, or place.
A Space in Printing.
Spacious, wide, or large.
Spaciousness.
A Spade, a kind of shovel to dig with.
A Spade, a red deer three years old.
The Spade-bone, or shoulder-bone.
Spadiers, or diggers in the Tin-mines in Cornwall.
I spake, or did speak.
A Span, the space between the thumb's end stretch'd out and the end of the little finger.
To span, or measure by spans.
A Spangle, a small thin piece of gold or silver.
A Spangle-maker.
Spangled, or set off with Spangles.
A Spaniel, a sort of dog.
A Land-spaniel.

A Water-spaniel.
The Spanish flie.
Spanish pick-tooth, *an herb.*
A Spanking lass, *one that is spruce*, or *tearing fine.*
A Spar, *a wooden bar.*
Spar, *or* Muscovy-*glass.*
The Spars *of a spinning-wheel*; also *certain stones found in lead-mines, like gems, but not so hard.*
Sparables, *or* sparrow-bills, *a sort of little iron nails.*
Spare, *thin, lean*; or *that may be spar'd.*
To spare, *to forgive*, or *favour*; *to forbear, to lay up*, &c.
Spare-hours.
The Spare-ribs *of pork.*
Sparingness, *savingness*, or *thriftiness.*
A Spark *of fire.*
A Spark, or *young gallant, that appears in a gay suit of clothes.*
Sparkish, or *spruce.*
Sparkishness.
To sparkle, or *cast forth sparks.*
A Sparrow, *a bird.*
A Hedge-sparrow.
A House-sparrow.
A Reed-sparrow.
Sparrow-mouthed, *that has a wide mouth from ear to ear.*
A Spat, spatter, *or* spattle, *a slice to spread salves with*, &c.
Spattling poppey, *an herb.*
To spatter, bespatter, or *dawb.*
Spatter-dashes, *or* spatter-plashes, *a kind of boots.*
The Spavin, *a disease in Horses, a swelling in the ham, that causes 'em to halt.*
To spawl, *spit much*, or *dawb with spittle.*
The Spawn *of a Fish, and to* spawn.
A Spawner, *the Female Fish.*
To spay, as *to spay a Mare.*
To speak, *say*, or *utter.*
A Speaker.
The Lord Speaker *of the House of Peers.*
The Speaker *of the House of Commons.*
A Spear, *lance*, or *javelin.*
A Boar-spear.
An Eel-spear.
King's-spear, *an herb.*
A Spear-head.
A Spear-man, or *Soldier arm'd with a* spear.
A Spear-staff.
Spear-mint, } *herbs.*
Spear-wort, }
A Specht, *or* speight, *a bird.*
Special, *particular, singular*, or *excellent.*
A Specialty, *a Law-term signifying, a bond, bill*, &c.
A Species, *a kind* or *sort.*
Specifical, *belonging thereto.*
A Specifick, or *specifick medicine.*
To specify, *particularize*, or *mention in express terms.*
A Specimen, *proof, essay*, or *pattern.*
Specious, *fair in appearance*, or *plausible.*
A Speck, or *little spot.*
A Speckle, or *pimple in the face.*
To speckle, or *spot.*
A Spectacle, or *publick shew.*
A pair of Spectacles, *to read, write*, or *work by.*
A Spectacle-case.
A Spectacle-maker.
A Spectator, or *beholder.*
A Speculation, or *contemplation.*
Speculative, *belonging thereto.*
Sped (*from to* speed)
A Speech, *discourse*, or *oration.*
Speechless, *that has lost the use of speech.*
Speed, or *haste.*
To speed, *to make* speed; or *to meet with success.*
Speediness, *swiftness*, or *dispatch.*
Speedwell, *an herb.*
Female speedwell.
Speedy, *quick*, or *swift.*
The Speedy-cut *in horses.*
Speeks, or *ship-nails.*
A Speight, *a sort of bird.*
A Spell, or *charm.*
A Spell *of work at Sea*; *a doing it by turns.*
To spell, *a word*; or *syllable*; *to gather the letters into syllables*, or *to divide the syllables into letters.*
A good or *bad* Speller.
Spelt (*from to* spell)
Spelt, *a kind of corn.*
Spelter *a sort of imperfect Metal.*
To spend, *waste, consume, lay out*, &c.
To spend, or *pass time.*
A Spender.
A Spend-thrift, or *prodigal spender.*
Spent, *consum'd, laid out, past over*, &c.
Sperage, or *asparague.*
Sperm, or *natural seed.*
Spermatick, *belonging thereto.*
To spew, or *vomit.*
A Sphere, *a round moveable Instrument, made up of divers circles*; *invented by* Astronomers, *for the more easie conceiving the motions of the Heavens, and representing the true situation of the Earth.*
Spherical, *belonging to*, or *round like a sphere.*
Spice, *several sorts of grocery-ware*, as *cinnamon, cloves, mace, nutmeg*, &c.
To spice, or *season with* spice.

A

A Spicery, *a place where spices are kept.*
A Spice, or *small fit of a disease.*
Spick *and* span *new*, or *brand new.*
Spicknel, *an herb.*
A Spider, *an insect.*
A Sea-spider, or *carvel, a fish.*
A Water-spider.
A Spider-catcher.
Spider-wort, *an herb.*
A Spigot *to put into the faucet of a tap.*
A Spike, or *iron-spike.*
Spike, or spikenard; as *oil of spike.*
Water-spike, *an herb.*
To spike, or *make sharp-pointed.*
Spikenard, *a sort of sweet smelling plant.*
A Spill, or *little gift of money.*
A Spill, or *splint.*
To spill *a liquor.*
To spin, *flax, thread*, &c. or *to turn round*, as *a top does.*
Spinage, *a pot-herb.*
A Spindle *us'd in spinning.*
A Spindle-maker.
The Spindle, *or nuel of a winding stair-case.*
The Spindle-tree, or *prick timber, a shrub.*
A Spink, or *chaffinch.*
A Spinner, *a small sort of harmless spider.*
A Spinning-wheel.
A Spinster, or *woman employ'd in spinning.*
A Spire, or *pyramid.*
A Spire *of corn*, or *grass.*
To spire, or *grow up into an ear*, as *corn does.*
A Spirit, *an immaterial substance*; or *the soul of a deceased person.*
Spirit, *liveliness, vigour*, or *courage*; also *the essence of several things extracted by chymical operations.*
To spirit away children, *to steal*, or *entice them from home, in order to send them to the* Indies, &c.
Spirited, *as*
High-spirited.
Low-spirited.
Spirits, *hobgoblins*, or *fairies.*
Spiritual, or *Ecclesiastical, in opposition to* Temporal; also *pious* or *devout.*
A Spirituality, or *care of Souls.*
The Spiritualities, or *spiritual revenues of a Prelate, those he receives as a Bishop, and not as a temporal Lord; such are the profits arising from his visitations, ordaining and instituting priests, prestation money*, &c.
Spirituous, or *full of spirits.*
A Spirt, or *squirt.*
To spirt *water*, &c.
A Spit, or *broach.*
A Turn-spit.
To spit *a joynt of meat.*
To spit, or *spawl.*
To spit, or *dig with a spade.*
A Spit-deep, *as much ground as may be digg'd up at once with a spade.*
A Spit-fish.
A Spitch-cock-eel, *a sort of large Eel, that is commonly roasted.*
Spite, *malice, hatred*, or *ill-will.*
To spite, *to bear a* spite, or *grudge against one.*
Spitefull, or *malicious.*
Spitefulness.
A Spitter, *one that* spits *and spawls.*
A Spitter, *brocket*, or *red deer, near two years old, when the horns begin to grow up sharp like a spit.*
Spittle, spit *out of the mouth.*
A Spittle, Spittle-house, or *Hospital.*
A Splatch *of dirt.*
Splay-footed, or *bandy-legg'd.*
The splaying, or *parting a horse's shoulder from the breast, caus'd by a slip*, &c.
The Spleen, or *milt*; or *a distemper in that part.*
A Spleen, *spite*, or *grudge.*
Spleen-sick, or *troubled, with the spleen.*
Spleen-wort, *an herb.*
Rough Spleen-wort.
Splendid, *stately, magnificent*, or *sumptuous.*
Splendor, *brightness, grandeur*, or *magnificence.*
Splenetick, or *spleen-sick, that has a distemper'd Spleen.*
A Splent, or *fracture of a bone*; also *a swelling in a horse's leg.*
Splents, *us'd by Surgeon's in the curing of broken limbs.*
Splents, or *harness for the arms.*
To splice *(a Sea-term) to make fast the ends of ropes one into another.*
A Splinter *of wood.*
Split, or *cleft.*
To split *asunder, to split with laughter*, &c.
Spoil, or *booty.*
To spoil, *waste, destroy, rob*, or *marr.*
A Spoiler.
A Spoke *of a wheel.*
I spoke *or* did speak.
Spoken, *or* spoken *of.*
A Well-spoken, or *eloquent Person.*
A Spokes-man, *he that speaks for another.*
Sponk, or *touch-wood.*
Spontaneous, *voluntary, free, or of its one accord.*
A Spool, or *spindle.*
A Spoon *to eat with.*
A Silver-spoon.

A

A Spoon-bill, *a bird.*
A Spoonful.
Spoon-meat.
Spoon-wort, *an herb.*
The Spooning *of a ſhip (a Sea-term) when ſhe goes right before the wind, without any ſail.*
A Sport, or *paſtime.*
To ſport *himſelf,* or *divert himſelf.*
A Sporter.
Sportful, *or* ſportive.
A Spot *of ground.*
A Spot, *blemiſh, ſtain, blur,* &c.
To ſpot, *to ſtain* or *dawb;* or *to mark with ſpots.*
Spotleſs, *without* ſpot or *blemiſh.*
A Spotter *of hoods.*
Spotty, or *full of ſpots.*
A Spouſe, *a bride,* or *bridegroom.*
A Spout *of a conduit,* &c.
A Water-ſpout.
A Rain-ſpout, or *ſudden fall of rain in a ſtream.*
To ſpout, ſpout *out,* &c.
A Sprain, *a violent contorſion of the* tendons *of the muſcles by a ſudden accident.*
To ſprain, or *get a ſprain.*
Spraints, *the dung of an Otter.*
A Sprat, *a fiſh.*
To ſprawl or *lye groveling along.*
A Spray, *ſprig,* or *little twig.*
Spray-wood.
A Spread, *or* ſpret, *a Waterman's pole.*
Spread, *and*
To ſpread, *ſcatter, lay open, divulge,* &c.
A Spreader.
A Sprig, or *young twig.*
Spriggy, or *full of ſprigs.*
A Spright, *ſpirit,* or *phantome.*
Sprightlineſs, *a being*
Sprightly, *lively, briſk, airy,* &c.

A Spring, *and to* ſpring *(in all ſenſes)*
The Spring-time.
A Spring-tide, or *great tide.*
Spring-water.
A Spring, *a net to catch Woodcocks.*
The Springer *of an arched gate (in* Archi-&ure) *the moulding that bears the arch.*
A Sprinkle, or *Holy-water ſprinkle.*
To ſprinkle, *daſh,* or *ſtrew.*
A Sprit-ſail, *the ſail that belongs to the* Bolt-ſprit *maſt.*
A Sprout, *of a tree,* or *herb.*
To ſprout, or *ſprout forth.*
Sprouts, or *young Coleworts.*
Spruce, *neat, fine,* or *gallant.*
Spruce-beer, *a ſort of phyſical drink.*
Spruce-leather, *for* Pruſſia *leather.*
Spruceneſs.
Sprung *(from to* ſpring)
Sprunt, *vigorous,* or *active.*
A Spud, *a ſhort ſcurvy knife.*
To ſpue, *or* ſpew.
Spume, or *fome,* as *the ſpume of gold* or *ſilver.*
Spun *(from to* ſpin)
Home-ſpun *cloth.*
Spunge, *a ſoft ſubſtance full of holes, and a great water-ſoaker, brought from the Iſle* Samos, *in the* Archipelago, *where grows under the rocks.*
To ſpunge, or *cleanſe with a* ſpunge; *alſo to hang upon, to eat and drink at his coſt.*
A Spunger, or *ſmell-feaſt.*
Spungineſs, *a being*
Spungy, or *like a ſpunge.*
Spunk, *a ſubſtance that grows on the ſides of trees.*

A Spur *for a horſe,* &c.
To ſpur, *to ſtrike with ſpurs;* alſo *to egg one on* or *put him forward.*
The Spur-leather.
To Spur-gall *a horſe.*
Spurge, *an herb.*
Spurge-laurel.
Spurge-olive.
Spurge-wort, *an herb.*
Spurious, *baſe-born,* or *counterfeit; that is not genuine,* or *of the right ſtamp.*
To ſpurn, or *kick.*
Spurry, *a kind of herb.*
A Spurt; as *to do all for a* ſpurt.
To ſpurt, *or* ſpirt *up.*
A Sputter, or *buſtle.*
To ſputter, or *ſpit faſt in haſty talk.*
A Sputterer.
A Spy, or *ſcout.*
To ſpy, *watch, obſerve,* or *deſcry.*

S Q

Squab, *young and fat;* as *a ſquab child.*
A Squab *rabbet,* or *chick ſo young that 'tis ſcarce fit to be eaten.*
A ſquab, *a ſoft cuſhion,* or *couch.*
To ſquab, or *ſquelch one.*
A Squabble, or *conteſt.*
To ſquabble, or *brangle.*
Squabbled Letters *(among Printers) when ſome lines are fallen out of order in a form before it is impos'd.*
A Squabbler.
A Squadron *of horſe,* or *of men of War.*
To Squander *away,* or *laviſh.*
A Squanderer.
A Square, *and to* ſquare *(in ſeveral ſenſes)*
Square-dealing.
To ſquaſh, *maſh,* or *beat flat.*
Squat, or *thick, and ſhort.*

To

To Squat, or *lie down*; *as a Hare*, or *Rabbet does*.
To Squawl, squeal, or *cry out*.
A Squawler.
A Squeak, *and*
To squeak, or *cry like a Pig*, &c.
Squeamish, or *queasy*.
Squeamishness, or *weakness of the stomack*.
To squeez, *press*, or *strain*.
A Squib, or *cracker*.
A Squill, or *sea-Onion*.
Squinant, or *Camels-hay*, *a kind of sweet rush*.
The Squincy, *or* Squinancy, *a disease*.
To squint, or *look* a-squint.
Squint-eyed.
A Squire, *or* Esquire.
A Squirrel, *a little beast*.
A Squirt, *to squirt water with*.
The Squirt, *a lask*, or *looseness*.
A Squirting, or *pitiful-fellow*.
To squitter, or *go to stool often*.
A Squob, *or* squab *to sit on*.

ST

A Stab, *and*
To stab, or *wound with a sword, dagger*, &c.
Stability, or *firmness*.
Stable, *steady, firm*, or *sure*.
A Stable *for beasts*.
A Horse-stable.
To stable, or *house Cattel in a stable*.
To stabilish, *or* establish.
A Stack, or *pile of hay, corn*, &c.
A Stack *of wood in* Essex *14 foot in length, 3 in height, and 3 in breadth*.
Staddles, or *young tender trees*.
A Staff, *to lean upon*.
A Crosier's-staff, *or* Bishop's-staff.
A Hunting-staff.
A Plough-staff.
A Quarter-staff, *a kind of weapon*.
A Spear-staff.
A Walking-staff.
A Staff, *a division of a Psalm*.
A Stag, or *male Deer*.
The Stag-beetle, or *great horn-beetle*.
A Stage, or *scaffold to act Plays on*.
A Stage-play.
A Stage-player.
A Stage, or *station in a journey*.
A Stage-coach.
A Stage-Horse.
A Staggard, *a young buck*, or *deer four years old*.
To stagger, *trip, reel*, or *to be in doubt*.
A Staggerer.
The staggers, *a horse disease*.
Stagger-wort; *an herb*.
Stagnant, or *standing water*.
To stagnate, *to lie still*; *as water does in ponds*, or *to want a free course*; *as the blood when grown too thick*.
Staid (*from to* stay.)
A Stain, *and*
To stain, *to defile, to die colours, to bespatter*, &c.
A Stainer.
A Painter-stainer.
Stairs, or *a pair of* stairs *in a house*.
A Stair-case.
A Stake *and to* stake (*in several senses*.)
A Beef-stake, or *slice of beef*.
A Mutton-stake, &c.
Stale, *old*, or *not fresh*.
Stale, *or horse-piss*.
To Stale, or *urine*; *as horses does*.
A Stale, or *balk in Elections*, or *a decoy in fowling*.
Staleness.
The stalk *of herbs, flowers, fruit*, &c.
A Bean-stalk.
To stalk, or *walk gently*; *as fowlers do*.
Stalkers, *a kind of fishing net*.
A Stalking-horse, *us'd in tunneling for Partridges*.
A Stall (*in several senses*.)
A Stall-boat; *a kind of fishers-boat*.
The Head-stall *of a bridle*.
An Ox-stall.
To stall, *to put into a* stall or *stable*; *also to glut*, or *cloy*.
Stallage, *Money paid for pitching* stalls *in a Fair*, or *Market*.
A Stallion, *a horse kept for the covering of mares*.
A Stammel, *or* stammel-jade; *a great flouncing Mare*, or *an overgrown bouncing Wench*.
The stammel-colour.
To stammer, *stutter*, or *falter in speech*.
A Stammerer.
A Stamp, *and to* stamp (*in several senses*.)
A Stamper, *one that* stamps *in walking*.
Stanch, *substantial, solid, grave*, &c.
Stanchness.
To stanch, or *stop blood*.
A Stand, *and to* stand (*in all senses*.)
A Standard, *banner*, or *ensign in an Army*.
The Royal Standard.
A Standard-bearer.
A Standard, or *model of measure, weight*, &c.
An Old Stander, *one that has lived long in a place*.
A Stander; *a Tree left for growth*.
A Stander-by, or *spectator*.
Stander-grass; *an herb*.
A Standish, *to hold ink*.
The Stannaries, or *Tin-mines in* Cornwall.
Stannary-men; *that work in those mines*.

A

A Stanza, or *staff, a certain number of verses.*
A Staple, *a principal mart,* or *publick storehouse for Merchandizes.*
A Staple-commodity.
Staple-inn, *one of the Inns of* Chancery, *which formerly belong'd to the* Staple-*Merchants.*
A Staple *for a lock.*
A Star *in the firmament.*
Star *of* Bethlehem, or *of* Jerusalem, *a plant.*
A Blazing-star.
The Day-star, *or* morning-star.
The Dog-star.
The Evening-star.
The North-star.
The Star-chamber Court *held at* Westminster, *to punish riots, forgeries,* &c. *and taken away by* 17 *Car.* I.
The Star-fish, *or* sea-star.
A Star-gazer, or *Astrologer.*
Star-wort, *an herb.*
Sea Star-wort.
The Starboard, or *right side of a ship.*
Starch, *a sort of composition.*
To starch, or *stiffen linnen with* starch.
A Starcher.
A Starched, *stiff,* or *formal person.*
Starchness, *affectedness,* or *formality.*
To stare, or *gaze upon.*
Stark, *altogether, quite,* or *beyond measure*; as, Stark mad.
Stark naked, *&c.*
A Starling, *or* stare, *a bird.*
A Starling *of a stone-bridge.*
Starry, or *full of* stars.
A Start, *and to* start (*in several senses.*)
To start, or *raise a Hare from her form.*
A Starter.
The Starting-place, *at horse-races.*
Startish, or *somewhat apt to* start *aside.*
To startle, *surprize,* or *fright one.*
To starve *for hunger,* or *cold*; or *to famish one.*
A starveling, or *hunger-starved fellow.*
State, *wealth,* or *grandeur.*
A State, *condition, rank,* or *degree.*
To state or *regulate a business, account,* &c.
To state, or *propose a question in its* state, or *due form.*
State-affairs.
State-policy.
Stateliness, *a being*
Stately, *magnificent, majestick, proud, haughty* &c.
The States *of the Kingdom.*
A States-man, or *politician.*
Staticks, *the Science of weights, and measures, a part of* Mechanicks.
A Station, *standing-place, post, rank, condition,* &c.
A Stationer, or *Paper-Merchant.*
The Company of Stationers, *which is of greater antiquity than the invention of Printing; but was not incorporated till the third year of Queen* Mary I. *now comprehending Book-sellers, Paper-stationers, Printers, Book-binders,* &c. *The Stationers at first dealt in Manuscript-Copies, Paper,* &c; *and probably took name from their particular* Stations, or *standing-shops; more especially about* Pater-noster *row, and St.* Paul's *Church-yard.*
A Station-staff, or *surveying-pole us'd in the measuring of land,* &c.
A Statuary, or *carver of* Statues.
A Statue, or *standing Image of wood, stone, brass,* &c.
The Stature, *size,* or *pitch of a person.*
A Statute, *Law,* or *Ordinance.*
The Statutes, or Statute-laws *of* England, *made by the King, and the three Estates of the Realm.*
To stave, or *break in pieces a vessel,* or *boat.*
To stave, *off,* or *keep off.*
Staves (*the plural of* staff.)
Staves-acre; *an herb.*
A Stay, *and to* stay (*in all senses.*)
A Stay-band *for an infant*
Stayed, *grave, serious,* or *sober.*
Stayedness.
A pair of Stays, or *bodice for Women.*
Stead, as *in his* stead; *to stand in good* stead, *&c.*
Steadiness, *a being*
Steady, *firm, constant,* or *sure.*
The Steal, or *handle of a spoon,* &c.
To steal, *take away privily, filch,* or *pilfer.*
A Stealer.
Stealth; as *to do any thing* by stealth.
A Steam, or *vapour.*
To steam, or *send forth* steams.
Stedfast, *stable, firm, fixed, unmoveable,* &c.
Stedfastness.
A Steed, or *horse.*
Steel, or *hard iron.*
A Steel *to strike fire with.*
To steal, or *harden himself in sin,* &c.
A Steel-box.
A Steal-buckle.
Steep, *of a difficult,* or *dangerous ascent*

To

To steep, or *soak.*
The Steeple *of a Church.*
Steepness *(from* steep; *)* *as the steepness of an hill.*
A Steer, or *bullock.*
To steer, or *guide a ship.*
The Steerage, or *place where the ship is steer'd.*
A Steers-man.
A Stem, *and to* stem *(in several senses.)*
A Stench, or *stink.*
A Step, *and*
To step, or *go by* steps.
A Foot-step.
A Step-father.
A Step-mother.
A Step-son.
A Step-daughter.
Stept *(from to* step.*)*
Steril, *barren,* or *unfruitful.*
Sterility, or *barrenness.*
Sterling, *or* Sterling-money, i. e. *current,* or *lawful money, so call'd from a certain pure coin first stamp'd in* England, *by the* Easterlings *or Merchants of East*-Germany, *by order of King* John.
Stern, *grim, crabbed,* or *morose.*
The Stern, or *hindermost part of a ship.*
The Stern-post.
Sternness, *austerity,* or *Crabbedness.*
A Stew, or *hot-house*; al-so *a fish-pond.*
To stew, or *boil over a gentle fire.*
A Stew-pan.
A Steward, *an Officer belonging to a Nobleman's house, a mannour, a ship,* &c.
The Lord high *Steward of* England, *an Officer formerly of very great power, now only appointed by the King, for the tryal of any Peer of the Realm; which being ended he breaks his wand, and puts an end to his own authority.*

Stewardship, *the office of a* Steward.
A Stews, or *common bawdy-house.*
Sticado's, *an herb.*
A Stick, or *little staff.*
A Printer's Composing-stick.
A Candle-stick.
A Fagot-stick.
A walking-stick.
To stick *(in several senses.)*
To stickle *hard in a business,* or *strive earnestly about it.*
A Stickler.
Stiff, *hard, benummed, rigid,* or *resolute.*
Stiff-necked, or *refractary.*
To stiffen, *to make,* or *grow* stiff.
Stiffness.
To, stifle, or *smother.*
Stigmatical, or *infamous.*
To stigmatize, *to brand with a hot iron; to set a mark of infamy on; to reproach,* or *traduce.*
A Stile, *to pass over, from one field to another.*
A Turn-stile.
Still; *as yet,* or *without ceasing.*
Still, or *quiet.*
To still, or *make* still.
A Still, or *alembick.*
To still, *or* distill, *waters,* &c.
A Still-born *Child.*
A Stilling, *gauntry,* or *stand in a cellar for hogsheads.*
A Stilletto, *an* Italian *dagger,* or *tuck.*
Stilness, *silence,* or *tranquillity.*
A pair of Stilts.
The Stil-yard, *or* steel-yard, *near the* Thames, *in* London, *a place where Steel, was very much sold, and where the society of* Easterling *Merchants sometime had their abode.*
A Sting, *and to* sting.

The Sting *of a fly, serpent, scorpion,* &c.
To sting, or *put forth the* sting.
Stinginess, or *niggardliness*
Stingo, *or* Yorkshire-stingo, *a sort of strong drink.*
Stingy, *niggardly,* or *miserably covetous.*
A Stink, or *ill savour.*
To stink, or *send forth a* stink.
A Stinkard, or *stinking fellow.*
Stinking-weed; *an herb.*
A Stint, *limit, task,* or *set measure.*
To stint, *bound, repress,* or *keep in.*
The Stiony, *a disease within the eye-lids.*
A Stipend, or *salary.*
A Stipendiary, *one that takes wages; a pensioner*
To stipulate, *covenant, bargain,* or *agree.*
A Stipulation.
A Stir, *noise, bustle,* or *tumult.*
To stir, *move, jog,* or *provoke.*
A Stirk, *or* sturk; *a young steer.*
A Stirrop, *to ride with.*
The Yeoman of the stirrop.
The Stirrop-leather.
Stirrop-stockings.
A Stitch *made with a needle,* &c: or *a pain in the side.*
To stitch, or *sow.*
A Stitcher.
Stitch-wort, *an herb.*
A Stithy, or *anvil.*
The Stithy, *a disease amongst Oxen, which causes the skin to stick so close to the ribs, that they cannot stir.*
A Stittle-back, *a fish.*
A Stiver, *a Dutch penny.*
Stoaked, *a sea-term for* stopped; *as the pump is stoaked.*
A Stoaker *in a brew-house.*

A Stoat, or *stallion.*
A Stoccado, *a thrust*, or *stab with a weapon.*
A Stock, *and to* stock (*in all senses.*)
A Stock-dove.
A Stock-fish.
The Stock-gillyflower.
The White Stock-gilly-flower.
Stock-still, *that does not stir*, or *budge.*
A Laughing-stock.
A Leaning-stock.
Stocks, *posts framed to build a ship upon.*
Stocks, or *a pair of* stocks *for Malefactors.*
A Stocking, or *pair of* stockings.
Silk-stockings.
Sirrop-stockings.
Woosted-stockings.
A Stocking-mender.
A Stocking-weaver.
A Stode, or *great company of horses.*
Stoical, *of*, or *belonging to the* Stoicks.
Stoicism, *the maxims and opinions of*
The Stoicks, *a severe sect of Philosophers, so call'd from the porch* (Stoa *in* Greek) *where* Zeno Citiæus *their first Master was wont to teach: They maintained fate, and did not allow passion; being always very grave and reserved.*
A Stole, *a kind of Priestly ornament.*
A Stole, or *wardrobe.*
The Groom of the Stole.
Stole, *and* stoln (*from to* steal)
A Stomacher *for Womens breasts.*
Stomack, *that part which digests the food; also the appetite*, or *a testy and refractary humour.*
To stomack, or *be angry.*
Stomackfull, *dogged*, or *peevish.*
Stomackless, *that has no* stomack, or *appetite.*
Stone, *in a quarry*, or *rock.*
The Stone *in the bladder*, or *kidneys; a disease.*
A Stone *of beef, in* London 8 *l. In* Herefordshire 12 *l.*
A Stone *of Wax*, 8 *l. Of wooll in* London 14 *l. In* Herefordshire 12 *l. In* Glocestershire 15 *l.*
To stone, *to strike*, or *kill with* stones.
A Blood-stone.
A Chack-stone.
A Diamond-stone.
An Eagle-stone.
A Fire-stone.
A Flint-stone.
A Grind-stone.
A Lime-stone.
A Load-stone.
A Mill-stone.
A Peeble-stone.
A Pumice-stone.
A Ruddle-stone.
A Sand-stone.
A Sleek-stone.
A Thunder-stone.
A Tomb-stone.
A Touch-stone.
A Whet-stone.
Stone-allum.
A Stone-bow.
Stone-break, or *saxifrage, an herb.*
A Stone-buck.
The Stone-colick, *a torturing disease.*
The Stone-cray, *a disease in hawks.*
Stone-crop; *an herb.*
A Stone-cutter.
Stone-dead, or *quite dead.*
A Stone-falcon, *a bird.*
Stone-pitch.
A Stone-smich, *a bird.*
A Stone-wall.
Stone-work, or *mason's work.*
Stone-wort, *an herb.*
Stony, *rocky*, or *full of* stones.
A Stook, or 12 *sheaves of corn.*
I stood, or *did* stand.
A Stool *to sit on.*
A Close-stool.
A Foot-stool.
A Joynt-stool.
To stoop, *incline*, or *bow down.*
A Stop, *and to* stop (*in all senses.*)
A Stop-gap.
A Stoppage, or *obstruction.*
A Stopper, or *Tobacco-stopper.*
The Stopple *of a bottle.*
Store, *abundance*, or *plenty.*
The Store, or *provisions of a ship*, &c.
To store, *to furnish with*, or *to lay up in* store.
A Store-house, *for victuals, armour, ship-tackle*, &c.
A Store-keeper.
A Stork, *a fowl.*
Stork's-bill, *an herb.*
A Storm, or *tempest of wind*, or *rain.*
To storm, *to chafe*, or *to be in a rage*; also *to attack a Town furiously.*
Stormy, or *tempestuous.*
A Story, History, *relation*, or *merry tale.*
A Story (*in building*) as *a house three* stories *high*
Story'd, or *reported.*
A Store, *a stinking sort of ferret.*
A Stove, *stew*, or *hot bath.*
Stover, or *fodder.*
Stout, *couragious, lusty, insolent*, or *sturdy.*
Stoutness.
To stow, or *lay up wares.*
Stowage, *the place where goods are laid up*; or *money paid upon that account.*
Stow-ball, *a kind of sport*
To straddle, or *stride.*
To straggle, or *wander about.* *A*

A Straggler.
Straight, *right, direct*, or *narrow*.
A Straight, *exigence*, or *great difficulty*.
A Straight, or *narrow arm of the Sea, shut up on both sides by the land*; as *The* Straights *of* Gibraltar.
To straighten, *to make straight*, or *narrow*; or *to put one hard to it*.
Straightness, or *narrowness*.
A Strain, *and to* strain (*in several senses*.)
A Strain, or *breed of horses*.
A Strainer, *to strain liquors*.
Straits, *or* streits, *a sort of narrow* Kersey-*cloth*.
Straitway, or *forthwith*.
A Strake, *the hoop of a cart-wheel, wherein the spokes are set*; also *the seam between two ship-planks*.
A Strand, or *high shore*.
A Strand, or *twist of a rope* (*a sea-term*.)
Stranded, or *run aground*.
Strange, *rare, wonderfull, unusual, foreign, shy*. &c.
Strangeness.
A Stranger.
To strangle, or *choak*.
The Strangles, *a disease in horses*.
Strangle-weed, *an herb*.
The Strangury, *or* strangullion; *a making of water by drops, with great pain and difficulty*.
A Strap, or *thong of leather*.
To strap one, or *lash him with a* strap.
The Strappado, *a kind of rack, to punish soldiers*.
A Strapping, or *bouncing lass*.
A Strategem, *a witty shift, or policy in War*.

Straw, *stubble*, or *litter for cattel*.
Pease-straw.
A Straw-hat.
A Straw-bed.
A Strawberry, *a fruit*.
The Strawberry-plant.
The Strawberry-tree, *a* shrub.
A Stray-worm, *an insect*.
To stray, *go a-stray*, or *wander*.
A Stray-sheep.
Stray-time *for cattel, after harvest*.
A Streak, *and*
To streak, or *mark with* streaks.
A Red-streak apple.
The Streaks *of a cart-wheel*.
The Stream, or *current of a river*.
To Stream *out*, or *flow out*.
A Stream-anchor.
A Stream-cable.
Stream-works, *in the tin-mines, when the veins of metal are followed by trenching*.
A Streamer, *a flag*, or *a pendant in a ship*.
A Street, or *pav'd way*, as Fleet-street, *in* London.
A Street-door.
A Street-walker.
A Streight, *or* straight.
Strength, *force, vigour*, or *power*.
To strengthen, *make strong*, or *re-inforce*.
Strenuous, *vigorous, stout, valiant, hardy, active*, &c.
Strenuousness.
A Stress, *endeavour*, or *effort*.
The Stress, or *main point of the business*.
To stretch, *or* stretch *out*, *to extend*, or *reach out*.
To be upon the Stretch *in running*.
The Stretcher *in a boat, on which the water-man* stretches *out his feet*.

To strew, or *spread*.
Stricken, or *advanc'd in years*.
A Strickle, strickless, *or* strike, *to strike, the measure of corn even*.
Strict, *exact, punctual, rigid*, or *severe*.
Strictness.
A Stricture; as *Brutes have some* strictures, *or sparks of reason*.
A stride, *and*
To stride, or *straddle*.
A Cock's stride, strine, or *tread*.
Strife (*from to* strive) *contention*, or *variance*.
Loose-strife, *an herb*.
A Strike, *a certain measure of Corn*.
A Strike *of flax*.
To strike (*in all senses*.)
A Striker.
A String, *and to* string (*in several senses*.)
A Bow-string.
The Heart-strings.
A Shoo-string.
Stringy, *having small* strings, or *fibres*.
A Strip, or *small piece of cloth*.
To strip, *to pull off one's cloths*; or *to spoil*.
A Stripe, *blow*, or *lash*.
To stripe, or *make* stripes or *streaks, in stuff, cloth*, &c.
A Stripling, or *youth*.
Stript, *or* stripped.
A Stritchel, *or* strickle *to strike off the over-measure*.
To strive, *endeavour, struggle*, or *contend*.
A Striver.
A Stroke, *and to* stroke (*in several senses*.)
The Strokings *of milk*, or *beastings*.
To stroll, or *rove up and down as*
A Strolling *set of stage-players*.
Strong, *firm, stout, forcible, vio'nt*, or *heady*.

Head-

Head-strong, or *obstinate.*
Strong-bodied *wine.*
Strong-limbed, or *well set.*
A Strong-dock'd baggage, *a lusty common strumpet.*
I Strove, or *did* strive.
Struck (*from to* strike.)
Planet-struck, *stunned*, or *amazed.*
A Structure, *fabrick*, or *pile of buildng.*
A Strude, stode or *flock breeding Mares.*
To struggle, *to strive*, or *contend earnestly.*
A Struggler.
A Strumpet, or *common whore.*
Strung, (*from to* string)
To strut, or *stalk proudly along.*
A Stub, or *stump.*
To stub *up*, or *grub up.*
A Stub-nail.
Stubbed, *short and well set.*
Stubble, or *short straw, left after the Corn is reaped.*
A Stubble-goose.
Stubborn, *self-willed*, *obstinate*, or *refractary.*
Stubbornness.
I Stuck, or *did* stick,
A Stuckle *of Corn.*
A Stud, *for a robe, watch-case*, &c.
A Stud, *in building.*
A Stud, *or* stode, *a great company*, or *breed of horses.*
Studded, or *set out with* studs, or *gems.*
A Student, *one that* studies *any Art*, or *Science.*
Studious, *much addicted to* study; or *very desirous.*
Studiousness.
Study, *and*
To study, or *apply one's mind to a thing.*
A Study, *a closet to* study *in*; or *a library.*
Stuff, *and to* stuff (*in several senses.*)
Houshold-stuff.
Kitchen-stuff.
Stuke, a *kind of morter fit for imagery, made of chalk and marble well pounded together and sifted.*
Stum, *the flower of wine, set in a ferment.*
To stum wine, *to put certain ingredients into sick* or *decayed wine, to revive it and make it brisk*
To stumble, *to trip, to make a scruple*, or *difficulty.*
A Stumbling-block, *an occasion of scandal*, or *offence.*
A Stump *of a tree, leg, tooth*, &c.
Stump-footed.
To stump, *bounce*, & *brag*, (*in a burlesque sense.*)
To stun *amaze*, or *astonish.*
Stung (*from to* sting.)
Stupendious, *prodigious*, or *wonderfull.*
Stupid, *blockish, dull*, or *senseless.*
Stupidity.
To stupify, or *make stupid.*
Sturdiness, *a being*
Sturdy, *bold, robust*, or *insolent.*
A Sturgeon, *a sea-fish.*
To stutter, or *stammer.*
A Stutterer.
A Sty, or *hog-stye.*
A Swine-sty.
A Pig-sty.
A Sty, or *little swelling upon the eye-lid.*
A Style, *a manner of expression*; or *an account of time.*
The Style, or *needle of a dial*,
To style *call, name*, or *term.*
Styptick, *astringent*, or *of a binding nature*; as *a* styptick *water, that stanches blood.*

SU

Suasory, *that tends to perswade.*
Subaltern, *or* subalternate, *that succeeds by turns*; or *is appointed under another.*
A Sub-Brigadeer, *an Officer next under the* Brigadeer.
A Sub-Chanter, *an inferiour* Chanter *in a Cathedral*, or *Collegiate Church.*
A Sub-Commissioner.
A Sub-Deacon.
A Sub-Dean.
A Sub-Delegate, *or subdelegate judge.*
To subdelegate, *substitute*, or *appoint another to act under himself.*
To subdivide, or *divide a second time.*
A Subdivision.
To subdue, *conquer, vanquish*, or *mortify.*
A Subduer.
Subject, or *liable.*
A Subject, *one that depends on a Soveraign Prince*; also *the argument of a discourse*, &c.
To subject, *subdue*, or *bring under.*
Subjection.
To subjoin, *annex, joyn*, or *add to.*
Sublimate, or *white mercury, a corrosive powder us'd by Surgeons to consume corrupt flesh.*
Sublime, or *lofty.*
To sublime, or *refine.*
A Sublimeness, sublimity, or *loftiness of style.*
The Sub-marshal, or *under Marshal of the Marshalsea.*
Submiss, or submissive.
Submission, *respect*, or *resignation.*
Submissive, *humble*, or *respectfull.*
To submit, *to be subject, to yield*, or *refer a thing*

to another's judgment.
Subordinate, or *inferiour.*
To subordinate, or *appoint under another.*
A Subordination.
To suborn, *to bring in a false Witness, to prepare,* or *instruct him under hand.*
Subordination.
A Suborner.
A Subpœna, *a Writ of citation to appear in a Court of Judicature, under the penalty of* 100 *l.*
To sub-pœna *a Witness,* or *cite him in such a manner.*
A Sub-Reader, or *under-reader, in the Inns of Court.*
To subscribe, *sign,* or *set one's hand at the bottom of a writing.*
A Subscriber.
A Subscription.
Subsequent, or *immediately following.*
Subserviency, *a being*
Subservient, or *helpfull.*
A Subsidy, *aid, tax,* or *tribute granted to the King, upon some urgent occasions.*
To subsist, *to hold out,* or *bear up.*
A Subsistence, or *livelihood.*
Substance, *being, essence, goods, estate, wealth, firmness,* &c.
Substantial, *belonging thereto.*
A Substitute, or *deputy.*
To substitute, or *appoint in the room of another.*
A Substitution.
To substract, *or* subtract, *to take one number out of another.*
Subtraction, *a rule in* Arithmetick.
A Subterfuge, *shift,* or *evasion.*
Subterraneous, *that is under ground.*
Subtil, *or* subtle; *thin, fine, shrewd, witty, cunning,* &c.
Subtilty.
A Subversion, or *ruin.*
To subvert, or *over-throw.*
A Sub-Vicar, or *under-vicar.*
A Sub-vicarship.
A Suburb, *that part of a City,* or *Town, which lies without the walls.*
To succeed, *to come in the room of another, to take place after; to go well forward,* or *be prosperous.*
Success, *a good,* or *bad issue of an affair.*
Successfull.
Successless.
A Succession.
Successive, *that follows one after another.*
A Successour, *he that succeeds another in a place.*
Succinct, *compendious, short,* or *brief.*
Succinctness.
Succory, *an herb.*
Gum-succory.
Swines-succory, or *hawkweed.*
Succour, *help,* or *relief.*
To succour, *aid, help,* or *relieve.*
A Succourer.
Succourless, *destitute of* succour.
Such, such as it is, *&c.*
Suck, as *to give* suck.
To suck, *or* suck *in.*
A Suck-stone, or *sea-lamprey.*
A Sucker.
A Sucking-bottle, *for Children.*
The Sucker *of a pump.*
Suckers of *trees; unprofitable shoots, that spring out of the root,* or *side of the stock.*
To suckle, or *give* suck.
A Suckling, or *sucking child.*
Sudden, *speedy,* or *unexpected.*
Suddenness.
Sudorifick, or *causing sweat.*
Suds, or *sope-suds.*
To sue, *press,* or *put in for a thing.*
To sue, or *prosecute, at Law.*
The hawk sues, or *whets her beak.*
To suffer, *bear, endure, permit,* or *tolerate.*
Sufferable, or *tolerable.*
Sufferance.
A Bill of Sufferance.
Long-sufferance, or *long-suffering.*
A Sufferer.
To suffice, or *be enough.*
Sufficiency, or *ability.*
Sufficient, *that suffices, able,* or *capable.*
To suffocate, *smother, choak,* or *stifle.*
A Suffocation.
A Suffragan, *a Bishop's vicar;* or *a Bishop that is subordinate to an Arch-bishop.*
A Suffrage, *voice,* or *vote at an Election.*
A Suffusion, *a pin,* or *web in the Eye.*
A Sug, or *sea-flea.*
Sugar, *the juice of* Indian *reeds, boil'd, clarify'd and bak'd.*
To sugar, or *sweeten with* sugar.
Loaf-sugar.
Powder-sugar.
A Sugar-baker.
A Sugar-box.
A Sugar-cane.
Sugar-candy.
A Sugar-loaf.
Sugar-Sops.
Sugary; as a *sugary sweetness.*
To suggest, *prompt,* or *put into one's mind.*
A Suggester.
A Suggestion.
A Suit, *a request,* or *a legal process.*

A Suit, *at cards.*
A Suit of *clothes.*
To suit, or *agree.*
Suitable, *agreeable*, or *convenient.*
Suitableness.
A Suiter, *a petitioner*, or *wooer.*
Sullen, *sowr*, *morose*, or *peevish.*
Sullenness.
To sully, *dawb*, *dirty*, or *defile.*
Sulphur, or *brimstone.*
Sulphureous, *belonging to* or *mingled with* sulphur.
Sulphur-wort, *an herb.*
Sultan (*i. e.* Earl, *or* Soveraign) *a title given to the Emperour of the* Turks.
A Sultaness, *a* Sultan's *Wife*, or *Empress.*
A Sultanin, *a* Turkish *coin worth about 7s. 10d.*
Sultry, or *excessive hot.*
Sumach, *a sort of shrub.*
Red Sumach.
A Summ of *Money.*
The Summ, or *substance of a discourse.*
To Summ *up*, or *cast up accounts.*
Summage, *or* sumage, *a toll paid for horse-carriage.*
Summary, *short*, or *brief.*
A Summary, or *abridgment.*
A Full-summ'd, or *well fledg'd hawk.*
Summer, *the hot season of the year.*
A Summer-house.
Summer-quarters.
Summer-weather.
A Summer, *a sort of beam.*
A Summer-tree, *full of mortises, for the end of joysts to lye in.*
To summer, or *pass the* summer.
To summon, *to cite to a Court of Judicature*, or *to demand the surrender of a place.*
A Summoner, sumner, or *Apparitor.*
A Summons.
A Sumpter-horse, or *pack-horse, that carries necessaries for a journey.*
A Sumpter-saddle.
Sumptuous, *costly*, *stately* or *magnificent.*
Sumptuousness.
The Sun, *the source of heat and light.*
The Sun-beams, or *rays of the* sun.
Sun-burnt, or *scorch'd with the sun-beams.*
Sun-dew, *an herb.*
A Sun-dial.
The Sun-rising.
The Sun-set.
The Sun-shine.
A Sun-shiny *day.*
To sun, *to set*, or *dry in the* Sun.
Sunday, *the first day of the Week, so call'd ever since the heathen* Saxons *dedicated it to the Idol of the sun.*
Palm-sunday.
Rogation-sunday.
Whit-sunday.
Sundry, *several*, or *divers.*
Sung (*from to* sing.)
Sunk (*from to* sink.)
Sunny, or *expos'd to the sun.*
A Sup; as *to take a* sup.
To sup, or *be at* supper.
To sup, *or* sup *up broth*, &c.
To superabound, *to be over and above.*
Superabundance, or *excessive plenty.*
To superadd, or *add over and above.*
Superannuated, *worn out with age*, or *past the best*
Supercilious, *proud*, *arrogant*, or *haughty.*
Superciliousness.
Supereminence, *singular excellency*, or *prerogative.*
Supereminently, or *extraordinarily.*
To supererogate, *to give*, or *do more than is required.*
Supererogation.
A Superfetation, *a second conception*; or *the breeding of young upon young.*
Superficial, *belonging to a* superficies; *outward light*, or *perfunctory.*
A Superficies, *or* surface; *the outside of a thing. In* Geometry, *an extent in length and breadth, without depth, whose bounds are call'd lines.*
Superfine, or *exceeding fine.*
Superfluity, *that which is*
Superfluous, *over-much*, or *more than needs.*
To superinduce, *to bring in over and above, to cover*, or *draw over.*
Superinstitution; as *when one clerk is admitted and instituted to a Benefice upon one title, & another is likewise instituted to it by the presentment of another.*
Superintendency, *the office of*
A Superintendent, or *chief overseer.*
Superiority, *a being*
Superiour, *higher*, or *above others in dignity.*
A Superiour (*in* Printing) *a small letter plac'd above a material word, which directs by a like letter to the marginal citation.*
Superiours, *Magistrates*, or *persons in any eminent station.*
Superlative, *of the highest degree*, *very eminent*, or *extraordinary.*
Supernal, *that comes from above.*

Supernatural, *that goes beyond the course of nature.*
Supernumerary, *above the usual number.*
To superscribe, or *write on the outside of a letter,* &c.
A Superscriber.
A Superscription.
To supersede, *to omit the doing of a thing; to forbear,* or *countermand.*
A Supersedeas, *a Writ to stay the doing of that which otherwise ought to be done, according to* Law.
Superstition, *idolatrous worship; vain timorousness,* or *idle scrupulosity, in matters of* Religion.
Superstitious, *addicted to superstition,* or *bigotted.*
To superstruct, or *build upon*; as to superstruct *one thing upon another.*
A Superstructure.
To supervene, or *come unlooked for.*
To supervise, or *oversee.*
A Superviser, or *overseer.*
Supine, *idle, careless,* or *negligent.*
Supineness.
A Supper, or *meal at night.*
The blessed Sacrament of the Lord's Supper.
Supper-time.
Supperless, *that has no* supper.
To supplant, *undermine, circumvent,* or *deceive.*
A Supplanter.
Supple, *soft,* or *limber.*
To supple, or *make* supple.
Suppleness *(from* supple.*)*
A Supplement, or *addition to an History,* &c.
Suppletory, *that serves to supply some imperfection.*
A Suppliant, or *humble petitioner.*

To supplicate, *beseech, entreat,* or *make humble request.*
A Supplication.
Supplies, or *recruits of military Forces.*
A Supply, *aid,* or *relief.*
To supply, *fill up, furnish, relieve,* or *succour.*
A Support, *help,* or *stay.*
To support, *bear up, maintain, aid,* or *favour.*
Supportable, or *tolerable.*
A Supporter.
Supporters, *images that seem to bear up a building.*
The Supporters *of a coat of Arms.*
To suppose, *think, imagine,* or *put the case.*
A Supposition, or supposal.
Supposititious, *put in the place of another, forged,* or *counterfeit.*
A Suppository, *a remedy apply'd outwardly to the fundament to loosen the belly.*
To suppress, *to keep under, to put a stop to, to conceal,* &c.
A Suppression.
A Suppresser.
To suppurate, *to matter,* or *run with matter*; as *a sore does.*
A Suppuration.
Suppurative.
A Supputation, or *reckoning.*
Supremacy, *primacy, supreme,* or *soveraign power.*
The Oaths of Allegiance *and* Supremacy.
Supreme, *highest of all,* or *soveraign.*
The Surbate, *a bruise under a horse's foot, occasion'd by travelling too long unshod.*

Surbated, or *seiz'd with the* surbate.
To surcease, or *give over.*
A Surcharge, *and*
To surcharge, or *overload the stomack.*
A Surcingle, *a Parson's girdle.*
A Surcoat, or *upper coat* also *a coat of mail blazon'd with arms.*
Sure, *certain, safe, stedfast, faithful,* &c.
Sure-footed, *that does not stumble.*
Sureness, *a being* sure.
A Surety, *a bail,* or *security*; also *one that undertakes for a Child.*
A Suretiship.
A Surface, or *outside of a thing.*
A Surfeit, or *surcharge of stomack, by immoderate eating,* or *drinking.*
To surfeit *himself.*
Surfeit-water.
A Surge, *billow,* or *wave of the sea.*
To surge, or *rise up in* surges.
A Surgeon, or Chirurgeon, *one skill'd in*
Surgery, *an Art,* or *manual operation, whereby we endeavour to cure the outward diseases of the humane body, by the help* or *assistance of the hands; in* Latine Chirurgia, *from the* Greek *words* Cheir, *a hand, and* ergon, *a work.*
The Surgery, or *place where Chirurgical operations are perform'd.*
Surliness, or *a surly humour.*
A Surloyn *of beef, a joint so call'd.*
Surly, *testy, morose,* or crabbed.
A Surmise, *and*
To surmise, *imagine,* or *have a suspicion of.*

To

To surmount, *surpass, excell*, or *overcome*.
A Surname, *the name of one's family*.
To surname *one*, or *give him a* surname.
K. William I. surnam'd *the Conqueror*.
To surpass, *go beyond, exceed*, or *excell*.
A Surplice, *a linnen-vestment worn by Clergymen that officiate at Divine Service*.
A Surplus, *or* surplusage, *an addition more than needs*.
A Surprisal, *or* surprise.
To surprise, *to take unawares*, or *amaze*.
Surprizing, *that causes* surprise, *strange*, or *wonderful*.
A Surrejoynder, *a second defence of the Plaintiff's action, opposite to the Defendant's* rejoinder.
A Surrender, *or* surrendry.
To surrender, *give*, or *yield up*.
Surreptitious, or *done by stealth*.
A Surrogate, or *Bishop's Chancellour*.
To surrogate, *substitute*, or *put in the place of another*.
To surround, *go round*, or *encompass*.
A Sursengle, *a long upper girth, to come over the pad*, or *saddle*.
A Survey, or *general view*.
To survey, *view, look about, oversee*, or *measure*.
A Surveyer, *or* surveyor, *of land*, &c.
A Surveyor *of the King's buildings, high-ways*, &c.
A Surveyorship.
To survive, or *out-live*.
A Surviver, *or* Survivor.
Survivorship, *or* Survivance,

Susceptible, *apt to take an impression*, &c.
To suspect, *fear*, or *mistrust*.
Suspectfull, *apt to* suspect, or *distrustfull*.
Suspence, *doubt*, or *uncertainty of mind*.
To suspend, *to hold in* suspence, or *to deprive of an office, for a time*.
A Suspension.
Suspicion, *mistrust*, or *jealousy*.
Suspicious, *that may be suspected*; or *apt to suspect*.
To sustain, *maintain and bear up*, or *to suffer*.
Sustenance, *food*, or *nourishment*.
A Sutler, or *camp-victualer*.

S W

A Swab, or *bean-cod*.
A Swabber, *a ship-drudge, that makes clean the ship*.
A Swad, or *pease-cod shell*.
To swaddle, *to swathe*, or *bind with swathing-clouts*; or *to cudgel one*.
To swag, *force down*, or *hang down*.
A Swag-belly.
To swagger, *boast, vaunt, huff*, or *play the hector*.
A Swaggerer.
A Swain, *a Country-clown*.
A Boatswain *of a ship*; *an Officer that manages the long boat and its crew*.
A Cock-swain, *that looks after the cock-boat*.
A Shepherd-swain.
A Swainmote, *a Court that takes cognizance of Forest-affairs*.
A Swallow, *a bird*.
The Sea-swallow, *a flying fish*.
A Swallow, or *gulph*, &c.

To swallow, or swallow *down*; as *to swallow a pill*.
To swallow, swallow *up*, or *devour*.
A Swallow-tail (*in Joiners-work*) *a particular way of fastening two pieces of timber strongly together*.
Swallow-wort, *an herb*.
I Swam, or *did* swim.
A Swamp, or swomp, *a little Dale, moorish valley* or *Pasture*.
A Swan, *a fowl*.
Swans-skin, *a sort o flannel, so call'd from its extraordinary whiteness*.
To swap, *barter, truck*, or *exchange*.
The Sward, or *rind of bacon*.
The Green-sward *of the earth*.
A Swarm *of bees, ants, lice*, &c.
To swarm, *as bees do*.
To swarm, *appear in great numbers*, or *to be full of vermin*.
Swarthiness, *a being*
Swarthy, *of a tawny complexion*.
A Swash, or *torrent of water*.
To swash, or *make fly about*.
A Swash-buckler, *a vain-glorious sword-player, meer braggadochio*, or *vapouring fellow*.
A Swath, or swarth, *a row of cut grass, barley*, &c.
A Swathe, *or* swathing-band.
To swathe *a young Child*, or *to wrap it up with swathing-clouts*.
Sway, *rule*, or *dominion*.
To sway, *bear* sway, or *govern*,
To sweal, or *melt away waste-*

wastefully; as *a candle does.*
A Sweap, *or* swipe *for a well*, &c.
To swear, *to take an Oath*, or *to give one his Oath.*
A Swearer.
Sweat; *an excrement of the body.*
To sweat, *to be in a* sweat or *to cause one to sweat.*
A Sweater.
The Sweating-sickness.
Sweaty, or *full of sweat.*
To sweep, or *cleanse with a broom.*
To sweep *away*, or *destroy in great numbers.*
A Sweeper.
A Sweep-net, or *drag*, *a sort of fishing-net.*
The hawk sweeps, or *wipes her beak.*
A Sweep-stakes, *one that gets all the stakes.*
The Sweepage, or *crop of hay in a meadow.*
A Sweeper.
A Chimney-sweeper.
Sweet, *pleasant to the taste*, or *smell*; *charming*, or *agreeable.*
A Sweet-bag, *to perfume clothes.*
A Sweet-ball.
The Sweet-bread *of a breast of veal*, &c.
The Sweet-brier *shrub.*
Sweet Cistus, *an herb.*
A Sweet-heart, or *lover.*
A Sweet-lips, or *liquorish fellow.*
Sweet-meats.
Sweet-natured, or *sweet-conditioned.*
Sweet-scented, or *perfumed.*
Sweet-smelling.
Sweet-spoken, or *eloquent.*
The Sweet-rush.
Sweet-William, *or* sweet-John, *a flower.*
To sweeten, or *make* sweet.
A Sweeting, *an apple.*
Sweetish, or *somewhat sweet.*
Sweetness.
To swell, *rise up*, *puff up*, or *bunch out.*
A Swelling, *bunch*, *bump*, or *unnatural gathering together of any corrupt matter in the body.*
To swelter, or *broil with excessive heat.*
Sweltry, *or* sultry *weather.*
Swept (*from to* sweep.)
To swerve, *decline*, *depart from*, or *go out of the right way.*
Swift, *quick*, *nimble*, or *rapid.*
A Swift, or *martin*, *a kind of swallow*, *with legs so short*, *that it cannot rise from the ground.*
Swift-footed.
Swifters, *certain ropes belonging to the masts to keep them stiff*, *and strengthen the shrouds.*
Swiftness.
Swill, or *hogg-wash.*
To swill, or *drink greedily.*
A Swill-bowl, or *lusty toper.*
To swim, *in the water*, or *in pleasures*; *to float*, or *sail.*
A Swimmer.
A Swimming, *of the head*, or *dizziness.*
A Swine, *hog*, or *sow.*
Swine-bread, *an herb.*
A Swine-herd.
A Swine-pipe, *a bird.*
The Swine-pox.
Swines-cresses, } *herbs.*
Swines-grass, }
A Swine-sty.
A Swing, *and to* swing (*in several senses.*)
To swinge *off*, or *chastise severely*, *with words*, or *blows.*
Swinging, *huge*, or *exceeding great*: as *a* swinging stomack.
A Swinger, or *a* swinging *lye*, &c.
A Swingle-staff, *to beat flax with.*
A Swipe; *an engine to draw up water*, or *to throw granadoes.*
A Switch, *rod*, or *wand.*
To switch, or *strike with a* switch.
A Swivle *of iron*, *that turns round about.*
A Swoling, *of Land*, i. e. *as much as one plough can till in a year.*
Swoln (*from to* swell.)
I Swom, or *did* swim.
A Swoon, *and*
To swoon *away*, or *faint.*
To Swop, swap, or *change one thing for another.*
A Sword, *a weapon.*
A Two-edged Sword.
A Two-handed Sword.
A Sword-bearer; *an Officer that carries the sword before a Magistrate.*
The Sword-fish.
Sword-grass, or *gladder*; *a kind of sedge.*
A Sword-hanger.
A Sword-player.
Swore, *and* sworn (*from to* swear.)
Swung (*from to* swing.)

S Y

A Sycomore-tree.
A Sycophant, *properly an informer amongst the ancient* Athenians *that gave notice of the transportation of figs contrary to their Law*: *Whence the word is taken to denote any false accuser*, *tell-tale*, or *pick-thank.*
Syder, or Cider, *a drink made of apples.*
A Syllable, *a sound formed of one* or *more letters.*
A Syllogism, or *logical way of arguing.*

Syllogistical, *belonging to such disputations.*

A Symbol *a badge, sign, token, cognizance, motto,* or *device.*

Symbolical, *belonging thereto.*

To symbolize, or *represent by* symbols; *as an eye* symbolizes *vigilancy.*

Symmetry, *a due proportion,* or *uniformity, of each part in respect to the whole.*

Sympathetical, *or* sympathetick, *that partakes of a sympathy.*

To Sympathize, or *act according to*

A Sympathy, (i.e. *fellow-suffering*) *the natural agreement of things; a conformity in passions, dispositions,* or *affections.*

A Symphony, *a melodious harmony,* or *musical consort.*

A Symptom, *an accident, that happens to a disease; a sign, a token discovering what the distemper is.*

A Synagogue, *a Congregation,* or *religious assembly among the* Jews; or *the place where they meet.*

A Syndick, or *chief magistrate of* Geneva.

A Syndickship.

A Synod, *Convocation, Council,* or *Assembly of Clergy-men.*

Synodal, *or* Synodical, *belonging to,* or *acted in a Synod.*

A Synodal, *a duty formerly paid by the inferior Clergy, to a Bishop,* or *Arch-deacon,* at Easter-*Visitation.*

Synonymous, *of the same name,* or *of the same signification.*

A Syringe, *a kind of squirt us'd by Surgeons to inject medicinal liquors into a sore.*

To syringe *an ulcer,* &c.

A Syrup, *a decoction made of the juice of plants,* or *fruits and sugar boil'd up to a due consistence.*

A System, *the body of any Art,* or *science.*

Systematical, *belonging thereto.*

T A

Tabby, *a sort of waved silk.*

A Tabby-cat.

A Tabby-petticoat.

A Taber, tabor, *or* tabret, *a kind of drum.*

The Taber and pipe.

A Taberer, *one that plays on the* taber.

A Tabernacle, *tent,* or *booth.*

The Feast of Tabernacles, *kept by the* Jews *for seven days together, in remembrance that their Fathers liv'd for a long time in tents, after their departure out of* Egypt.

A Table *for meat, to write upon,* &c; *also an* Index, or *collection of the Chapters,* or *principal matters in a book.*

To table, *to board, to entertain,* or *be entertain'd at table.*

A Table-basket.

Table-beer, or *small beer, that which is usually drank at meals.*

A Table-bed.

A Table-book.

A Table-cloth.

A Table diamond.

Table-plate.

Table talk, or *discourse at table.*

A Tabler, or *boarder at table.*

Tables, or *a pair of* tables, *to play at.*

A Table-man.

A Tablet, or *little table*

A Tabret, or *taber.*

Taces, *an armour for the thighs.*

A Tack, *hook, buckle,* or *clasp.*

Tacit, *not express'd*; as *a tacit consent,* or *approbation.*

Taciturnity, *silence,* or *a reserved humour.*

A Tack, or *little nail.*

To tack, or *fasten with tacks.*

To tack about (*a sea-term*) *to bring the ship's head about, so as to lye quite the other way.*

A Tack-wind.

Tackles, *small ship-ropes to heave in goods,* &c.

Tackling, or *furniture.*

Kitchen-tackling.

Ship-tackling.

Tacks, *certain great ropes that serve to carry the clew forward, and keep the sail close by the wind.*

A Tadpole, *a young frog,* or *toad.*

Taffety, *a sort of silk.*

Striped taffety.

Tuff-taffety.

A Taffety-tart, *a tart made of puff-paste.*

A Tag *of a lace,* or *point.*

To tag, or *set on a tag.*

A Tag-rag, or *beggerly fellow.*

The Tail *of a beast, comet, gown,* &c.

The Plough-tail.

Tailed, *that has a tail.*

A Tailer, *one that cuts out, and makes up suits of clothes.*

A Tainct, *a kind of small red spider, that infests cattel in the summer.*

A Taint, *blur,* or *spot.*

To Taint, or *corrupt.*

To take (*in all senses.*)

Taken.

A Taker, or *reciever.*

A Talbot, *a kind of hunting-dog.*
A Tale, *an idle story*, or *a reckoning.*
A Tell-tale, *make-bate*, or *whisperer.*
A Tale-bearer, or *spreader, of reports.*
A Talent, *a certain summ of money, among the ancients*; also *a natural endowment*, or *faculty.*
The Talent of silver, (*among the* Hebrews) *contain'd about* 375 *l. and that of* Gold 4500 *l.* The *lesser* talent *among the* Greeks, *was worth about* 175 *l. and the greater valu'd at* 233 *l. Sterling.*
A Talisman, *a magical image*, or *figure, made under certain Constellations, according to the keeping*, or *wasting of which the person represented by it, is preserv'd*, or *wastes away.*
A Talismanist, *one that makes* Talismans, or *gives credit to 'em.*
Talk, *a kind of transparent mineral, of which a curious white wash is usually made.*
Talk, or *discourse.*
To talk, or *hold a talk.*
It is Town-talk.
Talk-worthy, *that deserves to be* talked of.
Talkative, *much given to talk.*
Talkativeness.
A Talker.
Talkt, *or* talked *of.*
Tall, *proper, high*; as *a tall person, a tall tree*, &c.
Tallage, *custom*, or *impost.*
A Talley, or *score kept on a cleft piece of wood mark'd with notches.*
Tallow, *made of the fat of beasts.*
Tallowish, or *full of tallow.*
Talness, (*from* tall.)
A Talon, or *claw of a bird.*
Tamarinds, *a sort of* Indian *fruit, the tree of which, is like a date-tree.*
A Tamarisk, *a kind of shrub.*
Tame, *gentle, submissive*; *cowardly*, or *mean-spirited.*
To tame, or *make* tame.
Tameness.
A Tamer *of wild beasts.*
To tamper *with one*, or *feel his pulse.*
The Tampin, tampkin, or *stopple of a great gun in a ship.*
Tamy, *a sort of stuff.*
To tan *in the Sun*, or *to dress leather.*
A Tan-house.
A Tang, *smatch*; or *ill taste.*
To tangle, or *entangle.*
A Tankard *to drink out of.*
A Silver-tankard.
A Tankard *to carry water from a conduit.*
A Tankard-bearer.
A Tanner *of leather.*
Tansy, *an herb.*
Maudlin-tansy.
Wild tansy.
To tantalize, *to deceive under a specious shew*; or *to make one eager for a thing, and yet not suffer him to enjoy it.*
A Tantalizer, *one that puts another into the condition of*
Tantalus, *the son of* Jupiter, *who (as the story goes) having killed, dressed and serv'd up his son* Pelops *at a feast made for the Gods*; *was set in water up to the chin, and surrounded with delicious apples bobbing him on the lips*; *yet had he no power to stoop to the one, to quench his thirst, nor to reach up to the other, to satisfy his hungry appetite.*
Tantamount, *that amounts to as much, equivalent*; or *of like value.*
To ride tantivy, or *full speed.*
A Tap *for a vessel, and* To tap, or *set a-broach.*
The Hare taps, *or* beats, i. e. *makes a noise.*
A Tap-house, or *storehouse for drink in an Inn*, &c.
A Tap, rap, or *blow.*
Tape, *a sort of thread-ribbon.*
Tape-lace.
Taper, *broad beneath, and sharp towards the top.*
A Taper, or *torch.*
A Wax-taper.
Tapestry, *clothes wrought with pictures of divers colours.*
Tapestry-hangings.
A Tapestry-maker.
To tappy, or *lye hid*, as *a deer does.*
A Tapster, *one that draws liquors.*
Taptoo, *a particular way of drumming*; as *to beat the* taptoo *in a garrison.*
Tar, or *liquid pitch.*
A Tarand, *a kind of buffle*, or *wild Ox.*
A Tarantula, *a venomous spider, ash-colour'd, speckled with little white and black*, or *red and green spots. 'Tis so call'd from* Taranto, *a City of* Naples, *where they abound, and its sting is said to be cur'd only by musick.*
Tardiness, *a being*
Tardy, *slow, dull, slack*, or *faulty.*
Tare, *or* darnel, *a plant that grows among Corn.*
Tare, *and* tret, *the first word*

word denotes the weight of box, straw, bail-cloth, &c. *in which* Goods *are pack'd up; the other is an allowance for waste in emptying,* &c.

A Target, *a kind of great shield.*

To tarnish, or *lose its brightness, as plate does*

A Tarpawling, *a piece of tarred canvass, commonly laid over the gratings in a ship to keep off the heat of the Sun and showers of rain.* Also *a downright Sailer,* or *common Seaman.*

Tarragon, *or* dragon-wort, *an herb.*

Tarras, *a kind of plaister,* or *strong morter.*

To tarry, *abide,* or *remain; to delay,* or *linger.*

Tart, *sharp,* or *smart.*

A Tart, or *little pie, made of fruit,* as

An Apple-tart.

An Apricock-tart.

A Cherry-tart

A Curran-tart.

A Gooseberry-tart.

A Plum-tart, &c.

Tartar, *the lees of wine, that stick to the sides of wine-vessels.*

Tartness, *a being tart,* or *sharp.*

A Task, *a piece of work set out, or appointed.*

A Task-master.

A Tassel, or *small ribban,* &c. *sowed to a book, to serve for a mark.*

A Tassel-hawk, or *male hawk.*

The Tassels *of a coach, the silk-cords that are fasten'd on each side the doors, and serve for a stay to those that sit therein.*

The Taste, *one of the five Senses.*

To taste, or *relish*

A Taster; *as the* King's Taster, or *Cup-bearer.*

A Taster, or *little cup, to taste liquors with.*

Tasteless, *that has no* taste, or *insipid.*

A Tatter, or *rag.*

A Tatterdemallion, *a shabby nasty fellow.*

A tattered, or *ragged housewife.*

To tattle, *prattle,* or *babble.*

A Tattle-basket, or *talkative person.*

A Tavern, *to sell wine in.*

A Tavern-haunter.

A Tavern-keeper.

Taught (*from to* teach.)

A Taunt, *a reproachfull,* or *scurrilous jest.*

To taunt, *rail,* or *revile.*

A Taunter.

A Taunt-mast, *a mast too high for the proportion of a ship.*

Taunt-masted, *that has such a mast.*

A Tautology, *a saying,* or *repeating of the same thing over again.*

To taw, or *tan leather.*

A Tawer, tawyer, or *tanner.*

Tawdry, *ridiculously, gay,* q. d. *made fine with*

Tawdry-lace, *such as is usually bought at* Audery-*Fair in* Cambridgshire.

Tawny, *of a tann'd,* or *swarthy complexion.*

A Tax, *tallage,* or *impost.*

To Tax, *impose a tax,* or *rate;* also *to censure, accuse,* or *charge one with.*

A Land-tax.

A Poll-tax.

A Tax-gatherer.

Taxable, or *liable to pay* taxes.

A Taxation, or *valuation.*

A Taxer.

A Taylor, or tailer.

A Tazel, *or* teazel, *a kind of hard burr, us'd by Clothiers in dressing clothes.*

T E

Tea, *a plant, and the liquor made of its leaves.*

To teach, or *instruct.*

Teachable, *apt,* or *willing to be taught.*

A Teacher.

A Teal, *a delicate fowl.*

A Team, or *set of horses,* or *oxen for a cart, waggon, plow,* &c.

A Team, or *flock of ducks.*

A Tear, *let fall in weeping.*

To tear, or *rend in pieces,* or *to rant and roar.*

A tearing Lass, *one that that is high-flown,* or *exceeding fine.*

To teaz, *vex,* or *disquiet one continually.*

A Teazel, teazle, *or* tazel, *the* Fuller's-thistle, or *Clothier's burr.*

A Teat, *nipple,* or *dug.*

Techy, touchy, or *froward.*

To Ted, or *strew grass.*

A Tedder, *or* tether, *a rope with which a horse's leg is tyed to hinder him from grazing beyond a set compass.*

To tedder, or *bind with a* tedder.

Tedious, *troublesome, irksome, over-long,* or *long-winded.*

Tediousness.

To teem, or *be with child.*

Teeth (*from* tooth) as *a good set of teeth.*

A Teil-tree, or *linden-tree.*

A Telescope, or *prospective glass.*

To tell, *say,* or *declare; to count,* or *reckon.*

A Teller.

Tel-

Tellers in the Exchequer, *four Officers, whose business it is to receive and pay all the Moneys upon the King's account.*

A Fortune-teller.

Temerity, or *rashness.*

A Temper, or *natural disposition.*

To temper, *moderate, allay, mingle,* or *season.*

An Even-temper'd *Man.*

A Temperament, *mixture of natural humours, constitution of body,* or *a medium in a perplex'd business.*

Temperance, *a vertue that moderates pleasures.*

Temperate, *moderate,* or *sober.*

The Temperateness, or temperature *of the air.*

A Tempest, or *storm of wind, hail,* or *rain.*

Tempestuous, or *stormy.*

Templars, or Knights Templar, *a religious Order instituted by Pope* Gelasius II. *and suppress'd by* Clement V. *They continu'd about* 200 *years, and had a particular Governour in every Nation. The* Master of the Temple *here, was summon'd to Parliament, and the chief Minister of the* Temple-Church *in* London *(formerly in their possession) still bears that title.*

A Temple, *Church,* or *place consecrated to Divine Service.*

The famous Temple *of* Jerusalem.

The Temple, or Templers *Inn, in* Fleet-street, *sometime the chief seat of the Knights* Templars *in* England; *upon the suppression of which Order, it was given to the Knights of St.* John *of* Jerusalem, *whose principal Mansion was St.* John's *Priory near* Smithfield, *and of whom certain eminent professors of the Law under King* Edward III. *obtain'd a perpetual Lease of this Temple, for the yearly rent of ten pounds: Then it was divided into three several Houses,* viz. *the* inner, *the* middle, *and the* outward Temple, *which last, afterwards was* Essex-house: *Their Church yet standing, was consecrated by* Heraclius *Patriarch of* Jerusalem, *A.D.* 1185.

A Templer, or *member of the* Templers-Inn.

The Temples *of the head.*

Temporal, *that continues for a certain time*; or *secular, in opposition to* spiritual; as,

The Lords Spiritual and Temporal *of the upper house of Parliament.*

The Temporalities of Bishops, *the temporal Revenues,* viz. *lands, tenements, and lay-fees, belonging to them, as they are Lords and Barons of Parliament.*

Temporary, *that lasts but for a while.*

To temporize, *observe,* or *comply with the times.*

A Temporizer, or *timeserver.*

To tempt, *prove, try, sollicit, entice,* or *seduce.*

A Temptation.

A Tempter.

Ten, *in number*; as *the ten Commandments.*

Ten-fold.

Tenable, *that may be held,* or *maintain'd*; or *capable of defence.*

Tenacious, *that holds fast, stiff,* or *self-willed*; also *close-fisted, covetous,* or *niggardly.*

Tenacity.

A Tenant, *one that holds or possesses any land,* or *tenement, by any kind of right*; as

A Tenant in chief, *that holds of the King in right of his Crown.*

A Tenant by Copy, or Court-roll, *that is admitted to lands,* &c. *within a Mannor, which time out of mind, have been demisable, according to the particular custom of such a Mannor.*

A Tenant at Will, *that holds at the Will of the* Lord, &c.

A Tench, *a fresh-water fish.*

To tend, *incline,* or *lead to*; *to wait on, look to,* or *take care of.*

A Tendency, *natural inclination,* or *drift.*

Tender, *soft, nice, delicate, feeble,* or *effeminate.*

Tender-eyed.

Tender-hearted.

Tender-heartedness.

A Tender, or *offer.*

To tender, *indulge,* or *favour*; or *to offer.*

Tenderness.

A Tenderling, *the horn of a pricket,* or *young buck.*

A Tendon (*in* Anatomy) *a similar nervous part annex'd to muscles and bones for voluntary motion.*

A Tendrel, *a young tender branch of a tree,* or *plant.*

Tendrels, or *small grisles.*

A Tenement, *messuage, house,* or *cottage.*

A Tenet, or tenent; *an Opinion that is maintain'd,* or *asserted.*

Tennis, *a sort of play.*

A Tennis-ball.

A

A Tennis-court.
A Tenon, *to be let into a mortise-hole*
The Tenor, *effect, substance, purport*, or *true meaning of a Writing*.
The Tenor *in musick*.
The Counter-tenor.
A Tent, *pavilion*, or *booth*.
A Tent-maker.
A Tent *for a wound*.
Tent, *a sort of red wine brought from* Alicant, *in* Spain.
Tent-wort, *an herb*.
A Tenter-hook, *a kind of nail*.
The Tenth *(from* ten.)
Tenths, *the yearly Tribute which Ecclesiastical Livings pay to the King*.
A Tenure, *the manner whereby lands and tenements are held of their respective Lords*.
A Terce, *a certain measure of Wine, Oil*, &c *containing the third part of a Pipe*, or *the fifth part of a Tun*.
Tergiversation, *(i. e.* turning the back, *) a boggling, dodging, shuffling*, or *flinching*.
A Term, *a particular word*, or *expression*; also *a fixed*, or *limited time*.
Term-time.
To term, *call*, or *name*.
The four Terms of the Year, *when the Courts of Judicature are open for all Law-suits*, viz.
Hilary-term, *which begins* Jan. 23, or *(if that be* Sunday) *the next day after, and ends* Feb. 12.
Easter-term, *beginning the* Wednesday *fortnight after* Easter-*day*, *and ending the* Munday *next after* Ascension-*day*.
Trinity-term *begins the* Friday, *next after* Trinity-Sunday, *and ends the* Wednesday *fortnight after*.
Michaelmass-term, *which is the longest, begins* Octob. 23. *(unless it be* Sunday) *and ends* November 28.
To terminate, *limit, bound, decide*, or *end*.
The Termination, or *ending of a word*.
Terminer, as *a Commission of* Oyer *and* Terminer, *i. e hearing and determining*, (or *the tryal of Malefactors*.
Terms, *conditions*, or *womens monthly courses*.
A Terrace *or* terrass, *a bank of earth*, or *an open raised gallery*.
A Terrace-walk.
A Ternary, or *three in number*.
Terrestrial, *belonging to the earth*; as *the* terrestrial Globe, *a Globe, on which the true situation of the earth is represented*.
Terrible, *dreadful*, or *horrible*.
The Herb terrible.
Terribleness.
A Terrier, *an auger*; *to bore with*, or *a sort of hunting-dog*.
To terrify, *strike a terrour into*; or *affright*.
A Territory, or *compass of land, belonging to a City*, or *Town*.
Terrour, dread, or *great fear*.
Terse, *neat*, or *polite*.
A Tertian ague, *that comes every third day*.
A Test, or *tryal of metals*, or *persons*.
A Testament, or *last will*.
The Old and New Testaments, *the two principal parts into which the Bible is divided*.
Testamentary, *of* or *belonging to a testament*
A Testator, *he that has made his* testament, or *last will*.
A Testatrix, *a female* testator.
A Tester *(in Money) a Coin worth six pence*.
The Tester, *or* testern *of a bed*.
The Testicles, *cods*, or *stones of a man*.
A Testification, *testifying* or *witnessing*.
To testify, *attest*, or *bear witness*.
A Testimonial, or *certificate under the hand of a Justice of peace*, &c.
A Testimony, *evidence* or *deposition*; also *(in* Scripture-Phrase) *a Law* or *ordinance*.
Testiness, *a being*
Testy, *morose, peevish*, or *apt to take pet*.
A Tether, *or* tedder *for a Horse's leg*.
A Tetrarch, *a governour of the fourth part of a Country*; as
Herod *the* Tetrarch (*Mat.* 14. 1.
A Tetrarchy, *such a government*.
A Tetter, or *ring-worm*.
Tetter-wort, *an herb*.
To tew, or *tug*.
The Text, or *very words of an author, writing*, or *book, without any comment*, or *note*.
A Text, *a portion of Scripture chosen for the subject of a Sermon*, or *discourse*.
The Text-hand, *in writing*, as
The German Text.
The Church-text.
A Text-letter.
A Text-pen.
A Textuary, *a book containing nothing but the* Text *without any notes*.
A Texture, or *weaving*.

TH

Than; *(in comparison)* as *he is elder* than *I.*
To thank, or *give thanks.*
Thankfull.
Thankfulness, or *gratitude.*
Thanks, *an acknowledgment of kindnesses* or *favours received.*
Thanksgiving.
Thank-worthy.
That, *so* that, *lest* that, *&c.*
Thatch, or *straw.*
To thatch *a house*, or *cover it with* thatch.
A Thatcher.
A Thaw, *and*
To thaw, or *melt as ice does.*
The, *as* the *one of them is living* the *other dead.*
A Theam, *an argument*, or *subject proposed to be treated of.*
A Theater, *a Play-house*, or *stage.*
Thee, *(from* thou*)* as *I fear thee not.*
A Theft, or *robbery.*
Their, *or of* them; as *'tis their folly.*
Theirs, *belonging* to them; as *this is theirs.*
Them; as *it was given to them.*
Then, or *at that time.*
Thence, or *from thence.*
Thenceforth, or *from thenceforth.*
Theological *of*, or *belonging to*,
Theology, or *Divinity.*
A Theorboe-lute, *a musical instrument.*
A Theorem, *a speculative principle*, or *rule in any Art, or Science, more particularly oppos'd to a problem, which relates to practice.*
Theoretick, *or* theorick, *belonging to*
Theory, *contemplation*, or *speculation the knowledge of an Art, abstracted from practice.*
There, *in that place.*
Thereabout, *or* thereabouts.
Thereat, or *at that.*
Therefore, *for that cause.*
Therein, *or in it.*
Thereof, *of that*, or *of them.*
Thereto, *or* thereunto, *to it.*
Thereupon, *upon that.*
Therewith, *or with that.*
These, *the plural of* this; as *these persons.*
They, as *they are afraid.*
Thick, *gross, close, muddy,* &c.
The Thick *of the* Forest.
Thick-set, or *close-set.*
Thick-skinn'd.
Thick-wrought, or *close-work'd.*
To thicken, *to make*, or *grow thick.*
A Thicket, *a place full of bushes and brambles.*
Thickness.
A Thief, or *robber.*
To thieve, *steal*, or *filch.*
Thievery, or *the practice of* thieving.
Thieves, *the plural of* thief.
Thievish, or *apt to steal.*
Thievishness.
A Thigh, *a part of the body.*
The Thigh-bone.
The Thill, *team*, or *draught-tree of a Cart.*
A Thiller, or *thill-horse.*
A Thimble, *us'd in sowing with a needle.*
Thin, *rare, light, subtil, lean,* &c.
To thin, or *make thin.*
Thin-bodied.
Thine, *belonging* to thee; as *this is thine.*
A Thing, *affair, matter*, or *business.*
Something, *or* somewhat.
To think, *muse, reflect on, imagine, suppose,* &c.
A Thinker.
Thinness (*from* thin)
The third, *in number.*
A Third, or *third part.*
A Third, or *tierce, in musick.*
To thirl, *drill*, or *bore.*
Thirst, or *drowth, a great desire to drink*, or *to possess any thing.*
To thirst, *to have*, or *endure thirst.*
Thirsty, or *dry.*
Blood-thirsty, *that thirsts after blood.*
Thirteen, *the number*, (q.d. three *and* ten)
The thirteenth.
The Thirtieth.
Thirty.
This; *as in this place.*
A Thistle, *an herb.*
Fullers-thistle.
Holy-thistle.
Milk-thistle.
Sow-thistle.
Thither, *to that place,*
Thitherto.
Thitherwards, *towards that place.*
Tho' *for* though.
A Thong *of leather.*
Thonged, or *tied with thongs.*
A Thorn, or *bramble.*
Black-thorn.
Box-thorn.
Buck-thorn.
Christ's thorn.
Ever-green thorn.
Goats-thorn.
Haw-thorn.
Hey-thorn.
White-thorn.
Thorn-apple, *an herb.*
A Thorn-back, *a fish*
A Thorn-back-dog, *a fish*
A Thorn-bush.
Thorny, or *full of thorns*
Thorough, *or* through; as *I went* thorough *that lane.*
A Thorough-change, or *absolute change.*
A Thorough-fare, or *passage through.*

Thorough-

Thorough-paced, *accomplish'd,* or *perfect.*
A Thorp, *a little Town,* or *Village.*
Those, as *those Men, and those Women.*
Thou, thou thy self.
To thou *one, to use* thou *and* thee *in speaking, as the* Quakers *do.*
Though, *or* although.
Thought (*from to* think.)
A Thought, *imagination, consideration, opinion,* or *intention.*
The Merry-thought *of a Capon.*
Thoughtfull, or *pensive.*
Thoughtfulness.
Thoughtlessness, *a being*
Thoughtless, *carelss,* or *regardless.*
A Thousand *in number;* as *a thousand pounds.*
A Thousand *of nails,* &c.
The Thousanth.
Thraldom, *or* thrall; *captivity,* or *slavery.*
A Thrave, or 24 *sheaves of Corn.*
Thread *to sow with.*
A Thread *in cloth, weaving,* &c.
To thread *a needle.*
Thread-bare, *quite worn out.*
Thready, or *full of threads.*
To threaten, *or* threaten *with.*
A Threatener.
Threats, or *menaces.*
Three, or *the number* three.
Three-corner'd; as *a three corner'd cap.*
A Three-footed *stool.*
A Three-forked *tail.*
A Three-headed *monster.*
Three-leaved *grass.*
Three-fold.
Threescore.
To thresh, or *beat Corn.*
A Thresher.
A Threshing-floor.
The Threshold *of a door.*

I threw, or *did throw.*
Thrice, or *three times.*
Thrift, *an herb.*
Thrift, or thriftiness, *savingness,* or *sparingness.*
A Spend-thrift, or *prodigal waster.*
Thrifty, or *frugal.*
To thrill, or *bore.*
To thrive, *to grow mightily, to become rich,* or *prosperous,* &c.
The Throat.
The Throat-band, *or* throat-latch *of a bridle.*
The Throat-piece, or *sticking-piece of a hog.*
The Throat-pipe, or *wind-pipe.*
Throat-wort, *an herb.*
Frog-throated, or *wide-throated.*
To throb, *pant, beat,* or *ake.*
A Throne, *a Royal Seat,* or *Chair of state.*
Thrones, *the third Order,* or *Rank of Angels.*
A Throng, or *crowd.*
To throng, throng *together,* or *make a throng.*
A Throster, *or* Silk-throster, *that winds, twists, and spins silk, to fit it for use.*
A Throstle, *or* thrush, *a bird.*
To throttle (*from* throat) *to choak,* or *strangle.*
I Throve, or *did* thrive.
Through, as *to walk* through, *about,* or *up and down the Town.*
Through-splent, *an horse-disease.*
Through-wax, *an herb.*
Throughout, as *throughout all the year.*
A Throw, *and*
To throw, *fling, hurl,* or *cast.*
A Thrower.
A Silk-thrower, *or* silk-throster.
Thrown.

The Throws, or *pangs of a Woman in labour.*
Thrum, or *woollen shag.*
A Thrum-cap.
A Thrum-mop.
To thrum, or *baste one.*
A Thrush, *a bird.*
A Thrush, *a disease in the mouth.*
A Thrust, *and* to thrust (*in several senses.*)
A Thumb.
To thumb *a book, to dawb it with the* thumbs
A Thump, *blow,* or *bounce.*
To thump, *knock,* or *beat with the fist.*
A Thumper, *a thumping,* or *whisking lye.*
Thunder, *a Meteor.*
To thunder, *to make a great and terrible noise.*
A Thunder-bolt.
A Thunder-clap.
A Thunder-stone.
Thursday, *the fifth day of the Week, on which the Idol* Thor *was worshipped by the ancient* Saxons *and* Teutonicks.
Holy-thursday.
Maundy-thursday.
A Thurse-lowse, *or* sow, *an insect.*
Thus, or *in this manner.*
To thwack, *together,* or *cram close.*
To thwack, or *bang one's sides.*
To lay on thwick-thwack, or *beat one furiously.*
Thwart, or *a-cross.*
To thwart, *cross, oppose, contradict,* &c.
Thy, or thine, as *thy Wife and Children.*
Thyme, *a sweet herb.*

T I

A Tib, *a poor sorry Woman.*
A Tick, *a sort of insect.*
A Bed-tick.

To

To go upon Tick, or *run upon trust.*
A Ticket, or *bill.*
To tickle (*in different senses.*)
A Tickler.
Ticklish.
Tick-tack, *a game at Tables.*
A Tid-bit, or *delicate morsel.*
To tiddle *one up*, or *sooth him up in his humour.*
The Tide, *the flux, and reflux of the Sea.*
A Tide *of flood*, or *ebb.*
To tide *it over*, or tide *it up into any place; to get thither by taking advantage of the tide.*
A Leeward-tide, *when the wind and tide go both together.*
A Windward-tide, *a tide that runs against the wind.*
A Neap-tide.
A Spring-tide.
A Tide-gate (*a sea-term*) *when the tide runs strong*
A Tidesman, *an Officer of the Custom-house attending upon a ship till the Custom of the fraight be paid.*
A good Tide, or *season.*
Evening-tide.
Twelfth-tide.
Whitsun-tide.
Tidings, or *news.*
Tidy, *handy, neat*, or *cleanly.*
A Tie, *and to* tie (*in several senses.*)
A Tiercel-hawk, or *male hawk, from the* French Tiercelet; *so call'd from its being a third part less than the female, in bigness and strength.*
Tiffany, *a sort of light silk-stuff.*
A Tiger, *a wild beast.*
Tight, *neat, whole, close*, or *well set.*
A Tigress, or *female Tiger.*
A Tike-worm, *an insect.*
A Tike, or *cur*; as *A* Yorkshire-tike.
A Tile, *and*
To tile, or *cover with tiles.*
A Pan-tile,
A Ridge-tile, or *roof-tile.*
A Tile-kiln.
A Tile-shard.
A Tiler, or *tile-maker.*
Till, or *untill.*
A Till, or *little drawer.*
The Till, or *shelf of a Printing-press.*
To till, or *manure the ground.*
Tillage, or *Husbandry.*
A Tiller, or *plough-man.*
The Tiller, or *helm of a boat.*
A Tilt, or *covering for a boat, to keep off rain*, &c.
A Tilt-boat, or *cover'd boat, such as those that constantly pass, and repass with the tide between* London, *and* Gravesend.
To tilt, or *stoop a vessel, when the liquor begins to be low.*
A Tilter, *a piece of wood for that purpose.*
To tilt *at one, to make a thrust*, or *pass with a sword*, &c.
The Tilts, *a kind of exercise, by running one against another with lances*, or *spears.*
A Tilt-yard.
Tilth, or *manuring*; as *a field out of tilth.*
Timber, or *wood to build with.*
A Timber-Merchant.
Timber-work.
A Timber-worm.
A Timber-yard.
A Timber of skins, i. e. *forty in number.*
To timber, or *make a nest*, as *a hawk does.*
Timbers of Ermine (*in Heraldry*) *the rows of Ermine in Noblemens robes*
Timbred, or *made of timber.*
A Well-timbred, or *well set Man.*
A Timbrel, or *taber.*
A Timbrel-player.
Time, *occasion, season, leisure*, &c.
Time, or thyme, *an herb.*
To time, *a business well, to compass it, at a convenient season.*
Timely, or *seasonable.*
A Time-server.
Timidity, or *fearfulness.*
Timorous, or *fearfull.*
Timorousness.
Tin, *a metal.*
To tin *over*, or *cover with tin.*
A Tin-candlestick.
A Tin-man, or *dealer in tin.*
A Tin-mine.
Tincel, *stuff*, or *cloth made of silk and copper.*
A Tincture, *colour, stain*, or *die.*
Tinctured, or *died.*
To tind, or *light a candle.*
To tind, or *make up a hedge.*
Tinder, *to light a match with.*
A Tinder-box.
The ting *of a bell.*
To ting, or tingle; *to make a noise*, as *a little bell doer.*
The tingling *of the ears.*
A Tinker, or *mender of old Kettles*, &c.
To Tinkle, or tingle.
Tinsel, or tincel.
A Tint, or *half a bushel.*
A Tintamar, or *confused deadly noise.*
A Tip, *and to* tip (*in several senses.*)
A Tip-staff, *an Officer that attends the Courts with a rod tipt with silver, and has the charge of Prisoners com-*

mitted

mitted to the Judge's Chamber.
To stand a tip-toe.
A Tippet, *a Doctor's scarf; or a neck-ornament for Women.*
An Ermine-tippet.
A Sable-tippet.
To tipple, *guzzle,* or *drink hard.*
A Tippler, *toper,* or *fuddle-cap.*
A Tippling-house, or *blind ale-house.*
Tipsy, *a little in drink.*
Tipt, *or* tipped, *with silver,* &c.
The Tirdles, tirtles, *or* treadles *of a sheep.*
A Tire, attire, or *dress.*
A Tire-woman.
A Tire, or *row of guns in a ship.*
The Tire, or *iron-band of a cart-wheel.*
To tire, *to weary,* or *to grow faint.*
Tiresome, or *irksome.*
A Tirwhit, or *lap-wing, a bird.*
'Tis, *for* it is.
The Tissick, *an ulceration of the lungs, accompany'd with a hectick feaver.*
Tissical *troubled with the* tissick, *short-winded,* or *pursy.*
Tissue, *or* Cloth of tissue, *cloth of silk and silver.*
A Tit, tom-tit, *or* titmouse, *a bird.*
A Tit-lark.
A Tit, or *little* Welsh *horse.*
To tit *over.*
Tithable, *liable to yield tithes.*
Tithe, *the tenth part of all fruits,* &c. *due to the Parson of the Parish.*
To tithe, or *take the tenth part.*
A Tither, or *tithe-gatherer.*
A Tithing, *formerly a Society of ten Families bound to the King for their peaceable, and good behaviour.*
A Tithing-man, *headborough,* or *constable.*
Tithymal, *an herb.*
A Titillation, or *tickling.*
A Title, *an inscription,* or *a mark of honour.*
The Title-page *of a book.*
A Title, or *right to an Estate.*
To title *a book, to give it* a title; also *to stick up titles of books newly set forth, to be expos'd to publick view.*
To titter, or *laugh wantonly.*
A Tittle, or *point set over a letter,*
Tittle-tattle, or *vain babbling.*
Titular, *that bears a title only.*

TO

To, to *and* fro, *&c.*
A Toad, *a venomous creature.*
A Land-toad, or *ruddock.*
The Toad-fish.
A Toad-stone.
A Toad-stool, *a sort of mushroom.*
Toads-flax, *an herb.*
Tobacco, *a well known plant, which probably takes name from* Tobago *one of the* Caribbee-Islands *in* America, *from whence it was first brought into* England *by Sir* Francis Drake*'s Mariners.* A. D. 1585.
Spanish Tobacco.
Virginia Tobacco, *&c.*
A Tobacco-box.
A Tobacco-pipe.
A Tobacconist, *one that trades in Tobacco.*
A Tod *of wool,* i. e. 28 *pounds.*
A Toe *of a foot,* or *shoo.*
A Toft, *a place where a Messuage has stood.*
A Toft, or *grove of trees.*
Together, *at the same place,* or *time;* or *without intermission.*
Toil, *hard labour,* or *fatigue.*
To Toil *and* moil.
A Toilet, or *dressing-cloth.*
Toilsome, or *laborious.*
A Token, *sign, note, mark, pledge, small present,* &c.
A Plague-token.
Told (*from to* tell) *inform'd; declared, counted,* &c.
Tolerable, *that may be born with,* or *indifferent*
Tolerableness.
To tolerate, *suffer, permit,* or *connive at.*
Toleration.
Toll, *tribute,* or *custom.*
A Toll-booth, *the place where* toll *is paid;* also *the chief prison in* Edenborough.
The Tollsey *of* Bristol, *a publick place where the Merchants meet,* &c. *as at the Royal Exchange in* London.
Toll-free, *exempted from all manner of* toll.
A Toll-gatherer.
Toll-money.
To toll, or *ring a bell, after a particular manner.*
To toll *one, entice,* or *incite.*
A Tomb, or *monument for the dead.*
A Tomb-stone.
A Tom-boy, *or* tom-rig, *a girl,* or *wench that ramps up and down like a boy.*
A Tome, *a division,* or *particular volume of a book.*
A Tone, or *accent of the voice.*

A

A pair of Tongs, *to take up coals, cinders,* &c.
The Tongue, *a little, but unruly member.*
Dogs-tongue, *an herb.*
Tongue-tied, *that has an impediment in his speech*
Tongued, *as*
Double-tongued, or *given to dissimulation.*
Ill-tongued, or *foul-mouthed.*
Long-tongued, *talkative,* or *blabbing.*
Silver-tongued, or *eloquent.*
A Tongue, *language,* or *speech.*
The Mother-tongue, or *one's native language.*
The Tongue, *of a ballance, buckle, sword-blade,*&c.
Tonnage, *or* tunnage, *a Duty paid to the King for goods imported,* or *exported in ships,* &c, *at a certain rate for every Tun-weight.*
Tonnage and Poundage, *first establish'd* 45 Edw. III.
Too, as *too little,* or *too much.*
I took, or *did* take.
A Tool, or *instrument.*
To toot, or *look a-skew.*
To toot, *or* tote, *to blow in a pipe,* or *horn.*
A Tooth; as *tooth and nail.*
A Gag-tooth, *that stands out beyond the rest.*
The Tooth-ach, *or* tooth-ake.
A Tooth-drawer.
A Tooth-picker.
A Tooth-wrest, *an instrument to draw teeth.*
Toothed, *that has teeth.*
A Toothing, *a corner-stone, left for more building.*
Toothless, *that has no teeth.*
Toothsome, *pleasant to the* tooth, or *palatable.*
Top, or *chief;* as *this is the* top-evidence.
The Top, or *highest extremity of a thing;* as *the top of a hill, house,*&c.
To top the sail-yards, or make 'em hang even (a sea-term.)
Top-heavy.
A Top-knot.
The Top-mast, *and* top-gallant-mast *of a ship.*
The Top-sail.
A Top *for a boy to whip.*
To top a tree, or *strike off its top.*
A Topaz, *a precious stone of a gold-colour.*
To tope, or *drink briskly.*
A true Toper.
Topical, *belonging to*
Topicks, *common places,* or *heads of discourse;* also *the art of invention,* or *finding out of arguments.*
Topographical *belonging to*
Topography, *the description of a particular place, in any Country.*
Topped, as *sharp-topped.*
A Topping, or *eminent Person.*
The Toppings *of a Coach-horse,* or *cart-horse.*
Topsy-turvy, or *upside down.*
A Torch, or *taper.*
A Torch-bearer.
Torch-weed, *an herb.*
I tore, or *did* tear.
Torment, *great pain,* or *grief.*
To torment, *put to pain; vex, trouble,* or *afflict.*
A Tormenter.
Tormentil, *an herb.*
Torn *(from* to tear.*)*
A Torrent, *a violent stream,* or *land-flood caus'd by rain,* or *snow.*
Torrid, *burning-hot, scorched,* or *parched;* as
The Torrid Zone, *the Countries under which, were erroneously suppos'd by the Ancients to be uninhabited, by reason of the excessive heat.*
A Tortoise, or *shell-crab.*
A Land-tortoise.
A Sea-tortoise.
A Tortoise-shell.
Torture, *rack,* or *exquisite pain.*
To torture *one,* or *put him upon the rack.*
A Torturer.
A Tory, *bog-trotter,* or Irish *robber.*
To tose, or *card wooll.*
A Tos, *and to* tos *(in several senses.)*
A Tos-pot, or *great drinker.*
Tost, *for* tossed.
A Tost, *and*
To Tost, or *broil before the fire.*
A Tosting-iron.
Total, *whole,* or *entire.*
To totter, *stagger,* or *reel.*
A touch, *and to* touch *(in all senses.)*
The Touch-hole, *and* touch-pan *of a gun.*
A Touch-stone, *to try gold.*
Touch-wood.
Touching, or *concerning.*
Touchy, *froward, morose,* or *peevish.*
Tough, *hard,* or *rude.*
Toughness.
A Tour, *journey,* or, *walking about a place;* as *to make the* tour *of* France.
Tow, or *hards;* the *course part of flax.*
To tow, *to hale a great ship,* or *barge with another Vessel; with an Engine;* or *with ropes drawn by men* or *beasts.*
Towage, *the towing* or *drawing in such a manner;* also *an allowance to the Owner of the ground next a river, where a barge,* or *vessel is towed.*

A Tower, *one that* tows *a ship, barge*, &c.
Toward, *or* towards.
Towardness; *or* towardliness, *a good disposition.*
Towardly, *gentle*, or *teachable.*
A Towel, *to wipe one's hands with.*
A Tower, *castle*, or *citadel.*
The Tower of London.
A Town, *a considerable space of ground cover'd with houses, inhabited by Men, and encompass'd with walls.*
A Borough-town, or *Corporation.*
A Country-town, or *Village.*
A Town-house, or *chief* Hall *of a Town.*
A Towns-man.
A Towr, or *fore-top of false hair.*
To towr, *soar*, or *fly high.*
To towz, *tug, tumble, ruffle*, or *rumple.*
To towz, toze, or *card wooll.*
A Towzer.
A Toy, or *trifle.*
To toy, *sport*, or *dally.*
Toyish.
A Toy-man, *one that sells childrens toys.*
A Toy-shop.
A Toyl, *bay*, or *snare to catch wild beasts.*

T R

A Trace, or *foot-print.*
To trace, *follow*, or *discover by the footsteps.*
To trace *over a picture.*
A Tracer.
The Traces, or *harness of draught-horses.*
A Track, trace, or *foot-print*; or *the mark of a cart-wheel in the ground.*
A Tract, *a space of ground*, or *time.*
A Tract, or *small treatise.*
Tractable, *that may be handled, order'd* or *manag'd*; *flexible*, or *gentle.*
Tractableness.
A Trade, *profession, employment, traffick, commerce*, &c.
To trade, or *traffick.*
Traded, as *a well traded Town.*
A Tradesman.
Tradition, *the successive delivering*, or *transmitting of doctrines*, or *opinions to posterity*; as *The* Traditions *of the Church of* Rome.
Traditional, *or* traditionary, *of*, or *belonging to* tradition.
A Traditionist, *one that stands for tradition.*
To traduce, *defame, slander*, or *disparage.*
A Traducer.
Traffick, *trade, trading*, or *commerce.*
To traffick, *deal, trade*, or *drive a trade.*
A Tragedian, *a writer*, or *actor of Tragedies.*
A Tragedy, *a sort of lofty play in which great Persons are brought on the Stage, the subject being full of trouble, and the end always doleful; so called from two* Greek *words* tragos *a goat, and* ode *a song; because the Actors usually had a goat given 'em for a reward.*
Tragical, *belonging to* tragedies; also *sad, cruel*, or *fatal.*
A Tragick Poet, *one well skill'd in the writing of tragedies.*
A Tragicomedy, *a play that is half* Tragedy, *and half* Comedy.
A Trail *in hunting.*
To trail, *draw*, or *drag.*
A Train, or *retinue of attendants.*
A Train *of gun-powder.*
The Train, *or* trail *of a gown.*
To Train up, or *bring up, instruct*, or *discipline.*
To train, or *exercise Soldiers.*
The Train-bands.
A Trainel-net, *or* tramel-net.
A Trainer *of Soldiers.*
Train-oil, or *whale-oil.*
A Tramel, or *drag-net.*
A Trammel, or *pot-hook.*
To trample, or *tread under foot.*
A Trance, *a rapture*, or *wandering of the spirit from its natural seat.*
Tranquillity, *calmness, stilness*, or *quietness.*
To Transact, *negotiate, dispatch*, or *manage affairs.*
A Transaction.
A Transacter.
To transcend, *surpass*, or *go beyond.*
Transcendent, or *extraordinary.*
To transcribe, *to write*, or *copy out from an original.*
A Transcriber.
A Transcript, or *copy.*
To transfer, *remove*, or *convey, from one place to another.*
A Transfiguration, *a change of* figure, or *shape.*
Transfigured; as *when our Saviour came to be transfigured.*
To transform, or *change from one* form, or *shape to another.*
A Transformation.
A Transformer.
A Transfusion, or *pouring out of one vessel into another.*
To transgress, (*i. e.* go beyond the due bounds) *to violate*, or *break a Law.*

A Transgression.
A Transgressor.
Transient, *or* transitory.
Transiently, or *by the by.*
A Transition, *(in* Rhetorick) *a passing from one point of discourse to another.*
Transitory, *that soon passes away, momentany, fleeting,* or *frail.*
To translate, *to remove from its place*; or *to render out of one language into another.*
A Translation.
A Translator.
Transmarine, *lying beyond sea,* or *foreign.*
A Transmigration, *or departing from one place to dwell in another.*
To Transmit, *convey,* or *make over.*
A Transmutation, or *Change.*
To transmute *Metals, to change their colour, form, &c.*
A Transom, or *overthwart beam in a house, ship, &c.*
Transparency, *a being* Transparent, *that may be seen through.*
Transpiration, or *the breathing of Vapours thro' the pores of the Body.*
To transplant, or *plant in another place.*
A Transplantation.
A Transplanter.
A Transport, or *excess of joy, or anger.*
To transport, or *convey from one place to another.*
A Transportation.
To transpose, or *put out of its proper place.*
A Transposition.
To transprose, or *change the manner of a style.*
Transubstantiated, or *changed into another substance.*
Transubstantiation, *the change of the Sacramental Bread and Wine, (according to the Papists) into Christ's real body and blood.*
Transverse, *overthwart,* or *a-cross.*
A Trap, *Snare,* or *Gin.*
To trap, or *catch in a trap.*
A Mouse-trap.
A Rat-trap.
A Trap-door.
To trap, or *set out with trappings.*
To trape, or *go idly up and down.*
A Trapes, *a meer Slattern,* or *dirty Slut.*
Trappings, or *harness for horses.*
Trapt, or trapped, *catched in a trap,* or *dress'd with trappings.*
Trash, *trumpery, or pitiful stuff.*
A Trave, *or* travise, *an Engine to shoo untamed Horses in.*
Travel or *pains*; also *the pangs* or *labour of a Woman in Child-birth.*
To travel, *to perform a journey,* or *to take great pains.*
Travels, *Voyages,* or *books on that Subject.*
A Traveller, or *wayfaring person.*
Travellers joy, *an herb.*
Traverse, *cross-wise,* or *in and out*; as *to sail by* traverse.
A Traverse-board, *on which all the points of the Compass are set down with marks for the hours the Ship has gone on every Point, in order to take an account of her Course.*
A Traverse (*in* Fortification) *is a little Moat border'd with a parapet, which the besieger makes quite a-thwart the Moat of the place to pass secure from* **Flank-shot,** *and bring his Miners to the Bastion.*
To traverse, or *go cross a Country.*
To traverse *an Indictment, to contradict,* or *invalidate some point of it.*
Traverses, *turnings and windings,* or *cross adventures.*
Travested or *disguised*; as *the Poems of* Virgil, *or* Ovid travested, i. e. *turn'd into burlesque verse.*
A Tray, *a kind of hollow woo len vessel, to put meat in,* &c.
A Butchers-tray.
A Milk-tray.
Trayterous, *belonging to*
A Traytor, *a person guilty of high-treason.*
Treacherous, *full of* Treachery, *perfidiousness,* or *unfaithfulness.*
Treacle, *a Physical composition.*
To tread, *go,* or *set foot to the ground*; *to stamp* or *trample upon,* &c.
A Treader *of Grapes,* &c.
A Yeoman-treader, or *usher.*
The Treadle *of a Weaver's Loom.*
Treadles, *or the* treddles; *excrements of Sheep.*
Treason, *perfidious dealing, treachery,* or *disloyalty.*
High-treason, *or* treason paramount, *an offence against the security of the Prince,* or *State*; *as to compass the death of the King or Queen; to levy War against them; to adhere to their Enemies; to coin false Money,* &c.
Petty-treason *is when a Clerk kills his Ordinary,* or *Superiour*; *a Wife*

her Husband; or a Servant his Master.

Treasonable, *belonging to, or full of Treason.*

Treasure, *abundance of riches, wealth, or precious things; a stock of* Money, &c.

To treasure *up, or heap up Riches.*

A Treasurer, *an Officer to whom any* treasure *is committed to be kept, and duely disposed of;* as *the* Lord-Treasurer *of* England.

The Treasurer *of the* King's Houshold, &c.

Treasurer-ship, *the Office of a Treasurer.*

A Treasury, *or* treasure-house, *where treasures are kept.*

A Treat, *entertainment,* or *collation.*

To treat *one,* or *give him* a treat.

To treat, or *use one kindly, to discourse of a thing, to manage a business,* &c.

A Treatise, or *discourse upon some particular Subject.*

A Treaty, *covenant,* or *agreement, between several Nations for Peace, Commerce, Navigation,* &c.

Treble, or *threefold.*

To treble *to make* treble; or *to put thrice as much.*

The Treble-part, *in Musick.*

A Tree *of (all sorts)*

An Apple-tree.

A Cherry-tree, *&c.*

A Fruit-tree, or *fruit-bearing tree.*

The tree of a Cross-bow, or Saddle, *&c.*

Treenels, *long oaken pins that serve to fasten the ship-planks to the timbers.*

Trefoil, or *three-leav'd grass.*

Bean-trefoil.

Hedge-hog-trefoil.

Snail-trefoil.

Shrub-trefoil.

A Trellis, *a kind of wooden lattice.*

To tremble, *shake* or *quake.*

Tremendous, *much to be feared,* or *dreadful.*

A Trench, or *Ditch to convey water.*

Trenches *in* Fortification *are Moats which the Besiegers make to approach the more securely to the place attacked.*

Trenched, or *fenced with trenches.*

A Trencher, or *Wooden plate.*

A Trencher-friend, or *belly-friend.*

A good Trencher-man, or *great eater.*

The Trendle *of a Mill.*

A Trepan, *an Instrument used by Surgeons for the curing of fractures in the skull.*

To trepan the skull, *to raise up the crushed and depressed parts of it with the* Trepan, *in order to take out the broken bones, clotted blood,* &c

To trepan *one, to bring him into a premunire; to ensnare, circumvent,* &c.

A Trepanner.

A Trespass, *offence, transgression, fault, wrong, dammage,* &c.

To trespass, or *commit a trespass.*

A Trespass-offering.

A Trespasser.

A Tress *of hair.*

A Tressel, or *three-footed Stool.*

A Tressel, or trestle *for a Table.*

Tret, *an allowance for waste, in the weight of goods.*

A Trevet, or *trivet.*

A Trey, *or* trey-point, *i. e.* three, *at Dice* or *Cards.*

A Trial *(from to try) a proof, essay, Law-process,* &c,

A Triangle, *a figure that has three* angles, or *corners.*

Triangular, *belonging thereto.*

A Tribe, *or* ward, *among the ancient* Romans, *of which they had 35 in the City of* Rome, *altho' there were but three at first.*

The Tribes, or *distinct families of the* Israelites *descended from the Patriarch* Jacob's *twelve sons.*

A Triblet, *a Goldsmith's tool, us'd in the working of rings.*

A Tribulation, *great trouble, anguish,* or *affliction.*

A Tribunal, or *Judgment-seat, properly the seat of*

The Tribune, *an Officer mong the old* Romans *who chiefly maintain'd the Rights of the Commons, and were two in number, like our* London-*Sheriffs*

Tributary, *that pays*

Tribute, *a tax, toll, custom, impost,* or *subsidy.*

A Trice, or *moment;* as *it was done in a* trice.

A Trick, *wile,* or *subtil device.*

To trick *one,* or *put a trick upon him.*

To trick *(in* Painting*) to begin the first draught of a Picture.*

To trick *up, trim,* or *set out.*

The Tricker *of a gun.*

To trickle *down,* or *fall down in small drops.*

Triennial, *that continues three years;* as *a triennial Parliament.*

A

A Trier, *assayer*, or *prover*.
To tri-tallow land; *to labour*, or *till it a third time*
A Trifle, or *bawble*.
To trifle, *toy*, *play the fool*, or *spend time idly*.
A Trifler.
To trig, or *skatch a cart-wheel*.
To trig *one*, *and to* toe one's trig *at nine-pins*.
A Trigger *to stay a wheel*.
Trigonometry, or *the Art of measuring triangles*.
A Trill, *and*
To trill, or *quaver in singing*.
Trim, *neat*, or *spruce*.
To trim (*in several senses*.)
A Trimmer, *one that* trims, or *carries it fair with both parties*.
Trinitarians, *or* Socinians, *an heretical Sect, that deny*
The Holy Trinity, i. e. *the distinction of three Persons in the* Godhead, viz. Father, Son, *&* Holy Ghost, *which are one and the same in essence and substance*, 1 John 5. 7.
Trinity, *or* hearts-ease, *an herb*.
The Trinity-house of Deptford-strond, *belonging to a Company*, or *Corporation of Seamen, consisting of a Master, Wardens and Assistants, authorized by the King's Charter, to take cognizance of those that destroy Sea-marks; to reform abuses among Sailers; and to regulate other matters relating to Navigation, and Maritime Affairs*.
Trinity-sunday, *the first* Sunday *after* whitsunday.
The Trinket-sail, *the highest sail in a ship*.
Trinkets, *toys*, or *gewgaws*.
A Trip, or *herd of goats*.
A Trip, or *short voyage by sea*.
A Trip, or *false step*.
To trip, or *make a trip*.
To trip *one up*, or *to* trip *up his heels*.
Tripartite, or *divided into three parts*.
Tripe, *the entrals of neat-cattel*.
A Tripe-house.
A Tripe-woman.
The Tripery, or *tripe-market*.
Triple, or *threefold*.
The Triple-tree, *or* Tyburn-*gallows*.
Trite, *common*, or *vulgar*; as *a* trite *argument*.
A Trivet, *an iron instrument with three feet, to set a pot upon the fire*.
Trivial, *common*, or *ordinary*.
A Triumph, *a solemn pomp*, or *shew, at the return of a victorious General from the Wars*.
To triumph, *to ride in triumph*, or *to rejoice in an extraordinary manner*.
Triumphal *of*, *or belonging to a* triumph; as *a triumphal arch*.
Triumphant, or *triumphing*; as *the Church triumphant*.
A Triumpher.
Trod (*from* to tread.)
To troll, *along his words*, or *speak very fluently*.
To troll, *or* stroll *about*, *to ramble up and down, in a careless*, or *sluttish dress*.
A Trollop, or *nasty slut*.
To troll *for fish with a particular sort of net*.
Troll-madame, *a kind of game at pigeon-holes*.
Tronage, *a custom*, or *toll, for the weighing of wooll*; *from* trona, *a beam to weigh with*.
The Tronator, *an Officer in the City of* London, *who weighs the wooll brought thither*.
A Troop, or *company, more especially of Soldiers on horseback*.
To Troop, or *get together*.
To troop *away*, troop *off*, or *run away*.
A Trooper, or *armed horseman*.
A Trophy, *properly a monument set up where enemies were vanquish'd with their ensigns, and other spoils hanging on it; a sign*, or *token of victory*.
Trophy-money, 4 d. *paid yearly by House-keepers on the Train-bands, for the charge of Drums, Colours, Scarves*, &c.
A Trope, (*a term of* Rhetorick) *from the* Greek trepo *to turn*; *an elegant turning of a word from its proper and genuine signification to another*; *as the word* Fire, *when we say*, the Fire of Persecution.
The Tropicks, *two Circles parallel to the* Æquator; *and equidistant from it*; *one of them passing thro' the beginning of* Cancer, *Northwards, and the other through the beginning of* Capricorn *Southwards*; *from whence they take their names*.
The Sun's arrival at the former June 11. *makes our longest day, and at the other* Decemb. 12. *the shortest day and longest night*.
A Trot, *and*
To Trot, *as an Horse does*.

An

An Old Trot, *or decrepit Woman.*
A Trotter, or *trotting horse.*
Trotters, or *Sheeps-feet.*
Trouble, or *disquiet.*
To trouble, *disturb, vex* or *molest.*
A Troubler.
Troublesome.
A Trough *to feed hogs in,* &c.
A Kneading-trough.
Trough, *(a* Sea-term) *the space between two waves*
To trounce, *harass,* or *punish one severely.*
A Trout, *a Fish.*
A Salmon-trout.
A true Trout, *or trusty Companion.*
A Trowel *to spread Morter with.*
Troy-weight, *of* 12 *ounces to the pound, for the weighing of Bread, Gold, Silver, Precious Stones, Drugs,*&c
A Truant, *an idle Boy that absents himself from School.*
A Trub, *or* trub-tail; *a little squat Woman.*
Trubs, *a kind of Herb.*
A Truce, or *Cessation of Arms for a time agreed upon by both Parties.*
A Truce-breaker.
A Truch-man, or *Interpteter,*
Truck, *a chopping,* or *swapping.*
To truck, *exchange,* or *barter one thing for another.*
A Truckle, *a little running wheel.*
A Truckle-bed.
To Truckle, *submit, or yield.*
Trucks, *a kind of Billiards.*
A Truck-table.
To trudge, or *trot up and down.*
True, *certain, sure, genuine, faithful, unfeigned,* &c.
True-hearted, or *sincere.*
True-love, *an herb.*
Trueness, or *sincerity of heart.*
A Truffle, *a sort of Mushroom, growing within the ground.*
A Trull, *a vile Strumpet,* or *Camp-whore.*
A Trump, or *trumpet.*
A Jews-trump.
A Trump, *and to* trump *at Cards.*
The Trump-Card.
Trumpery, *old baggage,*or *paltry stuff.*
A Trumpet, *a musical Instrument.*
A Trumpet-marine.
A Speaking-Trumpet.
To trumpet, *divulge,* or *spread abroad.*
A Trumpeter.
Put to his Trumps, *or to his last shifts.*
A Truncheon, or *Battoon.*
To trundle *along,* or *roll along.*
A Trundle-bed, or *truckle-bed.*
A Trundle-tail, *a wench that runs fisking up and down with a draggled tail.*
A Trunk *(in all senses.)*
Trunk-breeches.
A Trunk-light *in a shop.*
A Trunk-maker.
Trunks, *or* troll-madame, *a sort of play.*
The Trunnions, or *knobs on the sides of a piece of Ordnance.*
A Truss, or *bundle of hay,* &c.
A Truss *for bursten persons.*
To truss, *tie up,* or *gird up.*
A Trussel, tressel, or *prop.*
Trusses *a sort of Ship ropes, to bind the yards to the Mast, or to hale 'em down.*
Trust, *Confidence, assurance, credit,* &c.
To trust, *confide in,* or *relie upon.*
A Trustee, *one that has Money,* or *an Estate, put into his hands in trust, for the use of another.*
Trustiness, *a being* Trusty, *true to his trust, faithful and sure.*
Truth, *that which is* true.
To try, *prove, assay, examine, endeavour,* &c.
The Ship tries, or *is* a-try, *when she has no more Sails abroad but the Main-Sail, or the Mizzen-Sail only.*
A Tryal, *or* trial.

T U.

A Tub, *a sort of Vessel.*
A Bathing-tub.
A Bucking-Tub.
A Kneading-tub.
A Powdering-tub.
A Washing-tub.
A Tube, *or* Pipe.
Tuberosa, *a kind of white flower.*
A Tuberous Plant, i.e. *full of bunches or knots.*
A Tuck, or *Rapier.*
The tuck of a Ship, *the trussing or gathering up of her quarter under water.*
To tuck, *turn,* or *gather up.*
A Tucker, or *fuller of Cloath.*
A Tucker, *a long slip of Linnen,* tuck'd, or *pinn'd along the top of a Woman's Stays.*
A Lace-tucker.
The Tuel, or *Fundament of a Beast (a term in Hunting.)*
Tuesday, *the third day of the week, so called from* Tuisco, *the most ancient and peculiar Idol of*

 the

the Teutonicks, or *old* Germans *and* Saxons, *to which this day was more especially dedicated.*
Hock-tuesday.
Shrove-tuesday.
A Tuft *of hair, grass, trees, silk, feathers,* &c.
A Tuft, or *crest.*
Candy-tufts, *a plant.*
Tufted, *that has a* tuft; *crested,* or *plumed.*
A Tug, and *to* tug, *pull* or *labour hard.*
Tuition, *Gardianship, protection,* or *patronage.*
A Tulip, *a flower.*
To Tumble, *roll, or wallow; to touse* or *rumple.*
A Tumbler, *one that plays tumbling tricks; also a kind of drinking-cup.*
A Tumbler-Dog.
A Tumbrel, *a dung-cart* or *a Cucking-stool.*
A Tumor, or *preternatural swelling in any part of the Body.*
A Tumult, *bustle, uproar, sedition,* or *mutiny.*
Tumultuary, *done in a* tumult, or *confused,*
Tumultuous, or *full of tumults.*
A Tun, *(among Sea-men) the weight of* 20 *quintals* or 2000 *pounds by which the contents,* or *different dimensions of vessels are usually express'd;* as
A Ship of 200 Tuns.
A Tun, or *pipe of wine, oil,* &c; *containing* 252 *gallons.*
A Tun of Timber, *is* 40 *solid feet.*
To tun, or *pour into a tun.*
Tun-bellied.
Tun-hoof, *an herb*
Tunable, *harmonious,* or *conformable to the rules of Musick.*

A Tune, or *musical air.*
To tune, or *set an instrument in* tune.
A Tuner.
A Tunick, *a sort of garment.*
Tunnage, *or* tonnage, *an impost paid for every Tun of Merchandizes exported,* or *imported in ships.*
A Tunnel, *or* funnel.
The Tunnel *of a chimney.*
A Tunnel *to catch partridges.*
A Tunneller, *a fowler, that takes partridges in such a manner.*
A Tunny, *a sea-fish.*
A Tup, or *ram.*
To tup, as *the ram* tups or *covers the ew.*
A Turbant, *a* Turkish *cap.*
A Turbot, *a sea-fish*
Turbulent, *troublesome, boisterous,* or *seditious.*
Turcism, *the Religion of the* Turks
A Turcois, *a precious stone of an azure colour.*
A Turd, *the ordure of men,* or *beasts.*
Turdy, *nasty, filthy, rude,* or *uncivil.*
A Turf, or *green sward.*
A Turk, or *native of* Turkey.
Turks-cap, *a flower.*
Turkey, *a large Country in* Asia, *and* Europe; *the dominions of the grand Seignior.*
A Turkey-Merchant.
The Turkey-company.
A Turkey, *a fowl.*
A Turkey-cock.
Turkish, *belonging to the* Turks.
Turmerick, *the root of an* Arabian *plant.*
A Turmoil, *bustle,* or *tumult.*
To turmoil, *toil,* or *keep a heavy do.*
A Turn, *and to* turn *(in all senses.)*

A Turn-coat, *one that has chang'd his party,* or *religion.*
A Turn-pike, *or* caltrop.
A Turn-sole, *a flower.*
A Turn-spit.
A Turn-stile.
A Turnament, *justing,* or *tilting, a martial exercise of* Gentlemen *encountering one another on horse-back with lances.*
A Turnep, *a root.*
A Turnep-ground.
A Turner, *that turns* wood, &c.
A Turning, *lane,* or *street, that turns to the right,* or *left.*
The Turnings *and* windings *of a river.*
Turpentine, *a clear and moist rosin issuing out of the* Larch-tree, *or*
Turpentine-tree.
Venice-Turpentine.
A Turquois, *or* turcois, *a precious stone.*
A Turrel, *a cooper's tool.*
A Turret, or *little tower.*
A Turtle, or turtle-dove, *a sort of pigeon that is very kind and chaste, living single after the death of its mate.*
A Turtle, or *sea-tortois.*
Tusan, *an herb.*
The Tushes *of a horse; the name of four particular teeth.*
The Tusks *of a wild boar; the great teeth that stand out.*
To tussle, or *rumple.*
Tutelar, or tutelary, *that protects,* or *performs the office of a Gardian.*
Tut-mouthed, *that has the chin and neither jaw, growing out too far.*
A Tutor, *instructer, gardian,* or *governer.*
To tutor, *instruct, reprove,* or *censure.*
A Tutoress, or *female tutor.*

A

A Tutorship, *the office*, or *employment of a* tutor.

Tuty, *or* tutty, *the flower of Copper, a light white stuff, which falls to dust as soon as touch'd, and is bred of the sparkles of brazen furnaces.*

T W

Twain, *into two parts*; as, the vail of the Temple was rent in twain, *Mat.* 27. 51.

A Twang, *a sharp sound*, or *harsh pronunciation.*

To twang *like the string of an instrument.*

To twattle, or *prattle.*

A Twattle-basket, *a twattling*, or *prattling gossip.*

A Twattler.

Tway-blade, *an herb.*

To tweag, *or* tweak; *to twitch*, or *pinch*,

A pair of Tweezers, *or* nippers, *to pull hair up by the roots.*

The Twelfth *in number.*

Twelfth-day, *or* twelfth-tide, *the festival of the* Epiphany, *or manifestation of Christ to the Gentiles; so call'd, as being the twelfth day exclusively from the Nativity, or Christmas-day.*

Twelve, or *the number twelve.*

A Twelve-month, *the space of a year.*

The Twentieth.

Twenty.

A Twibill, *an iron-tool, us'd by Carpenters and Pavers.*

Twice, or *two several times.*

To Twifallow *ground*, or *till it over again.*

A Twig *of a tree.*

A Lime-twig.

The Twilight, (q. d. double-light) *a space of time in the morning just before Sun-rising, and in the evening a little after Sun-set.*

A Twin, *one that is born with another, at the same birth.*

Twin-brothers.

Twin-sisters.

To twine, or *twist.*

To twine *about*, or *embrace one.*

A Twinge, or *gripe.*

To twinge, *gripe*, or *cause a very sharp pain.*

To twinkle, or *sparkle, as some stars do.*

To twinkle, or *wink often.*

A Twirl, *and*

To twirl, *to run round*, or *to turn about.*

A Twist *of a rope.*

The Twist, or *inside of the thigh.*

To twist, *twine*, or *wreath*

To twist, or *eat greedily.*

To twit, or *hit in the teeth.*

A Twitch, *and*

To twitch, *pinch*, or *pluck.*

To twitter, *tremble*, or *shiver for fear.*

Twittle-twattle, or *idle talk.*

Two *in number.*

A Two-edged *sword.*

A Two-handed *sword.*

A Two-leaved *door.*

Two-fold, or *double.*

Two-penny-grass, *an herb.*

T Y

A Tye, or *band.*

To Tye, *to bind*, or *fasten*; or *to oblige.*

The Tympan *of a Printing-press, the parchment frame, on which the sheet is pinn'd, in order to be pull'd off; the word in* Greek, *signifies a* drum.

The Tympany, *a kind of dry windy dropsy, that causes the belly to extend and sound like a drum*, or *taber.*

The Type, *the figure*, or *mystical shadow of a thing.*

Typical, *belonging thereto*

Typographical, *relating to the Art of* Printing.

Tyrannical, *acting like a* tyrant, *imperious*, or *cruel.*

To tyrannize, *to play the* tyrant, *oppress*, or *lord it over one.*

Tyranny, or *cruel oppression, the practice of*

A Tyrant, *a Soveraign Prince, that abuses the Royal Power in oppressing his Subjects; a cruel Governour*, or *Usurper.*

V A

A Vacancy, *the time during which a Benefice*, or *Office is* vacant; also *a time of leisure.*

Vacant, *that is at leisure*, or *that is not fill'd up*; *as a vacant living*, or *office.*

A Vacation, or *ceasing from ordinary business*; also *the time between the end of one term, and the beginning of another.*

The long Vacation, *between* Hilary *and* Michaelmass-*term.*

A Vaccary, or *cow-house.*

A Vacuity, *or* vacuum (*in* Philosophy) *a space void of air.*

A Vagabond, *an idle wanderer*, or *straggler.*

A Vagary, *or* figary.

Vagrant, *wandring*, or *roving.*

A Vail, or *covering for the head.*

To vail, or *cover with a* vail.

To

To vail the bonnet, *put off the hat*, or *strike sail.*

Vails, or *profits arising besides the salary*, or *wages.*

Vain, *fruitless, unprofitable*, or *frivolous.*

Vain-glorious.

Vain-glory.

Vain-speaking.

Vainness.

A Vale, *or* valley.

A Valediction, or *farewell.*

A Valedictory Oration, or *farewell-speech.*

Valentines *in the Church of* Rome, *Saints chosen as Patrons for the year ensuing, on the festival of* St. Valentine *a* Roman *Bishop*, Feb. 14. *Among us young Men and Maids chosen for sweet-hearts*, or *special loving friends.*

Valerian, *a flower.*

Garden-valerian.

A Valet, *servitour*, or *mean servant.*

A Valet de Chambre, *one that waits upon a person of quality in his bed-chamber.*

Valetudinary, *sickly, subject to sickness*, or *often indisposed.*

Valiant, *stout*, or *courageous.*

Valiantness.

Valid, *done in due form, firm and ratify'd.*

Validity.

The Vallance, *or* Vallence *of a bed.*

A Valley, or *dale surrounded with hills.*

Valorous, *valiant*, or *magnanimous.*

Volour, or *courage.*

Valuable, or *of considerable value.*

A Valuation, or *estimation.*

Value, *worth*, or *price.*

To value, *set a value on, prize*, or *esteem.*

A Valuer.

A Vambrace, or *armour for the arm.*

The Vamp, or *upper part of a shoe.*

To vamp, or *new* vamp; *to trim*, or *trick up.*

A Vamplate, *or* gauntlet.

A Van, *or* fan, *to winnow Corn with.*

The Van, *or* van-guard *of an Army.*

A Vane, fane, or *weather-cock.*

To vanish, *disappear*, or *come to nought.*

Vanity, *vainness*, or *levity.*

To vanquish, *overcome*, or *subdue.*

A Vanquisher.

Vantage, *that which is given over and above just weight and measure.*

A Vant-courier, or *fore-runner.*

Vaporous, *full of vapours*, or *that sends forth vapours.*

A Vapour, *moist fume; steam*, or *smoak that easily dissolves into water.*

To vapour, *huff*, or *boast.*

A Vardingale, *a kind of whale-bone circle formerly worn by Women, about their hips.*

Variable, *subject to variation, changeable, fickle*, or *inconstant.*

Variableness.

Variance, *enmity, difference, dispute*, or *contest.*

A Variation, *change*, or *alteration.*

Variegated, *streaked*, or *diversify'd with several colours.*

Variety, or *diversity.*

Various, *divers*, or *several.*

A Varlet, *a pitiful drudge*, or *sorry wretch, the word was us'd* 20 Rich. II. *for Yeomens servants*

Varnish, *a compound of gum, spirit of wine*, &c. *to set a fine gloss upon wood*, &c.

Cheek-varnish.

To varnish *tables, stands*, &c; *to lay a* varnish *upon them.*

A Varnisher.

Varry, *or* verry (*in* Heraldry) *argent and azure*, i. e. *white and blew colours intermix'd.*

Varvels, *little silver-rings about hawks legs, on which the owner's name is engraved.*

To vary, or *alter.*

A Vassal, or *slave*; or *a tenant that holds his land of another, by homage and fealty.*

Vassalage, *subjection*, or *the condition of a* vassal.

Vast, *huge, great, spacious*, or *immense.*

Vastness.

A Vat, *or* fat, *a kind of vessel.*

A Barley-vat.

A Cheese-vat.

A Dying-vat.

A Vavasour, *a person of honour, anciently next to a Baron.*

A Vault, or *arched building.*

To vault, or *arch a Church cellar*, &c.

To vault, or *leap.*

A Vaulter.

A Vaunt, *and*

To vaunt, *boast*, or *brag.*

A Vaunter.

A Vauntlay (*a term in* Hunting) *as when hounds are set in a readiness, where a chace is like to pass, and cast off before the rest of the kennel come in.*

U B U D

Ubiquitarians, *a Sect holding, that Christ's Body is every where present*

sent, as well as his Divinity.
Ubiquity, or *a being in every place at the same time.*
An Udder, or *tet.*

VE

Veal, or *calves-flesh.*
A quarter of Veal.
To veer more cable, *to let more of it run out.*
The Wind veers, i. e. *changes often, sometimes to one point, and sometimes to another.*
The Veering, or *oblique course of a ship.*
Vegetable, *that has life and growth*; as *herbs, plants, and trees.*
Vegetable, or *plants.*
The Vegetation, or *growth of a plant.*
Vegetatives, *that quickens*, or *causes to grow.*
Vehemency, *a being*
Vehement, *fierce, violent*, or *impetuous.*
A Vehicle, *that which serves to carry*, or *convey a thing*; as *broth is a proper* vehicle *for this remedy.*
A Vein (*in several senses.*)
To vein *a mantle-piece, to paint it marble-like, with* veins.
Veined; as *big-veined.*
Veiny, or *full of* veins.
The Veiny-piece *of beef*
Vellam, *the finest sort of parchment, made of calves-skin.*
Velvet, *a sort of silk-stuff.*
Mock-velvet.
A Velvet-brush, or *rubber for a hat.*
A Velvet-cap.
Velvet-flower, or *floramour.*
A Velvet-gown.
A Velvet-heart.
To vend, *sell*, or *set to sale.*
Vendible, *saleable*, or *to be sold.*
Venerable, *reverend*, or *worthy of respect.*
To venerate, *revere*, or *honour.*
Veneration, or *respect.*
Venereal, or venereous, *belonging to the sports of* Venus.
Venery, *carnal copulation*, or *lustfulness.*
Venery, or *the Art of hunting.*
Vengeance, or *revenge.*
Venial, or *pardonable.*
Venison, *the flesh of wild beasts that have been hunted.*
A Venison-pasty.
Venom, or *poison.*
Venomous, or *poisonous.*
Vent, or *air*; as *to give*, or *take* vent.
A Vent-hole.
A Vent, or *sale of Commodities.*
To vent, or *wind, as a spaniel does.*
Venter (*a* Latin *word for belly*) *as a brother by the same* Venter, *that is by one Mother.*
A Venture, *attempt, hazard*, or *risk.*
To venture, *put to a venture, run the risk of*, or *expose to danger.*
A Venturer.
Venturesome, or venturous, *bold*, or *apt to venture.*
A Venu, or *veny, a thrust*, or *touch in fencing.*
Venus, *the Goddess of Love, and Beauty*; also *the evening-star.*
Venus-comb, Venus-hair, Venus-looking-glass. } *herbs.*
Veracity, or *speaking truth.*
Verbal, *by word of mouth.*
Verbatim, *in the same words*, or *word for word.*
Verbose, *full of words*, or *talkative.*
Verdant, or *green*, as *a verdant meadow.*
Verdegrease, *the green rust of brass*, or *copper, hang'd for some days over strong vinegar.*
A Verderer, or verderor, *a judicial officer of the King's forest, sworn to keep the assizes of it*; *to enroll the Attachments of all manner of Trespasses committed there*; *and to take care that the* Vert *be well maintain'd.*
A Verdict (*q. d.* vere dictum, i. e. *a true report*) *the* Jury's *answer, upon any cause committed to their examination, by a court of Judicature.*
Verditure, *a sort of green colour us'd by Painters.*
Verdure, *the greenness of fields, meadows*, &c.
A Verge, *rod, wand*, or *mace, carried before a Magistrate.*
The Verge, or *compass of the* Royal Court, *formerly of* 12 *miles extent, within the Jurisdiction of the Lord Steward of the King's Houshold.*
A Verger *of a Cathedral*, or *Collegiate Church, an Officer that ushers in the Dean, Preacher*, &c. *with a silver-wand.*
Vergers, *certain Officers that attend the Judges with white wands in their hands.*
A Verification, or *verifying.*
To verify, *prove*, or *make good.*
Verily, or *truely.*
Verity, or *truth.*
Verjuice, *a liquor made of sour and unripe grapes.*
Vermilion, *a kind of red colour made of brimstone and quick-silver.*
Vermin, *hurtfull beasts*, or *insects*; *as rats, mice, worms*,

worms, lice, &c.
Vernal, *belonging to the Spring.*
A Verrel, *or* verril; *a little ring at the small end of a handle, cane, &c.*
A Verry, *or* varry *in blazonry.*
Verse *in opposition to prose.*
A Verse *in a Chapter.*
A Versicle, *or little verse.*
Versification, *the way of making verses.*
A Versifier, *or verse-maker.*
To Versifie, *or make verses.*
A Version, *or translation out of one Language into another.*
Vert, *or green-hue (a Forest-law word) every thing that grows, or bears a green leaf in a Forest, and is capable of covering a Deer.*
Vertical, *as the vertical point called* Zenith; *that point of the Firmament which is directly over our heads.*
A Vertigo, *giddiness, dizziness, or swimming in the head.*
Vertue, *in opposition to* Vice; *honesty, good Principles, &c.*
Vertuous.
Vervein, *or holy-herb.*
The Vervels, *or* varvels *of a Hawk.*
Vervise, *or plonkets, a kind of cloath.*
A Verule, *or* verrel.
Very, *as the very same.*
A Vesicatory, *or blistering Plaister.*
Vespers, *or Evening-Prayers in the Church of* Rome.
A Vessel, *an Utensel.*
A Wine-vessel.
A Vessel, *or Ship.*
A Vest, *and Tunick; a kind of Garment.*
To vest, *or invest one with Supreme Power.*
A Vestment, *or Garment.*
A Vestry, *a Room adjoyning to a Church, where the Priest's Vestments and Sacred Utensils are kept;* also *an Assembly of the Heads of a Parish usually held in that place.*
A Vestry-clerk, *that keeps the Parish-Accompts, &c.*
A Vestry-keeper, *or Sexton.*
Vestry-men, *a select number of chief Parishioners, who choose Officers for the Parish, and take care of its concernments.*
Vesture, *a garment or cloathing;* also *admittance to a possession and the profits of it.*
A Vetch, *or* fitch, *a sort of pulse.*
Bitter vetch.
Crimson-grass-vetch.
Hatchet-vetch.
Kidney-vetch.
Milk-vetch.
Wild-vetch.
Yellow wild vetch.
A Veteran, *or old Soldier.*
To vex, *trouble, torment, incense, or teaz.*
Vexation, *or disquiet.*
Vexatious, *that causes trouble, &c.*

U G.

Ugliness, *a being*
Ugly, *deform'd, indecent, base or shameful.*

V I.

A Vial, *a thin glass bottle.*
The Vibration, *or shaking motion of a Pendulum.*
A Vicar, *or Deputy; the Priest of a Parish, where the tithes are impropriated.*
A vicarage, *or* Vicaridge, *the Cure or Benefice of a Vicar.*
A Vicarship, *or Vicar's Office.*
Vice, *a habit contrary to Vertue, Wickedness, Lewdness, &c.*
Vicious, *given to vice, depraved, corrupt, lewd, restive, &c.*
Viciousness.
The vice, *or spindle of a press.*
A Vice, *an instrument used by several sorts of Artificers.*
The Vice-chops.
The Vice-pin.
Vice *in compound words imports a subordination, or the supplying of another's place;* as,
A Vice-Admiral, *or second Admiral.*
A Vice-Chamberlain, *or under-Chamberlain.*
A Vice-Chancellour, *and* Vice-Chancellourship.
A Vice-Commissary.
A Vice-gerent, *or Deputy.*
A Vice-Roy, *or Deputy-King, one that Governs a Kingdom instead of the King;* as
The Vice-Roy *of* Naples.
A Vice-Treasurer, *or under-treasurer, &c.*
Vicinity, *or Neighbourhood.*
A Vicissitude, *change, or turn; the interchanging or succeeding of one thing after another.*
A Vicount, *or* Viscount.
A Victim, *or Sacrifice, properly a Beast killed in Sacrifice after a Victory.*
A Victor, *Conqueror, or Vanquisher.*

Victorious, *that has got*
A Victory, or *Conquest*
To Victual, or *lay in Stores of Victuals for Ships, Camps, &c.*
A Victualler, *or provider of Victuals; also a Ship that carries Provisions for the Fleet.*
A Victualling-house, or *Ale house.*
Victuals, or *Food; all manner of Provisions for the mouth.*
A Vie, *or* vye *at Cards.*
A View, *sight*, or *survey.*
To view, or *take a view of.*
A Viewer.
A Vigil, *the eve*, or *day next before any Solemn Feast.*
Vigilancy, *a being*
Vigilant, *watchful, careful, mindful*, or *diligent.*
Vigorous, *lively, lusty, stout*, or *full of courage.*
Vigorousness.
Vigour, *sprightliness, strength, force*, &c.
Vile, *filthy, lewd, mean, base*, or *of no account.*
Vileness.
To Vilify, *abuse* or *set at nought.*
A Village, or *Country-Town.*
A Villager, or *Inhabitant of a Village.*
A Villain, *properly a man of servile and base degree, who is a meer bond-slave to his Lord; also an arrant Rogue, or pitiful sordid fellow.*
Villainous, *base, wicked*, or *infamous.*
Villany, *baseness*, or *lewdness.*
Villenage, *the meanest sort of tenure belonging to Lands* or *Tenements, whereby the Tenant is bound to do all manner of servile work for his Lord.*

Vincible, *that may be overcome.*
To vindicate, *defend, maintain*, or *justifie.*
A Vindication.
A Vindicator.
Vindictive, or *revengeful.*
A Vine *that bears Grapes*
The wild-vine.
A Vine-bud.
A Vine-dresser.
A Vine-fretter, or Vine-grub, *a kind of worm that gnaws the Vine.*
Vinegar, *i. e. eager*, or *sour wine.*
Beer-vinegar.
Elder-vinegar.
White-wine-vinegar.
A Vinegar-bottle, or *cruet for Vinegar.*
A Vinegar-maker.
A Vinegar-Man, or *seller of Vinegar.*
A Vinegar-yard, or *place where Vinegar is made.*
A Vinet, *a kind of border* or *flower in Printing, set at the beginning of a Book* or *Chapter.*
Vinew, *mouldiness, hoariness*, or *mustiness.*
Vinewed, *mouldy*, &c.
A Vineyard, or *place where Vines grow.*
A Vineyard-plot.
Vinous, *that has the taste* or *smell of Wine.*
Vintage, *Vine-harvest*, or *the gathering of grapes*
A Vintager, or *Vine-reaper.*
A Vintner, or *Tavern-keeper.*
A Vintry, *a noted place for the selling of Wine.*
A Viol, *a Musical Instrument.*
A Viol-maker.
To violate, *to break*, or *infringe*; or *to deflour.*
A Violater.
A Violation.
Violence, or *force.*
Violent, *forcible, vehement, boisterous, impetuous toilsome*, &c.

A Violet, *a Flower.*
Corn-violet.
Dames-violet.
A Violin, or *little V.*
A Bass-violin.
A Violist, *one well skilled in playing on the Viol.*
A Viper, *a kind of venomous Serpent.*
Vipers-grass.
Viper-bugloss.
A Virago, *a stout*, or *manly woman.*
A Virgin, *or Maid.*
The Blessed virgin Mary.
Virgin-honey.
Virgin-parchment, *made of the skin of a young Lamb*, &c.
Virgin-wax.
Virgins-bower, *an herb.*
Virginal, or *Maiden-like.*
Virginianclimer, *an herb.*
A pair of Virginals *a sort of Musical Instrument.*
Virginity, or *Maidenhead.*
Virile, or *Manly.*
Virility, or *Manhood.*
Virtually, or *effectually.*
Virtue, *efficacy, energy*, or *power.*
A Virtuoso, *a Learned and Ingenious Person, more especially, well skill'd in natural Philosophy.*
Virulency, *Poison*, or *Venom (in a figurative sense)* as *the virulency of his pen is notorious.*
Virulent, *sharp*, or *biting*; as *a virulent tongue*, &c.
A Visage, *face* or *countenance.*
A Viscount, *or* Vicount, (*q. d.* vice-count) *a person of honour, next to an Earl.*
A Viscountess, *a viscount's Wife.*
Viscous, *clammy*, or *slimy.*
The Viser, *the sight of a head-piece*, or *helmet.*

Visibility, *a being*
Visible, *that may be seen, apparent, clear,* or *manifest.*
The Visier, grand Visier, *or* prime Visier, *the principal Statesman among the* Turks, *next in dignity and power to the* grand Seignior.
A Vision, *apparition,* or *phantome*; also *a divine revelation in a dream, such as the Prophets had of old.*
A Visionary, *a fanatical pretender to* visions.
A Visit, *and*
To visit, *to go,* or *come to see a friend, place,* &c.
A Visitation, *or* visiting *of a Diocess, by the Bishop every three years,* or *by the Arch-deacon once a year, to inspect matters relating to the several Churches and their Rectors,* &c. Also *the* Divine *visiting of a Nation,* or *particular Persons with some signal judgment,* or *affliction*; as
The Visitation, or *great sickness in* London *A.D.* 1665.
A Visiter, or *maker of visits.*
A Visitor, *one that has a right to* visit *a Convent.*
Vital, *of life, that has life in it; that gives and preserves life.*
The Vitals, or *vital parts.*
To vitiate, *deprave,* or *corrupt.*
Vitriol, *a kind of mineral salt, somewhat like rock-allum.*
Vivacity, *liveliness,* or *sprightliness.*
The Vives, *kernels that sometimes breed in a horse's throat, and puts him in danger of being choaked.*
To vivify, *quicken,* or *revive.*
A Vixen, *or* fixen *a fox's cub;* also *an arrant scold,* or *brawling wench*
Viz. (*for* videlicet) *to wit.*
A Vizzard, *mask,* or *false face.*

U L

An Ulcer, *a running sore in the soft parts of the body accompany'd with putrefaction.*
To ulcerate, *to cause,* or *to break out into an ulcer.*
An Ulceration.
Ulcerous, or *full of ulcers.*
Ultimate, *final, last,* or *utmost.*

U M

An Umber, *a fish*; also *a kind of sad yellow paint.*
The Umbles, or numbles, *of a deer.*
An Umbrage, *shadow, appearance,* or *mistrust.*
An Umbrello *to keep off the Sun,* or *rain.*
Umpirage, *the Office of*
An Umpire, or *arbitrator.*

U N

Un, *a negative particle put for the* Latin *in,* as,
Unable, *impotent,* or *incapable.*
Unableness, or *inability.*
Unacceptable, or *disagreeable.*
Unaccepted, *that is not well received.*
Unaccessible, inaccessible, or *not to be come at.*
Unaccountable, *that cannot be accounted for.*
Unaccustomed, or *unusual.*
Unaccustomedness.
Unacquainted with, *ignorant of*; or *not having any skill in.*
Unacquaintedness.
Unactive, *that is not active.*
Unaddicted, *not addicted* or *not given to*
Unadvisable, *that ought not to be advised.*
Unadvised, *inconsiderate, imprudent, indiscreet* or *rash.*
Unadvisedness.
Unaffected, *without affectation*; also *that is not mov'd,* or *concern'd.*
Unaffectedness, *plainness,* or *simplicity.*
Unalienable, *that cannot be alienated.*
Unallowable, *that ought not to be* allowed, or *endur'd.*
Unallowed, *that is not permitted.*
Unalterable, *that cannot be alter'd,* or *chang'd.*
Unaltered, *without alteration,* or *that is not chang'd.*
Unamazed, or *undaunted*
Unamazedness.
Unanimity, *a being*
Unanimous, *of one mind,* or *of one accord.*
Unanswerable, *that cannot be answer'd.*
Unanswered, *that is not,* or *has not been answer'd.*
Unappeasable, *not to be appeased.*
Unappeased, *that is not yet appeased.*
Unapprehensive, *that does not apprehend,* or *perceive.*
Unapproachable, or *inaccessible.*
Unapt, or *unfit.*
Unaptness, or *incapacity.*
Unarmed, *destitute of Arms.*
Unasked, *that has not been* asked, or *demanded.*
Unassured, *that has no assu-*

assurance, or *doubtfull*.
Unasswaged, *that is not appeased*.
Unattainable, *that cannot be attain'd*.
Unattempted, *that has not been tryed*, or *experimented*.
Unavailable, *that profits nothing*.
Unavoidable, *inevitable, that cannot be avoided*.
Unawaked, *not awake*.
Unawares, *unthought on, unexpected*, or *unlooked for*.
To unbar, or *remove the* bars *of a door, window*, &c.
Unbecoming, or *indecent*.
Unbefriended, *destitute, of friends*.
Unbegotten, *not begotten*.
Unbelief, *infidelity*, or *incredulity*.
An Unbeliever.
Unbelieving.
To unbend, *losen*, or *slacken*.
Unbent, or *unbended*.
To unbeseem, or *be unseemly*.
Unbeseemingness, or *indecency*.
Unbesotted, *reduced to a sound mind*.
Unbewailed, *not lamented*.
To unbewitch, or *free from inchantment*.
Unbiassed, *not drawn to any side; impartial*.
Unbidden, *that is not commanded*, or *invited*.
To unbind, or *unty*.
Unblamable, *void of blame*, or *innocent*.
Unblamableness.
Unbloudy, *done without bloud-shed*, or *that has cost no bloud*.
Unboiled, *not boiled*.
To unbolt, or *undo the* bolt *of a door*, &c.
Unboned, *that has the bones taken out*.
Unbooted, *that has got his boots off*.
Unborn, *not yet born*.
To unbosom *himself, to declare his mind freely*.
Unbought, *not bought*.
Unbound, or *untied*.
Unbounded, *boundless*, or *that has no bounds*.
To unbow, or *make straight again*.
To unbowel, or *take out the bowels*.
To unbrace, or *ungird*.
To unbridle, or *take off the reins*.
Unbroken, *not broken*, or *untamed*.
To unbuckle, or *unclasp*.
Unbuilt, *not built*.
To unbung, or *take off the* bung *of a vessel*.
To unburden, or *unload*.
Unburied, *not buried*.
To unbutton, or *undo the buttons of a coat*.
Uncalled, *not called*.
Uncanonical, *not Canonical*, or *not conformable the Canon*.
Uncapable, *incapable*, or *unfit*.
To uncase, or *take out of the case*.
Uncaught, *not catch'd*.
Uncertain, *not* certain, *inconstant, irresolute, fickle*, &c.
Uncertainness, *or* Uncertainty.
Uncessant, *incessant*, or *continual*.
To unchain, or *let loose from the* chains.
Unchangeable, *not subject to change*.
Unchangeableness.
Uncharitable, *void of charity*, or *inhumane*.
Uncharitableness.
To uncharm, or *take off a charm*.
Unchaste, or *incontinent*.
Unchastness.
Unchewed, *without being chewed*.
Unchristian, *unworthy of a Christian*, or *contrary to the Principles of Christianity*.
Unchipped, *not chipped*.
To Unchurch, or *exclude from the Catholick Church*.
Unceiled, *without cieling*.
Uncircumcised, *not circumcised*.
Uncircumcision.
Uncircumspect, or *unwary*.
Uncivil, *or* incivil; *rude*, or *unmannerly*.
Unclad, or *uncloathed*.
To unclasp, or *undo a clasp*.
An Uncle, *the father's*, or *mother's brother*.
Unclean, *unchaste, impure*, or *filthy*.
Uncleanness.
Uncleansed, *not* cleansed, or *not made clean*.
Uncleft, *not* cleft, or *not divided*.
To unclose, *or* disclose.
Unclothed, *stript of clothes*
Uncombed, *not combed*.
Uncomeliness, *a being*
Uncomely, *indecent*, or *unseemly*.
Uncomfortable, *destitute of comfort*; *sad*, or *deplorable*.
Uncomfortableness.
Uncommon, *not* common, *not usual*, or *rare*.
Uncommonness, or *rarity*.
Uncommunicable, *not to be communicated*.
Uncompounded, *not compounded*, or *simple*.
Unconceivable, *not to be conceived*.
Unconceivableness.
Unconcerned, *not concerned*, or *not troubled*.
Unconcernedness, or *indifferency*.
Unconcluding, *or* unconclusive,

clusive, *that concludes nothing.*

Uncondemned, *not condemned.*

Unconfirmed, *not ratifyed.*

Unconformable, *that refuses to conform.*

Unconformed, *not conformed.*

An Unconformity *of Religion.*

Unconquerable, or *invincible, that cannot be overcome.*

Unconquered, *not subdued.*

Unconscionable, *that has no conscience; unreasonable.*

Unconscionableness.

Unconsecrated, *not consecrated.*

Unconstant, *or* inconstant.

Unconstrained, *not forced without* constraint, or *free.*

Unconsumed, *not wasted.*

Uncontemned, *not despis'd*

Uncontrollable, *not to be controlled.*

To uncord, or *undo the cords*

Uncorrected, *not corrected,* or *not amended.*

Uncorrupt, or *uncorrupted.*

Uncorruptible, *or* incorruptible, *not subject to corruption.*

Uncorruptness, or *incorruption.*

To uncover, or *take off the* covering.

To uncouple, or *disjoyn.*

Uncourteous, discourteous, or *uncivil.*

Uncourteousness, or *discourtesy.*

Uncouth, *foreign, barbarous, harsh, not to be understood; from the old* Saxon *word* uncuth, *i. e.* unknown, *as a stranger is that lies but one night in an Inn.*

Uncreated, *not created.*

To uncrown *a King, to deprive him of his* Crown *and Dignity.*

An Unction, or *anointing.*

Unctuous, *oily, fatty,* or *greasy.*

Uncurable, *or* incurable, *that cannot be cured.*

Uncured, *that is not cured.*

Uncut, *not cut.*

Undaunted, *not* daunted, *void of fear, stout,* or *bold.*

Undauntedness.

Undeceivable, *that may be undeceived.*

To undeceive, *disabuse,* or *make one sensible of his mistake.*

Undecent, indecent, or *unseemly.*

Undecided, *not determined.*

Undecked, *not adorned.*

Undefended, *destitute of defence.*

Undefiled, *not polluted, pure,* or *without spot.*

Undefrayed, *not discharg'd,* or *not paid.*

Undeniable, *that cannot be denied.*

Under; as *under ground*

Under-age, *non-age,* or *minority.*

To under-bid, *to offer less for a thing than it is worth.*

To under-bind, or *bind underneath.*

An Under-Brigadeer, or *Sub-Brigadeer.*

An Under-Butler.

An Under-Caterer.

An Under-Chamberlain, or *Vice-Chamberlain.*

An Under-Chanter, *or* Sub-Chanter *of a Cathedral.*

To under-gird, or *underbind.*

An Under-girdle.

To undergo, *suffer,* or *sustain.*

An Under-Governour.

Under-hand, *private,* or *secret;* as *under-hand dealings,* or *sinister practices.*

Underived, *not derived.*

To under-lay *a shoo,* or *clap on a new sole.*

The Under-leather *of a shoo,* &c.

A Under-Lieutenant.

An Underling, or *inferiour; one that acts under another,* or *only by his orders.*

An Under-Marshal, or *Sub-Marshal.*

To undermine, *dig under,* or *supplant.*

An Underminer.

Undermost, or *lowest of all.*

Underneath, or *below.*

An Under-Officer.

To Under-pin *a house.*

An Under-Prior *of a Convent.*

An Under-Prioress.

To under-prop, or *set a prop under.*

An Under-Secretary.

To under-sell, *to sell a thing for less than it is worth.*

A Under-Servant, or *servant of a lower rank.*

An Under-Sheriff.

Under-sold (*from to* under-sell.)

To understand, *know,* or *perceive; to receive advice of,* &c.

Understanding, *intelligence,* or *correspondence.*

The Understanding, or *intellect.*

Understood, *known, perceived,* &c.

To undertake, *to take upon him, attempt,* or *answer for.*

Undertaken.

An Undertaker.

I Undertook, or *did undertake.*

The Under-Treasurer, *or* Trea-

Treasurer of the Exchequer, ***an Officer subordinate to the*** **Lord-Treasurer**, ***whose business is to chest up the King's Treasure, and to note the content of Money in every Chest.***

To Undervalue, *to set a low price upon*, or *to slight.*

I Underwent *or did undergo.*

The under-wheels *of a Coach*, &c.

An Under-wood, *or* Copse, *a Wood that is felled*, or *lopped every nine or ten years.*

Under-written, or *subscribed.*

Undeserved, *not merited.*

Undeterminate, indeterminate, or *indefinite.*

Undetermined, *not determined*, or *not decided.*

Undevout, or *irreligious.*

Undied, *that is not died*, or *has no tincture.*

Undigested, or *indigested.*

Undiligent, or *negligent.*

Undiminishable, *that cannot be diminished.*

Undiminished, *not lessened*, or *not impaired.*

Undiscerning, *that has no judgment* or *discretion.*

Undischarged, *not discharged*, or *not paid.*

Undisciplined Troops, *not Disciplined*, or *not duely Exercised.*

Undiscovered, or *not disclosed.*

Undiscreet, indiscreet, *imprudent*, or *unwise.*

Undiscreetness, or *indiscretion.*

Undisposed *of*, *not yet disposed of.*

Undisprovable, *not to be excepted against.*

Undissolvable, *or* indissolvable, *that cannot be dissolved.*

Undissolved, *not dissolved.*

Undistinguishable, *that cannot be distinguished.*

Undistinguished, *not yet distinguished.*

Undistinct, indistinct, or *confused.*

Undisturbed, *not troubled.*

Undivided, *not divided.*

To undo, *unty*, *loose*, *make*, *void*, *destroy*, &c.

An Undoer.

Undone.

Undoubted, *not to be doubted*, or *questioned.*

To undraw, or *draw back Curtains*, &c.

An Undress, *and*

To Undress, or *pull off his cloaths.*

Undried, *not dried.*

Undue, *illegal*, or *irregular.*

Undutiful, or *disobedient.*

Undutifulness.

Uneasiness, *a being*

Uneasie, *not* easie, *difficult*, or *inconvenient.*

Unedified, *that is not edified.*

Unedifying, *that does not edifie.*

Uneffectual, *or* ineffectual, *that does not take effect.*

Uneloquent, *that is not eloquent.*

Unemployed, *not employed.*

Unendowed, *that has no* dowry, or *cost bestowed upon it.*

Unequal, or *uneven.*

Unequality, *or* inequality.

Unerring, *that cannot err*; *infallible.*

Unestimable, *or* inestimable, *not to be sufficiently valued.*

Unevangelical, *not conformable to the Gospel.*

Uneven, or *unequal.*

Unevenness.

Unevitable, inevitable, or *unavoidable.*

Unexcusable, *or* inexcusable.

Unexecuted, *not executed.*

Unexampled, *that has no example*, *president*, or *parallel.*

Unexpected, or *unlooked for.*

Unexperienced, *that is not* experienced, or *well vers'd.*

Unexpert, or *unskilful.*

Unexplicable, *or* inexplicable, *that cannot be explained.*

Unexpressible, *or* inexpressible, *not to be expressed.*

Unextended, *not extended.*

Unextinguishable, *or* inextinguishable; *not to be quenched.*

Unextinguished, *that is not extinguished.*

Unextirpated, *not rooted out.*

Unfair, *not* fair, or *unjust.*

Unfaithful, *not* faithful, *disloyal*, *treacherous*, or *false.*

Unfaithfulness.

Unfalsified, *not* falsified, *not disguised*, or *not corrupted.*

Unfarced, *not* farced, or *not stuffed.*

Unfashionable, *not conformable to the fashion.*

Unfashioned, *that has no shape.*

To unfasten, or *undo.*

Unfeasible, *that is not* feasible, or *that cannot be done.*

Unfeathered, or *featherless*, *that has no feathers.*

Unfed, *that has not been fed.*

Unfeign-

Unfeigned, *sincere or upright.*
Unfeignedness.
Unfenc'd, *not fenced*, or *not fortified.*
Unfertile, infertile, or *unfruitful.*
To unfetter, or *free from fetters.*
Unfinished, *not finished*, or *imperfect.*
Unfit, *incapable, inconvenient*, or *improper.*
Unfitness.
Unfixed, *or* unfixt, *not fixed.*
To unfold, *to undoe the folds*, or *to explain.*
An Unfolder.
Unforced, *free from force*, or *compulsion.*
Unforeseen, *not foreseen.*
Unformed, *without* form, *rude*, or *indigested.*
Unfortified, *destitute of any Fortification.*
Unfortunate, *unhappy*, or *unlucky.*
Unfound, *not found.*
Unfree, *not free*, or *ungenteel.*
Unfrequency, *a being*
Unfrequent, *rare*, or *that happens but seldom.*
Unfrequented, *not frequented* or *not resorted to.*
Unfriendliness, or *want of friendship.*
Unfriendly, *unworthy of a friend*, or *disobliging.*
Unfruitful, or *barren.*
Unfruitfulness.
To unfurnish, or *take away the furniture.*
Ungainful, or *unprofitable.*
Ungainly, *oddly*, or *aukwardly.*
Ungarded, *not garded*, or *not fenced.*
Ungarnished, *not decked*, or *not trimmed*; *whose* garniture *is taken away.*
Ungathered, *not yet gathered*

Ungenteel, *ignoble, rude*, or *uncivil.*
Ungenteelness.
Ungentle, *not gentle; cruel, rigorous*, or *crabbed.*
Ungentleness.
Ungenerous, *not generous*, or *base.*
Ungilt, or *ungilded.*
To ungild, or *take off the gilding.*
To Ungird, or *undo the girth.*
Ungirt, or *ungirded.*
To unglue, or *undo the glue.*
Ungodliness, or *impiety.*
Ungodly, *impious*, or *irreligious.*
Ungovernable, or *unruly.*
Ungovernableness.
Ungraceful, *unhandsome* or *unbeseeming.*
Ungracefulness.
Ungracious, *void of grace, untoward*, or, *lewd.*
Ungraciousness.
Ungrateful, *that do's not return thanks*, or *acknowledge a favour done.*
Ungratefulness, or *ingratitude.*
To ungravel, or *take away the gravel.*
Unguent, *Ointment*, or *Salve.*
Unhabitable, *not fit to be inhabited.*
Unhabitableness.
Unhallowed, or *profane.*
Unhaltered, *that has the* halter *taken off.*
Unhandsome, *ill-fashioned, ungenteel*, or *unseemly.*
Unhandsomeness.
Unhappiness, or *misfortune.*
Unhappy, *unfortunate, unlucky*, or *shrewd.*
Unharmonious, *without harmony*, or *jarring.*

To unharness, or *take off the harness.*
To unhaspe, or *undo the the hasps.*
Unhealed, *not healed*, or *not cured.*
Unhealthful, unhealthy, or *sickly.*
Unhealthfulness, *or* unhealthiness..
Unheard *of, not heard of, surprising*, or *extraodinary.*
Unheeded, *not regarded.*
Unheedful, or *unwary.*
Unheediness, or *heedlesness*
Unheedy, *negligent, heedless*, or *careless.*
To unhinge, or *take off from the hinges.*
Unholy, *void of holiness, ungodly*, or *profane.*
To Unhook, or *take off from the hooks.*
Unhonest, *or* dishonest.
Unhoped *for, not* hoped *for*, or *unexpected.*
To unhorse *one*, or *throw him from off his horse.*
Unhospitable, *or* inhospitable, *not given to hospitality*,
Unhurt, *that has receiv'd no* hurt, or *dammage.*
Unhusbanded, or *untilled.*
An Unicorn, *a Beast like a horse, said to have one horn on the forehead.*
Uniform, *of one form, regular, having all parts alike.*
Uniformity.
Unimaginable, *that surpasses imagination.*
Unimitable, *or* inimitable, *not to be imitated.*
Uninhabited, *not inhabited*, or *not dwelt in.*
Unintelligible, *not to be understood.*
Unintermitted, *that has no intermission.*
Uninvited, *not invited.*
Union, or *Concord.*
Union-pearls, *the best sort of* pearls, *that grow in couples.*

To

To Unjoint, *or undo the joynts.*

Unison (*a Musical Term*) *when two notes, or strings agree in the same tone.*

An Unit, *or number one,* (*in* Arithmetick.

Unitable, *capable of being united.*

To unite, *or join together.*

Unity, *a being united together*; also *concord,* or *agreement.*

Unjudged, *not judged.*

Universal, *the whole, all without exception, all together.*

Universality, or *generality.*

The Universe, or *the whole World.*

An University, *a nursery of Learning and all sorts of liberal Sciences*; as *the famous Universities of* Oxford *and* Cambridge.

An University-man.

Unjust, *not just, wrongfull,* or *unreasonable.*

Unjustice, or injustice.

Unjustifiable, *that cannot be justify'd.*

Unked, or unkward, *lonely,* or *solitary.*

To unkennel *a fox,* or *to drive him out of his den.*

Unkind, *that shews no kindness, uncivil,* or *disobliging.*

Unkindness.

Unkissed, *not kissed.*

To unknit, or *un to knitting*

Unknowingly, or *ignorantly.*

Unknown, *not known,* or *not understood.*

Unlaboured, or *untilled.*

To unlace, or *undo a lace.*

Unladen, or *unloaded.*

Unlamented, or *unbewailed.*

Unlaudable, *or* illaudable; *not commendable.*

Unlawfull, *not* lawful, *illegitimate,* or *illegal.*

Unlawfulness.

To unlearn, or *forget what one has learnt.*

Unlearned, *illiterate,* or *ignorant.*

Unlearnt, or *unlearn'd*

To unleash, or *undo the* leash *in order to let go the dogs in hunting.*

To unleave, or *pluck off the leaves.*

Unleavened-bread, *that is made without* leaven, or *yest.*

Unless, or *except.*

Unlicensed, *not licensed.*

Unlike, *not like,* or *different.*

Unlikeness, or *improbability.*

Unlikely, *not likely,* or *not probable.*

Unlikeliness, *diversity, disparity,* or *difference.*

Unlimited, *not circumscrib'd,* or *not bounded.*

To unline, or *take off the lining.*

To unload, or *disburden.*

To unlock, or *open that which is shut with a lock.*

Unlooked *for,* or *unexpected.*

To unloose, *untye,* or *resolve.*

Unlovely, *that is not amiable,* or *agreeable.*

Unloving, or *unkind.*

Unluckiness, *a being*

Unlucky, *unfortunate, shrewd,* or *mischievous.*

Unmade, *not yet made,* or *not finished.*

To unman, *himself, to degrade,* or *debase himself.*

To unman *a ship, to take the guns,* &c. *out of her.*

Unmanageable, *that cannot be well* managed, or *governed.*

Unmanliness.

Unmanly, *unworthy of a Man,* or *effeminate.*

Unmannerliness, *a being*

Unmannerly, *incivil,* or *uncourteous.*

Unmanured, *not cultivated,* or *not tilled.*

Unmarried, *not married,* or *single.*

To unmarry, or *dissolve marriage.*

To unmask, *to pull off the mask,* or *to discover.*

To unmat, or *take off the mat.*

To unmatch, *to sever,* or *to make uneven.*

Unmeasurable, or *immense.*

Unmeasurableness.

Unmeet, *indecent,* or *unfit.*

Unmerciful, *that shews* no mercy, *hard-hearted,* or *pitiless.*

Unmercifulness.

Unminded, *neglected,* or *not regarded.*

Unmindful, *forgetfull,* or *negligent.*

Unmindfulness.

Unmingled, *or* unmixed, *that is not mixt, simple,* or *pure.*

Unmolested, or *undisturbed.*

Unmoored, as *a ship that has her anchors weighed, and is ready to set out to Sea.*

Unmoveable, *that cannot be moved.*

Unmoveableness.

Unmoved, *not moved.*

To unmuffle, or *pull off the muffler.*

To unnail, or *draw out the nails.*

Unnatural, *void of natural affection,* or *inhumane*; also *preternatural,* or *monstrous.*

Unnaturalness.

Unnavigable, *not navigable,* or *that cannot be sailed on.*

Unnecessary, *not requisite,* or *superfluous.*

Unneedful, *needless,* or unnecessary.

Un-

Unnoble, or *ignoble*.
Unoccupied, or *unemployed*.
Unorderly, disorderly, or *confused*.
Unpaid, *not paid*.
Unpainted, *not painted*.
Unpaired, *not disposed of in* pairs.
Unparallelled, *that cannot be match'd*, or *incomparable*.
Unpardonable, *not to be forgiven*.
Unpared, *not pared*.
Unparted, *not separated*.
Unpastured, *not let into pasture*, or, *not fed*.
Unpatient, or impatient.
To **unpave**, or *pull up the pavement*.
Unpeaceable, *not peaceable*, or *unquiet*.
To **unpeg**, or *draw out the pegs*.
To **unpeople**, dispeople, or *destroy the People of a Country*.
Unperceivable, *not to be perceived*.
Unperfect, or imperfect.
Unperfectness, or *imperfection*.
Unperformed, *not perform'd*, or *not accomplish'd*.
Unperishable, or *incorruptible*.
Unpestered, *got clear from trouble*, *disengaged*, or *disentangled*.
Unpleasant, unpleasing, *disagreeable*, or *harsh*.
Unpleasantness.
Unpliant, or *inflexible*.
Unpliantness.
Unplowed, *untilled*, or *unmanured*.
Unpolished, *not polished*, *rough*, or *rude*.
Unpolled, *not shaved*.
Unpolluted, *not defiled*.
Unpossible, or impossible.
Unpracticable, or impracticable; *that cannot be practis'd*, or *done*.
Unpractised, *not practised*, or *not put into practice*.
An **Unprejudicate** *Opinion*.
Unprejudiced, or *void of prejudices*.
Unpremeditated, *not studied before-hand*.
Unprepared, *not prepared*, or *not made ready*.
Unpreparedness.
Unpressed, *not pressed*.
Unpretended *to*, *that to which no* pretension, or *claim is laid*.
Unprisable, or *unvaluable*.
Unprofitable, *that yields* no profit, or *useless*.
Unprofitableness.
Unpronounced, *not uttered*.
Unproper, or improper.
Unproportionable, or disproportionable.
Unproportioned, *not proportioned to*.
Unprosperous, or *unsuccessfull*.
Unproved, *not proved*, or *not tried*.
Unprovided, *not* provided or *not furnish'd with*.
Unprovident, *that has no fore-sight*, or *imprudent*.
Unpruned, *not* pruned, or *not lopped*.
Unprovoked, *without any* provocation, or *not exasperated*.
Unpunished, *not punished*.
Unqualified, *not* qualified *that has not requisite* qualities, or *unfit*.
Unquenchable, *that is never quenched*.
Unquenched, *not quenched*, or *not extinguish'd*.
Unquestionable, *not to be* question'd, or *not to be doubted*.
Unquestionableness.
Unquiet, *restless*, *turbulent*, or *troublesome*.
Unquietness.
To **unravel**, *undo*, or *disentangle*.
Unreadiness.
Unready, *not* ready, or *undress'd*.
Unreasonable, *void of reason*, *not consonant to it*; or *immoderate*.
Unreasonableness.
Unrebukable, or *unblamable*.
Unrebuked, *not reprov'd*, or *not censur'd*.
Unreclaimed, *not* reclaimed, or *not reduc'd to reason*.
Unrecompensed, or *unrequited*.
Unreconcilable, or irreconcileable.
Unreconciled, *not reconciled*.
Unrecoverable, or irrecoverable.
Unrecovered, *not recovered*.
Unredeemable, *that cannot be redeemed*.
Unredeemed, or *not redeemed*.
Unreformable, or *incorrigible*.
Unreformed, *not* reformed, or *redressed*.
Unregarded, *disregarded*, or *slighted*.
Unregardfull, *unmindfull*, or *negligent*.
Unrelenting, *not* relenting, or *inflexible*.
Unremediable, or irremediable, *that cannot be remedied*, or *helped*.
Unremoved, *not removed*.
Unrepairable, or irreparable.
Unrepaired, *not repaired*.
Unrepealable, *that cannot be repealed*, or *abolished*.
Unrepealed, *not abrogated*, or *not dissannulled*.
Unreprovable, or *blameless*.

Un-

Unreproved, *not reprov'd*, or *not rebuk'd*.
Unrequited, *not rewarded*, *not recomponced*, &c.
Unresisted, *not oppos'd*.
Unresistable, or irresistible.
Unresolved, or *irresolute*.
Unrespectfull, *inofficious*, or *disobliging*.
Unrestored, *not restored*.
Unrevealed, or *not disclosed*.
Unrevenged, *not revenged*.
Unreverent, or irreverent, *that shews no reverence*, or *respect*.
Unreverentness, or irreverence.
Unrevocable, or irrevocable, *not to be revoked*.
Unrewarded, *that has had no reward*, or *recompence*.
To unriddle, *undo the* riddle, *discover*, or *explain*.
To unrig, or *take away the rigging*.
Unrighteous, or *unjust*.
Unrighteousness.
To unring, or *take off a mare's ring*.
To unrip, or *unsow*.
Unripe, *not ripe*, or *not come to perfection*.
Unripeness.
Unript, or *unripped*.
To unrivet, or *undo the rivets*.
To unroll, or *undo a roll*.
To unroot, *root out*, or *grub up*.
Unruliness, *a being*
Unruly, *intractable*, *untamed*, or *refractary*.
To unsaddle, or *take off the saddle*.
Unsafe, *not* safe, *not secure*, or *dangerous*.
Unsaid, or *recanted*.
Unsalted, *not salted*.
Unsaluted, *not saluted*.
Unsanctified, or *unhallowed*.
Unsatiable, or insatiable, *that cannot be satisfied*.
Unsatisfactory, *that gives no satisfaction*.
Unsatisfied, or dissatisfied.
Unsavouriness, *a being*
Unsavoury, *tastless*, or *insipid*.
To Unsay, *to deny what was said*, or *to recant*.
Unscaled, *that has no scales*.
To unscrew, or *undo the screw*.
Unscriptural, *not prescribed in the Holy Scriptures*.
To unseal, or *take off the seal*.
Unsearchable, *that cannot be found out*, or *comprehended*.
Unsearchableness.
Unseasonable, *out of season*, or *untimely*.
Unseasonableness.
Unseemliness, *a being*
Unseemly, *unbecoming*, or *unhandsome*.
Unseen, *not seen*.
Unsensible, or insensible, *that has no sense of*.
Unsent *for*, *not sent for*.
Unseparable, or inseparable, *not to be parted*.
Unserviceable, *of no use*, or *unprofitable*.
Unserviceableness.
Unset, *not set*.
Unsettled, *not* settled, or *not established*; *instable*.
Unsettledness.
To unsew, or unsow.
To unshackle, or *strike off the shackles*.
Unshaded, *not cover'd with a shade*.
Unshaken, *not shaken*, or *immoveable*.
Unshamefaced, *not* shamefac'd, *hardy*, or *bold*.
Unshamefacedness.
Unshapen, *without* shape, *form*, or *fashion*.
Unshaved, or unshaven; *that is not shaved*.
To unsheath, or *draw out of the sheath*.
Unshod, *without* shoes, or *bare-footed*.
To unshoo, or *pull off the shoos*.
Unshorn, *not shorn*, or *unpolled*.
Unshut, *not shut*.
Unskilled, *not versed in*.
Unskilfull, *unexperienced*, *ignorant*, or *raw*.
Unskilfulness.
Unsincere, not sincere, or *not upright and cordial*.
Unsinning, or *free from sin*.
Unsnared, or *got out of the snare*.
Unsociable, *not sociable*.
Unsociableness.
Unsodden, or *not boiled*.
Unsoiled, or *not dirtied*.
To unsolder, or *undo the solder*.
To unsole, or *pull off the soles*.
Unsolid, *void of solidity*, or *soundness*.
Unsollicited, *not sollicited*.
Unsought, *not sought for*, or *unlooked for*.
Unsound, *not sound*, *corrupt*, or *unsincere*.
Unsoundness.
To unsow, or *undo what is sow'd*.
Unspeakable, *not to be utter'd*, or *express'd*.
Unspent, *not us'd*, or *not consum'd*.
Unspoken *of*.
Unspotted, *without spot*, or *blemish*.
Unstability, or instability.
Unstable, instable, *unsteady*, *unconstant*, or *wavering*.
Unstained, *unspotted*, or *undefiled*.
Unstayed, *unsettled*, or *dissolute*.
Unstayedness.
Unsteadiness, *a being*
Unsteady, *not* steady, *uncertain*, or *fickle*.
Unstedfast, *not firm*, *inconstant*.

constant, or *changeable*.
Unstedfastness.
Unstirred, or *not moved*.
To unstitch, or *undo the stitches*.
To unstop, *remove or open the stoppage*.
Unstopt, or *unstopped*.
Unstrained, *not strained*, or *not forced*.
Unstrung, *that has no* strings (*speaking of a Musical Instrument*.)
Unstuffed, *not stuffed*.
Unsubdued, or *unconquered*.
Unsuccessful, *successless, that has no good* success, or *unfortunate*.
Unsuccessfulness.
Unsufferable, *insupportable*, or *intolerable*.
Unsufficient, or insufficient,
Unsummed, *as Hawks feathers not come to their full length*.
Unsure, *uncertain*, or *unsafe*.
Unsuitable, *unfit*, or *improper*.
Unsuitableness.
To unswathe, or *undo the swathing-bands*.
Unsweet, *not* sweet, or *unsavoury*.
Unsworn, *that has not taken his oath*.
Untainted, *uncorrupted*, or *unspotted*.
Untaken, *not taken*, or *not apprehended*.
Untameable, *that cannot* be tamed, or *mastered*.
Untameableness.
Untamed, *not tamed*.
To untangle, or *disentangle*.
Untasted, *not tasted*, or *not touched*.
Untaught, or *not instructed*.
To unteach, or *teach the contrary to what was taught before*.

Unteachable, indocile, or *unapt to learn*.
To unteam Horses, or *take 'em out of the Team*.
Untemperate, *or* intemperate.
Unterrified, or *undaunted*
Unthankful, *not thankful*, or *ungrateful*.
Unthankfulness.
Unthinking, *inconsiderate, unwary*, or *indiscreet*.
Unthought of, or *not looked for*.
An unthrift, *spend-thrift*, or debosshee.
Unthriftiness, *a being*
Unthrifty, *not given to* thriftiness, *prodigal*, or *profuse*.
Unthriving, *that does not thrive*, or *succeed*.
To unthrone, dethrone, or *put out of his Throne*.
To untile, or *pull off the tiles*.
Untill, *or* till.
Untilled, or *unmanured*.
Untimed, *not well-timed*, or *done out of season*.
Untimeliness, *a being*
Untimely, *unseasonable, over-hasty*, or *that happens before due time*.
Untired, or *unwearied*.
Unto, *or* to; as *he said unto him*.
Untold, *not declared*, or *not counted*.
Untolerable, *or* intolerable, *not to be tolerated*, or *born*.
Untoothsome, *not pleasant to the* tooth; or *not palatable*.
Untouched, *that has not been touched*, or *meddled with*.
Untoward, *perverse, obstinate*, or *cross-grain'd*.
Untowardness.
Untractable, intractable, or, *unruly*.
To untrap, or *pull off the horse-trappings*.

Untired, *not* tried, or *not examined*.
Untrimmed, or *undecked*.
Untrue, *not true, false*, or *unfaithful*.
To untruss, *ungird*, or *untye*.
Untrustiness, *a being*
Untrusty, *unfaithful*, or *perfidious*.
An Untruth, or *falsity*.
To untuck a *Gown, Bed*, &c.
Untuneable, *out of tune, jarring*, or *harsh*.
Unturned, *not turned*.
To untwine, *or* untwist, *to undo what has been twisted*,
To untie, or *undoe a knot*, &c.
To unvail, *to take away the vail*; or *to reveal*.
Unvaluable, *that cannot be valued*.
Unvanquished, or *unconquered*.
Unvariable, *not subject to variation*, or *change*.
Unvariableness.
Unversed, *not well* versed, or *not experienced*.
Un-uniform, or *not uniform*.
Unviolable, *or* inviolable.
Unusual, *uncommon*, or *extraordinary*.
Unusualness.
Unutterable, or *unspeakable, that cannot be expressed*.
Unwalled, *not fenced with a Wall*.
Unwarrantable, *that cannot be* warranted, *maintained*, or *justified*.
Unwariness, *a being*
Unwary, *heedless, inconsiderate*, or *imprudent*.
Unwashed, *not washed*.
Unwasted, *not consumed*.
Unwatched, *not watched*, or *not observed*.
Unwatered, *not watered*.
Unwavering, or *that does not*

does not waver, *firm, or unmoveable.*
Unwearied, *untired*, or *indefatigable.*
Unweariedness, or *indefatigable diligence.*
To unweave, or *undoe the Woof.*
Unwedded, or *unmarried.*
Unwelcome, *not welcome*, or *disagreeable.*
Unwholsome, *not wholsome*, or *unhealthy.*
Unwholsomness.
Unwieldy, *that cannot be well managed; over-heavy*, or *unactive.*
Unwilling, *not* willing, or *having no inclination.*
Unwillingness.
To unwind, *to undoe what has been wound up, disentangle*, or *disengage.*
Unwise, *imprudent*, or *indiscreet.*
Unwished *for*, *unhoped for*, *unexpected*, or *unlooked for.*
Unwittingly, *without ones knowledge*, or *inconsiderately.*
Unwonted, *unaccustomed*, or *unusual.*
Unwontedness.
Unworkman-like, *not like a work-man*, or *not artificially.*
Unworn, *not yet worn.*
Unworthiness, *a being*
Unworthy, *that has no* worth, or *merit; base*, or *infamous.*
Unwoven, *unweaved*, or *not woven.*
Unwound, (*from to un*wind) *not wound up*, or *not wrapt up.*
To unwrap, or *unfold.*
To unwreath, or *untwist.*
To unwring, or *undo that which is* wrung *together.*
Unwrinkled, *that has no wrinkles.*

Unwritten, *not* written, or *not committed to writing.*
Unwrought, *unmade*, *raw*, *rude*, or *unpolished.*
Unyielding, or *inflexible; that does not* yield, or *give way.*
To unyoke, or *free from the yoke.*

V O

A Vocabulary, *word-book*, or *little Dictionary.*
Vocal, *belonging to the voice.*
A Vocation, *Calling*, *Employ*, or *Course of Life.*
Vogue, *popular applause*, *esteem*, *reputation*, or *sway.*
A Voice, or *sound that proceeds from the mouth*; also *a suffrage*, or *vote at Elections.*
Void, *null*, *invalid*, *vacant*, *empty*, or *destitute of.*
To void, *to depart*; *to discharge*, or *cast forth*, &c.
Voidance, *a want of an incumbent, upon a Benefice.*
A Voider *a kind of vessel to carry away the remains at Table.*
Voidness, *a being void.*
Volatil, (*a Chymical term*) *apt to evaporate*, or *resolve it self into Air.*
A Volley, *a great shout*, or *a general discharge of Musket-shot.*
Volubility, *a round delivery*, or *ready utterance.*
Voluble, *that speaks with great fluentness.*
A Volume, *the size*, or *bulk of a Book.*
Voluminous, *that consists of several volumes*, or *bulky.*

Voluntary, *of his own accord*, *without compulsion* or *force.*
A Voluntary, *that which a Musician plays extempore.*
A Volunteer, *one that serves* voluntarily *in the Wars.*
A Voluptuary, or *voluptuous person.*
Voluptuous, *sensual*, or *given to carnal pleasures.*
Voluptuousness.
A Vomit, *prescrib'd by a Physitian.*
To vomit, *spew*, or *cast up.*
Vomitory, *that provokes vomiting.*
A Votaress, or *female votary.*
A Votary, *one that has bound himself to the performance of a Religious Vow.*
A Vote, or *Suffrage.*
To Vote, or *give his Vote.*
To Vouch, *assert*, *maintain*, or *defend.*
A Voucher.
To Vouch-safe, *to condescend*, or *to grant graciously.*
A Vow, or *Solemn Promise.*
To Vow, or *make a Vow.*
A Vowel, *distinguished from a Consonant*, *without which the latter cannot be sounded.*
A Voyage, or *Journey*, *more especially by Sea.*
A Voyager, or *Traveller.*

U P

Up, up and down, &c.
To upbraid, *twit*, *cast in the teeth*, or *reproach.*
An Upbraider.
Upheld, *from*
To uphold, *support*, or *maintain*,
An Upholder.

An Upholster, *to hang rooms*, &c
The Upland, or *high ground.*
An Uplander.
Upon, *or on*; as *upon that day.*
Upper, as *an upper room.*
Uppermost, *or* upmost; *highest*, or *on the top of*
Upright, *erect and straight*; or *sincere and honest.*
Uprightness, *integrity*, or *sincerity.*
The Uprising, or *first rising out of bed.*
An Uproar, *rout*, or *tumult.*
The Upshot, *event*, *issue*, or *success of a business.*
Upside-down, or *topsy-turvy.*
The Up-sitting *of a Woman after Child-birth.*
An Upstart, or *novice.*
Upward, *or* upwards; as *to fly upward.*

U R

Urbanity, or *civility.*
An Urchin, *a hedge-hog*, or *a dwarf.*
A Sea-urchin.
Ure, *or* use; as *brought in* ure, or *accustomed.*
A Ure-ox, *a kind of buffle*, or *wild ox.*
The Ureters, *two conduits through which the* Urine *passes from the reins to the bladder.*
To urge, *press*, *insist upon*, *incense*, or *exasperate.*
Urgent, *earnest*, or *pressing.*
An Urinal, *or* urine-glass, *to make water in.*
The Urinary *passage.*
Urine, or *chamber-lye.*
To urine, *to piss*, or *make water.*
An Urn, or *pitcher.*

U S

Us; as *he loves us.*
Usage, *custom*, or *treatment.*
Usance, *a month's* use *of a Merchant's bill of Exchange, before the summ of money expressed in it, becomes payable.*
Double Usance, *two months allow'd for that purpose.*
Use, *and to* use *(in all senses.)*
Use-money, *interest for the principal summ of money lent for some time.*
Usefull, *profitable*, *advantagious*, or *serviceable.*
Usefulness.
Useless, *of no use*, or *unprofitable.*
An Usher, *properly the door-keeper of a Court*; also *an under-master in a School.*
An Usher, *or* Gentleman-usher, *that attends upon a Lady*, &c.
The Usher of the Black-rod, *who is Gentleman-usher to the King, the House of Lords, and the Knights of the Garter; and keeps the Chapter-house-door, when a Chapter of the Order is sitting. This Officer is so call'd from the black rod he bears in his hand, with a gilt lion on the top, and all Noblemen call'd in question for any Crime are first committed to his custody.*
Ushers of the Exchequer, *four in number, who attend the chief Officers and Barons of that Court.*
To usher *in*, *introduce*, or *bring in.*
Usquebagh, *a sort of* Irish *strong liquor.*
Usual, *common*, *ordinary*, or *accustomed.*
Usualness, or *commonness.*
An Usufructuary, *one that has the use and profit of a thing, but not the property and right.*
An Usurer, or *lender for gain.*
To usurp, *to take wrongfully to his own use that which belongs to another.*
An Usurpation.
An Usurper.
Usury, *money given for the* use *of money*; or *an unreasonable and unlawful gain extorted upon that account.*

U T

An Utensil, or *necessary implement*; *any thing that is fit for* use.
Utility, *profit*, *benefit*, or *advantage.*
Utmost; as *to do one's utmost endeavours.*
Utter, *total*, or *entire.*
Utter, or *outward* as;
An Utter-Barrister, or *young Lawyer admitted to plead without the* Bar.
To utter, *speak forth*, *pronounce*, or *tell*; also *to sell*, or *expose to sale.*
Utterance, *a delivery in speaking*, or *a sale of Goods.*
The Uttermost, *farthermost*, or *most remote.*

V U

Vulgar, or *common.*
The Vulgar, or *common sort of People.*
Vulnerary, *belonging to*, or *good to cure wounds*; as *vulnerary plants.*
A Vultur, *a bird of prey.*

UX VY

Uxorious, *that is over-fond, of*, or *dotes upon his Wife*.
A Vye, *at cards*.
To vye, *dispute*, or *contend*.

WA

A Wad, or *bundle of pease*, or *straw*.
Wad, *course flannel*, or *cotton*.
To wad, or *line with* wad.
Wadable, *that may be waded over*, or *forded*.
To waddle, or *go side-long*; as *a duck does*.
The Waddles, or *stones of a cock*.
To wade, *in the water, over a river*, &c.
To wade into, *to penetrate* or *dive into a business*.
A Wafer, or *wafer-cake*.
A Waft, *a sign made to come on board a ship that is in some imminent danger; such as a coat, ship-gown*, &c. *hung out in the main shrowds*.
To waft, or *convey by water*.
Wafters, *passage-boats*; or *frigats to convoy merchant-men*.
A Wag, or *wanton youth*.
To wag, *stir, budge*, or *shake*.
A Wag-tail, *a bird*.
To wage, *to carry on War*, or *to prosecute the Law*.
A Wager, or *pledge*; as *to lay a wager*.
Wages, *a salary*; or *money given for any kind of service*.
Waggery, *wantonness*, or *merry pranks*.
Waggish, *wanton*, or *toyish*.
To waggle, *joggle*, or *move up and down*.
A Waggon, *a sort of cover'd chariot*.
A Waggoner.
A Waggon-maker.
A Waif, or *stray*, i. e. *lost goods claimed by no body, which belong to the King, unless challeng'd by the owner, within a year & a day*; also *goods that a thief drops*, or *leaves behind him when over-charg'd*, or *close pursued*.
To wail, bewail, or *lament*.
Wails, or *marks in the skin, after beating*.
A Wain, or *cart*.
Charles-wain, *a northern constellation*.
A Wain-man, or *carr-man*.
Wainscot (*in* Joyners *work*.)
To wainscot *a room*.
A Wair, *a piece of timber two yards long, and one foot broad*.
Wait, or *ambush*; as *to lye in* wait *for one*.
To wait, *to stay for*, or *to attend*.
A Waiter, or *waiting-servant*.
A Waiting-maid.
The Waits, *a sort of musical instrument*.
The Wake, or *smooth water that a ship makes a-stern, when under sail*.
To wake, or *watch*.
To wake, awaken, or waken *out of sleep*.
Wakefull, or *watchfull*.
Wakefulness.
A Wakeman, *the chief magistrate of* Rippon *in* Yorkshire.
Wake-robin, *an herb*.
Wakes, *certain Country-feasts still kept in some parts of* England. *They were usually celebrated for several days after the Saint's day, to whom the Parish-Church was dedicated, and probably took name from the custom of watching and praying*, or *awaking from sleep, at the several vigils of the night, on the eve of those festivals*.
A Wale-knot, *a kind of knot us'd at sea, by tying a rope with three twists, so that it cannot slip*.
A Wale-reared ship, *so termed, when built straight up, after she comes to her bearing*.
A Walk, *and*
To walk, or *go*.
A Walker.
A Night-walker.
Walkers, *Forest-Officers, appointed by the King, to take care of a certain space of ground*.
A Walking-staff.
A Wall *of a town*, or *house*.
To wall *in*, or *enclose with a wall*.
A Brick-wall.
A Mud-wall.
A Partition-wall.
A Stone-wall.
A Wall-creeper, *a bird*.
A Wall-eye, *in a horse*.
Wall-eyed.
The Wall flower.
A Wall-louse, or *bug*.
A Wall-nut, *a fruit*.
Wall-pepper, Wall-rue, Wall-wort, } *herbs*.
A Wallet, *a kind of sack*, or *satchel*.
A Wallop *of fat*.
To wallop, or *bubble up in boiling*.
To wallow, *roll*, or *tumble*.
Wallowish, *insipid*, or *unsavoury*.
A VValnut, *or* wall-nut.
To wamble, or *rise up*, as *boiling water does*, &c.

A

A Wambling, or *qualm in the stomack.*
Wan, or *pale.*
A Wand, *rod*, or *switch.*
To wander, *straggle*, *stray*, or *rove up and down.*
A Wanderer.
The Wane, or *decrease of the moon.*
To wane, or *decrease in such a manner.*
Wanness, or *paleness.*
Want, *lack*, or *need*; also *poverty*, or *penury.*
To want, *to be wanting*, or *to stand in need of.*
A Want, *a North-country word for a mole.*
A Want-louse, *an insect.*
Wanton, *unchaste*, *frolicksome*, or *nice.*
A Wapentake, or *hundred*, *a division of a Country*; *so call'd*, *because the Inhabitants were wont to give up their* weapons *to the Lord in token of subjection.*
War, *and*
To war, or *make* war.
A Man of war, or *armed ship.*
A War-horse.
To warble, *trill*, or *quaver in singing.*
The hawk warbles *her wings*; i. e. *crosses 'em together, over her back.*
A Ward, *and to* ward (*in all senses.*)
A Warden, *or* gardian; *one that has the keeping, or charge of persons*, or *things*; as
The Lord Warden *of the* Cinque-ports.
The Warden, or *chief keeper of the* Fleet-*prison.*
The Wardens *of the Companies*, or *Societies in* London, *&c.*
A Church-warden.
A Warden-pear, *a large sort of pear.*

A Warder, *one that keeps gard in the daytime.*
The Warders of the Tower, *certain Officers, who are cloath'd like the Yeomen of the King's gard, with red jackets, and black velvet-caps, and have charge of the Prisoners committed thither.*
A Wardmote, wardmote-*Court*, or *inquest*, *a Court kept in every Ward in* London.
A Wardrobe, *a place where a Prince's*, or *Nobleman's* robes *are kept.*
The Master *and* Yeoman *of the King's* Wardrobe.
The Wards *of a lock.*
The Court of Wards and Liveries, *relating chiefly to* Wards. *i. e.* Heirs *of the King's Tenants during their nonage*, &c. *It was erected by King* Hen. VIII. *and suppress'd* 12 Car. II.
Wardship, or *gardianship.*
A Ware, *or* wear *in a river.*
Ware, or *merchandize.*
A Ware-house.
A Ware-house-keeper.
Warfare, or *military affairs.*
Wariness (*from* wary) *prudence*, or *precaution.*
Warlike, *military*, or *valiant.*
Warm, *hot*, *vehement*, or *eager.*
Luke-warm.
A Warming-pan.
Warmness, *or* warmth.
To warn, *to admonish*, *advertise*, or *give notice*; *to cite*, or *summon.*
A Warp *of cloth in the loom.*
To warp, *cast*, or *bend.*
To warp *up a ship* (*a sea-term*) *to hale her to a place, when the wind is wanting, by means of a* hawser, or *cable and an anchor bent to it.*

A Warrant, *order*, *authentick permission*, *power*, &c.
To warrant, *maintain*, or *secure.*
Warrantable, *that may be warranted.*
A Warranter, or *voucher.*
A Warranty, *a covenant by deed to secure a bargain against all opposition.*
Warren, *a place privileged by prescription*, or *by the King's grant*, *to keep beasts and fowl of* Warren; *as hares*, *rabbets*, *patridges*, *pheasants*, &c.
A Warrener, *or* warren-keeper.
A Warrier, *or* warriour, *a Man of Arms*, *well vers'd in warlike affairs.*
A Wart *on the finger*, &c.
The Wart *in the middle of a flower*, &c.
Wart-wort, *an herb.*
Wary, *prudent*, *cautious*, or *circumspect.*
A Wary-angle, *a kind of magpye.*
Was; as *I was with him.*
A Wase, *a wreath of cloth*, &c; *to be laid under a vessel that is carry'd on the head.*
Wash, or *hogg-wash.*
Wash, *us'd by* Glovers, Goldsmiths, Painters, *&c.*
A Wash, or *ten strikes of oisters.*
To wash, *wet*, *rinse*, or *cleanse with water.*
A Wash-ball.
A Wash-bowl, or *wash-tub.*
A Wash-house.
A Washer.
A Washer-woman.
The Washes, or *marshes*

of

of Lincoln-shire.
A Wasp, *an Insect*.
Waspish, *touchy*, or *fretful*.
Waspishness.
A Wassel, *a Country-drinking-match*.
A Wassel-Bowl, *filled with spice-ale*, &c.
Wassellers, *a Company that make merry, and drink together*.
Waste, *and to* waste, *(in several senses)*
A Waste, or *Desart place*.
The Waste, or *middle of the Body*; also *that part of a Ship, which lies between the Main-mast and the Fore-castle*.
A Waste-Belt.
A Waste-Coat.
Waste-Cloaths, *(a Sea-term) certain cloaths hung about the Cage-work of a Ship's hull, to shadow the Men from the Enemy in a Fight*.
Long-wasted.
A Waster, *Consumer*, or *Spender*.
Wastfull, *prodigal*, or *profuse*.
Wastfulness.
A Watch, *and to* watch *(in several senses.)*
A Scout-watch.
A Watch-Candle, or *watch-light*.
A Watch-man.
A Watch-Tower.
A Watch-word.
A Watch, or *little Clock*.
A Watch-Case.
A Watch-maker.
Watchet, *a kind of blew colour*.
Watchful, *that stands on his guard, vigilant, heedful*, or *careful*.
Watchfulness.
Water *of all sorts*; as,
Cistern-water.
Holy-water, *used by* Roman-Catholicks *in their Devotions*.
Pump-water.
Rain-water.
River-water.
Rock-water.
Snow-water.
Spring-water.
Well-water.
A Water-Bailiff, *an Officer that has the oversight of Fish brought to* London, *and the gathering of Toll, that arises from the River* Thames: *He also attends upon the Lord-Mayor; marshals the Guests at his Table; arrests persons on the* Thames, *by Warrant from his Superiors*, &c.
A Water-Bank.
Water-born, as *a Ship is said to be, when she is just above ground, and begins to float*.
Water-colours, as to *Paint in water-colours*.
A Water-course.
Water-cresses } *herbs*.
Wild water-cresses. }
Water-flag. }
Water-fowl.
A Water-gage, *a Sea-wall*, or *Bank to keep off the Water*; also *an Instrument to gage*, or *measure the quantity* or *depth of any Waters*.
Water-germander, *an herb*.
Water-gruel, or *Potage made of Water and Oatmeal*.
A Water-hen.
The Water-Lilly-flower.
A Water-mill.
A Water-nut.
Water-pepper.
A Water-pot.
A Water-shoot, *that springs out of the Root*, or *Stock*.
A Water-Snake.
A Water-Spaniel.
A Water-Spider.
A Water-Spout.
A Water-swallow, *a bird*.
A Water-trough.
Water-willow, *an herb*.
Water-works.
A Watering-pot, *to water a Garden*.
Waterish or *full of water*.
Waterishness.
Watery, or *moist*.
A Waterman, or Wherry-man, *that rows a* Boat, *Barge*, &c.
To Wattle, *to cover with hurdles*, or *grates*.
Wattles, or *Folds for Sheep*.
The Wattles or *gills of a Cock*.
A Wave, *Surge*, or *Billow of the Sea*.
To wave *up and down*.
Wave-loaves, or Wave-Offerings, *certain loaves which the* Israelites *were enjoyned to give as the first fruits of every year's increase*.
To wave, or *decline a business*.
To waver, *to float to and fro*; or *to be uncertain what to do*.
A Waving, or *making a Sign for a Ship* or *Boat to come near*, or *keep off*.
To waul, or *cry as a Cat does*.
Wax *to Seal with*, &c.
Ear-wax.
Virgin-wax.
A Wax-Candle.
A Wax-Chandler.
A Wax-Taper.
To wax, *to do over*, or *dress with wax*.
A Way, *Road*, *Passage*, *means*, *manner*, *method*, &c.
A By-way.
A Cross-way.
The King's high-way.
A Wayfaring-Man, or *Traveller*.
The wayfaring-tree, or *wild-vine*

To way-lay one, or *lie in wait for him.*
A Way-layer.
Wayward, *froward*, or *peevish.*
Waywardness.
A Waze, or *wreath of Straw.*

WE

We, we our selves; &c. as *we love, we teach*, &c.
Weak, *feeble, infirm*, or *impotent.*
To weaken, or *make weak.*
A Weakling, *a Child that has little or no strength.*
Weakly, or *crazy.*
Weakness.
Weal, as *the Common-weal*, or *publick benefit.*
The weald, or *woody part of* Kent.
Wealth, *store of Riches, Goods*, &c.
A Common-wealth, or *State*; or *a popular Government in opposition to a Monarchy.*
The chief Common-wealths *in* Europe, *are those of* Venice, Genoa, Holland, & Switzerland.
A Common-wealths-man, or *stickler for a Common-wealth.*
Wealthiness, *a being*
Wealthy, *abounding in wealth, very rich*, or *potent.*
To wean *a Child*, &c.
Weapons, *all sorts of Warlike Instruments, except Fire-arms.*
Weapon-Salve, *a kind of Salve said to cure a wounded person by applying it to the Sword* or *other* weapon *that made the wound.*
Weaponless, *destitute of weapons*, or *arms.*
A Wear, or *dam in a River.*

A Wear-net, *or* weel.
Wear, *any thing that is worn.*
To wear, wear *out*, &c.
Wearable, or *fit to be worn.*
A Wearer.
Weariness, *a being weary.*
Wearisome, or *tiresome.*
Wearisomeness.
Wearish, or *unsavoury.*
Weary, *tired*, or *faint.*
To weary, *make weary*, or *tire.*
The weasand, or *throat-pipe.*
A Weather, or *gelt sheep.*
A Bell-weather, *a weather-sheep, that leads the whole Flock, with a collar of* Bells *about his neck.*
Weather-mutton, *the flesh of weather-sheep.*
The Weather, or *disposition of the Air.*
Weather-beaten, *properly said of a Ship, that has endur'd the stress of bad weather, and many Storms.*
A Weather-cock, *or* Vane, *that points out on what quarter the wind blows.*
A Weather-glass, *to shew the change of the weather, with the degrees of heat and cold.*
Weather-wise, *skilled in foretelling the disposition of the weather.*
To weather *a* Hawk, or *set her abroad to take the air*,
To weather, *double*, or *pass by a Cape*, or *point of Land (a Sea-Term.)*
The Weather-coiing of a Ship, *when being a-hull, her head is brought the other way, without losing any Sail; only by bearing up the helm.*

The weather-gage *at Sea*, or *advantage of the Wind*
To weave *cloath, silk, hair.* &c.
A Weaver, or *woollen-cloath-weaver.*
A Linnen-weaver.
A Ribbon-weaver.
A Stocking-weaver.
A Silk-weever.
A Web *of cloath*, &c. *that is wove.*
A Cob-web.
A Web, or *Sheet of Lead.*
A Web, or *Pearl in the Eye.*
A Webster, or *Weaver.*
To Wed, or *Marry a Wife.*
A Wedding.
A Wedding-dinner.
A Wedding-garment,
A Wedding-ring.
A Wedding-song.
A Wedge *to cleave with.*
A Wedge, or *Ingot of Gold.*
Wedge-wise, or *in form of a wedge.*
Wedlock, *or* Marriage.
Wednesday, (*q. d.* Wodensday) *the fourth day of the week, so called from its being dedicated to* Woden, *the God of War, among the ancient* Saxons; *the word signifies* Fire, or *Furious.*
Ash-wednesday, *the first day of Lent, taking name from the ancient custom of repenting in Sacck-cloth, and Ashes*; or *from that of eating nothing but a Cake baked under the Embers.*
A Weed, *a rank*, or *wild herb.*
To weed, or *root out Weeds.*
A Frier's weed, or *habit.*
Choke weed.
Rope-weed

Sea-

Sea-weed.
A Weeder, *one employ'd in grubbing up of weeds.*
A Weeding-hook.
A Week, *the space of seven days.*
The Week, or *cotton of a candle*, or *lamp.*
Weekly, or *every week.*
A Weel *to take fish in.*
To weep, or *shed tears.*
A Weeper.
A Weesel, *a little wild beast.*
A Weevil, *a small black worm that eats up corn.*
A Weigh *of cheese*, or *wooll*, i. e. 256 *pounds.*
To weigh, *to poise*, or *to be of weight*; *to examine*, *consider*, *judge of*, &c.
A Weigher.
A Weight, *poise*, or *burden*; also *a matter of moment.*
Weightiness, *heaviness*, or *importance.*
Weights *to weigh with.*
Gold-weights.
Avoir-du-poise-weight, *containing* 16 *ounces in the pound.*
Troy-weight, *that has but twelve ounces.*
Weighty, *heavy*, or *important.*
To weild, or wield.
Welcome, or *acceptable.*
To welcome, *to bid*, or *make one* welcome.
To weld; *as* Smiths *do iron.*
Welfare, *health*, or *safety.*
Well, very well, well enough, well and good, &c.
Well-advised, or *considerate.*
Well-affected, or *well-minded.*
Well-beloved, or *dearly beloved.*
Well-born, or *well-descended.*
Well-doing.
Well-favoured, or *well-featured.*
A Well-meaning, or good *intention.*
A Well meant *zeal.*
Well-nigh, *very near*, or *almost.*
Well-set, *compact*, or *lusty.*
Well-tasted.
A Well-traded *Town.*
A Well-wisher *to a party*, &c.
A Well, or *pit to to hold water.*
A Draw-well.
A Well-hook.
A Well-spring, *as* Epsom-wells.
Tunbridge-wells, *&c.*
Welsh-men, *the natives of* Wales, *descended from the ancient Inhabitants of Great* Britain.
The Welt *of a garment*, or *shoo.*
To welt, or *make a* welt.
To welter, or *roll in his blood.*
A Wench, *a young girl*; *light houswife*, or *strumpet.*
A Servant-wench.
To wench, *to keep wenches company*, or *go a whoring.*
A Wencher, or *whore-master.*
A Wen, *a kind of hard swelling.*
I Went, or *did goe.*
I Wept, or *did weep.*
Were (*from* to be;) *as I wish he were gone.*
A Were-wolf, Man-wolf, or VVolf-man, *a kind of Sorcerer, said to transform himself into the nature and seeming shape of a wolf by virtue of an inchanted girdle*, &c.
The West, *a quarter of the World.*
North-west.
South-west.
The West-country.
The West-wind.
Western, or *westerly.*
Wet, *moist*, *liquid*, or *rainy.*
To wet, or *make wet.*
Wetness, or *moisture.*

W H

A Whale, *a huge sea-fish.*
Whale-bone.
A Wharf, *a yard near a river*, or *creek to hold wares brought to*, or *from the water.*
A Wharf-porter.
Wharfage, *the fee due for loading*, or *unloading goods at a wharf.*
A Warfinger, *the owner of a wharf.*
A Wharl, or whern, *to put a spindle on.*
To wharl *in the throat.*
What, for *that which*; *as mind well what I say.*
Whatever, or whatsoever.
Whay, or *thin milk.*
Whayish.
A Wheal, or *pimple.*
A Wheal-worm.
Wheat, *the best sort of grain.*
Beech-wheat.
Buck-wheat.
Black-wheat, *a weed.*
French-wheat.
Indian-wheat.
Red-wheat, or *Zeland*-wheat.
White-wheat.
A Wheat-ear, *a bird.*
Wheat-harvest.
A Wheat-plum.
Wheaten, or *made of wheat.*
To wheedle, or *draw in craftily by fair words*, &c.
A Wheedler.
A Wheel, *of all sorts.*
The Ballance-wheel *of a clock.*

A

A Cart-wheel.
A Coach-wheel.
A Crane-wheel.
A Spinning-wheel.
A Water-wheel, *to draw up water.*
A Wheel-barrow.
A Wheel-wright, or *wheel-maker.*
Wheel-work.
To wheel *about*, or *turn about.*
Wheelage, *a duty paid for Carrs and Waggons.*
To wheez, or *rattle in the throat.*
A Whelk, wheal or, *push.*
To Whelm, whelve, or *cover.*
A Whelp, *puppy*, or *young cub.*
To whelp, or *bring forth* whelps.
Whelpish, or *like a whelp.*
When, as *when you will.*
Whence, *or* from whence
Whencesoever.
Whenever, *or* whensoever.
Where; as *where you please.*
Whereabout, *or* whereabouts.
Whereas.
Whereof, for *at which.*
Whereby, or *by which.*
Where-ever, *or* wheresoever.
Wherefore, or *for which cause.*
Wherein, or *in which.*
Whereinto, or *into which*
Whereof, or *of which.*
Whereto, *or* whereunto; *to which*
Whereupon, or *upon which.*
Wherewith, or *with which.*
Wherewithal.
A Wherl, wharl, *or* whern, *for a spinning-wheel.*
A Wherret, *a flap on the chaps*, or *box on the ear.*

A Wherry, *a small boat*
A Wherry-man.
A Whet, or *mornings draught.*
To whet, or *sharpen tools.*
A Whet-stone.
Whether, or *which of the two.*
A Whetter (*from to* whet.)
Whey, *or* whay.
Which; as *I know not which it is.*
Whichsoever.
A Whiff, or *puff*; *as a whiff of Tobacco.*
To whiffle, *trifle*, or *prevaricate.*
A Whiffler, or *whiffling fellow.*
A Whiffler, *one that plays on a Fife before a Company of Soldiers*; also *a young Freemen that attends upon the Company*, or *Society to which he belongs.*
Whig, *whay*, or *very small beer.*
A Whig, *a fanatick*, or *a factious fellow.*
Whiggism, *a fanatical*, or *rebellious humour.*
While; as *while they were talking.*
To while off, or *put off a business.*
Whilst, or *whilst that.*
A Whim, *or* whimsey.
A Whim-wham, or *meer bawble.*
To whimper, or *begin to cry*; as *a Child does.*
A Whimsey, *a capricious humour*, or *conceit.*
Whimsical, or *fantastical.*
Whin, *or* petty-whin, *a kind of shrub.*
Whin-berries.
To whine, *whimper*, or *speak with a dolefull tone*
A Whiniard, *a kind of crooked sword.*
To whinny, or *neigh.*
Whins, or *furze.*
A Whip, or *scourge.*

To whip (*in several senses.*)
A Whip-staff, or *helm-handle with which the steersman governs the Ship.*
A Whip-saw.
A Whipster, *one that takes delight in whipping.*
Whipt, *or* whipped.
A Whirl, *put on a spindle to spin with.*
To whirl *about*, or *turn swiftly about.*
A Whirl-bat, *or* hurlibat.
The Whirle-bone *of the knee.*
A Whirl-pool, or *gulph.*
The Whirl-pool, *a sea-fish.*
A Whirl-wind.
A Whirligig, *a kind of top for boys to play with.*
A Whisk *made of osier.*
To whisk *off the dust.*
A Whisk, *a sort of neck-cloth for a Woman.*
Whisking, *swinging*, or *great.*
A Whisper, *a soft still noise*; as *when one speaks low.*
To whisper *one in the ear.*
A Whisperer.
Whist! or *peace!*
Whist, *a game at cards.*
A Whistle, *and*
To whistle *with the mouth*
A Whistler.
A Whit, or *little matter*; as *not a whit.*
Whit-wort, *an herb.*
The White colour.
Milk-white, or *exceeding white.*
The White *of an egg*, or *of the eye.*
A White, or *mark to shoot at.*
To white, *whiten*, or *make white*
White-lead.
White-lime, *a kind of wash us'd by* Plaisterers.

To **white-lime**, or *do over with white-lime.*
White-liver'd, *sneaking*, or *cowardly*.
White-meats, *made of milk*; as
A White-pot, *a mess of milk bak'd in an earthen pot with eggs, bread, sugar*, &c.
White-wort, *an herb.*
Whiteness.
The Whites *in Women.*
Whither, or *to what place*
Whithersoever.
Whiting, *to white houses with.*
A Whiting, *a fish.*
Whitish, or *somewhat white.*
A Whitlow, *a sore at the finger's end.*
A Whitler, or *bleacher of linnen.*
The Whitsun Holy-days.
Whitsunday, (q. d. *white sunday*) *so call'd from the admission of the* Catechumens *cloath'd in white robes to the Sacrament of Baptism, on the eve of this solemn Festival; which was instituted to commemorate the descent of the Holy Ghost upon the Apostles in the shape of fiery cloven tongues.*
Whitsuntide, *the season of the same Festival.*
A Whittail, *a bird.*
The Whitten-*tree.*
A Whittle, or *little knife.*
To whittle, or *cut sticks*, &c.
Whittled, or *cup-shot.*
To Whizz, or *make a noise; as liquor pour'd into the fire.*
Who; as *who goes there?*
Whoever, *or* whosoever.
Whole, *all, entire, solid, safe*, or *sound.*
The Whole, *with respect to its parts.*

Whole-chase-boots, or *large riding boots.*
Whole-footed *birds*, &c.
A Wholesale-man, *that disposes of commodities by whole-sale*
Wholeness, *a being whole.*
Wholesome, *healthful, sound*, or *profitable.*
Wholesomeness.
Whom; as *that Man whom I spoke to.*
Whomsoever.
A Whoop, or *pewet, a bird.*
To whoop, or *hollow.*
A Whore, or *harlot; a lewd Woman that prostitutes her self for gain.*
An Ammunition-whore, or *camp-trull.*
To whore, or *go a whoreing.*
A Whore-house, or *bawdy-house.*
An Whore-master, whore-monger, or *hunter of whores.*
Whoredom, or *fornication.*
Whorish, *belonging to whores*, or *given to whoredom.*
A Whorlbat, *a kind of gauntlet with straps, and leaden plummets, us'd by the ancient Heroes in their solemn games and exercises*, &c.
A Whortle, *a shrub.*
Sweet-whortle.
A Whortle-berry.
Whose; as *whose book is this?*
Whosesoever.
Whose (*Ps.* 107. 43.) for *whosoever.*
Whosoever, *or* whoever.
To whurr, or *snarl, as a dog does.*
Why, or *for what reason.*

WI

Wicked, *debauched, impious, lewd*, &c.
The Wicked, *reprobate persons.*

Wickedness.
Wicker, or *osier.*
A Wicker-basket.
A Wicker-chair.
A Wicket-door, *a little door within a gate.*
To go widdle-waddle, *like a duck.*
Wide, *large, great, spacious*, or *vast.*
Wide-kneed *breeches.*
To widen, *to make*, or *lye wide.*
Wideness; as *the wideness of cloth.*
A Widgeon, *or* widgin, *a foolish bird*; also *a simpleton, foolish* or *silly fellow.*
A Widow, *a Woman depriv'd of her Husband.*
A Widower, *a Man that has bury'd his Wife.*
Widowhood, *the state of a widow*, or *widower.*
Widow-wail, *a shrub.*
The Wick, *or* week *of a candle.*
To wield, *handle, manage*, or *sway.*
A Wife, or *married Woman.*
A House-wife.
A Wig, *bun*, or *little cake.*
A Wig, *or* periwig.
Wild, *savage, furious, hair-brain'd, extravagant*, &c.
Wild-fire, *made of gunpowder*, &c; also *a kind of S.* Anthony's *fire, a disease.*
A Wilderness, or *desart.*
A Wilding, *a sort of fruit.*
Wildness.
A Wile, or *cunning shift.*
Wilfull, *wedded to his own will, obstinate, stubborn*, &c.
Wilfulness.
Wiliness, *craft*, or *subtilty.*
Will, *and to* will (*in all senses.*)

Will with a wisp, *or* Jack in a Lanthorn, *a fiery Meteor*, or *exhalation that appears in the night, commonly haunting Church-yards, privies and fens, as being evaporated out of a fat soil: It also flies about* Rivers, Hedges, &c. *and leads those that follow it quite out of the way.*

A Will-jill, *scrat*, or *inconsiderable Hermaphrodite.*

Willed, *as*

Ill-willed, *of an envious*, or *ill-humour'd Temper.*

Self-willed, or *obstinate.*

Willingness, or *readiness.*

A Wilk, or *Sea-Snail.*

Williams, *or* Sweet-william, *an herb.*

A Willow, *or* willow-tree.

Willow-weed, *an herb.*

Wily, *full of* wiles, *crafty*, or *subtil.*

A Wimble, *a sort of piercer.*

A Wimple, *a kind of muffler worn by Nuns.*

To win, *gain, get* or *obtain.*

To wince, or *kick with the hind feet, as a horse does.*

Winches, *a kind of Engine to draw Barges up the River, against the Stream.*

The Wind, *an agitation of the Air, a vapour of the Body*, &c.

The East-wind.

The West-wind.

The North-wind.

The South-wind.

A Fore-wind.

A Quarter-wind.

A Side-wind.

A Trade-wind, *a wind which in some Parts blows constantly at certain seasons, and promotes Trading-voyages.*

A Whirl-wind, *a boisterous wind, Storm*, or *Hurricane.*

Wind-bound, or *stopt by contrary winds.*

The Wind-colick, *a disease.*

A Wind-Egg, or *addle Egg.*

A Wind-fall, *of fruit*, or *of an Estate.*

The Wind-flower.

The Wind-gall, *a soft swelling on the joynt of a horse's leg next the foot; occasioned by over-riding.*

A Wind-mill.

A Wind-row, or *rank of mow'd grass, ready to be cock'd.*

Wind-taught, or *stiff in the wind (a Sea-Term.)*

Wind, or *breath*

To wind, or *blow a horn.*

The Wind-pipe.

Winded, *as*

Broken-winded.

Long-winded.

Short-winded.

The wind, or *scent.*

To wind, or *have one in the wind.*

To wind, *turn, twine, twist*, or *wreath.*

A Wind-Beam *of a house.*

To wind *a Ship*, or *bring her head about.*

A winder *of Wooll*, &c.

Windiness, (*from* Windy.)

The windings *and turnings of a River.*

A Winding-sheet, *to wrap up a dead Corps.*

A Windlass, *or* windless, *a draw-beam in a Ship.*

Windles, or *blades to wind Yarn on.*

A Window *of a room.*

A Bay-window.

A Glass-window.

A Lattice-window.

Window-shutters.

A Windward Tide, *a* Tide *that runs against the Wind.*

Windy, *full of Wind, exposed to the wind*, or *flashy.*

Wine, *made of grapes*, or *other sorts of fruit.*

Canary-wine, or *Sack.*

Claret-wine.

Cherry-wine.

Curran-wine.

Malmsey-wine.

Muscadel-wine.

Rasberry-wine.

Rhenish-wine.

White-wine.

Wormwood-wine, *&c.*

A Wine-bibber.

A Wine-Cellar.

A Wine-conner, or *wine taster.*

A Wine-cooper.

Wine-flies.

A Wine-Merchant.

A Wine-Porter.

A Wine-press.

A Wing *of a Bird, Rabbet, Army*, &c.

Winged, *that has wings.*

A Wink, or *winking.*

To wink, blink, or *twinkle*; or *to make a sign with the eyes.*

A Winner, or *gainer.*

To Winnow, or *fan Corn.*

A Winnower.

The Winter, or *winter-season.*

The Winter *of a Printing-press.*

To winter, or *pass the Winter.*

Winter-Cherry.

Winter-green, *an herb.*

Winter-Quarters, *for an Army*

A Winterly *day.*

Winy, or *like wine.*

A Wipe, *jeer*, or *flout.*

To wipe, or *make clean with a cloath*, &c.

A Wiper.

A Wiping-clout.
Wire *made of Metal*, as
Copper-wire.
Gold-wire.
Silver-wire.
Wires *for a Woman's headdress.*
Wire-strings, *for Musical Instruments.*
To Wire-draw, *to draw out* Gold *or* Silver-*thread*; also *to entice*, or *decoy.*
A Wire-drawer.
Wire-drawn.
Wisdome, or *prudence.*
Wise, *prudent*, or *discreet.*
A Wise-acre, *or* Wise-man *of* Gotham; *a fool, ninny*, or *half-witted fellow.*
A Wise-man, *or* Cunning-man; *a Wizzard*, or *conjurer.*
The Seven Wise Men of *Greece*, viz. *Bias Chilo, Cleobulus, Periander, Pittacus, Solon*, and *Thales.*
A Wise, *manner*, or *means*; as *he did in this wise.*
A Wish, *and*
To Wish, or *desire.*
A Wisher.
A Well-wisher.
A Wishly look, or *amorous glance.*
A Wisp, or *wreath, on a Woman's head, to carry a pail on.*
A Wisp, or *bundle of Straw.*
Will, with a wisp, *a Meteor.*
Wist, as *bad I wist*, or *bad I known.*
To look wistly, or *earnestly upon one.*
Wit, *Ingenuity*, or *Sagacity.*
To wit, viz. *that is to say.*
To be out of his wits, or *distracted.*

To out-wit, or *over-reach.*
A Witch, or *Sorceress.*
To Witch, or *bewitch.*
A Witch-elm, *a tree.*
Witchery, *a bewitching.*
Witchcraft, or *the black art.*
With, as *I was with him.*
A With, or *withy twig.*
Withal, *with what*, or *at the same time.*
To withdraw, *draw back*, or *retire.*
A Withdrawing-room.
Withdrawn.
To vvither, *fade*, or *decay.*
The Withers *of a horse, the joyning of the shoulder-bone below the crest.*
With-held *from*,
To with-hold, *detain, stay*, or *stop.*
A With-holder.
Within, or *on the in-side.*
Withiwind, or *bind-weed, a kind of plant.*
Without, or *on the out-side.*
To withstand, *resist, oppose*, or *be obstinately bent.*
A Withstander.
Withstood.
A Withy, or *willow.*
Witless, or *void of wit.*
A Witness *of any Deed, a giver of evidence*, or *the evidence it self.*
To witness, or *bear witness.*
An Ear-witness.
An Eye-witness.
Wits, *Sense, judgment*, or *Reason, as to have his wits about him.*
A Wittal, or *contented Cuckold, that* wits, or *knows himself to be so.*
Witted, as *dull-witted.*
Half-witted.
Quick-witted.
Wittingly, *knowingly*, or *diligently.*
Witty, or *ingenious.*

A Witwall, *a Bird.*
Wives (*from* Wife) as *wives must be bad, whe good* or *bad.*
A Wizzard, *Magician*, or *Sorcerer.*

WO

Wo, *Calamity*, or *Misery.*
Woad, *an herb like Plantane of great use for the dying of a blew colour.*
Bastard-woad.
Garden-woad.
Wild-woad.
Woaded, or *steeped in woad.*
Wofull, *doleful, sad*, or *lamentable.*
A Wold, *a Champain ground, hilly, and void of woods*; as
Stow *in the* wolds, *a Town in* Glocestershire.
A Wolf, *a ravenous Beast*; or *a corroding ulcer.*
A Sea-wolf.
A Were-wolf, *or* Wolf-Man.
Wolf-bane } *herbs.*
Wolfs-milk }
Wolves as *a herd of Wolves.*
Wolves-teeth, *a sort of teeth in Horses, that grow sharp-pointed, so as to prick the Tongue and Gums, as they are eating.*
Wolvish, *belonging to*, or *partaking of the nature of* Wolves; *greedy*, or *ravenous.*
A Woman, (*q. d.* womb-man) *a female Man; the word* Mon *or* Man, *in* Saxon (*as* homo *in* Latin *signifying both Sexes.*
A Waiting-woman.
A VVork-woman.
Woman-hood, *the state or condition of a Woman.*

Womanish, *belonging to a* Woman; also *soft* or *effeminate.*
The VVomb, *matrice,* or *mother in a Woman.*
The VVomb-passage, womb-pipe, or *neck of the womb.*
VVomen, *the plural of* VVoman: as *given too much to the love of Women.*
VVon (*from* to win.)
To wonder at, *admire*, or *be surpriz'd.*
The Seven VVonders of the World, viz. 1. *The pyramids of* Egypt. 2. *The* Mausoleum, or *tomb of* Mausolus, *King of* Caria, *built by Queen* Artemisia. 3. *The Temple of* Ephesus. 4. *The Walls of* Babylon. 5. *The* Collossus, or *huge image of the Sun at* Rhodes 70 *cubits*, or 105 *foot high.* 6. *The statue of* Jupiter Olympius. 7. *The* Pharus, or *watch-tower, erected by* Ptolemy Philadelphus.
VVonder-working, *astonishing*, or *surprising.*
A VVonderer.
VVonderfull.
VVonderfulness.
A VVonderment, or *astonishment.*
VVondrous, *marvellous*, or *admirable.*
I VVon't, *for I will not.*
VVont, or *custom.*
VVont, or *accustomed*; as *we are* wont *to do so.*
VVonted, or *usual.*
To woo, *court*, or *make love.*
A Wooer.
VVood, or *timber growing in*
A VVood, *a large piece of ground, cover'd with trees and shrubs that grow naturally.*
Brush-wood.
Pock-wood, or *holy-wood.*
Sear-wood, *in Forests, dead boughs cut off from trees.*
An Under-wood, or *copse.*
A VVood-bill.
VVood-bind, *a shrub.*
A VVood-cleaver.
A VVood-cock, *a bird.*
A VVood-culver, or *wood-pigeon.*
A VVood-fretter, *a sort of worm.*
A VVood-house.
A VVood-knife.
A VVood-land, or *woody place.*
A VVood-lark, *a bird.*
A VVood-louse, *an insect.*
A VVood-man, *that looks to the King's Wood in a Forest.*
A VVood-monger, *Timber-merchant*, or *seller of wood.*
A VVood-pecker, *a bird.*
VVood-roof, } *herbs.*
VVood-sage, }
The VVood-sere, *an insect.*
VVood-sorrel, *an herb.*
A Wood-stack, or *wood-pile.*
A Wood-ward, *a Forest-Officer that walks with a forest-bill, and takes cognizance of all offences committed therein.*
A Wood-yard *for timber-merchants.*
Wooden, or *made of wood.*
Woody, or *full of woods.*
A Wooer, or *suiter.*
The Woof *in a* Weaver's *loom.*
Wooll, *that grows on sheep.*
Wooll-blade, *an herb.*
A Wooll-driver, *one that buys* wooll *of the sheep-masters, and carries it on horse-back to markets, &c.*
Wooll-gathering; *as your wits are a wooll-gathering.*
A Wooll-pack.
A Wooll-winder, or *packer of wooll, that winds, or bundles up the fleeces; sworn to do it truly between the owner and the buyer.*
Woollen, *made of wooll.*
A Woollen-draper.
Woolly, *belonging to wooll.*
Woosted, or *crewel.*
Woosted-stockings.
Wop-eyed, or *blear-ey'd.*
A Word (*in several senses.*)
To word a thing, or *express it in words.*
A By-word, or *proverb.*
A Watch-word.
A Word-book, or *vocabulary.*
I Wore, or *did* wear.
Work, *and to* work (*in all senses.*)
Checker-work, or *inlaid work.*
An Out-work, *in fortification.*
A Horn-work.
Needle-work.
Tent-work.
A Work-day, *or working-day.*
A Work-house.
A Work-man, or *Artisan.*
A Master-work-man.
Workmanship.
A Work-woman.
A Worker.
A Fellow-worker.
The Master-worker *of the mint.*
Workt, *or* worked.
The World, *Universe*, or *the people that dwell therein.*
A VVorld, *a great number*, or *great quantity.*
Marvel of the world, *an herb.*
VVorldliness, *a being worldly.*

A VVorldling, or *world-ly-minded man.*
VVorldly, *belonging to the* world, *sensual*, or *covetous*, &c.
VVorldly-minded, or *addicted to the World.*
A VVorm, *an insect.*
A VVorm, *an iron-tool, to unload a gun.*
A Belly-worm, or *maw-worm.*
A Chur-worm.
A Dog-worm, or *worm in a dog's tongue, which makes him mad, if not taken out.*
An Earth-worm.
A Glow-worm.
A Hand-worm.
A Palmer-worm.
A Ring-worm, or *tetter.*
The Silk-worm.
A Sloe-worm, or *blind-worm.*
A VVood-worm.
VVorm-grass, *a kind of plant that kills worms.*
VVorm-eaten.
The Worm-eating *of trees*, or *fruits.*
VVorm-seed, *a sort of powder to destroy worms in the humane body.*
To worm *a dog, to take a* worm *from under his tongue.*
To worm *a cable, to strengthen it by winding a small rope between the strands.*
To worm, or *wriggle into one's favour.*
The VVorms *in Children*; also *the bots a horse-disease.*
VVormwood, *an herb.*
Sea-wormwood.
VVormwood-wine.
VVorn *(from to* wear.)
To worry, *tear in pieces, and devour*; or *to tear one.*
VVorse *(from bad)* as *he is worse than ever he was.*
VVorship, or *adoration.*
Idol-worship.
Your VVorship, *a title of dignity.*
To worship, or *adore.*
VVorshipfull, Right-worshipfull, *&c.*
A VVorshipper.
VVorst; as *he is the worst of Men.*
VVorsted, *or* woosted.
To worst one, *to overcome*, or *get the better of him.*
VVort, or *new drink.*
VVort *in composition, signifies an herb*; as Liver-wort, spoon-wort, *&c.*
VVorth, *value, desert, esteem*, or *price.*
To be VVorth.
VVorthies, *worthy*, or *illustrious personages.*
The nine VVorthies, *of whom three were* Jews, *viz.* Joshua, David *and* Judas Maccabæus; *three Gentiles*, Hector *of* Troy, Alexander *the great and* Julius Cæsar; *and three Christians*, Arthur *of* Britain, Charles *the great of* France, *and* Godfrey *of* Bouillon.
VVorthiness, or *merit.*
VVorthless, or *of no value.*
VVorthy, *of much worth, deserving, vertuous, generous*, &c.
Praise-worthy.
Thank-worthy.
VVoven *(from to* weave.)
VVould to God!
I VVould *(from to* will.)
To would, or *strengthen the mast, by binding it about with ropes.*
Wound *(from to* wind.)
A Wound, *hurt*, or *sore made by a Weapon.*
To wound, or *cause a wound.*
A Love-wound.
VVound-wort, *an herb.*

VV R

VVrack, *a sea-weed*; also *ruin, spoil*, &c.
A VVrack, *or* Ship-wrack *is properly, where a ship is lost at Sea, and no person escapes alive out of it; then the goods brought to land by the waves belong to the King: But if any person comes safe to shore, it is no* wrack, *and if a dog or cat be left living, the goods are the owners still, provided they be claim'd within a year and a day.*
To wrangle, *brangle*, or *brawl.*
A VVrangler.
To wrap *up*, or *fold up.*
The Wrappers *that cover a ream of paper.*
VVrath, *anger*, or *indignation.*
VVrathfull.
To wreak, or *vent his anger on one.*
A VVreath, *a garland*, or *a twisted cloth, to carry a milk-pail*, &c.
To wreath *about*, or *twist about.*
A VVren, *a little bird.*
A VVrench, or *sprain.*
To wrench, or *get a wrench.*
To wrench *open a door*, &c.
To wrest, *wring, snatch, distort, pervert*, &c.
A VVrester.
To vvrestle, *to use* vvrestling; *to struggle*, or *strive for the mastery.*
A VVrestler.
VVrestling, *a sort of exercise.*
A VVrestling-school.
A VVretch, *a poor* vvretch, *an unfortunate*, or *forlorn creature.*

VVretched, *miserable, wicked*, or *scurvy*.
VVretchedness.
To wriggle *like a Snake*.
To wriggle, or *insinuate himself into one's favour*.
VVright, as *a Cart-wright*
A Ship-wright, or *Ship-Carpenter*.
A VVheel-right, or *wheel-maker*.
To wring, *press, squeez, pinch*, or *put to pain*.
A VVrinkle, or *fold of the skin*.
To wrinkle, or *make wrinkles*.
The VVrist, *that part which joyns the hand to the arm*.
A Wrist-band *of a shirt*, &c.
Writ, (*from to* write.)
The Holy-vvrit, or *Holy Scriptures*.
A Writ, *a written Order*, or *precept relating to Law-business, from the King*, or *a Court of Judicature*.
Original Writs, *Writs, issued out under the Prince's name*.
Judicial Writs *that come from a Court of judicature, with the name of the chief Judge of that Court*.
To write, *form characters, pen, set down in writing*, &c.
A Writer.
To vvrithe, *twist*, or *wrest*.
Writing, or *the art of fair writing in all the usual hands*.
A Hand-vvriting.
Short-hand-vvriting.
A Writing-Master.
A VVriting-Scholar.
A VVriting-School.
VVritings, *Papers*, or *Deeds of an Estate*, &c.
VVritten, or *put in writing*.
VVrong, *false*, or *preposterous*.
Wrong, *injury, damage* &c.
To vvrong *one*, or *do him wrong*.
VVrongfull.
I vvrote, or *did* vvrite
VVroth, *Angry*, or *in a Passion*.
VVrought, or *work'd*; as Wrought-Brass.
VVrought-Silver, *&c*.
VVrung (*from to* wring)
Wry, *crooked*, or *distorted*.
To wry *the mouth*, or *set it a-wry*.
VVry-legg'd.
VVry mouth'd.
VVry-neck'd,
A wry-neck, a *Bird*.

VV Y

A VVydraught, a *Water-course*, or *Water-passage*.

Y A

A Yacht, *a small sort of Ship*, or *Pleasure-Boat*; as
The Royal Transport-Yacht.
A Yard, *a measure of three foot, which King* Henry I. *is said to have ordain'd by the length of his own arm*.
A Yard-Land *or* verge of Land; *the quantity of which is various, according to the Custom of several places; from fifteen to forty Acres*.
A Yard, *or* Sail-yard of a ship, *the Timber cross the Masts, on which the Sails hang*.
The Main-yard, or *yard belonging to the Main-mast*.
A Yard, *or* Court-yard, *adjoyning to a House*; also *a Man's Privy Member*.
Yarn, or *spun wooll*.
The Yarn-beam *of a Weaver's Loom*.
Yarn-windles, or *blades to wind yarn on*.
Yarrow, or *milfoil, an herb*.
To Yaw, or *work as a Ship does, when she goes in and out with her head*.
To yawl, *bawl*, or *cry out*.
To yawn, or *gape*,

Y E

Ye, as *ye shall* be *oblig'd to do it*.
Yea, or *yes*.
To yean, *ean*, or *bring forth Lambs*.
A Year, *or* Solar-year, *a space of time measured by the Sun's Course, consisting of* 12 *Months*, 52 *Weeks*, or 365 *Days and* 6 Hours.
A Lunar-Year, *containing* 12 *Revolutions of the Moon*, or 354 *days*.
A Leap-year *has one day more than the others, and happens every fourth year; because the six odd hours in that space amount to* 24, *or a whole day; always added to the Month of* February, *which in such* Leap-years *contains* 29 *days*.
A New-years-gift, *a Present usually made by one friend to another, on the first day of the new year*.
A Yearling, *a Beast a year old*.
Yearly, *that happens*, or *is done every year*.
To yearn, *to be mov'd with Pity* or *Compassion*; also *to bark as Beagles do at their prey*.
The yelk, or yolk *of an Egg*.
To yell, or *make a dismal*

mal howling noise.
Yellow } *colours.*
Yellow-bay }
Yellow-haired.
A Yellow-hamber, *a bird.*
Yellowish, or *somewhat yellow.*
Yellowness.
The yellows, *or* yellow jaundice, *a Disease.*
To yelp, *to cry like a Dog,* or Fox.
A Yelt, or *young Sow.*
A Yeoman, *a Wealthy Country-man, that has an Estate of his own;* also *an inferiour Member of any Company,* or *Corporation.*
The Yeomanry, or *Body of yeomen,*
Yeomen of the King's House, *a sort of inferiour Officers, between a Serjeant and a Groom;* as *The* Yeoman *of the* Chaundry.
The Yeoman *of the* Scullery.
The Yeoman *of the* Stirrup.
The Yeomen of the Gard, *a sort of Foot-Gards, that wear red jackets, and black velvet-caps, trimm'd with ribbons of several colours: They follow the King with Halbards, when he walks on foot, and march by the side of his Coach when he rides.*
A Yerk, or *jerk.*
To yerk, *jerk,* or *whip;* or *to wince as a horse does.*
A Yerker, *or whipster.*
A Yerker *out, a yerking,* or *wincin horse.*
Yes, ye, *or* ay; *as answer* yes, *or* no.
Yest, or *Leaven commonly used to make dough rise,* as
Ale-yest.
Beer-yest.
Yesterday, or *the day before.*
Yester-night, or *last night.*
Yet, as yet, or *till this time.*
An Yew, or *ewe, a female sheep.*
The Yew-tree.

Y I

To yield, or *bring forth, as the Earth does;* also *to afford, grant, give up, surrender,* &c.
Yielding, *pliant,* or *submissive.*
Yieldingness, *complaisance,* or *condescension*

Y O

A Yoke *for Cattel,* &c. also *a double Rope reaching from the Helm, along the Ship's sides to help the steering.*
To yoke, or *put to the yoke.*
The yoke-elm, *a tree.*
A Yoke-fellow *in* Wedlock, *a Husband,* or *Wife that bears the same yoke.*
The yolk, or *yellow part of an Egg.*
Yonder, or *there;* as *yonder he is.*
A Younker, or *youngster.*
Yonkers, *young fore-mast-men in a Ship.*
You, *as he will write to* you.
The Hawk youks, i. e. *sleeps.*
Young, *youthful, tender, new,* &c.
The young, or *young ones of any living Creature.*
A Young-beginner.
A Youngling, *or novice.*
A Youngster, *a brisk* or *airy young man.*
Your, as *'tis your own fault.*
Yours, as *this is yours;* *I am* yours, i. e. *your Servant* or *Friend.*
Youth, *the state of young persons,* or *the persons themselves,*
A Youth, *young man,* or *stripling.*
Youth-wort, *an herb.*
Youthful, *belonging to* youth; or *being in the prime of one's years.*

Z A

A Zany, *a Buffoon,* or *Jester, (after the* Italian *way) that professes to create* Laughter *by unseemly speeches, mimical gestures, ridiculous actions,* &c.

Z E

Zeal, or *ardent affection.*
A Zealot, *a great stickler in matters of Religion.*
Zealous, or *full of zeal.*
A Zechin, *a Gold-Coin, worth about* 7s. 6d.; *so call'd from* La Zecha *a Town of* Venice, *where the Mint is settled.*
A Turkish Zechin, *valu'd at* 9s. *Sterling.*
Zedoary, *an* Indian *root like ginger, but more sweetly scented, and of a bitterish taste.*
The Zenith, *or vertical point (in* Astronomy) *an* Arabick *Term, signifying that point of the Heaven, which in any place, is directly over one's head.*
A Zereth, *an* Hebrew *measure of nine inches.*
A Zest, *an Orange,* or *Lemmon-chip.*
To Zest, *(among* Confectioners) *is to cut the peel of such fruits from top to bottom, into small slips, as thin as can possibly be done.*

ZO

The Zodiack, *an imaginary Circle in the Heaven, taking name from the* Greek *word* Zoon, i.e. *an animal, because 'tis adorned with twelve* Signs *or Images, most of which resemble living creatures. It crosses the* Æquator *in two points,* viz. *in the beginning of* Aries *and* Libra, *and the* Ecliptick *Line passes through the middle of it.*

The Sun *goes about this Circle once every year, and the* Moon *once in a Month: The former never swerves from the* Ecliptick, *but the* Moon *and the rest of the Planets wander up and down, for the space of eight degrees on each side; upon which account, the breadth of the* Zodiack *is supposed to take up 16 degrees.* *See* the Signs of the Zodiack.

Zones, (*i. e.* Girdles) *are certain spaces, or parts of the Earth, distinguished by several names, according to the different temperature of the Air, and are five in number,* viz. *one* Torrid, *two* Temperate, *and two* Frigid.

The Torrid Zone *lies between the two* Tropicks *of* Cancer *and* Capricorn, *taking up* 47 *degrees of Latitude, that is to say,* 940 *leagues,* or 2820 *miles. 'Tis called* Torrid, *i. e.* parched, *or* burning-hot, *from its excessive and constant heat, caused by the continual course of the* Sun, *between the* Tropicks; *insomuch that the Ancients erroneously believed it to be altogether unhabitable.*

The Temperate Zones, *are one Northern, and the other Southern: The former, (in which we live) extends it self between the* Tropick *of* Cancer *and the* Arctick *Circle, and the other between the* Tropick *of* Capricorn, *and the* Antarctick Circle; *so that they apparently owe their name, with the advantages of the Climate to their Situation between the extremities of the* Torrid *and* Frigid Zones; *and each of 'em takes up* 43 *degrees of Latitude; about* 860 *leagues, or* 2580 *miles.*

The Frigid Zones, *likewise one on the* North, *and the other on the* South, *are situated in the farthermost parts of the World; that is to say, the Northern between the* Arctick Circle *and the* Arctick *Pole, and the* Southern *between the* Antarctick *Circle and the Pole of the same name. So that each of them contains* 23 *degrees and a half,* 470 *leagues, or* 1410 *miles.*

These two Zones *are call'd* Frigid, *i. e.* exceeding cold *or* frozen, *because being extremely remote from the Sun's Course in the* Zodiack, *they partake but little of its heat, recieving its Rays oblique and without reflection; upon which account, the ancient Greographers and Historians, could not imagine them to be at all Inhabited no more than the* Torrid Zone *for its vehement heat; but their mistakes are now sufficiently discovered.*

Zoophytes, (q. d. *plant-animals*) a Philosophical *Term, denoting things that are as it were of a middle nature, between Plants and Living-creatures, as Spunges,* &c.

FINIS.